A Biography of Edward Marsh

EDWARD HOWARD MARSH, K.C.V.O., C.B., C.M.G.

At Gray's Inn, 1938

A BIOGRAPHY OF EDWARD MARSH

BY

CHRISTOPHER *Vernon* HASSALL

Harcourt, Brace and Company

New York

CONTENTS

ILLUSTRATIONS

PREFACE

EDWARD MARSH was a scholar. He was also, and for many years, a great deal more, making active appearances where men of academic temperament do not normally feel at home—such as dancing his way through every ball of the London season, travelling on foot to the source of the Nile, playing mah-jong with the King of Portugal or bézique with the Aga Khan for sixpenny stakes. So it is advisable at the start to pinpoint the central being. He will only be imagined aright if seen as a scholar whose other qualities combined, sometimes for years at a stretch, to lead him away from his natural bent. He was, of course, an aesthete of acute perception and an ornament of society with an inexhaustible fund of small talk; one, moreover, for whom no talk could be too small. Owing to these contrasts in personality his conversation was often an engaging blend of ambrosia and small beer. Concinnity of mind, perhaps the most striking element of his nature, while making a harmony of these differences, also made it impossible for him to be pedantic. His lightness of touch was so deceptively feather-light that it never seemed to carry the weight of authority.

The man of marked ambition (such as is most often the subject of a biography) goes from one limited aim to the next, always holding the longer aim in view. He sets a course for himself, brushing things and people out of the way to either side, and it is easy enough in that case to distinguish between what is relevant, lying within or near the groove of his career, and what is outside it and dispensable. With a man of more passive nature discrimination is not so simple. If he is so far from being a man of action as to manage very well by means of a happy gift of letting things happen to him, he will almost certainly leave behind him a story rather lacking in momentum. Instead of a prominent guiding line there will be an infinite number of little strands of interest radiating in all directions, and if a biographer should start paring away the inessentials, as he must, he must be careful where he stops, or he will discover that the man himself whom they composed has

ix

mysteriously gone as well. So when one recalls Sir Sidney Lee's dictum 'Character which does not translate itself into exploit is for the biographer a mere phantasm' one is brought up against the crux of the problem. Apart from intrepidly opening a pink umbrella in the face of an enraged rhinoceros, the exploits of Sir Edward Marsh were few and far between. His adventures were largely crises of the sensibility, but on occasion he was caught up in historical events and appeared a figure as it were suddenly dwarfed by his setting. Those larger affairs must at least be sketched into the picture. More in scale was the movement known as *Georgian Poetry*, which has taken its place in literary history. That history, or rather his own view of it from his editorial chair as it unfolded, is too important, and has been too often misunderstood, for it not to be allowed now and again to divert the reader's attention from the central theme. But in the main it is a question of giving shape and coherence to what is evanescent. Granted we accept the scholar as an abiding presence (as fully one of the 'sons' of A. W. Verrall as those Jacobean poets were 'the sons of Ben'), then the loose-flying threads of gossip and good talk can without risk of wrong impression be taken for what they were—no less the stuff of his life than Catullus and the Greek dramatists.

To mirror the passing show, reflecting it truthfully (which is to say almost unconsciously), was another of his qualities. Often one feels the man *was* what he was watching, in the way that one thinks of a looking-glass as *being* the reflections carried on its face. But here again the scholar in him made the vital difference. He had just enough detachment to make him selective and critical in his comment when he came to putting his pen to paper. He was so eminently communicative and sociable that when alone in the privacy of his room he felt the need to go on talking. The letter-writer wrote as he talked. Hardly less useful to the biographer is his interlocutor. If a man reveals himself in his letters there is also something to be deduced from the tone of address that others adopt towards him. The reader will find I have included passages of correspondence which are none the less necessary for being apparently inessential.

As opportunity served he responded by serving it brilliantly in return. With him the governing factor (in so far as there was one at all) was never the thing he wanted to do but the person that he wanted to be with. He let himself be guided by his insatiable need to be needed. Whenever he began to feel he was no longer necessary he experienced a gradual and painless kind of disenchantment and looked elsewhere for a cause to serve. His friends in this special class slip unobtrusively into the scene of his life, stay for a while, then as it were drop back into the solitude of their own biographies, combining in a group, or giving place to one another, with criss-cross and perplexing alternation. It is a panorama of friends going to and fro and of shifting reflections (two or three of the characters never finally going out of the picture) and, throughout them all, the one unchanging figure—the fastidious and exacting master of pure scholarship. Perhaps the only positive decision he ever took in his life was, paradoxically, a negative one—*not* to accompany Lord Gladstone to Pretoria in 1909. For the sake of future advancement (as things were at the time) he was tempted, but as will be seen he preferred to stay in the service of Sir Winston (then, and throughout this book, Mr.) Churchill. Personal attachment made the decision. Had he chosen otherwise, and been out of England during Lord Gladstone's term of office abroad, there would have been no *Georgian Poetry*, very little patronage of painting, if any worth noting, and both the work and life (perhaps even the duration of life) of Rupert Brooke would have been other than they were. The association with Winston Churchill recurs like a refrain. It is the one strand, excepting only Brooke, which was never dropped, and on looking back it serves to bind together nearly fifty of his years.

So when in 1938 he published his autobiography, and called it *A Number of People*, the title was most apt, but it seemed a pity that the author himself could hardly be counted as one of their number. After the opening chapters he abandoned the chronological sequence, thereby saving himself the distastefully egotistical labour of unfolding the story of his own achievements. He had his share of vanity, but it was not enough to make him do with a clear conscience what his modesty forbade. Although the book was dedicated to me in the belief that it had saved me a lot of biographical exertion in the future, the truth was that for all its wit and charm the main problem had been evaded and the task was still to do. It was as entertaining as anyone could wish, but only as far as it went. It fell short of what some readers had looked for, chiefly because so much of what really mattered in his life had been done 'off-stage' and in mutual confidence among friends. It was not for him to do more than leave the evidence undestroyed.

The word patronage suggests a condescending gesture of philanthropy made by the greater toward the less. Edward Marsh did not see it in that light. For him the impulse to patronize came from an awakened sense of his own limitations. The young artist might be a crude and 'scrubbed boy', but if he showed signs of creative promise then that offset every disadvantage, transformed the relationship, and made of the patron a devoted servant. He asked little more of life than the satisfaction of being able to foster the spark wherever he found it, and he had an instinct for detecting its presence—rather more through something in the man than in his work—long before it was evident to anyone else. Under the heading of patronage, as he understood it—a word he seldom used, but he provided no alternative—might come anything from settling the optician's account, paying for a honeymoon, applying a hot poultice, or providing a bed for the night, to pointing out with nagging severity that the writer had not properly expressed his meaning, or dropping the hint to a painter that perhaps it was time he looked elsewhere than to Renoir for inspiration.

'I have never had what anybody in his right mind could describe as Money,' he once said. Even so, a patron must have funds of a sort, if not actually Money. He had a small reserve which, thinly spread, was enough. A full account of its peculiar origin was found in his bedroom at Walton Street after his death. On top of the wardrobe stood his massive Greek Lexicon; on the chimneypiece was an array of tiny oddments, such as Chinese buttons carved into the likeness of mice, foreign coins; in the grate his many pairs of shoes (his one extravagance) stood in a row, stretched in their trees, and under the bed were three boxes. One, such as is normally used for the delivery of vegetables, contained framed photographs of Brooke, Baring, Churchill, Henry James, and others; the second, an imposing despatch-box with small brass handles and bearing the royal cypher in crimson and gold, a relic of the Admiralty in the days of Gallipoli, was locked, and found to contain nothing but a first edition of Joyce's *Ulysses*; the third, covered with perished red leather, was also a despatch-box. This I recognized, though I had never looked inside. The Prime Minister Spencer Perceval was carrying it when he met his death in the lobby of the House of

Commons. It contained a copy of *Bell's Weekly Messenger* for
May 17, 1812, giving all the circumstances of the tragedy which
had occurred six days before and was to lead a hundred years later
to the benefit of British art.

The minute attic with its sloping roof, too low to stand up in
even if there had been room to stand, was a glory-hole of shabby
Victorian novels, engravings of Perceval, old suitcases full of
brown envelopes stuffed with letters, damaged frames, shivers of
broken glass, and what was labelled 'The Rupert Trunk'. In this
was a file of notes for political speeches from the Old Vicarage,
Grantchester, several copies of a pamphlet called *Sexual Ethics*,
native baskets and oddments from Tahiti, the khaki tie Brooke
was wearing when he fell ill, the handkerchief from under his pillow,
dried sprigs of olive from his grave, his pocket Shakespeare, and
various pre-war magazines. And round about, loose or in bundles,
lay old letters dumped in their thousands in an area about
four feet wide by six. These miscellaneous papers were the main
source material of this biography, and to them were added extracts
from Edward Marsh's own letters copied as they were gradually
called in from all traceable sources over a period of about five
years. Overriding the chapter headings of this book there is a
larger pattern which may be helpful to the reader if it is given here
in broad outline.

This is a life which fulfilled itself in a sequence of six phases
with its central and turning point being reached in November of
the year 1915. The first of these phases (Chapters 1–5) ends in
September 1896, and gives some account of Marsh's education at
Westminster and Cambridge against the background of his
attachment and resistance to his mother. Oswald Sickert stimulates
his interest in painting and the drama; A. W. Verrall lays the
basis of his scholarship; the philosophers Bertrand Russell and
G. E. Moore influence his attitude to life, and Robert Bridges
becomes his first acquaintance among the contemporary poets.
With the death of his mother and the beginning of his official
life in the Civil Service we enter the second phase (Chapters
6–8), which comes to an end in December 1911. Edmund Gosse
introduces him to literary London; Neville Lytton encourages him
to start as a collector of classical paintings; he begins his association
with Winston Churchill (1905) and Rupert Brooke (1907); the
purchase of his first modern work of art coincides with the

publication of Brooke's first volume, and he first appears as a patron of the arts of literature and painting at the age of thirty-nine.

The third phase (Chapters 9–13) incorporates the whole of Churchill's term of office at the Admiralty, Brooke's short public career, and the six months following the poet's death. *Georgian Poetry* is founded (1912) and many new poets enter the circle, while the young painters from the Slade keep their patron in touch with the latest movements in contemporary art; Flecker, D. H. Lawrence, de la Mare, and others, are prominent in his life; the deaths of Brooke and Howard Marsh, his father, lead to a closer relationship with Henry James, and this central period is brought to an end with the departure of Mr. Churchill for active service in France. Chapters 14–16, ending in August 1924, comprise the fourth phase. During this time his work in the service of Mr. Churchill is interrupted and resumed (1917); the brothers Nash and Spencer, also Graves and Sassoon, are among his especial friends; he writes his journal letters of visits to the Front; a long dispute with Brooke's mother is brought temporarily to an end with the publication of the Memoir (1918) and the first collected edition of the poet's works; he continues the Georgian series, and with the fourth issue (1919) begins to lose his influence with the younger poets. After the last Georgian anthology (1922) he turns to scholarship, especially the emendation of texts (Byron, Jane Austen, Proust, etc.) and begins his work as a translator with the seven-year labour on the Fables of La Fontaine. During the fifth phase (Chapters 17–18), ending May 1941, he becomes the theatrical first-nighter; suffers a grave misadventure in Corsica (1928); ends his official services to Churchill (1929); completes the work on La Fontaine (1931); retires from the Civil Service (1937); begins intensive literary association with Churchill and Somerset Maugham; writes his reminiscences (1938); translates the Odes of Horace (1940); then evacuates Gray's Inn where he had lived for forty years. In the final phase (Chapter 19), which ends in January 1953, he is at first homeless for five years; he translates *Dominique* (1946), settles at Knightsbridge, translates two works of Princess Marthe Bibesco, continues practising his special brand of book-doctoring, and is still engaged on a section of Churchill's *History of the English-Speaking Peoples* at his death.

If the reader, having come to the end of the book, should turn back to this summary, I hope he will be amazed to discover how completely (in spite of its familiar names and occupations) it fails to convey the slightest impression of what Edward Marsh really was. Only private letters, such as Pope called so happily 'the very *déshabille* of the understanding', and the little and often trivial vicissitudes of the daily round, can give any true picture of this man who, were he to see that outline, would recognize and endorse the facts, then yawn and pour himself a double whisky and soda. There are biographies (fewer nowadays than formerly) which have shown that their subjects did the State much service but were apparently never alive. In writing of a contemporary, especially if he was a friend, it is necessary first, I believe, to have come to terms with a world in which he is irremediably no more. There is nothing so hampering to a writer as setting out to reconstruct a man's life in a spirit of such reverence and caution that it is as if the subject himself had already promised to read the proofs (though in this present instance, if in no other, what an asset that would be!). For the sake of hitting the truth, I think one should have enough respect for one's subject to risk being disrespectful. Fortunately Edward Marsh is continually making the gesture of knocking himself off his high horse. From time to time he elegantly debunks himself, which has saved his biographer the trouble of doing anything of the sort. The best way to commemorate a benevolent scholar to whom so many artists have been indebted is to avoid that brand of memorial portrait which is blurred by its own thick varnish of dully super-human virtue, and try to present, as best one can, a fellow creature with all his foibles and pettinesses, no less than his honours, still thick upon him, and in his habit as he walked. 'In a word,' said Pope in another of his letters, 'what is Man altogether, but one mighty inconsistency?' For this I only need to let him quote himself and my subject will do all that is required.

I am very much aware of my coming by accident of birth at the tail end of a long line of writers whom Eddie Marsh befriended, and happening to be not only among the least of them but that one to whom chance has given the most advantageous place for undertaking this task. What I have managed to do I regard as done on behalf of those others who, if circumstances had been otherwise, would have accomplished this business better than I. It is to them, the writers who have survived their patron, that I consider this book dedicated, not only out of fellow feeling, but in the fond hope, I must confess, that they may the more readily hesitate before denying it their indulgence. To the great many who have done so much to help in various ways I make acknowledgement elsewhere. They would all agree, I am sure, that this book will have done something worth doing (such as Marsh himself would most approve) if his example as a patron brings home to the reader, perhaps with a new emphasis, the very real responsibility which modern society still has, and will always have, towards its creative spirits who by the very nature of their work can derive but small benefit from the world which they interpret and enrich.

C. H.

Hampstead, 1958

Chapter One

DEATH AND BIRTH
(1812–1879)

Our own age can boast of some fine specimens, such, for
instance, as Bellingham's affair with the prime minister. ...

DE QUINCEY: *On Murder Considered as One of the Fine Arts*

A T a quarter-past five in the afternoon of Monday, May 11,
1812, the Prime Minister, Spencer Perceval, accompanied
by Lord Osborne, reached the top of the stone steps which
led to the lobby of the old House of Commons. He had left his
cloak and stick with an attendant at the foot of the stairs and
was now carrying nothing but a small rectangular despatch-box
covered in red leather. It hung lengthwise, swinging from a small
brass ring looped on a finger of his left hand as with the right he
threw open the door of the lobby and stood aside to give his friend
precedence. Lord Osborne bowed and stood back to let the Prime
Minister enter first. There was the sound of a shot. From within
the lobby a man was seen to advance a few paces into the room
and fall forward on his face at the feet of a certain William Smith,
M.P. for Norwich. Smith had not seen who had just entered, for
his back was to the door, but on turning round he heard the words
'Oh, I am murdered', uttered barely audibly as someone fell. He
stooped and raised the man's head and recognized the Prime
Minister. By the time they had carried him out of the smoke to
the sofa in the Speaker's room he was dead. The surgeon who was
fetched by a runner from Great George Street made a hurried
examination and declared that a ball of 'unusually large size'
had penetrated the very centre of the heart.

The room was crowded when the shot was heard. For a moment
there was silence, then a voice shouted, 'Where is the rascal that
fired?' and General Isaac Gascoyne, who had been writing a
letter in the committee room adjoining, and had rushed in at the
sound of the disturbance, was seen forcing a man on to a bench by

the fireplace. The intruder was giving no resistance. He seemed to
be in a state of terrible agitation, but he managed to answer the
shouted enquiry by calling over the General's shoulder: 'I am the
unfortunate man.' The doors into the House of Commons and
into the Speaker's apartments, and the way out to the head of the
steps, were at once bolted and no one was allowed to leave. All
eyes were turned to the group at the fireplace. Someone asked the
man why he had done this appalling thing. He answered quietly:
'My name is Bellingham. It is a private injury. I know what I have
done. It was a denial of justice on the part of the Government.'
Then there was a move to take him into the body of the House for
cross-questioning, but first he was searched. In his breeches
pocket was found a loaded steel pistol with a screw barrel and a
bundle of papers folded like letters. His other weapon, a smaller
pistol, he had already surrendered.

Two Messengers led the prisoner to the bar of the House, where
there was the utmost confusion. Peers came running in from the
Lords and strangers ran down from the Gallery, and the prisoner,
involved in the crush, was pressed violently back against the wall.
For several minutes the Speaker, though he had taken his Chair,
was unable to command attention. To prevent further commotion
he directed that the man be taken through the side doors and
upstairs into what was called the 'prison room', and that a select
group of members should go ahead of the Sergeant and prepare
to conduct an enquiry. He also gave orders that the doors leading
into Westminster Hall and the street should be locked.

In the prison room Bellingham was stripped of his coat, waistcoat, and neckcloth, and held pinioned by the arms while two
Members who were magistrates conducted the proceedings. The
prisoner was observed to be a tall, large-boned man of about
forty, with a narrow face and aquiline nose. Michael Angelo
Taylor, the senior magistrate in charge, invited General Gascoyne
to speak first. To everyone's surprise he said he had met the man
before. Bellingham had called on him three weeks previously, and
had described himself as a timber merchant. It seemed that he
had been under arrest in Russia and had been refused compensation for the loss of property at sea. It was Gascoyne himself who
had advised his visitor to make representations to a member of the
Cabinet. Joseph Hume, the expert on window tax, spoke next.
He told how on hearing a shot he had run into the lobby from the

Commons and found himself forcibly propelled towards the fire-place. There he came up against Bellingham, who was being jostled this way and that, while his arms were held by the General. It was Hume who had snatched the small pistol from his hand, and he described how on searching the man it was found that a 'pocket extraordinary' had been sewn into his tunic for the concealment of his weapon. At last called upon to speak, Bellingham said no more at this stage than that the General had twisted his arm so ferociously he feared it would be broken. Then Mr. Phillips of Longsight Hall, near Manchester, related how he was standing by the fire and ran forward and supported Perceval's head after he had fallen. Mr. Phillips gathered him into his arms, where he died almost at once. At this the prisoner began to weep, and was heard to murmur, 'I wish I were in his place.' After Mr. Jordan of Old Brompton had claimed that he was the first to secure the prisoner (the General having arrived a moment later) Bellingham was again ordered to speak and this time to explain himself. 'I am a most unfortunate man,' he was saying, 'and feel I have sufficient justification for what I have done,' when Lord Castlereagh entered and asked him whether he was prepared to make his defence in public trial. 'Since it seems best to you that I should not now explain the causes of my conduct,' replied Bellingham, 'I will leave it until the day of my trial when my country will have an opportunity of judging whether I am right or wrong.'

He was then removed to the Secretary of State's office, and the rabble outside was heard singing for joy and loudly applauding the assassin. As he climbed into the carriage to be taken to Newgate the mob opened the opposite door while others climbed on top and tried to knock a hole in the roof. The prisoner was therefore taken back into the House and not again brought out until a detachment of Life Guards had formed a protective semi-circle in Lower Palace Yard.

In his cell at Newgate Bellingham gave more information about himself. He was born at St. Neots in Huntingdonshire and had a wife and three children living in Liverpool. He had spent most of the afternoon which had just passed in the company of his land-lady, admiring the exhibits in the European Museum. They stayed, much entertained by the interesting curiosities, until after four o'clock, when he suggested they should take a stroll. This they did, enjoying the mildness of the weather, until he parted from his companion at the corner of Sydney Alley with the excuse that he was going 'to buy a prayer book'. He walked alone and at leisure to the House of Commons. As for his fire-arms, he had bought them some time before and had practised with them every day for a fortnight on Primrose Hill. 'For eight years,' he said, 'I have never found my mind so tranquil as since this melancholy but necessary catastrophe.' He then asked that a message be taken to his landlady in Milman Street, for he desired to wear his best clothes at the trial.

Meanwhile the body had been removed to Downing Street, where Nollekens the sculptor was admitted under orders to superintend the making of a death mask, and Lord Redesdale, the dead man's brother-in-law, had driven to the Manor House at Ealing with the task of breaking the news to the widow. At the time of the outrage Mrs. Perceval was taking tea with Mrs. Ryder, wife of the Secretary of State, close by in Great George Street. The surgeon who was summoned to the House must have gone hastening by her very window. After hearing the news she neither wept nor spoke nor seemed to hear a word that was uttered in her presence, and she remained in this trance-like condition of suspended feeling until the noon of next day. Alarmed by this inability to release her pent-up grief, members of her household tried to excite her to some show of emotion by repeating to her slowly the terrible news and enlarging on the tragic consequences to the family, but to no avail. It did nothing to dispel their anxiety when they considered that Mrs. Perceval was pregnant with her twentieth child. At length it was decided to take her to the room in Downing Street where her husband lay in state. There at last she broke down.

It was now Monday, and the Lords and Commons were met. The Duke of York read a message from the Prince Regent, then Lord Liverpool rose to deliver a second message from Carlton House, but could not speak for tears. He resumed his seat and handed the document to one of the Lord Chancellor's clerks, who read it in his stead. It was resolved that on the following day the entire House of Lords should wait upon the Prince Regent at Carlton House. In the Commons Lord Castlereagh, seconded by Canning, moved that a loyal address be sent to the Regent, and went on to make a proposal concerning the welfare of the bereaved

family. He moved that the widow should receive £1,000 a year
for the duration of her life, and that a sum of £50,000 be granted
to the Regent for him to hold in trust for the twelve surviving
children and their descendants. 'It would not be proper,'
he said, 'to make a grant to the family of Mr. Perceval which
might cease upon the death of an individual and leave the rest
destitute.'

Although nobody wished to show himself wanting in sympathy
for the bereaved, Castlereagh's proposal, involving so great a sum,
was not at once approved. What tipped the balance was a speech
by Mr. Lushington in which he described Lord Arden weeping
by the body. 'You are gone—you are gone to Heaven,' he had
cried out in his distress. 'You are gone . . . but your children——?'
Here Mr. Lushington paused and a voice at the back of the House
called out, 'His children are his country's!' After this, when Mr.
Huskisson rose to suggest the payment of a special annuity for the
eldest son's education there was no murmur of opposition. Next
morning the Lords, dressed in black, and led by the Dukes of
York and Cumberland, walked in slow procession to Carlton
House, where, after being informed of the various financial recommendations, the Prince Regent made a short speech. 'It is a most
beneficial mode of disposing of the public money,' he said, 'and
one most gratifying to my feelings, in marking with peculiar
distinction the family of an individual whose talents and virtues
have been snatched by an act of unparalleled atrocity from the
service of his country.' And so it came about that Spencer, the
eldest boy, Edward Marsh's grandfather, was able to continue his
studies at Harrow, and Marsh himself, on the death of an uncle
almost exactly a century later, found himself the heir of one-sixth
of Castlereagh's grant.

On May 15 Bellingham was tried by Sir James Mansfield in the
presence of the Duke of Clarence. The only witness who made
some attempt to defend the prisoner's character was a maid-
servant in the Milman Street house where he lodged. She declared
that on the day of the incident Bellingham had attended both
matins and evensong at the Foundling Hospital Chapel. Sir James
was not impressed. The prisoner himself, when invited to speak,
remained on his feet for an hour. He began by thanking the
Attorney-General for effectively disposing of the plea of insanity
which the defending counsel had been so foolish as to put forward.

He told how in 1804 he had been seized in his carriage at the Russian frontier by orders of the military governor at Archangel. A merchant ship owned by him and his partner had been lost in the White Sea, and although he had taken the precaution of having it insured at Lloyd's Coffee House he had received no compensation. On getting no sympathy from the British in Russia he became violent and abusive in his protests, as he admitted, and was thrown into prison without trial. On his return to England he consulted one authority after another, beginning with the Marquess Wellesley, and at last was advised to petition Parliament. This he set about doing after his third appeal to the Prince Regent had elicited no reply. He then called on his own M.P., General Gascoyne, the Member for Liverpool, who advised him to get the sanction of a Cabinet minister. This led to an interview with Spencer Perceval, who saw no good reason to support his claims. 'I have no malice toward the Mr. Prime Minister,' said the prisoner. 'In fact had it been Lord Granville who had entered at that moment *he* would have received the ball.' He went on: 'It is a melancholy fact that the warping of justice, including all the various ramifications in which it operates, occasions more misery in the world, in a moral sense, than all the acts of God, in a physical one, with which he punishes mankind for their transgressions, in confirmation of which, the simple but strong instance before you is remarkable proof. . . . I submit to the fiat of my fate, firmly anticipating an acquittal from a charge so abhorrent to every feeling of my soul.' Before giving sentence of death, the judge summarized the enormity of his crime: 'You have been found guilty of the murder of a person whose suavity of manners disarmed hostility and rancour. By his death Charity has been deprived of its warmest friend, Religion of its best support, and the Country of its greatest ornament.'

Ever since the time of Richard II the Perceval family had been concerned with the collection of revenues. Spencer Perceval himself was a son of the Earl of Egmont by Catherine Crompton who was later created Baroness Arden of the county of Cork. The Earl is reported by Horace Walpole as having never been seen to laugh 'though he was indeed seen to smile, and that was at chess'. His fanatical love of tradition was carried to such a pitch that when building himself a mansion near Bridgwater he had it designed so as to be defensible by crossbows and arrows 'against the time in which the fabric and use of gunpowder shall be forgotten'. His second son, Spencer, was born in Audley Square in 1762 and named after his mother's brother, the Earl of Northampton. After completing his studies at Harrow and Trinity College, Cambridge, he married Jane Wilson, daughter of the lord of the manor of Charlton, the village where the Earl of Egmont had built a characteristically old-fashioned mansion, and where his children were to spend their early years. A timely and persuasive political tract brought Perceval to the notice of Pitt, and in April 1796 on the death of one of the Members for Northampton he was granted the seat by special writ. After he had made his first speech in Parliament Richard Brinsley Sheridan rose to welcome the new Member, asserting that 'this was a speech of great talent, great ingenuity, and considerable force'. The newspaper next day was no less encouraging: 'His delivery wanted dignity, but he spoke, however, with great ease and grace, and his clear and musical voice joined to the benevolent softness and unaffected placidity of his manners made a deep impression on the House.' By 1807 he had risen to the position of Chancellor of the Exchequer, and when the Duke of Portland died in 1809 he was appointed to succeed him as First Lord of the Treasury and Prime Minister. At the time of his death he was in his fiftieth year. Together with the tragedy at Westminster the newspapers were reporting a French retreat in the Peninsula. The literary news was the publication of the first instalment of *Childe Harold*. In painting they were advertising a Wilkie exhibition in Pall Mall.

ii

In 1811, seven months before his death, the Prime Minister had sent his eldest son at Harrow the complete set of Bell's Edition of the Poets, each volume of convenient pocket size and embellished with an elegantly engraved frontispiece. The covering letter was dated from the Manor House at Ealing: 'The possession of the Poets which I conceive to be a very great Treasure for you and to make almost a library in itself may afford you much valuable amusement, if you consult them freely.' He advised the boy to read the epistles and satires of Horace 'which Pope did not translate but imitate' and compare them with the originals, and to do likewise with Dryden's transcriptions from Juvenal.

Nay, it will not be time flung away if after having read, or while you are reading, a Book of Virgil or of Horace you look at Dryden's translations of the one and Pope's of the other. This will improve and enrich your knowledge of the English language which, at least, is the language that you will have most occasion in life to employ and which perhaps is generally too little attended to in schools. Not that I would have you attend to *that* in preference to the learned languages, but *neither* should be neglected. Remember this is the last year of your schooling and that I have always told you more may be done in the last year than in any of the five years which have preceded it. From your Mother's account of the heat in which she has twice found you I fear that football is upon the whole a more favourite pursuit with you than your books.

The boy (Spencer Perceval II) did not inherit the family gift in matters of finance. He was notoriously spendthrift, but his father's injunction to cultivate a love of English literature was duly respected and obeyed. The realization that those fifty little volumes, contained in two boxes, were the last gift he would ever receive from a parent so untimely lost may have added a pious zeal to his study of their contents. The younger Spencer was responsible for a quotation made in a speech to the House of Commons which became famous for its aptness and wit. The day before a debate on the delicate question of Queen Caroline he was consulted by Lord Brougham on how reference might be made to George IV without actually mentioning him by name. Perceval at once drew his attention to the description of Death in the second book of *Paradise Lost*, and this, when reference to the monarch could no longer be deferred, was slipped into the stream of Lord Brougham's discourse:

> . . . *what seem'd his head*
> *The likeness of a kingly crown had on.*

Some time before 1830 Spencer Perceval met the Rev. Edward Irving, the son of a tanner of Annan, and immediately came under the spell of his zealous and unconventional personality. Three years later Irving was excommunicated by the Church of Scotland. He died in 1834, leaving a group of 'apostles', with his friend Perceval among them, to found the religious body which styled itself the Catholic Apostolic Church, known popularly as the Irvingite faith. Ritualism, symbolism, and a belief in the gift of tongues, were prominent features in its form of worship, and Perceval set forth its principles in a treatise which he distributed

personally in all the drawing-rooms to which he managed to gain
admittance. The *Greville Memoirs* for 1836 record his failure to
button-hole the Duke of Wellington, also his interview with
Lord Holland when two lusty pages were posted outside the door
with strict orders to 'rush in if they heard Lord Holland scream'.
In accordance with his faith the author was excessively modest.
'I am aware', he would say on presenting a copy of his tract, 'that
it is not well written. The composition is not perfect, but I was not
permitted to alter it. I was *obliged* to write it as I received it.'
While in Scotland Irving brought Perceval and Carlyle together
(Irving was among the first to recognize Carlyle's genius) and it
was probably through the same friend that on a visit to Skye
Perceval called at Dunvegan Castle during the 1820s and met
Anna MacLeod of MacLeod, whom he subsequently married and
took with him to his headquarters in Rome, where he was sent
soon after the wedding to serve as the Irvingite 'Angel' in Italy.

There were ten children of the marriage. Jane, the youngest of
seven daughters, named after Jane Wilson of Charlton, Prime
Minister Perceval's wife, was born in 1836. By the time she came
to England in her early twenties she was fluent in Italian and
French, and something of an authority on Italian art. Though not
herself a convert to her father's beliefs, the evangelical form of
religion which became the mainspring of her life was also the
source of her extraordinary strength, and nobility, as well as nar-
rowness of character. About seven years after the founding of the
Children's Hospital in Great Ormond Street she joined forces
with its founder, Miss Wood, and she was working there as the
matron of a ward (one of the first of many women to be inspired
by the example of Florence Nightingale) when in the autumn of
1859 her father died. Mrs. Villiers (the grandmother of Victor
Lytton, who was to be a lifelong friend of Jane's only son) wrote
in sympathy to Anna, the widow: 'Who was so humble and sweet
tempered, so clever and fascinating as that dear fellow?' She was
afraid that none of the Compensation Grant might come to the
rescue of the bereaved family. 'I dread the evils of real poverty
being added to your troubles. That was dear Spencer's weak side.
He was not *practical*, but how could he be so? Had he calculated
pounds, shillings and pence he would not have been Spencer
Perceval. He took the text of the lilies of the field somewhat literally, and I admired him for so doing. There are enough, goodness

knows, to look after the world's pelf. Still I should grieve that you, dearest, or any of his, suffered any of the cankering cares of real destitution.' The worst did not happen. The second Spencer's share of Lord Castlereagh's grant accrued to his wife for herself and her children, and from it she made a handsome donation to the Alexandra Hospital for Children with Hip Disease, in Queen Street, which her daughter Jane founded in 1867 and to which she devoted her life.

Apart from the benefit to the medical amenities of London, the new hospital was to bring about a transformation in the life of its founder. In 1869 she was thirty-three. The fashionable age for marriage had passed her by, but she had no regrets. The children in her care were family enough, or so it had seemed for several years. Any other kind of life or occupation was unthinkable. After the struggle to leave home in the first place and take up a profession, Jane was not going to give up the ground she had won. It was at this time that a new housesurgeon was called in for consultation and taken on the staff.

Frederick Howard Marsh was Miss Perceval's junior by three years. He was born at Homersfield, Suffolk, in 1839, the second son of Edward Marsh, an impoverished farmer who 'left very little impression on the minds of those who knew him best'. Marsh was fortunate in his marriage. Maria Hayward came of a Norwich farming family, and after the death of her first husband she married Marsh, who was her junior by eleven years. The anonymous author of the Memoir of her son, the distinguished surgeon, gives her credit as being the source of qualities which were observed in her descendants.

> She was tall and good-looking, able and shrewd, and hated every form of pretence and sham. She had the power of summing up people in a single sentence and of saying what was very difficult to answer. She must, however, have exercised this dangerous faculty with much discretion, for her advice was in great request, more especially with her newly married neighbours, for she was also a consummate housekeeper.[1]

Her second son took it upon himself to change his name from Hayward to Howard. He had studied medicine under Sir James Paget, to whom he owed his upbringing and the benefit of his first post at St. Bartholomew's Hospital. At the age of twenty-nine he was

---

[1] *A Memoir of Edward Marsh, F.R.C.S.* John Murray, 1921.

already considered an authority on diseases of the bone and had begun lecturing. His success as a teacher was largely due to his custom of illustrating with an anecdote each new technical point he made, so that the students (among whom was Robert Bridges, who preferred to become a poet) never lost sight of the human and practical application. He was no innovator, but his remarkable talent for clear exposition and apt illustration was soon to make him one of the leading surgical teachers of his day.

At this time, however, Howard Marsh was poor, having no private means, and conscious of his relatively obscure origin compared with that of the Miss Perceval with whom he was falling in love. Their work was the bond they shared. Outside the hospital they were strangers, and the years which were to come did little to lessen the difference between them. Miss Perceval had an august and rather formidable mother and two sisters, now living at Lowndes Street, who could be seen in Hyde Park on Sunday mornings riding in a handsomely caparisoned barouche with a footman on the box. She was cosmopolitan, and looked upon Italy as her second home; she was widely read in English and Italian literature, and at all times of doubt or stress could turn to the Church for spiritual support. Her admirer shared none of this. His work was everything. There he had imagination, extraordinary precision of thought, and even a dry sense of humour. Away from it he was a man of few words, lacking in sentiment, with a temperament alien alike to the fervently religious and the intellectual worlds where Jane seemed equally at home. It was something to his advantage that he did not also have the world of fashion to contend with. If good fortune had not endowed Miss Perceval with natural graces her positively aggressive lack of personal vanity might have proved a considerable handicap. Throughout the fashion for crinolines she considered them absurd to the point of wickedness, and continued to present her natural proportions to her acquaintance when a woman who was not distorted according to the vogue was thought wantonly eccentric. Spared the embarrassment of trying to live up to a great lady of fashion, Mr. Marsh was nevertheless discomfited when he observed her standing in the presence of a piece of sculpture by Michelangelo, having lost her accustomed poise so far as to be shedding tears. This seemed to him irrational, as indeed it was. Ten years later he was to discover his small son in a similar condition with no apparent cause for grief beyond a volume of Milton open in his lap.

In the spring of 1870 Howard Marsh married Jane Perceval in St. George's, Bloomsbury. They took lodgings in 38 Guilford Street, where a year later their first child, a daughter, Mary, was born. They were still colleagues at the Alexandra when on November 18, 1872, a son was born, whom they named Edward after his paternal grandfather of Homersfield, and Howard after his paternal grandmother, preserving the corruption of the name by his father. Eight months later when the mother was again with child the infant Mary died. Jane was soon delivered of a second daughter, whom they called Margaret. They had no more children. Determined to avoid a repetition of Mary's tragedy, they moved the two surviving children into the country on the slightest suspicion of an epidemic in the metropolis. It was to be one of these visits out of town which finally confirmed the bent for imaginative literature in the little fair-haired boy whom his mother, to match his baby sister Maggie, had decided to call Eddie.

On his seventh birthday he was sitting alone by the window of his bedroom in the new house, 36 Bruton Street, London, with the Bible on his lap lying open at the first chapter of the Gospel according to St. John. 'Hallo,' he suddenly said aloud, 'I can read!'

Chapter Two

MOTHER AND SON
(1880–1891)

EDDIE's home education, which Howard Marsh left entirely in the hands of his wife, had 'a *Sandford and Merton* tinge about it' as he said in after times, and was about thirty years out of date. The parents had little opportunity of making friends outside the hospital, so that Jane's benevolent but outmoded methods by which every subject somehow became diverted into a homily on one of the Ten Commandments were never modified by contact with new ideas. There was no social life for them beyond an occasional call on the aunts at Lowndes Street or Ealing, and an annual invitation to the garden party in the grounds of Fulham Palace. There Eddie first discovered strawberry ices, which he thought a special invention by the Bishop of London, and was much put out when he later found them being sold indiscriminately on the front at Whitby. It may have been on the same holiday that he was looking into the window of a curiosity shop when it seemed as though the potential wonders of poetry were flashed upon him. On a dirty slip of paper which was stuck to the inside of the glass a single stanza was written in a childish scrawl:

> I pointed out the blessing
> That Civilation be.
> He wished he were a Heathen
> Asitting by the sea.

He had started visiting the day-school run by two ladies, Miss Scripps and her sister Miss Fanny, down the road in Bruton Street. His private lessons at home soon gave him a sophisticated outlook beyond his years, so that he could not restrain a smile of superiority when in an English class Miss Fanny pronounced *Et tu, Brute* as if it were French; and he felt obliged to complain to the senior mistress when in a 'List of Words Spelt differently

13

but Pronounced Alike' he found included as a pair—*Engine* and *Indian*. He was disconcertingly teachable, and after his first term of Latin not only won full marks in the paper but in the oral test revealed that he had committed a good deal of the Latin Primer to memory, thereby anticipating the syllabus for next term.

His life was bounded by the Scripps Academy and the hospital. To him the Alexandra was a playground. His earliest memories were of being chased by the patients, 'the little Hip-hoppers' as he called them, up and down the wards. It was his only recreation, for he was never given any toys except a paint-box and a packet of 'comic' playing-cards. Reading the books which his mother with scrupulous supervision allowed him was both his moral instruction and his play. He was seven when she started him on poetry by reading Shakespeare aloud, but he was not permitted to 'see' it until a copy of Dr. Bowdler's edition had been procured. After his first year with Miss Scripps, bed-time was at nine and it was always preceded by a period of reading which started punctually at eight. His introduction to non-dramatic verse began with *L'Allegro*, which he had to learn by heart, omitting the slightly dubious preamble in which Zephyr 'fills' Aurora with the 'buxom Euphrosyne'. *Lycidas* followed, and some time in his ninth year his mother read him the first book of *Paradise Lost*, which he has recorded as the first major aesthetic experience of his life. Jane was a beautiful reader and greatly skilled at what was called giving 'expression'. She used to say that if she had been a man she would have chosen the profession of an actor. That she might have been an actress was of course out of the question. Fiction began with the Waverley novels, *Marmion* and *The Lay of the Last Minstrel* being thrown in by way of contrast, all of which led him to the conclusion that Scott was as good as Shakespeare. So Scott was judiciously given a rest and Jane 'performed' the whole of *Hamlet*, enacting the Ghost to telling effect, in a desperate effort to redress the balance. He was then given Mr. Mackay's *Thousand and One Gems of Poetry* and told to learn Southey's *Cataract of Lodore* as a memory test. For this he was rewarded with half-a-crown, but it was on his own initiative that at the age of twelve he committed to memory the first four books of *Paradise Lost*, which must be a record in the annals of precociousness. He was still at the Academy down the road when Shelley was put in his way, and he has described how he read Swinburne's *Triumph of*

Time 'twice or thrice in such an ecstasy that it never occurred to me to consider what it was about—not that I could say very clearly now'. At the age of ten he was considered too advanced for Miss Scripps and indeed already beyond the junior standard of a public school. For the end of term play he was cast as Portia but forbidden to appear on the grounds of 'over excitement'. It was not known at home that he had fallen in love with Shylock's little sister, who for some obscure reason presented him with a small pair of iron pincers as a token of her esteem. Eddie found the gift inappropriate and suffered but few pangs of separation when the morning walks began across St. James's Park to his new school at Westminster.

He entered Westminster as a day boy at the unusually early age of ten, with an Exhibition worth thirty pounds a year, and for at least two terms thought the word meant that he must hold himself in readiness for exhibition to visiting parents as an exceptionally clever boy. Three years later, a few weeks after his thirteenth birthday, he would have had somewhat better grounds for this agreeable opinion of himself, had he wished to entertain it, for in December 1885 he finished translating all five acts of the *Andria* of Terence into English prose. His first ambitious essay in translation already showed something of that gift for racy colloquial speech which he brought to the service of La Fontaine, his second big task in translation, almost half a century later.

In the year when he was devoting so much free time to his Roman comedy Uncle Norman Perceval came into his life. There were several relations to whom he had to be civil on occasion. At the Manor House at Ealing, the old Perceval home, three of the Prime Minister's daughters were still living, and at Lowndes Street there were his grandmother MacLeod and two of her daughters, including Helen, the favourite aunt, who looked like a Muse in a drawing by Rossetti. Norman was the youngest of Jane Marsh's brothers. From the start his life had gone awry. He had resigned a commission in the Army after an impulsive marriage in the colonies (in Java, it was supposed, though no one knew for sure) and had settled with his wife in West Kensington, there to be 'bored as nearly to extinction as a human being can be without being actually extinguished', and his only known occupation after leaving the service was the secretaryship of an obscure institution for providing old soldiers with jobs as window-cleaners. His wife, Aunt Bessie, was loved by the little Eddie, who was touched by her demonstrative affection and amused by her easygoing ways. In return for his providing a link with the family whose adult members were not accustomed to doing him the honour of a call, Uncle Norman would take the boy to meals at his favourite haunt, the Rag, and show him the sights of London, among them the National Gallery where one day he planted him before Turner's *Fighting Téméraire*. 'That's a very *dangerous* picture!' exclaimed Eddie in an awed whisper, and began his career as an art connoisseur. But Uncle Norman did more than this. For many another boy of Eddie's age an occasional spree round the sights would have been fun and no more. For Eddie Marsh, whose life had so far been unusually circumscribed, it was a first bewildering glimpse of the great world.

The year 1887 was of special consequence. It began with a visit to Bournemouth, where his mother called upon Lady Taylor, the widow of Sir Henry Taylor, author of *Philip van Artevelde*, a poetic drama much admired in its day. When Mrs. Marsh and her son were shown into the drawing-room Aubrey de Vere was just leaving. De Vere, the friend of Tennyson and Browning, had been an ardent supporter of Taylor's verse dramas, and no doubt he had called to condole with his friend's wife. It was suggested that Eddie should stand on a footstool and perform the *Cataract of Lodore*, or any piece of Milton de Vere might choose to mention. This was a rash offer, and probably to everyone's relief it was declined and the poet went his way. A trivial incident, but the boy remembered it as the first time he had ever seen a poet face to face. A little later his mother took him for his first visit to the theatre, a performance of *The Mikado* at the Savoy, and shortly after he was shown Irving and Ellen Terry in *The Merchant of Venice*, the play which he had last seen done under the direction of Miss Scripps. Sarah Bernhardt in *Phèdre* he saw more than once. He was to discover that in the case of French literature his mother's moral standards were slightly lowered so as not to rule out altogether such authors as Racine and Molière.

In June, having already reached the top form at Westminster at the age of fourteen, he was the youngest commoner present in the Abbey for the Queen's first Jubilee, and together with his companions led the shouts of *Vivat Regina*. His arrival in the seventh form about three years before the customary age had brought him another privilege of more enduring value. There is no doubt that the four years he spent as one of the pupils directly under the headmaster, the great scholar Gunion Rutherford, substantially influenced his life. He was always acutely susceptible to the personal influence of anyone he really admired. Milton was inevitably associated in his mind with his mother, and all the more closely for the ever-increasing resistance he felt impelled to put up against what was by far the most dominating aspect of her character—her religion. And now Rutherford, with his ardour which seemed to lift an ordinary school lesson right out of the narrow bounds of the classroom into life itself, became the guiding influence. He was renowned for his pointed Johnsonian pronouncements delivered in a broad Scottish accent—'I thought people were *born* knowing the date of the battle of Leuktra!' With his reverence for the classics as living literature, he was the embodiment of high scholarship, and his subject of course was Greek. By comparison with the time spent on Greek, Divinity was perfunctory, and Latin a miserable poor relation. A newcomer to his class either observed him with awe and proceeded to become one of his disciples, or languished for want of a teacher and a subject more fitting to his temperament. Of the former kind was Eddie Marsh, not at first for the subject's sake, but because he was impressed by the man; and with him was J. S. Phillimore, who in the final examinations beat him by only one mark and went on to become Professor of Greek at Glasgow. In Marsh and Phillimore Rutherford soon recognized two pupils who would repay special and even loving attention. One of his remarks, though made in reference to classical scholarship, might have been given as a motto for Marsh's whole life. He certainly never forgot it. 'Nine-tenths of the Tradition may be rubbish, but the remaining tenth is priceless, and no one who tries to dispense with it can hope to do anything that is good.'

By the end of the summer term 1887 the boy had acquired through Uncle Norman a taste for aesthetic and slightly raffish pursuits, and through Rutherford a religion of scholarship weighing heavily on the other side of the scale. But the year's events were not over with the discovery of Greek. In July he was taken ill. He had shot up several inches in the last year and had become a blonde and lanky creature with an erratic voice on the point of breaking. He had outgrown his strength, and possibly the excitements of Bernhardt, Irving, Rutherford, Swinburne, and a domestic upheaval occasioned by the family's move to a bigger house, 30 Bruton Street, all compressed within a few months, had overtaxed his mind. He was gawky, clumsy, spotty, subject to fits of ill-temper, and already in a weakened condition, when mumps complicated by German measles, a particularly virulent infection in those days, sent him to bed, where he remained for most of the summer holidays, unable to shake off the languor which had followed so sudden and so sharp an attack. It was decided not to send him back to Westminster for the autumn term. Instead, lodgings were taken for him at Cold Ash, near Newbury, where Howard Marsh was consulting surgeon at the local hospital and so could look in on the boy from time to time. Jane had her work at the Alexandra, but there was a family acquaintance living near by, a widow with two sons of her own, who was willing to adopt the child for the period of his convalescence, though for fear of lingering infection she could not at first have him under her own roof.

Laura Denniston had come back from India the year before in order to make ready a home for her husband, an official in the Indian Civil Service, who was about to retire. She did not know of his death on board just before sailing until she saw his replacement announced in a newspaper. She was a woman of considerable charm who matched the easygoing ways of Aunt Bessie with a mind cultivated in literature beyond the attainments of Jane Marsh herself, and the atmosphere of her home was less fervently evangelical than at Bruton Street. With her even Sundays were tolerable. The day she called round at the lodgings with a volume of Jane Austen under her arm was a landmark for Eddie Marsh even greater than the evening when he saw his first page of *Paradise Lost*. What was perhaps most remarkable about Mrs. Denniston was her disinclination to subject a child's reading to any kind of censorship. At home *The Heart of Midlothian* had been banned because of the seduction of Effie, *David Copperfield* for the fate of Emily, and several pages of Byron were sealed with sticking plaster; but here, at the house called Highfield at the top of the hill—once the requisite number of days for quarantine had passed—Eddie was shown a little attic filled to the roof, as it seemed, with novels and the works of Elizabethan dramatists, new names to him, Massinger, Webster, Ford; and up there, as if he had stumbled on a gold nugget, he found *The Faerie Queene*. Any of these he was allowed to read, even on a Sunday, when at home he would have been fumbling laboriously at his missionary needle-work. Opposition to his mother's view of life grew stronger and more daring. Mrs. Denniston did not seem to share his mother's opinion that the End of the World was at hand, nor was it a wish near to her heart that her son Gilbert should be martyred by Antichrist so as to be among the first of the elect at the Second Coming. This was indeed a strange departure from what Eddie had come to regard as the natural thing, but as yet he showed no leanings towards agnosticism. On the contrary, it may have been another result of these weeks at Cold Ash that on returning to London he asked to be taken to St. Alban's, Holborn, where the ritual was High Church and the renowned Father Stanton ex-horted his hearers in vehement sermons, almost hurling himself bodily from the pulpit.

At St. George's, Hanover Square, where he had been attending both matins and evensong every Sunday, he had devised and perfected a form of defence against tedium which he called 'sleeping without jerks'. He could put away his consciousness at will, like a pocket-handkerchief, somehow control his movements while asleep, and wake up with a promptness and complete lack of heaviness which gave the impression that he must have been awake all along. This gift he retained throughout his life, though he confined its practice to the after-luncheon snooze which under no circumstances would he ever forgo. In one movement he would open his eyes, sit up, take his watch from his pocket, look at it, and if it was a little too early, drop off again as if he had suddenly received a blow on the head. Since he passed on this strict regimen of an after-luncheon 'coma', as he called it, to Winston Churchill (and it may be imagined some measure of his knack in the conscious control over the senses), the pious but uninspiring preacher during the 'eighties in Hanover Square may be said to have performed a national service.

He went back to school for the Easter term (1888) and was allowed to revisit Cold Ash for the holidays. It took Jane Marsh some time to realize that Laura Denniston's influence was in conflict with her own. Not that anyone was deliberately concealing anything, but certain books had fallen into Eddie's hands which were returned with thanks before he could read them, and a gentle remonstrance by letter was necessary, while at home the regulations were tightened. 'I really am in earnest about novels,' Jane had written to her son at Cold Ash. 'You have read too many while you have been there, and I think you cannot have done so with quite a clear conscience, knowing my wishes so well. The life of Charlotte Brontë is not very useful reading at your age.' Uncle Norman was reprimanded for taking his nephew to an unsuitable play at the Haymarket, and Howard Marsh himself was discouraged from ever making another attempt at spending an evening out with the boy when he got back after seeing William Terriss in *The Bells of Haslemere* and found himself thoroughly in disgrace. This by now was no unusual thing. Husband and wife had begun to find that the bond of their work among the crippled children was no longer enough. It had become the custom after dinner for the family to sit and converse in separate rooms, Maggie with her father and Eddie with his mother; for all their differences of opinion, they were never more close to each other than now, she never doubting that her son would one day by heaven's grace come round to her religious way of thinking, and he quite agreeable to believing for a little longer that a miracle might happen. Never for a moment did he resent her strict surveillance of his reading. It only meant that while away from home he felt himself under an obligation to curb his curiosity in the attic at Highfield. The emotional tie between them was very great. With his father he was tongue-tied and ill at ease.

During the second visit to Cold Ash Mrs. Denniston drove over to Yattenden, and Eddie, now getting on for fifteen, went for a walk through the meadows with Robert Bridges, who wanted to know all about the Mr. Marsh whom he had known at Bart's. Eddie took note of his loose-fitting clothes, brightly coloured tie, and the slight impediment in his speech. Asked to name his favourite poem, he replied 'Shelley's *On a poet's lips I slept*', and felt encouraged when Bridges declared that he seemed to have surprisingly good taste for one so young. When they got home from the walk Bridges brought out some manuscripts by a friend of his, a Jesuit priest. The boy remembered the line 'O look at all the fire-folk sitting in the air!' but never saw it again until 1918, when Bridges sent him the poems of Gerard Manley Hopkins in print.

The next eighteen months were spent in arduous preparation

for the university. He was pinning his hopes on Oxford, but his mother had already foreseen the choice, and confided in Dr. Rutherford, urging him to plant in her son's mind the seeds of a preference for Cambridge. The High Church atmosphere at Oxford might confirm deplorable tendencies in that direction which were already only too apparent. Rutherford was disturbed on other grounds. Eddie was listless in class. Phillimore was having it all his own way in the rivalry. Some deep-seated unrest or anxiety seemed almost to be changing the boy's character. It was suggested that perhaps his serious illness, coming as it did at the beginning of his adolescence, had caused a more drastic interruption in his development than anyone had so far supposed. It was some months before these misgivings came to a head. Meanwhile an epidemic of influenza suited Eddie perfectly, and he was sent with his sister to Cold Ash for the Christmas holidays.

By the time he left London at least one source of his disquiet had come to an end, though it meant a loss to the family. Ever since the move to a larger house in Bruton Street it had been difficult for his parents to make ends meet. They had not confided in him, he was still a child in their eyes, but he had overheard remarks, and the constant and vexatious little economies left him in no doubt. The situation had become serious, when Anna Perceval died at the great age of ninety-eight and bequeathed to her married daughter a share of what Eddie called the 'murder money' which she had come into on the death of her husband. Born in 1792, Anna MacLeod enjoyed the distinction of having been befriended when a little girl by Walter Scott, who had mentioned her in his Journal—'my favourite Nancy [Anna] MacLeod'. She had always been a moral support to Jane Marsh through the years when gradually mounting difficulties at home had given Jane the need of a confidante, and she had always taken an active interest in her grandson's education. In the last month of her life she wrote to him, 'Have you seen the popular Edition of Macaulay's Works published by Longman, 5 vols.? You had better look at it before you make your intended purchase', and she enclosed the money. The strong personality which had held the family together was now gone, but with Eddie coming to the university age the money was providential. Jane could now take the children abroad, which she had longed to do. But for the boy in his present condition she feared Italy might be too stimulating.

A cruise in the Norwegian fjords would probably be more advantageous, and without the distractions of sightseeing she might be able to regain some of the ground she had lost in her religious dispute with him. He was growing away from her, and from Christ. So with the prospect of a sea trip after his last term at school Eddie once more escorted his sister to the little red-brick house on the top of the hill at Cold Ash.

Although he still could not altogether shake off the extraordinary languor which had taken hold of him, he seemed to revive under Laura Denniston's care. On Christmas Day 1889 he began a commonplace book and for the next few weeks amused himself by ornamenting its pages. He entitled it *The Paradise of Dainty Devices*. For the frontispiece he had to go to Winchester Cathedral, where he made an ink drawing of Jane Austen's grave, and on the opposite page he copied out the long inscription. There followed a water-colour drawing of the hills above Newbury seen through the bare branches of a tree, with an apt quotation from a Shakespeare sonnet beneath; a chorus from *Atalanta* on the page adjoining; his own translation of a sonnet by Petrarch; a joke, 'There is nae luck aboot the hoose when E.H.M.'s awa', a drawing of Mrs. Denniston's house (a small, square, two-storeyed building) with four complimentary lines from *The Faerie Queene* to match it; a garish tulip blossom painted above the phrase 'Motley's the only wear', and a parody of Milton addressed to Mrs. Denniston's elder boy, beginning 'Gilbert, of virtuous father virtuous son'. Perhaps the best item was a minutely detailed water-colour sketch of the drawing-room with a fire blazing in the hearth and beside it a bamboo table with an oil lamp and a few blobs to represent books. The flowers in the buff carpet stand out like handfuls of livid strawberries. He seems to have regretted his incapacity to make them merge with the background, for he wrote at the side 'The carpet is a libel'. Also in the margin he recorded: 'The books on the table were *Poems and Ballads*, Browning (vol. iii), *Goblin Market*, *Asolando*, Rossetti, Tennyson, *The Mill on the Floss*.'

Mrs. Denniston must have observed in Eddie one rather curious difference from the time when she had first met him immediately after his illness. His voice was softer and less distinct, as though he had injured his vocal chords, yet his laugh could be as resonant as ever. He had acquired two voices. As he himself remarked,

'Two voices are there. One is of the sea, but that's the one I
don't use', and many years later he was to claim that he had organ
tones enough at his command 'but I could never manage to use
them in conversation in what seemed to me a natural manner, and
if my choice lay between squeaking and gibbering like a ghost in
the streets of Rome and growling like Hamlet's father I preferred
the former. Perhaps this is because I can't hear myself talk—my
voice sounds to me quite normal.' But it was far from normal. His
speech sounded like a witty aside written in faded pencil. The
illness which had left him with a mode of expression strangely
appropriate to his unusual personality (though at first it might
give a misleading impression of weakness of character) had at the
same time affected his physical constitution in a more serious
way. The disease had determined the colour of his personality and
the course of his life so fundamentally that one cannot wish it to
have been otherwise, although the result was a disability. So early
in life did it happen, and the knowledge of it came so gradually,
there are no grounds for supposing he grieved that he was to be
incapable of the act of love, or minded at all that he was destined
from then on to live and die as chaste as the day he was born.
It enabled his affections to grow more intensely in the mind,
and as a result he cultivated a capacity for friendship which,
untroubled by physical desire, could develop into a devotion
characteristically feminine in its tenderness.

He was in Bruton Street again in the first week of February
1890, and Jane Marsh wrote in her Journal: 'E is getting more
and more interested in Browning. I am reading him too. There is
much to admire, but in his teaching there is something lacking, a
something that is lacking in the teacher himself. Does he feel the
need he has, his wife has, men and women have, of a Saviour? Is
he not all-sufficient to himself? Does he not believe that human
nature is all-suffering so as to form the perfect man?' Her sister
Helen was ill, still overwhelmed by the recent loss of her mother.
'Is it God's will she should recover? Perhaps she may yet survive
me. To depart and be with Christ is far better in itself, but if we
can serve God by living and suffering longer on earth that must
be—for us—better still.'

In the Easter holidays she drove with Eddie down to Ealing
to call on the old Percevals. On the way back she ventured to
ask him why he was doing less well at school and received an

unsatisfactory reply. 'I am far from happy about him,' she confided to her Journal. 'May God keep him from self-love and love of pleasure and from making his own will the only law he obeys. I can only pray and hope.' At the end of the term Rutherford gave him a bad report. 'He will not do things as duties,' he wrote. 'He will not act on principle.' In November a friend of the family invited him to Oxford. There was no reasonable way of preventing the visit, and he came back enthusiastic about all he had seen. His mother was perturbed. 'His faults will be fostered at Oxford which is more of a mutual admiration society than Cambridge.' She got no help from Howard, who did not care where the boy went so long as he kept out of mischief. With no Anna MacLeod to turn to, Jane had recourse to her Journal. 'I bring the matter before Thee and spread it out before thy Throne.' She went on to reflect on her boy's situation. 'I wish he had more principle and a stronger character, and that he were not so easily led. He has the wilfulness and obstinate clinging to his own way that weak characters have, just because it is for the moment his fancy, not because it is right and good—and then he is young for his age. It will be a great crisis in his life when he goes to College.' And at the foot of the page she scribbled, 'Am reading Thoreau, an American as queer as Whitman.'

During December she corresponded with Dr. Rutherford. He was of the opinion that Cambridge was the more likely place to induce the boy to work. 'Oxford might lead him to only a literary career which I deprecate strongly. . . . Let him try for a scholarship. If he fails, then Oxford. It would injure his career if he entered unwillingly and without the prestige of success.' Later in the month Jane saw him off at King's Cross. He wrote next day to say there were only four, not sixteen, open scholarships at Trinity (the college where his great-grandfather the Prime Minister had studied) but the papers so far were fairly easy. Meanwhile the school report was to hand, and Jane commented on the headmaster's remarks. 'He speaks of E's literary inclination and friendships as things he should throw off. Mr. Rutherford is very clever at discerning character and I do hope E will profit by his advice.'

Only now did Jane realize that Laura Denniston was to a great extent the cause of the trouble. By her conversation and frequent letters she had distracted Eddie from the even and sheltered course of his development. It was too late now to forbid him her companionship without widening the rift between the boy and herself. The very next day, however, she was given new hope. The boy's scholarship papers were said to show brilliant promise. Dr. Montagu Butler, the Master of Trinity, wrote direct to the successful candidate. 'Your translations are always pointed, intelligent, and interesting. Perhaps you will be able with further experience to give them rather more simplicity.' The news arrived on a Saturday, and next day the family, excluding Howard, to Jane's grief, attended seven o'clock Holy Communion at St. George's. The idea was to give thanks, but on the way home Eddie made it abundantly clear that he had gone solely to give worship. 'He maintained it was *he* who had won the scholarship,' Jane wrote in the Journal, '*not* the Almighty, and that a large measure of praise and glory was being misdirected.'

There were two more terms at Westminster. By the time he was due to leave he had won the Phillimore Translation Prize and another for Latin Verse. Then the trip to Norway began. By an odd coincidence a book which for years had been strictly banned by Jane was found in the cabin, left behind by a previous passenger. As a special holiday concession Eddie was allowed to read *Vanity Fair*, but the result was unfortunate. Nothing would induce him to go up on deck and admire the Norwegian scenery. He was reading. His mother's Journal pronounced the excursion to have been only a moderate success.

Returning in the middle of September Jane and Eddie spent the inside of a day at Cambridge, visited his rooms at Trinity, Room K in New Court, then went to the shops to buy furniture, of 'good, sound William Morris type'. Early in October they were back unpacking crates of chattels, arranging ornaments on the chimneypiece, interviewing the bed-maker, dragging into position the three wicker chairs and the bed like a cot open down one side with wooden bars along the back.

Eddie was agreeably surprised. The furniture was less hideous than he had feared. He glanced round, a man of possessions, and his own master. One sees him alone among his new acquisitions. He is aged nineteen, and five foot eleven in height. He is coltish and lanky but with broad shoulders and a square, rather big head covered thickly with fair hair brushed well off the forehead. The brow is broad, eyes wide apart, a strong and straightly jutting nose dominates the face, but a weak, rather prim upper lip looks a little odd above the assertive, masculine jaw. His eyebrows are a shade darker than his hair, and they turn up stiffly at the outer corners, giving him a witty and spry expression. He wears a high stiff collar, and subfusc tie pulled very tight, and a tweed suit with the short lapel of the period. A distinctly handsome youth, ready with sociability and eager for it, in spite of his omnivorous reading. He holds his head tilted up. There is about him the alertness of a thoroughbred. He has a way of looking about him like someone just stepped from a railway train and confidently expecting to be met by the friend of his choice.

Two days later, in Bruton Street, Jane brought her diary up to date.

On Wednesday I left him alone to begin his undergraduate career. Oh Heavenly Father, watch over him and keep, I humbly pray Thee, to Thine own Honour and Glory, that which I have committed again and again unto Thee. Guide him by Thy Spirit even though he knows it not, and O Lord, draw him unto Thyself. His *heart* seems far from Thee and far from humbly seeking Thee. Give him good friends, such as fear and love Thee, and grant that he may acknowledge Thee as the giver of all the talents he possesses and use them all to Thy Honour and Glory. Preserve him in purity, give him grace to withstand temptations. Help me to pray day by day and by night for him and especially to remember him at the Holy Feast.

A week went by and she had not received a word of news from Cambridge.

Have been quite alone today. My thoughts have been much with Eddie. I feel barren and unfruitful. Oh for the gift of the Holy Ghost! Lord, breathe on me and let my dry bones live. Wherefore tarriest Thou so long, my loved Lord? What seed I had of God that have I sown in my son's heart, and now he is gone from me. Very completely is the growth of the seed hid from my eyes.

When at last he came back for a Sunday he was accompanied by another freshman, R. C. Trevelyan. He talked enthusiastically of his other new friends, Bertrand Russell and Oswald Sickert, both his senior by a year. He had not only taken to smoking a pipe, but to smoking it all the time. In her Journal that night Jane wrote: 'Why should I have to fight my way to the door in my own house?'

The undergraduate who at Trinity had begun to feel so adult and emancipated found no easing of the childhood restrictions when he got home for his first vacation. As the new year 1892 came in, Maggie and he were both upstairs asleep while in the drawing-room below their parents celebrated the occasion with restraint in the company of a select gathering which styled itself District Friends of the Poor.

Chapter Three

THE *CAMBRIDGE OBSERVER*
(1892–1893)

BEFORE going up for his second term, R. C. Trevelyan came to stay at Bruton Street. He was an ardent Tennysonian and had bought a map which showed all the houses in the London area where Tennyson had stayed. He prevailed on Eddie to join him on a round tour of the Tennysonian haunts. They would go on foot, it would take the inside of a day, but the problem was how to eat. 'There is such a thing as a pub,' Eddie scribbled on a postcard, his earliest surviving communication with a poet. When Trevelyan arrived for the jaunt Oswald Sickert turned up unexpectedly, so the three of them set out together, and the main topic of conversation was Oswald's new venture, the *Cambridge Observer*. He was to be the editor, his brother Walter had promised to contribute drawings, and Eddie Marsh was engaged as the theatre and music critic. The field of Eddie's experience in music was bounded by the household music at Cold Ash, where Laura Denniston had often played on the enormous black grand piano which practically filled one end of the drawing-room. Jane Marsh was tone deaf and her son was hardly qualified for his new job. This did not deter the critic, but if his musical contributions to the new magazine were perfunctory he would be able to make up for it by spreading himself on subjects more fitted to his powers.

The inaugural number came out in the first week of May 1892. Sickert contributed an article on Zola, and his colleague, who signed himself 'M', saw his work in print for the first time in the form of a short review entitled 'Mr. Stevenson's New Book'.[1] 'Modern travel writing has reached the stage of impressionism,' he wrote, and argued that modern writers described things not as they are, but as they happen to strike them. 'Mr. Stevenson sees with the eyes of his time but writes in the mellow language

---

[1] *Across the Plains.*

of literature. . . . For writing of this kind there are two essentials —grace of manner and a delicate sensitiveness. Mr. Stevenson combines a perception perhaps less keen but more refined and straightforward than Dickens, with a gift for charming auto-biography which makes him as adorable as Thackeray. . . . His style is of an unforced ingenuity which makes each phrase a vivid and illuminating picture.' The critic praised the character studies drawn 'with a humorous sympathy like Sterne's' and ended: 'The weird and beautiful *Pulvis et Umbra* strips the idea of man to an abhorrent nakedness only to show how wonderful and consoling are his imperfect virtues. Its conclusion is like the Rainbow after the Deluge.'

His first extended article, which appeared on May 10, was an account of the first performance in England of Ibsen's *Doll's House*, which he had attended in London with his mother. Eddie felt so strongly about the play that he consulted Sickert on how he could do justice to the work without shocking and alienating the subscribers. 'First the ethical side—readers will think it's all safe,' Sickert replied, 'then the transition to a sudden blast which will dash the sheet from the hand, and then your boat can be guided boldly through the waves of a pure artistic criticism.' In her private Journal Jane Marsh wrote: 'A very powerful play, and moved me strangely. The tragedy of too many a woman's life. Ibsen seems to have an insight into the true nature of marriage, the spiritual union it *should* be to make the bodily more *tolerable*.' But the dramatist's solution showed none of 'the patience of the divine. Women *must* not, dare not, try to overcome by flight— that is selfish.' She should have practised 'self-abnegation', wrote Mrs. Marsh. The theme of the play had touched her closely. Nora had come alive to her situation with a sudden shock, she reflected. She was lucky. Most women in her position 'discover their woe as it is ground into them daily and hourly in the pitiless and pitiful trivialities of life; they live without violent catastrophe because they keep before their eyes the Sacrifice Eternal of the Son of God'. She found the characters less consistent than Shakespeare's. 'And yet there *is* something of Shakespeare's talent in portraying human creatures so vividly.' She concluded that perhaps Ibsen's greatest asset was his power to make every word in the dialogue contribute to the whole impression. 'I shall go through a course of Ibsen, for he gives one lots to think about.'

To 'M' in the *Cambridge Observer* there had dawned a new age of the drama.

What more do critics want? Why do they talk as if the *Doll's House* were a revolutionary experiment, dangerous to the existence of the stage—as if the wickedness of the writer was too great to be made harmless, even by his excessive stupidity? It is quite true that the *Doll's House* completely condemns every play that has been produced in England for three generations; but this is not by opposing the existing dramatic ideal, but by realizing it so perfectly as to make the failure of previous attempts unmistakable. The recent history of the English drama is curious and pathetic. So long as the principal dramatists were, in the first place, great poets, like Marlowe and Shakespeare, or great wits, like Congreve and Sheridan, the drama was inevitably mixed up with literature. It hardly occurred to anyone that there might be a quite distinct art of writing for the stage. But just at the moment when eighty years of mediocrity had freed the dramatic ideal from the superfluities with which it had been loaded by the excessive genius of the old writers, and so, strange as it seems, had actually created a new art which was merely waiting for a new talent to practise it, then—let us hope, only anticipating us by a little —a new play was suddenly brought over from Norway, in which the thing was already done; and that without the preliminary dreariness of the century in which we had done our best to laugh or to cry over the productions of Lytton and Boucicault (I may be excused for knowing no more instances) and the nameless celebrities of today.

He had heard that the third act had been condemned as 'unnatural' by some critics, because the dénouement would not have occurred so soon (that same night) or, if it had, Torvald would never have accepted it as final. 'M' did not agree. 'The answer to this is that every art has its conventions, which it is forced to observe; and that until it is thought desirable to keep an audience in a theatre for a month or so at a time the art of play-writing must put up with artificiality of condensation.' And then he dealt with another objection. 'Some people refuse to discuss anything about the *Doll's House* except what they consider to be its ethical tendency. But, of course, the real question for criticism is not whether a play has good ethics, but whether it has any ethics at all. Unfortunately it seems rather probable that Ibsen wrote "with a purpose", but even if this is so, Providence has a way of taking care of great artists, even when they are themselves on a wrong line.' At the same time he pointed out that society was

agitated at this moment by doubts on the sanctity of marriage, so
that the dramatist who treated this very theme without any bias
of practical teaching would surely be at fault. After blaming the
players for grossly over-acting he concluded, in agreement with
his mother, that perhaps the play's most novel quality, not in aim
but in achievement, was the dialogue—'so perfectly natural that
each of the short, clear sentences, as it comes from the mouth of
the actors, seems the one thing that in the circumstances was
inevitable'.

Sickert was happy to discover that the article on the *Doll's
House* was considered unusually daring and that as a result his
magazine had become a rallying point for the increasing number
of Ibsen supporters. From the start he had suspected that Marsh
would be an asset, and partly to encourage him as well as for his
own sake he sent a copy of the first number of the magazine to his
family friend Oscar Wilde, and asked him if he might bring his
young critic round to Tite Street next time they were in London.
On getting an encouraging reply he sent the letter to Trinity for
Marsh to keep as a memento of his first appearance in print.

> My Dear Oswald,
>
> Thank you for your charming letter and for the new venture as
> well. I wish that in the latter there had been more about that delicate
> artist in language Robert Louis Stevenson and less about mysterious
> things called Boating and Billiards and Cricket—However even these
> may be subjects for criticism if you take grace of movement and
> gesture as your standpoint. From the point of view of art the athlete
> may be civilized but from no other. Come and see me when term
> is over and bring your friend Edward Marsh, who has a charming
> name—for fiction.
>
> > Sincerely Yours,
> >
> > Oscar Wilde.

The meeting with Wilde never came about. The man with the
charming name for fiction regretted this all the more when two
years later he attended with Sickert the opening night of *The
Importance of Being Earnest* and pronounced it 'the greatest thing
since Sheridan'. He would have had an appropriate anecdote
ready to amuse the author. When a small boy he had always
thought his own name 'stupid' and for some inexplicable reason
had longed to be rechristened Ernest. One day an old lady in
Hyde Park patted him on the head and asked his name. 'Guess,'

he had said, and to his astonishment she replied 'Ernest'. A few weeks later his father gave him a birthday present of Webster's Dictionary of proper names and to his horror he discovered that an alternative spelling of his favourite name was originally 'ear-nest', which he interpreted, not as an adjective, but as 'ear nest', the nest which earwigs, as he supposed, had the beastly habit of making in one's ears, a disclosure which reconciled him for good to the less sensational Edward.

His next extended article for the *Cambridge Observer* was a review of Paul Verlaine's *Chansons pour Elle*.

Of all literary personages Verlaine is perhaps the most interesting to a student of the human comedy; for no other has been so pure a type of the artist. It is seldom that a poet is nothing more than a poet; usually he has also either extraordinary powers of thought, like Browning, or an overwhelming personality, like Shelley, or a strong moral prepossession, like Wordsworth; or some such quality, which introduces another, perhaps a disturbing element, into work which we might expect to find merely artistic. Verlaine invariably treats life and thought as other poets do occasionally—Browning, for instance, in *Fifine*; Shelley in the *Cenci*; Wordsworth, in some of his short poems—simply as a mine of beauty, such as sound is to a musician. It is not that he looks on thought as a mere vehicle for language; that would make his art not more but less complete; he is an artist in thought itself. He embraces philosophies and beliefs because they are beautiful; but (and here is the main difference, in this connexion, between him and Keats) his choice is instinctive rather than deliberate; he is a lake shone upon by a rainbow, a magnet attracting all beauty from his surroundings to himself.

The article included his own translation of one of the *Romances sans Paroles* and ended with a tribute to Verlaine's earlier, religious poems. For poetry of this kind, he argued, sincerity and simplicity of language were the first essentials, and the verse must seem unstudied, even imperfect, so as to 'cause the same kind of feeling that we have when we hear an old peasant use some imaginative phrase that he owes to his plain life in the midst of nature'. Of Verlaine's earlier poems he observed: 'The reason why they are so much better than any other religious poetry that has ever been written, except Isaiah's and Miss Rossetti's, is that the purpose at the back of them is not in reality religious but artistic. Verlaine's religion is only his particular kind of paganism. . . . One wonders if this will be his last word; probably, for he will not live long.'

On May 31 he reviewed a new drama of Swinburne's. 'I am sorry
to see so little to care for in any work of Mr. Swinburne's; but it
is exceedingly hard to guess what was the use of writing such a
play as *The Sisters.*' In an earlier review of a performance by Sarah
Bernhardt in Sardou's *Cléopatre* he had deplored the style of
playwriting fashionable in France, with its lifeless symmetry, so
that even Bernhardt could do little with it. On November 8 he
touched on this again.

> The revival a short time ago of the *Duchess of Malfi* by the Independent
> Theatre was the most significant dramatic event in England since
> the first performance of Ibsen. It ought not to be. Considering that
> we have a dramatic literature, compared with which that of Athens
> is tame and meagre, it seems strange that we should have to be
> thankful for a performance of one of the greatest of English tragedies.
> But the traditions of France have taken so firm a hold on our stage
> that some of us (or let us say, some of them) cannot tolerate the
> virile energies even of the greatest literary age of the world.

The articles on music were peculiarly lively, to compensate
the reader, perhaps, for lack of substance. 'Mr. Phillips sang
Schubert's *Gesang des Harfners* (ii) very creditably. But what on
earth induced him to follow immediately on this with a composition called *Vittoria* by one Carisissimi, we are unable to guess. He
who can calmly put such a song by the side of Schubert and Goethe
must glory in his lack of sensibility. Imagine the sensation of
seeing the third act of *King Lear* and then hurrying off in a hansom
to the Empire to hear a second-rate comedian sing some patriotic
abomination!' Of Mendelssohn's string quartet in D major he
remarked in the same article: 'To hear Mendelssohn abused has
often pained us, but never did he seem to *merit* such unmitigated
blasphemy as on this occasion.' Next week he complained that he
could hardly breathe during the Wagner concert because of the
'endless jets of gas and no ventilation', but gave his reader a long
meditation on illustrative art. 'Wagner's music is to a large extent
descriptive, and this is one reason that he fails as an artist. He
describes sensations which require a knowledge of the form and
colour with which they are associated for us to understand them
properly.' What seemed to have gone down well was the overture
to *Tannhäuser.* 'You felt that the performers themselves were
carried away by it. They had no time to yawn or look round and
throw in a note here and there in a casual sort of way.' (This

throwing in of a note here and there suggests a species of concert such as one would dearly wish to attend.) 'The music seemed self-created and the performers to perform in obedience to the commands of sounds that already existed. Altogether a triumph, at the close of which the conductor retired kissing his hands to a well lined avenue of exhausted performers.' In November he heard Sullivan's latest work *Haddon Hall* with a libretto by Sydney Grundy and found nothing to enjoy but the Highland Fling. The fault, he maintained, was Grundy's. 'There is, as we have said, one Gilbert, and Sir Arthur is his prophet—no one else's.' But it wasn't until January 1893, when he heard the unlucky Mr. Ingram at the local music club, that he let himself go.

The concert concluded with the best performance of the vilest work I ever listened to. Anything more devastating than Liszt's arrange-ment of Verdi's *Rigoletto* as a pianoforte solo it is impossible to conceive. This sort of thing is the rankest abuse of the piano that a man can be guilty of. Its ridiculous aspect is merged in a feeling of intense disgust. The horrid quivering 'harpy' movements, the meaningless, shrill trills up in the treble, the ridiculous runs and rhapsodical chords, the Quixotic devilry of the thing—all are infinitely hideous. One has no time to laugh at one absurdity before another crowds its way in. It was Mr. Ingram who selected this abomination to play, and he played it with a reverence and an affection that it is difficult to exaggerate. Every note was caressed, except where, from exigencies of the composition, it was impossible to do anything but touch it lightly and skip or fly along the keyboard. At the conclusion of a performance that was a blasphemy of music, the club applauded loudly, and Mr. Ingram commenced an encore.

There were three more essays in dramatic criticism before the journal came to an end after a brief career of eleven months. In January he was bored by Beerbohm Tree's presentation of a verse drama called *Hypatia* at the Haymarket. Only his 'delight in suffering martyrdom' had made him applaud it. 'Mr. Tree is, as usual, exceedingly conscientious, but his efforts are somehow not so successful as usual.' The critic deplored the neglect of scansion in the speaking of verse in the contemporary theatre. He agreed that the situation was, if anything, worse at the Lyceum where Irving in a revival of Lear 'deliberately turns nearly all his lines into prose by the simple method of changing the accent, dwelling on elided syllables, and inserting a profusion of the inarticulate noises with which he has enriched the language of our stage'. In the case of *Hypatia* it did not matter, however, that the verse was turned into prose, for the author's poetry was not 'particularly good', being written in a language made of an odd mixture of natural conversation and an obsolete literary dialect. 'Such a line, for example, as *I'll try to keep her there for one short hour* with the baldness of *keep her there* and the conventionality of *one short hour* is not on the whole impressive.' Mention of the Lyceum gave the critic an opportunity for pronouncing Ellen Terry 'a consummately great actress', but the rest of his comments were severe. They prompted the editor to ask 'M' to devote an article to his views on Irving. It appeared on February 7, 1893.

A recent performance at the Lyceum, when the leading lady was indisposed and her part was taken by an actress whose un-questioned ability to 'recite ballads about the Indian Mutiny with very suitable emphasis' hardly qualified her to be under-studying Ellen Terry, left the critic sufficiently un-bewitched by the spell he was accustomed to in that theatre to reflect with detachment on the actor-manager and his policy. There was a discrepancy, he thought, between the Lyceum's popular reputa-tion for theatrical culture and the spectacular display of showman-ship it invariably offered which was indeed its real attraction. He asked himself what the plays were which best served Irving's personality and won the highest acclaim from his admirers. He listed them and gave the foremost place to 'the riotous romping farce of *Richelieu*'.

Romping gave me the key I wanted. Mr. Irving is in reality a grown-up schoolboy; he loves to exceed, to exuberate in every direc-tion, to be the hero of a sensational story, to have hair-breadth escapes, to dress up, to fight, to make old jokes, to insist on obvious irony.

All these things he does, and I do not wish to deny that he does them in a very remarkable way. You cannot see him walk down Bond Street without feeling that he could do nothing without being remarkable; and there is no disputing the elegance of his figure, the beauty of his hands, the distinction of his countenance. Everyone is thrilled by *The Bells*, everyone admits that the caricature of Louis XI is striking caricature. Moreover, there are some parts in the great plays that suit Mr. Irving: he is almost perfect as Benedick, and does no great violence to Shylock; but the actor who revels in *Richelieu* ought to let *Lear* and *Macbeth* alone.

His last essay in dramatic criticism was on a subject exactly to his taste, the opening of Ibsen's *Ghosts* at the heroic little Independent Theatre. The acting was poor and the conditions unfavourable.

> The Athenaeum Hall, 73 Tottenham Court Road, is just what it sounds like—a dirty room, neither large nor small, with a good deal of red velvet, sea-green walls almost covered by large mirrors, and a skylight. Invitations had very judiciously been sent to about half as many people again as the hall would hold, so that the gangways were crowded, and consequently everyone at the back had to stand; and some were perched on shelves up the walls where the best way of seeing what was going forward on the stage was to look in one of the looking-glasses. Thus the audience had every temptation to be in a bad temper, yet nobody went away. . . . I have been told that at the first performance of *Rosmersholm* the house was filled with the habitual students of the British Museum Reading Room. [For *Ghosts*] they were mostly good-humoured, well-dressed people, who looked as if they were accustomed to being amused, and were neither invidiously artistic nor obtrusively earnest.

The cast was not admired. The Mrs. Alving was 'untidy and suburban; she has a foolish little laugh and an irritating little trick of dusting her face with a pocket-handkerchief', and she was handicapped by a ridiculous wig. The Oswald (Lewis Waller) was not up to it. 'A very difficult part, but to shout and gasp is to go out of one's way to spoil it.' The critic pointed out that Ibsen's plays belonged to 'the comparatively new art of writing for the stage', so it was especially interesting to compare the impression drawn from reading them in the study with their effect in the theatre. In the case of *Ghosts* what one felt most in reading the play was the force of the idea behind the situation, the sins of the fathers being visited upon the children, but 'when one actually sees the mother and the son on the stage the feeling is changed to one of personal sympathy, the drama becomes more human'. Though the end of the first act in his opinion was artificially contrived so as to make an effective curtain he nevertheless pronounced it 'unquestionably one of the most striking scenes that have ever been written'.

In March the *Cambridge Observer* collapsed. With articles by Lowes Dickinson (reviewing the first appearance in English of *Peer Gynt*) and A. W. Verrall, and drawings by Walter Sickert, it was well worth the sixpence. Its pages were enlivened with remarks like: 'Buy Tosti's *Goodbye* and you will have more thumping sentimentality than you can get in any other form at the price. There are oceans of it—for two shillings net.' Eddie Marsh's poems, whether original or translated from Gautier or Victor Hugo, were nothing special, but the practical journalism was of immense value to the development of his critical faculties. Forty years were to pass before he wrote another review of a dramatic performance, and he wisely never put pen to paper again on the subject of music.

'Of course "theatre" is the thing he looks forward to most,' his mother wrote in her Journal when the youth came back after his first term at Cambridge, 'and so I suppose we must give him a fair amount.' Not all the credit must go to Oswald Sickert for educating the playgoer. He had certainly discovered one of the first Ibsenites, but his confidence in Eddie Marsh had results of another kind. The *Cambridge Observer* lasted long enough to be responsible for an open rift at Bruton Street between mother and son.

Chapter Four

CAMBRIDGE
(1892 retraced—1895)

I N October 1892 Sickert's magazine was still flourishing. Laura Denniston had moved to Oxford so as to be near her son, who had gone to the university, but the neighbourhood of her home had become Eddie's favourite place of retreat. He had found rooms in a small Tudor house called Grimsby Farm and there for a few weeks he stayed, reading Greek philosophy, before going for the first time to stay with Bertrand Russell's family at Haslemere. Whenever his Cambridge magazine had wanted a report on a play, he had taken his mother with him. It was an excuse for them to be amicably together without much risk of the religious controversy that he wished at all costs to avoid. There seemed to be no way of his discussing the subject without her being hurt. On one occasion they attempted an ordinary outing and visited the British Museum, lingered among the Roman busts and tried to recapture the intimacy they had once enjoyed. Jane Marsh could think of little to write in her Journal beyond 'Brutus looks idiotic, Marcus Aurelius a heavy British farmer'.

It was soon after Eddie's return to Cambridge for the last term of 1892 that Sickert suggested he should ask leave of absence for a long week-end and go to Paris at the expense of the *Cambridge Observer*. Sickert would furnish him with letters of introduction to theatrical friends of his brother Walter, then the chief attraction of next month's issue would be an article by 'M' on the *Comédie Française*. Eddie made no demur, but he thought it would be advisable to pay his parents the compliment of asking their permission. The answer which came back at once consisted of one word—'Impossible'. He wrote again. The second reply only added that, contrary to what he might suppose, both parents for a change were in full agreement. 'I have felt as lead,' Mrs. Marsh wrote in her Journal, while in Cambridge there occurred one of

those incidents in a young man's life over which his more mature
self draws a veil of oblivion, unless of course he has grown into an
accomplished rake, in which case the affair is casually dismissed
and forgotten as being but one lapse among so many. In the
instance of a man who was to become a model of decorum and,
as Max Beerbohm described him, 'undoubtedly one of the
ornaments of his time', it was rather as if a man should release in
a single night all the Dionysiac impulses of a lifetime and then
settle down for his remaining span to an existence of unruffled
tranquillity. How, or precisely where, or in whose company,
Eddie got first morbidly bemused, then fighting drunk, he would
never divulge. He was probably quite alone, at least at the start,
and set about it with all the calculation of a desperate man who
has at last made up his mind to some ostentatious gesture of
protest only just short of self-immolation. Nor is it recorded how it
became known to the college authorities so that he was temporarily
suspended. His sense of the ridiculous stopped short at this one
episode in his life which was doubtless an escapade no sillier than
the sort of thing he would have shrugged off with a laugh, or
forgotten altogether, had it not been for the distress it caused his
mother, who had unwittingly brought it about. She kept up her
Journal a few months longer, then stopped it for good. 'E writes
to me regularly, but there is no real intercourse in our correspondence.' And when the family festival came round a few weeks
later, her entry was brief and joyless. 'Xmas Day being Sunday we
indulged in quietness.'

Before the end of term he was reinstated in college and a
semblance of peace was restored at Bruton Street, but not before
two of his friends had intervened. It was perhaps natural that
Sickert should feel bound to go to London and give his account
of how the whole affair had come about. More significant, and
doubtless more telling, was the intervention of Mrs. Verrall. She
was a comparatively new friend and one of particular importance
in the eyes of the parents, for she was known to them as the wife
of Eddie's tutor in Greek. Since her husband was by far the
greatest influence in Eddie Marsh's life (it would not be too much
to say that he finally determined the nature of his character and
the direction of his gifts) it is necessary here to do more than mention him by name.

Arthur Woollgar Verrall was the son of a solicitor, and was

born in Brighton in 1851. He won a Foundation Scholarship to
Cambridge, bracketed with Walter Leaf from Harrow and
Henry Butcher, the translator of the *Odyssey*, from Marlborough,
a triumvirate of scholars such as perhaps had never before appeared
at one time. Verrall's first publication, an edition of the *Medea* of
Euripides, appeared when he was thirty, and his restorations of
the text wherever readings were in question soon earned him a
high place in Greek scholarship. His second volume was a group
of essays on the Odes of Horace. More than half a century later
Eddie Marsh was to produce the standard translation of the
Odes, but Verrall instilled into him far more than a love of Latin
poetry. In 1889, two years before Eddie arrived at the university,
Verrall became a tutor at Trinity and he and his wife instituted
the custom of Tuesday and Friday dinner-parties and afternoon
croquet tournaments at their house in Selwyn Gardens. In such
ways Verrall got to know his pupils as individuals, and for as
many as proved worthy of him he changed the whole current of
their intellectual lives. What impressed them on closer acquaintance seems to have been a noble simplicity of character combined
with a most unusual subtlety of mind. They observed that in spite
of his pervading sense of humour he was never afraid of losing
dignity and consequently never lost it, and they were infected by
the scope of his literary enthusiasms, which extended from
Aeschylus to Jane Austen and the latest show in town. Above all
Eddie was won over by his lightness of touch and the style of his
wit, such as when he was chairman at a smoking-concert and
apologized for not having prepared a speech 'owing to a succession
of incalculable circumstances over *whom* I had no control', or
when a pupil remarked, 'Well, Mr. Verrall, I must avow that in
my opinion Edna Lyall is the first of contemporary novelists', and
after a pause for breath he replied, smiling, 'Well, if you think so,
my dear, you are quite right to *avow* it, you know.'

But it was in the lecture-room that he made the greatest
impression on his pupils. He was one of the first dons at Cambridge
to insist on treating the Classics as works of art, and for Eddie his
lectures on the *Choephori* were an experience never to be forgotten.
For fear of breaking the spell of the discourse by taking notes he
would put a dot with his pencil under each Greek word that
Verrall examined, and afterwards discover that the exposition
had been so clearly organized that he never failed to remember

what the dots meant. He has left his own account of Dr. Verrall
in the lecture-room.

> He used to sit in a subdued frenzy of impatience, waiting till every-
> one was settled down, and if the noise of settling down went on a
> moment after he had hoped it was over, there was an agony, shown
> only by his martyred face and in the drumming of his pencil on the
> desk. Then in the silence the high rich shrillness of his voice came
> streaming out under the closed eyelids in his ivory face. We are not
> likely to see anything more resembling the phenomenon of inspira-
> tion. I find my mental picture has completed itself with curls of pale
> blue smoke from a tripod.[1]

But more revealing are his comments on Verrall's critical
method. 'He forced you to criticize, taking no literary reputation
or judgement for granted.' With him common sense was always
the first test.

> He had the most scrupulous sense I have ever known of the value of
> exactness in language. There was nothing academic in this; no one
> took more pleasure in novelty or audacity of expression if on close
> inspection it was justified and held water; but he would never
> tolerate an approximation to the meaning required.

Eddie Marsh might have been writing of himself.

Earlier in the year he had met Walter Sickert. 'He would very
much like to see you at his studio,' Oswald wrote. 'Anyone who is
at all inclined to see things his way, and who is likely to see what
he is after, is a help and pleasure to him.' Eddie's first encounter
with contemporary painting occurred in April 1892 when the two
Sickert brothers met him for luncheon at their favourite midday
haunt, the Café Royal, then took him back to the studio to show
him Walter's latest work. He began to cultivate his eye.

Shortly before the Michaelmas term, after a few weeks with a
reading-party in Yorkshire, Robert Trevelyan wrote to say he had
looked in at Eddie's rooms in Trinity and found his bed-maker
sitting at his writing-table and eating bread and marmalade. By
way of reproach Eddie sent the woman a loaf and a pot of
marmalade and wrote to Trevelyan, whose report of a romantic
encounter which had failed to develop set Eddie meditating on
the subject of women.

[1] *Collected Literary Essays by A. W. Verrall*, edited by M. A. Bayfield, M.A., and
J. D. Duff, M.A. (Cambridge, 1913). The volume included a Memoir by F. M.
Cornford to which E.M. contributed his reminiscences.

Why is it harder to fall in love with women the more real they are? It is easiest with purely imaginary ones, such as Beatrice Esmond or Balzac's duchesses, next easiest with people who really existed long ago, such as Mary Queen of Scots or whoever you please, next with an actress in a part and hardest of all with actual women in real life. I suppose it's chiefly want of imagination, because we can't see in the women we meet what the writers saw in the people they wrote about.

You'll be glad to hear I have an anecdote which is the strongest possible argument for the Return to Nature. If a little child, fresh from the Ideas, approves of it, who is to object? We had a kid staying with us in Yorkshire (3½ years old) who happened to come into my room one day when I had nothing on, and professed great pleasure at the sight. 'Oh I like to see you like that,' he said. 'You look so pretty'—and next day at lunch he asked me in a loud voice, 'Why don't you come down naked? You really must *not* wear clothes.'

On December 9 he was back in London with plans to go to the Royalty Theatre to see the first play of a new dramatist, Bernard Shaw. Sickert wrote on the same day saying that he had met William Archer at Cambridge, who had seen 'M's' Ibsen articles in the *Cambridge Observer* and was confident they had done much to further the cause. Archer told Sickert he had just finished another translation, which was due to come out in the new year. It was called *Peer Gynt*. Sickert had just been to Ascot, and he described the Guards officers 'standing around in the pride of their scarlet uniform and the women magnificent and athletic-looking, talking of bay mares and steppers'. 'I expect you will be at Shaw's play tonight. Sanger[1] will be there, and Archer.' Eddie always remembered the first night of *Widowers' Houses* when the author —'willowy, long faced, a lot of red hair'—appeared before the curtain, lifted his hand for silence, and told the audience (which was booing and hissing) that he was in full agreement with their verdict, but if they came back next time they would see him do better.

Early in 1893 Sickert wrote again, having visited the exhibition of paintings at the Grafton Gallery as the critic of his magazine. There he had met his brother Walter, who drew his attention to the work of Alexander Roche, a member of the Glasgow school of painters. 'If you look closely at the work,' Walter had said, 'you'll

1 Charles Sanger, the mathematician, one of the Cambridge circle and the particular friend of Bertrand Russell.

see how nicely the patches of colour suit one another, but if you look at it from a distance the colour becomes dirty and meaningless. Just the opposite happens with a *real* colourist—Steer, for instance. There are some pictures that the Secretary should hand to visitors on a *plate* for them to look at.' Oswald had begun writing his first and only novel, a story of calf love based on his own experience, called *Helen*. It was the first literary work which Eddie criticized in manuscript, and when it came out in Fisher Unwin's series of little oblong books in yellow paper covers it bore the first dedication in his name. At this early stage of composition Sickert was girding against the inescapable influence of Zola, Dickens, and Balzac. 'After you have exhausted all known sensations, you come to your own, if you have any—the tyranny of all the different sensations an ordinary fairly well-informed modern has to undergo before he is left to himself!—that is what comes of being born at the top of all the centuries.' And some months later he wrote: 'It is from your corrections at the side that I am learning (I hope I am, slowly) to write a little better, and as I am very conscientious about thinking the objections out, your trouble is not lost. . . . I owe you such big thanks because you help me in what is very near my heart. . . . I know that every sentence ought to read as if the author had been intensely interested in it while writing.' It was spring and Oswald was afflicted with what the eighteenth-century called the Spleen and a young man of the 'nineties the Hump. He had been seeing the painter Wilson Steer, a fellow victim who had said it was due to 'the season of the year, when Nature is happier than man. It's rather degrading when you think that a compound rhubarb pill can make you contented with life.' Walter Sickert was painting in what he called his meadow, 'somewhere between Cumberland Terrace and Regent's Park, far away from the districts of gentility he hates so much, where he is liable to meet a man with a moustache and tennis racquet who, if he knows him, wants him to come in and have a whiskey and pipe, or if he doesn't, looks at his coat and thinks it's too short or long behind'. Eddie, meanwhile, after seeing himself in print in the *Cambridge Observer*, had begun to discover his limitations. 'If you can't or *won't* write more poetry,' wrote Sickert, 'then you must do solid criticisms on actors and actresses, criticisms which will astonish by their insight and convince by their validity—this you can do perfectly well.'

When Sickert's magazine came to an end for lack of support Eddie settled down to work with rather more conscientiousness for the first part of the Classical Tripos, which he was due to take in the winter term. Jane and her son were going to the play again, but at home he still felt under restraint. In July he wrote to Trevelyan from Grimsby Farm:

I've just got free from the bondage of London, and have finished my first day of work here, which has consisted in pouring a stream of indigestible facts about Roman literature through my sieve of a memory. My flesh crept to such a degree on Monday night, when I woke up and began to think about the Tripos, that I think it must have moved on about an inch all round. I stayed in London a day or two longer than I ought for the sake of a superior French company which came over to do *Rosmersholm*, *The Master Builder*, and a play of Maeterlinck's. It's bossed by a M. Lugné Poë, who seems to be a descendant of Edgar Poe's—a very beautiful man with a pale face and black hair, who reminds me of a portrait of some poet, I can't remember who—perhaps Poe himself—he acts very respectably and quite revolutionized my idea of *The Master Builder* by making him into an American with a straggling beard and a drunken complexion —the rather vulgar, arrogant manner he put on in certain parts made the character seem much more consistent than it did under the suavity of Lewis Waller. It's a fascinating play, but you have to give yourself up to the charm of looking on, without trying to understand. Have you ever read Maeterlinck? It's useless to try and explain what he's like if you haven't—the play has to be acted through a gauze curtain, in a kind of sing-song—in the mixture of great simplicity with an entire rejection of realism it seems to me to go back to the Burne-Jones and Morris kind of thing. The Independent Theatre is the worst managed concern in the world, I should think. The performances generally begin 20 minutes late, after the curtain has gone up two or three times, to encourage the audience. You're never safe from the irruption of a cat in the most moving scenes, the actors aren't ready to come on at their cues, or the curtain stays up at the end of the act. The man who is called the Acting Manager is the greatest crack I ever met with in a responsible position. I went one day and asked for a dress circle seat, and after fiddling about with a book he looked up and said, 'You see this theatre is so confusing—there are orchestra stalls, and balcony stalls, and dress circle'—so that I had to help him myself. The best of all was that after the 2nd act of *Rosmersholm*, which he had been watching, he came and asked me if that was the end of the play! I took the Verralls to see *Rosmersholm*; he admired it immensely. It's very curious that he never is, or lays himself out to be, in the least moved by a play, but simply keeps his eyes open to see the cleverness or stupidity with which it is written. So far as he goes, I suppose there could be no better critic.

While her son was at Cold Ash, undistracted by mundane pleasures, Jane Marsh considered the moment auspicious for making one last effort to persuade him to put right what she felt sure was the great wrong at the heart of his unrest. She began her letter by saying she simply could not see why every topic excepting religion should be freely discussed between them, 'but so it is—therefore it is with some little hesitation that I write to you—but I do feel you may justly think me careless about what is to me the one important thing in life if I keep perpetual silence on the subject.' Eddie had said that controversy was no use, belief must come from one's own internal conviction or not at all. She based her main argument on the miraculous transformation of the disciples 'from ordinary men into a band of heroes' after the Resurrection, and ended what must have been the longest letter of her life with a pointed reference to *Rosmersholm* and one last exhortation.

It is very difficult for me to see how a man can admire Christ and acknowledge that he lived the life he did, and yet reject his explanation of it. We know that all others who have deceived themselves or have been impostors have infallibly betrayed themselves before the end. . . . For myself if Christ's revelation of God is not the true one I see no help for Man, no possibility of deliverance from his impure nature, no hope of gradual evolution into perfection—his nature at this day after 5,000 years and more is just the same as in the days of the Flood, and I see no better ending for us all than with Rebecca and Beata in the Mill Race; but if the revelation is true what boundless possibilities are opened out, what unimaginable glory awaits mankind, what inexhaustible fulfilment of our wildest hopes of joy! If it is true who need complain of anything which happens to him in this short life when such an eternity—which holds at this very moment the past and future as well as the present perfected in the thought of God—is given to him to partake of in union with God? . . . Dear E, I do not fear that if you care to seek you will not find, but I *do* fear that in the happy carelessness and brightness of your youth you should not care to seek and that you should wake at last when it is too late. . . . It is very wonderful that God should come to exalt such a creature as man is—in some aspects a brute beast made to be taken and destroyed. . . . If what Christ says of Himself and what St. John says of Him is true, come then to his side, virtue and triumph wait for you, you will overcome with Him. . . . Stay where you are and the battle will go against you to the end.

If she had feared that Oxford would confirm his leaning towards Anglo-Catholicism, Cambridge seemed to be turning him away from religion altogether. Certainly the friends who were influencing him were agnostic, but there was surely more to it than that. If it were possible for a man to be temperamentally incapable of any kind of transcendental belief Eddie Marsh was he. His was a rational, eighteenth-century cast of mind, and one could no more expect him to believe in a pattern of events contrary to natural laws than in the merit of a poem in which the parts were held together by some quality in common other than a sequence of logical thought.

Almost by the same post a letter from Sickert arrived to distract him from higher things. He had been to Paris and gone back-stage at the *Comédie Française*. 'It was amusing and exciting. The actresses behaved charmingly behind the scenes, quite simple and pleasant—the men of course were beastly, pompous, self-conscious, strutting about in a business-like way, as if they had anything different to do than the women—I wanted to kick them.' Roger Fry had come into Oswald's life through Walter. 'He has rather a strange way of combining realism with ideal composition and I should not think it would work out in the end.' Sickert had been dancing late, and had become enamoured of two fair sisters. 'I took them home in a four-wheeler over Putney Bridge, going through into Notting Hill very sweet in the dawn.' And a little later he wrote from Pembroke Gardens with more news of painters. 'Walter has come home and is staying here; Nellie [his wife] is left behind in Paris being painted by Whistler for the second time; he says Dégas is doing splendid work although he is growing blind—landscapes guessed out of grease spots on the table cloth.'

After the new year 1894 Eddie heard that in the first part of the Classical Tripos he had done less well than was expected of him. As a result, Henry Jackson, his tutor in philosophy, advised him to concentrate on pure scholarship. This was valuable and timely advice, for Eddie was nothing if not a natural scholar of

language. He was at a loss among abstract ideas. From now on he
determined to concentrate on the work which brought him closer
to Verrall. In July he was one of a reading-party in Wales with
Erskine Childers, who was to become a tragic figure in the Irish
troubles many years later. 'Childers has turned us all into fisher-
men,' Eddie wrote to Trevelyan. 'I had my first try yesterday and
became perfectly brutal when I'd seen three trout knocked on the
head. I was quite ready to put a wum on the hook, if I'd been
asked. I got one fish out of the water, but (by no fault of mine) it
awoke to its position before I could land it and rejoined its wife
and family.' Bertrand Russell was also of the party, and he has
recalled that Eddie was known among his reading companions as
'The Strange Grey Shape', owing to his exsanguinated appearance
at breakfast after sitting up with his book till the small hours.

Meanwhile a constant stream of letters from Sickert, who had
gone down from the university and was job-hunting in London,
made it difficult for Eddie to keep his mind on the academic
situation which so badly needed to be restored. The letters began
in January.

'There is going to be a new quarterly called the *Yellow Book* to
come out in March. Walter, Will Rothenstein, Steer, Beardsley,
are drawing, and a man called Harland is literary editor. . . .
Talking to Harland I mentioned you! I don't think Harland's a
good man; rather a raucous voice and no tact.' Sickert had just
met Rothenstein, who had given a dance at his studio. 'The belle
was Miss Pearsall Smith, she had on a dark green voluminous
dress which looked almost navy blue, with enormous floppy sleeves
and skirt, a sort of recollection of Rothenstein's *Souvenir of Scar-
borough*. George Moore was there, and I *saw him dance*.' Also there
was a Mr. Studd who had bought Whistler's *White Girl* at Goupil's
for £1,000. 'Studd has had a charming letter from Whistler which
ends: "If you think of leaving the picture out of the family at your
death I must beg you not to leave it to any gallery in England."'

It was one of Sickert's hobbies to keep his Cambridge friend
in touch with artistic occasions in the metropolis. In November he
reported another gathering of painters where he met George
Moore again. Sickert, who was now, at least for the time being, an
author himself, could not understand why *Esther Waters* had been
so favourably noticed in the papers. By this time his own *Helen*
was in print, after Charles Whibley, Frank Harris, Henry Harland,

and Eddie Marsh, aged twenty-one, had each in turn read the proofs for him. 'I walked down Piccadilly as though the whole of London belonged to me,' Sickert had written, 'then realized how poor were the opening chapters.'

The first book to be dedicated to Eddie Marsh was no furore. At the party in November Sickert asked George Moore what he thought of it. 'I cannot make up my mind,' he said, 'whether it's very bad, very good, or nothing at all.' Moore then got Walter into a corner and said George Alexander had been badgering him for a play. Walter sat listening with his other ear to some talk about the Society of Illustrators. Moore pulled him round. 'You have a most insatiable curiosity. If you could hear what those men are saying it would not interest you, so listen to ME.' 'There's not a more close or loving observer,' wrote Oswald of his brother. It was also true of himself. He declared himself determined to introduce Eddie to editors 'so that you can become *the* dramatic critic'. In May another Ibsen play burst upon London. 'I'm not very much taken with *The Wild Duck*,' wrote Sickert, 'the play seems the most Ibsenish of them all; the symbolism, the intense conversations, all exaggerations of characteristic virtues.'

Eddie had no ambition to become '*the* dramatic critic' and after a few more months Sickert gave up the struggle to induce his protégé to take up journalism. Verrall's personality and example had tipped the balance towards scholarship, and Eddie made up his mind to concentrate on his work for the second part of the Tripos. In March 1894 he was again at Grimsby Farm, where he wrote his first letter to Bertrand Russell. In company with his sister he had just called on a lady of advanced views who was conducting a campaign to induce daughters to rebel against parental tyranny.

She wanted to make my sister revolt, and accordingly asked me to bring her to lunch last Wednesday, which was exceedingly kind. My sister also seemed to make friends, and was most enthusiastic when we went away. I don't know if she'll revolt or not. Mr. Pearsall Smith is a dear old boy. I think he was very sarcastic to me, but I'm not really sure if he was or not. Among other things he said I talked exactly like old Jowett, which I don't believe. What funny grammar they talk to one another. . . .

The most interesting thing is that I've been seeing a certain amount of Robert Bridges, he's a charming man with thick dark hair which grows like thatch and a very attractive impediment in his speech, he reminded me curiously of Verrall, though he's much bigger all over and his face has funny bumps like Furness. I went for a walk with him on Friday; he talked in a very interesting way, though not quite as Coleridge talked to Hazlitt; after lunch he got a headache or something and seemed to get somehow much older (he's 49) and talked about his own plays a good deal. He had a perfect right to, as of course I was interested, but it was very funny how openly he praised them. He said, 'I think I've given blank verse all the pliability it's capable of in the *Humours of the Court*, don't you?'— 'The *Feast of Bacchus* is amusing from beginning to end, it's sure to find its way to the stage, and when it gets there it'll keep there.' This isn't vanity in the least, he's quite free from that. I'm just going over there to church. I hear he's trained the choir with remarkable success.

An undated letter to Trevelyan belongs to the same time.

I've been getting on very well with Bridges. I went to Oxford for the day with him last week, he seems to me to be the biggest man I've ever known anything of, perhaps equal with Rutherford. I can't think of anyone else who's thoroughly serious, thoroughly humorous, and thoroughly consistent, except Sickert perhaps, and even he doesn't seem to be exactly 'great' at present. I don't know what he'll be at 40. Bridges is soon going to bring out an edition of Keats, which he says will be very interesting as it will explain *Endymion* as an allegory—he told me a few things about it—the 4 books are the 4 elements, 1 earth, 2 underground, i.e. fire, 3 water, 4 air. The reason why Arethusa, for instance, comes in, is that her myth is the only one in which a being passed through all four stages—the real point of the last book is the identification of the spiritual love with the sexual. When we were at Oxford we went to the Bodleian, which is a delightful place. Lady Shelley has recently given them a fine collection of Shelley MSS. By the way one of the poems that is exposed is 'The sun is warm, the sky is clear' and not 'light', as it is in some editions, making light—light—and delight all rhyme in the same stanza. . . . I've been working very hard but without much result, and I feel as if I was getting very stupid; whenever the thought of the Tripos comes into my head I pray that the hills may cover me.

R. C. Trevelyan had written to ask him about the effect of Maeterlinck on the stage.

The great thing about Maeterlinck is the sound, the rhythm of the sentences, which is most beautiful when they are spoken by artistic French actors. *L'Intruse* was a complete failure on the stage —I don't care for it so much as for some of his things. *Pelléas and Mélisande* was delightful to listen to. I'm afraid the beautiful M. Lugné Poë is gone for good and won't come back, the theatre was so dreadfully empty, though all the decent critics were greatly pleased. I haven't seen Archer's articles, but Shaw praised the company highly.

He went on to say that the main literary event had been the publication of Verrall's *Euripides as a Rationalist*. 'I don't think I've ever read anything so *clever*. I won't tell you anything about it, as that would spoil it. It's as difficult to leave off reading as any book I've read.'

In the summer he paid his first visit to Germany, staying at the Pension Scherrer in Heidelberg as the only Englishman among a number of students from Paris. He had been persuaded to go there by his new friend, Maurice Baring, who was living near by. 'Please bring with you a volume of Verlaine,' Baring wrote, 'Sickert's article on Zola, a vol. of Musset, and all Miss Austen. I pay no fines.' Baring had come up to Trinity from Eton a year before, and was soon to go down again without any regrets because of his failure to pass his first examination. They had been introduced by Baring's friend Hubert Cornish, who brought him one evening to Eddie's rooms in New Court. 'He seemed an unremarkable youth, shy and shambling, with prominent blue eyes, and nothing to say for himself, and he sat on the edge of his chair, only uttering from time to time an abrupt high cackling laugh, between a neigh and a crow.'[1] To Eddie, whose life so far had been somewhat circumscribed, Baring seemed an extraordinarily precocious man of the world, and his sense of humour, of which perhaps a peculiar form of false logic was the basis, opened up for him new vistas of wit, as if a character out of *Alice in Wonderland* had come into his life.

It is difficult to convey the quality of personal charm, and most of Baring's own books are non-conductors of that peculiar unexpectedness in turn of thought and phrase which had such an appeal for his friends. When someone remarked as an interesting fact that since the sale of plover's eggs had been made illegal very few had been laid, Baring interjected: 'Naturally plovers won't take the trouble to lay eggs if nobody's going to eat them.'

[1] *A Number of People.* Wm. Heinemann, 1939.

In a post office in Florence he asked for postage stamps, and on being handed a sheaf, put them tentatively to his nose, with 'Are they fresh? They are for an invalid.' Another remark of his which for Eddie never lost its bloom was made when they had just got into an empty railway-carriage—'Let's shut the door so as to make it more difficult for people to get in.' And his letters to Eddie were full of characteristic touches. 'I've come to the conclusion that the secret of time is in German prose. You say everything you want to say in one sentence which doesn't leave off till you've said everything.' And during the prolonged summer of 1895: 'The Gulf Stream has got caught somewhere near England. The Park is overgrown with hibiscus and it's dangerous to go south of Battersea because of the pythons.' Of the funeral of Sir Henry Ponsonby in the same year—'We had to walk a mile to the church, slow march, crowds of people lined the hedges, one felt like Richard III and expected to be stoned. The Queen had been most nice and pointful, telegraphing every five minutes. One of the telegrams was *Beethoven or Chopin. Not Saul. V.R.*' And of a cantankerous friend in the same letter: 'He is so argumentative he won't even let me agree with myself. I eye him in an acrid manner and contradict with calm.' From Copenhagen, where he found the climate upsetting, he wrote: 'It makes me feel like a *Master Builder* who has been fed on rainbows.' In 1899, when Eddie was in the Colonial Office (the Boer War having broken out), he wrote, 'I hope the African Dept. of the C.O. has murdered sleep and felt that not all the perfumes of Arabia will sweeten their little hands', and giving news of a mutual friend who was a notoriously copious author, 'Arthur Benson wrote two books last week.'

He wrote to Eddie in Latin, French, German, pidgin English, pidgin Greek, and in baby-language with letters an inch high, or one line to a page written microscopically at the bottom, and at all times in what was called the Baring-Ponsonby private language (being chiefly the invention of Baring's aunt, Lady Ponsonby). Many of the 'expressions', as they were called, came to be used by Eddie throughout his life in ordinary conversation among his friends, and at least one word, 'pointful', has entered the language. Most of Baring's letters would be incomprehensible without a special dictionary. An example, at random, is a description of a musician introduced to Baring in Florence by Vernon Lee. 'He was not a bit pale ale[1] or Heygate[2] or Brahms[3]. This letter is very type-drawers[4] but what can one do with such grub-Johnson[5] note-paper?' Eddie did not find these verbal quips, nor practical jokes, as tiresome as they are to some people. Indeed he remembered with delight being given a quinine pill disguised as a bon-bon. 'I bit into it eagerly,' he would say relating the incident, 'and my features went off in all directions. "Oh Maurice, it's agony!" I cried, whereupon he said, "It's nothing to what it will be a week from now."' Yet another of his attractive qualities in Eddie's eyes was his aristocratic disdain of money. This too had its anecdote. One day Eddie felt bound to protest. Baring replied there were many aspects of life in which he was positively cheese-paring in his economy. 'Tell me *one*,' demanded Eddie, and the instance given was: 'You can't say I'm extravagant about under-clothes.' Finally there was his habit of breaking into snatches of impromptu song, of which perhaps the favourite example was

> Lord Salisbury's my only friend,
> Oh come in *TO-O-O* the mountains!

One of Baring's first ventures on arriving at the university was to found a magazine called *The Cambridge A.B.C.*, which survived for four weekly numbers during the month of June 1894. Aubrey Beardsley specially designed the cover for the modest fee of ten guineas, and Carr-Bosanquet and Baring shared the editor-ship. In the second number (June 9) appeared a dialogue called *A Game of Croquet* featuring Oscar Browning, Ethel Smyth, and Eddie Marsh, under appropriate pseudonyms. The opening stage direction described Edith Staines (Smyth) and Ethelbert Swamp (Marsh) engaged in colloquy on the croquet lawn. The scene is 'St. Oscar's' College. 'Miss Staines is dressed in South American leather buck-jumping breeches and a St. Andrews' golf-kit. She is discussing the rhythm of Baudelaire's poems with Mr. Swamp, an intellectual-looking gentleman with a pince-nez; his hair curls outwards from his collar, he bears a striking resemblance to M. Emile Zola.' Mr. Swamp's contribution is nugatory. He invites Miss Staines to open the game, then as she takes aim is heard humming 'a couplet of his own composition (in the manner of

---

[1] Sloppy.   [2] Obsequious.
[3] Superior, in the sense of condescending.
[4] Lower middle-class (official) in appearance.
[5] Severely practical and economical.

Verlaine) in a delicate falsetto'. The satirical point of the piece has faded like an old photograph, but it serves to show that Mr. Swamp was a sufficiently well-known figure among his contemporaries at Cambridge to be honoured with a caricature.

After meeting Maurice Baring, Eddie combined the high serious-ness of his scholarship and the intensity of his aesthetic life with a love of irresponsible pleasure in which several of his friends were unable to follow him. Henceforward there was always one part of his life which was a mental escapade. It may be argued that a man cannot initially acquire any basic quality of mind from outside, though it can be brought out and developed by his environ-ment; and yet in the case of Eddie Marsh, to regard him as an 'original', a man of genius born with marked characteristics and habits of mind, would be to mistake what is perhaps the secret of his individuality. He was always wide open to impressions. In Blake's words 'he became what he beheld,' so that it might almost be possible to break up and reduce his character to its component parts, giving them names—Jane Marsh, Denniston, Rutherford, Verrall, Russell, Baring—and others who have not yet entered this story. What was most individual in him was his unconscious ability to be infected by such contrasted influences and then to make of them that harmony which was his own unique personality. There was one friend, who came up in his second year, whose influence, less easy to define, was considerable and beneficial as a counterweight to the first intoxicating impact of Baring. It is possible that the influence in this case worked both ways, and that Eddie's confessions on the nature of his friendships did something to help G. E. Moore formulate one aspect of his moral philosophy which he set out in his *Principia Ethica*, which came out in 1902. Moore, Eddie, and his friend John Barran, formed a private study group for reading the classics together.

In August 1894 Eddie wrote his first letter to Moore from the Pension Scherrer at Heidelberg. Moore had sent him a frank letter warning him against his tendency to attach exaggerated importance to interests of inferior value. Among these was a habit of gossiping about the more superficial qualities of his acquain-tances. 'The good advice,' Eddie replied, 'made me feel a little uncomfortable (for if your eyes are tender they are also piercing).'

I'm leading such a funny life here that even after three weeks of it I'm sometimes overcome with sudden laughter, for instance when I realize that I've spent the last couple of hours playing dice to see who shall pay for the quantities of cider we've been drinking, or when I find myself planning a childish lie to tell the Frau Professor in explanation of my being out after 10 (you must understand I'm having a St. Martin's Summer of being a schoolboy which I never was at Westminster—very curious). I don't think anything ever happened to me more interesting than this time of almost complete detachment from my ordinary way of life, and the opportunity of seeing how much of one's usual character is accident and how much is essential. The chief thing that I recognized was the way in which my feelings towards my new companions immediately began to run in the old channels. It seems so strange that there should be people who don't know the two ways of caring for people, the one mainly through the senses, the other through the mind. Do you remember the terrible argument we had about it with George Trevy?[1] Before I'd been here a week I found that quite without any choice of mine I was great friends with a German boy of 17 with whom I haven't an idea in common, who has beautiful eyes like Verrall's and a manner which happens to charm me, and that I was always glad to be with him and to listen to whatever he chose to say, however uninteresting I should have thought it from anyone else; and also with an exceedingly clever Frenchman, whose exterior leaves me quite untouched, but to whom I can say anything that comes into my head with the certainty of being understood, and whose conversation is a perpetual delight to me; and also that there were some people who might or might not have any number of good qualities, but whose presence would always afflict me because of the ugly coarseness of their looks and manners.

The thing that surprised me was the way in which I turned out not to have any moral prejudices at all about the way in which other people ought to behave, and very few about how I ought to behave myself. . . . I don't say that I go to brothels or like German pictures any more than I did in England, but I drink quantities of beer, talk smut, and say that I'm going for a walk when I'm going to a brasserie with all complacency. How can one possibly object to people behaving in the way they've been brought up to? One immediately feels that it would be the extreme of bad taste not only to try to reform them but even to hold aloof from their occupations.

All this comes under the heading of talk about people. That was the only point in your good advice that I couldn't accept. Surely there isn't anything in the world so interesting as people's characters —and if so, why not talk about them? Do you call Russell an old

[1] G. M. Trevelyan, elder brother of Robert.

woman when he explains to you someone whom he has studied? It always seems to me one of the most brilliant displays of intellect I'm acquainted with. Of course if you simply mean that one ought not to talk gossip I agree with you and admit that I do it too much.

A month later he was still at Heidelberg. Of Moore's reply, which must have been critical of his behaviour, Eddie remarked: 'You mustn't be so ironical another time or I shall expect your letter in terror.'

I shan't excuse myself by saying that the Cambridge side of me is dormant, tho' that is perfectly true, as one's real friends don't belong to one side or another, but are part of one's consciousness which one carries about everywhere. I will rather say that I 'object to the weariness of composition' like a dear old lady in the journal of the Psychical Society who got someone else to write about the ghost. That's always the true and best explanation.

I've got a confession to make, I had boasted of my capacity to tell lies without knowing what it was. The only time I was put seriously to the test I failed dismally. I still think that when people ask about things that aren't their business, and you know that they'll be troublesome if you tell them the truth, you have a right to lie, especially if the secret is shared by others; but it's exceedingly difficult. To be sure there are certain words (such as *Stadtgarten*) which appear to me to have a double meaning; in the instance given, the first is 'public garden', the second *Tingeltangel* or rowdy concert in a public house, and I have little difficulty in saying that I'm going to the *Stadtgarten* when the first meaning is only the ostensible one. But it's beyond doubt that you have more morals than I have. In other respects I've been a perfect angel in the last month. I soon got tired of drinking too much beer; and since I've known enough German to carry on a more or less rational conversation we don't talk smut any more.

He had been to the opera at Mannheim. 'The musical taste of the average German doesn't seem to be better than ours; for instance they have the same habit of beginning to clap as soon as the voice part of a song is over, without waiting for the symphony, and the theatre is much fuller for Meyerbeer than for *Fidelio*.' A fortnight before he had written to Bertrand Russell after hearing he would be unable to come and join the party in Heidelberg.

I'm very sorry not to see you, though in some ways it's a good thing as I'm not in the least either solemn or suitable. I'm not going to give you an account of all my wickedness, as I'm tired of doing that. I resolved to write to all my friends and see who'd be shocked first, beginning at the most likely end with Barran, G. Trevy, Conybeare; to my utter astonishment they contented themselves one after another with telling me not to get fat, and the first person who thought of being horrorstruck was Moore.

To Russell he enlarged on the experience of opera-going. 'The performances aren't quite satisfactory, as the actors are so dreadful to look at.' *Fidelio* in particular had given him food for thought. 'Fat women are in a sad dilemma—either they must have their bodices all of the same stuff, in which case they look as if they were going to burst, or they must have an interval of some other stuff in which case they look as if they had!' He had scandalized everyone by falling asleep in the middle of being drawn round the sights of Frankfurt in a fly, and he concluded his budget with: 'Write me a postcard now and then when your brain is for the moment off the boil.'

Russell's reply showed that he did not envy Eddie's household of Frenchmen. 'I don't quite understand your not liking Frenchmen,' Eddie remarked in his next budget to Haslemere. 'Is it simply because they are unchaste? It is very disgusting—all the ones here for instance fornicate pretty regularly from 16 years old, and talk about it in a way that would sicken me in England—but it's merely a matter of education.' Eddie's wide latitude of tolerance was not accepted by either of his philosophers, and next year G. E. Moore was to raise the issue again. For the present, since Bertrand Russell was not taking it very seriously, Eddie proceeded to describe a copy of *Zion's Herald*, an American magazine he had found in the pension.

I was absolutely stupefied by the sublimity of its funniness. For instance there was a young lady who was explaining that when she was in Europe the great ocean always washed away her recollection of her country's imperfections, and 'indeed' she went on 'the flapping of the Eagle's wings may often be heard in my conversation'. I began to wonder what I should say if she made such a statement to me. I could only think of Alice's answer 'That must be very curious' —and finally an advertisement that looks like poetry tho' it is not.

TORTURED
DISFIGURED
HUMILIATED
By unsightly skin and blood diseases
Is there hope of cure?

CUTICURA RESOLVENT
Is the greatest of skin purifiers
As well as of blood purifiers
Because of its peculiar action on the pores
Entirely vegetable, solvent, and effective—

I don't know if 'Entirely vegetable' etc. appeals to you as it did to me—the metre becomes so *stately* at that point.

On October 1, shortly before leaving for England, he wrote again to Russell.

I shall write you a very serious letter some day, for the sake of my character, but till then, I'll go on being frivolous if you like. My last great adventure was meeting Oscar Browning accidentally at the station—he was on the way to Elfiel to buy German champagne, and had come here for German cigars. I brought him for a night to the Pension—he made a great impression on everyone and was very jolly. Almost the first thing he told me was that the Duchesses of York and Teck are going to pay him a visit at Cambridge next term—which, as he remarked, would give people a great deal to talk about, but it wasn't his fault, as they'd practically invited themselves.

By October 23 Eddie was back at Trinity, playing fives, and reading thirty pages of Zola a day. 'I saw Miss Pearsall Smith on Saturday at the Richter concert, and we discussed the comparative fascination of space and economics. She had such a pretty green cloak with fur trimmings.'

I had such a funny scene with my bedmaker the night you left. I was in my bedroom and heard a timid voice calling me. 'Well?' I said. 'Isn't this a sad affair, sir? . . . about your table, sir.' 'Well?' 'Weren't you surprised to find the leaf still in?' 'Very much, why was it?' 'Didn't the gentleman tell you, sir?' 'What gentleman? What's happened?' It turned out she'd broken a bit of the wood just as Jeremy Booth came in with a pipe of mine. Wasn't it extraordinary how she couldn't tell me straight out? I hope when my wife dies, or anything like that, I shall always have someone to make my troubles ridiculous by their exaggerated concern.

During the month he attended a meeting of the Apostles, the select society founded by F. D. Maurice of which Eddie and his close friends were initiates. In the previous term Eddie had read a paper on *The Ring and the Book*, and it was now Moore's turn. Eddie wrote to Russell, who had by now gone down:

> Have you heard about Moore's paper on Friendship? There's not much to say about it, as it was a specification of one's own ideal more or less, without much practical bearing. Of course our poor old friend copulation came in for its usual slating, one would think from the way people talk about it in the Society that it was a kind of Home Rule Bill that has to be taken some notice of but which everyone thinks a bore. . . .
>
> It's great fun seeing so much of Verrall as I do now (I go to him for composition again). The other day I asked him the meaning of something in the Shelley we had to translate. 'I'm sure I can't tell you, my little dear,' he answered, 'you pays your money and you takes your choice.' That kind of thing makes me very cheerful. . . . Thanks for the photograph, though you look rather bumptious.

During this term he travelled to London for his first visit to Edmund Gosse at Delamere Terrace. At this time Gosse was aged forty-five, the friend of Swinburne and Stevenson, the most agreeable and amusing host in literary London. Maurice Baring could not have done his friend a better turn. Eddie had already shaken hands with Gosse at a tea-party of Mrs. Verrall's but this did not prevent Baring from bowing stiffly with the remark: 'Let me introduce Mr. Marsh, my hanger on. We needn't pay any attention to him.' Eddie wrote at once to Robert Trevelyan.

> Baring took me to supper with Edmund Gosse on Sunday—he's a most amusing man—his conversation is described in Stevenson's essay on Conversation under the name of Purcell, do you remember? He was in the teakettle mood when I was there. I met Harland the editor of the *Yellow Book*, whom I thought an awful little man, tho' next day, on getting accustomed to his manner, I made up my mind he was likeable on the whole. Next Sunday I hope to go to supper with the even more distinguished Bridges. Talking of poets, I met John Davidson for a few minutes the other day—all I could see was that he seemed a genial and lighthearted little man, with a nice Scotch accent.

The meeting with Davidson had occurred at Cambridge when Baring invited John Lane, the publisher, and some of his friends to dinner and provided his guests with a printed menu three inches long and headed *Of this small paper edition five copies only have been printed.*

ii

Russell, Sickert, and R. C. Trevelyan had gone down. By staying up an extra year for the second part of the Classical Tripos, Eddie met a new generation of freshmen at Trinity among whom he made new friends who were to play an important part in his life: Victor Lytton, Desmond MacCarthy, and Reginald Balfour.

The year 1895 began with news of Sickert, who had found a job with a firm of advertisers. Meeting his brother Walter in the street he had complained that he had no time for writing. 'You needn't bother about it,' said Walter. 'You'll be kicked out of the business soon enough.' In May Oswald walked into Eddie's new room at Trinity, admired the nasturtiums in the window-box, and noticed the floor littered with little strips of paper ready for use as markers. Later in the month Sickert sent a report from London. 'Walter is in Venice wearing white kid gloves.'

> I wanted to tell you of what Copper Smith has been doing; you know everybody was rather horrid when Oscar [Wilde] was sold up, some of his friends went and bought things for nothing and scrambled about. Copper, who does not know him at all, spent what money he could in buying his books, had them done up in a parcel without looking at them, ready to send back to him when he came out.

In August Oswald Sickert was in Dieppe, where he had spent his childhood, and was again reminded of Oscar Wilde. He was about seven years old at the time he was recalling, staying with his sister and his brother at his mother's old school.

> Then a little later the school stopped and we took the house for the summer, and I remember Oscar reading us his poems in the meadow in front of the house, and playing with Lea and me. Once when he was reading his poems dear old Miss Slea, the schoolmistress, 'Aunty' we used to call her, interrupted him and said: 'No, my dear fellow, not like that. Now begin again. . . .' Then another year we had a house on the Route d'Arques, and Nelly and Walter (the first year of their marriage) had a dear little house, and Walter used to put his pictures out of the window to dry them. Then one day Whistler arrived, and he used to be at odd corners, standing upright, immaculate, dainty, doing little water-colours as another man would roll a cigarette; then Dégas came too, and I shall never forget the gentleness and the charm of his personality.

At the turn of the year Eddie had been on a walking-tour in

Switzerland with Bob Trevelyan and G. E. Moore, who were to be his main correspondents in the ensuing months. In the spring Trevelyan heard from Roger Fry of a spot near Naples, and wrote assuring Eddie that if he stayed with him in July he would be free to come and go. 'I, wrapped in the contemplation of the Ideal, would be as indifferent to your comings and goings as Buddha in his ascetic stage to the journeyings of the finest ants in and out of his nostrils.' Eddie managed to resist the temptation on account of the books he had to get through before next term. 'I've been reading one of the most entertaining books I've come across— De Quincey's autobiography. Reading simply the text, one thinks it's written as completely at random as a book could be—but when you come to the footnotes you find there have been un-suspected possibilities of divagation which he has honourably avoided.' Trevelyan's reply showed signs of impatience. 'I am sure you will find your wife at the top of a bookshelf. Men are fated beforehand to take their wives from strange places. Adam found his in himself, many find theirs in other people's beds, while a relation of mine found his in his cook.'

In March Eddie was again at Grimsby Farm. He had just done some playgoing in London and had taken Moore to a matinée of *Frou-frou*, 'of which', Moore writes,[1] 'I remember nothing but the figure of the husband (the principal character) and that his wife was continually saying to him, "Oh James, you are wonderful!" On that occasion I was introduced to Marsh's mother and his sister, and even in the short time I saw his mother I admired her extremely and understood, I think, how "superior she was to the common run" as Marsh himself says in one of his letters.' After the occasion in question Moore wrote to apologize for his country clothes. 'Of course neither I nor my people minded a scrap what you came to see us in,' Eddie replied, 'but I'd be careful *who* I came to see in a cap, people would think it funny.' Eddie was going to see Bridges next day. 'He'd be a capital man to Boswellize when one got the knack.' Bridges wrote, however, to put him off. 'I have a cricket club meeting after dinner this Wednesday.' When the meeting did take place Eddie brought with him Verrall's book on Euripides. Soon afterwards Bridges sent to Grimsby Farm a long and erudite account of his views on the book, which was the start of a lifelong correspondence.

[1] Letter to the author, August 17, 1954.

Moore, who was in Switzerland, and not enjoying himself, had once again written in criticism of certain of Eddie's friends who seemed to be encouraging the more frivolous side of his nature. Eddie replied from Haslemere, where he was the guest of Bertrand Russell. (Moore was not his only critic. Trevelyan also in a mood of dejection had remarked: 'You have surrendered your birthright.') Eddie noted a verbal correction in Moore's letter, and declared it was considerate of him to have altered the epithet for his friends from 'wicked' to 'polished', and went on: 'I prefer your style of plain narrative (as a succedaneum to breakfast, where there are so many other claims on one's attention) to your style of complicated diegesis.' He then threatened to copy out a passage from a dissertation of Russell's which he had been reading, but feared Moore would understand it perfectly 'so that there would be no revenge'. Moore had been disgusted by some of the young people he had met abroad. Eddie made his comment:

> I wish you could get over your horror of incontinent people. I'm sure it's exaggerated. I went wrong myself in the opposite direction, and am considerably ashamed now to think of the conversations I heard and joined in with enjoyment—it was very odd the complete *bouleversement* of my ordinary way of looking at people which took place as soon as I went abroad (and changed back when I got home); their morals, being all of a piece, seemed to me as good as any other morals, and I believe I only noticed the depravity of their *manners* because some of them were better than others. . . . This was interrupted by lunch of which I had great need after Russell's identification of the Point with the Soul.

It was probably during this visit to the Russells that Eddie met Lionel Johnson.

> When Russell and the others went to bed, L.J. asked me to stay up with him: he was born with insomnia, he told me, and had never been able to sleep, in his cradle or since; so we settled down to talk. His conversation was enthralling, but alas very little of what he said has stuck in my memory. One topic was the novels of George Meredith, which he put very high; but he owned that after giving a week of his life to the first chapter of *The Egoist* he had come to the conclusion that it had no meaning whatever. Later in the night he discoursed with eloquence on the *Summa* of St. Thomas Aquinas, which he exalted as the most wonderful structure of thought that the world had produced; and—this is my last fragment—he said that he

had never in his life been able to do a mathematical sum of any kind. At about five or six in the morning he poured himself out a tumblerful of neat whisky, after drinking which he said that now he would be able to sleep; so I went to bed, leaving him curled under a rug in a big armchair, 'upgather'd like a sleeping flower'—he looked so young and delicate and defenceless.[1]

It was a brief encounter yet it made a big enough impression on Johnson to prompt him two years later with the idea of dedicating his poem *Windermere*[2] to his acquaintance of one night.

Eddie wrote again to Moore on the day he left England for Hildesheim in company with his mother and sister, and
polished
expected to be joined by 'the wicked [*sic*] and clever Maurice Baring'. On his way abroad he posted a letter which he felt represented a distinct stage in his academic career. It was a long list of emendations for correction in the next edition of Sir Richard Jebb's *Philoctetes*.

His destination was a small house in the Weissenbergestrasse, a two-storeyed, square, grey house with a flat roof, the residence of Dr. Timme, Baring's tutor in German. In leisure hours it was Eddie's custom to go with Baring to the *Biergarten*, listen to the band, drink beer and eat *Butterbrot* and play what they called *The Game*. It would start by one of them saying, 'Who is this by, in *The Game*?' Whereupon the other player would be allowed two guesses at the authorship of a quotation, and a third on the strict condition that it followed *immediately* after the second. They kept the score in a notebook, and it was found that Baring could never guess a line out of *Lycidas* while his opponent was invariably caught out by *Adonais*. On the other hand Baring seemed to have an unerring ear for Zola's prose style but lost several marks one afternoon for attributing one of Milton's best lines to the poetaster Montgomery. Eddie for his part made a bad mistake which appreciably affected Baring's life. 'Who is this by in *The Game*?' Baring started one day, and quoted three lines of his own.[3] 'Shakespeare,' said Eddie, as he snatched his third guess. 'It was not that I took myself seriously,' Baring wrote years afterwards

---

[1] From a letter to Mr. Adrian Earle, March 1943.
[2] *Ireland, and Other Poems* (1897).
[3] Sank in great calm, as dreaming unison
Of darkness and midsummer sound must die
Before the daily duty of the sun.

in his memoir, 'but the mere fact of E. making such a mistake convinced me that mistakes *in my favour* were possible.'[1] It was the start of his ambitions as a poet.

To this stay with Dr. Timme belongs one of the Baring remarks that Eddie particularly treasured. Baring was late, as usual, for breakfast, and Eddie, also as usual, was punctual. 'Oh do come on,' cried Eddie, as Baring at last entered in his dressing-gown. 'You know you don't like a cold egg.' Baring stopped by his chair, looking piqued. 'Well, of course I don't like a BITTERLY cold egg!' Eddie meanwhile was not being unmindful of Moore's friendly warning against wasting his substance on frivolous pastimes, and on August 29 he wrote to Moore during his second Continental opera season:

It's a rather delicate question how long after getting a letter one ought to answer it. If we hold with Plato that all true pleasures except those of smell consist in the restoration of the normal condition, it is clear that we should reply by return of post; for he out of whom the first letter has passed will desire to receive the compensating one with as little delay as possible, and if we leave him till he has given up all hope, grown accustomed to the pain and in fact forgotten all about it, the answer will presumably give him no pleasure at all. But I'm rather inclined to think that the true delights are the unexpected ones, and that one considers a prompt answer merely one's due, like the affection of one's parents or the payment of one's scholarship allowance, or a merited eulogy. It's always distressing to disagree with Plato, but I can't say I enjoyed your letter any the less because I had to wait for it.

My reason for not answering at once was a more practical one— I've been waiting till I'd heard a little more Wagner. Mottl has been doing the *Ring* at Karlsruhe and I've now heard all but the *Götterd.* which is to be played tonight.

Of course I've 'got beyond' the Oscar Wilde idea that art and morals have no connection at all—indeed I now think the first essential for any work of fiction is that it should have an adequate moral basis; but I don't think I go quite as far as you, as I think to expect the moral basis to be 'true' comes to the same thing as expecting it to meet one's own views. Morals are such an extremely complicated affair that I think any *Anschauung* would do, so long as it was consistent, because it is just as impossible for any one view of morals to be wholly false as to contain the whole truth. At least if

---

[1] *The Puppet Show of Memory*, p. 162. It may be noted here that his elegy on Lord Lucas appeared in the third (1917) volume of *Georgian Poetry*.

you want to convince me of the contrary you must explain away *Antony and Cleopatra*. What I find unsatisfactory about Wagner is not that his morality seems to me false, but that I can't make head or tail of it. What on earth is the meaning of the *Valkyrie*? Why does Wotan punish Brünnhilde? and in *Götterdam.* what is the sense of the outrageous incident of the potion? If I wanted to combat Verrall's ideas about Euripides I should do it by writing a book on the same lines about the *Ring*.[1] The character of Wotan seems to me at present to be a proof of Wagner's sheer imbecility as a dramatist. And then the intense vulgarity of the conception of Fricka, both in general and in every detail! As a satire on τὸ τί ἦν εἶναι bourgeoise[2] it would be extraordinarily felicitous; but that the great goddess of marriage should be so conceived is as strange as if Georges Ohnet[3] had accidentally produced Mrs. Elton[4] because that was as near as he could get to a lady. It isn't possible that Wagner's intention was satirical, is it? if so, how do you explain the triumph of Wotan? I don't agree with you about the *Rheingold*, it's true there are plenty of incidents, but they really are so puerile—they might do to read in an epic, but on the stage Alberich's transformations and above all the part where the giants cover Freia with the treasure (by the help of towel horses) seems utterly meaningless. And $2\frac{1}{2}$ hours at a stretch is far too much.

But the music is surely sublime. I've never been so much impressed with anything as the 1st scene of the *Rheingold*, the 1st and 3rd acts of *Valkyrie*, and the end of *Siegfried*. Of course I'm perfectly helpless at a first hearing, but I'm looking forward to the most intense pleasure at the third. *C'est riche mais ce n'est pas raffiné* comes into my mind every now and then, I must admit, but what is refinement by the side of such power and magnificence.

> Who would not give all these for twop-
> -ennyworth only of beautiful Soup?

In fact I'm *a posteriori* converted to Music Drama (though I still can't

---

[1] Mr. G. E. Moore's comment on this passage is as follows: 'The answer to your first query is, I think, that Marsh thought he could make as good a case for thinking that Wagner in the *Ring* did not mean what he seemed at first sight to mean, but something much more profound, as Verrall had made for so thinking in the case of Euripides; and that this would refute Verrall, because it was so obvious, in Wagner's case, that he did only mean what he seemed at first sight to mean and not anything more profound. But how on earth Marsh could have made as good a case in the instance of Wagner, as Verrall made in that of Euripides, I cannot guess.'

[2] The 'essence' of bourgeoisie.

[3] Georges Ohnet, author of *La Grande Marnière*, the French dramatist popular at the time, often made fun of by Marsh and Baring for his vulgarities.

[4] Mrs. Elton, the character in *Emma*, emphatically 'not a lady'.

The Rt. Hon. Spencer Perceval, 1762-1812

A posthumous portrait by G. F. Joseph painted from the death mask by Nollekens

Father

Howard Marsh
Master of Downing

Mother

Jane Marsh

Eddie Marsh at Bruton Street

Eddie Marsh at Cambridge

upset my theoretical objections) and I think that if the drama were as good as the music Wagner's operas would be the finest things in the world.

But I've followed the thread of my discourse long enough. I prefer 'debate' to 'exposition in turn', so we'll leave the discussion of the 'motifs' till we meet. . . .

I should like to be able to account by heredity for my blind worship of the French and all their attributes. I don't believe I've got a French ancestor nearer than Charlotte de la Tremouille who married the Earl of Derby in the 17th century! It's very bad for my best nature to be here. I'm so incomparably the best tempered, best natured, least narrowminded, most industrious, and most chaste, of all the pensionnaires. And besides all this I'm so irreproachably modest that all these qualities make me beloved instead of detested —in fact there's not a person in the house who doesn't think it a crying shame when anybody else helps himself to my tobacco.

In September he went back to Trinity for his last term and the second part of the Tripos. Robert Bridges came to luncheon in his rooms one day in November, but there were no other social events. He was in Rome for Christmas. On New Year's Eve a letter from Moore arrived which he considered disappointingly brief. He replied in kind:

Not a word shall you find about the many beautiful and interesting objects, especially to the classical student, to be found in this celebrated city, which beggar alike description and word-painting. (You don't know how hard it is to write with such subtle badness as that sentence exhibits.)

He recognized in Moore a scholar and thinker of a far more serious purpose than himself and a friend whose genuine concern for him was one of the chief benefits of these last years at Cambridge. The emphasis in *Principia Ethica* on the value of human relationships (the ideal friend as comely in body as in mind and spirit) as a desirable part of a man's aesthetic life among works of art, shows that for all their differences they had much in common. Perhaps it would be more exact to say that Moore confirmed in Eddie a natural bent towards a conception of Platonic friendship bound up with the experience of art which otherwise might never have developed as it did. It would be absurd to underline the influence of Baring, who broadened his view of life, without acknowledging Moore, who certainly deepened it. It was a younger generation than Eddie Marsh's, men who went up to Cambridge in the first few years of the new century, who were to form what was called the Bloomsbury group, a circle of creative artists whose conception of the function of art and the nature of the good life was largely derived from *Principia Ethica*. Roger Fry alone was their senior in age. Yet the climate of thought which centred in Moore and Russell in the middle 'nineties found no more characteristic product than Eddie Marsh. He remained apart from Bloomsbury, not so much because of his being himself no creative artist, but because he was a man who could function to best effect among the arts as an amateur. He lived in the heart of the artistic world of his time, but he saw to it that he was only a spectator and critic. He chose to belong no less to the *beau monde*, but moved from one order of society to the other with the ease of a man walking out of the elegant drawing-room into the bohemian studio of his own house. His proper place was in both, yet he belonged nowhere, always feeling at home, yet always a guest, as if having no private life but what he was invited to share in the private lives of others.

When his last term was over and the examination behind him (he was the first student to take the new subject in the Tripos syllabus called Pure Scholarship) he returned to Bruton Street with his books and furniture, and with only a vague idea of what he wanted to do in life. By now this seemed to be clarifying itself into 'something connected with the Foreign Office'. Looking back in after times on his sojourn at the University he came to realize that the clear and serene air in which he saw it was by no means an enchantment lent by distance. An earlier generation, racked with religious doubts, and abandoning its 'belief in Jonah's Whale with the agony of losing a limb' had bequeathed to its successors what Eddie came to regard as a cheerful and confident agnosticism. Compared with the young men he was to meet or hear tell of in years to come he considered his companions singularly blessed in their freedom from the obsession of sex. 'We had no known "affairs",' he wrote, 'and I can only remember two of my intimates even falling in love.' His friends were tingling with intellectual curiosity, accustomed to arguing round and about, in the firm belief that Truth was only just round the corner; they worked hard at the immediate task with little thought of their 'careers'; they were keen politicians, mostly of the Liberal persuasion, aware of the stresses in the world outside but not unduly disturbed by them; they were ardent students of literature, both English and foreign, holding the sister arts (except, perhaps, music) in somewhat chilly respect, and to sport they were almost wholly indifferent. They lived with a high degree of plainness, entertaining one another chiefly at breakfast, generally on buttered eggs, dining almost every evening in Hall and meeting afterwards for the consumption not of alcohol but cocoa. 'Taken altogether,' he declared forty years later, 'it seems now to have been a very civilized form of life.'

As the year 1895 came to an end, closer to his heart than the prospect of that 'something connected with the Foreign Office' was his anxiety to restore what he could of the happy, bygone relationship with his mother.

Chapter Five

TRANSITIONAL
(1896–1898)

I T was January 1896; the result of his final examination was a
First Class honours with Star. The hopes of Rutherford and
latterly of Verrall had been fulfilled. Academically it had
been an almost model career. In his first year he had won the
Freshman's Prize, which is worth recording since it provided the
only instance of his wantonly committing an act in doubtful
taste. He chose for his prize three volumes of Zola in order to give
the dons a lesson in broadmindedness and, as he said, 'Europeanize
their outlook'. They expostulated, but he held his ground, still
infected with the rebel spirit which a month or two before had
driven him to the bottle. And in his last year he had won the
Senior Chancellor's Medal, which also led to a discourtesy,
though this time accidental. On the letter from the Master gently
but sternly pointing out that he should have attended the
ceremony of presentation he wrote: 'This was the worst thing that
ever happened.'

He was now at Scoones's, the crammer for Civil Service candidates in Garrick Street, where Baring was already a student,
struggling to make up his academic deficiencies. In January
Jane Marsh wrote from Rome, where she had seen the new year
in with her family. (She did not at all agree with the guide-book
which had informed her that the work on the ceiling of the
Sistine Chapel was 'second-rate'.) She and Howard were pressing
Eddie to try for a Fellowship of his College. An alternative plan
was to find some friend who would be willing to nominate him
for the Foreign Office. Eddie was in no mood to force the issue
where his career was concerned, and he had no inclination to look
beyond the next exam. He fostered no ambition beyond the
immediate objective. Whatever came his way as an honourable
occupation he would welcome and thrive on as best he could.
At Easter he was in his favourite retreat at Cold Ash, reading

Molière, Pascal, Alfred de Vigny (whom he described as 'a kind of French Wordsworth') and Marshall's Political Economy. His landlady struck him 'as one of those rare beings who are absolutely contented with their lot. She does not have to read Marshall', he said in a letter to Moore. 'I like reading Political Economy though I do not understand a word of it yet. To approach the Law of Diminishing Returns was almost as great a moment as the entry into the Sistine Chapel—it was a thing I had 'heard as much of and could as little conceive. (Don't tell Sanger, but I found the Sistine Chapel less of a disappointment.)'

Moore had just left a reading-party in Cornwall and he wrote to Grimsby Farm. His companions had not all been equally congenial.

It may be a very serious, because a very ridiculous thing, to have a philosophic mind, but I cannot refrain from asking what enjoyment means. If it means pleasure, as I imagine it ought to, I should then say that my pains in those three weeks decidedly overbalanced my pleasures. I am disposed to hope that I am peculiar in a propensity to be always bored (not to mention more criminal sources of misery) but I cannot convince myself that it is not the same with everyone. I seem to see it in their looks (as Sidney saw what he felt in the moon's) whatever they may say. . . . Yet with this persuasion, forced on me by my own experience, that the pains of life much overbalance the pleasures, I am not a pessimist. I think that most things are more valuable than pleasure, and certainly I would rather know I was in pain than enjoy the greatest pleasure. And though I see little hope of obtaining, or anyone's obtaining, in this life that complete satisfaction in contrast to which almost everything actual seems painful, yet I am afraid I believe in something better which I can neither prove nor understand. How very solemn! I wish I had the tongue of Mephistopheles.

The first concern of Eddie's answer was to explain the character of the younger Trevelyan, with whom Moore was out of sympathy; then he came to the larger issue.

As for the question of pleasure etc. (I think enjoyment is a better word, it seems less specialized) you know I find it so difficult to look at anything 'valuable' except as enjoyable that I can hardly discuss it. I mean that the element by virtue of which goods are good seems to me always to be an element of enjoyment. My own idea is that the positive pleasures of life far outweigh the positive pains, especially in recollection. The damnable thing is the ineliminable feeling of dissatisfaction, not with the particular pleasures as they come, but with one's existence as a whole—the shadow of an all too earthly despair—that comes over one in all the entractes and poisons everything. It's not exactly boredom. I don't think, really, that I'm often bored—but the sense that I am tied, for the whole of my one chance —which, being what it is, is too many by one—to this lost, evaporated 'me'.

Moore wrote again on April 17:

What you (and others) say about enjoyment makes me feel very uncomfortable: it does seems as if pleasure had much more to do with good than I can possibly see. . . . Your other remarks are very profound, and I'm afraid I haven't quite got to the bottom of them.

But they seem rather to confirm my view, for surely that feeling of dissatisfaction, which you acknowledge, is much the most important thing there is? Can you rate highly particular pleasures except by their reference to that? I think that is what I chiefly mean by being bored, and I suppose I have it more constantly than most.

Moore's comments on Desmond MacCarthy, another of his companions in Cornwall, about whose morbid habit of self-deprecation Eddie had expressed concern, reflect on Eddie as well.

I can't take MacCarthy's morbidness seriously, with him, as with your modesty, it seems to me mere words, put out because he knows he has the ability to produce thereby a good aesthetic impression, but not at all proceeding from any misery of feeling; and surely morbidness proper can only be of the feelings. I should like to know what this distrust of intellectual fitness is, if you think it is really solid and serious. If it comes out in self-deprecation I shouldn't have thought it could mean much—certainly no disease.

One of the aspirants to the Diplomatic Service at Mr. Scoones's establishment was George Graham, who one day was to become ambassador to Belgium. He took a liking to Eddie Marsh, but deplored the impression he gave of a somewhat uncouth Cambridge intellectual. It was during a bicycle-ride from Margate to Canterbury in this spring of 1896 that Graham expounded the whole duty of a man about town, pointing out that it was not enough for a Civil Servant to be blessed with a cultivated mind, he should also be the glass of fashion. 'A man who is correctly dressed is always given the benefit of the doubt,' he maintained, 'because at first glance he is found likeable whatever may be thought of him later.

To start with,' he went on, having dismounted and gained his companion's full attention, 'you are wearing the wrong apparatus on your nose', and Eddie put up a hand to his pince-nez. Graham assured his friend that the correct thing was an eye-glass. He then proceeded to indicate the subtle wrongness of his tie, his jacket, his trousers. There was apparently nothing about him which was not dismissed as either bohemian or provincial. Graham himself must have been a man of enviably correct appearance or Eddie would never have so readily set about reorganizing his wardrobe. The eye-glass, especially adopted as part of the decoration of a façade, became a feature of his personality. It gave his countenance hauteur and, in conjunction with the tufted eyebrows, a slightly magisterial sternness which often misled at a first encounter, seeming to hold the stranger at arm's length.

It was characteristic of him that once he was convinced that the enthusiasm of a friend whom he respected was well grounded he espoused the same cause and carried it further than its original champion. Throughout the Edwardian decade to come he was indeed the glass of fashion. But as yet it was not beyond him to say 'lunch' for 'luncheon', or pronounce 'valet' as if it were a French word, or be guilty of other such departures from the accepted idiom which in after years would have been impossible from his lips. Eddie Marsh, as he was known to the world for half a century, was coming into being, but was not yet fully evolved.

In July, while still working at Scoones's, he appeared in his first London season, attending balls almost every night until four and sometimes five in the morning. 'I refused a most delightful ball for Thursday,' he wrote to Victor Lytton, 'and mother gave me five shillings as a reward.' Jane Marsh, he confessed, was shocked by his worldly behaviour, and had even complained when he succumbed to the latest craze and attended a 'bicycle breakfast' in Battersea Park 'which seemed to me *the* most beneficial thing I could have done'. Among quieter pleasures he had spent some days with the Cornishes at Eton and met Neville Lytton, Victor's younger brother, and A. C. Benson ('I almost sobbed at the beauty of his writing on the blackboard') and he had gone several times to enjoy the flowers in Hyde Park, 'which seems rather a mild dissipation for an heir of all the ages—still it's nice to form friendly relations with the London County Council'. In all this excitement he had lost Lady Lytton's signed copy of the poems of Wilfrid

Blunt, and by a roundabout means was having a new copy sent to the poet for signature. 'When it comes I shall lend it to the cook to give it an appearance of maturity and then send it innocently to your mother.'

A fortnight before he was due to sit for the Civil Service examination he withdrew to the academic peace of Cambridge and took as his companion Reginald Balfour, who had come up to Trinity in his fourth year. One of Balfour's aims in life at this time was to support Jane Marsh in her efforts to bring Eddie back to Christianity. Having never raised the subject herself since her last fruitless attempt three years before, it seemed providential to Jane Marsh that one of Eddie's contemporaries, endowed with all the brilliance of his other friends, should be not only sincerely religious but anxious to bring Eddie to a state of grace. They met or corresponded throughout this year, beginning in January when Eddie had issued a challenge with the statement, 'The use and origin of Evil is the rock upon which all Theology splits.' In August, after they had drawn closer together at Cambridge, Balfour recommended him to read Stopford Brooke's *Life of the Rev. F. W. Robertson*, an astute move, for the human interest in the book caught Eddie's imagination and provoked him into the first and only serious discussion on religion in his life. He learned from this book that faith comes through the Holy Spirit. 'But how does the Holy Spirit come in the first place?' he asked Balfour. 'The greatest obstacle to communion with God,' Balfour replied, 'is a man's want of uprightness and steadfastness in his daily life.' Eddie granted that 'life is not without duty and unworldliness', then again asked how the Spirit comes to a man. Balfour answered from his own experience:

In my own case the 'spirit' came to me quite against my will. I had conceived quite a contempt for it. 'Righteousness' was the thing I was always thinking about and I did not care what the motive was. And then quite suddenly (and without any visible cause except re-reading *Ecce Homo* and still more Matthew Arnold's Comment on Christianity in *St. Paul and Protestantism*) I was filled with an intense feeling of loyalty to Christ.

But will this be any help to you? I suppose not. I doubt if you will ever get there. I think perhaps your mind is differently shaped. But I am convinced that one day, and possibly soon, if you make a real effort, if you think of the effects and of the essential worth and motive of every act and word of yours, as I did for eighteen months, you will find yourself in an unconscious harmony with the divine will. . . . I do hope you will try to hold fast to the idea that life is not without religion. . . . I am half afraid to tell you that I am beginning to believe in the divinity of Christ in a more special sense than I believe in my own or your divinity. And so far as I personify God at all it is in Christ's person. But what does it matter? To believe in a first order of the Universe is the supreme act of faith for our generation and to live in harmony with that first order is its highest duty. You are beginning to do both. Go on and prosper.

The correspondence could go no further. It had ended with Balfour content to have reassured himself that his friend at least had 'some vague sense of the divine in life'. Meanwhile MacCarthy alone of his friends was unimpressed by Eddie's qualms about the future.

To tell you truth which may shock you I don't take much interest in your exam. I can't understand why *you* do. Since when have you thought yourself the stupidest and worst informed of intelligent persons? I believe it's only an excuse for having no plans for the future. I am, and have been, for 18 months, acutely conscious that I am only quite a small hippopotamus, and so will never be able to do anything big, *but*—and that's just all the difference between us. . . . You should imitate the shark and never doubt that you are well filled out. I am sure you have three rows of teeth and could dance a minuet.

He sat for the Civil Service examination early in August, then left with Baring for the opera season at Bayreuth. 'It seemed wicked to spend the afternoon in a *theatre*,' he wrote to Lytton, 'especially when one has spent the morning in *bed*.' While he was abroad Jane Marsh had a heart attack and a house on Richmond Common called Holly Lodge was rented for her convalescence. Here Eddie arrived at the beginning of September. After five years at Cambridge and several months with Mr. Scoones it was difficult to believe that the last of the exams was over. His thoughts turned with gratitude to the Verralls, to whom he sent an account of his new existence. Every morning he walked to Richmond with his sister and her Skye terrier 'to buy a stamp or a penny notebook. . . . Richmond is an odd place to come to in these days of vastly improved facilities for locomotion.'

I'm at last enjoying what almost seemed would never come—the chance of reading without the prospect of being examined in what

I read. What do you think I began with? *Sir Charles Grandison.* I've read about one third with the deepest interest, for which I can't quite account to myself. I love what the Barings call an *archhager* (the g is hard), it means a long long story, without point, told with the utmost fulness of detail, like *Hermann and Dorothea*—but even for such a taste I should have thought Sir Charles would be too much. Richardson has an art, of which I don't quite see the secret, of making his people and incidents perfectly real—one is dying to know all the little secrets that Harriet is dying to know, however sure one's better self is that they'll turn out to be quite uninteresting—for instance there is a long dialogue in which Sir Charles makes his sister confess that she has a love affair, which he knows all about all the time. 'Name your man, sir,' says Miss Grandison at last. 'Not *my* man, Charlotte —Captain Anderson is not *my* man,' says Sir Charles—and I had the most lively feeling of satisfied curiosity. So it's Captain Anderson, is it? tho' the Captain hasn't been mentioned before. The way in which the characters express themselves is a perpetual delight—you would have thought they all talked exactly alike, but it comes out, in an indication here and there, that this is not so. Sir Charles says for instance, 'My first duty is to inter the venerable remains (I must always use this dialect, sir)'; and Miss Byron remarks that she is expressing herself as Miss Grandison would when she says that Sir Charles is as penetrating in business as a sunbeam.

I bought myself a delightful Montaigne and read about a third of *Sebonde* with the greatest pleasure my first evening here, but I've been unlucky with it—next morning I began the life of F. W. Robertson (which I've just finished) and somehow he has taken possession of my mind so completely that I simply can't go back to Montaigne, his irony and worldliness seem so far away and impossible that I have to read a sentence three or four times to see what it means and then throw the book away in mere boredom—whereas I can sympathize with Sir Charles' immoral platitudes just because they are serious. I hope however that such a good influence can't have such fearful results for long. How splendid Robertson was—are there any Brighton traditions about him that you know? But he leaves the question of religion very nearly as dark as I have always found it. He admits that it can't be got by thinking, which I'm glad of, it must come to the spirit—but the next step seems to lead him into a vicious circle —he says you must just be as good as you can in daily life, in a humble spirit and it will come, but when somebody does this and complains that nothing happens, he says, 'Ah, yes, routine is no good without the spirit.' And then I can't see how one *is* to be better than one is already—my own aspirations have taken a rather comical

form, getting out of bed when I'm called, and cutting myself down
to two pipes a day. By the way that's another of my difficulties. I
shall never feel serious till I leave off laughing at myself—and if I
don't laugh at myself where's the fun in being alive?

Another book he has disaffected me with a little is the *Souvenirs
d'enfance et de jeunesse* of the virtuous Renan, the prudent Renan,
Renan who is best of all—it's a delightful book but towards the end
one gets a little tired of always hearing him call himself 'the polite'—
I almost feel that there burns a truer light of God in Robertson's
vexed, beating, stuffed and stopped up brain, than in Renan's
serene and self-satisfied *esprit*—but this is unfair—it's only because
Renan writes from the mountain tops where is the throne of truth,
which Robertson saw only afar off in the cloudy air and would have
reached if he'd lived. (By the way I hope you recognize all the
quotations about here, or you'll think I'm practising for an extension
lecturer.) I think Renan's ideas are really firmer than Robertson's—
his 'Courage, courage, Nature!' has as little in it that may be
self-delusion as any optimism can.

Have you heard about Roger Fry's engagement to a Miss Coombe,
an artist, very pretty, and a few years older than he, without a penny?
I met his sister at Bertie Russell's the other day—the living
Jane Eyre!

Roger Fry's romance had been furthered by Eddie's not being
at home when R. C. Trevelyan called at Bruton Street earlier in
the year. Trevelyan wrote after calling to say: 'I had for you a rose
of Shiraz, the direct descendant of the one which intoxicated
Hafiz when he looked on it, and led his spirit forth like wine on
the turnpikes of imagination into a land of luminous horizons. As
it was I took it round to Fry who fell violently in love with it and
fell to painting it.'

On September 21 he came home after ten days with the Lyttons
at Berkhamsted to find the news awaiting him that he had won
second place in the Civil Service examination, beaten by only a
few marks by a candidate who had taken twelve subjects to his
eight. Instead of sitting back to receive the letters of congratulation
he soon found himself writing to all his friends to tell them what
had happened on the evening of the 24th. The family was seated
at dinner. Jane Marsh was relating an anecdote which amused
her, when she broke off in the middle of a sentence, quietly leaned
forward, and rested her head on the table. Within five minutes
she was dead.

'I know you will be sorry for me,' he wrote to Trevelyan. 'You always seemed to understand her so well. She and I had been such particular friends lately. She knew all about me and it was ages since we'd had a quarrel.' And to Moore: 'There's something in the certainty of a love like hers for me that one can never get in any friendship. . . . You knew her very little, but many people seem to have seen even from a slight acquaintance how superior she was to the common run.' To Victor Lytton he confessed feelings of terrible remorse. He had never shown the love he felt. 'It was only this morning that I began to feel how large a part of every nice thing was the prospect of telling her about it.' A year later he wrote to him again on the same theme. 'All young people must be warned that they will never regret sacrifice for their parents.' Alarmed by the distress in his letter Desmond MacCarthy came down from Cumberland to Holly Lodge. There is no need to explain why this sudden blow struck Eddie Marsh with such especial force, compounded as it was of grief and overwhelming remorse. The conflict with his mother was over, and in a way difficult to describe she had won in the end. She became to him a flawless image. More than one of his friends observed that he was almost possessed by her, and seemed unconsciously to assume some of her mannerisms: her rather stiff, upright bearing, the backward tilt of the head as she walked, her demonstrative affection; and the tender solicitude he had always shown for anyone in distress seemed now to have increased in its readiness and warmth. He was already very like her in appearance. Nothing will better illustrate his feelings at this time than his correspondence with MacCarthy two years later, in January 1898. MacCarthy's mother had confided in Eddie her sorrow at what she considered her son's neglect. Unknown to her, Eddie intervened by writing to her son. He said he had once behaved just as Desmond was doing. 'Now she is gone I would have given anything to be different and to have accommodated my idea of loving her to hers of being loved by me. I have persuaded myself that she really knew it was all right, but still, if only I had been different! and your mother is different from mine in a way that makes her feel it much more, she is more dependent and (in a way) more emotional and more excitable.' He then confessed that he had just written to her.

I tried to explain how it is that kind of thoughtlessness comes about

and how little it indicates a real deficiency in love. I told her all
about how I used to be myself. I also told her it was partly her fault
to torture herself as she does about little things. If you are in the
least bit tempted to think her unreasonable and to persist in looking
at things in the way that's natural to *you*, do consider how miserable
you'll be at having done so when you have lost her and what a rich
reward you'll have then for any half hours devoted now to merely
doing what you don't feel exactly an impulse to do. . . . When I see
such a relationship in danger of being the least bit injured by any
thing that could be avoided I can't bear not to rush in and give
warning, when I know so well all about it. Your mother has such a
tremendous capacity for suffering, as well as happiness and, when she
is unhappy, instead of melting or freezing, she *burns*.

Two days after the funeral Howard Marsh accompanied his
son to Whitehall and left him at the entrance of the Colonial
Office, where he started his public career as a junior clerk in the
Australian Department under John Anderson, who was destined
to become a Governor of Ceylon. But Eddie's mind was in a
turmoil of speculation on those very themes which Balfour had
raised in his correspondence, and the moment he was granted
his first leave of absence he travelled north to Braemar, where
Balfour had begun the theological studies which were soon to
make him a convert to the Roman Catholic faith.

ii

Before the eventful year 1896 came to an end Marsh had for the
first time been addressed as 'a patron and lover of art'. R. C.
Trevelyan (who was about to be Roger Fry's best man) had
written to him asking for the contribution of a guinea to promote
Fry's exhibition of painting in Cambridge. 'The exhibition will
combine beauty and entertainment in the most judicial proportions. The nude will not be included unless it be beautiful, but
not the beautiful unless it be nude.' Trevelyan was counting on
him to rope in MacCarthy and Balfour—a small service which
was duly performed. He spent Christmas in company with
Balfour among the Lytton family. 'Word making and word
taking' was all the rage as a parlour game, and various elaborate
kinds of Patience. In January Eddie wrote to Mrs. Verrall:

Lady Lytton has an idea that the whole family ought to live up to
Reggie Balfour and when everybody has a fit of the giggles at meals,

which usually happens, she says, 'Treat it as a disease, my dears, and drink a glass of water.' Once we were all talking on the principle of laboratory aboratory boratory, and when Reggie asked me to pass the Chablis hablis ablis blis lis is, she said, 'I say, you are rather silly, aren't you?' which became the 'phrase' of the visit.

I've read the new Ibsen, which I think is the best since Hedda, tho' as I read it aloud in a tearing hurry and excitement I haven't quite taken it in. Meredith doesn't stand a 'monumental edition' so well as Stevenson. It's astonishing how big print and the consciousness of its costing 10/6 a volume brings out the weaknesses of a book. If only Meredith didn't always leave out such a lot of the matrix of his book (is that the right metaphor?) there's always so much undigested machinery (that's *certainly* wrong) I mean a whole fringe of vague and incomprehensible people and events.

I went to Mr. Gosse's New Year party where there was a Punch and Judy show, a regular street one. . . . Mrs. Gosse was very flurried, rushing about to break up conversations and redistribute her guests. . . . With all 'reasonable' messages (that's what *you* put) to Dr. Verrall.

Later in the year he stayed with Baring in Oxford, and one evening he was peacefully conversing among friends when the door opened and Baring entered with someone's head tucked under his arm. 'Gentlemen, gentlemen,' cried the tuft of hair, 'this is not the posture in which I should have chosen to be presented to you.' It was Donald Tovey. Baring and Marsh had planned to go to Bayreuth, but when Baring's father died he handed his ticket to Tovey, so that Marsh found himself listening to his first full cycle of the Ring accompanied by an almost complete stranger. In September he described the adventure to the Verralls.

For the first three days I was alone and rain poured in torrents and they did *Parsifal* very badly, and I wished I was dead and had never come; but after that everything became heavenly—beautiful sunny days to walk in the pinewoods, capital performances (on the whole) of opera which are I should think as good as anything in the world —and a perfect companion. This was a young gentleman whom I had met once before, and knowing that he was going to have the seat next mine I was rather terrified. Tovey is his name, and he is the son of Tovey, the new Clark Lecturer. I wonder if you knew or know about the family. Donald, the son I know, is a musician—he has a brother called Duncan, who said when he was six years old, 'It's rather funny, in our family, my brother has a genius for music, and I have a genius for poetry'. *He* is now an actor in Penley's

Company. But about Donald it is perfectly true, and there seems to be every hope of his turning out simply glorious. We used to go into the woods and compose concertos, symphonies, etc., for which he made notes in an enormous 'sketch-book', explaining to me as we went along. He talked about music all day in the most instructive manner. One of the most amusing things was to hear him discoursing to a little man called Hughes (son of 'Tom Brown') whom we came across, with a chirpy polite little voice, like a canary bird. Donald would say 'dramatic music is to pure instrumental music as painting is to architecture' and the little man would interject, 'Ah, dear me, dear me, is it really?' with a tone of gratified, sympathetic surprise. Donald himself is a curious character. He has every virtue and one defect that is utterly inconsistent with the rest. Morally he is honest, affectionate, modest, self-confident and persevering—intellectually he is profound, acute and sure—but with all this he has a mania for making the most *infâme* school-boyish stiff and pointless jokes which he admitted were worthless—and for repeating anecdotes from Mark Twain whom he admitted to be an author beneath consideration. By no tears or entreaties could I prevail on him to mitigate his output of this humour, tho' he became more and more apologetic about it. This was all the stranger as he had plenty of real wit and humour as well. He complained once of the ignorance shown by artists of all arts but their own, saying that in *Abt Vogler* Browning had written a most glorious poem about music and attached to it the name of a man who is notorious to all musicians as an abject charlatan, and he said it was just the same as if Beethoven had written a magnificent 'Martin Tupper symphony'. Don't you think it's a delicious idea? Getting to know Tovey is much the most interesting thing that has happened to me lately.

Soon after his return he spent a week-end with Mrs. Humphry Ward. 'I didn't know her before, I thought her delightful in every way, I've now read *Marcella* as I thought the proud position of never having read any of her books was becoming untenable. To my surprise I found them absorbingly interesting. I've got through two books that are "undertakings"—Boswell and *La Guerre et la Paix*. I don't know which is the greater treat. There is an amazing new book by H. G. Wells called *The Invisible Man* which quite cures one of wishing one were invisible, and some of the stories in Bourget's *Voyageuses* are very good indeed I think.' He had been going to the theatre with Baring. 'You should see Forbes Robertson in *Hamlet* if you get a chance. He has no charm (to me) and compared with what the part requires very little passion—but he says the lines with more point and *nuance* than anyone I have ever heard.'

One evening he came home to find a travelling box in the hall bearing a label with a familiar name, so he rushed hopefully upstairs to the spare room, only to find it empty. 'With that indifference to my inferiors which marks the upper classes,' he wrote to G. E. Moore, whose unexpected arrival he had confidently inferred, 'I had neglected to inform myself of the cook's name!' In such stray fragments he was apt to exhibit in his letters one facet or another of his character. Another example comes from his correspondence with Victor Lytton on *King Poppy*, the poem written by Lytton's father, 'Owen Meredith'. 'I think perhaps there's too much of the classical French eighteenth-century element in my mind, as it has been educated, for me to take allegorical poetry quite in the right spirit. I'm too much concerned that it should all work out neatly, that there should be a complete correspondence of the type with the thing typified.'

He saw the new year in (1898) with Gosse at Delamere Terrace. It was the occasion of his second meeting with Henry James. He had first made the great man's acquaintance a few months before in the same house. Dinner being over, and the ladies having retired, they found themselves after the reshuffle seated next each other for the port. After a brief exchange James began to show curiosity about the age of his young neighbour. Eddie Marsh always looked much younger than he was and now, at twenty-four, was doubtless looking eighteen. 'Just so, just so,' said James, when Marsh confessed his years, 'but you look so delightfully young. What an advantage that is, to combine the appearance of juvenility with the experience of maturity—in a word the Flower of Youth with the Fruits of Time.' On this second encounter Marsh again found himself beside Henry James, but this time jammed up against him in a small upstairs room where a not very successful performance of marionettes was being staged to beguile the interval before the new year bells. 'An interesting example, my dear Marsh, of Economy,' James whispered in his ear. 'Economy of Means—and—and—Economy of *Effect*.' While waiting for the change of scene Marsh told him that he had planned to pay his first visit to Paris in a few weeks' time in the company of Neville Lytton. 'Do not allow yourself,' said James, 'to be put off by the superficial and external aspect of Paris; or rather (for the *true*

superficial and external aspect of Paris has a considerable fascination) by what I may call the superficial and external aspect *OF*
the superficial and external aspect of Paris.' Marsh laughed.
'Surely, Mr. James,' he exclaimed, 'that's carrying lucidity to
dazzling point.'

The trip to Paris did not take place until April. Before
leaving, his pioneer work in the *Cambridge Observer* brought him
an unexpected honour. Gosse and William Archer were organizing a letter of congratulation to Ibsen on the occasion of his
seventieth birthday, a tribute from those in England 'whom your
executive skill has stimulated and your intellectual intrepidity
encouraged'. The message accompanied the gift of a silver loving-
cup and was signed by forty-one persons of whom Eddie Marsh
was by many years the youngest. So far he had done little more
than talk, commanding attention by his elegance of address and
by his reputation as one of the most accomplished scholars to have
come out of Cambridge for several years. And now by courtesy of
Edmund Gosse he had gained a foothold in literary London.

Chapter Six

LATE VICTORIAN
(1898–1902)

AT the end of April he left England with Neville and Constance Lytton and their mother, the plan being that he should stay a fortnight alone with Neville at his *pension* in the Rue St. Jacques, then rejoin Lady Lytton and her daughter at the Casa Tiepoletto on the Grand Canal in Venice. Neville had left Eton two years before and instead of going to the university had decided to give himself a course of art in Paris. His father, when ambassador in Paris, had submitted some of the boy's work to Bonnat, who had declared it showed promise and had undertaken to keep an eye on his progress if ever he should consider taking up painting as a profession. Lady Lytton saw Neville and Eddie installed in their lodgings, left with them a few useful introductions, including a letter to the elder Coquelin, the actor, then moved on to Italy. Marsh's first impressions were sent to Victor, Neville's elder brother. There were several Americans in the *pension*. 'They say "How-d'you-do-very-glad-to-meet-you-Mr. Marsh." When they do this to Neville he says simply "Thank you" which takes them aback.' Before leaving London. Marsh had paid another visit to Mrs. Humphry Ward and found her in high hopes of her new book *Helbeck of Bannisdale*. He had also supped at Delamere Terrace and talked about Stevenson's life in Samoa with the novelist's step-daughter Mrs. Strong, 'a nice cheerful little person, not what Neville would call *distingué*, but charming to live with. It was extraordinary to think one was talking to the person who had written down the *Weir of Hermiston*.' Having reached Venice he wrote again to Victor, describing the main event during his fortnight in Paris, a visit to Coquelin. Its purpose was to enlist his support in getting a painting by Neville accepted for exhibition.

You've never been told about our visit to Coquelin have you? How we went in our clawhammer clothes (new expression, shall be explained presently) and made up our minds to stay 20 minutes, changing our minds to 10 minutes as we got further up the staircase. However the interview began as if it was going to last all day, and had to be forcibly broken off after an hour by engagements. He and Neville made great friends over his pictures, which are many and very good. There are a lot of portraits of himself in different parts, and when he came to one he liked specially he said, '*Tenez voilà comme c'est moi*'—and put on the expression of the picture so that we saw him in his repertoire all to ourselves. Then he began talking plays, and we discussed Cyrano—he practically acted the death scene, to show how fine it was, and said it was greater than Macbeth —we were so much carried away that we admitted it was much greater. His 'diction' is so perfect that the conversation was no harder to follow than an English one, and we didn't have to say much and think we only made about two mistakes each. We were so *épatés* when he said he would call at the studio that afternoon that we could only gasp the address and could hardly say thank you. The visit was very short but each second more charming than most people's five minutes, and he offered to give himself no end of trouble about the salon picture in case Neville found out nothing from Bonnat next morning. However as you know he found out a great deal! Clawhammer comes from the American pension, where an evening coat is called a clawhammer coat. Hence clawhammer gloves, boots, carriages, gondolas, anything smart.

As soon as he was back at his official duties in Whitehall he began a series of weekly letters to Neville which lasted for nearly four years. His letters were full of amusing comments and scraps of information. In June he saw Calvé in *Carmen*. 'I never saw a more intense piece of acting than her terror in the last scene, and her death is indescribably horrible, she falls on her face in a most ignoble and trivial attitude with an odd kind of jerk which leaves one of her legs sticking up above the other.'

He was learning the piano, and after dining with the Blunts at Crabbet Park had played some Schumann to Wilfrid Scawen Blunt and his family and was happy to have perpetrated only one wrong note. This was his first meeting with the poet, his wife Lady Anne Blunt (Byron's granddaughter) and his daughter Judith, who was soon to marry Neville Lytton. He had installed a piano in one of the front rooms at Bruton Street. 'As the windows look at me with dumb reproach I am saddened at the thought of the inhabitants whose lives I daily wreck, tho' they don't like to make a fuss about it, and don't even bang their baths to make me stop playing, as one would expect', and he was keeping up with Gosse, who had recently got him into the Reform Club. It had been redecorated, 'papered in a style even more hideous than my room at the office, but when I said I could hardly bear it Edmund answered that he liked it so much because it was bright without being tasteful, and reminded him more than it used of railway waiting-rooms, where he had passed many hours of pleasing meditation'. Gosse amused him one day by pointing to an advertisement in a newspaper, *Messrs. Gunter send their celebrated Invalid Turtle to all parts of the Kingdom*, remarking, 'I conceive of it travelling with a lacklustre eye.' One evening Marsh met Gosse coming away from the private performance of a new play by Swinburne and asked him if he had enjoyed it. 'Well,' said Gosse, 'we were as nearly bored as enthusiasm would permit.' Gosse also talked of his cook at Delamere Terrace who had deplored his proneness to frequent bouts of illness, saying, 'And it's no wonder, him sitting all day with his stomach pressed against a desk!' Another evening Marsh listened with some distaste to Henry Arthur Jones and Anthony Hope paying each other what he considered unmerited compliments, but the dramatist's description of George Moore as 'a boiled ghost' gave him something to carry away. Hope made an unfavourable impression owing to 'his pretentious manner (partly author, partly handsome middle-aged young man) due to his success with young ladies'. On another occasion Marsh found Alma-Tadema at the Terrace, 'a fat, stumpy little man, with a rather fine face which has got coarsened'. The painter was a voluble raconteur of amusing but badly connected stories. One of them was worth passing on to Neville. On entering a village in Shropshire a stranger was stopped in his progress down the High Street by a funeral procession. He made bold to draw aside one of the mourners. 'Whose funeral?' he asked, and was told, then 'What complaint?' he went on. 'Oh, no complaint,' said the other. 'Everyone's delighted.'

Maurice Baring was often a fellow guest with Marsh at Delamere Terrace. He broke a silence at table one evening with a dogmatic pronouncement. 'There are only two kinds of biscuit. Mixed biscuits and *unmixed* biscuits.' One of his stories at this time was: 'Did you hear of one of the Queen's uncles who used to make loud responses in church out of his own head? "Let us pray," said the clergyman. "By all *means*," said the Duke, reverently.'

Baring had recently spent a week-end at Chislehurst as a guest of the Empress Eugénie. 'One night a bat got into the passage and there was a fearful crisis, so the next night, when one actually came into the dining-room, and was only perceived by Maurice and the Empress, she said to him in a whisper "*Ne dites rien*" and nothing happened.' On June 1 the small talk in Marsh's budgets to Neville Lytton gave place to something more substantial.

I had a very interesting talk with Edmund Gosse today. He had just come back from a short holiday during which he had bicycled (art new to him) in a hillish country, so that as he expressed it he had been for a week under the sway of fear, the most rousing of the passions.

What he wanted to talk about was a visit to Mrs. R. L. Stevenson that morning, the first time he had seen her since Steve and she started for Samoa eleven years ago. I have never known anything about her to speak of, and was very much interested to hear. He said she was one of the strangest people who had lived in our time, a sort of savage nature in some ways, but very lovable—extraordinarily passionate and unlike everyone else in her violent feelings and un-restrained way of expressing them—full of gaiety, and with a genius for expressing things picturesquely, but not literary. I think RLS must have caught some of his ways of feeling things from her. Gosse said she had told him today how when she was out of sorts she used to be driven almost mad by seeing the monstrous rapidity with which vegetation grew in Samoa, how a thing that began to come up one day would be three feet high the next. I thought this very Stevensonian, a good deal of the uncanny part of *Pulvis et Umbra* (the thing I said to you in Paris, do you remember?) might have been written in such a mood. As for facts, she is a Spanish American, and met Steve at Barbizon, she afterwards got a divorce from her husband, who was a brute, in order to marry Stevenson. She is now dreadfully ill, and suffers a great deal. Gosse told me a lot of little things about RLS very interesting and amusing to me as being about him, such as how he came to dine with them the last time before going away, and sat at dinner in a long scarlet shawl. Gosse had reminded Mrs. Stevenson this morning of a visit he paid them at Braemar, when suddenly a fire broke out close by, and Gosse and old Mr. and Mrs. Stevenson rushed out to see it, but Stevenson and his wife were ill at the time and couldn't go out, so they were left with their noses against the windowpanes. Mrs. Stevenson said she perfectly remembered what a shame it seemed to her and Louis that there should be a fire, and they not able to go and see it. The father and mother were a pair of dear respectable canny old Scotch folk, very much upset at first when Louis couldn't turn his hand to anything, and pained at having produced a person so painfully below the average—though they got to be tremendously proud of him afterwards; and Gosse said it was simply wonderful how they adapted themselves to Mrs. Stevenson and never showed that they thought her in the least odd, though of course she was totally contrary to all their ideas. Louis was always most diffident and modest about himself, and never ceased to be surprised when anything nice happened to him.

The next gathering of special interest at Delamere Terrace took place early in October.

George Moore the novelist was there, and Lloyd Osbourne (Stevenson's stepson, who helped write *Wrecker* and *Ebb Tide*) and his wife. The wife is by far the most *rasoir* woman I ever met, she is a highly trained American girl who has studied zoology and said the battle of Omdurman reminded her of Xenophon's *Anabasis*. I discovered even before dinner that her favourite subject was New Mexico, and I was not surprised at Edmund beginning the table conversation with trying to keep her off it by saying, 'Mrs. Osbourne, let me entreat you to instruct Mr. Moore on the subject of New Mexico. It is a constant source of worry to Mr. Moore's friends how little he knows. We are always trying to put him in the way of information.' She at once began a lecture on the subject. Later on Edmund's fury got beyond his control, and when she said the French had as much right to Fashoda as we had he said, 'My dear lady that is nonsense. I can't entertain the idea for a moment, and I'm sure you haven't studied the subject.'

George Moore told a rather amusing story of how an English play that he had translated into French was once received at the Odéon, and he heard it was to be rehearsed the same day as *Midsummer Night's Dream*, so he went to the theatre and said to the doorkeeper in his best French accent, '*J'ai une pièce reçu à l'Odéon, et je voudrais assister à la répétition.*' '*Vous dites, Monsieur?*' G.M. repeated his sentence and was again not understood. Damn the fellow, he thought, and said it again. '*Ah, laissez Monsieur passer,*' said another doorkeeper. '*C'est peut-être Shakespeare.*'

During one of his visits to Yattenden, while he was at Cambridge, Marsh had learned that the minor poet Canon Beeching, Rector of the local church, was for some reason at variance with Robert Bridges. Marsh met the Rector only once while on a walk with Bridges and his wife, and he has described how the ladies exchanged civilities while Bridges played with his enormous dog and Beeching stood apart 'looking rather like my idea of James the Less'. Marsh was amused to report Gosse's version of the situation when next he wrote to Paris.

> The other day the conversation turned on the village of Yattenden in Berkshire, which both I and Edmund know, and he was very amusing about it. The chief inhabitants are the poet Robert Bridges and his wife, the architect Waterhouse, and the rector Mr. Beeching, also Mrs. Beeching. The villagers live a peaceful life of subjugation to the artistic ideals drummed into them by these personages—but the personages themselves, though all connected by marriage, are continually quarrelling with each other. Bridges, who is Mrs. Beeching's uncle, uses the curious privilege of a relation to come and abuse her through the Rectory windows, and when Beeching comes out on the lawn to remonstrate he reminds him that they are not on speaking terms. Mr. Beeching is a delightful person. I remember once hearing a sermon of his which he began by saying that he was going to bring forward and answer all the serious arguments against the Christian religion. He then proceeded to marshal all the arguments with great logical force, but when the time came to refute them there was a long pause after which he left the pulpit, saying he would go on with the sermon next Sunday. But next Sunday's was on quite a different subject.

Gosse was away early in December, but shortly before Christmas he met Marsh at the Reform Club.

> Edmund wasn't at the Club yesterday, he only came back today from visiting his stepmother, an old lady of 87, who is quite mad in some ways and extremely on the spot in others. For instance she takes him into her orchid house and says, 'That is the odontoglossus dolicocephalus, it won't flower till February' (such being the case), and then breaks off to say 'Let me see, dear, did your dear Father marry anyone else before he married me?' which, as Edmund says, seems to put him in such a dubious position. One evening she made him read out loud a commentary on the Apocalypse (she's morbidly religious) and when he'd been reading for about an hour an explanation of the 5 big horns and the little horn, or whatever it is, and his brain was reeling and tears started to his eyes, she sweetly said, 'I hope *you* like it, dear, it seems to *me* simply bewildering.' One day she said, 'Who was that nice respectable man who used to live at Hesketh Crescent?' 'Surely,' said Edmund, 'you can't mean my eminent friend Mr. Henry James?' 'Yes, is *he* married?' 'Not that

I know of.' 'What a shame, that a respectable man like him shouldn't be able to get a wife. I haven't quite made up my mind to marry again, but if I did he's just the sort of man I should choose.' Edmund wrote to H.J. about this. He was simply delighted, and wrote back a letter beginning 'My beloved stepson'.

When next he wrote it was the first week of January 1899. He had again seen the new year in at Delamere Terrace.

The Gosse party was extremely amusing. Edmund was in his funniest mood, circulating through the room and shuffling the guests at intervals of 2 minutes. The entertainment was a conjurer, they had taken great pains to get one who was a gentleman—and though I shouldn't have said he was quite that, he was extraordinarily wonderful. I do love a conjurer. He told E. afterwards that it was customary for the master of the house to sign a statement that he had never seen such a skilful and brilliant performance, and produced a form to be filled up. E. wrote (as he couldn't condescend to have his phrases dictated to him) that the whole company agreed they had never witnessed an exhibition so ingenious and superb. After the conjurer there was supper with crackers and paper caps— it was very rowdy and reached its climax when E. started to complain that a lady had covered him with scent from a squirt. I sat next to Max Beerbohm, Tree's brother—he is most amusing and original and it's difficult to believe he has such a banal brother. He told me a delicious story. An actor called Arthur Playfair and his wife took a small theatre for an autumn season, and in order to have at least one supporter in the audience they gave a seat to their parlourmaid in the front row of the upper circle, hoping that she would at least be a centre of friendly feeling towards the play, and perhaps might even lead the applause. The piece fell rather flat, and they went home to supper, where they were waited on by the parlourmaid. 'Well, Jane, how did you like it?' 'Well, Sir, the little first piece wasn't so bad, but that long play—Lor', 'ow I did 'iss!'

We had been made at supper to drink something called a 'wassail-bowl' made according to a 17th century receipt, in which the chief ingredient appears to have been crab-apples and the only thing it was exactly like was Halviva. Well, when I spoke to Henry James after supper, the only subject I could think of to begin a conversation was this comparison; and it set him off on a long account of how he always prepared for a voyage by getting some stuff sold by the chemist at the end of St. James's Street in cases containing 12 bottles. At this point Maurice came up saying, 'I'm sure you're talking about remedies for sea-sickness.' 'Yes,' said James, with ever-increasing emphasis, 'we were discussing that charming, that *alluring*, that *fascinating* subject.'

By the 18th he had stayed at Oxford with Tovey.

Donald himself is one of the most extraordinary people I know, exactly like a genius in a book. I don't think you'd like him at all, unless you took some trouble to understand him, but I saw a great deal of him at Bayreuth and got accustomed to him. He is the incarnation of Brahmsness,[1] and lives almost entirely by the intellect. When he talks to one he gives the idea that he looks on one exclusively as a listener and not in the least as a human being. I mean I never feel as if he saw the very slightest difference between me and anybody else. When we went to bed he came into my room and talked music while I undressed, an odd idea occurred to me that I might have been the most beautiful woman in the world and he would have gone on pouring out his ideas in exactly the same way without noticing. It's very interesting to know *one* person like that, but I shouldn't like everybody to be so. I had an extremely funny journey back with him and Miss Weisse next morning—one other person in the carriage, a perfectly commonplace middle-class man. At first Miss Weisse and I talked to each other in an ordinary sort of way, only rather more interesting than what one usually hears in a train —and as she speaks in a beautifully distinct schoolmistress voice I could see the man thinking we were rather curious. Then suddenly Donald, who had been meditating and moping in the corner, began to sing, in an unearthly kind of murmur occasionally swelling into a roar; and then without a moment's notice he burst into a lecture on Bach, with floods of the most recondite information.

In his last two years at Cambridge Marsh had often been a guest to tea at Leckhampton, the home of Mr. and Mrs. Frederick Myers. It was there that he had expressed a great admiration for James's *The Turn of the Screw* which his host did not share. 'My dear Marsh,' exclaimed Myers, 'do you mean to tell me that you seriously believe in the possibility of the Lesbian vice between the ghost of a governess and a little girl of six?' Mrs. Myers' mother was the Victorian hostess Mrs. Tennant, who lived in London. Another of Mrs. Tennant's daughters had married H. M. Stanley, the explorer, who one day crossed the room and greeted Marsh with 'I see you're looking neglected, so I've come to talk to you', which Marsh was to recall for its curious similarity to the explorer's

---

[1] Baring word for 'superior quality'.

greeting on a more historic occasion in the jungle. His letter of January 26 described a visit to Mrs. Tennant.

I began badly by arriving long after I was asked but still before the ladies had left the dining-room, and I had to wait upstairs for about five minutes first looking at Millais' audacious picture of Mrs. Myers in a scarlet dress and bright sky-blue necklace, but then fatally drawn to an enormous looking-glass, where I stood staring at myself, at first with fair complacency but, as I heard the ladies padding up the stairs, wondering which they would say—'Here's just an ordinary person' or 'Who is this hideous little abortion?' However when they arrived my legs ceased to totter, and I got on all right except for realizing every now and then that my mouth was fixed in a stark grin, and *would* not come loose. It was one of Mrs. Tennant's usual lion-hunting parties—first of all the people I didn't talk to—Le Père Didon and Mrs. Patrick Campbell (very miarish and effective), and Arthur Benson spreading a delicate charm through the atmosphere. (I'd never seen him behave before—I don't mean that I had only seen him *mis*behave, but that I don't think I've ever been in the room with him and I realized for the first time how delightful it's at any rate *possible* to think him.) Then there was Cambon, the new French Ambassador, who gave me two of the most heavenly handshakes I've ever experienced—*the* very most charming Frenchman I've ever seen, with white hair and graceful youthful attitudes, *effleurant* the backbone of life, in murmured sentences of the most polished diction. The Lady Jeune, whom you just escaped going to stay with in the summer, a kind-looking brisk woman, grey hair and rouge, who rattled off more words in a minute than I've ever heard, and ended by asking me to come and drink a cup of tea some Sunday afternoon which I think I will—and Miss Mary Kingsley, a bony retiring old maid (exactly like Mrs. Sidgwick, only without even so much of the look of *bien-être* which marriage has given her)—do you know her story? She spent years of her life tending an invalid mother at Cambridge, never leaving the house except to wheel a bathchair for an hour in the sun—and when her mother died she went among the bloodthirsty tribes of West African savages, whom she dominated by sheer pluck and good sense, and whom she described in a book of the highest scientific value—isn't it extraordinary? I also had a kidglove[1] attempt at a flirtation with a sort of Captain Rose girl, very pretty in that sort of way, familiar without being sympathetic—for instance we discussed dancing, and she said that if I at that moment put my arm round her waist and waltzed round the room there'd be quite a scandal, and that she

[1] Baring word for 'half-hearted'.

couldn't help wondering, when a man put his arm round her waist to dance, what her waist was given her for, though she was sure that was *one* of the reasons—I wasn't an absolute failure, but I couldn't help feeling how much better you'd have managed it. I've scarcely left room for my anecdotes after all—one is Landseer bringing his landlady to see one of his 'masterpieces', she looked at it a long time, and all she said was, 'I hope you're not going to ask me to take anything, sir, but if you do, I hope it will be a little brandy and water.'

On February 1 Neville Lytton was married to Judith Blunt in Egypt. Marsh was to have been best man, and Lady Anne, the bride's mother, had offered to pay the fare, but he was obliged to stay in England for the marriage of his sister to Frederick Maurice on the same day. As in the case of the Verralls, Marsh was fortunate to find in the wife a friend who became as dear to him as the husband. The daughter of Wilfrid Blunt, and the great-granddaughter of Byron, in appearance a subject for Gainsborough (Neville always seemed to be haunted by that master's style whenever he painted her) was to become a cherished acquisition in Marsh's life. Of Neville he wrote to her, 'I never get tired of the colour of his mind', and of them both, 'I think N. and you are the only people who don't have occasional fits of unaccountable disagreeableness', and in a joint letter he addressed a few lines to Neville individually: 'I have no duties, no pleasures, worth thinking of in the same day as your company—whereas you have one supreme pleasure, and many duties growing out of it—it seems to me as if not your but *my* guardian angel would be better pleased if I *showed* less avidity. It's merely a question of manners.' In this spirit he was to conduct all the intense friendships which succeeded one another throughout his life.

While the Lyttons were still in Egypt he described for them a violently musical occasion at Hubert Parry's house in London.

Monday was also Gwen Parry's birthday, and I went to her party to play games, hunt-the-slipper, General Post, etc. It was the most dangerous party I ever was at, and the evening was a series of hair's-breadth escapes. Everyone was fearfully rough, and enormous Sir Hubert Parry roughest of all. There was one dreadful moment when he was pounding and plunging along blindfolded, on all fours, between two rows of chairs—and by a wild impulse a fragile girl called Nora Martin, height about 4′ 6″, flung herself head foremost on the floor in his way. Dozens of stout arms seized her round the waist and rescued her, but in another second she would have been certainly destroyed. The same girl, in the Lancers, was flung horizontal, across the room, and hit another lady across the knees with such force that she felled her to the ground, however no bones were broken. The most wonderful thing was Parry playing the music for Musical Chairs, he made it so intensely exciting that the players got absorbed listening and went mechanically round and round, quite forgetting to sit down when he stopped.

Overheated by the hilarious party, he caught influenza and ten days later wrote from his bed.

Please begin by wasting lots of rheumatism[1] on the thought of my semi-transparent hands with difficulty guiding the pen, and the spiritual expression of my face whiter than the pillows on which it is propped, or you'll never get through this letter. As a matter of fact my 'Flu has been almost pure delight. The first day and a half were one long slumber, the second night some 'failure of the sleeping powers'—at least I didn't get off with any impetus, and kept stopping between the stations (the feeling is exactly like that). In one of the runs, by the way, I had such a vivid glimpse of you, in your most *echt* Paris clothes at a bookstall in an enormous American railway station called 17 Kensington Ontario. We were going to join our regiment. Next day I kept awake more, thus getting a glorious start and whizzing through the night without slacking down once (do you know the feeling of being too weak to escape from the clutches of a simile, I'm so afraid I shall have to go on describing myself as a train all through this letter).

He was in such a frail condition that he would 'fall off his chair at the mere thought that a feather might blow in at the window'. On February 22 he reported a strange encounter.

Edmund one day brought Hall Caine down to the smoking-room at the Club to amuse me and Vic. Luckily H.C. thought he'd been brought as an object of worship, so everyone was pleased. He's such a ridiculous man, figures himself on being like Shakespeare (he is rather) and has long *mèches* of red hair sticking out behind—he has a most self-conscious manner, and says everything in a measured voice, as if it were a very important pronouncement, which he had been at great pains to get exactly right, on some frightfully difficult subject. However all the things he said were so banal that neither Vic nor I could remember a single one afterwards, though we had both been on the look-out for things to repeat.

[1] Baring phrase for an expense of sympathy on mistaken grounds.

At the end of the month he went to Paris, where Lytton had a studio in the Rue Denfert-Rochereau, and brought back to London two portraits, one of himself and the other of Ruth Balfour. Lady Lytton had arranged for him to show them to G. F. Watts at his house in Kensington. At this time Watts was aged eighty-two. A letter of March 2 described the interview.

Ruth was shown first, and the first thing he said was that it was very French, but you had plenty of time to get out of that. Then my portrait appeared (which I will call E.). 'Ah,' he said, 'he ought to do.' Then he looked at them both and said 'Now R. is *better* than E. but E. is more *promising*. R. *couldn't* be made better than it is, but E. shows that he sees the way to doing something of a better kind.' Then he went on to say that the two men who became in the end more '*du premier coup*' than anyone else—Velasquez and Rembrandt —both began by painting very carefully and 'tightly'—he said Velasquez' earliest pictures were even tighter than E. and not so good! and that to paint like that at first was the surest way to get on. 'I *know* what I say is true. I've been thinking about it for years.' Then he began looking at Ruth again, and evidently thought it charming. 'That's *beautiful*, I wouldn't have it touched for worlds', but that the difference was that you'd tried to do R. *cleverly* and had tried to do E. *well*—he evidently didn't think E. quite successful— he made a gesture-of-the-hand in the neighbourhood of the cheek, and said 'all that doesn't matter' implying that it wasn't right—he said you hadn't tried to make a picture of it, and that that was quite right. I told him that all he'd been saying was really almost exactly what you thought yourself—and that you'd made up your mind not to do any more sketchy portraits but to take great pains and finish things. He then showed us one or two of his own early drawings, to illustrate what he meant, especially one tremendously careful outline drawing of Lady Tennyson's profile, done in 1858 (or was it '48, I think not) and said with great emphasis, 'I was so desirous of getting it right I did it with my shoes off.'

In the same letter he gave an account of his feelings when slightly at a loss among a group of ladies presided over by Lady Charles Beresford, 'one of the quaintest people I ever saw, a stout, short little figure, in a gown.'

Can you imagine Mrs. Noah out of a Noah's ark, but *d'un chic*? The gown was just that shape, straight and the same breadth all the way down, a pretty bright grey with regiments of thin red lines round all the trimmable places, and a bright red soufflé hat on auburn hair—about 50 years old, an ugly, clever, comical little face, rouged up to the eyes—more like Mrs. Bancroft than anyone else, do you know her? Both she and Lady Jeune were very amusing and the three women kept up a ceaseless flow of talk—all rather Brahms to me, as I've never been exactly in that sort of society before, and couldn't quite cope with it. Conversation on every sort of subject—the *very* smartest people, the budget, gossiping secrets about politics in general, money, Kaffir stocks, copper-mines, the Queen having said Princess Christian was painfully thin, did I know of anyone who wanted a genius of a French cook, because there were two looking out for places?—Mrs. Walker's income and how she never had money enough for anything—Lady Charles' stoutness—her first words were, 'Oh my dear I'm banting. Nothing but cold beef for me'—I can't explain smart society to myself, it's in a way so vulgar, and yet so different from middle-class vulgarity, a much more amusing and goodnatured kind.

Certainly the unaffected simplicity of Jane Marsh and her home had done nothing to prepare him for his entry into the *beau monde*. Her want of personal vanity was to some extent inherited by her daughter. The occasion of her presentation to the Queen was always quoted by Marsh as an illustration of a family trait which, after he had met George Graham, at Scoones's, he considered he had overcome. After the presentation there was a party at Bruton Street.

Friday Helen[1] was presented, and I went to her drawing-room tea. Driving up I found the approach to the house blocked by two enormous dustcarts, and grimy men in huge sou'westers staggering up the area steps under loads of scavenge—of course they must needs choose that very day and hour for accomplishing their task of purification. Inside I found things more cheerful. Helen looking to great advantage and surprisingly intact (I thought people were always torn to pieces at 'drawing-rooms'). She'd had one small misadventure—very characteristic. I hope it will teach her to be more vain—she had put on her train just as it came out of the box, without ever looking to see how it looked, so that when the flunkey unrolled it the moment before she was going to make her curtsy, it turned out to be neatly packed with silver-paper! The Lord Chamberlain stopped the band, which was just beginning to play, and the flunkey got rid of the paper as if by magic.

I had a dream on Sunday morning, which I must tell, not for its own sake, but because it's the first time that a thing which seemed

[1] Helen Marsh, christened Margaret.

to me brilliantly clever in a dream has ever turned out on waking (not to be brilliantly clever but) to have some point. I dreamt I was reading the preface to one of Walter Scott's novels, in which, showing some disregard for dates, he gave a description of your grandfather's style of conversation[1] and he said he used always to accent all his little words, so that his sentences seemed like dogs running with small steps on their hind legs. I don't think I'd ever seen this said of anybody, certainly not of your grandfather, and I do think it's a rather good description of what a sentence would sound like with all the syllables equally accented.

So absorbing was his concern for human creatures that he seldom felt moved to describe the appearance of things inanimate, but a haystack on fire near the house in the country where he was staying was an exception. 'It really was a gorgeous sight, huge supple flames leaping up and waving about with jagged edges, just like the petals of parrot-tulips, and above a great pillar of Titian-fire-coloured smoke, full of sparks, going straight up for some way, and then bent and blown aside by the soft but steady wind, and shading off into beautiful greys as it got away from the fire.'
Later in March Tovey reappeared on the scene.

Do you remember my account of my musical genius friend Donald Tovey? He's in London just now, and Charlotte Cornish wrote and asked me to look after him. This is rather difficult, as I don't like to ask him here, because none of my family know one note from another, and he's apt to be the most fearful bore on any subject but music; and when I take him to my clubs I live in terror of his bursting into a Bach fugue when the waiter is giving him potatoes. Besides which he has the most elaborate and conspicuous system of manners—when I took him to the Savile he turned round as we left the dining-room and made a low bow to the other members, turning the palms of his hands towards the ceiling.

In April Victor Lytton asked for Marsh's opinion of an essay he had written on the Irish poet 'A.E.' (George Russell). When Marsh was introduced to Yeats at Delamere Terrace on the 23rd it provided an interest in common. He wrote to Victor on the following day.

Neville may have told you I met Yeats at Edmund's last night. (P.S. I haven't said how absolutely fascinating I thought him.) He was kind enough to walk far out of his way with me in the pouring

[1] Edward Bulwer-Lytton (1803-73).

rain! and I summoned up courage to tell him of the article! He seemed really delighted to hear of it, as he said Russell hadn't been recognized at all, and he was very anxious that he should be. I mischievously raised the question of the two Standish O'Gradies, and it was rather amusing to hear the other side—of course to Yeats the poet is the real S. O'G., and Norman Moore's one the tiresome double. I told him Betty had made you leave out the allusion to 'A.E.' being concerned in the 'Horace Plunket movement' and he said it was a pity, as it would have been interesting.

Before he came Edmund had been giving an amusing account of Yeats's lecture the night before on the Ideal Theatre—how Yeats occasionally fell into an abstraction at the end of a sentence, and started out of it to resume the thread of his discourse. There was a discussion afterwards and a certain lady had asked beforehand that she might be called upon to speak—but when she got up her presence of mind deserted her, and nothing could be heard save the beating of her heart, so she had to resume her seat. Yeats told us of a new play he is writing, which is to be very remote from ordinary life, so much so that 'all except three of the characters have eagles' heads'. Did you see, or did I tell you, or did you otherwise know, that Yeats is 'Ulick Dean' in [George Moore's] *Evelyn Innes*? He said that all his friends were shocked at his not being indignant at the moral character thus attributed to him—but he said, 'I tell them that I don't see why I should be indignant, because people are responsible for their *opinions*, but Providence is responsible for their morals.' After supper he was made to read to us some things out of a new volume of his poems published on Saturday, they seemed most beautiful in sound, tho' I never can understand poetry read out. He read them in an extremely monotonous voice, with very strong emphasis on all the accents—it was rather effective, but I think it's possible to read in a more natural way without sacrificing the music of the verse.

When next he wrote to Neville and Judith he had been to the fair at Earl's Court with Philip Burne-Jones and Geoffrey Locker-Lampson. They began by mistaking genuine Zulus and Matabeles with assegais for English people dressed up, so 'missed the suitable alarm'. The Swan boat afforded some excitement, but the best was to come.

After screeching ourselves hoarse on the Switchback we went to the Waterchute, which is a most terrifying spectacle. Down the precipitous side of a dark and beetling eminence, about as high as the Dome des Invalides, the boat darts into the water, and quite

Edward Marsh, from a drawing
by Violet Duchess of Rutland,
1910

Edward Marsh, 1900

Edward Marsh (*in rear seat*) motoring with Winston
Churchill in Uganda, 1907

Edward Marsh at Ambleside,
September 1912. A snapshot
by Elliott Seabrooke

hidden by its own spray ducks and drakes along the surface at cannon-ball speed. It seemed what the newspapers call 'almost providential' that it wasn't dashed to bits. Undeterred by the sight, however, an intrepid mass of the nobility and gentry was seething toward the turnstile which admits to this experience and after squashing for twenty minutes we got our turn. As a matter of fact it is all over before one notices that anything is happening and I hadn't time to scream till we had slowed down at the other extremity of the lake. For physical agony it's nothing to the Switchback.

On April 5 Howard Marsh had broken the news that he was engaged to marry one of the sisters at St. Bartholomew's Hospital, Miss Violet Dalrymple Hay, the daughter of a distinguished soldier in the Regular Army. Judith Lytton was the first to be given the news. 'I winced and whistled backwards,' Marsh wrote, lightheartedly, but he was filled with dismay at the thought of his father marrying again. The wedding took place on July 18. In a forlorn attempt to bridge the gulf between him and his son, if only for a moment's trifling exchange of opinions, Howard went up to Eddie's room with three 'going away' hats and asked him to advise on which he should wear. Eddie Marsh attended the ceremony in no appropriate spirit.

> The clergyman told us that the real reason why thinking people rejoiced over the marriage was that it meant the inauguration of a new Christian home! as if 30 Bruton Street had hitherto been a notorious haunt of evil livers. He was also very Jingo in tone, and said that the necessity of defending the Empire was one great reason for having children. I gave my next-door neighbour the giggles by whispering 'Why drag in the Transvaal?'

For some weeks the humour in his letters was barbed with cynicism. 'The last two days I've been disgustingly irritable. I'm getting an absurd habit of losing my temper in the privacy of my bedroom, waves of passion surge up in my throat if I find my clothes haven't been properly folded. I suppose I ought to "take more exercise" and must get a pair of dumb bells.' Meals at home among the new family acquaintances were a trial. 'The man gave me some pleasure by saying when some unusual word came up, "I don't think I ever heard it spelt, I mean I don't think I ever saw it pronounced"—and the woman by saying, when the subject of mince pies was suggested by the menu, "We don't make our own mince pies but we cure our own tongues." I could only wish the cure had been more radical. Early in the evening I made up my mind to get drunk, so from an animal point of view I had a fairly pleasant evening.' It was some time before a full appreciation of his stepmother's qualities overcame his aversion to this marriage, and enabled him to realize that the family circle had been considerably enriched.

By now Frederick Maurice and his wife had moved out of Bruton Street and found a home in Woolwich. For all his affection for his sister, Marsh's first visit to her did nothing to dispel what by now was a cynical attitude to the married state. He didn't think her new abode was a change for the better. 'Too many things in it—a row of books on a shelf just below the ceiling and a pyramid of sugar basins in the grate—however I suppose this is inevitable during the period before wedding presents begin to get broken or disappear.' On top of everything else the weather was too hot. 'I feel like a blancmange on the rack!' In the evening as he finished his letter, moths from Berkeley Square and St. James's flapped round the oil-lamp at his elbow. And now he was weighed down with a sense of tedium. 'The lady who lives over the stables next door has been SINGING, with that power which is alas so often divorced from refinement.'

Throughout his life he took peculiar delight in carrying out relatively menial commissions. To him they were not acts of virtue, but a form of indulgence, and the more tiresome they might be to persons of baser mould the more he seemed to enjoy them. It was very difficult not to take advantage of him when that was the very thing he asked for. The Lytton correspondence contains pages of reports which read as though the writer were the agent of a small country estate. Not to include at least one example would be to give the impression that his pleasures were solely aesthetic or social. In his July letter to Judith Lytton he related his efforts to buy a replacement for the new reflector of her camera, which had arrived broken in the post.

I went to the photograph shop this morning in righteous indignation, and had rather a funny scene—I expounded my grievance to the man who had sworn that the reflector should arrive intact. He was rather stupid and showed the radiant good temper so offensive in a person who is in the wrong. His first set of arguments was that they couldn't be responsible for the post, that 'the lady might have her own ideas as to what was loose packing and what was not', that they were continually sending glass to South Africa, and that their packing-people were 'so used to packing that they didn't think anything of it at all'—'Yes,' said I, 'they're so used to it that they don't think of it nearly enough.' (But one's neatest scores are always thrown away on shopkeepers, and one has to console oneself by putting it down to their want of education.) He then proposed that you should *send back the packing materials!* in order that they might get compensation from the General Post Office—but I pointed out that this would be giving you trouble which you hadn't done anything to deserve—so he asked 'then what do *you* propose that we should do?' 'Give us another reflector, of course.' But it turned out that this would involve sending back the whole thing to have a glass fitted and he suggested that you could easily get one in Paris. 'All right,' I said, 'only you ought to pay for it.' 'All right,' he replied, 'I'll give you the shilling directly.' At this revelation as to the value of the article in dispute I rather spoilt my argument by bursting out laughing— (I had somehow imagined that it was a sort of enormous cheval-glass, such as Neville might use, when you weren't retouching, for doing a full-length auto-portrait) and I didn't think it worth while to go on arguing, so after he had promised to scold the packers I walked off with a parting oath which left him as imperturbable as ever.

When reporting to Judith Lytton a further stage in the Camera Question he included his observations on reading Mackail's *Life of William Morris.*

I have at last finished Morris's Life—to my surprise I like the Socialist side of him better than the artistic. I like the idea that perfection would be for everyone to lead a simple life with pleasurable and artistic work to do—and I think it essentially possible, i.e. that there is nothing in the *nature* of things to prevent it—tho' I don't see how we can ever get to it now, considering the turn things have actually taken. On the other hand his artistic ideals are rather anti-pathetic to me (tho' I admit they are consistent with his social ones). He is all for general decorative effort as against salient points—for instance he considered art as properly subordinate to architecture; didn't care much for easel pictures, to which he preferred an illuminated border in a manuscript; thought it a mistake to make a face the most important part of a design; and in poetry avoided strikingly happy lines or phrases, which he thought an interference with the general run of the whole. On all these points my taste is the other way, I suppose because I prefer interpretation to abstract beauty. I think Nev prefers abstract beauty to interpretation, but I'm sure he would not go so far as Morris. As M's artistic ideals were entirely his own, while his Socialism is derived from Ruskin, I'm come to the conclusion that he doesn't really mean very much to me—and I can't really care for him as a man, he was too self-sufficient and independent, and tho' no doubt he had strong affections he doesn't seem to have given them so much importance, compared with other things, as I should like.[1]

When the married couple came back from Egypt Marsh at last broke away from the parental home and took rooms at 3 Gray's Inn Place, sharing the rent with Neville and Judith, who had agreed to make it their London *pied-à-terre*, and almost every week-end he stayed with them at Rake Mill near Milford in Surrey. But in October his official work came to the forefront. He had been sitting up late, drafting telegrams to the colonies, directing them to send troops to South Africa. 'I have not changed my mind that these disasters are deserved punishment for national ὕβρις,' wrote R. C. Trevelyan, 'I think we have about suffered sufficient penance. I cannot however see there is much in this talk of the existence of the Empire being at stake. Even in the event of our losing the whole of South Africa, I cannot see that that would be fatal, though everyone says it would.'

Writing from Paris, Baring felt bound to warn his friend in London that there was growing hostility to everything British. 'If I ever believed that such a thing as a war could happen—and a war between France and England—I could believe its happening as a result of this Dreyfus case.' In a footnote to these alarms he told how Balfour, who was about to become a Roman Catholic, had succeeded in engaging him in religious controversy. 'Buddha and St. Francis pale before him. He has permanently upset my

---

[1] At the same time Marsh wrote to Edmund Gosse, who was on holiday in Norway, giving his views of the book. None of Marsh's letters to Gosse written before 1912 have survived, but Gosse's reply is interesting. 'When I had finished it I said to Nellie, "I don't at all regret that I never got to know Morris any better." His character was in the book as he was to me in life, antagonistic, unsympathetic. I think mainly because it was so *incoherent*. You may say what you will, but all that socialistic business was very silly; I don't for a moment suggest it was insincere, but it was irrational and unintelligent; it did not belong to the carpets and the Kelmscott Press and the tapestry kings and queens. Suppose I was suddenly to take up anti-vivisection, or you were to become a ministering Swedenborgian! It wouldn't fit in—and the socialism doesn't fit in to Morris. The work, too, for one who knows, is not quite true. Throughout the early volume Mackail is simply the mouthpiece of Burne-Jones' prejudices, in the second he is simply the mouthpiece of his own extreme boredom. One thing I resent is the continual description of Rossetti, who is very unkindly and unfairly spoken of and ignored. You could have carved twenty noticeable human beings out of Rossetti. Morris seems to me to make up rather less than one.' (*August 17, 1899.*)

opinions. This came about by *my* unsettling some of his.' With these rumours of precarious relations with France and the threatened disintegration of the Empire, Howard, his wife, and Eddie Marsh celebrated the arrival of a new century with Neville and Judith Lytton, lifting the convivial glass in the drawing-room at Bruton Street.

ii

In January Victor Lytton (who during the past months had been helped by Marsh in his academic work) announced the approach of his final examination for the Diplomatic Service. 'Shall I send you Wordsworth? I believe he's a very bracing author,' Marsh wrote. 'I also recommend you to go about with a loaded revolver.' Baring, who had scorned Marsh's offer of help in reading the proofs of his article on Victor Hugo, now discovered cause to repent. 'He has been made by the printer to say that Gray's *Elegy* is admitted by critics to be one of the best loved poems in the French language,' Marsh reported to the Lyttons in satisfaction. 'Maurice has been making friends with Sarah Bernhardt who is very pro-English and told him she had vowed *jamais, au grand jamais*, to act before a Boer audience. I shouldn't think this form of self-denial will cost her much.' Marsh had been to the pantomime with Edwin Lutyens (Victor's brother-in-law) and failed to appreciate the new style of stage illumination.

First of all on entering the theatre one is almost knocked down by an overpowering smell of Cherry Blossom and from time to time we were either blinded by the sudden glaring up of the whole stage with electric light or deafened by the roar of 50 trumpets. The sense of touch was assailed by blasts of pitch cold draught caused by the scene-shifting, and for the sake of completeness I quite expected that a spoonful of cayenne pepper would be thrust into my mouth as I went out for the entr'acte. Dan Leno was amusing.

In March Baring wrote again from Paris. He had attended the first night of *L'Aiglon*. 'The audience sobbed and yelled.' In Madame Bernhardt's dressing-room he met Sardou, Anatole France, and Jules Lemaître, and when Rostand entered 'all kissed the palpitating genius'. The work was considered more 'human and interesting' than *Cyrano*. 'Sarah, it is universally admitted, never acted better and never looked so young. She looked charming, very thin, very fresh, very slight, but very manly. . . . What will the world be without her?' In the same month Baring wrote again. 'I went to see Anatole France yesterday morning. Jaurès and Zola were there. Anatole badly bitten with Dreyfus disease still which obscures his judgement on things of the present day. *L'Aiglon* has become an entirely political thing. Rostand himself is a Dreyfusard—by the irony of things. . . . Zola sat in the corner, observing the cobwebs and thinking of obscene occurrences and not saying a word.'

Since September 1896 Marsh's work in the Colonial Service had gone smoothly enough but for an energetic campaign he had conducted to right the alleged wrongs of a policeman in Fiji called Ensor, who complained of unjust treatment at the hands of the Governor, Sir John Thurston. Marsh's dispatches were mounting in number and severity when the Governor suddenly died. This significant turn of events inspired Marsh's immediate superior with a quatrain which caught on in the department.

> Who killed Sir John Thurston?
> I, answered Marsh,
> With my language so harsh—
> I killed Sir John Thurston.

In spite of this he was promoted in the spring of 1900 to the position of Assistant Private Secretary to Joseph Chamberlain. At this time there was no Appointments Board for the posting of officials in the Colonial Office, and it was Marsh's function, with the assistance of an unpaid colleague, to interview candidates, examine the qualifications, and make submissions for appointment to the principal, Lord Ampthill. The first of Marsh's two colleagues, Oliver Howard, a son of George Lord Carlisle, took no interest whatever in literature or the arts, but it was he who put the finishing touch, or perhaps the penultimate touch, to that character whose evolution into a public figure familiar in London we have watched through the last years of the nineteenth century. To Marsh it seemed that Howard's vitality and quickness of temper marked him as an Elizabethan hidalgo, born out of his time; but it was his favourite recreation, the making of ancestral pedigrees of fearful complexity and unerring precision, which revealed more of the true man. He was a stickler for exactitude in demeanour, address, accent, the social idiom of his day and age, and with pained look and sibilant indrawn breath he registered censure of any lapse in proper usage. So far from resigning office or falling upon his colleague bodily Marsh discovered through Howard a new field of arbitrary rules for the exercise of that part of his nature which respected nothing so much as properly informed skill in the niceties of custom. For him an arbitrary rule endorsed by tradition was endowed with a peculiar beauty of rightness. This extended to minutiae. What seemed a mantelpiece was nothing of the sort. It was a chimneypiece, and only in spheres beyond the pale could the word 'lunch' be used as a noun. Oliver Howard instilled only the principle, not its literary application. Howard was what nowadays one might regard as an embodiment of the subtle distinction between things U and non-U, that code of usage where lack of breeding is betrayed by infinitesimal but fatal flaws. As with the other standards in art or manners which Marsh acquired from the friends he esteemed, so in this he lived to outstrip his model and become the arbiter.

On June 18 a small crowd gathered outside the Colonial Office in Whitehall, a horse-drawn fire-engine came to a halt and helmeted figures vanished intrepidly through the doorway. Billows of smoke poured from an upper window. Eddie Marsh had been instructed to destroy all drafts of telegrams to South Africa and the conflagration had got out of control.

Before taking his winter holiday he called at Delamere Terrace, where he found the elderly painter Alfred Parsons.

Parsons was asked if he knew Ruskin, he said he had only seen him once, and then a pretty young lady was there so Ruskin had taken no notice of him. They went for a walk on a moor, however, and Ruskin said there was a blight on all the heather that year—pointing out that each bell had a little hole in it near the stalk, round which the texture of the flower was withered. Parsons asked why this was, and Ruskin explained that it was a curse of God, in revenge for the misdoings of man. Some time afterwards Parsons had occasion to make a study of heather, and he observed that the bees couldn't get at the honey through the opening of the bell, and were obliged to make a little hole near the stalk, hence the phenomenon! I remarked that this justified the ways of God to man, as it would have been rather unfair of him to visit humanity with a curse which Ruskin would be the only person to notice.

In November Marsh travelled alone to Berlin and was joined
in Dresden by Victor Lytton. From Berlin he wrote to Judith,
describing his Alma-Tadema marble bathroom and the telephone
apparatus by his bed which he was 'much too nervous to use'. He
had seen two plays by Hauptmann. 'When I go to a play by
myself I always feel so terribly alone with God, and daren't be
pleased with anything not up to the highest standard.' He had
also been to *Lohengrin*.

Jean de Reszke's the only living tenor. We had a Bayreuth celebrity,
whose only merits were that he presented an ample surface for the
reflection of magnesian light, and that he made the vocalization of
Elsa appear, when heard immediately after his own, comparatively
suave. She was fairly pretty and not fat—but how tired one gets of the
everlasting Elsa get-up—flaxen wig, arms, and the Wagnerian tea-
gown—and how one sympathizes with actresses like Calvé who are
cursed for trying to look a little different from the usual representatives of their parts. An Elsa with black hair would be a comfort
for once. I think the opera was given *dans son entier*, there seemed
much more of Ortrud, poor woman; she comes on again and again,
now in satin, now in rags, now in velvet and now in widow's weeds,
but always in the same spirit of gesticulation and obstructiveness—
and always to be 'foiled again'. One wonders if she wakes up in the
night and thinks what a ghastly fool she is. Poor Telramund too, who
is knocked down three times with his feet towards the footlights, very
much foreshortened. The scenery was rather good and the chorus
much better than in London. The swan fortunately makes no
attempt at feathers, like the poor English one which only succeeds
in looking half plucked. It is frankly one of the cardboard embossed
kind used for holding ices, only of course much larger. German
theatre manners and customs are rather amusing—for one thing there
is hardly any applause, and I haven't yet seen the curtain go up at
the end of an act. Then between the acts nobody smokes, the whole
audience goes up to the foyer and walks solemnly round and round
in a string, husbands and wives arm-in-arm, while every now and
then someone drops out of the procession to have a glass of beer or
eat a plateful of ham, tongue, or raw salmon at the buffet.

Of the sights in Berlin only one keenly aroused his interest.

It is worth while to see the highest and final manifestation of any
quality, and it would be impossible to beat the 'Hohenzollern
Museum' as an expression of the *positive* quality of want of humour for
which our language doesn't yield an appropriate name. The glass

cases round the walls contain baby-clothes, Coronation robes, evening gowns, uniforms, widow's weeds, and cerecloths, worn by dead Emperors and Empresses and Kings and Queens—leaves of clover picked by the Empress Frederick, pencils sharpened by the Emperor William and the skin of the pony on which the present Emperor learned to ride. Two entire rooms present nothing but the ribbons which once tied the wreaths sent by public bodies to imperial funerals. One can't help feeling a certain respect and pity for the poor dead royalties who after all were human beings and who are not responsible for being made fools of by their living descendants, and it's with the oddest mixture of awe and *fou rire* that one walks through the Galleries.

From Dresden he sent a description of the plot of *Il Trovatore*. 'Did you ever hear anything more harrowing? and isn't it extraordinary to reflect that such a story was seriously set to music by a man of genius who is still alive?' While still in Dresden he wrote to Neville: 'I suppose the Queen will be dead by the time you get this. I am very sorry about it, and all the English ladies in Dresden are in tears.'

On June 26, 1901, Edmund Gosse invited Marsh and Baring and Victor Lytton to celebrate his last evening in Delamere Terrace before the move to his new London home. It was a hilarious occasion. 'Maurice carved the mutton, standing and first pulling up his sleeves to show there was no deception and solemnly bowing to the audience after each slice.' And he did his parody of Dr. Warre, the headmaster of Eton, preaching in Lower Chapel. 'And you boys—whatever you may be in after life —*whether* you may be great statesmen—or *whether* you may be lawyers—or *whether* you may be writers—or *even* if you're only engin*EERS* . . .' and the peroration 'The sins that drag us down, the sins that drag us down and which we *loathe*—the sins which we hate and which we *loathe* and which in fact we DEPLORE'. Afterwards Baring accompanied Marsh back to Gray's Inn Place and produced from his pocket the manuscript of his verse drama *The Black Prince*, which he left behind for detailed criticism. This was the first poem of importance that Marsh was invited to scrutinize in manuscript. It was ten years before the next.

In his copious correspondence with the Lyttons there is only one isolated poetical opinion: 'If you call le Gallienne a minor poet you might just as well call a street-lamp a minor planet!'

The theatre too was seldom referred to, though from Berlin he wrote of watching Réjane. 'I certainly prefer a rather quieter style, but it carried me away and was quite as terrific as Duse, even if a little more theatrical. There was one moment when both her tears came off at once and flashed through the air, which was one of the most passionate things I've ever seen.' Nor did the social scene particularly engage his correspondent's interest, though as soon as the mourning for the Queen was over Marsh could not resist informing his friends that he had for the first time enjoyed the privilege of 'opening the ball'. It was not, however, the smartest assembly of the season. 'There was a mixture of chalk and cheese, large cliffs of the former with here and there *des petits Suisses*, by which I mean excellence without fashion,' and in March 1902 he attended a royal levée at St. James's Palace, ending the day with Stephen Phillips and Tree at His Majesty's Theatre.

> Prepare to meet thy Sovereign! . . . The levée was a most wearisome performance and I don't know whether to laugh or cry when I think of the manner in which some 1,500 of the educated classes spent their morning. I rather liked my uniform when finished, especially my Jemimas which are very elegant, and my cocked hat, with a nice curly black ostrich feather over my eyes, making me feel like a Shetland pony. It took about an hour to get round, through the successive pens in which one is shut up with the same little group of people—what with the fog and the crowd, it was like nothing so much as going through locks in an underground railway turned into a river. And when one reached 'The Presence' one was rushed through with just time to make one's bow to the red bored stolid sovereign and none either to look at the sight or (thank goodness) to make a fool of oneself. My only approach to misadventure was that during the first long wait I found that my sword kept slipping out of its scabbard! I *could* not make out what was wrong and was just beginning to be terrified of what might happen, and at the same time quite without courage to confide my perplexity to any of the complete strangers who surrounded me—when the man next to me began to make a fuss and ask me to make room for him to adjust his garters which were coming off. This emboldened me to consult him about my own difficulty and a gigantic guardsman in front of me, whom I shall ever bless for putting me in countenance, turned round and said that *his* sword had once come out as he was passing before the King! The man with the garters kindly put mine to rights, and entering into conversation turned out to be Dr. Howard,

Lord Strathcona's son-in-law. We struck up a friendship and went
round together.

Luckily I have a really farcical subject to turn to—*Ulysses!*
Davis classed it as a 'tragedy bouffe', which is an excellent description. It is really rather a clever idea of Tree's to attract enormous
audiences to the theatre by the promise of an intellectual treat, and
once there keep them amused by the lowest form of buffoonery.
There is a fat old man, and a comic swineherd, who are more
degraded than anything in *Charley's Aunt*—and rapturously applauded. The only good thing is the ghosts in Hades, which are really
beautiful at moments. I don't pretend to judge the play as very little
was audible, and what I caught was so badly delivered that one had
to imagine it in print before one could see what it was really like,
but even then it is full of lapses. One rather amusing line was when
Penelope, in giving a list of the ties that bind her to Ulysses, says that
they 'have watched, like gardeners, a growing child'. I couldn't make
up my mind whether it was a higher duty to give pecuniary support
to the Poetic Drama or to refuse it Beerbohm Tree.

His sole link with the Coronation ceremony was his brother-
in-law Frederick Maurice, who acted as an usher in the Abbey,
showing Sarah Bernhardt to her place, and arranging together
in a pew the motley trio of Sir Thomas Lipton, Marie Corelli,
and the composer Saint-Saëns. Marsh acted however in a semi-
official capacity at the reception afterwards given by his Chief at
the Colonial Office.

My only Coronation festivity has been the Joseph Chamberlains'
reception on Monday which was more of an anxiety than a pleasure.
Mrs. Chamberlain told me to introduce everybody to everybody
without knowing or caring who or what they were, and I did a good
deal in this way, and was only just saved by my better angel from
such solecisms as presenting the Duke of Abercorn to the Duchess of
Marlborough as Sir Gordon Sprigg. One Colonist told me that he
had no doubt I was Mr. Chamberlain's son—'No,' I said, 'only his
Private Secretary.' 'Ah well, no doubt it's that intimate association
which has produced the likeness.' I said I thought it was only the eye-
glass, but he said it went deeper than that. The end of the party was
rather amusing, it melted away about 12.15 to the members of the
family, the Private Secretaries, and one imposing lady who planted
herself solidly on the sofa and proclaimed that she was ashamed of
staying so late but that her husband had gone down to supper, and
when that happened there was no telling when he would reappear.
Mr. Chamberlain who was standing with Monk Bretton said, 'Who

is that woman? she seems to have got stuck.' I told him what she had just said, and he remarked, 'I suppose her husband is getting drunk downstairs.' I then made what I thought the most obvious and practical suggestion, that Monk B. should offer to take *her* down to supper—at which Mr. Chamberlain roared with laughter for five minutes. In the end Mrs. Chamberlain somehow got her out of the room.

I walked out for exercise down the Strand and Whitehall which were swarming with Austin Birrell and the people of the greatest nation on earth. The impression on my mind was that all those who are so plain that they are usually kept indoors had been let out for the occasion in patriotic hats, and with a bit of plush to smarten them up. I don't know why I mentioned Birrell except that he was the only person I had ever seen before, or could imagine seeing again. The newspaper posters were all 'Coronation contretemps—Archbishop faints' or 'Dr. Temple breaks down—Gorgeous Scene' but it seems he didn't faint, he only had some difficulty in rising from his knees. I dined at Bruton Street and walked out with Helen and Freddie to see a few illuminations which were not very good. There were very elaborate police regulations for getting about, the oddest was that if you wanted to cross a street you mustn't do so directly, but go as far as possible at right angles to your direction and then return. Luckily this wasn't needed as there was no great crush.

Marsh was not infrequently at this time mistaken for a member of the Chamberlain family. His first suspicion of this was when a parting caller at the office shook him warmly by the hand with 'I'm a Birmingham man myself'.

With the advent of the Edwardian era the surviving Lytton letters come to an end. In the main they had been devoted to domestic preoccupations of great but ephemeral importance, pages which look to the stranger's eye like a small fragment of Jane Austen's world in late Victorian dress, examined under a microscope and treated with that serio-comic mixture of detachment and sympathetic concern natural to a man of lively curiosity without family responsibilities of his own, never omitting of course the occasional spice of an anecdote—'Lord Salisbury is getting very shortsighted, and the other day the King showed him his last new photograph, and asked what he thought of it—"Ah, poor Buller," said Lord S.' His position of detachment gave him the advantage as a judge of character and he was often in one way or another redressing the balance.

I think your opinion of Mrs. Fry is one of your rare mistakes. She is so completely out of the common that the question of beautiful or ugly scarcely seems to me to arise, but if I were forced to use one word or the other I believe I should after all say beautiful, there are certain positions of her head in which the lines of her face compose so finely—and certain positions of her figure which are simply *du Luca Signorella*. Her personality is out of my ken altogether, I feel it as something mysterious and grandiose made human by her frank and generous humour. Her aloofness and impenetrability give way at once on any common ground of fun—I have met very few women who seemed to have more of the dignity and less of the limitations of their sex. Don't imagine you can dispose of all this by saying that her few teeth are brown.

But one topic of common interest with his friends which from time to time is touched on briefly in these letters is so important that it must be considered on its own. By far the greatest contribution which Neville Lytton made to Marsh's life was the continuation of his education in the graphic arts, which had been initiated by Uncle Norman and at Cambridge carried a further stage by Oswald Sickert and Trevelyan, the close friend of Roger Fry. Lytton was always ready to hear about painting, and Marsh's anxiety to be a fitting companion for a painter sharpened his critical eye.

iii

Lytton was a traditionalist. Marsh's initiation during the 'nineties into the new movements in art came too soon and was too desultory to fire his interest. He needed to start afresh and on traditional lines, so as to acquire a sound basis of experience among the visual arts. Through Lytton he discovered the early English water-colourists, and in 1901, at Lytton's prompting, made his first purchase, a Girtin in monochrome of a sloping hill with what might be two shepherd's huts to one side and an irregular row of trees. Lytton had turned to the work of Cotman, Girtin, and both Alexander and J. R. Cozens, in reaction against the contemporary influences from France. At this time the early English water-colour tradition was almost as neglected by painters as it was unfashionable among collectors. Through his desire to follow his friend's development with full understanding Marsh discovered one of his own greatest gifts, the perceptive eye and responding sensibility, and his activities as a patron were to remain confined to that sphere of art, the English schools, where his interests were first engaged.

During the period 1898-1902 there were several significant references to his experience of pictures.

I had a longer look than ever before at his [Neville's] favourite Gainsborough [he wrote to Judith] and for the first time felt its peculiar beauty—it's another instance of his being *always* right. I wish I had his quickness and power of seeing things at the first go off, it literally takes me five or six minutes hard looking before I even begin to see the real beauty of a picture.

And after visiting a Turner exhibition in the same year: 'I've invented a new way of looking at supremely lovely pictures —to look hard at a beautiful bit, then shut one's eyes and try to remember it, and then open them again to find out how much lovelier it is than one's mental picture.'

His reading of the *Life of Morris* had helped him to understand the aim of the Pre-Raphaelites.

Burne-Jones's method of making every part of a picture equally important was evidently deliberate, as Morris held strongly the theory that that was the right way to paint—and I think he probably imposed it on B.J. as he seems to have been the stronger and more original of the two.

You know the two kinds of dreams, one in which everything is as distinct as life only more delightful, and the other when everything is dim? All B.J.'s pictures are dream-like, but they are mostly the misty kind of dream—in this one[1] all is misty except the woman's face which is painted with extraordinary intensity and has the reality of life and the mystery of dreams both together.

In May 1899 he discovered the work of Charles Conder.

Did we see a Conder at the New English? or did we not? Either way I remember you didn't know about him—there is a little ex-hibition of his things, mostly fans painted on silk, with one or two landscapes in oils. I think he's rather a *dentiste*. In drawing and senti-ment he hasn't much that he couldn't have got either from Watteau or Aubrey Beardsley, but he seems to have an absolute mastery over colour, which is quite his own. His eye has room for every colour and tone, but over or rather within them all he puts the subdued and shimmering lightness of mother-of-pearl (I don't mean he uses those

[1] *Love among the Ruins.*

colours, but he has that evanescent radiance—my goodness, how
difficult it is to find words for such things) and he has a knack of
mixing up all the different scales of colour—for instance imagine a
Monet tree in the midst of a Turner mist—without ever making a
mistake. I wonder what you would think of him.

While in Berlin he had seen the Rembrandts. 'Luckily there
are no feathers or one would be knocked down and *never* get up
again. There was one especially of Potiphar's wife complaining
to Joseph after which one never wants to see a picture again.'
The Fragonards in Paris he found unexciting. 'At first sight they
are simply very superior chocolate box, but after a bit I began to
see, or perhaps persuade myself, that they are graceful to the point
of dentistry.' In 1900 he paid his first visit to the Grafton Gallery
to see a South African exhibition. 'It was touching to see Alma-
Tadema's delight at finding pictures demonstrably worse than
.his own.' But his first encounter with Bernhard Berenson in 1901
failed to develop. 'We didn't get into any quite satisfactory vein
of talk, just offering each other the subjects of Time and Death
and Judgement, as if they were cold meats on the sideboard of
Miss Austen's dinner, without helping ourselves.'

He was one day to be the connoisseur who walked alone, but
for the first ten years Lytton was always at his side when he bought
a picture. In 1900 he acquired *The Summit of Cader Idris* by Richard
Wilson; there followed *The Lady in Brown Silk* attributed to Lely
and subsequently ascribed to Pieter Borsseler, and the handful of
other early paintings which he hung on what he called his
National Gallery Wall. They were the exception to the rule. His
water-colour drawings gradually increased in number: *Harlech
Castle* in a misty brown silhouette by Girtin, *The Tanning Mills* by
Crome, the view of Richmond Bridge by Sandby, and wounded
soldiers reading a notice-board by Dadd, bought among others
through Robert Ross from the William Bell Scott Collection.
Although he had met Steer, Rothenstein, Sickert, and Fry several
years before, his was a backward-looking eye. If he was ever in
any doubt as to whether he would make headway as a collector
with the small financial resources he had at his command, all
doubts were dispelled in 1904. He had been corresponding with
Robert Ross on behalf of Neville Lytton, who was ready for a
one-man show at the Carfax Gallery in Ryder Street, and for a
year or so now Ross had been on the watch for bargains in Eddie

Marsh's period, roughly 1780-1830. On March 19 he wrote to say
he had a proposition which for the time being must be kept
strictly secret. He explained that a personal friend (he could not
yet divulge the name) wanted to dispose of a complete collection
of English drawings. There were two hundred of them and the
price was 'absurdly cheap'. He was asking £2,400, which worked
out at £12 each, and Ross contended that he could sell many of
them individually for £40 any day. He gave a rough inventory.

> There are six or seven magnificent Gainsboroughs, about three if
> not more superb Cozens J.R., six A. Cozens, and a set of particularly
> fine and interesting Romneys, several Blakes certainly worth £35-40
> each at the least, Cotman and Girtin are well represented by very
> choice examples, particularly the former. The collection is weak in
> Turners, but there are three *very fine* ones (two early and one 'full'
> period) and I know no such set of Wilsons in private hands. Would
> you consider the collection?

Marsh replied that he would inspect the collection if he was
allowed to bring Lytton with him. Then Ross wrote again: 'My
reason for approaching you was a chance remark of yours that
you were rather looking out for something important and did
not want to waste money over an unimportant picture however
charming. I did not imagine you were a Pierpoint Morgan.'

It was not until May 10 that Marsh and Lytton saw the collection. They found that it included Blake's exquisite *Har and Heva
Bathing*, and the portrait of him by his wife; also drawings by
Reynolds, Crome, Rowlandson, Rysbraek (from the Walpole
collection at Strawberry Hill) and Zuccarelli. The owner's name
was at last disclosed; it was Herbert Horne who was going to settle
in Florence in order to work on Botticelli. On May 18 the bargain
was concluded.[1] Marsh appealed to his father, who was now
Professor of Surgery at Cambridge, and persuaded him to advance
some of Jane Marsh's money which was due to come to the
children on his death. This was of course the residue of the
'murder money' which had come to her on the death of Anna
Perceval in 1889. Howard Marsh agreed to lend the sum at a
low rate of interest. He knew that his son had nothing but his
Civil Servant's salary for living on and repaying the loan, but Uncle

---

[1] He never spent more than £80 on a single picture. For the reader interested in
the fluctuations of value it may be added here that in 1905 he bought a Turner, an
Edward Dayes, and no less than six Girtin drawings for £92 9s. 6d.

Norman had just died, and Eddie was due to receive a share of the 'murder money' in his own right.

Norman Perceval had worked out an elaborate system on the principle of a family tree showing the relative entitlements of each living descendant of his grandfather. Though himself a younger son, the family fortune by a series of premature deaths and bequests had accumulated in his hands, and according to his elaborate scheme of distribution one-sixth was due to his nephew Eddie Marsh. The news reached Eddie on his thirty-first birthday in 1903, in a letter from his brother-in-law. The capital residue of Castlereagh's grant which remained in the family then amounted to £14,600. After other investments were taken into account Eddie Marsh's expectation could be estimated at about £4,000, which would come to him in instalments on the decease of certain relatives. Over the next fifteen years the successive payments fell due by what seemed to him a peculiarly happy sense of timing on the part of Fate.

As yet he had brought his critical assistance to bear upon only one contemporary painter other than Lytton. When Roger Fry held his London exhibition in April 1903 Marsh bought an example of his work, called on him at his studio in Willow Road, Hampstead, and followed it up with a letter. 'I can't tell you what pleasure your letter gave me,' Fry answered. 'I had no vaguest dream that you would be likely to care for my things in that sort of way. Your criticism of the *Shillingley* really started me off again on it. . . . I may perhaps take it in hand once more and get it more perfectly modulated.' So by the early years of the new reign Marsh had made his first efforts in the private criticism of prose, poetry, and painting. But Sickert, Baring, and Fry were his contemporaries. At least a decade would have to pass before mature age and experience gave him the confidence and the authority which he needed for his main achievement in this aspect of his life, the recognition of talent in creative artists at the outset of their careers.

Chapter Seven

EDWARDIAN
(January 1903–May 1910)

WHEN Eddie Marsh left Bruton Street in 1899 and took rooms with the Lyttons in Gray's Inn Place the agent of the property supplied a servant. She was a Derbyshire woman aged thirty-seven who had come to London so as to live near her husband's work. Mr. Elgy died in 1906 before Marsh had become sufficiently acquainted with his servant for her to divulge the nature of his occupation. Mrs. Elgy herself was a countrywoman with the wholesome air about her of a rambling farm-house miles from anywhere and smelling of new-baked bread. Her life in Holborn made no impression on her. She remained a villager. It took Marsh some time to discover that she was anything more than a useful pair of hands, but as the years went by he became aware that she was one of the most remarkable women in all his acquaintance. She was his housekeeper, cook, maid, valet, butler, and confidante, although barely able to read and write except in her own peculiar but serviceable brand of phonetic spelling.[1] So her devotion to her employer had no basis of admiration for his true qualities. He was a mystery to her, and she left it at that. The gradual proliferation of pictures on the walls remained more of a joke than a puzzle to her, and each new acquisition was greeted with some genial or downright disparaging remark. For some while it was only the quantity that exercised her mind, but when at last the contemporary works began to appear her howls of derisive laughter were so unaffected that for a while Marsh himself would suspect that he might have made a mistake. His first Matthew Smith, the torso of a woman reclining among dark red shadows, was greeted with 'Looks as if she's been 'aving a *blood-bath*', and Ethel Walker's portrait of two little girls against a stippled background, with 'But why are the poor mites

[1] A fair specimen is the sentence from a postcard of complaint sent to her employer while she was on holiday: 'i no nobudy and nobudy noes me.'

114

lost in a snow-storm?' By some quaint dispensation of Fate the charwoman who was to become the beloved châtelaine at Raymond Buildings was an artist, and the cooking with which her employer regaled his guests and his own impeccable appearance in Whitehall or the theatre stalls were to be her masterpiece.

Early in 1903 he left 3 Gray's Inn Place and moved round the corner to 5 Raymond Buildings, a top flat on two floors approached by a spiral of fifty-nine stone steps. He wanted more wall space, but his main reason was his desire to live where a hansom could drive up to the door. This certainly proved a convenience in hours of daylight, but at the end of the *cul-de-sac* which abutted on Theobalds Road there was a lodge gate like the entrance to a college which was closed at sundown, so the vehicle bringing back its solitary passenger in the small hours during the London season would have to come to a halt in the main road.

He was still a regular attendant at Gosse's salon, which was now a weekly gathering in Hanover Terrace. Thomas Hardy would be there on occasion, a withdrawn figure that seldom spoke, but Max Beerbohm would drop a remark worth carrying away, such as his description of Pinero's eyebrows as 'the skins of some small mammal just not large enough to be used as mats'. Howard Marsh's Professorship of Surgery at Cambridge (1903) meant that from now on his son had somewhere to stay for his visits to the Verralls. It was at this time that he dropped in unexpectedly on G. E. Moore[1] when he was sitting with a group of students, and attributed the want of give-and-take in conversation to the philosopher's principle that unless one was going to say something that was both true and of some consequence it was idle to speak at all. Marsh's conversational gambits struck no responsive chord in the breast of anyone present. He left disconcerted to discover that he had drifted so far away from an old friend, but consoled by the knowledge that this slight failure of his was due to an austerely self-denying ordinance which, so he fancied, made social intercourse impossible. On this incident Mr. G. E. Moore has remarked: 'I used to give a breakfast party nearly every Sunday morning. If I remember right, Marsh came in once after breakfast, and he must have found us a very silent party. I think that why he did must have been because we were embarrassed by feeling that he did not quite fit in. I don't believe that

[1] Moore was a Prize Fellow at Trinity from 1898 to 1904.

I ever gave such instructions as he said I did to my so-called "disciples". Lytton Strachey was probably one of the number.'[1] One can imagine the disquieting impact of a breezy young graduate eager to coruscate with anecdotes from the metropolis. It illustrates a certain insensitiveness in Eddie Marsh which led him into difficulties more than once. He was apt to see his friends solely as they stood in the innocence of his own vision, never conceiving of them as they might look in the eyes of one another. He could be tactless. At times when even acute intelligence was not enough he could suffer a lapse in the simple faculty of social imagination, and as on that Sunday morning in Cambridge prove insensitive to atmosphere. At this time (1903) he had unwittingly set Gosse, Baring, and A. C. Benson at odds. Gosse was never slow to take offence, so Baring forgave the culprit on the grounds that he had been subjected to too severe a test, but he gave his warning a characteristic twist. 'It would be a pity if you never saw me again.'

In 1903 Alfred Lyttelton took over the Colonial Office when Joseph Chamberlain resigned, but this brought about no change in Marsh's position. By then Oliver Howard had been posted abroad and the new unpaid assistant was Conrad Russell (a cousin of Bertrand Russell) a colleague somewhat less exacting than Howard. The change of Chief prevented Marsh from going to Italy for an Easter holiday with Victor Lytton. 'It is very kind of you to offer to buy me things in Florence,' he wrote, 'and if you come across a Botticelli for a few lire I don't say but it wouldn't come in very handy, but it must be genuine, not a Botticini or an Amico di Sandro.' In June there was time for a visit to Assisi, and when he got back the orders were to clear the files of redundant papers which had accumulated during the Chamberlain regime. The task involved examining and tearing up about twelve thousand old letters, a process punctuated with shrieks of laughter at some of the suggestions put forward by correspondents. Not all of them seem so outrageous today, judging by the list in his letter to his new friend Pamela Lytton.[2]

> . . . Schemes for scattering conciliatory pamphlets among the Boers from balloons, for arranging the railways of Australia in the shape of a Union Jack, for making eggs imperishable, for Old Age pensions,

[1] Letter to the author.
[2] In 1901 Victor Lytton (2nd Earl of Lytton) married Miss Pamela Plowden.

for rechristening England the Homeland and its inhabitants the Homelanders, for curing dysentery and the bites of bees and wasps, for the proclamation of a solemn silence of an hour throughout the Empire during the funeral of Queen Victoria after which all clergy, churchwardens, and municipal councillors publicly to take the oath of allegiance.

And there was a category of papers called the Lunatic Bundle, which included a picture-postcard (since identified as a view of Hampstead Heath) on which the correspondent had written 'Armenian mission hidden by foliage'. He concluded his letter with an account of the latest spectacle at Drury Lane.

It is unspeakably amusing, and the great scene, the submersion of the villain by a flood, is thrilling. The peculiarity of the play is that all the sympathetic characters are engaged throughout in crime. It is unknown to me by what instinct the audience recognize poor Mrs. Beerbohm Tree from the first, as they unmistakably do, for the villainess—for it is not till nearly the end that she turns what Arthur Balfour would call 'the balance of criminality' distinctly in her favour, by adding murder to the scores of forgeries and fraudulent impersonations in which, up to that point, she has been run closely by the heavy father and the 'the poor but honest' heroine. I am haunted by the sight of Mrs. Tree as she is left at the fall of the curtain, sitting penniless and forsaken on her luggage at Charing Cross, having just missed the boat-train which all the other characters have caught.

In the following January Marsh was on holiday in Milan, where he was kept in touch with the office by Conrad Russell.

Office boy wanted: polite, attentive, quick; one who does not whistle Hiawatha preferred.

Now I've caught you! I see you tried to engage a successor to me in my absence, but I suppose failed, seeing the ridiculous conditions you made.

Russell had been approached for the post of cartographer to John Buchan. 'No one knows what this means. Do you know who it is?' Marsh enlightened him, and Russell wrote again. 'Have just dined with John Buchan. He began talking of you of his own accord. 'Pon my word I thought he overdid it.' 'By the way,' he pleaded in a postscript, 'please don't write in Latin again because I don't understand a word of it.' Conrad Russell is important to this story for the sake of a single remark. 'If I were making a list of Sayings that have Influenced Me,' wrote Marsh in his memoir, 'I should have to cite a casual remark of his—very insignificant it may sound, but it was one of those moral commonplaces which strike with a new and illuminating force when they are spoken by someone of whose whole being they are the natural outcome. "I think," he said, "that one's first duty is to make life as pleasant as one can for the people one is thrown with."'

Early this year he was with Russell in Mantua and the holiday was ruined by their making an arduous pilgrimage to a house to see the Veronese paintings and being rudely denied admittance by the butler. 'I cannot describe him,' he wrote irritably to Pamela Lytton, 'unless you can imagine a Free Trade loaf propagating itself by the method of excrescence like a cactus.' He consoled himself by re-reading the works of Swinburne and sending his comments to Gosse, who found himself in agreement.

> Your phrase about Swinburne's 'nonsense' pleased me very much indeed. It is just the right word. There has always been, with so much splendour and exaltation and beauty, that to say. Shelley began it, I think, but it now pervades all new poetry. Especially the French and Yeats. But Swinburne most of all.

At a house-party given by the Poynder family at Hartham during December Marsh was introduced to a man who was to be one of the major figures in his life. On this occasion he merely exchanged a few words with Winston Churchill. From the only reference to that fateful week-end, a sentence in a letter from Conrad Russell, to whom his colleague had described the party, one would never guess that it would lead to affairs of pith and moment. 'What an account of Hartham!' exclaimed Russell. 'It's not fair on women that such an irresistible young spark as you should be about.'

The years of waiting for the big opportunity were coming to an end. And his promotion was timely. Within four months of making the move to Raymond Buildings, and taking Mrs. Elgy along with him, he was promoted to First Class Clerk, and he shifted his place to the basement of the Colonial Office, where he found himself the secretary in charge of the West African Department. The remaining months of 1905, which included an Italian walking-tour with Conrad Russell, passed without comment or event until in December he received a letter, one among the constant influx of invitations, which he carefully preserved as a memento of the party in Arlington Street which transformed his career.

13 *Dec.* 1905 *Tuesday*   16 *Arlington Street S.W.*

DEAR MR. MARSH,

If you feel inclined, *do* look in here tomorrow evening from after dinner—or late.

The George Curzons are dining here, and I have a little party of friends—lots of your especial friends. So do come.

Yours very sincerely

VIOLET GRANBY

Mr. Balfour had resigned office. Campbell-Bannerman was forming a Liberal Ministry, and had proposed that Winston Churchill should take the office of Financial Secretary to the Treasury. Personal experience in the affairs of South Africa, however, gave Churchill a definite preference. Only that morning the newspapers had announced his appointment as Parliamentary Under-Secretary for the Colonies under Lord Elgin. At the age of thirty-one he was a junior Minister of the Crown, and he had just written the Life of Lord Randolph Churchill which was still in manuscript.

ii

When Marsh entered Lady Granby's drawing-room his acquaintance from the Hartham week-end was the first person he met. 'How do you do,' he said with exaggerated courtesy, and added 'which I must now say with great respect.' Churchill looked him up and down. 'Why?' he asked. 'Why with great respect?' and Marsh explained, 'Because you're coming to rule over me at the Colonial Office.' Later in the evening he happened to notice that Mr. Churchill was seated on a sofa beside Mrs. Leslie, and kept looking pensively in his direction. They were obviously talking about him. Mrs. Leslie, who was Churchill's aunt, knew Eddie fairly well and she was no doubt being asked a number of searching questions.

When he was sent for next morning and informed that the new Minister had asked for his appointment as his Private Secretary, his first reaction was one of misgiving, and he quickly left the office, hailed a hansom cab, and called on Lady Lytton. She too had been a guest at Lady Granby's party. The widow of an Ambassador to Paris, who had known Lord Randolph and his family in their childhood, she was the best person to consult. Marsh confided in her that he was uncertain of success in his new appointment. Should she not ask Mr. Churchill to think again? He gave three reasons for his misgivings. Not only was he older than his new Chief by nearly three years, but so different from him in character as almost to be his very antithesis; moreover at Hartham Churchill had seemed, for all his obvious brilliance, rather truculent in manner. On Marsh's making this last point Lady Lytton put in a remark which he never forgot. 'The first time you meet Winston you see all his faults, and the rest of your life you spend in discovering his virtues.' She did not tell him, or perhaps she did not know, that it was largely on the recommendation of her own daughter-in-law, Pamela Lytton, one of Churchill's oldest friends who was also at the party, that the new Under-Secretary for the Colonies had made his choice of a right-hand man.

Still not reassured, Marsh went that night to dine alone with Churchill in Mount Street. They sat up late, and he came away with most of his doubts removed. 'He is the man for me,' he said to himself, as he left the house. Before going to bed he wrote to Pamela Lytton. Not much of it was news to her.

> I must tell you what has happened, it's so thrilling for me—the man who ought to be Winston's Private Secretary is very ill and can't come back to work for six months or so—and W. has asked for me! I've just been dining alone with him, he was perfectly charming but I can see what he will expect from his P.S. and it's *simply* terrifying—all so utterly beyond my capacity. If I could only faintly hope to give satisfaction I should be bird,[1] as it will be intensely interesting, but I'm so awfully afraid of being a kidglove.[2] I expect I've told you how much I admire him, so I shall do my best. Do pray for me.

By the same post he wrote to Neville's sister, Lady Constance Lytton, who was one day to be a heroine in the cause of Women's Suffrage. Her answer represents the general attitude of his friends to this new development.

> How movingly exciting about your new job. I have a theory about secretaries that they should be the opposite poles in type from the *secretaryee*. Father's life-success in secretaries was Sir George Colley:

[1] Baring word for 'blissfully content'. [2] Baring alternative to 'wet blanket'.

there couldn't well have been two more opposing types—a love of literature lurked in both of them, but I think that was the only point duplicated.

My spectator's experience since then has tempted me to make a law out of that example, and I think you and Winston Churchill will add another proof of it to my list. You say he'll expect much— but so will you, and when you both live up to each other's standards, as I expect you will, you'll be a quite splendid, taut combination of forces.

Almost immediately he was plunged into the drama of politics, assisting his new Chief in laying plans for the contest with Joynson-Hicks for the seat of Manchester North-West. On the opponent's side was the profit that could be made from Churchill's recent desertion from the Conservative to the Liberal camp, as against which there was Churchill's powerful advocacy of Free Trade, which in industrial Manchester would stand him in good stead if he played his cards well. Before the new year Marsh and Churchill took rooms in the Midland Hotel, and on the first evening they went for a walk, finding themselves in the poor district: 'Fancy living in one of these streets,' said Churchill, in an access of compassion, 'never seeing anything beautiful, never eating anything savoury, never saying anything *clever*!'

The election campaign was hectic. Marsh wrote to Pamela Lytton saying it was unlike anything he had ever seen before. 'When we are back from the evening meetings I always have to write for two or three hours.' The final result was a resounding Tory defeat. The cause of Free Trade was immensely strengthened by a campaign which Lord Mottistone has described as 'one of the most remarkable electoral performances of our time'. As confidential assistant to the new Minister at this vital stage of his career Marsh had managed to stay the pace and ably acquit himself at the first real test. From now on he was less diffident.

His own account of Mr. Churchill's speech on the retirement of Lord Milner, which occurred this year, shows that already it was his custom to hear his Chief rehearse in private the delivery of his speeches, for he has recorded his surprise at the unfavourable impression in the House made by an argument which in the office had seemed wholly innocent of antagonism or condescension towards its subject. He attributed this unforeseen result to a difference in manner of delivery; the public occasion had called forth the speaker's innate forcefulness. It is obvious that criticism of the logical arrangement of a case, and the lucidity of its presentation, by a star pupil of A. W. Verrall with an expressive gift of his own, would be of service to a practical man of affairs and orator in the great English tradition. And no doubt it was something of a stimulus to Mr. Churchill to have at hand so perceptive an audience of his pungent remarks. In fact it was an extraordinarily happy coincidence that his Private Secretary should have been the one man who appreciated above all else the thing well said. As a sounding-board for his ideas in the process of dictating a memorandum or the first draft of a speech, the objective and academic view of his right-hand man must often have been a most useful complement to Churchill's creative mind. For Eddie Marsh the lucky coincidence lay in this, that a man whose private life away from Whitehall was largely devoted to the encouragement of literary genius should find himself in official hours at the beck and call of one of the great stylists among historians. Soon after the Manchester election *The Life of Randolph Churchill* was published and the author gave his secretary one of the first copies. It was after reading this, the book he admired most of all Churchill's books (though his favourite single passage came to be the description of the Armistice at the end of *The World Crisis*) that he realized he was associated not only with a politician but with a considerable man of letters, such as he might first have met, not in his hours of duty, but at Hanover Terrace in the company of Gosse and Henry James.

He kept only one memento of those days in the Colonial Office among his papers. The Colonial Secretary at this time was Lord Elgin, who had been Viceroy of India. He and Mr. Churchill regarded each other with what Marsh has euphemistically described as 'qualified esteem', and he preserved an exasperated letter (doubtless a relic of several such incidents) in which Lord Elgin vigorously protested against the Under-Secretary's minute scribbled on a draft of a despatch. The letter ended: 'I must formally request you not to place these remarks on papers which have to pass through me back to the office. It does not tend to edification! In this case I suggest you should paste a paper over your remarks on the draft despatch, and I hope you will not object to do so.' On high affairs of State Eddie Marsh was not only reticent, he was mum. Fortunately for one born with a talent for gossip he was not really a political creature. It was greatly to his convenience that Civil Servants were not expected to have strong political allegiances of their own. He was a man of personal loyalties rather than of politics. One day someone asked him his political colour when Mr. Churchill was standing by. He had taken breath for some noncommittal reply when Mr. Churchill chipped in, 'I hope he's a fully qualified Winstonian.' The interruption was timely and perfectly true.

In August 1906 their correspondence began. Mr. Churchill wrote from Deauville with instructions for his mail. He was on holiday before attending the Army manœuvres at Breslau as a guest of the Kaiser. 'I have been very wild out here and very dissipated. I have made a little money—had made a lot! You had better not show this to D. as it stands or my moral influence with him might be impaired.' Marsh must make it his business to placate certain creditors. 'I shall be back Oct. 8 and not before; but if that does not satisfy them let me know and I will pay them at once. But they may just as well wait a little longer, having already waited so long. I hope you are frisking and the British Empire slumbering in the calm sunlight of the Parliamentary recess.' Then on August 23: 'Will you ask Marlborough to lend me his Yeomanry horse plume and leopard skin? I want both for the Breslau parade; and will you send them by the next messenger. That Mercury should also bring my guns . . . I have today bought a lot of nice French books.'[1] On the 31st he wrote in ten numbered headings from the Villa Cassel in Switzerland. High on the list and underlined was 'Will you send me the copy of Clemenceau's speech against Socialism'; another item was, '7. Uniform. The peaked hat sent by Hamburger and Rogers is much too small for me. Foolish people never took the trouble to enquire the size but tried to guess it.' So now he wants another 'with as big a peak as possible to protect my face from the sun'. He enclosed a despatch on the subject of Nigerian roadways: 'Will you have a fair copy typed out, being very careful to see that my corrections and inter-locutions are followed exactly and then forward the fair copy with the corrected one to Lord Elgin.'

---

[1] The bills which Marsh received from two booksellers in Paris involved in all 267 volumes: the complete works of Maupassant, Balzac, Musset, Voltaire, Lamartine, Chateaubriand, Michelet, Sévigné, the Correspondence of Louis XVI and Marie Antoinette, and *Manon Lescaut*.

During these first exchanges with Churchill he was planning an autumn holiday in Italy with Edward Horner and his sister Katharine, who lived at the Manor House, Mells, Frome. As it was Horner's first Italian visit the itinerary was worked out with painstaking detail. Marsh's love of making plans was almost greater than his pleasure in carrying them out. After six alternative routes, timings, and costs of the journey at every stage, he became a little self-conscious.

It is like the song called 'Choosing an Encampment' that was sung by the African Pigmies who came to London last year. Gilbert Russell asked the interpreter what the words meant and found it was *Chorus*: 'This would be a very good place for an encampment', then solo, by the grumpy old man: 'But any other place would do just as well.'
Will you look out my places on the map and see how they look? Sterne says in the *Sentimental Journey*: 'There is no place that looks better on the map than Montreux', but he was disappointed in its actual self. This never happens with Italian towns.

Later in the month he went with Victor Lytton to his family home at Knebworth. The seventeenth-century edifice overlaid with the plaster and pseudo-Gothic gargoyles of the last century was to be his favourite home from home for many years to come. He soon wrote again to Horner from Shere, where he was staying with Lady Arthur Russell in company with Mrs. Hughes, widow of the author of *Tom Brown's Schooldays*, 'which will never be forgotten while the Boy's and Empire's Own Paper keeps up its circulation. She is rather a nice old witch, beetling but benign, with fine white hair carefully trained up in the fashion of the 18th century to form a tableland planted with black lace.'
After the Italian trip in September the correspondence with Horner was resumed.

I dined yesterday with G. M. Trevelyan who has become very nice, he was always interesting. I must make you known to each other. I tried him with hard questions about *Modern Love* but he wasn't much good at any of the recondite points. I have been making a brown study of that poem and strenuously kept myself from consulting George's book[1] till I had made a fair attempt on my own. The consequence was that when at last with a sigh of expectant relief I read his analysis I didn't find much extra light. . . . How beautiful

[1] *The Poetry and Philosophy of George Meredith* by G. M. Trevelyan.

it is, Edward, the two I like best after the Swan and the last of all, are the one with the error of 'taste' and 'I play for seasons not Eternities' both of which I have learned by rote, and the first four lines of 'Out in the yellow meadows'. By the way George seemed quite sure that the full brown flood is the sunset. I am now reading *Harry Richmond* with the greatest delight. I have just got to where he is rescued by Capt. Jasper Welsh, a sublime character. . . . I've been dining with Neville and Victor. V is very much excited about a new discovery for taking alcohol out of wine, beer, etc., and leaving them just as nice as they were before. If true, this is the most millennial thing I ever heard of, but I can't help fearing there will prove to be some little difference which is *the* difference. 'The little more and how much it is, the little less and what miles away' (I can't help quoting it like this as I now can't remember what the real word is instead of miles—leagues? yards? what *is* it?).

In his picture-collecting he had just made three contemporary purchases of an unadventurously traditional kind, a long rectangular painting of Arab horses in a glade by Neville Lytton, and two works by Charles Geoffroy (the French painter who was staying with the Lyttons)—a village church in water-colour not unlike Cotman, and a study in oils of ploughland and white cumulus clouds. The next letter of November 21 talked of a luncheon with his Chief.

Winston had a jolly luncheon today, Duchess of Rutland, Raymond [Asquith] and Lady Susan Townley who is one of the most charming and amusing women I know. We had a very interesting discussion as to whether it was better for a husband to be in love with his wife or vice versa (assuming that reciprocity was so rare as not to be worth considering). Violet Granby and I were all for being in love ourselves, the rest thought the wife should always be the one in love. Winston's view was that the husband should always be the rich one —evidently he was thinking of the Marlboroughs—we went on to consider whether you could be in love with someone if they lost their nose. Winston took the noble line, everyone else thought the difficulty would be almost insurmountable. V.G. said she lived by her eyes.

John Burns came to Winston's room in the afternoon, and burst into a rhapsody about Norah Lindsay with whom he has been staying for a week at the Ian Hamiltons'. 'That fay,' he said—'there is no word for her but fay—when she sits at the piano with a few flowers between you and her she shines out of what you call the gloom like a spirit!' Winston said 'H'm, 'm'.

Winston's speech on sodomy among the Chinese was a great success; as he said he 'smote the Radicals hip and thigh from Sodom to Gomorrha'. The word catamite, which as no doubt you know, is the Brahms word for a b——, was a great puzzle to the MPs, hardly anyone knew it, and in the proofs of the speech for Hansard Winston was made to say that it was very difficult to know by looking at the Chinamen whether or not they were Amalekites.

In his letter of December 21 he gave Horner his reason for catholic taste in art and described a visitor to the Horne collection, about half of which was now arranged on the walls at Gray's Inn. He began with an account of *The Gondoliers*.

It is fairly well performed, except by the hero who is grotesque, and the heroine who sang one particular false note which burst into the chorus as a comet might burst into the solar system and shook the entire audience to the roots of its diaphragms. As for the opera itself both music and words are perfect. I know my artistic swans are always geese to you, and if ever we see it I am prepared for your confessing to a slight disappointment. I think that what really gives me most pleasure is the feeling that the artist has squeezed out *everything* that there is in his subject and then arranged it perfectly. This is the reason for my intense admiration for things that strike you as rather trivial such as Miss Austen's novels and *Alice in Wonderland*. Of course on a small scale the feat must be much easier both to perform and to recognize.

I had a less successful evening yesterday with my new friend X. We went to a very stupid piece *called* the *Vicar of Wakefield* (the piece really *was* nothing of the kind, see *Through the Looking Glass*) and he came home with me afterwards. Have you ever noticed the distinction between bores who make you want to cry and those who make you want to scream? I am afraid that to me X is one of the latter. I am a beast to say so, as you know what a perfect angel I think him in many ways. But really, the things he says! Here is a specimen, when I showed him my sea picture by Cotman—(you must imagine me feebly muttering between each sentence)—'Eddie, why is a picture better than Nature? . . . I mean, would you rather live by the seaside or have a picture of the sea in your room? . . . But why is that picture any better than a coloured photograph? (Here I murmured something inconclusive about a *mind* being concerned in a picture.) Oh yes, a mind! of course a Christian would say there was a mind concerned in the photograph, but I don't believe all that'— and so on. I never before met with a character I liked so much, combined with such an antipathetic mentality. He told me his object in life is to influence people for good, but he can't make up his mind whether to spread out his influence thin over 'millions'—or give it in strong doses to a small circle of intimates.

One item of news which might have been mentioned in this letter seemed at the time too trivial to report. In mid-November he had been to stay with his father at Cambridge to hear his old friend Dr. Verrall lecture on the *Eumenides* and to watch a performance of the play given by the Amateur Dramatic Club. A young man had entered upon the scene, tall, slim, with a long neck, a pallid, almost girlishly good-looking face, and a bright red wig. He wore *papier-mâché* armour with a short cloak of red, blue, and gold. Striding to centre he put a property trumpet to his lips and someone in the wings blew a fanfare as Eddie Marsh, seated between Dr. and Mrs. Verrall, for the first time set eyes on Rupert Brooke. After the show he was taken on stage and introduced to the cast. Brooke was nineteen, a freshman at King's who had just come up from Rugby. Only a few words were exchanged. There was nothing about the occasion worth telling Edward Horner.

In January 1907 Mrs. Elgy furnished the spare room at Gray's Inn with the William Morris bed, a relic from Cambridge, and a few odds and ends picked up at second-hand shops in Holborn, and Edward Horner had the honour of being the first guest. A plan was worked out which became the regular routine for occupants of the spare room. On the way to Whitehall in the morning Marsh would leave the spare latch-key and a note of welcome with the porter at the Lodge in Theobalds Road. The guest would then call for his key and leave his bag for the porter to carry along the pavement and up the many stone steps later in the day.

Early in April the letters to Horner began again. The first was addressed from the Colonial Office.

Winston has gone home early so there is time for a little jaw. I must tell you an anecdote about him. He was lying in bed this morning in gestation for his great speech on the Land Question, the telephone rang by his side, so he listened for some time, saying Hullo, hullo, *hullo*, getting more and more impatient. At last a voice said 'Yes?'

'Christ dam' your soul,' shouted Winston. 'Why do you keep me waiting?'

Upon which a gentle voice, which he recognized as Mrs. Spender's, asked, 'Is that Mr. Churchill?'

'*No!*' roared Winston, replacing the receiver. Wasn't it simply *glorious* presence of mind?

The Neville Lyttons were now living at Forest Cottage, near Crawley, where Marsh had just been for a week-end, sitting all day in the studio, reading aloud *Joseph Vance* while Neville painted Judith.

The only excitement in the neighbourhood is an old woman holding a subordinate post in Judith's day nursery, who has locked herself in for eleven days with a plentiful supply of gin which she persuaded a little boy to fetch for her on the pretext of wanting it for a solution to wash her feet. The police are earnestly studying the law books for a precedent.

In his letter of the 16th he subdued his natural modesty so far as to report a rare compliment to his reputation as a conversationalist. He had received 'what I at first took to be a letter from a lunatic':

a very shabby ½ sheet of notepaper deeply scored on both sides and all round the edge with a very sharp pencil—it turned out to be from Lady Elcho, written in the train, and contained the most overwhelming compliment I have ever received. She is going to have a small dinner party for the purpose of really good general conversation. Cynthia[1] and she are the only ladies, the men are Mr. Balfour, Butcher, H. G. Wells and (alas) Sir Oliver Lodge. 'Cynthia and I feel that you will help us in *all* the right ways.' I shall go with my heart in my mouth, and my tongue, I fear, anywhere rather than in my mouth. You must forgive my vanity for narrating this dewdrop.[2]

The Imperial Conference had started, and Churchill's onetime adversary General Botha, representing the Transvaal, was among the Colonial statesmen whom Marsh was welcoming in London.

I attended the first meeting of the Colonial Conference—an historical occasion no doubt but I feel it won't really make much difference in my life, unless I live long enough to describe it to my great-grandchildren. That is the worst of seeing history in the making, the finished article is so much more enticing. Last night Mr. Balfour asked Winston to introduce him to Botha and said 'I feel honoured in making your acquaintance'.

---

[1] Cynthia Charteris, Lady Elcho's daughter, later Lady Cynthia Asquith.
[2] Baring expression for a gratifying (because considered not unmerited) compliment.

On April 20 he wrote of another political meeting.

> I am having a solitary evening, and have just exhausted the enter-
> tainment of changing my pictures, i.e. putting a fresh set out of my
> boxes into the frames with practicable backs, so I will write you a
> tedious and brief letter.
>
> Winston made an excellent speech about the Land Question this
> afternoon at Drury Lane theatre. The stage represented a village
> green overshadowed by treetops without any treebottoms—the
> trunks having been omitted to make room for the Members of
> Parliament and miscellaneous supporters clustered round an
> incongruous green baize table and Jack Poynder in 'the' chair.
> The only person at all in keeping with the scenery was Masterman
> who sat under a thatch roof sniffing a bunch of jonquils and did very
> well as the village idiot. . . . My companion was my acquaintance X,
> one of whose remarks I will write down *verbatim*. 'I don't admit the
> existence of evil, *qua* evil. "Not-good" is as far as I can go.' I must
> add this observation seemed to me to be quite uncalled for by the
> trend of the conversation.
>
> The 1900 Club dinner was a fine sight, but otherwise dull. Mr.
> Balfour extremely so, except for the highly comical effect of an in-
> stantaneous echo, rather louder than his own voice, which made him
> seem to be prompting someone in the top gallery.
>
> I am at last beginning to get some invitations *not* 'to meet the
> Colonial Premiers', it was so dull to have nothing in prospect but
> parties with a purpose, which are worse than parties without a
> purpose. However the clouds are darkest before the dawn, and on
> Tuesday I shall have to attend a ball given not only *to* Premiers but
> *by* a Premier! I don't suppose I need stay very long.

And now an exciting plan was in the wind. The Under-
Secretary for the Colonies was arranging to visit south-east
Africa in the autumn and had asked his Private Secretary to
accompany him on the excursion. Now that the Conference was
over, all activity in the office was devoted to that end.

During this month of April Raymond Asquith wrote to tell
of his engagement to Edward Horner's sister, Katharine, and
accepted the offer of 5 Raymond Buildings as his first London
home after his marriage, for the weeks while Marsh was away.
'You deserve a new beatitude all to yourself,' he wrote. 'If you
will let me know what form the operative clause is to take I will
have it drafted forthwith by Hugh Cecil and inserted by John
Buchan in all the Bibles of the Upper Classes.' Edward Horner

and Marsh were ushers at the ceremony in July. Pamela Lytton received a full account of the event.

> Mrs. Horner and Katharine were in tears. Ann standing over them with smelling salts, the rest of us loitering about clasping handfuls of a special sort of patent rice warranted not to hurt the bride which began to melt and be uncomfortable so we couldn't help eating it to get rid of it for something to do, till at last when Raymond did appear scarcely anyone had any left to throw at him.

At the reception Mr. Balfour had made a speech. 'He merely clapped his hands and said "Ladies and Gentlemen, I give you a toast—Katharine and Raymond"—but it was said in such arresting and vibrant tones that several people including me burst into tears—it was a marvellous display of oratorical genius.' He ended the letter with a confidence. 'Pamela, there is nobody but you to whom I would dare confess, without pretending it was a joke, how tremendously I have enjoyed "the season" and how flat I feel now it is over.' The season had been unusually lively, and he had sent a description of his late nights to Conrad Russell, who was now in New York. Marsh's sociability had always seemed excessive to his former colleague in the office, and he had once argued that he drank champagne because it 'made him more amusing'. 'It only makes you *think* you're more amusing,' retorted Russell. Marsh then put it to Russell that he would get more pleasure out of balls if he took a more active part on the floor. 'You can't think how funny you look, flying *round* and *round* the room like that!' was Russell's comment. His reply from New York, however, was of sterner sort. He complained that Marsh seemed to have no interest save in what he called the marriage market.

> The life you lead simply strikes me dumb. It is damaging to the character, and unless you have very much more moral fibre than I have you will go down hill. When you write to me 'Lady X is a dear little woman' I feel very nervous, because I know she is a vulgar old bitch with the brain of a squirrel.

'Beware of the Smart Set!' he warned in a postscript, but Marsh continued to find in the social life of Edwardian London the main delight of his leisure hours. There were occasions when Mr. Churchill and he would meet at the same *soirée*, and they devised a pastime for the intervals when they happened to be standing together within sight of the ballroom door, watching the ladies make their entrance. On the basis of Marlowe's line 'Was this the face that launched a thousand ships?' they would assess the beauty of each newcomer as she appeared. '200 ships, or perhaps 250?' the one might remark tentatively, gazing ahead as he made his reckoning. 'By no means,' the other might reply. 'A covered sampan, or small gunboat at most.' Among the very few who scored the full thousand in the opinion of both assessors were Lady Diana Manners, and Miss Clementine Hozier whom Mr. Churchill was to marry.

On less fashionable evenings, and especially at concerts, his companion was often Donald Tovey, who had recently pleased him with the observation, 'The weather is so cold that it's impossible to tell anything but the truth.' The substance of one of Tovey's letters became the basis of his analysis of the fourth symphony of Brahms, and it was their attendance of a performance of that same work at the Queen's Hall (when they were obliged to sit apart and afterwards go their ways without exchanging comments) which in a letter next day prompted a fair example of Tovey's impatience with the current style of programme notes.

I thought the behaviour of the audience was the excusable result of the tone of the programme analysis. I'd be hanged if I'd read a poem of which I was told that 'if not apparently beautiful or inspiring its technical merits are such as to repay careful study'. What blatant impudence for an analyst to criticize the work that it's his business to put fairly before the public, even if it were a very bad work. It seems to me about as gross as if the conductor himself were to make a speech saying, 'Ladies and gentlemen, the work I am now going to conduct is more intellectual than emotional, so you'll have to lump it!' The wonder to me was that the audience didn't leave in a body before it began.

Marsh's life was always to be a pattern of contrasts. If he had just been listening to Brahms, or elegantly revolving under the chandeliers of Londonderry House, it was soon to be his unlikely portion to arrive footsore and blistered at the source of the Nile.

In September he started learning horsemanship with Wilfrid Scawen Blunt as his instructor and his mount one of the Arab greys from the stud at Crabbet Park. The plan was that he should join Mr. Churchill at Malta. 'Bring with you squeezer pens in plenty,' Churchill wrote from abroad, where he was drawing up a report on the French manœuvres. 'I only have a few nibs left and can write with no other.' And Lady Randolph, whom Marsh had met at Blenheim, wrote from her home at St. Albans, 'Bless you, dear Eddie. Be happy and enjoy yourself, and look after my Winston—he is very precious to me.'

iii

The French boat which took Marsh to Malta was infested with flies, which had come aboard with the cattle whose carcasses were destined to replenish the island's supply of beef. On October 2 he set foot in Africa and walked in the Moorish quarter of Tunis —'an interminable and labyrinthine arcade', he called it in his letter to Horner. 'Tobacco kiosks and *art nouveau* theatres all within a few miles of the ruins of Carthage!' The rendezvous at Valetta took place as planned. 'We had a most rewarding evening, ingratiating ourselves with intransigent Archbishops.'

They left Malta in H.M.S. *Venus* and on October 9, 1907, anchored off Famagusta, where Mr. Churchill and his party landed and received the addresses of the Greek and Turkish spokesmen amid more flag-waving, jostling, and shouting than had been anticipated, and the ceremony was frequently interrupted with raucous cries of 'Hurrah for Union' from the Greeks, who were frantically waving their national flag. The mayor on behalf of the Greeks begged Mr. Churchill to hand the island over immediately to the King of Greece; the Moslem leader urged him with equal fervour to do no such thing; then in clouds of dust the cortège of carriages, bumping into each other at the sharp turnings, took the visitors to see the old Venetian city. Later in the day they all left by train for Nicosia accompanied by Sir Charles King-Harman, the High Commissioner. On the platform there were more Enosis demonstrations, which prompted Mr. Churchill formally to announce to the crowd that he would be more impressed by sound argument than flag-waving.

The official discussions in the Legislative Council did not take place until the fourth day of the visit, by which time Mr. Churchill had rested and spent many hours with Marsh at his elbow in the presence of the High Commissioner and his advisers. At the Council itself, since every sentence had to be interpreted immediately on delivery into the two languages, oratory was impossible and progress slow. Not only the question of union with Greece but the matter of the island's tribute to the Sultan of

Turkey came high on the agenda. After the assembly Marsh was. fascinated by the procession of persons to be presented: the Mufti and his attendants, among them the sheikh of the dancing dervishes in a tall brown fez; an Armenian priest in blue robe and poly-gonal hat; and a Franciscan friar in subfusc habit, a delegate from the Roman Catholic community. Later in the day the construction of roads, bridges, railways, and especially re-afforestation were the topics for discussion, then on October 13 the *Venus* weighed anchor, to the confused sound of more screams and shouts for union, and sailed into the calm of the Mediterranean, bound for East Africa.

On October 26 the *Venus* crossed the Line, and an entertainment given by the crew in the form of a sing-song was interrupted by Father Neptune, who delivered a short address of welcome to Mr. Churchill and his friends, and distributed among them various nautical decorations made of damp cardboard (Neptune having unfortunately slipped into a canvas bath on his way to the investiture). Next day he reappeared and presented Mrs. Neptune. 'An august figure hitherto unknown to mythology!' Marsh observed, as she bowed before him and dropped her wig in his lap. Mr. Churchill (who was already a freeman of the Southern Seas and so exempt from molestation) then had the pleasure of watching his Secretary being seized from behind by four deck-hands, lathered all over with a froth made from the white of egg, 'shaved' with a jagged piece of wood and pitched backwards into the bathing pool. This of course was not at all the Private Secretary's idea of fun. He had been commissioned to write a series of descriptive articles for the *Manchester Guardian*, but of this episode all his readers in England were given was, 'The ceremony lasted most of the afternoon', which was hardly up to the standard of racy *rapportage* they had been led to expect.

On the 28th they dropped anchor in the Bay of Mombasa and that same evening dined on the verandah at Government House, a small one-storey building set among all kinds of flowering trees. As they ate and talked they caught sight of little weaver-birds flashing to and fro among their plentiful nests. Next morning work began with deputations arriving from the planters and com-munities around. The development of the fertile coastal strip was the most pressing matter in hand, but also such themes as coffee, rubber, sisal, roads, railways, harbours, came up in turn for consideration. The visitors were shown the prisons in the

Portuguese fort, 'homicides working their sewing-machines', observed Marsh, 'with all the benevolent serenity of the pirate in *Peter Pan*'. For dinner that evening there was a special menu at the Mombasa Club. Marsh felt duty-bound to partake of *Pouding Manchester* and *crême Churchill*, declined a helping of *Joynson-Hicks sur croûte-toast*, but made up on the *Glace Blenheim*.

The torrential rains had broken the railway line, so the departure was delayed for more than a day. When at last they set out for Nairobi Marsh tried to learn the names of the curious trees and shrubs which he saw from the carriage window. There were mango trees, misshapen baobabs as if stricken with elephantiasis in their trunks, euphorbias like candelabra, and a tree the name of which no one could pronounce, with scarlet flowers at the end of every leafless bough. After a night on the train they alighted at Simba for a lion hunt. Before leaving England Marsh had asked Mrs. Patrick Campbell what she would do if she heard he had been eaten by a lion. 'I should laugh first,' she said, 'and then be very, very sorry.' Now was the moment. Wart-hog, waterbuck, and buffalo revealed themselves in the near distance on the Athi plain, ice-capped Kilimanjaro heaving itself upward in the background under an empty blue sky—but no lion. What did appear, uncomfortably close, horned, armoured, prehistoric, or like 'a railway engine which had come off the line', as Marsh noted in a momentary flash of apprehension, was a rhinoceros.

For the first and last time in his life, infected as usual by his environment, Marsh evinced what he called 'a passionate desire to kill animals'. By the evening it had worn off, but not before it had provided him with a story of the hunt. With that instinct for preservation against dangers from his own kind only natural in a man already exposed to real dangers from the animal kingdom, Mr. Churchill asked his Secretary if he would mind *not* carrying a gun. Marsh had quoted Milton's description of the animals in Eden from *Paradise Lost*, and this contribution was considered to be enough. The native hunters proceeded in line up a slight incline, while Mr. Churchill followed behind with Marsh, who would not be left out of it, equipped with nothing more lethal than a pink umbrella which at this juncture was folded but held in readiness. After a few minutes of stealthy approach, the word *Faro* (rhinoceros) was passed down the line, and walking farther to a place of vantage, they saw the creature about a hundred yards ahead, asleep under a tree. After various manœuvres in accordance with the direction of the wind, Mr. Churchill took aim and fired. The monster rose cumbrously to its feet and like a battering-ram charged straight for Eddie Marsh, who, being unarmed, was rooted to the spot in petrifying alarm. He had the good sense to hold his ground, and instantly conceived a plan of action, 'to stand firm with my finger on the trigger of the umbrella', as he put it, 'planning as a Happy Thought to jump aside at the last moment and open it upon her with a BANG'. The monster had but thirty yards more to go when in mid-career it faltered and sank to its knees, suddenly overtaken by the fatality of its wound. In the past Mr. Churchill had observed Marsh's way of crossing a London street (which was to step without hesitation off the pavement and trust to the vigilance of the drivers to avoid mishap) and by way of reproof he had more than once quoted a proverb which he had picked up from his nurse—'Where there's no sense there's no feeling'. On this occasion of the Great Escape he not only magnanimously withdrew the stigma (as a tribute to his friend's presence of mind) but directed that henceforth he should carry fire-arms. This was no simple matter, for the up-to-date guns were already distributed, and all that remained was an obsolete weapon which had been left behind by a settler, who had quitted those parts in haste for Australia, and which for some reason was not known by a brand of manufacture but by its rather humiliating nickname of Michael. When another rhinoceros hove in sight, and Marsh was invited to shoot, the thought crossed his mind that his shot might not have the force to penetrate a flank so stoutly armoured, and might rebound with deadly error and penetrate one of the natives or even Mr. Churchill. However, he took the risk and was immediately lost sight of in a cloud of acrid smoke. Before long a second opportunity presented itself. Both creatures fell, but such was the fusillade the credit was not easily assigned. 'Without an autopsy,' he remarked in relating the affair, 'I could never prove that I had hit them.'

The special train resumed its journey and on November 4 the travellers drove through the streets of Nairobi, which were lined with warriors, their hair matted with red or yellow earth, brandishing spears adorned with ostrich feathers. There followed days of intensive work, receiving deputations, broken by a visit to the hill station of Fort Hall, where the Kikuyu tribe staged a

demonstration of welcome. A short before-luncheon ride to the
Tana river so fascinated Mr. Churchill that he decided to ride on to
Embu, where he took the District Commissioner by surprise and
stayed the night, together with three companions of whom Marsh
was one. After three hectic days in Nairobi the journey began
again along the track of the Uganda railway, the train coming to
a halt for the hours of darkness so that the party would not miss
any of the scenery. On November 17 they reached Port Florence
on the shore of Lake Victoria, where they were met by the
Kavirondo people in their thousands, dressed in what seemed to
be nothing but glistening coils of brass wire and outsize sun-
bonnets plumed with feathers. This brought the East African part
of the tour to an end.

They crossed the lake by steamer and landed at Entebbe, a
city of palm and purple-flowering solarum, overlooking a lake
dotted with low-lying islands all greenly overgrown, and reminding Marsh of Stevenson's island in the South Seas. After two days
they set out inland by rickshaw. As they approached Kampala
the roads began to be thronged with white-robed folk who crowded
round and applauded, at which point Marsh learned that the
correct thing was every so often to call out what sounded to him
like 'Way wallia wally', which meant 'Well done, everybody'.
At length the procession stopped at the foot of a hillock surmounted
by a pavilion set up at the end of a pathway of rushes freshly
strewn. At the entrance sat King Daudi Chewa, a boy of eleven
dressed in a flowing black robe fringed with gold and a small
white cap. Around him stood the Council of Regency, several of
them sporting the Uganda medal of 1898. Mr. Churchill and his
party entered the pavilion, tasted syrups from tiny bowls, and
were presented. In the afternoon the first Governor of Uganda[1]
was installed and took the oath before a great concourse of people.
On the following day they inspected the church missions, where
they were amused to hear the dusky children in print frocks
singing 'Oh dear, what can the matter be?' and other familiar
ditties from the English nursery.

Later that day the young Kabaka staged the most elaborate of
all the war-dances or tattoos, and all the while, close to where the
guest of honour and his friends were seated, a giant warrior, his

---

[1] The previous style of the chief British Administrator was H.M. Commissioner.
This change marked a new and important stage in the history of the Protectorate.

naked body smeared all over with a white substance as if he were trying to portray a marble statue, held his formidable pose. Champion of the warriors, he stood chained to a companion lest the sound of the drums and the war-cries should rouse him from his ceremonial lethargy and provoke him to some savage and inhospitable act of violence. When the dance was over there were refreshments in the new palace, a small villa with Victorian furniture and loyal engravings of Queen Alexandra and Westminster Abbey, while only a few yards away stood the conical hut with thatched roof sloping to the ground which would still have been the royal residence but for the coming of Western ways; and all the time in a smaller hut near the front door of the King's villa, a band of some dozen musicians, unseen and unremitting, kept up a gently rhythmical drone of drums in their sovereign's honour.

On leaving Kampala they went by steamboat to Jinja, where the Victoria Nile flows out of the lake over the Ripon Falls. From there they proceeded on trek, escorted by a section of the King's African Rifles, a doctor, a young explorer who was making for Mount Elgin, and the usual troupe of carriers, among whom was the amiable Josiah, personal attendant upon Eddie Marsh. At intervals of twelve miles or so the local chief had cleared a patch of ground and erected tents of rushes against the coming of the strangers for the night. They made their way on foot, for there was only one mule (laden with luggage) and two punctured bicycles which had to be carried. After reveillé the main party would start off, having dressed and shaved by candlelight, while the tents and bedding were packed and distributed among the carriers, who yelled and fought until each man was reconciled to the shape and weight of his appointed load. There were never more than two marches in the day, between ten and fifteen miles each, the sultry mid-days being passed in siesta under trees or in an improvised encampment, and each day's trek ended with supper and talk round a camp-fire. During the second day of the trek Marsh wrote to Lady Lytton. On borrowed writing-paper he scribbled 'not a bit of it' under the London address and added 'Nakabugu, Uganda'.

MY DEAR PAMELA,
      What a life this is. You wouldn't know me if you saw me, emerging from my tent at 4.30 a.m. in a shirt, and 'shorts', and 'putties', with

brown arms and knees, and swearing in Swahili. I am forgetting my rifle! for I have become, so far as looks go, a mighty hunter before the Lord, and it doesn't matter if I seldom hit, and never in a vital place. Won't Raymond Buildings look funny, when ½ Neville's pictures are displaced to make room for horns and heads. I must give a series of dinner parties for the sake of seeing my friends' faces. Except that I don't see how I am ever to find time to see my London friends again. I have made about 100 new ones out here, and I foresee that they will all dribble home on leave, one a week, and claim my undivided attention, except of course in office hours. They are rather a mixed lot—sailors in great numbers, a few soldiers, a few officials, and a lot of wild bushranging buccaneers whose manners and appearance I do my best to copy under a running fire of sarcasm from Winston. He has been simply magnificent out here, and leaves everybody gaping with admiration at his quickness and power of seeing what ought to be done and how to do it. I can never get over the wonder of it myself. And nothing ever pumps him dry. I left the 'banda' to come out and write to you—a banda is a great big straw hut where one has dinner in the middle of the camp, and I can hear him fascinating all the men in it with his conversation.

I am writing in my tent, and it's rather difficult, as I have only one candle. We are on 'safari', which is the pretty East African word for expedition—'sofari sogoodi' Winston says at the end of a day's march. There are ten of us, and we have 350 native porters! who walk along the road with our tin boxes, beds, etc. on their heads. The country is most beautiful, and so far I have nothing but praise for the climate. I shall probably be chattering with fever in a day or two, but meanwhile it's the most glorious life I ever led, and how I am ever going to settle down again among the Lady Cunards etc. of the other world, I can't imagine. Yesterday we stood at the source of the Nile! which is a sight I never expected to see six months ago.

It was during another of the midday halts, a little over a fort-night later, that Marsh scribbled a letter to Cynthia Charteris, and by some circuitous postal wonder it was eventually delivered at Stanway, the beautiful grey Cotswold house with the Inigo Jones gateway.

Uma River Camp
Uganda
Dec. 11th '07

DEAR CYNTHIA,

This is a very disinterested letter as you can't possibly get it in time to answer before I get back. I suppose you are crouched over a fire. I am in a tent under a torrential sun, in the costume of the country, which consists of a khaki shirt and shorts, with brown legs and arms, which I cultivated at the cost of great pain and inconvenience, but which are now the joy of my life and the admiration of all beholders. We are now on what is called here safari, it means the same as trek. We are woke up by bugles every morning at 4, and start any time before 6, with a train of between 3 and 400 black porters each carrying one of our loads on his head—(one can't help feeling that it is a great personal convenience to belong to a dominant race). We walk anything from 12 to 25 miles in the morning, and afternoonly pitch our moving camp a day's march nearer home. Luncheon is always delightful, supplying as it does a long felt want—and after it we sleep heavily till tea time, after which we smoke round the camp fire, which looks pretty and doesn't add appreciably to the heat—then to bed at 10 after a gay and early dinner. Do you think it sounds an agreeable life? I forget if you are fond of big-game-shooting—I like it very much, but I don't shoot the big game, I only shoot at it. We saw a herd of elephants the other day but as they were all ladies we left them alone according to the chivalrous custom of this country. However we got 4 white rhinoceros the next day, a very rare species, and just about as white as my hat, which I suppose is why they are called so.

I haven't had any letter from England dated since the end of October, so I have no notion what is happening. I hope for a mail at Gondokoro 3 days from now, an exciting prospect. I heard alarming accounts of Violet [Asquith] but I hope it was nothing serious. Is Mr. Asquith going to be Prime Minister? I hope so. It's too hot to write any more, my very brain is melting.

The object of the trek was for Mr. Churchill to follow the proposed route for a railway connecting the three lakes, Victoria, Chioga, and Albert. It lasted from November 23 to December 14, and the last lap was a march of one hundred and seven miles, which they accomplished in six days. They had seen the source of the Nile, and the Ripon and Murchison Falls, and had come at last to Gondokoro, which was to be their last glimpse of Uganda. Although incommoded by blisters from the sun Marsh had relished every moment of this rough-going part of the journey. As Mr. Churchill remarked afterwards, 'Eddie stripped himself naked and retired to the Bush, from which he could only be lured three times a day by promises of food.'

They now boarded a boat and Marsh took pen and paper and tried to describe the country they had passed through for the *Manchester Guardian*. 'Every now and then there came a stretch of luxuriant forest with curtains of flowering creepers hanging from the trees, and whole ballets of butterflies dancing near the pools of rush-grown water. Sometimes an accident of the ground gave us a magnificent view over immense plains and distant mountain ranges, but often for miles together the road lay between walls of grass at least as tall as ourselves.' And he talked of the elephants. 'Mr. Churchill only saw a herd of about a dozen cows and as these may not be killed he gained nothing but a strange impression of these enormous and ancient creatures, some of them possibly contemporaries of Shakespeare, flapping their tremendous ears and placidly wandering, each with a little egret on her back, among the primeval pastures.'[1]

There were several stops before Khartoum: the Belgian station of Lado, Fashoda, Tanflebha, where the women standing in their doorways welcomed the travellers with a curious high-pitched yodel, Tonga Island, where they watched the bee-eaters, and Mashra-Zeraf, where Marsh saw Mr. Churchill shoot a fine specimen of waterbuck. On Christmas Eve they reached Khartoum. Here Marsh despatched his servant to prepare a bath. But Mr. Churchill had got there first. Back came the servant— 'There's a European in the bath,' he explained with deference.

They visited Cairo, the temples of Luxor, and the Assouan Dam, which was in process of being heightened, but sightseeing was no fit occupation for a band of hardened explorers. They were back in London by the end of March. Campbell-Bannerman was ill and on the point of resigning the Premiership. His death followed suddenly. Mr. Churchill was to be included in the Cabinet, and while his actual post was still in question he expressed a slight disinclination to accept the Local Government Board. 'I refuse,' he assured Marsh, 'to be shut up in a soup-kitchen with Mrs. Sidney Webb.' When Mr. Asquith announced his Government in April, Winston Churchill had accepted office in the Cabinet as President of the Board of Trade. He invited Marsh to accompany him. 'After all,' he said, 'you were the *Bwana Balozi* [the big noise] in Uganda.' As they had passed through a village the natives had decided that Eddie *must* be the leader, for he was 'much the fiercest in appearance', a compliment he treasured when told of it by a native bearer, and one which Mr. Churchill was in no hurry to let him forget.

[1] *Manchester Guardian*, January 11, 1908.

iv

Before attaining full qualification for his seat in the Cabinet Mr. Churchill was obliged to face the ordeal of a by-election in Manchester. This would have passed without incident but for the suffragettes. Their opposition was, however, less spectacular than in 1906, when Sylvia Pankhurst, hustled from the Free Trade Hall into a side-room, reappeared at the back having climbed out of the window into the street. Demonstrations were a daily occurrence in a fierce campaign which resulted in the return of Joynson-Hicks and the defeat of Churchill. The set-back was grave but only momentary, for the same evening as the results were made known a telegram arrived from the Liberals in Dundee. So Mr. Churchill and his Secretary travelled by the night train to try their fortunes in another field.

While in Manchester Marsh had received a letter from the new Prime Minister's young daughter Violet. The family was on the point of moving into 10 Downing Street.

> An 'interesting' house of the most accepted type, pitch dark, with highly official, wholly uninfluenceable furniture (different Prime Ministers having lived and died in every chair) and not a bathroom or a bookshelf anywhere (how *can* they have neither washed nor read?). When we have had these put in, the Glamour of the Great Shades will begin to assert itself—but so far it's dim. . . . One nice thing is a garden full of daffodils (and a detective) which you must come to tea in every day. . . . Your Chief has asked me to tea with you and him in the Board of Trade which will be fun if it happens.

From Dundee Marsh replied, describing how Mr. Churchill and he were sharing a suite in a small hotel with 'only two armchairs which are moved from room to room. If you ask for coals a man comes in with a lump in each hand', and two election jokes had reached their ears. One was 'Your Winston will cost you more', and the other 'Dear coals, dear beer, and £100 a week for *dear* Winston'. The by-election in Dundee, however, resulted in a Liberal victory, and Mr. Churchill journeyed south to fill his chair in the Cabinet beside the Government's Elder Statesman, John Morley.

In the summer there were two Churchill weddings, and Marsh had so timed his holiday that it would begin with the festivities at the first of them,[1] which took place at Oxford. From there he

[1] John Churchill and Lady Gwendeline Bertie.

went with Mr. Churchill to Burley-on-the-Hill, near Oakham, the noble country mansion of Frederick Guest, one of his Chief's cousins. In the middle of the night Marsh was rudely awakened by a pounding on his bedroom door and the sound of cries that the house was on fire. Without staying to gather up any of his belongings he rushed downstairs in his pyjamas and reached the terrace only a few moments before his room collapsed. The staff and guests assembling in the garden were soon joined by the stalwarts of the local fire-brigade. Mr. Churchill in a fireman's helmet and a dressing-gown directed operations with despatch and gusto, but the fire had been fanned by a dry wind and soon was out of control. Marsh rushed to the nearest room where he knew there were books and threw them out on the lawn, only to discover when dawn broke that he had salvaged the servants' library. Two of the guests, himself and F. E. Smith, lost everything they had, and were fitted out with clothes in the Rectory near by. Two tie-pins which had belonged to Spencer Perceval, his uncle's gold watch, and many other personal treasures of his were destroyed, so that never again did he feel quite so elegantly and richly attired. When what was apparently a young curate walked into Raymond Buildings, Mrs. Elgy wept.

On August 20, shortly before his marriage to Miss Clementine Hozier at St. Margaret's, Westminster, Mr. Churchill wrote a letter of thanks for his Secretary's wedding gift, the complete works of Sainte-Beuve.

> Few people have been so lucky as me to find in the dull and grimy recesses of the Colonial Office a friend whom I shall cherish and hold to all my life. Yours always, W.

The main threads in his web of relationships were beginning to reveal themselves. In November of this year another of these began to develop. An exchange of postcards between Marsh and Rupert Brooke at King's, making plans to meet in Cambridge at a gathering of the 'Apostles', coincided with the beginning of a closer friendship with the Churchills. The Apostles Society, once the arena for Russell, Moore, and Marsh himself, was due to meet on a Saturday night. Marsh would try to get away after dinner with the Verralls, and he planned to walk over to breakfast with Brooke in college on the Sunday morning. They had probably met once at the Verralls' since their first meeting two years before when Brooke was disguised as the Herald. They were not yet on terms of Christian names and the transactions of the select undergraduate society were their only common ground.

In February 1909 Marsh began sending his news to Cynthia Charteris, who had gone to Canada on an official visit with her parents. On the 28th he had just dined with Mrs. Patrick Campbell, whose play was about to come off.

> But is she down-hearted? No. Mrs. Tree came in in the middle and sailed up to the table saying 'How-do-you-do, you won't be able to take your eyes off my hat.' It was one of the new shape which you may not have seen—something between a beehive and a mudpie. Mrs. Campbell had one too, so there at once began a rivalry between the two hats. 'Shall I tell you the romance of mine?' said Mrs. C. 'I got it to fascinate a man who's in love with Lily Elsie.' 'And the romance of mine,' said Mrs. Tree, 'is that it cost seven and twopence.' Apparently she had made it herself. It reminded me of the flower bed in *Punch* that the gardener said 'looked as if someone had done it 'isself'.

He had been staying at Belvoir, a fellow-guest with Mrs. Tree's daughter Viola, who was later to become so close a friend. 'Viola, alas, has now reached the stage of not being allowed to sing, which marks such an important advance in the career of a singer.'

In order to keep in touch with Horner he had begun his weekend visits to Oxford and been admitted into the brilliant circle at Balliol: Charles Lister, Patrick Shaw-Stewart (both of whom were shortly to play a tragic role in Brooke's life), Julian and Billy Grenfell, and Ronald Knox. All these and their friends would foregather in the vacations at Mells as the guests of Sir John and Lady Horner, and Marsh, their senior in age but none the less a kindred spirit, would be of their number whenever time allowed. Of these it was Shaw-Stewart, tall, freckled, red-headed, with ice-blue eyes, whom Marsh especially befriended and was always ready to welcome at Gray's Inn. Perhaps the most brilliant of this legendary Eton-Balliol group, Shaw-Stewart was also, in an unconventional way, the most striking in looks, with prominent cheekbones and a nose, as Marsh recorded, 'so long that when Lady Marjorie was drawing his profile and found her pencil going farther and still farther down the paper she grew, as she said, "almost frightened"'. His sense of humour was of the extravagantly affected kind which Marsh especially enjoyed, as when

Shaw-Stewart sent a telegram to the Admiralty which ran: 'If you have any beautiful thoughts concerning dinner next Thursday I am prepared to consider them', or when after enjoying several weeks of Mrs. Elgy's hospitality he left a cheque for £50 on Marsh's plate at breakfast. Edward Horner was shocked to hear of this when Shaw-Stewart told him. Eddie must have taken offence. 'You must have *known* he wouldn't accept it,' he protested. 'I'm not so sure,' said Shaw-Stewart. 'VERY FEW people refuse cheques for £50.'

In March Max Beerbohm exhibited his drawings at Goupils, including a caricature of Mr. Churchill in his office at the Board of Trade with Marsh a willowy, monocled figure obsequious at the door. Max sent a ticket for the Private View. 'You will be glad to see that you may, if you like, arrive at 10 and not *stir* from the place till 6.' Marsh bought the drawing but left a note complaining of the artist's treatment of his nose. On the 13th Max wrote again.

> I knew already who was the impulsive purchaser of the drawing. For on Saturday when I went into the Gallery on my way to Waterloo, to see how my drawings looked, and saw a cheerful little scarlet wafer confronting me, I asked one of the attendants if he knew who was the buyer, and he replied in a professional whisper that it was 'Mr. Marsh, the young gentleman whom you have drawn standing against the door'—and I was of course much flattered by the 'young gentleman's' action. I think it shows a beautiful spirit of forgiveness in you, and if at any time you should like the nose carefully redesigned and drastically remodelled command me!

In April Brooke was planning to stay for the first time at Raymond Buildings. They had tried to meet in January for another gathering of the Apostles, but Marsh was held up in London. He was reading *Jean Christophe*, 'easily the best novel in the world'. On March 26 he wrote again to Brooke who was in Devonshire.

> My dear Brooke, or may I say Rupert and will you do likewise?
>
> I am delighted that you will come on the 23rd, Shakespeare's birthday, oh frabjous day—I will keep it jealously—so if you want to change it, or could stay more than one night, let me know in goodish time.
>
> I feel out of it not knowing about Poor Professor Saintsbury's Latest[1]—what a good name it would be for a play, I shall suggest it

---

[1] Brooke was writing a review of Saintsbury's *The History of English Prosody* for the *Cambridge Magazine*.

to Barrie. Is it his History of Metres? and is he poor because *it* is? or has he committed suicide by swallowing his artificial teeth, like poor Professor Churton Collins?

I have just heard of a superb John drawing which I shall buy if I can go and see it before it is snapped up—I have only got one, and *must* have another before you come, or you will think my collection stick-in-the-mud.

But Brooke had to change the date, asking to come a day earlier and saying he was mourning for 'Mr. Swinburne and the Independent Labour Party'. Marsh had just come back from a holiday in Avignon, having sat in the corridor all night across France reading *Paradise Lost*. 'I am in mourning for Swinburne,' he wrote, 'but not the Labour Party.' On April 22, their first of so many evenings together in London, they met at Brooks's for dinner and went to the play. It happened to be Rupert's second visit to the theatre that day and he had little energy left for his first tour of the pictures at Gray's Inn. He stayed the night and struck up a friendship with Mrs. Elgy next morning. It was six years before his death to the day.

In May Marsh spent a week-end at Brooke's cottage, The Orchard, between the bridge and the church at Grantchester, and they did not meet again until August. Marsh was then at Mells, and he suggested driving over with Edward Horner to Clevedon, Somerset, where Brooke was staying with his parents. 'I expect you will hate my Radical family,' Brooke wrote. 'There is a book of Lord Avebury's here, about Life, which I read aloud at tea, and when we laugh they think us irreverent.' (His friends Hugh Dalton, Gerald Shove, and Francis Birrell were already staying there.) He could not read the name of the friend who was going to drive Marsh over from Mells. 'Not *the* Homer, dare I hope, the Writer?' Horner drove up to the door on the appointed day and for the first time Marsh set eyes on Mrs. Brooke, a woman of strong and forthright character, not without nobility, and closely resembling her son in appearance—her face was extraordinarily like his with the addition of a mass of tiny wrinkles.

Just before the Clevedon visit Marsh had accompanied his Chief on an inspection of the Labour Exchanges in Alsace. Mr Churchill was contemplating the adaptation of the German system in England. Unemployment Insurance was also to be one of his innovations at this time, and Old Age Pensions (his department performed the functions later taken over by the Ministry of Labour), all of which was to lead in a few months to a controversial Finance Bill which shook the Country with its imposition of an income-tax ranging from 9*d.* to 1*s.* 2*d.* in the pound. While on the Continent Mr. Churchill took Marsh a tour of the battlefields of the Franco-Prussian War and expounded to him the deployment of forces and fluctuations of fortune in that fateful campaign of forty years before. At Strasbourg the German officials were amazed by Marsh's free-and-easy manner in the presence of his Chief. They asked him in genuine concern why he did not spring to attention and click his heels when Mr. Churchill entered the room.

Soon after his return Mrs. Elgy packed his trunk for a trip to Russia with Maurice Baring, where he was to be the guest of Baring's friend, Count Benckendorff, the Russian Ambassador to London. Granville Barker's plays were published the day before he left England. 'I've scurried through *Waste* and found it almost unintelligible,' he wrote to Brooke. 'It's written more like Aristotle than anything else. What it can have been like on the stage I *can't* imagine.'

The Benckendorffs lived in two small adjoining houses in the village of Sosnovka, about a day's journey from Moscow. Baring and Marsh shared a room and talked late into the night. There were frequent draughts from the presiding samovar, and a duck-shoot at dawn. On the way home they spent a day in Moscow, then visited the Hermitage at St. Petersburg and the Embassy, where they made the acquaintance of Harold Nicolson, whose father was the British Ambassador. When Marsh got back he went to Cambridge, where Howard Marsh was now Master of Downing College and still occupied the Chair of Surgery. Brooke came up to town in October to see *King Lear*, so that when Marsh wrote on November 5 Russia was no longer news.

Do tell me your news and whether you got the Shakespeare prize.[1] Have you read Frank Harris's book?[2] I'm going to begin it tonight— Desmond [MacCarthy] tells me it's most exciting. There are too many good new books. I've just finished Belloc's last but one, in time for his last—but if he goes on bringing out a new one every fortnight I'm afraid I shan't be able to keep up. *Marie Antoinette* is very good

[1] The Charles Oldham Shakespeare Prize at Cambridge, which Brooke was awarded in December.　　[2] *The Man Shakespeare.*

reading, and magnificent in parts—especially the last chapter, but crammed with all his usual crankiness about 'the Faith', on Jews, the Hohenzollerns, the infamy of all modern politicians etc. It's no use reading him with a grain of salt, one ought to have a large salt cellar at one's elbow and take table-spoonfuls. He has an amusing way of providing for readers of different social grades, for instance to give an idea of the size of the reporter's box in which the Royal family were put when they escaped from the Tuileries on the 10th August, he says the readers if wealthy may think of an opera box, if poor, of a ship's cabin. On this system one might cater for very large audiences and yet make each individual think his interests had been specially considered, and write books in parallel columns, one for clergymen, one for doctors, one for children, etc. His newest book is called *On Everything.* I think the public might treat it as a kind of 'blocking motion', say for a year, and inhibit him from publishing a book on anything in particular.

I don't suppose you will take an interest in Miss Stawell's book about Homer, on account of the classical nature of the subject, but it's charming—unfortunately, as I've read both the *Iliad* and the *Odyssey* in the last 12 months it's chief effect on me is the unpleasing one of showing me how little I know about either. Max's new essays are perfectly delightful—if you ever read novels, do try *The First Round* by St. John Lucas, the man who did the *Oxford Book of French Verse.* I think it simply fascinating and couldn't bear its coming to an end. *Ann Veronica* is interesting but the end is as stupid as a *deus ex machina* in Euripides according to Verrall. He can't really think that if a girl runs away with a poor married man whose wife won't divorce him the natural consequence is that the wife should immediately die, the man begin making £10,000 a year by writing *good* plays, and the girl's family forget the past. Such is not what Belloc (I don't know why) calls 'what fools call the logic of events'.

I'm going to stay at Downing for the Sunday of the week when the *Wasps* are acted—the 27th I think—so I shall look forward to seeing you there.

Brooke made no reply, so he wrote again.

Do let me find a note at Downing Lodge to give me a P.S.M. on Sunday. This is on the analogy of the P.S.A. Society which means Pleasant Sunday Afternoons; but for years I never would let Winston accept invitations to speak for it because I thought it meant the Prevention of Sodomy with Animals.

At Cambridge he made a new young friend whose first essay in fiction had struck him as showing considerable promise. Soon

E. M. Forster was staying in the spare room at Gray's Inn, and a few days later wrote to say that after Marsh had gone off to start his morning's work at Whitehall he had visited

> the National Gallery, the National Loan Exhibition of Medici prints, a china Exhibition, and an Exhibition of Irish Industries where I bought three pairs of stockings, three of socks, three pen-holders, a jar of honey, half a pound of butter, and a book of poems. Today I am feeling a morsel tired, but have read *Nan*—wonderful, unquestionably great, there's nothing else one wants to say about it. Have also read a lot of Frank Harris, who irritates, but I shall read him all. Perhaps what you told me about him prejudices me, but the conceit, and so often the superficiality, do bob up right and left. How *can* he say that *Lear* is the first attempt in all literature to paint madness? Or, after his sneers at conventional morality, simply absolve Shakespeare from the 'imputations' of the Sonnets? Such lapses are unpardonable in a critic who boasts of his scientific equipment—they reduce him to the level of me, and I tell you what, he's not really half as nice.

In December E. M. Forster joined Horner and Shaw-Stewart as an occasional holder of the spare latch-key to Gray's Inn and he was left in Mrs. Elgy's care when Marsh went for a few days to the Lyttons at Knebworth. Brooke had never been to Drury Lane, so Marsh took him there to see *The Whip*, and to *The Importance of Being Earnest* at the St. James's, before leaving for Dundee to make preparations for Mr. Churchill's contest in the General Election.

At Dundee he heard from Brooke, who was wanting to come up again for a night in London. Mrs. Elgy had to have several more spare keys cut, and for a few days her hands were full, with Brooke in Marsh's bed and Forster in the spare room. 'Will you be free to take me to gape at any London wonder, in my rustic way, on Tuesday night?' Brooke asked. He had just seen Shaw's *Blanco Posnet*. 'It was very mournful, I thought, to see the beginning of senile decay in that brilliant intellect.' By now he had taken himself to the New English exhibition and 'felt quite sick and faint with passion at the beauty of a painting by John'. He was writing from Rugby, where it was term-time. Next day he would have to deputize for his father (who was house-master of Field House) at school prayers. Meanwhile at Dundee Marsh was genuinely alarmed at the prospect of what the suffragettes might be going to perpetrate. Moreover there was trouble over a leakage in the Press. 'Mind you send me my letters with the utmost regularity,' Mr. Churchill had written, 'or you will never regain the affection which you have lost by your brutal usage of my Oldham speech. I am expecting you to write to the Chief of Police at Oldham and to the editor of the Oldham paper on the rapidity with which they produced a report of my speech.' In mid-January 1910, a few days before the poll, Marsh wrote to Brooke from Dundee.

I'm having a dog's life but it's fairly amusing. Four nights out of the last five in the train—speeches at Birmingham, Leamington, Derby, Glasgow, and Inverness—the wildest enthusiasm everywhere —we all think more than in '06, and are expecting a terrific majority. Winston has been brilliant everywhere—luckily for him he is no longer reported at length so he can say the same things again and again, consequently I am becoming almost as familiar with them as Mr. Clutterbuck was, after 18 years of married life, with the appearance and manner of Mrs. Clutterbuck—but even so I some-times get quite carried away—there are occasions when as I sit on the platform I wish for a little needlework—but there is always the excitement of wondering which peroration it will be. The thing that amused me most was when Winston said he had read one of Mr. Austen Chamberlain's speeches 'which the Conservative papers for once had the mood—and the humour—to report in full'. When I congratulated him afterwards he said he hadn't meant it! so he must have been speaking, as the Evangelists wrote, under the verbal inspiration of the Holy Ghost.

At Leamington we made the acquaintance of your candidate Lord Clonmell, a perfectly delightful fellow. Winston and I both fell head over ears in love with him—he said Alfred Brooke was working for him but not you—I hope you will be well enough to lend him a hand before the poll.[1] He said one injudicious thing in his speech which amused us very much—that the working classes must no longer lie and rot like sheep in their pens, as they had done for the past 100 years! the workmen present didn't appreciate this descrip-tion any more than sheep would have done, had any been present! Otherwise he spoke very well—and at luncheon made us shriek with laughter by the story of his bet with Lord Denbigh about his gamechickens—it was at once so guarded and so technical—'If Ld D could prove that any of my gamechickens had been taken from their *walks* during the *last three years* to fight *in this constituency*'! It

[1] Brooke was in Switzerland, recovering from blood-poisoning.

called up a delightful picture of the gamechickens being taken out daily for a stroll by an old woman, except when they left the constituency for martial pursuits. I do hope he gets in.

I've hardly had a minute to read—I'm getting slowly through Hogg's Life of Shelley again, an intensely amusing and delightful book in the good parts, but with every now and then a tract of wild balderdashy unintelligible letter from the youthful poet, which one daren't skip from the fear, quite unfounded, of missing something good. *Deo gratias non sic omnes (juvenes poetae)*. Compliment.[1]

I've also read an Anthony Trollope, do you know and like him? I think he's just the person to amuse the languor of an invalid, as he is to soothe the overwrought and fretted P. Secretary in the muddled intervals of an election campaign—his unobtrusive but thorough psychology, his urbane and amusing wit, his explaining picture of the time so near yet so far (I was brought up in the tail end of it) make him the most delightful and unexacting of entertainers. My book was *Phineas Finn*.

I haven't read *Villa Rubein* and got it for you not from any conviction of a subtle likeness between Galsworthy and Peacock but because he was the only author represented in the shop at whose name your chiselled lip wouldn't have curled with scorn.

I should never dare to write you a letter like this if you were in your usual health—why is it thought nice for invalids to get long dull letters? I apologize for being unable to free myself from the trammels of this superstition.

We poll on Tuesday (doubling majority at the very least—or so we think) then we fly off for 3 more days of speechifying in Cornwall, then to Dorsetshire, and after that if things are going well Winston proposes to take me to Menton or some such place for much needed rest, so I probably won't see you for ages—send me one of your postcards to say how you are.

I spend nearly all my days, when not on the platform, writing telegrams—Mrs. Churchill is putting it about that I telegraphed to the Editor of the *D. News* to send some more champagne, and to the wine merchant 'May God defend the right'—but this isn't true.

The polling day brought a Liberal victory. Within a week Mr. Churchill was the new Home Secretary, and once again he took his Private Secretary with him. In the same month of February Sir Francis Hopwood suggested to Herbert Gladstone, who was

---

[1] Brooke's first volume of poems was not published till nearly two years after this (December 1911). The first poem which Brooke showed Marsh was 'Day that I have loved', published in *The Westminster Gazette* (June 1, 1910). This 'compliment' was based on having seen the manuscript of that poem, probably late in December 1909.

due to take up his new position as the resident in Government
House, Pretoria, that Marsh would be the best man for him as
confidential secretary and master of ceremonies. The invitation
reached Marsh unofficially through Dorothy Gladstone,[1] the new
Governor's wife, who was Marsh's close friend and most likely to
persuade him to an acceptance. For Marsh this was an important
cross-roads. On February 5, 1910, he wrote reluctantly declining.

> First there is Winston, he has been niceness itself about 'not standing
> in my way'—but he has got accustomed to me, with all my faults,
> and though he said nothing to influence me till I had made up my
> mind, I knew that he would rather keep me. And then you know how
> much I love my friends here and how well the life suits me . . . it
> would mean breaking with almost everything that I have cared
> about up till now, and I can't face it.

This was not accepted as final, and the offer was repeated with
the term of office reduced to the limit of one year. Marsh wrote
again.

> It would mean chucking Winston for good, and that would simply
> be too great a wrench. We have got peculiarly attached to one
> another in the four years we have been together, and I do want to
> stay with him so long as he is in office—after that he has always said
> he will try to get me something decent, and I must take my chance of
> that. If Africa only meant taking a year off, I would come like a shot,
> but it would mean losing Winston for ever, as of course he would
> have to establish a new relation at once, and I really can't face it.

Before the Gladstones left England Marsh stayed with his
father at Downing and had talks with A. C. Benson, Francis
Cornford, and Lowes Dickinson. Brooke was at Rugby, working
as a temporary house-master in place of his father, who had died
during the holidays. Charles Frohman had started his repertory
season at the Duke of York's theatre, and from Downing Marsh
wrote to Brooke, telling him of the Galsworthy sensation.

> *Justice* is the chief topic of conversation in all walks of life, and there
> is a raging controversy. I am tremendously for it, not having yet
> acquired enough Home Office *esprit de corps* to feel the resentment it
> inspires in my colleagues, who say no doubt rightly that it takes a
> whole series of incidents some of which are impossible, and some of
> which might quite conceivably happen but never do, and makes out

---

[1] Youngest daughter of the Rt. Hon. Sir Richard Paget.

that they are typical. The only aesthetic criticism I have heard which I think has much validity was from Sir Frank Swettenham who arrived in time for the second act, the Court Scene, and at the end of it found himself so completely in possession of the story that he couldn't conceive what could have happened in the first act. There is a great deal in this but I think the answer is that the audience must first form their own judgement on the action which passes before their eyes, and then see what 'justice' makes of it. There is no doubt that it is an exceedingly able play and the acting and 'production' are beyond praisè. *Misalliance* is a terrible frost—both revolting and dull. . . . One is so battered and bothered by the interminable flow of *les paradoxes d'auteur* that all interest and pleasure are exhausted long before the end. I asked Granville Barker whether he couldn't possibly persuade GBS to shorten it. He said no, that was quite hopeless and the only thing he could think of was to put an announcement in the newspapers that the audience were recommended not to assemble till 9 o'clock.

The Meredith play[1] seemed to be very delightful—I missed a great deal of the dialogue because I was far back and that wretch Maurice Hewlett, whom I used to like, talked incessantly in the seat just behind me, but what I heard made an effect of beauty in language which reminded me of nothing I have ever heard but a performance I once saw of *The Way of the World*. The *mise en scène*, which I believe is mainly due to Will Rothenstein, is simply exquisite. . . . I had a splendid evening at the Albert Hall fancy-dress ball. I went as Leicester or Sir P. Sidney, whichever you please.

While in Cambridge he was confronted with a delicate problem in his human relations. There had been a long silence from Gosse, and A. C. Benson now disclosed the reason. Gosse had vowed never to have him in his house again. Some months before, it was explained, Marsh had taken Mrs. Gosse in to dinner and in the heat of his discourse with the fellow-guest on his other side had turned his back on Mrs. Gosse and neglected her for the rest of the meal. Such was the complaint which Gosse had confided to Benson. Marsh pleaded innocence, but on his return to London he found a letter from Benson urging him to take the initiative in putting things to rights.

It is very easy to think that other people ought not to cherish their dignity and honour, when an old friendship is at stake; and not so easy to discard them when one is inside a situation. . . . It is easier

1 *The Sentimentalists.*

for you to make advances because he is older and because rightly or wrongly he thought that his wife's dignity was compromised.

He replied that for him to make the first move would imply an admission that he was in the wrong. 'There is in Gosse a Puritan touch, the impulse to improve other people at all costs which obscures to him the real motives of his assaults,' he wrote, and complained that Gosse was 'in a lofty mood about it all, which is truly aggravating'. Benson then suggested going direct to the injured party herself. This Marsh did, but he reported that after putting his case he had asked her 'to scold her husband and make my peace'. Small wonder that there was no result. 'It isn't that I won't, but that I *can't* re-enter into a satisfactory relation with Gosse on the basis that my being a rude cad is to be overlooked and that he is to pull my nose whenever he likes.' He then happened to meet Gosse in the street. 'Arthur Benson looked quite well when I saw him last,' Marsh began, hoping he was thereby raising the subject tactfully and providing a cue, but Gosse mistook the motive and turned on his heel without a word. Why should he apologize where there was no consciousness of wrongdoing? Benson replied:

> Your reasons are excellent and conclusive, but I hope that some day you will be able to kick them out. I believe in instinct, not in reason. When reason is right, nine times out of ten it is impotent, and when it prevails, nine times out of ten it is *wrong*! But possibly you *are* acting on instinct. The whole thing seems to me pathetic rather than silly.

Marsh then took the bull by the horns and wrote to Gosse. He said he had offered to explain on the spot, before the dinner-party was over, but Gosse had refused to let him speak.

> You refused, and an angel from heaven would have resented your attitude, as I own I did. There can never have been a more absurd falling out. . . . The only thing I don't want is a unilateral forgiveness from you. This I must say, as I do not think it would work well in the result. I hope you will send me the magic words 'all is well' to the Home Office. I should return with gladness to my once valued place among your friends.

They were reconciled, but in Marsh's mind their relationship was never the same again. Perhaps he was never quite free of a slight feeling of self-reproach, for there is little doubt that his benefactor's grievance was not unfounded. Marsh always found it difficult to 'talk sideways', and this was not the only occasion when his habit of swinging his shoulders round to address his neighbour more directly gave an impression of discourtesy.

On May 5 he began the letters to Lady Gladstone[1] which make a chronicle of the last year and a half of his life in Edwardian London.

[1] Herbert Gladstone was created a peer before leaving for his new appointment.

Chapter Eight

THE BEGINNING OF PATRONAGE
(May 1910–December 1911)

THE Gladstones were seen off for South Africa by the Prime Minister's family, and among the friends was Eddie Marsh, who a week later began his correspondence with the new Governor's wife. She had expressed a wish to be kept in touch with London society.

> The only piece of news I have heard (except Dangerous Illness of the King, which broke out in the evening papers tonight, I do hope it won't come to anything) is that Cynthia and Beb[1] are at last allowed to be engaged—it isn't announced but they are to be married this year I believe—Elcho has written her a long super-paternal letter of eight sheets saying that he hopes she realises the difference between tubes and omnibuses on the one hand and motors and taxis on the other, the evanescence of imaginary grand passions etc. I am delighted that it is settled as I'm extremely fond of Beb, though of course I think he is the lucky one of the two.
>
> As I was leaving Waterloo on Saturday I met Elizabeth,[2] who invited me to luncheon at 1.45. I arrived punctually and found that the meal had begun and there was no place for me. Don't you think it is rather precocious, at her age, (1) to ask a young man to luncheon, (2) at the wrong time, and (3) to forget all about it? Anyhow, she had a place laid for me next her, and she talked so brilliantly that I was never more shocked when her governess who was on her other side suddenly rebuked her with great severity for sitting with her leg tucked up under her—the realisation that she is really a 'little girl' was almost too abrupt. Lord Kitchener was there, briefer and gloomier than ever—I was at the other end of the table, but Beb told me the only thing he had said during the meal was that the Emperor of Japan had taken him for a day's hunting and that the sport was catching ducks in butterfly nets.

Within fifteen days King Edward was dead. On May 20 Marsh wrote again.

---

[1] Lady Cynthia Charteris and Herbert (Beb) Asquith.
[2] Elizabeth Asquith, later Princess (Elizabeth) Bibesco.

The funeral procession this morning was wonderful, and I have just come back from the service at Westminster Abbey. Like the song in *Alice*, it was long but very very beautiful. I suppose we should know by now if any of the nine monarchs had been blown up—Lady Connie Hatch who came here for the procession told me she had said to her maid how dreadful it would be if there was a bomb, and the maid said, 'Oh, will there be many of *them*, my Lady?'

I suppose you have heard endless stories about the King's death and everything connected with it? I shall be lucky if I tell you anything you don't know. One of the most curious stories, which is quite true, is that on the Thursday, the day before he died, he was to receive Jack P.[1] as Governor of New Zealand, and somebody else as Agt. Gen. for W. Australia. Lord Sheffield's mind set to work on these names and produced 'the Agent Gen. for Newfoundland'. So when the W. Australian arrived the King said, 'I've never actually set foot in your interesting Colony, but I've twice seen its shores.' The A.G. who knew he had never been anywhere near W. Australia, looked bewildered—Hopwood saw what had happened, and told the King who he really was. The poor King was so terribly upset at having made such a gaffe that he had a violent fit of coughing and turned quite black in the face—and this was really the beginning of the end. Jack P. said when he got home he was sure he was a dying man.

Queen Alexandra, when told on the Friday that Mrs. Keppel, who had seen the King on Thursday, was to come back at 5 o'clock, said 'she will be too late' and immediately sent for her and took her into his room—but he was already unconscious. I am almost sure this is true, and if so I think it very wonderful and beautiful to hear.

The cock-and-bull stories that are going about as to the King having been killed by the Liberals are too amazing. The Queen Mother is supposed to have taken the P.M. and McKenna into the room and said, 'Look at your work'!! Muriel Lady Helmsley assured Pauline as a fact that Winston had gone to the proclamation in a red tie!

I know nothing about the political situation and don't suppose there is yet much to be known. So far as I can make out King George is very reasonable and well meaning about it.

Sunday, May 22nd

I was prevented from finishing this in time for the mail, and now I am at Penrhos (the Sheffields) on the island of Holyhead, a nice quiet visit, sailing in a tiny yacht or walking in spring woods. I will

---

[1] John Dickson-Poynder (Lord Islington), appointed Governor of New Zealand 1910, married Anne Dundas. She joined him a few weeks after he had taken up office.

go on with my other visits about which there is more to tell. Last
Sunday I was at Hartham, where Anne had just come back from
seeing off poor Jack, in the depths of depression, at Marseilles. The
Asquiths were there—the P.M. putting his foot into it, with his
robust good sense all the time. Once when Anne was between me
and him at dinner she turned round to me and said, 'Do people ever
say things to you that immediately start internal haemorrhage inside
you?' Mr. Asquith had just told her that he thought it was high time
New Zealand was put under Australia.

Margot was very funny—she and I and Basil Machwood arrived
together and were having tea with Pauline, when suddenly the Duke
of Beaufort appeared at the other end of the hall—Margot was
furious and began whispering almost spitting to Pauline, how *could*
Anne invite a man like that to a little intimate party at such a time?
it was too bad and would spoil everything. After dinner she sat on his
knee! I had never seen him before, he is like a mediaeval wooden
figure, over life-size, carved by someone who didn't know anatomy.

Margot told me how awful it was for her losing Anne—how nearly
all her friends were dead and Anne was much the most valuable she
had left. That is all very well but my good woman why do you send
her away?

My other visit was Belvoir, I think I told you about my last going
there. This time the most interesting guest was Melba. She refused
to sing, but I sang to her instead, and had a great success with her,
and she told the girls I was very handsome. This is the second time
I have been thought handsome this year, so I was becoming rather
vain, but this tendency was corrected by a dear old lady on the H.O.
stand at the procession who mistook me for X.

The Duchess of Rutland is furious, why do you think? because
Cynthia isn't going to marry John Granby! She can't bear anybody
getting married except her own children. Diana[1] was more beautiful
than ever, her complexion is easily the most wonderful I've ever seen.
The only thing that spoilt my visit at all was that the Duke was
evidently quite convinced I had killed the King—and even the
Duchess couldn't clear her mind of a faint suspicion.

When Marsh next wrote he had just received a letter from Lady
Gladstone dated the day of the King's death. 'I wonder when you
heard the news,' he wrote, 'by wireless, I suppose. I couldn't help
thinking about all your poor new clothes, and wondering whether
you had anything on board that you could land in—or if you had
to wait in your cabin while yards of crepe were hurriedly brought

---

[1] Lady Diana Manners.

out from Cape Town in a lighter!' He had been for a week to Brussels and Antwerp, looking at pictures with Victor Lytton, whose home at Knebworth was undergoing alterations. 'Pamela's sitting-room is now finished—it is hung with some old bead tapestries, a worked pattern of trees and fruit on a background of gold and silvery-white beads—I never saw anything of the kind before, and seldom anything so lovely.' The unbroken summer had produced a sultry, orchid-house atmosphere, and Patrick Shaw-Stewart, Horner, Lister, the Grenfell brothers, and himself were all going to sleep under the stars in the garden at Sutton Courtenay; at Whitehall the Home Office was crowded with visitors—'I can't keep awake in the deputations, and am in terror that I shall have a nightmare and wake screaming.' On June 17 the London season began.

It is a good thing balls will begin soon. Lady Alice Shaw-Stewart has one on the 28th, which is called 'a conjuror' and Lady Manners on the 30th—after that there will be heaps—otherwise the problem of 'what to do with our girls' would become serious. One solution was found at Lady Wenlock's last Wednesday, quite the funniest party I ever went to. It began with ordinary music and conversation till 12, after which everyone went away except about 20 of the choicest spirits, and we had the following programme—

(1) Russian dances.
(2) Lancers.
(3) Gymnastics, inspired by Rex Benson—the girls lifted up to the ceiling, the men climbing on each other's shoulders and hurtling through the air which was thick with bodies.
(4) Oranges and Lemons.
(5) Nuts in May.

After which the proceedings ended with—what do you think? Hymns (*Fight the Good Fight, Onward Christian Soldiers*, etc.). The funniest thing was that there was a little Italian, who stayed to the end—one of the judges in the horseshow. I am sure he will publish his impressions of English society in the *Corriere della Sera*, and end up by remarking on our ingrained Puritanism, which impels us to end any party, however frivolous, with a short divine service.

Yesterday Lady Plymouth's concert was a great contrast to Portland Place, all Schumann, divinely played by Donald Tovey and others—3 pieces, lasting about ¾ of an hour each—there was great decorum and a good deal of unobtrusive sleeping. Norah was sitting next me in a horn quintet, and made me laugh by suddenly whispering in a plaintive tone, after a great pow-pow *pow*, 'Eddie, I think motors have spoilt me for the horn.'

By the end of June the time of mourning was coming to an end and at a *soirée* just out of town the new reign was ushered in by the Household Brigade.

The account of your depressing arrival was very amusing. Is it true that you are going to have a Poiret exhibition of your coloured clothes that you can't wear?

London is getting quite amusing. The mourning comes to an end at midnight tonight, and we shall begin dancing at 12, as if at the end of Ramadan. It is at Lady Manners'. Her invitations were very non-committal—'Do come in after dinner on Thursday' and were evidently meant to be kept in evidence, to be produced not in but *at* Court. There is to be singing etc. first, but as the clock strikes the Household Brigade will come rolling in and we shall have fun. Meanwhile Lady Alice Shaw-Stewart's ball, after endless alarms and fluctuations, finally took place last Tuesday at Roehampton House under the name of a supper-picnic. Nobody knows to this day who actually gave it, she or Mrs. Arthur Grenfell, whose house it was in— A kind of Roundrobin dance, of which the responsibility can't be fixed. Anyhow it was glorious fun, and went on till past 3. A capital ballroom, delightful garden, and heaps of motors—so getting away was easier than from the ball the Levers had there. I didn't go to that, but Beb told me he had come home in a motor omnibus with 20 other people, all of whom quarrelled all the way as to who should be dropped first—in the end the victory was won by a determined man who lived at Shepherd's Bush, quite 3 miles away from anyone else.

Everyone is very pretty this year—Lady Kathleen Thynne has become quite gorgeous, and Miss Shaw-Stewart is lovely—Nan Lyttelton has become a beauty, her colouring is wonderful. I am looking forward to Moira Osborne, who was such a pretty little girl —she wants to come out but nobody knows, so Lady Gwendolen says she has got no invitations—like the starling in Sterne, who said 'I can't get out, I can't get out'. The only new girl of any consequence whom I have seen is Bridget Colebrooke, who walks in beauty like the night—wonderful black hair and eyes shining in the dusk of her face. She is rather too much for me—I told her how I loved the ball and how all my friends were there—'I'm not enjoying it so very much,' she said, 'of course I've been dancing all the time but there are none of my special friends here.' Wasn't that rather damping? Laura Lister was looking lovely, but as she cut my dance I will not enlarge upon her.

Anne[1] is spending her last week at Hartham—she has a party on Monday, and starts on Friday week with Pamela who goes with her as far as Teneriffe. I'm afraid she is getting more and more miserable. She went to luncheon with the King and Queen last week, whom she barely knew, and hadn't been there ¼ of an hour before she was doing Lady Minto receiving them in Canada! it seems to have been a tremendous success, wasn't it clever and brave of her.

I went to Knebworth for last Sunday, there were Margot, Lady Willoughby, Duchess of Leeds, Lady Cunard, Lionel Earle, Charles Lister and Jasper Plowden. Pamela had had difficulties about it because Margot and Lady Cunard had both said they would come if they could bring two young men—P. said yes, and all the 4 young men refused! At the last moment she lost her head and telephoned for Winston and Clemmie, quite forgetting about Lionel! but luckily they couldn't go. I had the narrowest escape from the worst floater of my life, it makes my blood run cold to think of it. We were all discussing at dinner whether the Manners's were natural or not, and some people began saying Marjorie was affected. I defended her, and was just going to tell how she came back from a visit to Lady X in dejection, saying, '*That's* what I ought to be like—quite dull, never taking or showing the slightest interest or feeling about anything'—I'd just got as far as 'Poor Marjorie, you should have heard her the other day when she came back from . . .' when either St. Michael or St. George put it into my head that her sister was seated at my side! wouldn't it have been awful?

Don't tell H.E. that I spend my official time writing gossip—I'm writing in Winston's room at the House, while the P.M. makes his important statement—and I've done all the work so my conscience is quite clear.

Friday, July 1st

At that moment Winston came in and official duties at high pressure followed—now the more peaceful earlier conditions of yesterday are repeated, and I must give you a sketch of last night.

I had an amusing invitation. On Wednesday I went to a play with Lady Plymouth, and as I said goodnight I asked if she had a concert on Thursday. Yes, she said, I hope you are coming—and then after a pause began tentatively (imagine her voice) 'm—the party isn't quite complete yet—m—can you think of anyone who'd like to come and—m—take in—m—m—Lady X?' I leapt into the breach and was amply rewarded by sitting between her and the Duchess of Rutland. Lady X was funnier than I'd ever known her—she got me to encourage her in venturing on a 'rich' pudding—and then said,

[1] Lady Islington.

'Now dear Mr. Eddie, I *know* I can trust you to tell me the exact truth, look at my face, is that too fat? Look at my neck, *look at the back of my neck*, is that?' etc. etc. Then she burst out, 'Do you know what I'd really like to do? Give up trying to look pretty, trying to make people like me, and live at home with a wonderful cook, and just eat and *eat* and EAT, and then have a box at the opera and sit in it like a kind of porpoise and then go home and have a wonderful supper.'! She *is* fun—she made us all roar with laughter at Knebworth by telling us about an American friend of hers who had written the 'most wonderful play, all in blank verse, full of the highest and noblest ideals—and the hero is a parrot and dies of cancer'.

After dinner a wonderful classical concert, with Donald Tovey and a quartet, Bach, Brahms, and Mozart—a little spoilt for me by Elcho's face of drawn misery on a sofa. The Lady Manners' ball was quite splendid, very small and nearly all friends—I didn't get to bed till 5! which is really ridiculous at my age, I *must* pull myself together, but at a ball I'm enjoying I never feel a minute over 25. Mary Vesey was there, looking much better—she had selected a tailor and taken Aubrey into the shop, where she kept her head long enough to say, 'I want you to make a suit for this gentleman', then her courage failed her and she rushed wildly out of the shop, with just enough presence of mind to point at the topmost bale of stuff on the counter saying 'That'. It turned out to be a magenta cloth shot with crimson.

By the way I made up a description of Billy Grenfell last night which I am proud of, 'the body of a Greek god and the face of a water-baby'—Billy has extraordinary charm, and sometimes says very good things, we were discussing a feat of drinking which had won fame at Oxford. 'When one comes to think of it,' said Billy, 'it's odd that there should be so much admiration for prowess in drinking, which after all is merely a domestic virtue.'

Before he came to write again a serious crisis had occurred which involved a public issue and two of his closest friends. The Suffragette agitations had resulted in the drafting of a Bill to give the Parliamentary vote to those women who were already entitled to vote in municipal elections, and in June it was brought before the House by a speaker from the Labour Benches. Lady Constance Lytton had worked indefatigably for the cause and it was therefore natural that the Bill should be of special importance to her brother, Lord Lytton. He was now Chairman of the Conciliation Committee for Woman Suffrage, and he was doing his utmost to further the campaign by enlisting the support of as many influential members of the Government as could be won over to his point of view. High on his list of course was Mr. Churchill, and he came away from a talk with the Home Secretary under the definite but mistaken impression that at least he would meet with no opposition in that quarter in the coming debate. As it happened, Mr. Churchill, though sympathetic to the Bill (in spite of the inconvenience he had suffered at the hands of militant suffragettes during two recent elections), was of the opinion that the measures proposed did not carry the matter nearly far enough, and when at last he rose in the House to say, 'Sir, I cannot support this Bill', several of his hearers were taken aback, and Lord Lytton was shocked 'by what seemed to him a personal betrayal. The dispute which followed in private placed Marsh in an extremely delicate position. On July 14 Mr. Churchill wrote to Lord Lytton, and Marsh accompanied his official statement of the facts with a covering note of his own.

Nothing in my life has pained me so much as the hideous breach between you and Winston, two of my dearest friends. Of course I know that you must sincerely believe you are in the right, and I have a kind of hope that if I can only persuade you that Winston has the same belief about himself and is guiltless of conscious 'treachery and hypocrisy' you will come to see that the facts, which so far as I know them are exactly and completely stated in the letter which he has sent you today, do not justify what you said at Welwyn.[1]

Winston's astonishment and indignation at your charges were absolutely genuine. It is impossible that anyone conscious of having played a double part could have spoken and behaved as he has done all day. And even if you will not take this from me, it is surely clear that no one would deliberately go in for a piece of treachery so certain to be immediately and disastrously exposed.

I wasn't present when he saw you five weeks ago, till just the end; but I remember how disappointed you seemed when you went away, and it is difficult to believe that he had then led you to think he would support the Bill.

Dear Victor, I can't help hoping that when your first anger at his opposition is over you will see the matter more nearly as I see it, with

[1] In the course of a speech at Welwyn which was reported in the Press, Lord Lytton had expressed his feelings on hearing Mr. Churchill's statement in the House the day before. Mr. Churchill then telegraphed Lytton, enquiring whether the report were correct. This was the beginning of the controversy.

every motive of deep affection for you both to keep me impartial; and if so, I think you will withdraw what you said last night?

I don't know if it is any good, my writing this—anyhow I hope it can do no harm, and I simply can't bear to sit still and try nothing.

That same day he wrote to Lady Gladstone. The dispute was now being vented in the daily Press, and he was at pains to represent Lord Lytton's point of view no less justly than his Chief's.

I could quite understand his thinking in his distressed and excited frame of mind, and without making allowance for human fallibility, that Winston has rather played fast and loose with the Suffrage movement, in the sense that after declaring in favour of its principle he has refused to support its practical proposal, without being able to suggest a satisfactory substitute—but from this to saying in public that Winston had first approved the *actual* Bill and then turned against it, is a tremendous step and I simply can't imagine how he has come to do it. . . . You can imagine the misery for me, seeing two of my best friends calling each other traitors and liars in the public Press. Nothing so odious and hurting has ever happened in my life, and I am afraid the consequences are irreparable. . . . It's the most disgusting form of misery I've ever experienced.

I must say the Suffrage debate was the best I've ever listened to. Winston's speech was brilliant, and really influenced opinion. His best sentence was about the cocottes. The Mothers of England would not have votes under the Bill, but the cocotte would—she would forfeit it if she married and became an honest woman—but she could regain it by divorce! The two most amusing speeches were Belloc's and Hugh Cecil's—Belloc said he was glad that one argument had not been used against the Bill in the debate—the intellectual inferiority of women. This argument, he said, he had only heard advanced by one limited class of his acquaintance—that of very, very young, unmarried men. 'The rest of us, as we grow older, come to look on the intelligence of women first with reverence, then with stupor, and finally with *terror*' (imagine his French *r*s). Hugh Cecil described his voting at Magdalen tower—'the process was serenely tranquil, austerely refined, by no means masculine. I did not come out reeling, panting, mopping my brow, saying "This is no woman's work."'

His private note to Lord Lytton arrived before the Home Secretary's memorandum. The reply was prompt but unyielding. It began on a note of personal esteem.

Your letter was kind and affectionate to me and rightly loyal to the Chief whom you serve. . . . I am absolutely wretched at what has happened . . . and when I write, speak, think about him I cannot bring myself to believe that it is the same Winston I have known for so many years and to whom I owe so much. I could write to you for ever to explain why it has hurt me so, but I want to try and forget it and so will say no more.

Marsh replied by return:

The one good in this nightmare is that you and I are still friends. I had a half fear that that might be swept away in the ruin—so in one respect your letter brought me happiness. Meanwhile I have to hear Winston, who is very miserable too, saying all day that he never could have believed it of Victor—and to think of you at Knebworth, never being able to believe it of Winston. It is all really a horrible muddle, and I also could write pages but it would be no use.

Meanwhile Marsh thought it advisable to let Mr. Churchill see a copy of his unofficial note of the 14th. The letter was replaced on Marsh's desk endorsed in Churchill's hand:

You are a good little boy, and I am very fond of you. W.

Marsh's subsequent visit to Lord Lytton's home did something to clarify the situation in his own mind, and Lytton followed it up with a long letter to Marsh (September 2) setting out his views on the memorandum, which had done nothing to alter his opinion. Mr. Churchill, for his part, took his stand not only on what he maintained he had said in the original interview, but also on a letter of June 11 in which, as he believed, he had made it clear that he had decided not to support the Bill, and he seconded that with Lytton's acknowledgement, which he regarded as proof that he had succeeded in conveying his meaning. It now seemed proper to Marsh to submit Lytton's last letter of critical comment on the memorandum to Mr. Churchill, who was on his way to Wales for a meeting with Lloyd George. Mr. Churchill acknowledged it on September 26.

I do greatly regret not having warned him and Brailsford[1] beforehand. But you know how long I was coming to my final decision as to speaking and how many things I had to consider.

'Want of consideration', 'neglect or levity' . . . all these were charges for which I would have defended or excused myself with all

[1] H. N. Brailsford, Secretary of the Conciliation Committee.

amity and patience. His imputations were of a very different order—that I was pledged to the specific form of his Bill, that I had entered upon the question into a fiduciary relationship with him and his associates. . . . I wish you had not sent me his letter; it has only revived a resentment which had gradually cooled into oblivion.

Yours always
W.

And there the situation remained suspended. It was some while before Marsh could feel he had at last brought about a true reconciliation.

ii

Throughout these months of abortive mediation much happened that was worth reporting to his correspondent in Pretoria. On the day (July 15) when the trouble came to a head and he confided in Lady Gladstone, the other main item of news was the departure of Lady Islington for Government House, New Zealand.

I got a delightful letter from you last Saturday—giving a most pleasing account of your interior. Do go on and make me acquainted with all the characters. Nunnerly must be a great man—I should never choose an A.D.C. without some apparently crushing physical infirmity, they are so much the best. Nunnerly, stone-deaf; and John Ponsonby who used to be with the Lochs at the Cape, with a cleft palate so that no one could understand a word he said—but he was invaluable and the most popular man in the Colony.

Anne's departure, a week ago today, was the most melancholy function I've ever attended—except perhaps the farewell party she gave the Monday before, when everyone stood about like mutes at a funeral. She was wearing the diamond chain for which Lady Kitty S. got up a subscription. It is very pretty, especially on a day-gown, but I must admit that in the evening among her other jewels it didn't look very expensive. The scene at the station was gloomy in the extreme, all the nicest people in London, all in deep black, all with reddening eyes and choked voices—Anne's poor beautiful face twisted out of recognition into a brave little would-be smile—Lady Claud Hamilton, whose son was going too, bolt upright and bellowing like a Madonna in a Pietà by Crivelli. The only gay person was the P.M., who cheerily compared the scene to an execution—there was a 'thinking chorus' of 'then you're the executioner' but no one dared to say it out aloud. Margot insisted on going to Plymouth, much against Anne's will. Julian Grenfell and Maurice went too; and

Pamela as far as Teneriffe, she will come straight back. I think everyone feels that we have lost something quite irreplaceable and that life in London will be like a statue with a broken nose. . . .

Do you know Nancy Cunard, Lady Cunard's little girl aged about 11? I went to *Figaro* the other day with them and between acts Nancy said in her high little squeaky toneless voice, 'The Count is exactly like George the Second. The Countess I should put a little later—about 1790.' What *are* the children coming to? Tonight the Manners's (Arlington St.) have what is now called a 'jolly', I am going as a Dutchman—it will be fun.

The July gaiety continued. He had gone as a Chinaman to Lady Cunard's ball in Cavendish Square and found his hostess in a leopard skin and a wreath, and Mrs. Hwfa Williams 'funny as an Albanian lady', but there was one ball to which he received no invitation. 'Eileen W. had one on Wednesday, but she didn't ask me! It is too stupid of her never to have forgiven me for *her* proposing to *me*!' This referred to a curious incident of the year before which several young women of the time were to remember for a long while to come. For all his popularity and readiness in conversation Eddie Marsh was something of an enigma, and even a challenge, to the young people of the fashionable London season who did not know him intimately. At one of the balls a number of them banded together and made a bet that none of them would dare sit out a dance with him and with every sign of sincerity make a proposal of marriage. They wanted to know what on earth he would say, and to discover how this ornament of society would demean himself in so delicate a situation. The young woman of beauty and breeding who accepted the challenge soon found occasion to be seated with Eddie Marsh among the potted ferns, and after a short and doubtless convincing preamble she came directly to the point, whereupon the wind was taken out of her sails by the promptness of Marsh's reply, which was, 'Yes, when?' It seems that after hearing the result her circle of friends were troubled with remorse for what only now struck them as a rather unworthy practical joke. Among a few of them the impression was that Marsh had fallen the victim of a trick and that his reply was given in earnest, but such a man would surely have expressed himself in other terms had he really been deceived. His answer was as false as the question, and an example of his quickness in repartee.

In July John Galsworthy wrote to congratulate Mr. Churchill on his speech advocating Prison Reform and to draw his attention to a letter in its support which would shortly be appearing over his name in *The Times*. Marsh and the Churchills had been to see *Justice* more than once, and now he was instructed to write to Galsworthy saying that the Home Secretary 'looked forward to anything else he might write on the subject'. Mr. Churchill's mother then conceived the idea of making the dramatist acquainted with her son, and she gave a dinner-party to which she invited Eddie Marsh. When the ladies had retired the conversation turned on didactic or propagandist art, and Marsh, who was sitting beside Galsworthy, put a direct question. 'If the Archangel Gabriel came down from heaven and gave you your choice: that your play should transform the prison system and be forgotten, or have no practical effect whatever and be a classic a hundred years hence, which would you choose?' Galsworthy did not answer at once, and his neighbour, who had fancied him to be more of a philanthropist than an artist, especially in present company, was impressed by his candour when he finally opted for the classic a hundred years hence.

In early August Mr. Churchill called at Naples on his way to Athens. From there, after disposing of business, he gave news of his doings. 'We have had a pleasant journey so far, though we had one rough night and I was very seasick. I am now better, and am, I think, getting accustomed to the less devilish forms of motion attendant upon marine adventure. You will be glad to hear that I visited the Monte Carlo Gambling Hell on four occasions and took away from them altogether upwards of £160.' At the end of the month Marsh wrote to Lady Gladstone before leaving for his own holiday in Italy. He had spent a week-end at Rousley with Julian and Billy Grenfell, and the Duchess of Rutland had drawn portraits of her guests. 'The Duchess did an extraordinarily good drawing of me in about 2 hours, just flattering enough to please me mightily, without being ridiculous.'[1]

He was back from Italy in October and going to the Follies with Rupert Brooke. This gave him an idea for his next letter to Pretoria.

There is a story that I want so much to send to the Follies. It is of a man who saved someone from drowning—a friend meets him and

[1] See illustration facing p. 96.

says, 'Oh, do tell me all about it'—'Oh,' says the hero, 'it was quite simple—I just swam out to him, turned him over to make sure he wasn't Lloyd George, and brought him back'—only I could never confess to Winston that I had sent it to Pelissier!

When Roger Fry gave his first exhibition of Post-Impressionist painters at the Grafton Gallery early in November Marsh's guest at the Private View was E. M. Forster. A recent letter of his had contained an unconventional request.

> I wish you would walk outside Sidgwick and Jackson's offices shouting nonchalantly 'Short stories are what *we* want'. They are considering mine, and even nibbling, but oh so feebly, and I am afraid that only those to which we refer as 'of a metaphysical nature' will be published. . . . If you love me do not telephone, as if I am in you will be talking to an imbecile, and if I am out the underpaid menials will muddle the message.

After the Private View Forster stayed the night at Gray's Inn and then wrote: 'Gauguin and Van Gogh were too much for me.' He had noticed that all round the gallery people were bursting into peals of laughter. Forster was just about to publish his third novel, *Howard's End*. When it came out shortly before Christmas Marsh hastened to send a copy to Gosse. This new work had convinced him that young Forster was one of the novelists of the future, and he counted on Gosse for an encouraging review. The quarrel with Gosse was over, but this time it was Marsh who took umbrage, for Gosse read the new book and would have none of it: 'I hardly remember such another disappointment,' and he cast a critical sidelong glance at what he must have suspected was Marsh's influence. 'I think it is due to the author's having listened to the people who (may have) said that he should give more "story" and that he should be coarse in morals and that he should coruscate in style. . . . I am now going to read a few chapters of Mrs. Gaskell to take the taste of *Howard's End* out of my mouth.'[1] The next budget to Lady Gladstone not only recommended the latest books but gave news of a new and happier stage in the Women's Suffrage quarrel. 'By the way Winston and Victor met at a dinner-party in Downing Street (I think the Asquiths had forgotten about the row). I'm thankful to say they shook hands and passed the time of day—I was so afraid they would cut each

[1] This letter is printed in full in *The Life and Letters of Sir Edmund Gosse* by Evan Charteris.

other—of course they will never really forgive each other, but it would have been beastly if they couldn't have met. . . . There are some good new books—especially a gloriously long Arnold Bennett called *Clayhanger*—and a very interesting curious and amusing book by a little friend of mine, Forster, called *Howard's End.*'

While he was still awaiting Forster's reviews with some anxiety there were developments at Whitehall that warranted his writing again.

We've been up to our necks in work at the Home Office mainly over the Shops Bill, which is intensely interesting. We are working on the old Bill and seeing about 3 deputations every day, getting the most thrilling revelations about 'how the poor live'. Did you know about it when you were at the H.O.? Winston is afraid he'll have to give up the universal ½ holiday by closing shops, and have a ½ holiday for shop assistants instead—the schedules of exemption will have to be changed a good deal, and he is trying to think of some way to make it easier for local opinion to get its way about early closing, otherwise I don't think there will be any very great changes—what a difference it will make to all the counterjumpers—it really is one of the things that are worth doing.

The Reformatory School scandal is giving a good deal of trouble —the Master's intentions and in a way his results, seem to have been good—but his methods were certainly brutal—I don't know yet how it will end as Charlie Masterman is still enquiring. He and I and Winston spent an amusing afternoon birching each other with the 'sealed pattern' birches, to see if they hurt. They didn't! but it will be awful if there is a birching scandal at the H.O. 'Brutal cruelty of a Minister to his Private Secretary'—or vice versa—I don't know which way they'll get hold of it.

When next he wrote, January 5, 1911, another General Election had passed and the nine-days-wonder of Sidney Street. A telephone call to the Home Office had given the news that a group of anarchists were firing on the police from a house in Stepney. Mr. Churchill could no more refrain from a personal visit to the scene of action than his Private Secretary could resist the invitation to accompany him. When the house caught fire and the Home Secretary ordered the fire brigade to take no action he laid himself open to criticism, and Press photographs of him in his top hat, directing operations, with Marsh standing at his side in a doorway which offered a meagre shelter from a rain of bullets, while orders were being passed to a couple of armed policemen and a detachment of Scots Guards, were thought to be gravely wanting in dignity. The technicians of a primitive species of newsreel were also quick to seize their opportunity, and at the Biograph Exhibition at the Palace Theatre Marsh was astonished to find himself exhibited in close-up, a spectacle greeted with howls of execration from the audience. Nevertheless he spent a quiet Christmas at Knebworth, and on January 5 (1911) he began his letter with an apology.

I was very good about writing till the Election, which sent everything to the winds, and me to the whirlwinds—really two elections with Winston in one year are more than enough for an ordinary young man—though if anyone could get accustomed to them I ought— this was my *fifth* in five years, I wish Baron de Forest would give a prize for the Private Secretary who has done most Elections in five years, instead of for such a tame feat as flying to Belgium. This time however I had a piece of luck that made up for many minor discomforts, did you see in the newspapers the ridiculous bets the Tories were making on the Stock Exchange? I got one on the terms that I should make a £1 for every seat in the Govt majority above 60, and lose one for every seat below—result, a chubby little cheque for £66 just in time to help me out with my Christmas and wedding presents and boxes.

I think the result was quite satisfactory from the political point of view too, though of course it would have been jolly to win a few seats. Winston is almost frightened at the strength of the Govt's position and the cloudlessness of the horizon, he thinks it too good to be true and that there almost must be some fearful invisible reef ahead, we shall soon see! The Tories are very unhappy, as they deserve to be after the reckless folly with which they played their cards. This is the first time I have really been a Liberal! as I think the Govt policy promises to be so much more sensible, moderate, and conservative than theirs.

I feel I ought to be able to make a good story of the siege of the Hounsditch murderers which I went to with Winston on Tuesday— but I find I can't cope with the newspapers. You can't imagine the extraordinary sensation it was to see a fusillade going on in a dim little London street—and still more to see the fire brigade standing by encouraging the burning house to burn. The murderers were wild beasts, there was no being sorry for them—though I'm glad to believe they weren't burnt to death, but shot themselves or were shot before. I expect Winston will bring in a pistol Bill, which seems a better way of dealing with the crux than trying to stiffen up the Aliens Act. The criminal aliens seem to be just the ones who have the money.

On the 18th he sent a second instalment on the affair.

I'm on the biograph, where I make a most gratifying appearance as almost the central figure of 'Mr. Churchill directing the operations', at the Palace, which is nightly received with unanimous boos and shouts of 'shoot him' from the gallery—why are London music-hall audiences so uniformly and so bigotedly Tory? you would have thought a stray Liberal must occasionally find his way in by accident—but it seems not. I didn't like to lead a counter-demonstration, which might have seemed egotistical—but I was so delighted to see myself skimming about with the ethereal fluttering grace which the biograph lends to human motion, that if I had given way to my instinct to applaud I feel I should 'literally have brought down the house'.

The truth is I'm getting bored to death with 'Sidney St.'—I wonder if you have been much exercised about it in S. Africa. I never remember a subject holding the town for so long together— there can't have been a meal in London for the last fortnight where it hasn't been the principal conversational course. I think the tide of opinion has now decisively turned in favour of the police and the Home Office. I went with Winston today to the Coroner's Court, where his evidence made a great impression on the jury—the verdict was everything that could be wished, and I expect it will practically squash criticism. By the way I hope you *are* interested in the affair—otherwise this will bore you sadly, but it's impossible to believe that anyone is thinking of anything else. We have a 'criminal aliens' Bill on the stocks and have been discussing it this afternoon. It is settled that the Home Secretary is to have the power in future to expel any alien convicted of a crime which under the present law gives the Courts power—which as you know they don't exert nearly enough—to expel him, and there is a provision for expelling aliens who are going to commit crimes before they commit them—but this is very difficult to draft and it isn't settled yet how it is to be managed. There is also to be something to prevent their having pistols, but this is also difficult—Thring has drafted a clause on which the Prime Minister's criticism was that if Sargent went out rook-shooting with a friend, and forgot to take out a licence, the police could go and rummage in his studio, find the box out of which he had taken his cartridges, and pack him off to America next day—of course this must be prevented by all means.

The next excitement was a visit with Wilfrid Blunt and Neville

Lytton to a prize fight. 'It was a horrible experience', so he turned to Parliament and the ballroom.

> Winston has made two quite excellent speeches, one on Home Rule and the other on the Parlt Bill. The best thing that has been said in the House was by Hugh Cecil—I haven't seen the newspapers so I'll risk your having heard it. That the P.M. if he had any Tempting to do, would be much too clever to take the form of a Serpent—he would do it as a retired Archangel of moderately progressive views. Very good, don't you think?
>
> I went to a ball last night, contrary to my new system of life, which is, not to go to balls. It was Lady Agnew's, in a *very* pretty house that Blow has built for her in Smith Square—the only thing I don't like is that the ceilings are painted blue to imitate the sky! It was a good ball, every sort of person there. Bridget Colebrooke gets lovelier and lovelier—I think without doubt she is the great beauty of nowadays—Diana Manners wasn't there to compare her with—wouldn't they be a wonderful couple as Day and Night?

After the Easter recess he found to his surprise that pressure of work was beginning to try his patience. 'The worst thing the Government has done is making Parliament meet again on Easter Tuesday after adjourning on Good Wednesday. My only comfort is that they will all kill themselves. The solution I foresee for the Constitutional difficulty is that the entire House of Commons will either go mad or die, thus leaving the House of Lords supreme.' He had spent Easter as a guest of the Sheffields at Holyhead.

> It is very eccentric to get out at Holyhead and not go on to Dublin —the porters won't believe that one really wants one's baggage! Winston and Clemmie were there. Winston lay in bed all the morning, and played Attaque with Venetia Montagu all the rest of the day, except when he was digging on the sands. That is what he likes best in the world—not digging in the usual way to make castles or mudpies, but to make dams and irrigation works. It was rather a shame that it got about, and he had to give it up because the cliffs were lined with people looking at him through opera-glasses. I played all the golf I could, and I did think I was conscious of a slight improvement.
>
> The thing that has amused me most today was in the *Daily Mirror*, which had a photograph of a little boy whose mother ties him to a telegraph post to prevent his getting run over. The *Mirror* interviewed a 'well-known motorist' on the subject who said quite seriously, 'The public little know what an anxiety children are to motorists. In my opinion they ought *all* to be chained up'!

A few weeks before this he had received auspicious news from Rupert Brooke, who was in Florence looking after an aged god-father, the Greek scholar Robert Whitelaw. For the first time in his correspondence Brooke showed signs of serious ambition to be a poet.

I spent two months [in Munich] over a poem that describes the feelings of a fish, in the metre of *L'Allegro*. It was meant to be a lyric, but has turned into a work of 76 lines with a moral end. It is quite unintelligible. Beyond that I have written one or two severe and subtle sonnets in my most modern manner—descriptions of very poignant and complicated situations in the life of today, thrilling with a false simplicity. The one beginning

I did not think you thought I knew you knew

has caused a sensation in English-speaking circles in Munich.

His experiences in Munich had revolutionized his politics. He now felt that German culture 'must never, never prevail! The Germans are nice and well-meaning and they try, but they are SOFT.' He was homesick for Grantchester, and on his return was going to move into the house almost next door, which was called The Old Vicarage. There, at the end of July, Marsh paid his first visit to the new home, having followed Brooke's instructions to come in 'primitive' clothes. 'One talks eight hours, reads eight, and sleeps eight,' he wrote. 'The food is simple and extremely unwholesome.'

Marsh returned from Grantchester to learn that the Germans had despatched a gunboat to the harbour of Agadir in Morocco, a provocative act which caused a redeployment of forces in the Cabinet. Winston Churchill was turning his thoughts to international affairs. The next letter abroad was dated September 15.

What a year we are having! it was amusing to find you wondering whether 50 peers would be created—when between your writing and my reading it had been absolutely touch and go whether we should have 500 or not. The debate was by far the most exciting thing of the kind there has ever been—that and the division—as nobody could have the slightest idea what would happen. G. Wyndham betted Winston that evening 4 to 5 on their throwing out the Bill! I am so glad it happened just when it did, so that the fun wasn't wasted—for next week it was all entirely forgotten and swallowed up in the strike. One day Sir Edward Grey said to Winston, 'What a remarkable year this has been—the Coronation—the great heat—

the strikes—and now the foreign situation'—'Why,' said Winston, 'you've forgotten the Parliament Bill'—and so he had—and so had everybody.

Well, we are not out of the wood yet. True, the Coronation is over, and so is the great heat (for the moment—since three or four days ago) but there *may* be another railway strike at any moment (though I hardly think there will) and there almost certainly *will* be a coal strike in October, and what that will mean no one can realize. But everything sinks into nothing compared with the great question —will there or will there not be a war? No one knows—but it looks very bad, and if the Germans *want* a war, there will be one—not otherwise. All accounts of the French Army are very good, and unless the Germans win in a month or so nobody can see how their finance is to hold out—so let's hope that if they try it on they'll be beat! I believe they didn't mean war to start with and that it is all bluff to get a patriotic vote at the elections—but that kind of thing may lead people further than they intend.

If there is *certain* to be a war some day, I suppose we may as well get it over now—but the idea is so ghastly that I feel like Mr. Micawber that if it is staved off this time something may turn up!

I have no gossip at all as I've hardly seen anyone that *is* anyone, for about a month. I went to Pamela at Broadstairs for three days, with Winston and Clemmie at an hotel—which was fun—did you see in the newspaper about W. building sand-forts? which he did quite wonderfully—'on Vauban's first system' as he proudly said. I wonder if the Germans heard that the Home Secretary was spending his holiday in personally fortifying the South Coast!

It was now apparent that although the War Office under Haldane had drawn up minutely detailed plans for the assembly and transport to the coast of an Expeditionary Force the Admiralty had no complementary scheme for its conveyance to France. With this among other major tasks before him, including the creation of a Naval War Staff, Mr. Churchill took office in October as First Lord of the Admiralty, and Marsh, who once more accompanied him in his progress, found he now had a naval colleague, Flag Officer David Beatty, who was to win renown in action at Jutland.

After a silence of several weeks he wrote to Lady Gladstone on November 30.

I have no excuse except a very good one, that I have been frightfully hard at work here ever since we came, Winston stays till at least 8 every day. . . . So all the usual writing times have been cut off. Even Sundays are no longer my own, as I have spent 3 out of the last 4 in the *Enchantress*. We have made a new commandment, 'The seventh day is the Sabbath of the First Lord, on it thou shalt do all manner of work.'

It is very obliging of you to think that Winston was taken away from the Home Office because he was making a mess of it! Quite the contrary. He had done himself no end of good by his dealings with the strike—and in fact become quite the National Hero—The Office was most depressed at losing him—he had of course annoyed some of the people at first, but I think everyone (including especially Brackwell) had got to like him—Froup had from the first, and more and more—and the King was more than pleased with him. The only reason for the change was, honestly, that the war scare had brought out the importance of the Admiralty more strongly than ever, and the P.M. and some of the important people in the Cabinet thought that the strongest possible man should come here—(I don't say this merely because I am W.'s young man, it's the diamond truth). The offer came as the greatest surprise to Winston—McKenna,[1] between ourselves, was terribly annoyed—but before the change was actually made he had found out that it wasn't W.'s own doing, so they are quite friends now. I don't know why McK. should have minded so very much, as he admitted that he had wanted to leave the Admiralty anyhow early next year, and specially wished for the H.O. I hear he is settling down there very well, and Froup tells me he is quite happy with him, though before it happened he looked on the change with consternation.

Winston is doing very well here, and strange to say he is becoming the idol of the Tory party. The sailors seem to like him very much— he has completely changed his character in some ways and has come out with a brand new set of perfect manners and a high standard of punctuality. Everyone seems honestly anxious to 'give him a chance' and the Service take a real pleasure in having for once a 'fighting man'—(in the sense of one who has actually seen war) as 1st Lord. Clemmie is of course a great asset, she is perfect in her part, and has suddenly become prettier than ever.

I'm very much disappointed at the dropping of nearly all the Shops Bill—it was settled yesterday that we could only have a Friday for it, so it has all been chucked except the ½ holiday, the mealtimes and perhaps the machinery for making voluntary closing easier. It's very sad, after all the trouble that has been taken over it—and I'm afraid poor Kipps and Mr. Polly will have to wait some time now

[1] Reginald McKenna, First Lord of the Admiralty, then Home Secretary.

before they get their 60 hours week. I haven't time to follow the Insurance Bill, it seems rather a hydra but most people seem to agree that it will all come right when it has been going for a year or two—and I don't suppose there will be an election before then!

The winter of 1911, which brought Marsh to the most responsible position of his public career, was important for two other events of such moment in his private life that in conjunction with his move to the Admiralty they amounted to a new beginning.

On December 4 Rupert Brooke brought out *Poems*, the only volume he was to publish in his lifetime. Now and again Marsh had been shown his contributions to the *Westminster Gazette*, but this collection came as a revelation. He realized his friend was a poet who must be taken seriously. On December 11 he wrote to the Old Vicarage, where Brooke was writing the dissertation on John Webster which was to win him a Fellowship at King's.

I've been living on your book since I got it a few days ago, and I must write and tell you. . . . I had always in trembling hope reposed that I should like the poems, but at my wildest I never looked forward to such magnificence. You have brought back into English poetry the rapturous beautiful grotesque of the 17th century. Marvell would have loved *Dust* and *Mummia* and Crashaw the *Shape of the Human Body* with its lovely ending following so naturally on that list of delicious absurdities. The fishy part of *The Fish* is as good as the prelude to the *Rheingold* (I rather wish the last two sections away, perhaps only because I'm not sure what they mean). The last three verses of *Town and Country* are superb, and the whole of *Dining-room Tea*, which I think is bracketed with *Dust*. I never read anything more attractive than the Queen and Tragic Lady song, and the *Jolly Company* ought to jump straight into every anthology. I am glad for the sake of the delightful title that you didn't find out what Ambarvalia[1] meant till too late (on the other hand you might have been saved from a rhyme[2] which might perhaps have been committed by Mrs. Browning, indulging in her art that licentious element which she so sternly repressed in her conduct—but by no one else). There are two lines[3] in that poem which might adorn *The Ancient Mariner*. . . . However I can't go on giving a list of all my favourites, I must just put in a good word for *Dead Men's Love* and then go on to a little abuse.

[1] *Lines written in the Belief that the Ancient Roman Festival of the Dead was called Ambarvalia.*
[2] 'star' and 'Ambarvalia'.
[3] And the air lies still about the hill
    With the first fear of night.

The Channel Passage is so clever and amusing that in spite of a prejudice in favour of poetry that I can read at meals I can't wish it away—but at the risk of your thinking me an awful borjois (as the man says in St. John Lucas's story) I must protest against the 'smell' line in *Libido* . . . there are some things too disgusting to write about, especially in one's own language. I wonder you didn't call *Dining-room Tea* 'pump-shipping in the drawing-room' and write 'the p' instead of 'the tea' hung in the air in amber stream. Surely the idea of the poem would have fitted in quite as well. Yet I'm sure you prefer it as it is (I hope this makes you very angry).

He went on to smaller details. 'I'm critical of your resolved feet [in the anapaests] and altogether I think you're rather free with them.' He concluded with, 'Well, Rupert, I think it's a splendid book, and I *am* glad you've written it', then referred briefly to the other main event of the month—'I've bought a delightful picture at Carfax by Duncan Grant, and one or two others,—how I'm to pay for them I don't know.' Brooke answered from Rugby on December 22. 'Your letter gave me great joy. It was very good of you to write. I horribly feel that degrading ecstasy that I have always despised in parents whose shapeless offspring are praised for beauty.' Several of his friends only admired the earlier poems, which depressed him.

I hobnob vaguely with them over the promising verses of a young poet, called Rupert Brooke, who died in 1908. But I'm so much more concerned with the living, who don't interest them. God, it's so cheering to find someone who likes the modern stuff, and appreciates what one's at. You can't think how your remarks and liking thrilled me. You seemed both in your classing of them and when you got to details to agree so closely with what I felt about them (only, of course, I often feel doubtful about their relative value to other poetry) that I knew you understood what they meant. It sounds a poor compliment—or else a queer conceitedness—to remark on your understanding them; but it's really been rather a shock to me, and made me momentarily hopeless, that so many intelligent and well-tasted people didn't seem to have any idea what I was driving at—in any poem of the last years. It opened my eyes to the fact that people who like poetry are barely more common than people who like pictures.

I'm (of course) unrepentant about the 'unpleasant' poems. I don't claim great merit for *The Channel Passage;* but the point of it was (or should have been!) 'serious'. There are common and sordid things

—situations or details—that may suddenly bring all Tragedy, or at least the brutality of actual emotions, to you. I rather grasp relievedly at them, after I've beaten vain hands in the rosy mists of poets' experiences. Lear's button and Hilda Lessways turning the gas suddenly on, and—but you know more of them than I.... And the emotions of a seasick lover seem to me at least as poignant as those of the hero who has 'brain-fever' . . . The 'smell' business I don't really understand. Four hundred poems are written every year which end 'the wondrous fragrance of your hair' and nobody objects. People *do* smell other people, as well as see and feel and hear them. I do, and I'm not disgusted to think so. . . . (Your suggestion for the recasting of *Dining-room Tea* shall receive consideration when I'm preparing the second edition!)

He neglected none of Marsh's minor points. 'I rather agree about one of the anapaests you pick out. . . . I was trying consciously to write on a much looser and more happy-go-lucky, Anglo-Saxon basis—like Lascelles Abercrombie.[1]' He ended by saying he was going 'to do scraps, reviewing, etc.'

I suppose you don't edit a magazine? I might review Elizabethan books at some length for the *Admiralty Gazette* or T.A.T. (Tattle amongst Tars) or whatever journal you officially produce? at least I hope you'll issue an order to include my poems in the library of all submarines.

In the public Press Edward Thomas (*Daily Chronicle*) foretold a poetic future for the author of this first book, but he was brief and guarded. Marsh had no doubts and was unstinted in his encouragement. It drew him closer to Brooke, and their common enthusiasm was the foundation of *Georgian Poetry*.

In the same week as Brooke's poems had come out Robert Ross asked Eddie Marsh to look in on an exhibition by young painters at the Carfax Gallery. For once he went alone, and the painting by Duncan Grant caught his eye. It was a Still Life of six tulips in a glass vase. He had never before bought the work of an artist who was not already established in reputation, and he did not realize that by including *Parrot Tulips* among his purchases he was opening a new chapter in his life no less important to himself and the world of painting than his encouragement of Brooke in the sphere of poetry. In an access of pride and excitement, and without the slightest suspicion of what it would lead to, he wrote and

---

[1] This would refer to Abercrombie's first book, *Interludes and Poems* (1908).

asked Neville Lytton to call at the Gallery and have a look at his acquisitions. Lytton wrote on December 17.

> I went to see your purchases from the Camden Town group and I quite see the point of the picture of the people leaning over the pier (Walter Bayes, is it not?) though it is not my style of picture, but I liked even better the picture next to it of a crowd on a shore; but I really must protest against the Tulips.
>
> It is a disgraceful picture. It has neither colour, drawing, nor composition. Its technique is atrocious and it is incompetent beyond measure. I hesitate to say thus all that I think because I am fully aware that you are the kindest and best patron that I have ever had or probably shall have. But think of the effect your choice will have on the young men that you are just taking up, such as Wyndham Tryon and Seabrooke. As a well-known collector and encourager of modern Art you have a responsibility, and I repeat that the Tulips are a *disgrace*. I quite understand that you should give the classic a rest and buy samples of romantic artists, but this is not art at all. Forgive my rudeness.

Elliott Seabrooke was staying at Raymond Buildings off and on during these weeks, and he may have been partly responsible for opening Marsh's eyes to the work of his contemporaries. In January Marsh sent him Lytton's letter, and he replied, 'I do think he's being very blind about your excellent tulip', and offered to try and persuade Lytton to think again, for Marsh had begun to fear that one of his oldest friendships hung in the balance. Seabrooke urged Lytton to write again in more moderate terms. Lytton readily obliged, but withdrew nothing of his former letter. 'There is nothing personal in my criticism of Duncan Grant's Tulip,' he wrote, 'and indeed I have seen some of his work at the New English that I have thought promising, and I have told Wyndham [Tryon] to let me know all about him . . . from all accounts he seems to be a very serious young man, and I am sure that he will recover from the Tulip before long.' Henceforth Eddie Marsh would have to look elsewhere for companionship and advice in picture-galleries. He was now determined to justify his opinion by making himself an authority on the new movement in Art. By the new year 1912 he had begun in a small way his great mission among poets and painters, but his relationship with Neville Lytton was damaged for good.

Chapter Nine

GEORGIAN
(January 1912–May 1913)

THROUGH the early months of 1912 the new First Lord was making constant visits to the naval units in home waters, and Marsh was often with him on board the *Enchantress*, the Admiralty yacht which was used exclusively for Mr. Churchill's tours of inspection. Not the least of Marsh's responsibilities was his function as unofficial liaison between the First Lord and Admiral Fisher, at present in retirement, who had taken him into his confidence and was counting on him to second his letters to Mr. Churchill with verbal support. At first the main topic in their correspondence was the making of new appointments in the rapidly expanding Navy. A note from Lord Fisher on February 2 shows that so far Marsh's efforts as an intermediary had been successful. 'My beloved Marsh, Heaven bless you and the Prime Minister and every other damned soul.' Later in the year Marsh was a guest at Kilverstone Hall, Norfolk, where Fisher succeeded in engaging his support in his campaign for the introduction of oil fuel, which was soon to revolutionize the Navy. 'You will just love the river here and the roses and the cook' was Fisher's inducement for the week-end. By October the oil question had become urgent, and on October 4 Fisher sent Marsh a memorandum *A New Navy: Why Coal Must Go, Why the Internal Combustion Engine is Vital* and supported it with a characteristically fervent note.

The enclosed written for some of our faltering colleagues may amuse you. Don't send it to the *Daily Mail*. It's written *currente calamo* as you will observe. On Nov. 26, 1910, every newspaper in America reported at length my words that the nation which first adopted Internal Combustion Propulsion would sweep the board commercially as well as pugnaciously! And I told them I had so said more than 10 years previously—not a single English newspaper put it in their columns except W. T. Stead in the *Review of Reviews* at the same time that I told them I had dined *tête à tête* with Woodrow

Wilson the night before (Nov. 25, 1910) and that he would be the new President.

Both events are coming true! The British Admiralty is going to see a German battle-cruiser going round the Earth without refuelling in 18 months from now, and all our wonderful marine engineers are simply servile copyists of a damned skunk called Diesel! and we haven't got a workman or a metallurgist who is capable to produce anything approaching the foreign article—I am going to become a naturalized Jew and go to Palestine as I think the end of the world must be near and the last trump begins there and I want to get in first somewhere!

Yours always,
FISHER

His more customary style of conclusion was 'Yours till charcoal sprouts'. By November 26 the matter of the new commissions was no longer developing as he wished. 'What does X's appointment to the Admiralty mean? What's he going to do? Can you tell me? He's a slimy sneak if ever one existed! Do let us keep clear of pimps and parasites.' It was at this juncture that Fisher retired to Naples like Achilles to his tent and did not relent until the Prime Minister and the First Lord with Marsh in attendance had followed him to Italy in the *Enchantress* and persuaded him to return. But he was no easy collaborator. On April 29, 1913, the fuel problem was too behindhand for his peace of mind. 'I don't want to make Winston's blood boil but really the procrastination in coming to terms about oil with the Californian man is *quite* DAMNABLE!' By contrast a brief minute of July 28 showed satisfaction on another issue. 'Mind Winston sticks to Jellicoe! I say that in every letter!'

While these affairs of moment (the expansion, manning, and modernization of the Navy with no time to lose) were engrossing Marsh's thoughts at Westminster, new friends were coming into his private life. Neville Lytton introduced him to George Mallory, a schoolmaster at Charterhouse (one day to become the hero of Mount Everest) who was engaged in writing a book on Boswell and wanted help in research.[1] It was many years since Marsh had acted as book doctor for Sickert's *Helen*. His work on Mallory's behalf (somehow he found time to make researches in the British Museum) revived his interest in the checking of proofs, and from

---

[1] *Boswell, the Biographer*, by George Leigh Mallory (Smith, Elder, 1912).

now on his table was seldom for long without its serpentine coils
of galleys. But for the importance of its consequences no social
occasion in these months can take pride of place before the
luncheon-party of January 29 (1912) at 3 Stanhope Street where
among the guests of Mrs. Hart-Davis, the elder sister of Duff
Cooper, was Francis Meynell.

Meynell was a friend of Harold Monro, who edited the *Poetry
Review*. Hearing Marsh enlarge on the merits of Brooke's poems,
he suggested that an article in the *Poetry Review* might reach a
greater number of readers than ordinary advertisement in the
publisher's list. If Marsh were agreeable to writing such an article
Meynell would put the editor in touch with him. The letter from
Monro which first brought together the future publisher and
editor of *Georgian Poetry* was dated February 6.

> DEAR SIR,
> Meynell tells me that you are enthusiastic about Rupert Brooke's
> poems, and that you have told him you are willing to write a review
> of them for the April issue of this paper. I want to make this the
> principal review, and the only one *signed*. . . . You will understand
> that when one book is selected for special attention in this way the
> article on it shall be rather in the nature of an appreciation than a
> criticism.

The article elaborated the points already made in his private
letter to Brooke and appeared in the April issue of the *Poetry
Review*. He was at Portsmouth with Mr. Churchill while Monro's
letter lay on his table at home, but he had not waited for the
official invitation. While still with the Fleet he wrote to Brooke
in Munich on February 4. By then he had already made a rough
draft.

> MY DEAR RUPERT,
> I wonder what you will think of this. Did you ever hear of the
> *Poetry Review?* I believe up till now it has been called something else,
> but anyhow it is the organ of the 'Poetry Reciters'—I am afraid it
> is rather an absurd publication—in the number I have seen there
> was an article beginning 'Let it be conceded at once, without cavil,
> that Mr. Ezra Pound's trumpet sounds the authentic note'[1] but it is
> beautifully printed, and I am told it has a circulation of 4,000
> copies! Francis Meynell told me the other day that the editor,

---

[1] Brooke had published a favourable review of Pound's *Personae* in the *Cambridge Review* of December 2, 1910.

Harold Munro (?), had a great opinion of your book, and wanted
to do you well—but as it is his daily business to compose panegyrics
he was afraid that if he wrote about you himself the readers would
only think it was the usual sort of thing, and pay no attention. (I
must say this is a very decent attitude.) The long and the short was,
that the pages of the *Review* were open to me! I was rather frightened,
never having written a line of any sort since I left Cambridge—but
anyhow, I thought, I can do better than say that Mr. Brooke's
trumpet sounds the authentic note—and I *might* be able to give you
a leg up—so I consented. I finished my lucubration today, and have
just sent it to be typewritten; so when it comes back I will put in a
copy with this, as it won't come out till April. At this moment I am
rather pleased with it, and I hope that on the whole you will like it
—and above all that it may induce some of the 4,000 to purchase.
I must say, my dear, that the more I study your poetry the more I
like it. I showed the book on Friday to Edmund Gosse and Austin
Dobson—and I was really delighted with their reception of it. E.G.
read a lot of it out loud, with every grace of diction—and after about
three poems said 'I declare *contra mundum* that he is a poet' and that
you were far the most interesting of the new people I had introduced to him (others were James Stephens, Frances Cornford, etc.
—both of which he liked very much). His special fancy, out of the
½ dozen or so he read, was for *Dust* and *The Fish*. I've since sent the
book to both. Austin Dobson, though less demonstrative and more
diffident of his critical powers, seemed almost as much pleased.
They asked me to convey to you the admiration of two elderly
poetasters. (By the way, Rupert dear, if you meet Gosse I beg you
for my sake to be nice to him—also he is a good backer and may be
useful to you! and a little kindness does wonders with him.) I steered
them clear of the ugly poems, but found to my surprise that they took
great exception to *Dead Men's Love* which I thought quite safe. They
took it as an out-pouring of youthful contempt on the love affairs of
persons past a certain age—and seemed to think you cast aspersions
on their own powers of——! I had not taken the poem in that sense
at all, and thought that when you said the scene was in Hell you
had meant it—and had imagined a kind of hell in which the tragedy
was to think one was alive and find that one wasn't. Which is right?
They wouldn't hear of my interpretation, so I said I would ask you.
Please answer as to this.

I was delighted to hear rather vaguely that you are now bursting
with health and had been revelling in the Riviera—I had a dismal
picture of you in my mind, broken and prematurely aged by excess
of milk and honey diet, mooning disconsolate in a depressing cosmopolitan watering-place. (The Riviera is the one goal of travel

against which I have an instinctive prejudice, and I can scarcely imagine you happy there.) It is splendid if you are really all right again and enjoying life. London has been rather exciting lately. I am pro-Reinhardt, with insignificant reservations—and this manipulation of large crowds seems to me perhaps the dawn of a new art. Perhaps on the other hand it will pall with repetition—the physical thrill that it gives is practically the same in *Oedipus* as in *The Miracle* —and the second time I saw *Oedipus* I was quite unmoved. *The Miracle* wears better—only time can show whether it is a mere sensation or a real enhancement of the drama. Meanwhile I am sorry you are missing the fun—Galsworthy's new play is an extremely good entertainment[1]—too good, it sent me away thoroughly pleased, but without any of that burning zeal for social improvement which I have hitherto felt for at least $\frac{1}{2}$ an hour after seeing one of his plays. The fact is that for fear of nullifying the effect of his play by dullness, he has made both his wastrel and his benefactor such fantastic and amusing characters that one forgets to be anything except amused. His appropriate punishment for this lapse from austerity is that the theatre is empty. I went to the third night, and I must say it provoked me to find that in the whole of London there are not enough people with sufficient curiosity to fill the theatre more than $\frac{1}{2}$ full for even three nights of a play by a man who is admittedly one of our first dramatists.

He recommended Compton Mackenzie's *Carnival*[2] and ended: 'I'm going to Belfast with Winston this week. Wait and see if I am killed, and if not write me a long letter.' The grave controversy over Mr. Asquith's Home Rule Bill for Ireland occasioned this flying visit to Belfast. E. M. Forster was already there. 'Do look us up if you have time,' Forster had written, 'bandages will be provided.' Many years after he recalled the occasion.

Our oddest meeting was in a Belfast hotel, in the midst of a raging anti-Churchill mob. The lift descended into the lounge—there was a rush at it, but out got a slim figure who advanced toward me saying, 'Have you read Wupert's [*sic*] new poem?' All Ulster retired.[3]

Later in the month Marsh wrote to Galsworthy, having heard that his play *The Pigeon* was coming off.

---

[1] *The Pigeon.*

[2] Marsh's recommendation of this novel led to Brooke's entering a competition in the *Saturday Westminster* for a review of the best recent work of fiction. It was awarded second prize (June 8, 1912) and it was largely responsible for his being sent by this paper to America.

[3] Letter to the author, April 7, 1954.

I can't resist writing to you to express my—well, indignation is not too strong a word—that there should be so few people in London to show appreciation of such an interesting and delightful work. In consideration of the excellent entertainment which with so much lightness of hand you have provided from beginning to end I should have thought that the public which 'goes to be amused' would have condoned the originality of your scheme, and even the beauty of the central figure! Besides everyone is supposed to like good acting, and you have given the company magnificent opportunities.

But before this, on the 12th, he had tried to enlist the support of Robert Bridges in his campaign for Brooke's recognition.

Would you look at a few of the poems in the book I am sending? It is by a very great friend of mine, about two years down from Cambridge (he is trying for a fellowship at King's with a dissertation on Webster about whom he has found out some interesting things— the tragic poet, not the American statesman and not the Dictionary!). I think he has such a great talent that I feel almost justified in asking you to take an interest in his work. If you have time to read it I beg you to begin with *Dust*, *The Fish*, *Town and Country*, and *Dining-room Tea*. My reason for making myself your cicerone is that he has printed some violent and disagreeable poems which if you chanced on them first would be sure to prejudice you against him! while if you come on them after reading the good ones I hope you may look on them as pardonable sins of youth.

A month had passed since Brooke received the draft of Marsh's review. He wrote at last from Rugby to say that work on his dissertation and other nervous strains had brought on a break-down. The doctor had said he was in a 'seriously introspective condition', and he had lost a stone in weight. 'Your letter and review gave me immense and slightly pink-cheeked pleasure. It is absurdly kind of you to face the terrors and pangs of parturition (at, you report, so advanced an age for a first confinement!) for me.' Either hidden genius, he said, or his studies of the masters of English—'me, and Trollope, and Crashaw, and the rest'—had given Marsh a practised wit and a clarity of style that would put the other reviewers to shame. As for his praise he felt 'passionately in agreement with it'. He went on to discuss *Dining-room Tea*, in which Marsh had felt the need of a central figure. Of Gosse he confessed respect in spite of 'an almost irresistible tendency to despise and hate anyone who was writing about Eng. Lit. before

1890. . . . Does he think my Muse one of those "decaying Maenads in a throng" who shout "a stumbling and indecent song" that I seem to remember he recently wrote about?' And on the poem *Dead Men's Love* his comment was: 'You're entirely right as to the meaning of it, in all ordinary meanings of the word meaning . . . a poem is essentially, I take it, tended by millions of strange shadows, just as poor Mr. W. H. was, and I'll not deny this was one of the shadows.'

'I'm so glad you liked my review,' Marsh replied. 'I hope the Virgin Mary was half as nice to Mrs. Zachariah about the birth of John the Baptist.' He withdrew his criticism of *Dining-room Tea.* 'I'm not sure that it wouldn't be better if you *had* meant what I thought—my feeling is that the group (as you put it) would be the better for a centre, still . . . you have a right to mean what you like and what, indeed, you say. As for *Town and Country* you have distinctly said what you do *not* mean.' This kind of objection was characteristic of Marsh. The letter ended: 'I should like to know if it would be too exciting for you or too depressing (you can *think* whichever you like, but please *say* too exciting) if I came and put up at the Rugby Inn for a Sunday?' Marsh went on the 23rd and took with him an album intended as an address book which Lady Diana Manners had given him for his last birthday. It was one day to contain poems in manuscript by almost all the poets of his time. On the 24th, after a country walk, Brooke copied into it his sonnet 'Oh Death shall find me long before I tire'. Almost exactly a year later Brooke sat beside Flecker after one of Mrs. Elgy's dinners at Raymond Buildings and watched him copying out into what was called *The Little Book* the serenade to Yasmin from his unfinished *Hassan.*

Marsh was beginning to see more of Hugh Walpole this spring, and his first letter, arising from the novel *Prelude to Adventure* (and a failure to keep an appointment) was written after his return from Rugby. 'Having the power of keeping things apart in my mind, and hence of distinguishing between your merit as a writer and your utter bloodiness as a man, I must write and congratulate you on your new book. . . . My criticism is that though you generally succeed in the difficult business of making it not melodrama you do sometimes topple off the tightrope in a phrase.' His next visit out of town was to Cambridge with T. E. Hulme, who took him to hear Ezra Pound read a paper in King's. Hulme was about to go to Germany for the Berlin Aesthetic Congress, where he met Brooke in November. Throughout the following year Marsh saw a great deal of him, attending his lecture on poetry at Kensington Town Hall, and on another occasion at the same place sat with him while Ezra Pound read aloud his poems. He was also to be found at Hulme's discussion evenings at Frith Street. On the one occasion he has recorded he was accompanied by Brooke and sat on the floor between him and Ezra Pound; the others present were Middleton Murry, who had brought Wilfrid Gibson, and the painters Wadsworth, Nevinson, and Gaudier-Brzeska. Of Hulme he had several anecdotes. 'There was a fashion at that time for ferreting out unexpected racial strains in the pedigrees of great men and crediting these with their qualities. Hulme was ridiculing this with his usual energy and finished up with comical gusto, "I decline to revise my opinions on the basis that Dostoievsky was an Italian."' Another rendezvous of Hulme's was the Café Royal, where he would often sit with Epstein, David Bomberg, and William Roberts (the last two found their first patron in Marsh) and Gaudier, who also became a visitor to Raymond Buildings. It must have been after just such a gathering that the strange encounter occurred which Marsh used to recall. Hulme was making water in Soho Square in broad daylight when a policeman came up. 'You can't do that here.' Hulme—'Do you realize you're addressing a member of the middle class?' at which the policeman murmured, 'Beg pardon, sir', and went on his beat. He would also describe how Hulme once emphasized a point in an aesthetic dispute by holding Wyndham Lewis upside down over the railings in Fitzroy Square.

Late in June Brooke returned from a second visit to Berlin and stayed the night in Raymond Buildings on his way home, curled up on the sofa because E. M. Forster was in the spare room. He left a note on the table. 'I was so angry at the amount of books here I wanted to read that I've taken one, *The Charwoman's Daughter*, having first made sure it wasn't a presentation copy.' In July he discovered he had been walking around with Mrs. Elgy's latchkey in his pocket and returned it with a new poem which he had written in Germany earlier in the year. It was already printed in the undergraduate magazine *Basileon* and entitled *The Sentimental Exile*. Under gentle pressure from Marsh he was to change the title to *The Old Vicarage, Grantchester*. 'Here's the hurried stuff,'

he wrote. 'Will you send it back to me some time? It's my only
copy.' A week later Marsh returned the magazine, having copied
out the poem.

> It's lovely, my dear, I see why [Lowes] Dickinson likes it best, and
> I think I agree with him, it's the most human thing you've written,
> the only one that has brought tears to my fine eyes. You say it is
> hurried, I do hope you'll polish it up *just* a little and make it perfect.
> (Personally I don't like 'blow—Oh', I mean one line beginning as
> the other has ended—but I know Horace does it!) I showed it to my
> two old pundits, Gosse and Dobson. They were enraptured and
> begged me to assure you of their continued admiration. A.D. said
> they were the best octosyllabics since Shelley, I think it was. Gosse
> wants you very much to leave out the couplet in brackets about
> shooting themselves which he thinks silly and out of key. Also he
> says why satanic? Why make them evil spirits when it's much nicer
> and more fun to think of them as good ghosts and good clerics? and
> he says if the clerics are satanic, Byron, Chaucer, and Tennyson
> must be too. Well, it's a lovely poem. I'm not sure the line I like best
> isn't 'From Haslingfield to Madingley'. You certainly have the art of
> using proper names. *Never* write anything so good again without my
> knowing. I should never have heard of it if G.L.D. [Dickinson] had
> not mentioned it in a postscript—and then where should I have
> been?

Brooke came to London in August, and wrote his name on an
envelope and affixed it with a drawing-pin to the dark green
outer door at the top of the spiral steps at Raymond Buildings.
He now had first claim on the spare room, which he filled with
his books and luggage and made the place his London home.
Mrs. Elgy was delighted, in spite of the extra work, for Marsh
was out all day and Brooke, she said, was a 'stoojius [studious]
type', who caused no trouble. His only peculiarity was his preference for having his meals served in the sitting-room and placed
on the floor, so that he could recline on a cushion and eat off the
tray. One of his first outings after settling in was to take Marsh
to meet John Middleton Murry and Katherine Mansfield, the
editors of *Rhythm*, round the corner at Gray's Inn Road. Marsh
took an immediate liking to them both and was soon to become the
patron of their magazine, which for a while in its hazardous
career was to be a vehicle for Georgian criticism. Middleton
Murry was about to take a cottage at Runcton, near Chichester,
where Brooke and Marsh joined him for a week-end early in

September and sealed a friendship whose record must come at a later stage of this chapter.

After staying with Elliott Seabrooke at Ambleside Marsh had no leisure time until September 17, when after dining out with Mallory and Duncan Grant he went with Brooke to fetch Wilfrid Gibson from his lodgings, to show him a spectacular fire which had broken out at King's Cross. It was Gibson's first visit to London, and here was a sight not to be missed. This proved to be one of the important moments in Gibson's life. He had never met Brooke before, and when the fire was under control all three went back to Gray's Inn for a talk, and the great friendship between Brooke and 'Wibson' (as he called him) began. It was two days after this, on the 19th, that Marsh came back late from the Admiralty. Brooke was sitting on his bed half undressed, and the conversation turned to the public's lack of interest in modern poetry. No one seemed to realize that there was a poetic renaissance. *The Everlasting Mercy*, published the year before, had reached thousands of readers (in fact Masefield was the most widely read poet at that time), but there were at least a dozen other writers of comparable merit whose work was undeservedly neglected. Brooke suggested that he might try playing a practical joke on the public which would at least draw its attention to poetry. He would write a book himself under twelve pseudonyms and issue it as an anthology selected from the poems of a dozen promising writers. Marsh's view was that there was no need to go to all that trouble when there must be twelve representative flesh-and-blood poets with material ready to hand. They began to count. As well as Masefield and Brooke himself there were of course Gibson, Davies, de la Mare, and Bottomley. They included A. E. Housman and Ezra Pound, and Brooke added his Cambridge friend Elroy Flecker, who had shown some promise. Marsh came out with the idea that Brooke should compile his anthology from the work of these writers, but he declined. It needed someone older and of more authority—but what could it be called? They believed that Victorianism in literature was gone for good and that a new era had begun. Marsh pointed out that the natural thing was to name eras after reigning sovereigns, the new reign was itself as new and hopeful as the renaissance in poetry, which train of thought led him to come out with what he afterwards described as 'my proud ambiguous adjective—*Georgian*'. But Brooke didn't like it. He thought it sounded too staid for a volume designed as the herald of a revolutionary dawn. He imagined that the book might provide a useful field for experiment, but Marsh argued that experiments were best confined to the poet's rough notebook; such an anthology must present only fully evolved and finished work if it was to win over an apathetic public. He was beginning to realize they had stumbled on a practicable idea, so that when Brooke proposed that he should be the editor he agreed on one condition, he must be allowed to remain in the background and not put his name to it; the Private Secretary at the Admiralty openly shepherding a group of poets might strike the uninitiated as a trifle absurd and so damage the cause. Finance was the next question. The obvious person to approach was the editor of the *Poetry Review*, whose office was at 43 Chancery Lane, within a stone's-throw of Gray's Inn, and who printed his magazine at the St. Catherine Press in the Strand. He would surely be sympathetic toward a scheme initiated by two men whose verse and criticism had already featured in his pages. But the *Review* would have no funds to spare. What if the anthology were a failure? It was now after midnight, but Marsh put off going to bed a little longer because he had thought of a solution. He told Brooke the story of his great-grandfather who had been assassinated in the lobby of the House of Commons, how the Perceval family had been granted a sum of money in compensation, and how one-sixth of what remained was still coming to him in irregular instalments which so far had been spent on modern pictures. But there was quite a lot of 'murder money' in hand. With this, if Monro were willing to act as publisher and carry the initial expense, he would be guaranteed against loss. This finally dispelled any shadow of doubt that the scheme was practical. In a fever of excitement they decided to telephone Monro first thing in the morning.

ii

Next day there was a luncheon-party at Gray's Inn. Brooke fetched Gibson, Monro brought his sub-editor Arundel del Re and John Drinkwater, and Marsh came back from the Admiralty. There was considerable opposition to the title 'Georgian Poetry', but nothing better could be thought of, so it was agreed to publish under that name before Christmas an edition of 500 at 3*s*. 6*d*. a copy, half the royalties to go to the *Poetry Review* (Monro's Poetry Bookshop was still only a vague scheme) and half to Marsh, who said he would distribute his share equally among the contributors. He was to be solely responsible for making the selection and for the accounting on behalf of the poets, and of course he gave assurance that he would make good any loss. Marsh could have had no inkling of the immense administrative labour he had so lightheartedly undertaken, for as yet the idea of a series was not thought of. As it worked out, however, the intermittent despatch of royalties to his contributors over the next ten years served to keep him in constant touch with the poets (the cheques were always accompanied by a letter) and thus he was able to keep them posted with news of one another. It became his rule to reserve this work for the last hour before bed, and sometimes when the vicissitudes of war delayed him at Whitehall it was an almost intolerable burden which he never confessed to until many years after it was all over. These occasional sums, small as they were, would often arrive at the critical moment, and if he had reason to suspect that the poet was in difficulties his share would be eked out with a fiver or so from the Perceval fund.

The first week-end after the Georgian luncheon he spent at Runcton, where he talked over the scheme with Katherine Mansfield and Middleton Murry. Work at Whitehall delayed operations until the 25th, when he made the first move by writing to Housman, Pound, Abercrombie, also to de la Mare, whom he invited to dinner at the Moulin d'Or to meet Gibson.

There's something I particularly want to talk to you about. I want to do something to make people realize the quality of the work that is done these days in poetry, and the idea, which has been evolved in the last few days in talks with 3 or 4 of the poets, is that I should bring out a small well-printed book, just before Christmas if possible, with specimens of the best poetry that has come out in the last two years. Lascelles Abercrombie is giving me the *Sale of St. Thomas* and so far I have had promises from Gibson, Rupert Brooke and Drinkwater. I'm asking Masefield, James Stephens, and Gordon Bottomley, and there will be one or two more. I hope you think it's a good idea. Of course I MUST have you, if I can possibly persuade you to let me have a few things out of *The Listeners*—that poem itself and *Arabia*, and two or three others. Do you think you could? and

make it all right with Constable? You might tell him that I shan't
make any money out of it and it will really be nothing but a good
advertisement for the book. . . . Monro of the *Poetry Review* wants to
publish it from his office. . . . Meanwhile let me know whether you
approve in principle and please say Yes.

On the 27th he wrote again.

It is very handsome of you to come into my plan. I think of beginning
merely with a short note saying that the book is issued in the belief
that there is going to be and already is a 'Georgian Era'—I haven't
thought out the wording yet, but there will certainly not be any
general or individual criticism—I merely want to throw the poems
hard at the public's head.

On the same day he wrote to Brooke, who had gone back to
Grantchester. 'The great scheme is going well. I saw Abercrombie
last night and he at once promised me the *Sale of St. Thomas*, and
with him and you and Wilfrid and Drinkwater it will be strange
if I can't get the others that I want, or at any rate enough. I'm
rather for having it published by the *Poetry Review* as I think that
is the likeliest way to avoid difficulties with the publishers.'
Brooke had taken away a new publication, *Casket Songs* by E. B.
Sargant, which Marsh wanted back at once. 'I must reread
Cuckoo Wood and see if I still like it. What did you think of it?'
(Brooke was lukewarm about it, but Marsh finally decided in its
favour.) He wrote again next day asking Brooke to get permission
from his publisher for the five poems he had chosen. 'Tell them
it's good advertisement and that *I* shan't make any money even
if there are profits. . . . I've found some thunderingly good things
in Davies' last book. I shall write today and ask for them. My
present terror is that the Poets will be 13! I must get round that
somehow. I had a good idea—to dedicate it to Bridges. . . . I
assume you would fall in with this, there can be no doubt he is
the head and front of English poetry at present?' Two days later
Brooke wrote to say he didn't rate Bridges so highly. 'I think
Yeats worth a hundred of him. But he's a fine figure so perhaps it'd
be all right.' Marsh had asked him to revise his long poem in
octosyllabics. 'Do you want it called *The Sentimental Exile* or
Grantchester?' Brooke asked. 'I'll sit and think but I fear it is too
old for revising. If a couplet or two could be taken out of the last
part and shoved in elsewhere it'd improve the balance—I fear
it'll have to remain its misbegotten self. I get so excited wanting to

scrap these poems and write you much better ones that'd fairly boom the book and obliterate poor Jan [Masefield] but I shan't.'

By that same post Marsh heard from Davies and Ezra Pound. 'I like your idea very much,' said Davies. 'As I would like to be represented by my very best work I must ask you to include *The Kingfisher* in *Farewell to Poesy* which is better than any you name.' Pound had been asked for his poem *The Goodly Fere* and one other (probably *Portrait d'une Femme* which had appeared in *Ripostes*). He wrote from Church Walk, Kensington. 'I'm sorry I can't let you have *that* poem as I'm just bringing it out in a volume of my own. Is there anything in the earlier books that you like? (not *The Goodly Fere* as it doesn't illustrate any *modern* tendency). Also I'd like to know more or less what gallery you propose to put me into. *Canzoni* is the only one that comes within your two years radius. I'm usually in on Tuesday evenings if you care to talk over the matter.' Marsh called and explained that there was nothing in *Canzoni* which he thought suitable. By the time a second volume was in preparation he had decided to confine the anthology to British writers, so that Robert Frost (who had been encouraged and recommended by Gibson) and Pound himself were never represented. Marsh and Pound remained friends until one evening at The Chantecler restaurant Pound brought from his pocket his version of Sappho's ode to Aphrodite and asked him whether he had learned the principles of the new system of quantitative verse and if so, were there any mistakes in his translation? Having read William Stone's paper on the subject and often discussed it with Robert Bridges, Marsh was in a position confidently to suggest several amendments in the versification. When the poem eventually appeared in the *Poetry Review* just as he had first seen it, he has recorded that this 'planted in me a lasting suspicion of his artistic seriousness', and they never met again. But in September 1912, brought together by their friendship for T. E. Hulme, there was no discordant note in their relationship, and Pound, who was to become a severe critic of the later Georgians, courteously expressed a hope that he would one day be represented in their pages.

On the same date as Pound's letter Marsh wrote again to de la Mare.

I very much want D. H. Lawrence's poem in the June *English Review*, 'Snapdragon', for my book. I don't know what you think of it. It's far from perfect, but like his two novels it seems to me to have elements of great and rather strange power and beauty. I've been trying to find out where he is, and now Mrs. [*sic*] Royde-Smith[1] tells me you are the best person to ask. If you know will you kindly direct and post this? and if you could spare the time to put in a line saying I'm a respectable person it might be a help—but don't bother.

Lawrence answered from Lake Garda, saying he would be very glad for his poem to be included in the anthology, 'which sounds very nice. I shall love to see the book. It will be quite profit enough in itself'—so he said, and doubtless meant it, but Lawrence and de la Mare himself were two of the contributors to whom the royalty system was to prove of most benefit. Two more answered on October 1: Bottomley, who was stricken with one of the haemorrhages which rendered him an almost chronic invalid, dictated to his wife a short note of consent, and A. E. Housman, who wrote from Trinity, Cambridge:

> If you want to get poetry out of me you must be either a relative or a duchess, and you are neither. As a brother and a snob I am accessible from two quarters, but from no others. Besides, I do not really belong to your 'new era', and none even of my few unpublished poems have been written within the last two years. I shall be very much interested in your book. One of the names you mention is new to me, and there are others of whom I have only read a little. You do not mention Chesterton: his *Ballad of the White Horse* is absurd in its plan and its conception and often cheap and brassy in its ornament, but it contains quite a lot of really magnificent verses which impressed me more than anything I have read for a long time. However, literary criticism is not what you were asking me for.

Chesterton no more 'belonged to the new era' than Housman, but the exclusive rule of youth had not yet been decided on, and out of deference to Housman, who was a friend of Marsh's father, Chesterton was approached and a section of his Ballad included in the book. Masefield was more cautious. He was in process of moving into a house in Well Walk and suggested tea and a stroll on the Heath. 'As to the scheme I would much like to talk it over with you, but I own that I am not very sanguine. Sir Ronald Ross had a scheme for a poetical monthly, *Musa Miscella*, which pleased me more, but let us meet and talk over

---

[1] Miss Naomi Royde-Smith, literary editor of the *Westminster Gazette*, in which some of Brooke's poems had first appeared.

yours.' As a tribute to the rival scheme, and a compliment to Masefield, a poem by Ross (best known for his service to humanity as the conqueror of malaria) was asked for, and Masefield himself, at last won over, wrote: 'I feel your book may be a useful fillip, as there has been nothing like it for some years.' Sturge Moore was even more sceptical at first, and remained so. 'My own belief is that what would really be best would be something far more catholic, not more specialized. A book representative of what is actually being produced, taking as little account of "how" as possible.' He suggested Flecker, 'certainly Yeats, and possibly Binyon', and he named a piece called *Dirge* by Marsh's old friend R. C. Trevelyan. Marsh replied that *Dirge* suffered from 'imperfect form'. Moore made a good answer.

> A perfect form may be beautiful, but we know so many impeccable ones that are not. A broken vase may be more beautiful than a new one uncracked, so may a broken form. Perhaps forms ought never to be repeated, perhaps every lyric should create a new form. *Lycidas* is a classical example of a rhymed poem with rhymeless lines. Success conforms to no standard. It sets a standard. Mere conformity is never a virtue. . . . I think we should not look on poets as little boys who have or have not done their exercise.

Lawrence, who was soon to argue the same case, would have been in complete agreement with Moore, but Marsh held his ground, and Moore was riled.

> As to your criticism about formally perfect—it is the very type of criticism which I abominate; that is it refers to a mechanical criterion as ultimate. There is no reason or commonsense in any such reference. . . . It's [the *Dirge*] not being what you call formally perfect is really in its favour and means that the writer's mind was more dominated by a real taste than by mechanical pedantry. . . . It is certainly far finer than anything of Bottomley's and I think as fine as the best of Bridges. . . . In fact I don't suppose I shall ever really forgive you if you leave it out.

He then made the inclusion of Trevelyan's poem a condition for the quotation of his own piece *Sicilian Idyll*, which Marsh particularly wanted. The dilemma was resolved by including both poems, but never again did Marsh give way to pressure.

When he sent Brooke an interim report on October 3 Lawrence's letter had not reached him, and Flecker, James Stephens, and Ronald Ross had not yet replied.

I shall take advantage of your grudging consent to the dedication! The other R.B. is to my mind the figurehead of English poetry on any fair adjustment of seniority and merit, and even if I thought Yeats a better man I should shrink from offering him a dedication from English poets. I somehow feel he would take it in the spirit of a lion receiving the homage of a dozen jackals. Masefield has been a perfect angel, he began very pessimistic but warmed to the idea and wrote afterwards to say he would keep back the publication of *Biography* in book form so that I could have it first! really most decent of him. I think it's a good poem. *Dauber* is splendid as a whole, but some of the writing abominably careless. I don't think he can ever have read it out loud to himself when once he'd finished it. . . . I'm afraid you weren't really in favour of *Cuckoo Wood*, but as Gibson and Abercrombie both liked it very much I thought my taste was sufficiently supported.

Brooke replied next day, on the point of passing through London for a week-end with the Murrys at Runcton Cottage. 'I find myself believing I can make a rival better selection from the same poets! Of course, I can't set up to advise you: but I can taunt.' To which Marsh replied forlornly by return, 'Don't make me too wretched about my selection.' He went on:

You *must* come on Monday whether the Tigers [Murrys] want you or not, as Walter de la Mare is dining with me[1] to meet Gibson (whose boils have come back, poor dear, so he may not be able to come, I'm just going round to see how he is) and Masefield said he would come if he could get away from his little girl who was to have her tonsils taken out on Thursday (this letter is becoming a Grub St. Bulletin).

Flecker wrote from Beirut on October 12: 'very glad to appear in the company of my old friend Rupert Brooke'. He made counter-suggestions about his poems for quotation (which Marsh did not accept) and went on:

Will you think it impertinent if I make one or two suggestions? One is that your anthology be the first to include, if it does not include already, the *Pirate Ship* of Richard Middleton which is a masterpiece.[2] I never knew poor Middleton who was murdered by the

[1] This was Brooke's first meeting with de la Mare, whom he made an heir of his copyright with Gibson and Abercrombie.

[2] Richard Middleton died prematurely in 1911. *The Pirate Ship* (*Poems and Songs*, Fisher Unwin, 1912) was not quoted in *Georgian Poetry* because the anthology was being planned as an encouragement to the living. It is interesting to note that there is a distinct relationship between Middleton's poem and Flecker's well-known *Old Ships* which the poet was to send Marsh in manuscript.

British Public, but his suicide this year was one of the tragedies of literature. I hope you have chosen de la Mare's *Arabia*. . . . I subscribe to the dedication to Robert Bridges cordially. But I shall dedicate my next book to Richard Middleton.

A week later Gibson wrote from the Old Vicarage, Grant-chester.

Rupert is hard at work on new poems and I am furiously jealous, though I am glad to realize one of my dreams at last by seeing a poet at work, I have so often wondered how it was done. I'd have written you a letter—but we haven't a penny stamp between us. . . . I only saw two poems of Rupert's that I liked though I rather marvelled that poems could be written because Monro wanted them, and to catch posts, and telegrams about them being sent off between the verses. It seemed queer—but never having seen poetry being written before, I didn't know—and anyhow from the spectacular point of view it was superb.

There were now seventeen contributors, including Monro himself, and James Stephens, the last to enter the fold, who had come in with a fervent plea that Seamus O'Sullivan should be invited to join him. Masefield had become enthusiastic. He gave a dinner-party in Well Walk so that Marsh could bring Brooke and introduce him to Mr. and Mrs. John Galsworthy, who wanted to hear all about the Georgian scheme. Meanwhile de la Mare continued to send in suggestions, but Marsh's anxiety to catch the Christmas market obliged him to close the list.

Thanks for your letter—I wish I had got it before as my MS is now with the printer, so I'm afraid I can't add. I don't know Hodgson's work at all, somebody did mention it but I was slack and forgot to get it. Monro showed me a long and very obscure poem by Locke Ellis the other day. . . . I never heard the name even of Freeman—though he sounds rather like Flecker who published first 36 *Poems* and then 42 *Poems* (what an odd fashion in nomenclature) of which I include specimens. . . . I should have liked to make it more complete, it will be horrid a few years hence to realize that I've left out half the best people.

He now thought it advisable to put the scheme before one of the older writers in his acquaintance whose critical opinion he respected. Maurice Hewlett was asked whether he approved the plan of giving so much space to the young and relatively unknown poets. Hewlett wrote on October 14:

I think you are right to keep it to Georgians, whatever uncertainty there may be about the note struck. *Is* a note struck at all? That's what interests me. In my judgement the only original notes sounded in our day have been Meredith's and the Irishman Yeats'—and they are plainly Ossianic—or began so. But Meredith I think was quite new. . . . A string I am always harping on about modern poetry is that invention is languid, and that all modern energy is diverted to technique. R. Bridges is a great example. There's a poet of great accomplishment practically without imagination. Try *Cupid and Psyche* or one of his plays. Binyon's nearly as bad. But I run on. All health to your Book.

Encouraged by this, Marsh began to write a Preface—'This volume is issued in the belief that English poetry is now once again putting on a new strength and beauty . . .' but he was annoyed by Hewlett's opinion of Bridges. It prompted him not only to protest to the writer but to decide that this was the psychological moment to offer Bridges the dedication. By the same post he wrote to Brooke listing his critical points on *The Old Vicarage, Grantchester*, the new title for *The Sentimental Exile*. Bridges replied from Chilswell on the 16th.

Of course I am very much interested in your 20th century poets, and you probably know me sufficiently well to guess that I am as much amused as gratified by your notion of dedicating the volume to me. It would be equally foolish and ungracious of me not to welcome the compliment; and my unworthiness, which is the only drawback, accentuates the friendliness of your goodwill. . . . You omitted to enclose your prospectus in your second envelope as well as the first! I have no doubt that you will do the thing as well as it could be done. Considering the condition of both home and foreign politics I would suggest that your introduction should be dated from the Admiralty. If this is not a part of your original plan thank me for the suggestion. . . . *P.S.* I see I have omitted to thank you definitely for your flattering compliment; and I should like to say that I am very proud of your contributors wishing to have my name in any way associated with theirs.

On November 5 the first proofs arrived and Marsh sat up correcting them until 2 A.M., a foretaste of the midnight work he would be doing for his poets in years to come. By now Monro in company with Gibson had found premises for his bookshop in Devonshire Street near Gray's Inn. The bookshop was to be its own publishing house, using the Arden Press, Letchworth, as its

printers, and from there the first pages of *Georgian Poetry* had just
been issued. The shop's premises, a small eighteenth-century
house in a side street off Theobalds Road, were not yet furnished.
The old building with the lecture-room above the shop and the
spare rooms at the top, where Gibson was the first to take a bed-
sitting-room, and T. E. Hulme and many other men of letters
were to be domiciled for a time, was solely Monro's enterprise.
Marsh had no connection with it whatever. In his eyes the place
was a publishing house. The valuable contribution to literature of
the Poetry Bookshop over thirty-three years has yet to be properly
recorded. The Georgians became a social group of which Monro
himself was never really a member, but the coincidence of the
anthology's appearance and the opening of his shop was of
enormous benefit to them both.

In the first week of November Brooke left England to stay with
his friend Dudley Ward in Berlin. 'When I lie awake o'nights,'
he wrote on the 9th, 'I plan advertisements for Georgian poets',
then he appended names of reviewers and their journals. 'I
forget all my other ideas; but they each sold some twenty-five
copies. I have a hazy vision of incredible *Reklam* seconded by your
potent wire-pulling and ingenious brain. . . . You'll be able to
found a Hostel for the Georgians on the proceeds.' He also suggested that Marsh should install 'an immense map (vide *Tono
Bungay*) and plan campaigns with its aid'. When Marsh replied,
he had just been to Cambridge for a few days and met the
philosopher Wittgenstein, who was being initiated or 'born', to
use the correct term, as one of the Apostles.

'Maynard [Keynes] says W. is an ultra metaphysician—his
passion is to push Russell's logic to ultimate refinements.' As to
Brooke's ideas on advertisements, 'you are Hooper and Selfridge
in one, you really must come back and organize my campaign.
. . . Noyes has promised an article in the *Fortnightly* (he is an
angel as he really rather minded not being in!).' He had gone for
his usual walk with A. C. Benson, and 'Housman was agreeable
in an arid manner. . . . I didn't feel that I could establish any
relation with him. He told me he wrote three-quarters of *The
Shropshire Lad* in 6 months and then dried up till lately.'

World affairs had begun to cast a shadow over the Georgian
adventure. 'My natural Pacifism is strongly reinforced by my
anxieties for the Book! a war would kill it dead.' When Brooke

replied on the 25th he had still more suggestions for advertisement, and enclosed a list of his friends[1] and their addresses to whom Marsh was to send copies of the book, for its publication was expected early in December. He also enjoyed copying out a few sentences from a virulent review of his *Poems* in the *Oxford Magazine*, of which one was: 'The book is full of bad taste and at times positively disgusting. . . .' 'Hulme has arrived in Berlin,' he wrote. 'I show him round and talk to him. He's an amiable creature and a good talker, though I don't think much of him as a philosophic thinker. But he has an extraordinary power of observation, and a good memory.'

While these talks were going on in Berlin Marsh was at Cambridge seeing *Oedipus* by the Marlowe Society, and sitting up late after the performance correcting the final page proofs of his anthology. On November 29 he told Brooke another of the contributors had come into his life.

> Flecker turned up at the Admiralty for a short time this morning, he has just arrived from Syria which bores him stiff, and he was off to see Raleigh and try to get a Professorship of Literature out of him. There is much to be said against his exterior, but I hope to see him more at length when he comes back, and to get over it. . . . I went yesterday to see Masefield receive the Polignac prize. De la Mare came up to me afterwards and said in a grieved voice, 'They've given him more than they gave me.' I was puzzled, and slightly flabbergasted at the seeming bad taste of this remark till he went on, 'They've given him an envelope.' I took Wilfrid and introduced him to Gosse, Hewlett, Newbolt, Sturge Moore, Masefield, de la Mare—I wonder if anyone has ever been introduced to so many poets at once.

Flecker's excuse for writing on reaching Cheltenham was his anxiety to retrieve 'some dull papers (the *Outcry* or something working-mannish)' from the Admiralty waiting-room. He had stayed long enough in Mr. Churchill's ante-room to interest Marsh in a play he had started while living in Corfu, and Marsh had offered to show it to Granville Barker. 'I am having the 2nd ac. of my play typed and shall send the 1st 2 acts to you in the course of the week with a synopsis of the third.' *Hassan*, which was eventually recast under Marsh's advice, was to cause the patron

---

[1] It included Geoffrey Keynes, Edward Thomas, Hugh Dalton, Rose Macaulay, Edward Garnett, Edward Shanks (then at Trinity, one day to be a Georgian contributor), Percy Lubbock, and the Woolfs.

almost more work than any other literary project he ever touched.
For the moment Flecker was more concerned for Marsh to use
his influence with A. C. Benson and the Cambridge Appointments Board to get him a job away from the Consular Service.
Benson replied to the enquiry saying he had once met Flecker—
'an interesting creature, with a sort of curious and rather attractive wildness about him. . . . To speak plainly, a man who writes
fine poetry, has married a Greek wife, and wants to throw up a
consular post, is difficult to place . . . the same sort [of difficulty]
as there would have been in placing Shelley.' That mail also
broughts Acts I and II of *Hassan* from Cheltenham. Flecker had
recently met Marsh for a luncheon so as to give him the manuscript, but in his fluster had come out with the rough copy in his
pocket. He soon wrote again from Neuilly-sur-Seine, where he
was enjoying an extension of leave. 'The hope of my life, which is
Hassan, is in your hands, my dear Marsh. I am longing to know
what Ainley thinks of it. . . . Do not scruple to tell me bad news
and bad opinions. My best love to Rupert, and many thanks to
you for your great kindness to one as unfortunate as Ovid!'
Brooke was home again on December 8. 'The bloodiest of all
bloody printers now say my book can't be ready till Saturday!'
was Marsh's greeting to him at Rugby. 'Isn't it damnable, and
Q.'s tiresome book[1] will take a good deal of wind out of my sails
—however I don't despond. . . . I've been seeing Flecker, whom
I like, and his wife is a nice pretty little woman.'

At this point Marsh was far too busy sending off advance copies
for review to give much thought to *Hassan*. Copies were sent to
newspapers abroad as well as to all parts of England and there
was a team of packers working at night at Gray's Inn, among
them Gilbert Cannan, who had recently joined the circle, Abercrombie, Seabrooke, Monro, and Brooke, who was again
installed in the spare room. The atmosphere was strained, the
main edition was held up at the printers and orders were accumulating. Marsh sent off a presentation copy to Lady Gladstone at
Government House, Pretoria. Knowing it would arrive too late
for the new year, let alone Christmas, he offered it as 'an Epiphany
present, if there is such a thing'.

You are the only person I am giving it to, everyone else is made to
buy it but as you are an exile an exception shall be made in your

[1] *The Oxford Book of Victorian Verse.*

favour. I hope it makes you feel blessed among women. I must mention that E.M. who signs the preface is the same who now addresses you, did you know I could write such good grammar? It's my first book, and probably only, so you must say it's a fine baby whether you think so or not.

I've been living mainly with poets and haven't got much news of the Smart Set. Has anyone told you of Diana Manners' floater at the Albert Hall Ball? Little else has been talked about, tho' it happened a fortnight ago. This is a kind of compliment, and is my excuse for spreading it as far as South Africa—i.e. she has got so much obloquy from it that she may as well have all the fame she can get as well. She was in Lady Sheffield's procession (so was I) the '12 dancing princesses' and had designed the dresses herself *exactly* alike, not a variation would she allow in any detail. (They were to be in white, with swansdown, like Pavlova in *Le Cygne*.) The night before the ball she was at a party and said to everyone, 'Have you heard this scandalous story that I'm going in black? not a word of truth in it.' Then she appeared at dinner in pitch black! Lady Sheffield said how do you do without the ghost of a pleasant expression, and had every dig at her that she could—and she has been almost universally condemned, though admired for courage! The Duchess's line is rather good. 'Poor little Diana, she was in *black*'—making out that from self-denial she had worn a dull dress so as not to look prettier than the others. I hope you hadn't heard this long story.

Marsh was present in his capacity as one of the 'twelve dancing Princes' whom Lady Sheffield had to enlist as escorts for her Princesses. Another member of the group was A. A. Milne who long afterwards recalled the occasion. 'We wore silver smocks with very tight tights and a golden wig—if you can imagine Eddie like this, particularly when he had screwed his eye-glass firmly into his eye and had stopped at my flat on the way to the Albert Hall to add the C.B. [not the genuine article until 1918] round his neck so as to make him look still more like a dancing Prince.' Mr. Churchill was there (for the dinner only) and Raymond Asquith 'whom I thought then, and have never ceased to think, the most brilliant man I have ever met. Oh! I was nearly forgetting Diana Manners. The women wore white ballet dresses, except Diana who wore a black one, having evidently made some slight mistake as to the arrangements.'[1] After that sidelight on the ball, Marsh's Christmas letter to Pretoria can be resumed.

[1] Letter to the author, April 14, 1954.

I suppose you will see a lot about Sir Francis Bridgeman's resignation as 1st Sea Lord, and may wonder whether there is anything mysterious. There is nothing whatever—the plain fact is that the poor old gentleman was frightfully worn out with office work and really quite useless even for peace—and Winston couldn't sleep for thinking what would happen if there were a war. Sir F., who up till then had been telling everyone that the strain was killing him and that he had a mind to resign, now of course says that he was perfectly well, but he *wasn't*. Even he doesn't say that he resigned from any difference on policy. Charlie B., who is Bridgeman's sworn enemy, has taken up the cudgels for him! in order to bang Winston; and some of the Tories have taken it up of course, and so has the *Daily News*! I told Winston the cry of 'The right to be First Lord though gaga' was like the 'Right to be Drunk' strike, now happily over. Well, I wish you a happy Epiphany. Write and tell me that you like my little book!

On the 20th there was a theatrical supper-party at Raymond Buildings at which two small plots came to fruition. Brooke had asked to be introduced to Cathleen Nesbitt, and the latter had wanted to meet Gilbert Cannan. All parties concerned turned up, and Henry Ainley also, to whom Brooke took an instant dislike. His first meeting with Miss Nesbitt was a landmark in his life. Marsh, who was to provide him with a wide reading public, began by putting him in the way of romance. Brooke was bemusedly happy when he returned to Rugby for Christmas. He wrote saying he had left the key on the hall table, 'small pieces of paper on the floor, and my heart all over the place'. He had looked in on Monro's bookshop, which had already run out of copies of the anthology. 'The most extraordinary people keep dropping in and spending immense sums.'

Before leaving Raymond Buildings Brooke had purloined a small Russian toy from the sideboard, thinking it was meant for him, or so he explained. 'You and Seabrooke and the eggs were phantoms on the horizon of my muddled consciousness. At one point you seemed to take something out of a box and say "*Buz buz buz* this *buz buz buz* Christmas present *buz buz* . . ." I remember vaguely thinking that you had said that Russian toys were your this year's Christmas presents . . . and vaguely saying—"Oh" . . . What else could a young man say with his eyes full of sleep and his heart full of Cathleen?' But *was* he meant to take it? He hoped so, for it was proving a success. 'A foreigner who shaved me was intensely

interested in it, and said, "It is very Beautifool" rather solemnly.'
In fact the toy was meant for Mrs. Elgy's nephew. Brooke's mistake
occasioned one of Marsh's best letters, but first he wrote querulously to de la Mare. It was Christmas Day, and he was at
Knebworth, sitting in his bedroom overlooking the park, which
was covered in snow, and the lake was frozen. 'The printers have
been abominably lazy and treacherous. They promised 500
copies for December 1st and performed 250 on the 16th and 250
yesterday. Meanwhile orders had poured in and all but 50 copies
were sold (or sent for review) when I left on Saturday. I'm furious
as I believe I could have sold most of the second edition for Christmas presents if they had kept faith.'

Then he wrote to Brooke about the Russian toy.

I now see exactly what the Queen of Sheba must have written as a
Collins:
Dear Solomon, I was terribly absentminded at dinner last night
and I am afraid you must have thought me rude as you *must* have
noticed that I wasn't listening to your delightful flow of proverbs—
the fact is I was so miserable at leaving Jerusalem that I could think
of nothing else. However it came back to me afterwards that you
must have told me to take away anything in the Palace that I specially
liked, so I told my maid to pack the hangings of the cedar house, I
hope this is all right. Yours ever, C. Sheba.
I'd left the toy behind very reluctantly, for fear of being shamed
into giving it to a child here! how vain is human precaution. . . . No
rain today so I'm just off to play golf, tho' my golf, from being a
joke, has gone on to be beyond a joke. Come back to Raymond Buildings as soon as you can.

On the last day of 1912 Brooke came up to his London *pied-à-
terre* and Marsh took him to *Hullo Ragtime* (which he saw ten times
before it came off), then brought him back to Raymond Buildings
for supper and to speculate on the results of their elaborate campaign for getting their anthology reviewed. After supper they
went out again and walked to the steps of St. Paul's, where they
were standing jammed in a dense throng as the bells rang in the
new year 1913.

iii

After breakfast next morning Brooke left for Cornwall and
Marsh went to stay with the Lyttons at Knebworth. They had to

dress up for dinner. Neville appeared as a courtier of Charles I, Jasper Ridley as Richelieu, and Marsh as a Turk. They played charades, and danced quadrilles. At Raymond Buildings the first important letter about his anthology was awaiting his return. It was from Maurice Hewlett. He was opposed to Abercrombie's recent work, contending that he had 'read Bridges on Milton not wisely. It runs too thin.'

> Bottomley is another Miltonian, but I like him better. *The End of the World* is very fine in conception. *Babel* is prose—and the end of it incomprehensible. What do the last lines mean? Rupert Brooke is a poet. I have no doubt about him. . . . *The Fish* ought to live—and so ought the man who can do Grantchester so divinely well. Nevertheless, *The Kingfisher* of Davies seems to me the best lyric you have. It is real music. Waller might have done it. De la Mare? Of course. He sings like a bird 'because he must'. Drinkwater is always rather too heavy. As if he found expression enormously difficult. He wants mastery. Sturge Moore is very perverse. I believe him to be the first of living poets. In such a book as this he is the first I should turn to —and on a bookshelf I should put my hand up to him instinctively. Now here he is charming, in parts—he has the air of the thing—and the intention—but he's muddled—he hasn't clarified his drama. The whole is ineffective. It wants brainwork.[1] James Stephens is good and I always like Gibson. Masefield might at any moment do—anything. With his technical skill and sense of rhythm he ought to reach the top. But I wonder. So far he seems to me a journalist—but his ear is perfect and it will be an awful shame if he doesn't justify it. The total impression I have is that your men are interested in strength rather than Beauty, have lost a good deal of sensation, and by reason of that make an imperfect fusion of their passionate natures. I believe that the fired sense and the fired mind have to burn together to produce great imagination. Abercrombie and Drinkwater in particular fail in this. They seem to make poetry entirely by ratiocination. The truest poets you have are Brooke, Davies, de la Mare. Lawrence will be good too, some day. . . . There's a very high level—a tableland of art with no cloud-kissing peaks.

Marsh sent on this letter to Brooke. 'I agree with nearly all of it except about Lascelles. (I have protested vigorously and quoted Horace's Ode on Pindar!) Flecker wrote to me from France, just starting for Beirut, agreeing with most of my criticisms of *Hassan*. He says he will have the third Act ready "in a month".' Brooke

---

[1] *A Sicilian Idyll* (first part).

replied: 'I hope, if these are his opinions, he will be persuaded to publish them in some paper with an extensive circulation.' He added that he had finished a play of his own.[1] Flecker had written on January 2 to say that Marsh's encouragement of *Hassan* had come 'just in time to console me. I honestly and without being merely amiable, agree in your criticism.' Marsh (who had been given the first two acts only) had said that the opening scene was poor. It should be rendered more 'exalted' by making Hassan himself more sharply defined as a character, the 'buffoonery' should be reduced, and more use made of the beggars. 'I'll leave out the further magic scene I had planned,' wrote Flecker, 'and give the beggars a better show.' A month later Marsh had to report that Granville Barker was too busy to read any new manuscripts. He now proposed sending the fragment to Drinkwater, who was in Birmingham working with the Repertory Theatre.

Brief entries in two pocket-diaries, minute books barely two inches square, give many clues to his crowded social life among the artists during the next eighteen months. On January 8 the official opening of the Poetry Bookshop took place. Marsh sat with Henry Newbolt, who made the inaugural speech, and Monro introduced him to one of his Georgian contributors, W. H. Davies. After dinner he called on Middleton Murry and Katherine Mansfield to describe the occasion over coffee. On the 10th he was with them again, reporting a conversation on painting he had had earlier that day with Sargent. Next morning he went to stay with Mrs. Verrall at Cambridge. A. E. Housman came to dinner and played anagrams with Marsh after the meal. Next day he spent the afternoon walking with A. C. Benson, and on the 14th, at Holmbury St. Lucy, the home of R. C. Trevelyan, he at last met Gordon Bottomley, yet another of his contributors. On the 15th Brooke came back to Gray's Inn. He had sent a telegram: 'Coming tomorrow my play awfully good', and followed it with a card saying that he wanted to finish his play at Gray's Inn under Marsh's eye. In his reply Marsh was sorry to report that Henry Ainley, to whom he had sent the unfinished *Hassan*, considered the play 'uncommercial', an opinion he strongly disagreed with.

Brooke arrived for luncheon with his friend George Mallory. Next morning Marsh and he called on Duncan Grant, lunched

[1] *Lithuania*.

with Mrs. Churchill, and dined in Soho with Gaudier-Brzeska, then Marsh went on alone to see Gaudier's work in his studio at Fulham. On the following day he was a guest of the Prime Minister at Downing Street with Yeats, de la Mare, and the Irish poet 'A.E.' After dining with Geoffrey Keynes, Brooke joined up with him for coffee with 'the Tigers' (their nickname for Middleton Murry and Katherine Mansfield). On the 18th Marsh went with Brooke to Ditchling to meet Eric Gill, and on the next day they had tea with W. H. Davies at his lodgings in Sevenoaks. They dined the following evening with Hugh Walpole, and next day Marsh accompanied Brooke on a book-buying expedition to the Poetry Bookshop. That evening they bought seats at a music-hall to hear Marie Lloyd. The 22nd was a special day for Brooke. Marsh was his host for luncheon at the Moulin d'Or, where he was joined by de la Mare and Davies; in the evening he dined with Yeats, got back to Gray's Inn at midnight, and sat up until the small hours talking over the ideas on poetry which Yeats had put forward in conversation. The 28th was another memorable day: after luncheon with Cathleen Nesbitt, who introduced St. John Ervine, they went to hear Shaw and Belloc in debate, and after supper at Gray's Inn Brooke read aloud his play *Lithuania*. The next evening they both dined with Masefield in Hampstead and heard him read aloud his latest narrative, *The Daffodil Fields*.

Meanwhile the Georgian anthologist was about to receive an unusual honour. A letter from Max Beerbohm complained of his trapesing up the stairs at Raymond Buildings only to find the outer door bolted against him. 'I wanted, and want, to set eyes on you: I have an idea for a caricature in which you take part and I can't remember the exact high-light on your monocle.' To avoid further mishap it seemed safer to arrange for a meeting at the office, where the artist could make his sketch while his subject went on with his work. The plan was approved.

MY DEAR EDDIE,

Capital, I will 'look' you 'up' at the Admiralty at four o'clock tomorrow, and am 'looking' keenly 'forward' to 'finding' you 'in'.

Yours very sincerely,

MAX.

On February 1 there was a visit to Charterhouse, where Marsh and Mallory read aloud to each other the new Masefield poem.

The 5th was a crowded day; in the morning at Portsmouth with Mr. Churchill for the King's inspection of H.M.S. *New Zealand*, back to London to hear, with Lady Cunard, *Rosenkavalier* on its first appearance at Covent Garden, both intervals spent talking with Sargent, then a late night session with 'the Tigers'. On the 7th Brooke came back for a night, and found that Bridges had at last written about the anthology (from Chilswell, February 6).

I heard an aesthetic philosopher talking, and very respectfully, of your 'Georgian' Book yesterday, and that reminded me that I had never written to you about it, except to thank you for sending it. I hope it is doing well. I think that you have certainly justified yourself, and that the book should do good in helping these writers to an audience. The bibliography at the end is exactly what the circumstances require. No one can find out where to get these books, for the shop will not help them at all. Also it struck me that putting the various poets together might enable them to see the value or lack of value of certain strangenesses that are common to the most of them. The book seems to me really rich in thought and diction. I was glad to be introduced to Lawrence. Also I knew Gibson only by a poem which I happened not to like—the extracts that you give are very remarkable. . . .

I do not wish to criticise, but I may say that I think I am mainly sympathetic with the psychological tendency of the 'school', which is generally, I suppose, a reaction against intellectualism. As far as a new moral position is deduced from this, I feel that the necessity of its being subordinated to aesthetic beauty is in danger of being lost sight of. I feel sometimes as if I were reminded of the Post-Impressionists' pictures. You know however that I am not offended by novelties and that I welcome any revolt against dull conventional bondage. I am really very much overwhelmed by the compliment of the dedication. I set it against the less pleasant experiences of old age.

Marsh replied from the Admiralty, saying he was glad 'to find that you don't think the book perfectly awful!'

I'm specially pleased at your liking Gibson. I think he is the most careful artist of them all. I wonder where you find the Post-Impressionism—I thought I had kept out all that kind of thing—but I suppose it has become so much part of the London air that one doesn't notice it.

On the same day Marsh and Brooke left for Cambridge, where they stayed at Downing for a Lamb Society dinner. (For the next

few weeks the diary is again the best guide.) Next day Brooke
introduced his friend Jacques Raverat, the painter. They lunched
with the Verralls, walked with A. C. Benson, called on Maynard
Keynes for tea, and after dinner at Downing A. E. Housman
dropped in and watched Brooke and Howard Marsh playing
billiards. On the 11th Marsh got away from the Admiralty in
time to give a luncheon in Soho to 'the Tigers', Davies, Brooke,
and Gilbert Cannan. In the evening Marsh and Brooke were at
Covent Garden for *Petrouchka* and supped afterwards with Roger
Fry, Francis Toye, and William Denis Browne.

One of Busoni's favourite pupils in Berlin, Browne was now
organist at Guy's Hospital. He had known Brooke at Cambridge,
and was the poet's junior by one year. It was probably on the
following day that Gibson met Brooke by appointment outside
the fire-station in Theobalds Road and found that he had Denis
Browne in tow. It was early evening, Marsh would be back from
the Admiralty, and they suggested taking Browne to call on him
and see the pictures. So began the friendship which Marsh came
to cherish second only to that with Brooke himself. Next day (12th)
Marsh gave Brooke luncheon at the National Club so as to
introduce him to Gosse, and in the evening they picked up
Browne and took him to *Hullo Ragtime*. On the 15th Marsh left
London to stay with Professor Sadler at Leeds for the opening of
a Gordon Craig exhibition. When he travelled south again, in
time to meet Browne at a concert, his companion in the train was
Michael Sadleir, the Professor's son, who had invited Marsh to
criticize some of his poems. Their discussion was left unresolved,
and while staying at Ambleside with Elliott Seabrooke Marsh
wrote a letter (February 22) to Sadleir which is of some consequence to the understanding of his attitude to tradition and
experiment in verse.

> I warned you I was going to write in defence of my ideas about
> poetical expression. I don't think I made you understand them in
> the train, because you said I was 'timorous', which could only mean
> that I was afraid of expression without authority and usage behind it.
> I don't think that is my failing, as I rejoice particularly in any bold
> and new use of language if I am satisfied that it really means what
> it is meant to mean, and also in any novelty of form if I find that it
> has and obeys a law of its own. I suppose we should agree that poetry
> *is* expression, and that if so it must have a meaning, and must convey

it; and it seems to me that the 'kritik' I was arguing upon in the train is a necessary deduction from those simple facts. Of course I'm far from thinking that I apply it correctly. The kinetic meaning of words is fairly clear, but about the potential (to which everyone would wish to give as wide a scope as possible) there *must* be differences of opinion, and perhaps I'm involuntarily less liberal about it than I should like to be—for instance in several of the most lovely Swinburne poems (such as the *Garden of Proserpine*) there are passages which seem to me kinetically such nonsense that their potentialities are lost upon me. Do you know the story of one of the Symbolistes, I forget if it was Mallarmé or another, who was writing a poem when a ray of sunlight fell upon his paper, and the word *palme* suddenly came into his head, so he put *palme* in the middle of his poem, hoping that it would convey his feeling about the sunlight to his readers? You will agree that this was going too far, but I thought your principles tended in that direction.

Shortly before the visit to Ambleside another poet had come into his life. At the instigation of Gosse, Siegfried Sassoon had sent a sheaf of his poems to Gray's Inn. Marsh was impressed and wrote at length.

I think it certain that you have a lovely instrument to play upon and no end of beautiful tunes in your head, but that sometimes you write them down without getting enough meaning into them to satisfy the mind. Sometimes the poems are like pearls, with enough grit in the middle to make the nucleus of a durable work, but too often they are merely beautiful soap-bubbles which burst as soon as one has had time to admire the colours. I believe there is a good as well as a bad sense in which there must be fashions in poetry, and that a vein may be worked out, if only for a time. The vague iridescent ethereal kind had a long intermittent innings all through the nineteenth century, especially at the end, and Rossetti, Swinburne, and Dowson could do things which it is no use trying now. It seems a necessity now to write either with one's eye on an object or with one's mind at grips with a more or less definite idea.[1]

Goblin Revel, the sonnet he particularly admired, reminded him of the dance of the grotesques in *Oiseau de feu*, an allusion which was lost on the young Sassoon, who had not yet discovered the Russian ballet. Sassoon replied that he would 'much enjoy a talk with you on poetry in general. . . . As you have observed I have passed through most of the influences. . . . *The Daffodil Murderer*

[1] From *The Weald of Youth*, by Siegfried Sassoon, p. 137.

was begun as a joke and finished in earnest. I don't see why
Masefield should have the monopoly in "powerful poems of forty
pages".' A little later he wrote again. 'Some day I will write some
good poems, and if I do they will be yours. . . . I am one of the
mugs who only finds a method by long years of groping.' After
they had met for luncheon at the National Club, and been joined
for coffee by Austin Dobson, Sassoon began to take his literary
life more seriously. 'I have quite made up my mind to live in
London a good deal in the future. I shall never do any decent work
buried alive among foxhunters. So I want you to help me find
somewhere to live.'

On March 1 Marsh came home from the office to discover a
note in Brooke's hand prominently displayed on the hall table.
'Don't be surprised to find me having a tea-party. Come in and
join us.' So in he went, and there were Brooke and Cathleen
Nesbitt sitting by the fire, and lying on the floor between them the
remains of a 'high tea' on a silver tray. At a breakfast-party next
morning attended by Browne, Gibson, Duncan Grant, Michael
Sadleir, and Albert Rutherston, Brooke again read aloud his one-
act play. In the evening he accompanied Marsh to dinner with
St. John Ervine, and late at night they walked the long way back
from Golders Green on either side of Yeats, who was in particularly
expansive mood. On the 5th Edward Thomas came to breakfast,
paying his only visit to Gray's Inn. It should have been a success,
but it was not. Thomas, not at his best in the mornings apparently,
gave a misleading impression of himself, and a chance remark of
his was taken by Marsh and Brooke (neither of whom had met him
before) as an unwarranted slur on Mrs. Elgy's powers as a cook.[1]

On the 8th news came from Cambridge that Brooke had been
awarded his Fellowship of King's for his dissertation on Webster,
and three days later a celebration dinner was given at Raymond
Buildings. Marsh took the head of the table facing Yeats, Brooke sat
between Mrs. Churchill and Violet Asquith opposite Jim Barnes,[2]
who sat with Cynthia Asquith. On the 15th Brooke left after a stay
of two months, and Middleton Murry took over the spare room and

---

[1] Writing of this occasion to Gordon Bottomley (undated, but during the second
World War) Marsh said: 'It must have been one of his less good days—he was unforth-
coming and constricted, perhaps dyspeptic, and seemed to look down his nose at both
of us as well as at the food, so it led to nothing. I wish we could have met him in the
country and known the man whom you describe.'

[2] James Strachey Barnes.

the front-door key. Brooke was soon arranging for Marsh to stay with his mother in Rugby. 'She is alarmed because she conceives of you as one demanding infinite spaciousness and elaborate entertainment. In vain I assure her that your range is enormous and that you move with equal grace in palace and hovel.' Marsh's second meeting with Mrs. Brooke, which occurred on the 22nd at 24 Bilton Road (the house to which she had moved after the death of her husband), went without a hitch, though they had little in common. The troubles to come were not casting the slightest shadow before. On the Sunday Marsh and Brooke walked to Dunchurch and back, and after dinner went through the principal reviews of *Georgian Poetry*[1] which Marsh had brought from London, and now spread out on the dining-room table. On the whole the Press was gratifying enough. They must have felt a glow of achievement, and for the first time was mooted the idea of a sequel to come out in the winter of 1914.

A few days after his return from Rugby there was a dinner-party at 10 Downing Street. It was decided that on May 10 the Prime Minister and the First Lord would sail for Malta in the Admiralty yacht *Enchantress*, the primary object being a meeting with Kitchener to discuss the future balance of British sea-power between the Mediterranean and the North Sea. It was understood that Mr. Churchill would want to take his Private Secretary, but Marsh was at once invited by Mr. Asquith to join the cruise as a friend of the family. After everyone had retired to bed, Marsh sat up until after one o'clock with Violet Asquith, whose lively interest in literature no less than in politics made her an especial bond between him and the family circle at Downing Street.

In a letter to Brooke Marsh included a political anecdote.

I don't know if you've heard about the rag in the House yesterday. Charles Masterman said the tactics would discredit a discredited Opposition—there was an awful row, and the Opposition began making out that he had said 'disgraceful', and the Chairman, who had been defending 'discreditable' as a Parliamentary expression, said for the sake of a quiet life 'of course if he had said "disgraceful" it would have been a very different matter'. So for the next ½ hour everyone on both sides amused themselves by bringing 'disgraceful' into every sentence, and got suspended. It was too ridiculous. I met Violet Asquith in the passage and said wasn't it fun 'disgraceful'

[1] See Appendix I.

being elevated to the rank of a swear word like 'bloody'. 'Yes,' she said, 'I expect Masefield will put it in every verse of his next poem.'

Before the end of the month Brooke was announcing his return to Gray's Inn. 'I'm going to tea that day with Cathleen Nesbitt in her dressing-room. Isn't that *too* romantic! I've never been into an actress's dressing-room in my life before!'

On April 16 Marsh was asked to accompany Brooke to a dinner-party in celebration of Violet Asquith's birthday. Brooke came down from a short stay in Birmingham with Drinkwater in time for the most memorable occasion of all his London seasons. His place at table was between Mrs. Bernard Shaw and Mrs. Masefield, while Marsh sat with Elizabeth Asquith on his right and Sylvia Gosse on his left. The other guests were Shaw, Masefield, Barrie, Gosse, Augustine Birrell, Walter Raleigh, Raymond Asquith, Lady Horner, and Lady Crewe. A fortnight later their young hostess accompanied Brooke and Marsh in a box at *Hullo Ragtime* (they had just come back from a week-end at Clouds with George Wyndham) and on the following evening they were again her guests to dinner in Downing Street and sat up late discussing the literary scene.

During these past weeks the friendship with Denis Browne had become more intimate. He had entertained Marsh in his lodgings in Shawfield Street, Chelsea, played over his latest compositions to him on the piano, and had also given him a private recital on the organ at Guy's. He had been taken to Pavlova's first night at Covent Garden, Forbes Robertson's *Hamlet* at Drury Lane, and to tea at the Admiralty, where he was presented to Mr. Churchill. Though Marsh was no judge of musical composition, an article on Scriabine in a recent number of *The Times* had impressed him with Browne's ability as an analytical writer, and he responded warmly to the gentle integrity of Browne's nature which was in sharp contrast to the restless brilliance of Brooke. Whenever Brooke was away Browne was the evening companion, or they would form a trio in Soho restaurants or at the theatre. Edward Horner, Shaw-Stewart, and Lady Tree and her daughter Viola were often in the picture, and an evening was spent with Alice Meynell and her husband, discussing the forthcoming edition of Francis Thompson on which they wanted Marsh's advice. While sitting in the window-seat helping Alice Meynell thread her new bead curtain Marsh expressed himself anxious to cut four lines out of the poem *The Hollow Wood*. 'I steel myself to a sacrifice,' wrote Meynell next day, 'that I know the Poet would have sanctioned under my considered approval.'

Two other friends and their literary struggles were now prominent in his life, John Middleton Murry and Katherine Mansfield, whom he chose as the main repository of Perceval's 'murder money' during this month. In mid-January Murry had asked him to stand surety for £100. The rent of his cottage at Runcton and especially the printing bills of his magazine *Rhythm* were making it almost impossible for him to live. By July he wrote to say his next venture, the *Blue Review*, was also failing. The first number of this now famous journal had sold barely eight hundred copies and the paper was losing £15 a month, and at this time the editor was still heavily in debt to the printer of *Rhythm*. Murry was now living in a cottage in Cornwall which he had rented from J. D. Beresford (another writer who had recently entered Marsh's circle) but it was not until he had come back to London that he discovered by chance that yet a further instalment of 'murder money' had come his way.

> When I went to my bath I dried myself on a towel which we had left behind in Cornwall and your letter come tumbling out. I don't know why you do these things, Eddie. Is it to heap coals of fire? I'm sure it isn't, but it hit me all of a heap. My normal state of mind towards you is one of fright because of all that money. . . . You see the real trouble is that no one has ever treated me as you have. It's outside my experience and it makes me nervous and afraid.

At this juncture Murry's financial prospects were nil, beyond a payment of £2 from the *Westminster Gazette* due at the end of the following week. The last (July) number of the *Blue Review* was a parade of Georgian talent, beginning with the first appearance in print of the serenade from *Hassan*. Denis Browne wrote on Wolf-Ferrari, and Abercrombie's article contained what must have been almost the first appraisal of D. H. Lawrence's first volume of poems, and together with Gilbert Cannan, Beresford, Walpole, Drinkwater, etc., Marsh himself appeared as a critic for the first time since his article on Brooke in the *Poetry Review*. A letter from John Middleton Murry to the present writer returns us to this point (April 1913) after giving his own reminiscences of Marsh and Brooke in the previous months.

I cannot remember the *exact* time when I first met Eddie Marsh—it was, I think, in the early summer of 1912. Certainly, it was through Rupert Brooke, who called upon Katherine Mansfield and myself in our flat in Gray's Inn Road early in May of that year. We had asked Rupert to contribute to *Rhythm*: first, he replied (from somewhere in Germany, if my memory is correct) to say that he would and then, when he returned to England, he called himself; I suppose to spy out the land. The visit ended by his inviting us to lunch, somewhere in Soho. Eddie was there. We were, at first, distinctly shy of him: he was so immaculate, so aloof behind his enviable monocle, so evidently from another sphere, that it was with a shock of pleasant surprise that we discovered in him a bubbling spring of dry and delightful humour. Rupert, having learned that *marrons glacés* were our favourite sweet as they were his, stood us a whole dish of them, which we munched appreciatively while he told us some very macabre stories. One that sticks in my mind was of a solitary old woman, whose habit it was to sit at the window of her cottage. Everyone was a bit scared of her: she had the reputation of a witch: so that the rare passers-by only glanced towards her, afraid to meet her eye. They just saw she was at her window, as she had been for years. Gradually her head began to droop: she no longer looked out of the window. At last her chin was quite sunk on her breast. And then someone plucked up courage to go right up to the window and look in. Her head was really all that was left of her. Her cats had eaten the rest.

However, we had enjoyed our lunch so well that we rather diffidently asked Eddie if he would care to come and see us. To our surprise, he evidently would, and he fixed the evening there and then. For one thing, I suppose we must have appeared rather unusual specimens of the literary fauna; for another, we had succeeded in enlisting the support of most of what were to be known as the Georgian poets, and since this was the moment at which Eddie was meditating the famous anthology which gave them their name, it was perhaps natural that he should make our acquaintance. Whatever his original motives, the one that came uppermost, after the friendship was begun, was plain kindness and generosity.

Not long after the beginnings of our friendship with Eddie, Wilfrid Gibson, with whom we had made friends at a distance—he lived at Hexham, whence he had sent us poems for *Rhythm*—decided to come to London, and asked us to find a cheap room for him: which we did, and sent him the address. Then we discovered that that particular house in Guilford Street was disreputable, and hunted for another. We found it just in time, for Wilfrid was on his way. We were, indeed, still negotiating with the landlord, when Wilfrid's train was due at King's Cross. So Katherine jumped into a taxi in time to catch him on the platform, and take him to the room, where I was waiting with the garrulous high-Victorian landlord. When we gathered in his room to clinch the agreement, his remark was memorable: 'You wonder to see so many photographs of the same woman in my room? She was my wife—a dipsomaniac, you know.' Then we took Wilfrid off to our flat in the Gray's Inn Road for tea. Afterwards, discovering that I had a whole golden sovereign in my pocket, I proposed a taxi-ride all over Hampstead and Highgate, to show Wilfrid the haunts of the poets. There was precious little of my sovereign left at the end. It must have given Wilfrid a false idea of our affluence.

However, at that particular moment, we were not badly off: in fact, we were living in a fool's paradise concerning the financial position of *Rhythm*. We quickly introduced Wilfrid to Eddie—*his* golden sovereigns, I remember, came out of a sovereign-purse: a forgotten article of furniture nowadays—and Eddie took to him as naturally as we had done, for his singular integrity. And both rejoiced with us at the news that a rising and apparently prosperous publisher who traded as Stephen Swift was taking over the financial responsibility for the magazine and giving us a joint salary of two pounds a week for editing it. That, we thought, gave us the opportunity of escaping from London. We promptly took a little house at Runcton, between Chichester and Selsey. Thither came Rupert and a brilliant friend of ours, Frederick Goodyear, also killed in the war, but unlike Rupert leaving no permanent memorial. Rupert and he got on famously, for Goodyear had an astonishing repertory of songs, which we sang at the top of our voices on our evening tramps through the marshes. Thither too came Eddie. Indeed one of my most vivid memories of him belongs to this time: of his standing cheerfully and patiently under an old apple-tree, while I stood on his shoulders to throw down the fruit to Katherine. He was so obviously not dressed for such an enterprise: but he insisted that it was safer than my climbing the tree, which he said he could see was rotten. A heap of leaves was burning slowly, and the smoke drifted low about us on that still evening of late September. Why should that memory of him be so vivid? Partly, I suppose, because of my shock of surprise when he told me to get on his shoulders: it was out of the range of things one associated with him. But chiefly because of the sudden glimpse it gave me of the essential sweetness of the man.

In Eddie's honour, Katherine put on her grey evening dress—
her only one—and I a dinner jacket, and we had a bottle of claret.
Though I can see it all vividly, and remember the odd sensation
of playing ladies and gentlemen, I have only the vaguest memory of
what we talked about; but there is a dim recollection that it was
about French literature: for I feel sure that it was on this occasion that
Eddie gave me a salutary shock by saying that he thought La
Fontaine the truest poet of all the French ones—an opinion which I
believe I have come to share. Anyhow, when he left us on the
Monday morning, he left with us the conviction that we had found a
friend.

Our fool's paradise quickly collapsed. Stephen Swift went bank-
rupt; and then we discovered to our complete dismay that though he
had taken over all the assets of *Rhythm* he had not taken over the
liabilities. The printer's bill had been left in my name. In short, I
owed them something over £400. Like fools, instead of closing down
the magazine, we determined to go on with it. All our hire-purchase
furniture was carted away, and we went back to London, much
sadder, but not much wiser. We found a room in Chancery Lane at
10s. a week; and then a time of real hardship began. Katherine
undertook to pay the whole of her allowance of £100 a year to the
printers for the old debt, and I agreed to settle the current bills of
another cheaper printer month by month. Everything depended
on what I could earn as a journalist. I suppose, for the next few
weeks, we must have lived on less than a pound a week between us:
and it was bitterly cold. We kept quiet about this preposterous
arrangement, knowing that any sensible friend would have dissuaded
us; and we lay for a time *perdu* in Chancery Lane. But it was not long
before sheer hunger, if nothing else, made us respond to Eddie's
invitations to breakfast, where we could lay a solid foundation for the
day. I fear we went as often as three times a week, if only to brace
ourselves to the appalling meals we inflicted on ourselves for the rest
of the time. And Eddie must have taken us out to lunch on many
of the non-breakfast days. My recollection is that, so far as substantial meals were concerned, we practically lived off Eddie for
those uncomfortable weeks.

One evening he turned up at our room in Chancery Lane and
asked if he might come out to supper with us. That really put us in
a hole. We had not enough money between us to take him to the
cheapest tolerable restaurant; and I suppose we looked our embarrassment. 'You do *have* supper, don't you?' 'Yes,' we said, 'but . . .'
'I want you to take me where you go. Didn't you say you went to a
place in Little Cold Bath Fields?' Alas, we did. It was a place where

they sold a hot meat pie for 1½*d*. and potatoes for ½*d*.; two of each made our normal supper. It was a horrible place: the forks were greasy, and the knives fastened to the table. And an inappropriate musical box, of the antique kind with a slotted brown metal disk, tinkled out ancient tunes. We told him he would hate it. Not at all, he said. He liked new experiences. So off we went. I can't say it was an enjoyable meal, though Eddie behaved as though he enjoyed it, even to the penny cup of 'coffee' which crowned it. However, we went back to our room, settled Eddie on the camp-bed; made a brew of some almost real coffee, and forgot all about our embarrassing dinner. I remember Eddie was very worried, or perhaps pretended to be. He had met, in our room, some evenings before, Gilbert Cannan, who was a friend of ours. We did not realize he had known Cannan before; but now we had all been invited to dinner with Gilbert and Mary Cannan at their house in Edwardes Square. Eddie had known Mary Cannan much better than he did Gilbert; but that was when she was J. M. Barrie's wife; 'I really don't know *how* I ought to behave,' he said, lifting his eyebrow. We laughed outright. Eddie not knowing how to behave struck us as a really comic notion. He was rather fond of pretending perplexity. Every week almost he had a new picture in his breakfast-room, and he was always saying: 'and now I'm not quite sure whether I really like it. But I certainly did when I bought it. Perhaps I am safer with old English water-colours'. His monocle would drop, and the characteristic expression, of a smile almost but not quite suppressed, would come on his face.

A few days after the meat-pie dinner, we received a letter from him with a cheque on Coutts' for £100, for *Rhythm*. It came out of the blue. Nothing quite so astonishing ever happened to us as that. Neither of us had ever handled a cheque of anything like that size before. And of course it put an end straightway to our rather appalling straits. It paid our printing bill for three months clear, and we could now use a decent proportion of what we earned, for ourselves. I remember we bought a bed that would hold us both instead of the camp-bed from which one or the other of us was constantly dropping on the floor. Even though we concluded, naturally enough but quite wrongly, that Eddie was a *very* rich man, our gratitude was enduring. Never again was anyone to befriend us in such a fashion.

And that was not all that Eddie did for us, and for *Rhythm*. He saw a way of helping both Wilfrid Gibson and us together. Wilfrid, if I remember aright, was keeping body and soul together chiefly by reviewing for the *Glasgow Herald*. It was atrociously paid, and he had to send the books back. It sounds fantastic, but I really believe he was paid a half-crown for reviewing a novel. To earn a pound a week on such terms was sheer slavery. I suppose we must have told Eddie about it. Anyway, one morning came a letter from him suggesting that Wilfrid should become assistant-editor of *Rhythm*, which would not be an exacting occupation. Eddie would provide a pound a week for his salary; and we must keep it a secret. Whether we did, I don't know; but I don't see how we could have done for long, for Wilfrid must soon have got to know that the magazine was not making enough to pay anybody at all.

In fact, *Rhythm* went on losing money, but not so catastrophically: the loss I think steadied down to about £10 a month. But since we were paying off the old printer's debt at the rate of £100 a year, even that was too heavy a burden. We had taken a little flat in the same building, at twice the rent of our hateful room. We had a bed-sitting room, and a kitchen, and a top-lit cubby-hole which served Wilfrid as an office. With a kitchen we could feed ourselves, which made a difference. Still it was hard going. But we received our callers with dignity. Eddie must have been the most regular of them. There came the Lawrences, back from Germany, just in time for the reviews of *Sons and Lovers*, to see the 'nice people' who ran 'the daft paper'. We cottoned to each other, and rashly promised to stay with them at Broadstairs, but couldn't go because we hadn't the fare. Eddie happened to be spending that weekend with Herbert and Cynthia Asquith at Kingsgate nearby. So he met Lawrence then, and through him Lawrence formed a friendship with Cynthia Asquith which lasted a good deal longer than most of his friendships. Eddie also explained to him why we couldn't come; and that produced a letter from Lawrence which was the real beginning of my more tumultuous friendship with him. It was one of the good offices Eddie was for ever doing.

Rhythm, finally metamorphosed for three months into the *Blue Review*, came to an end in July 1913. It would have ended long before but for Eddie. Its intimate association with him was commemorated by our using as the frontispiece to the first number of the *Blue Review* Max Beerbohm's caricature[1] of Eddie confronting Winston Churchill: '*A Study in Dubiety*: Mr. Edward Marsh wondering whether he dare ask his Chief's leave to include in his anthology of Georgian Poetry Mr. George Wyndham's famous lovely poem: "We want eight and we won't wait."' The next number contained a brilliant essay by Eddie himself on the exhibition of Max's

[1] See illustration facing p. 224.

caricatures: in which he drew a fine and illuminating distinction between Max's methods as parodist and caricaturist.[1]

The end of Middleton Murry's account has anticipated a stage in our main story, which broke off in mid-May after an evening with the Meynells. Browne had taken his place as the musician among the Georgians, and the voyage of the *Enchantress* on her special mission to the Mediterranean was now imminent. For Marsh there was only one slight shadow in this prospect. He would be away when Brooke packed up his things at Gray's Inn and left for America. Naomi Royde-Smith, then literary editor of the *Westminster Gazette*, had prevailed upon J. A. Spender, her senior editor, to send Brooke to Canada and the United States with all expenses paid, and the promise of a £4 fee for each article of a series giving his impressions of travel abroad. A review in her magazine of Compton Mackenzie's last novel *Carnival*, as well as other contributions which had appeared over the past few years, chiefly on her Competition Page, had given her to suspect that the results might be of rather special interest to her readers. She was asking her editor to take a risk, for so far Brooke's exercises in prose were extremely meagre (chiefly confined to journals in Cambridge) and but for the Georgian anthology, which was now in its fourth edition, and a book of poems which had made no very great impression, he was unknown to the public. Marsh had advised him to go, promising to keep him in constant touch with London affairs. Brooke was due to sail from Liverpool on May 22, twelve days after the Prime Minister's departure on the

---

[1] 'No one in England, except Rossetti, has reached such mastery in the two arts of pen and pencil; (and even this compliment must be strengthened if we are to believe Mr. Chesterton, who has just told us surprisingly that Rossetti was only successful in both because he was not very good at either). This is the more remarkable because his method of parody and his method of caricature are so distinct. His parodies are written from within. He seems to possess his victims like the imp of some severely logical nightmare, guiding them into strangely familiar surroundings, in which they remain themselves, only more so. He gets into their skins like a refined Sally Beauchamp, and jerks them into odd characteristic attitudes. He is a hypnotist, who shows up his subjects politely and cheerfully drinking methylated spirit in the belief that it is ice-cream-soda. Roughly speaking, no "Max" disengages himself: we have only Messrs. A, B, and C, in their habits as we know them, but a little off the rails. In his caricatures, on the other hand, he is entirely the outside observer and critic. There is far more exaggeration and distortion; and though there is equal subtlety, it is shown rather in choosing a point of departure than in keeping up a perfidiously faithful companionship. And everywhere we are conscious of Max—a grave, ironic, penetrating, Olympian sprite.'—*Blue Review*, June 1913.

Enchantress. On the 7th Marsh took Gibson to a Donald Tovey concert, then brought him back to Gray's Inn for a farewell supper to Brooke (and incidentally himself), the guests being Cathleen Nesbitt, Violet Asquith, Gilbert Cannan, and Henry Ainley. Browne, who had to stay at home to write an article, was taken to *Rheingold* at Covent Garden the following evening as compensation. This was Marsh's last evening in London for some while. Brooke stayed the night and was given a complete set of Jane Austen as a parting present. Next morning, May 9, Marsh went by train to Southampton. The realization that Brooke would not be in England on his return must have made it feel like the end of a chapter, as indeed it was.

Chapter Ten

BROOKE ABROAD I
(May–September 1913)

ON May 9 the *Enchantress* sailed from Southampton with the Prime Minister, Mrs. Asquith, her step-daughter Violet, Mr. and Mrs. Churchill, Admiral Moore, and Marsh in his capacity as Private Secretary to the First Lord. On arrival in Venice they went sight-seeing in a gondola. Some days later they visited the palace of Diocletian at Spoleto (Split), and drank beer under giant plane-trees at Ragusa (Dubrovnik); on the 16th they anchored in Corfu, where at last there was time to dash off a letter to Brooke.

There's nothing in the world duller than a travel letter written by me—but I expect this is nearly my last chance of catching you before you start so I must send you a few last words. Do take care of your precious self and have a glorious time, to make up to me for your not being in England! and try not to stay away for too long. I shall feel the want of you. I hope you'll send me your news whenever you can —and remember that I want you to make every possible use of me while you're away. I'm keeping Violet up to sending you introductions for New York—it's difficult to get anyone to do anything on a yacht,' but if not in time they can be forwarded.

We really are having a wonderful journey, the company is excellent—I'm getting very fond of Margot, excitable and easily upset, but a very good sort and says excellent things in the midst of her outpourings. Talking of 'principle' the other day she told me she liked people to have a few bars in their character '*very far apart*, but *iron*'. Last night we touched on the topic of unnatural vice, she said she never could see the sense of it as 'they can't even produce a paper-parcel between them, and *I* think the only point of that sort of thing is to have rows of jolly little children'.

Yesterday we enjoyed rural delights in Vallona bay, on the Albanian coast. Winston organized seine-fishing, expecting miraculous drafts—but in four goes we only caught 4 fish. We had a splendid picnic luncheon, Winston kept quoting Gray's *Ode to Spring*, 'At ease

reclined in rustic state' etc. When he came to the bit about the May
flies, 'Their airy dance They leave in dust to rest', the 1st Lieut.
thought it was 'Their arid aunts'. Such a good principle of family
life, to leave one's arid aunts in dust to rest. I always do it.

I wonder if you got my postcards, which I've sent off from all
sorts of unlikely looking little post offices. Cattaro was an extraordinary place—a series of bays one inside the other like Chinese
boxes, and the mountains round them getting bigger and
bigger.

We have a plan for going to Athens tomorrow for luncheon and
dinner, we telegraphed that the P.M. wanted to come strictly as a
tourist—*c'est le mot*. But even a few hours in Athens are better than
nothing.

Well, my dear, we are just going ashore so goodbye—and bless
you with all my heart.

They saw the Parthenon, and Mr. Churchill, indignant at the
sight of so many fragments of tumbled columns lying around which
still looked serviceable, came out with the idea that a posse of
blue-jackets from the *Enchantress* might be detailed to set them up.
The archaeologist in attendance was discouraging, but Marsh
has noted in his Memoir that nevertheless the simple repair
suggested on this occasion has since been carried out to the satisfaction of all scholars. 'Surely,' he observed of this excursion, 'to
have seen Athens gives a man what Swift calls Invisible Precedence
over his fellows.'

After Greece came Sicily, where the Prime Minister, having
brushed up his Thucydides for the occasion, regaled his party
with a brilliant review of the Sicilian Expedition, and from the
stage of the Greek theatre at Syracuse Marsh declaimed Housman's
parody of an Attic tragedy. To the astonishment of his companions in the remotest seats of that vast auditorium—he was
audible. 'It was a wonder,' he remarked afterwards, 'that the
offended shade of Aeschylus didn't send an eagle to drop a tortoise
on my head.'

On May 22, while the *Enchantress* was putting into Valetta
harbour at Malta, Brooke was being seen off at Euston by Denis
Browne, whose parting gift, as a gentle hint, was a box of writing-
paper. Later that day he sailed from Liverpool in the *Cedric*,
having tipped an urchin who called himself 'William' to wave him
off from the quay. Marsh and the First Lord were walking round

the docks at Malta. There Mr. Churchill and Admiral Moore remained while the *Enchantress* left for Palermo with the rest of the party. Mr. Churchill rejoined them at Palermo two days later, and among the mail he brought with him was Brooke's first letter written from Rugby a few hours before his departure. 'I commend into your keeping all England, especially Wilfrid, Cathleen, The Nine Muses, and the Spirit of Wisdom and Goodness. . . . I would send Violet Asquith my love if I didn't think it lacking in respect.' He had availed himself of Marsh's introduction to Granville Barker, who had spoken encouragingly about *Lithuania*, and he had instructed his mother to write to Marsh if she wanted to 'know about my literary affairs'.

After two days the *Enchantress* left Palermo and sailed to Sardinia. Recalling the pleasures of this trip afterwards, Violet Asquith was reminded of the card-games on board every night after supper. Eddie Marsh, she was amused to observe, took his bridge very seriously, and regarded the occasions when Mr. Churchill was his partner in the light of a mixed blessing. The First Lord's unconventional mode of play was liable to introduce an element of surprise. 'I can still hear Eddie's cry of pain,' she has recorded, 'when Winston, having "led up to" and sacrificed his partner's king, declared "Nothing is here for tears. The king cannot fall unworthily if he falls to the sword of the ace"—a dictum which left Eddie's tears over his fallen king undried.'[1]

On the 29th the *Enchantress* paid a flying visit to Ajaccio, where Mr. Churchill and Marsh called at Napoleon's house and in the upstairs room stood together 'for a full minute in silent cogitation'. Within a few days they were home again and dining at 10 Downing Street, where Marsh won 5s. 6d. off the Prime Minister at bridge, then went to Shawfield Street to relate his adventures to Denis Browne. The last stages of the cruise were described in a letter to Brooke written at Terling Place, Lord Rayleigh's house in Essex.

I got your letter after I had given up hope. Luckily Winston stayed at Malta while the rest of us went on to Girgenti and Palermo, and brought it with him, so there was more joy over it than over those just letters which had been posted up to time. It was dreadfully

---

[1] *Eddie Marsh*, Sketches for a Composite Portrait of Sir Edward Marsh, K.C.V.O., C.B., C.M.G., ed. Hassall and Mathews (Lund Humphries, 1953).

The Apple Gatherers by Stanley Spencer

A Study in Dubiety

Mr. Edward Marsh wondering whether he dare ask his Chief's leave to include in his anthology of Georgian Poetry Mr. George Wyndham's famous and lovely poem: " We want eight and we won't wait."

A cartoon by Max Beerbohm

(*a*)   Eddie in search of Talent
(suggested by Beardsley's
Algy in search of Ideals)

(*b*)   The artist in the house
E. M. and Paul Nash

disappointing to find no poetry in it, I did think at least you would have finished *Aeterna Corpora*.[1]

The cruise was a tremendous success till the end. We got to Athens at tea time and left after luncheon next day, but we saw the Acropolis 1) by daylight 2) by moonlight and found it a bit of all right. Sicily was divine and we had a day at Sardinia and 2 hours at Ajaccio. The party very harmonious on the whole, and at the end I found I liked everybody better than I had when I started—especially Margot whom I fell into desperate love with. The P.M. is excellent company, and his polished phrasing is a constant joy—I learnt by heart such a good sentence of his on the last day. He was asking my advice about tips etc. and wondered whether he ought to do anything for the Doctor, who had attended their maid Coats. 'I understand he has twice diagnosed her—once for ptomaine poisoning and once for cardiac debility—in both cases I believe falsely—but the *vis medicatrix naturae*, which is fortunately strong in Coats, triumphed over both his diagnosis and his remedy.'

We got back yesterday week, since when I haven't had one minute to write. I meant to begin giving up balls etc. this year, but have so far been to 4, including 'Versailles' at the Albert Hall, which was a heavenly sight, especially Diana Manners with a black page holding an umbrella over her, and a delightful one at Derby House, in knee breeches (in which I fancy myself) for the King and Queen. I enjoyed Winston's Birthday Dinner, where I sat next the Astronomer Royal and asked him whether Mars was inhabited and how much chance there was of the earth either falling into the sun or leaving the Solar system, and other elementary questions—he was very reassuring on the whole, I hope not merely from bland official optimism.

I've done some concerts etc. with Denis—he hasn't got any work yet but people are always holding out prospects to him and I expect some of them will come off. I got a letter yesterday from poor Flecker. He is in Switzerland, after breaking down at Beirut and 'almost perishing' on the voyage. He has given up 'the infernal East' and means to settle in a small cottage and write. His new book is just coming out—'I am immensely proud of the volume, which is about twice as good as the 42 poems, and I feel it ought to redeem me from the stigma of minor poetry for ever.' I'm sure I hope so! He sends you his love.

There was an alternated *Rhythm* luncheon, only Jack [Middleton Murry], Wilfrid [Gibson], and Hugh Walpole—who is very well

[1] A sonnet later entitled *Mutability* and eventually finished when Brooke was in the Pacific Islands.

satisfied with the work he has done in Cornwall, and is now enjoying himself for a month in London. Katherine Tiger [Mansfield] is in the country. She got turned out of an omnibus the other day for calling a woman a whore. She really ought to remember she's a lidy. The provocation was that the woman said that all suffragettes ought to be trampled to death by horses. Katherine tho' not a suffragette protested, and the woman said, 'You with your painted lips!' Rather a squalid little story.

There's a good deal of talk about the Laureateship. Monro wants to have a public meeting and charge 1*s*. to debate whether it should be abolished—he wants to have an unofficial laureate chosen by the poets, which he says they have in France. This seems absurd and I hope he won't have a meeting as it would be sure to be ridiculous. I like the idea of the Laureateship myself, and there's no fear of having another stewmer like Alfred Austin. I believe the P.M. will offer it to Bridges. Maurice Baring said what fun it would be if it were offered to Gosse, and what a struggle he would have between the duty of accepting and the duty of refusing.[1]

I've just begun D. H. Lawrence's new novel *Sons and Lovers*, which is so far a masterpiece—I do hope he keeps it up. He has got a lovely

[1] In an earlier letter Brooke had said 'The chief topic which excites America is, who (if anybody) is to be Poet Laureate. All the papers have immense articles, with pictures of Masefield and Noyes. They mention everybody as possible, except me and Wilfrid. Even Will Davies. I'm going down to the Stock Exchange tomorrow, where I hear they're betting on it.' Marsh, who was regarded as the man of special influence, received many suggestions by post. A friend in Ireland wrote to say he was forming a small society for the purpose of putting forward Alice Meynell as the new Laureate. He had heard that Bridges was expected to decline the honour and that Yeats was being backed by Gosse, while Mrs. Meynell's own candidate was Abercrombie. In Flecker's last letter (June 5) he had said: 'I wish they would make Rudyard Kipling Poet Laureate like sensible people. I have a horror of them giving it to that fellow Watson.' And Brooke writing in a Canadian railway train exclaimed: 'I say, do just see that the Laureateship is kept. It would be a frightful scandal if it were abolished. Why not Bridges? I hope Violet'll see that it's all right. Kipling'ld be fine too.' He wrote to Gosse in somewhat the same vein, and Gosse's reply (September 7) shows that he had been in conflict with Marsh, having disapproved of Marsh's candidate, who, of course, was Bridges. 'Oddly enough—but this is a secret—Thomas Hardy wished for it—and was disappointed. I was very keen that it should be kept up as an office, it is so stupid to do away with old amusing things because they are incongruous. All amusing things are incongruous.' Aggrieved by this opposition Marsh organized a meeting between Gosse and Bridges at Hanover Terrace, and then on July 24 wrote to congratulate the new Poet Laureate: 'You must be overwhelmed with letters, but I can't refrain from telling you how supremely pleased I am that you are Laureate as well as laureate which you have always been. The Prime Minister told me in the Mediterranean last May, before there was any question of a vacancy, what he would do if there were one—so my only fear was that you might contemn it. But you did not, and you have restored the post to what it was for most of the nineteenth century—a national recognition of Poetry in the person of a worthy representative.'

style and it's infinitely more sane and solid than his other books. I had practically no time for reading on the yacht, but I got in Beresford's new book[1] which was a bitter disappointment, it's merely a 2nd rate Wells I think (good things in it, of course) and I read Woolf's book[2] which I thought beautiful. Morgan Forster's coming to Raymond B. for the night of the dinner—I had been told he had run completely dry, but I'm glad to hear from him that he is writing. *I*'ve written nothing but a lot of anagrams to amuse the P.M. and Violet, who adore them.

Lord Randolph Churchill once, getting into the clutches of a bore at his club, rang the bell and said to the waiter, 'Would you mind listening to the end of this story?' and left the room. I'm afraid you may long ago have given this letter to a negro to finish. However do answer as much of it as you get through. I sent you a valedictory epistle from Corfu, but I don't think you can have got it before you left. I wonder if you will see Noyes. I hope he is better. If you come across Lord Murray of Elibank in a false beard give him my love.

Meanwhile Brooke's letter written at sea had shown him trying not to take his discontents too seriously. 'I think I will drown myself at thirty, or turn schoolmaster speedily. I do not care for the fate of a poet.' On June 15 Marsh wrote from Cambridge.

Here I am at the old place again, but I miss the undergraduates who are all gone down. Arthur Benson dined here last night, and Jane Harrison this evening. I went to luncheon at Downing with my Da—all sere-ish yellowish leaves. I went to the Fitzwilliam! (it reflects great credit on Cockerell) and read a little in the backs. It all reminds me of a contemporary of mine called Arthur Paley who was blamed for not taking part in the life of the place and said, 'But what *does* one come to Cambridge for except *absolute* peace and quiet?'

I had a fairly good London week—Monday a concert with Denis, Tuesday dinner with the Sturge Moores which was disappointing—I did think at least there would be Tagore! but there was only a poor little governess, pathetically pretty and prettily dressed, who was introduced as 'our governess' and never spoke, but kept running round the table to fill up my wineglass, which made me rather hot. There was no good talk—but Moore said a thing that I shall remember against him. The tedious old question came up of whether one would rather be blind or deaf, and he said deaf of course, because one could get practically everything one wanted from books!

Wed. I dined with Lady Hamilton, a fusion of fashion and

[1] *Goslings.*
[2] *The Village in the Jungle,* by Leonard Woolf.

intellect, the latter represented by Roger Fry, Charles Whibley, and Yeats whom I talked to after dinner. He told me of George Moore making friends with a woman and saying, 'How I regret, for your sake, that I'm impotent', and that this year's Academic prize is to go to James Stephens for *The Crock of Gold.* Thursday I won 15*s*. 7*d*. at bridge, Friday I went to a magnificent performance of *Aïda*, picked up Denis for supper, and then went to a ball at Norfolk House and met Violet, who had come early and said she found 'an unamalgamated mass of men and women like vinegar floating on oil', a good description of the beginning of a ball.

Yesterday I lunched with who do you think, the old Fred Pollocks 'to meet' the new American Ambassador. I sat next his son, who had a little conversational mishap. A bore called Lord Ferrer, on his other side, mentioned Miss Austen (by the way, Rupert, *how are you getting on with Miss Austen?*), so I asked Frank Page if she was much read in America? 'Not much,' he said. 'I've read her myself, but the truth is the Americans read books to be amused, and tho' there are amusing things in Miss Austen it must be allowed that the total impression left by her books is sad. For instance, *The Mill on the Floss*'——Here my good breeding gave way, and 'But that's by George Eliot' burst from my lips. He went a sort of mud colour—and then said, 'I've got mixed up. Wait a minute and I'll tell you what I meant'—rather a sweet way of taking it. I called my tact out of abeyance, and gave the subject a slight twist which saved what remained of the situation.

Are you following our politics? I've just remembered that I dined with the Asquiths the night we came back from the yacht, and he said he had just had a conversation with Illingworth which was very amusing, 'as he had a good deal of dry humour'. I now realize that the topic had been X's investment of Party Funds in Marconi. Asquith has a wonderful gift of detachment.

Lawrence's book was rather disappointing, after its beautiful beginning. It's a very serious work, but I thought the hero's passions became too obscure and eccentric to be really interesting. It's very long and I've read nothing else except today a translation of the *Rhesus* by Gilbert Murray which has a very fine line—'Unhood the eagle of thine eye' said by someone waking up Hector. I must see what it is in the Greek—I've only just heard that Rosalind Murray is engaged to one Arnold Toynbee, did you know?

On June 22 after a dinner of the Cambridge Apostles with G. E. Moore presiding and speeches by Robert Trevelyan and James Strachey (who embarked on 'a poisonous attack on the

Society which rather missed fire through his breaking down and
having to be revive'd with brandy'), Marsh sat down to make his
account of the occasion the start of a letter which contained news
of the first rumours of opposition to Georgian Poetry.

Bob Trevy made the most amusing speech but it owed everything to
his curiously infelicitous delivery. Most of the people made jokes about
you, but none very good. Morgan Forster stayed the night with me
but I didn't have much talk with him as about a dozen came home
with us and stayed till we dropped. He didn't tell me anything about
what he is writing.

I went to the Poetry Bookshop and bought all the most recent
verse but I don't think it's up to much. Hodgson's *Eve* is very disappointing, it turns out to be a nursery rhyme, in the exact style of
Little Miss Muffet, as such it has a certain charm, but I can't think
it's an appropriate manner for the subject. . . . Wilfrid tells me
there's a movement for a 'Post-Georgian' anthology, of the Pound-
Flint-Hulme school, who don't like being out of G.P. but I don't
think it will come off. I had to speak severely to Monro about one or
two things he has said in the new *Poetry and Drama*—one was 'Bad
popular poets like Tennyson, Lewis Morris, and Kipling—' (just like
that—with no elaboration of what he meant) which is pure mud-
throwing, like Pound's insult to Abercrombie.[1] He agreed at once,
and said pathetically that he was quite alone in the world, and always
had to write in such a hurry that he had no time to think, and there
was no one to keep him straight! The other thing was still more
typical, he had put solemnly that 'we understand it is probable that
the Laureateship will be abolished'. I asked him why and he said
because he hoped it would be. I pointed out that this didn't constitute
probability, and he said it was human nature to think that what one
hoped for was probable!

This is Lord Spencer's house [Althorp], one of the real Stately
Homes of England, with the *most* wonderful pictures—12 Vandycks,
2 supreme Rembrandts, several Gainsboroughs and about 20 Sir
Joshuas, many of them his very best. Lord S. is a very amusing
character, with lots of old-fashioned pronunciations like yaller for
yellow. He carries them into modern life and calls G.B.S. 'Barnard
Shaw' like Berkeley Square, and Sir Ernest Cassel 'Cussel' giving it
the German vowel. He has a delicious little petulant way of saying
things, there was a bird this afternoon which kept saying *Cracaw*,

---

[1] In the *Poetry Review*, Vol. I, No. 77, November 1912, Brooke had published a letter,
written at Monro's invitation, in answer to an article by Pound, whose offence was no
worse than the inclusion of Abercrombie's name in a list without comment.

Cracaw, Cracaw—and he said, 'I do wish the birds would be quiet—I don't mind *ordinary singing*, but this one makes such a tiresome noise.' I don't know if it sounds funny unless you know him.

It's now midnight, I've been playing lawn tennis all afternoon, five sets, all with vantage games—51 games altogether—so I've got pains in my legs, and am rather drunk from assuaging my thirst with champagne.

His last letter of June was written, as usual on a Sunday, from Ridgehurst, the home of Edward, elder brother of Sir Edgar Speyer.

—'the wrong Speyers', as Diana Manners said yesterday when I told her where I was going for Sunday. By the way, she was very funny, we were lunching with her sister Letty Charteris when up drove an enormous Victoria drawn by two huge white horses and containing Marjorie Anglesey's baby, about 10 days old, airing in her nurse's arms. We all went out to see her (rather disappointing as it must be admitted that she doesn't yet look quite so nice as, with her advantages, she doubtless will hereafter). When we got back Diana said the nurse had a very bad name to drive in a Victoria with—*Horsefall!* but the *other* nurse's name was so dreadful she couldn't even tell what it was. I got her to whisper it and it was *Miss Carry*. But to come back to the wrong Speyers, I should think they are the most musical people now alive. The house is swarming with musicians. Fanny Davies, Donald Tovey, Fleury (the greatest living flautist) and several others. I can tell you it has been a treat, Bach, Schumann etc. from morn to dewy eve. Do you know Donald? He is a very old friend of mine, but I find his humour more and more trying. Almost everything he says is a joke really, but sometimes it is very difficult to tell whether it is or not, and then if one asks he says 'obviously', which is a dreadful snub. For instance, that's what he said when he mentioned a publication called *Who are you?*—and I said, 'Is that the same as *Who's Who?*' which I thought an innocent question. However he told me a very funny story about J. G. Frazer, which I think you would have told me if you'd known it—so if you do, I'll tell it you as a punishment. It appears that F. is great at mechanical devices, among them a sliding door by which he can make his drawing-room into two. When not wanted, the door is made to fly up into the story above, where it makes one bedroom into two. Once there was some celebration at Cambridge, and an influx of distinguished foreigners who were quartered on the dons. Frazer sent up the door, put two married couples into the two bedrooms, and slept in the drawing-room himself. In the middle of the night he felt cold and cheerless in the vast room, got out of bed and pushed the knob which brought the door down—never realizing the consequences till he sent up in the morning to find out why neither of the married couples had appeared at breakfast—I hope you didn't know this.

I've had rather a jolly week, except the one evening which I attempted to spend in a manner worthy of my higher self by dining with the Walter Leafs—heavens, what a set of stewmers they had collected! It would be disloyal not to mention that I attended the State Ball and was received by Their Majesties with their usual affability, but I can't conceal from you that it was rather a squash. Poor Philip Sassoon gave a well-meant entertainment which was not so successful as it deserved. I arrived late, and after being kept a few minutes on the landing was admitted into a place like the Black Hole of Calcutta. The door was shut behind me, the light which it admitted having shown for a second the flash of stars and tiaras, revealing the fact that all the Ambassadors and Duchesses in London were present, but all that could be seen afterwards was a beautiful little Norman Wilkinson scene, representing a heavy iron nail-studded door which flapped in the draught—and Lillah McCarthy beating against it and moaning inaudibly. Poor Mr. Balfour said, 'I'm deaf myself, but I'm sure that even people who *can* hear can't hear this.' The play was Maeterlinck's *Death of Tintagiles*. If you know it you will realize that it is not the sort of thing to hold the attention of a fashionable London audience after a superb dinner. There was the most fearful fidgeting and bumping together of Guardsmen at the back of the room struggling for a little air to breathe. I stood next Sybil Sassoon who was in despair, and kept whispering, 'You can't imagine the anguish I'm suffering'—and 'Never again will I ask a soul inside the house.' Afterwards there was a little play by Masefield, I believe the first he ever wrote, called *The Sweeps of* '98, a humorous incident of the Irish rebellion. It was a little better, but hardly worth doing. I felt very sorry for the Sassoons, who had got Granville Barker to produce, Norman Wilkinson for the scenery, Vaughan Williams for the music, Lillah, Maire O'Neill, Arthur Wontner etc. to act and must have spent thousands—but it was very ill-judged.

Another night I went with Denis to the Ballet, *Scheherazade, Faune, Sylphides*, and the new Debussy *Jeux*. All the papers and most people hate it, but don't you believe them, it's *delicious*, I went thoroughly meaning to dislike it, so it isn't *snobisme* on my part. I was enraptured from the moment the curtain went up. It's a Post-Impressionist picture put in motion—Karsavina and Shollar in little indeterminate white garments—tripping and sliding about like specially unlifelike automata, with the most exquisite grace, skill and humour. The charm is quite inexplicable, except that it is obviously the cleverest thing in the world—it has almost brought me round to Matisse's pictures! I didn't understand Nijinsky's dancing, but hope I shall next time.

Early in June Marsh was on the *Enchantress* again, this time at Dover, with Mr. Churchill and Admiral Jellicoe, entertaining the French Minister of Marine. Dining at the Russian Embassy next day he took in a Lady in Waiting to the Czarina who observed that he talked French '*en perfection*', a dewdrop which he hastened to report to Brooke in his next letter written at Stoke Poges. 'Fancy staying a whole Sunday and not going to the churchyard. I did rehearse the Elegy to myself in the bath, meaning to say it later on the spot, but I played tennis instead.' He launched another shaft in his persistent quarrel with Brooke over his sonnet *Channel Crossing* with its unsavoury theme of sea-sickness, but this time the offending piece was only glanced at in a quotation. 'Do you know the game, for instance, you say, "Three charabancs on the Brighton beach", and the answer is "Brake, brake, brake, on thy cold grey stones, O sea"? Mine is, "Rupert Brooke ought to choose more elevated subjects for his poetry." It is a line from Browning. Can you guess it? It's, "Ah, but a man's grasp should exceed his retch."'

The social gossip of the day centred on Lady Sackville's libel case against Sir John Scott, and the principal literary topic was the threatened failure of Middleton Murry's courageous venture, the *Blue Review*. It looked as though Gibson's sub-editorship was coming to an end. Already he was making plans to join Abercrombie in Gloucestershire and concentrate on his verse, which to his surprise was becoming remunerative. His *Daily Bread* had just reached its third edition, and an American magazine had sent him ten pounds for his poem *Flannan Isle*. Gibson's well-being was a matter of constant concern to Brooke, and Marsh took pains to keep him informed, but to Marsh Flecker's book was the main excitement. It was read aloud at meals in Gray's Inn. Mrs. Patrick Campbell and Cathleen Nesbitt listened to it as Mrs. Elgy carried round the coffee; Marsh's new friend Mark Gertler (a young art student at the Slade, introduced by John Currie and Gaudier-Brzeska at a concert in the Albert Hall) was regaled with passages from *The Golden Journey*, after he had looked round the pictured walls where one day his own best works were to find a place. In the two years that followed it was his talks with Gertler and Currie at Gray's Inn or in their studios that more than anything else formed Marsh's taste in contemporary art and confirmed the revolution which Neville Lytton had deplored after the purchase of Duncan Grant's *Parrot Tulips*.

Shortly before the 13th there arrived a letter from Brooke written in the sleeper of his train to Montreal. His description of a fat woman snoring in the berth beneath him, assumed by the attendant to be his wife, provided Marsh with the opening gambit of his next letter (Hill Hall, July 13).

I got your delightful letter from the train to Montreal this week. It's my duty as a friend to warn you that mischief is brewing.

> BROOKE—*On the 9th July, at Ashford Hill, Newbury, the wife of R. C. Brooke, of a daughter.*[1]

Evidently the Fat Lady seen in the Train has nipped over to England and is foisting her bastard on you—so beware.

The great event of the week is Flecker's book, *The Golden Journey to Samarkand*, published by Goschen. I do think he has been and gone and done it! He has set out to make beauty, and has made it—a rare achievement, usually it only comes on the way to other things. I read the book, in floods of tears, on the way to the Admiralty! There's a preface in which he says that what English poetry now wants is the ideal of the French Parnassians, 'to redeem it from the formlessness and the didactic tendencies which are now in fashion'. It ends with a good arrogant sentence: 'Those who are for ever seeking for what they call profundity of inspiration are welcome to burrow in my verse and extract something, if they will, as barren as the few cheap copy-book headings to which they once reduced the genius of Browning. . . .'

It is a difficult book to quote from, because all the effects are so led up to, and depend so much on the context. There is a poem called *Gates of Damascus*, in which the watcher of each of the 4 gates describes what his gate leads to. . . .[2] Wilfrid has read the book and thinks it beautiful but doesn't like it for that reason. He first said the beauty was merely 'an ornament,' but I drove him from that position by proving that in each case the beauty *was the poem*, not

---

[1] Newspaper cutting pasted into the letter.

[2] He here quotes eight lines beginning '*The dragon-green, the luminous, the dark, the serpent-haunted sea*'. Another passage beginning '*O traitor pines*' he prefaces with 'very like *Lycidas*, and none the worse for that'.

something stuck on—he then said he preferred people to find beauty in places where it wasn't, rather than where it was—on which I remarked with asperity that I supposed he would like the *Ode to the Nightingale* better if it were the *Ode to the Crow*—to which nice knock-down argument he found no answer. Tho' I fear he is not convinced.

Monro has at last sent me £60 profit on *G.P.* so after paying myself back for disbursements I had £3 each to send to the contributors (I gave you yours in anticipation before you went, didn't I?). It might have been £4 each, as he is keeping back £18. The £78 are on the 1st 5 editions and the 6th is selling well—so there will be some more presently. . . .

I haven't had a very describable week—three nice dinners, a Russian Opera with Denis and a ballet with Jim Barnes account for my evenings—I lunched on Wednesday with Cathleen—and she came to supper with me the same evening which was in one way an awful failure as I asked 9 people and only 4 came! Pamela Lytton and Maurice Baring among the chucks, with *no* excuse, whereas dear Mrs. Campbell came in spite of having acted twice that day. She was extraordinarily amusing so I hope C. enjoyed it, tho' I was much too damped and depressed by the chucks to be very happy or at all at my best myself.

I don't see what use I can be to Cathleen! as I don't know her well enough for her to tell me her troubles. She *seems* very happy, and is living a healthy life in the country—so I hope she's all right.

I've enjoyed my Sunday very much, it's a *most* lovely William and Mary house, surrounded by glorious country—most beautifully furnished, and luxurious *à la limite du luxe*, as the *Arabian Nights* would say. It belongs to Mrs. Charles Hunter, sister of Ethel Smyth, and for some reason very rich—she's a tremendous friend of Sargent, Henry James, etc. The party is a mixture of Society and Bohemians, including Edith Wharton whom I like very much, and Percy Grainger who has been playing like an angel. I've played 9 sets of tennis and am absolutely worn out. Percy Grainger is just about my form, and we had three singles. I won the first, he the second, and then he won a 'conqueror's' after being 8 all, which was very Homeric and fatiguing.

Victor Lytton sent me down with 100 pp. of proofs of his life of Bulwer Lytton corrected by Edmund Gosse and by a man at the British Museum whose career is to correct proofs. He came rather a howler over a sentence in a letter in which B.L. describes Victor Hugo as a *monstrum, informe* but *ingens*—the poor pro corrected it to *informé* but *ingénu*—thus giving away his Latin on the one hand and his French on the other! Even after these two workers in the field I have gleaned so many misprints that I'm afraid I shall have to volunteer going through the whole—about 1,000 pp.

I must end with a good story of Edith Wharton's. An American lady engaged a servant at a registry, a Scandinavian girl, just arrived in New York with excellent characters from Norwegian situations. The first day she said, 'I'm having a little dinner tonight and shall expect you to cook it.' Answer, 'No cook.' 'Then you must get the rooms tidy.' 'No sweep.' 'Then you must help me to dress and do my hair.' 'No do hair.' 'Then what *do* you do?' Answer, 'Milk elk.'

At Hill Hall Edith Wharton was very severe with Marsh over his recommendation of *Sons and Lovers*, saying she would never trust his opinion again, and she was amazed that he could approve such bungled work. Marsh was adamant, however, and continued to spread what he called the 'gospel'. It was now that he received from Lawrence an acknowledgement of his share of *Georgian Poetry* royalties. 'What a joy to receive £3 out of the sweet heavens. I call that manna. I suppose you're the manipulating Jehovah. I'll sing you a little Te Deum.' He went on: 'I should like to see you very much, I suppose you won't be Margate way? (Don't be insulted, at any rate.)' Marsh replied that by coincidence he would be staying a week-end with Mr. Asquith's son Herbert and his wife at Kingsgate in a week's time, and he added that one of his fellow-Georgians, W. H. Davies, whom he had converted to *Sons and Lovers*, wanted his autograph. Lawrence replied at once, asking Marsh and his host to tea at his lodgings in Percy Avenue, Broadstairs, and remarked of Davies: 'I should like to meet him. He feels so nice in all his work.' In a guarded footnote, for he was not yet married to Frieda, he said: 'My wife is looking forward to seeing you also.'

The invitation was reversed, and when Herbert and Cynthia Asquith received the Lawrences to tea at Kingsgate on July 20, it was an historic occasion. Marsh and Cynthia Asquith remained among his truest friends and benefactors to the end of his life. Years later Lady Cynthia vividly recalled the encounter. 'The moment a slender, lithe figure stepped lightly into the room we both realized almost with the shock of a collision that something new and startling had come into our lives. I don't believe anyone could have been in Lawrence's presence for two minutes without being struck by his difference from other people. It was not a difference of degree; it was a difference of kind. Some electric elemental quality gave him a flickering radiance. Apart from this strange otherness, one could see at once that he was preternaturally alive. With his broad, jutting brow, and clear, sensitive, extremely blue eyes—very wide apart—he looked half faun, half prophet, and very young. He had not yet grown the tawny beard with which most people remember him.'[1]

The same evening Marsh wrote to Brooke.

Patrick [Shaw-Stewart] always laughs at me for finding a poet wherever I go (especially Davies at Knole!)[2] and this time it has really been a miracle. Hearing that D. H. Lawrence was in England, I sent him his Georgian cheque care of E. Garnett, who I knew was a friend of his—and got an answer from Kingsgate, Broadstairs, saying that he didn't suppose I ever was in this part of the world—whereas lo and behold I had been engaged for weeks to come here to Beb and Cynthia Asquith for this Sunday. So I went to see them and brought them to tea, where they were a tremendous success. He looks terribly ill, which I am afraid he is—his wife's German, they seem very happy together. She rather hurt my feelings by saying that she simply couldn't believe from my appearance that I cared for poetry!

I've distributed and (I hope) sold a good many copies of Flecker —Gosse wrote me a letter full of temperate and dignified praise, and next day his feelings got the better of him and he supplemented it by a postcard of incoherent enthusiasm. I hope the book will be well reviewed. I'm very keen on the scheme for you and Wilfrid, Lascelles and Drinkwater to bring out a poetical serial. I hope you are coming into it. I've been trying hard to think of an alternative title to 'The Gallows Garland'[3] (which I fear will win the day by its absolute fitness and rightness) but without success, though by the way I thought of titles for other things—for instance, if Father Terry wants to make his Palestrina performances a real success at the Westminster Cathedral, it occurred to me that he should call them Hullo Plainsong. I've asked Denis to suggest it to him.

I went one day to the new Stravinsky Ballet, *Le Sacre du Printemps*, at last the Russians have been too much for me—Denis adores it and I told him I would believe he liked it if he could assure me that

---

[1] *Remember and be Glad*, by Cynthia Asquith, pp. 133-4.

[2] The home of Lord Sackville near Sevenoaks, the town where Davies had lodgings. Marsh had already met him at the opening of the Poetry Bookshop.

[3] The Gallows was the name of Abercrombie's cottage near Ryton, Dymock, Gloucestershire. The scheme developed into the quarterly *New Numbers*.

he would enjoy hearing a canary, a slate pencil, a motor whistle, and a paper bag all at once. The physical pain in my ears was so great that it got between me and everything else. Poor little Pilz, who does a cataleptic trance at the end of it, had hysterics last time it was done, so I'm told it can't be repeated. I went with Denis on Friday to see Mrs. Campbell in *Mrs. Tanqueray* (the old Tank woman she calls it), it was the first time he had seen it, or her—she was simply glorious.

I met Yeats at luncheon with Lady Hamilton yesterday, he is full of a marvellous automatic writer about whom he is not allowed to publish anything, except that she writes for an enormous variety of obscure spirits who give dates and particulars of their lives which he afterward verifies in old *Timeses* etc. at the British Museum. He claims that she puts her fist through Religion and her toes through Philosophy—but it's difficult to judge on the slender evidence he is permitted to divulge.

When he got back to Gray's Inn he found Brooke had written to him from Ottawa, asking him to perform the functions of an agent, and to place his poems where he could for the fee of two guineas each. And he was homesick. 'I make up little minor pitiful songs, the burden of which is that I have a folk-longing to get back from all this luxury to the simplicity of the little places and quiet folks I knew and loved. The very beautiful one has a chorus—

> *'Would God I were eating plovers' eggs*
> *And drinking dry champagne*
> *With the Bernard Shaws, Mr. and Mrs. Masefield,*
> *Lady Horner, Neil Primrose, Raleigh, the Right*
> *Honourable Augustine Birrell, Eddie, six or*
> *Seven Asquiths and Felicity Tree*
> *In Downing Street again.'*

He enclosed two poems, 'the first fruits of my exile. Poor stuff, and more is on the way.' Marsh answered from Mells, where he was staying with Edward Horner's family.

I like the two poems, especially *Doubts*[1]—so does Wilfrid, who wants them both for his *New Numbers* (that is the title that now finds most favour) but of course I shall send them to Knox if he applies. By the way you imply that I have more poems of yours to dispose of. You say they are to be 2 gs. except *Wisdom in Women* which is one, but I

---

[1] *When she sleeps, her soul, I know.* The other poem was probably *He wonders whether to Praise or to Blame her.*

have no others—unless you mean me to get two guineas for the lines on Dinner at Downing Street? I'm still longing for the completion of *Aeterna Corpora*.

This is the Horners', a small party, only Venetia [Montagu], Felicity [Tree], Lord Haldane and Duff Cooper, a charming youth whom I don't think you know. I'm worn almost to the bone by four singles with Edward, following on a long four this morning which Duff and I won against Edward and Felicity at 10–8. The house and garden are perfect, you must come here some day—there's a swimming-bath which would appeal to you.

I can't tell you how glad I am the Season is over, it got bloodier and bloodier—the onestep—turkeytrot—bunnyhug or fishwalk or whatever you choose to call it—carried all before it, and my general dislike of its vulgarity, combined with my particular dislike of being on the shelf as a nontrotter—hugger—or walker, worked me up into a fine frenzy of disgust and socialism. Pamela Lytton, one of my oldest friends, admitted she had avoided my eye at balls for fear of having to talk to me and so lose five minutes of the joy of hugging some alien bounder! For the English gentlemen are at a hopeless discount, thank God that none of them are really good at these vile manœuvres and their rightful place is taken by the scum of two continents. You will probably sympathize with me when I say that for me the lid was put on it by finding Ethel Levey, whom I had seen kicking the chandelier at the Hippodrome, dancing and supping as a guest at Lady Wenlock's. Seen at close quarters she is terribly coarse and flashy—and her singing, in a room, where some subtlety is required as well as breadth, seemed hopelessly inartistic. I'm getting rather sick of ragtime, but I still think that such things as Willy Solar's singing of Dixie are artistic achievements. Ethel Levey throws rhythm to the winds, and uses the songs merely to exploit her great big ugly enormous bass voice. A few more such evenings and I shall have no noble and picturesque Toryism left for you to explain away. The negrification of Society will soon be complete—and black faces will be an essential part of evening dress.

Denis and I agreed that it would be unfair to use the 3rd edition of *Hullo Ragtime* as a bait to lure you back—it's completely spoilt. Nothing left of the old except Bonita's husband and the Wedding glide—and the only tolerable novelty is a *rather* but not very funny parody of Russian dancers. Denis let me in badly over the *Sacre du Printemps*. I told you in my last letter how he loved it and I hated it the first time. He gave me a lecture, and said my mistake had been to listen too much to the music—and that just as oxygen and hydrogen, tho' disgusting separately, made a delicious compound (is this scientifically correct, I don't know) so the cacophonous music and the ungracious gestures melted into a perfectly harmonious whole. With the ductility which is the defect of my docility, or the docility which is the quality of my ductility, I went again, followed his instructions, and succeeded in being ravished with delight. Next day I went to D. (who in the meantime had seen it again) and told him of my conversion, expecting to be told I was a good boy. Not a bit of it, he had completely changed round and the whole ballet was one vast mistake! Denis has written an excellent article on it which appeared in yesterday's *Times*. They seem very much pleased with him now and I think they are really going to give him some work, which will be better than writing for the poor *Blue Review* for nothing.

In his next letter, written at Ockham Park, Woking, Marsh gave the news that the seventh edition of *Georgian Poetry* was going to press, and that on July 30 D. H. Lawrence had been introduced to W. H. Davies and Gibson at a luncheon-party in Raymond Buildings. 'It's very sad you aren't here to meet Lawrence, you would like him.' One evening before this J. C. Squire had paid his first visit to see the pictures and had left behind an ode to Francis Thompson which, unlike his later work which was to find honoured place in *Georgian Poetry*, seemed unworthy of the promise its author had shown elsewhere. But this was not the only problem in Marsh's correspondence.

The Poet Laureate has done the dirty on me, I got a letter from a young Abingdon resident, saying that Mr. Bridges had recommended him to send me his poems for judgement and advice as to publication. I wrote him a very nice civil letter, advising against publication, and making a detailed examination of the poems which I couldn't keep from becoming more and more like Macaulay's essay on Robert Montgomery. I thought there were only two possible ways in which he could reply. Either, 'Sir, I return the fragments of the insults with which you have endeavoured to desecrate my sacred muse'—or 'I must thank you for the thoroughness with which you have performed the doubtless painful task of opening my eyes to the fact that my poems are worthless.' Instead of which he answered— 'Thank you very much for your kind letter, with every word of which I agree. A friend has put it in my power to publish my poems immediately.'

I went to luncheon with Mrs. Lavery one day after which Mrs. Pat Campbell and Harry Ainley read out Flecker's poems—with great effect.

I'm staying with Lady Lovelace, who is a very old strong-minded woman, with certain prejudices which detract from her merit as a hostess—one is that smoking is strictly forbidden except in the smoking-room (I'm now risking everything on my bedroom being on the opposite side of the house from hers) and another that there are no baths, one of her chief theses being that Surrey is being drained of the water it needs in order to gratify the disgusting middle classes in their insane passion for washing. Otherwise she is rather jolly. It's a dull party, with one bright spot—Eric Maclagan, whom you once met at Yeats's (and who greatly admires your poetry) and his new wife *née* Helen Lascelles—they are charming. There is also a German Professor called Schick from Munich, who has the sweetest and most appreciative of natures, and is one of the most thundering bores I've ever met. He pours out ceaseless floods of information mostly rather elementary. I've avoided talking to him myself but whenever I've overheard him he has either been lecturing on *Beowulf*, or explaining that the name of Cologne is derived from Colônia Agrippîna, or something like that. He was asked here to see the Byroniana. His naiveté is extraordinary, we played a game after dinner to prevent him talking—writing out lots of things beginning with the same letter—he was so delighted when any name he had heard of was read out—ach, Petrarch, *very* good—ach, Peebles, a town in *Scot*land, yes, excellent—ach, Pericles, colossal!

During the next week two of Brooke's letters arrived at once. The earlier was addressed from a hotel near the Niagara Falls where he had arrived on July 24. 'Funny to think that this noise has been continuously sounding and that I'm hearing the *same* noise as George Washington and Poe and Goldie Dickinson, only a little later on.' At Toronto he had found an Arts and Letters Club, 'and, Oh Eddie, one fellow actually possessed my "Poems". Awful Triumph! . . . One man said to me, "Mr. Brooks (my Canadian name) Sir, I may tell you that in my opinion you have Mr. Noyes skinned."' The other letter, from Lake Superior, enclosing an envelope to Gosse on which Marsh was to attach the correct suffixes to his name 'in something like my handwriting', expressed his bewilderment at Canadian methods of advertising. 'One said, "Ten thousand biscuits are made every year in our factory." Isn't that a dreadful picture? It has depressed me all morning.' Marsh answered from Pixton Park with news of Gertler, Browne, and Flecker.

Rupert, I've got *two* letters from you since I wrote last Sunday, I think you're *the* most wonderful correspondent—far better than me, as travel-letters are at least 5 times more difficult to write than stay-at-home ones. I must change my time for writing to you—the small hours of Monday morning are the worst imaginable—I'm always dog-tired with tennis and drunk with champagne. Such at any rate is my condition at this moment. . . . I had a most delightful dinner at R. Bdgs. on Tuesday, John Currie, the painter who dined at one of the Rhythm dinners—and his mistress, an extremely pretty Irish girl with red hair called Dolly Henry—Mark Gertler, a beautiful little Jew like a Lippo Lippi cherub—Michael Sadleir—and Denis —they were tremendous fun. Michael started on Friday for America, where he's going to work for six months with a publishing firm. Denis is off tomorrow to motor up to Cumberland with Alan Gray, and stay there for some time. He had another article in *The Times* yesterday and I think they now want anything he will send them, his thing on Stravinsky having had a great success. Talking of *The Times*, I've made Bruce Richmond promise to put in a proper review of Flecker's book, they had only given him 2 lines in the column which (luckily) doesn't preclude a subsequent review. The book is already going into a 2nd edition, which is wonderful. He writes that he has finished rewriting his play *Hassan*, and that he 'has tremendous hopes of it and will undoubtedly have a terrible disappointment'! he is a queer fish. Bob Trevy has taken Boccaccio's villa near Florence and asked Wilfrid and Abercrombie to stay with him in October, which will be jolly for them—Wilfrid comes to see me every morning for a bath now that he is quit of the poor *Blue Review*. . . . Beb [Asquith] very foolishly took upon himself to enliven the party by telling Cynthia I had told him as a great secret that I was engaged to Lady Margaret Sackville! I've had great difficulty in disposing of this—luckily before she had used it as an item of news for her correspondence.

On August 17 he paid his first visit to Lascelles Abercrombie's cottage, The Gallows, in the village near which less than two years later, in Gibson's cottage, he was to compose the first draft of his memoir of Brooke. The day after arrival he wrote to Brooke, recording his first impression of *The End of the World* that one day was to be the end-piece of *Georgian Poetry*'s second volume.

Here I am at last, it's the most delicious little house, black and white, with a stone courtyard, and crimson ramblers, and low-beamed rooms. Mrs. Abercrombie is a delightful woman, *bâtie sur les grandes lignes*, rather βοῶπις[1], rather Madonna, not exactly

---

[1] An attribute of the goddess Hera—'ox-eyed'.

beautiful, but very fresh, and very reassuring, extremely humorous and intelligent, perfect wife-and-mother. I've spent most of this morning with her cutting up French beans and peeling potatoes, I love domestic occupations. There are 2 charming little boys, David aged 3, and Michael, who is very beautiful, about one. Michael is the charmer—he sits in a pen in the dining-room, made of wooden rails, with an abacus let into the side, and full of stuff animals. The bathroom is a shed out of doors, with a curtain instead of a door, a saucer bath which you fill by means of an invention of Lascelles' (who was a scientist before he was a poet) a long tube of red india rubber, with a funnel at the end, which you hang on a pump on the other side of a path—cold water alas! otherwise I have nothing but envy of Wilfrid coming to live here. I came down on Friday evening (having packed Winston off to Switzerland) and went yesterday for a longish walk with L.A.—it's lovely country, and we climbed a high hill from which we should have seen all the Kingdoms of the Earth, but for a thick haze. He's a great beer drinker, and made me swill 'mild' at every pub, it's delicious and sustaining, but fuddling. Also he won't let me go to bed before one, so it's 'the strenuous life'. He's writing some plays, but the only thing I've seen is the beginning of a long poem called *Zagreus* which he insisted on reading out loud at the moment when I'd got up, at midnight, and said I really must go to bed. I didn't understand one word of it, so can't tell you what it's about. I hope he isn't going to be permanently obscure.

Your Mother sent me yesterday the proofs of your first two Westminster letters, my dear they are simply brilliant—the Abercrombies thought so too. There was only one correction to make. What is the American for 'you bet your boots', they had left out the word. I had to put in 'boots' simply—I hope it isn't disastrously unidiomatic.

Monday. Lascelles read out last night the beginnings of two plays (about ½ each) *The End of the World* and *The Staircase*, both magnificent, especially E. of W., in which a Dowser comes to a pub in a secluded valley and explains that the comet which they see in the sky is rushing on the Earth. You can imagine the splendid poetry and rhetoric he would pour out on such a theme. In the 2nd act, not yet written, it will turn out to be a false alarm. I am afraid of anticlimax, but his characters are so good that he may pull it off. *The Staircase* is a low-life drama, rather in the manner of *Blind*.[1] I am so glad, as *Zagreus* had depressed me.

They are rather uneasy about Drinkwater as a contributor to *New Numbers*, as they think he only means to send them what he can't get paid for by magazines! I should think it would be best to chuck

---

[1] A dialogue from *Interludes and Poems* (1908).

him and get Flecker or (or and) Bottomley, if he is able to write—
I hear he is better.

There is very little going on here, the discussion of the pox, arising
out of the Medical Congress, is the chief thing. One or two papers
called it syphilis, and some went so far to write of venereal disease,
but the *Daily Mail*, which was full of it, never got beyond 'The Hidden
Plague'—I thought of writing them a letter about the small-hidden-
plague and chicken-hidden-plague.

After lunching alone at the National Club Marsh had slipped
on the entrance steps and injured his foot. Brooke's school and
college friend Geoffrey Keynes, who happened to be in London,
was just starting his distinguished career as a surgeon, and
through Gibson, who became a self-appointed male nurse at
Raymond Buildings, Keynes was called in to examine the
patient, which resulted in the receipt of his first professional fee.

It was now that Lawrence answered a letter in which Marsh had
urged him to pay more attention to poetic form. 'I think you will
find my verse smoother,' he wrote from Germany, 'not because I
consciously attend to rhythms, but because I am no longer so
criss-cross in myself. I think, don't you know, that my rhythms
fit my mood pretty well, in the verse. . . . I have always tried to
get an emotion out in its own course, without altering it. It needs
the finest instinct imaginable, much finer than the skill of the
craftsman.' This was the beginning of a controversy that three
months later was to become perilously near a quarrel and a
breach in relations. At the luncheon with Davies in Raymond
Buildings Marsh had read aloud some passages from *The Golden
Journey*, and so Lawrence ended this first round with, 'Remember
skilled verse is dead in fifty years—I am thinking of your admiration of Flecker.'

On the 26th Marsh wrote again to Brooke, paying tribute to
Keynes, 'I've had all the resources of medical skill and a fascinating bedside manner lavished upon me.'

I'm expecting to get back to work tomorrow, hopping with a big
stick. It hasn't hurt the least, and has been quite pleasant. I hoped
to do a lot of reading, but the recumbency shuts my eyes almost as
surely as if I were a wax doll that can say Papa and Mamma, so I
drowse all day. Wilfrid has, as you might expect, been an Angel in
the Flat.[1] I haven't asked people to come and see me, for fear they

[1] *Cf.* Patmore's poem *The Angel in the House.*

wouldn't! but Wilfrid brought W. H. Davies in this morning—and Currie came yesterday. I have conceived a passion for both him and Gertler, they are decidedly two of the most interesting of *les jeunes*, and I can hardly wait till you come back to make their acquaintance. Gertler is by birth an absolute little East End Jew. Directly I can get about I am going to see him in Bishopsgate and be initiated into the Ghetto. He is rather beautiful, and has a funny little shiny black fringe, his mind is deep and simple, and I think he's got the *feu sacré*. He's only 22—Currie I think a little older, and his pictures proportionately better, he can do what he wants, which Gertler can't quite yet, I think—but he will. They both admire Cookham[1] more than anyone else. Gertler was to have taken me to see him (at Cookham) tomorrow, but it's had to be put off. Gertler has had a temporary setback in a picture he is painting. He takes tremendous interest in Christ, and wanted to paint him disputing with the Drs. It is apparently unheard of for a Jew to paint Christ, so to get his models (his brother, and some Bishopsgate Rabbis) he made them think it was only going to be just any young Jew with any old Jews—he writes today that they have found out, and won't sit any more! Isn't it curious.

I shall be buying some pictures soon! I think I told you I was inheriting £200 from a mad aunt aged 90, it turns out to be nearer four hundred than two! So I'm going to have my rooms done up and go a bust in Gertler, Currie, and Cookham. . . . Wilfrid's Muse suddenly returned to him yesterday, and after sitting at tea with me and Currie in a (literally) be-Mused condition he rushed off and wrote a long poem. I haven't seen it yet.

At the end of July Brooke had reached Winnipeg. He celebrated his twenty-sixth birthday with a picnic on the shore of Lake George, then went on to the Rockies and at Calgary wrote the letter that reached London in the first week of September. He was being looked upon chiefly as a 'political expert' and he was making 'vast speeches in favour of Winston's naval policy', and urged Marsh to bring Mr. Churchill out on the *Enchantress* for an inspection of the Panama Canal so that they could all meet and talk. His poem *Dust* was appearing as his representative piece in Canadian magazines, but he wrote: 'I've left Pegasus in a horse-van at Port Arthur, which reminds me that I don't think I should value Flecker's poems so highly as you seem to. . . . I expect I'd find him too fluid. Give him my love.' Then he went on:

---

[1] Stanley Spencer, who lived at Cookham.

England—I dreamt, last night, that at Vancouver I got sick of the trip and came back to England, and landed at Grantchester (you should have seen how we drew up at the Boathouse), and wired to you that I was going to stay a night with you in London, and caught the 4.55, and, oh! woke. Would you have been there?

Five days later he sent a picture-postcard from Lake Louise: 'I'm in Heaven (and quite time too!).'

The proofs of two of his letters to the *Westminster Gazette* had just come in. 'How can you call them painstaking drearinesses!' Marsh wrote from the Admiralty. 'They are extraordinarily good and amusing.' The main news was theatrical. He had taken Mrs. Patrick Campbell to the first performance of Shaw's *Androcles and the Lion* and found it 'pure joy—the papers have in general been extremely stupid about it.[1] I thought the switching backwards and forwards between farce and drama and high thinking were miraculously well managed. I was laughing one moment and crying the next, with hardly ever a jar, and the bits which aim at moral beauty achieve it, for once. . . . Flecker has sent me his play, rewritten, finished, and immensely improved— I now think it might have quite a chance.'

Flecker's health had broken down in Beirut, and in May he had moved to Leysin, Switzerland. He was awaiting Drinkwater's verdict on his first two acts. On June 6 he wrote to Marsh for the return of the MS. since he had lost his own copy, he said, and felt in the vein for work. 'I am going to cut the farce clean out— or modify it greatly, and be less heavy with the oriental expressions.' Marsh passed on the request to Drinkwater in Birmingham, which obliged him to read the play before sending it back. This was no doubt what Flecker had intended. This news and more comments from Gray's Inn were a great encouragement to him. 'The farce with the Jew has gone clean out at once,' he replied reassuringly. He had sent to Geneva for a toy theatre to work with, although he had already stated (June 6) that he wasn't going to 'worry over much about the requisites of the stage. A lot of rot is talked about literary plays not succeeding . . . I am only

---

[1] Lillah McCarthy, writing from the Kingsway Theatre, urged Marsh to support a counter-attack in the public Press. 'It really is very disheartening that the British Public should be ready to jump at phantom straws when they swallow camels. . . . Now that this idea of scoffing at religion has been started in connexion with *Androcles* it is extremely difficult to eradicate it.'

going to try and keep *Hassan* interesting; then if it's good enough the stage can adopt it or adapt itself to it.'

Meanwhile Flecker received a fanfare of praise and a list of critical notes from Marsh about his latest book of poems. This volume contained what was to be the concluding lyric passage of *Hassan*, and the last line Marsh criticized. He thought it should read: 'We take the golden road to Samarkand.' Flecker replied: 'I cannot—with all deference—get to like the golden road as much as the golden journey—I wouldn't mind Golden *Track* so much. . . . I am glad you liked the *Gates of Damascus*, I consider it my best work.' Early in July Marsh sent him his £3 share of the latest profits on the anthology, and with it Flecker decided to pay for the typing of his play. On August 5 he reported 'Hassan is finished' . . . and he had come round to Marsh's view and decided on 'the Golden Road'.[1] Within a few days Marsh was giving an account of the reaction to the new poems among his friends. 'I wish I had been at the luncheon party to hear Ainley spout the *Gates of Damascus*,' wrote Flecker. 'It would be a still greater joy to hear him in the part of Ishak on the stage.' After seeing the revised version Marsh still thought the action slow-moving in places and considered the ghosts at the end 'impractical', but he was greatly impressed and passed on a note of encouragement from Gosse. Within five weeks the poet had lost his high spirits, disheartened at the prospect of an indefinite sojourn in Switzerland for his health. 'Your comfortably calm letters are my only joy.' He was wanting Marsh to send books and place his poems in a London magazine. 'Alas, you too will cease to love me if I importune you.' Marsh had told him that two of the poems (*Phaeacia* and *The Sacred Incident*) were far below the level of the rest, and the poet readily acknowledged he had only left them in for want of better material. With this reservation it is clear that at this time Marsh regarded Flecker's achievement more highly than Brooke's. Within a month Brooke was to enter the South Seas, where his best work was written.

During the past three months there had been a lot of activity in the Georgian circle. In June *Peacock Pie* came out, and Marsh wrote to de la Mare.

---

[1] In the 1913 volume (*The Golden Journey to Samarkand*) the last line ran: 'We make the Golden Journey . . .' In the final version of the play (printed 1922) the line reads: 'We take the Golden Road to Samarkand.'

I've waited to write until I had time to read it twice and let it sink in. There are exquisite things in it, and no one else could have written them, or anything like them. *Dick and the Moon* is perhaps the one that takes me most of all, another great favourite is *The Little Green Orchard*, and there are several others that run them close. *The Ship of Rio* is delicious, and so is the one about the three farmers— 'Axcusing silver' is an inspiration! (There are some that I don't see quite enough point in . . . praps it's my fault?)

In July R. C. Trevelyan returned his Georgian royalties so as to enlarge the share of his fellow-contributors and gave news that Bottomley had started a play.[1] Marsh at once wrote to Bottomley, asking to see the work as soon as it was done. 'Lawrence, another Georgian, has distinguished himself with his novel, *Sons and Lovers*. It begins splendidly.' Bottomley's answer reported painfully slow progress, he was seriously ill. 'If only we had a Ministry of Fine Arts,' he complained, 'and if only it were under your control'; while from James Stephens (whom Marsh had not yet met) came a note, urging him to keep an eye out for a newcomer called Ralph Hodgson, 'good, not great, but nobody else is great either, and very few are good'.

Early in September preparations began for a trip to Barcelona, where Marsh planned to meet Jim Barnes for a walking-tour in Spain. Mrs. Elgy was to be left in charge of the alterations at 5 Raymond Buildings, which were undertaken solely to make room for more pictures. The walls were to be repainted a neutral tone as a background, and what had been the boxroom was now to be the spare bedroom. These improvements were the first fruits of the piece of good news given in his letter to Brooke of August 25. The instalment of 'murder money' amounting to about £400 was going to fall due to him in October. This legacy arrived at the very moment when his young painter friends, Currie and Gertler, were confirming his daring purchase of the Duncan Grant and it was beginning to dawn upon him that his future as a collector lay in the patronage of contemporary British art.

At this time, ceding Graham's point that the pince-nez which had graced his countenance for twenty years was a 'vulgar' appendage, he abandoned it for good, still keeping the monocle for special scrutiny, and took to horn-rimmed spectacles, which had become the fashion. In his person he was looking

---

[1] *King Lear's Wife.*

several years younger than his age (his forty-first birthday was due in a few weeks). He tended more and more to talk with his hands, the right hand nervously gesticulating with his monocle for emphasis, the left hand extended like a conductor restraining the violas, his whole body tensed. Every night, no matter how late his return, he dealt with the correspondence which was for him an essential, and perhaps the central, feature of his private life, and since he contrived never to be alone by day it meant that he was in converse with somebody or other by pen or word of mouth throughout his waking hours. In the body of the day and often for much of the night he was at work at Whitehall, assisting the First Lord in the task of organizing the expansion of British sea-power, against the clock, as it already seemed; participating too in the opening chapter of the airplane's development as an instrument of war. In Mr. Churchill's office a new terminology was coming into being—technical terms such as 'flight', 'seaplane', etc., were coined and put into currency.

In the first week of September Marsh posted to Flecker a lengthy criticism of the completed *Hassan*. He was not entirely happy about the end. 'I think your other criticism just,' the poet wrote, 'but I love my ghosts. . . . Do send me some picture-postcards of Spain.' He was so cheered by Marsh's letter that he sent it on to his close friend Frank Savory. 'I enclose a letter from my Maecenas Eddy Marsh, Winston's secretary. . . . Don't you think the criticism is rather good?' On the 6th builders invaded the top floor at Raymond Buildings and dumped their paraphernalia in the hall. Marsh was already on his way to Paris.

Chapter Eleven

BROOKE ABROAD II
(October 1913–June 1914)

MARSH joined up with Barnes at Barcelona and they went off to see a bullfight. Their holiday itinerary took them to Tarragona and Montserrat, into France by the Valley of the Cerdagne and back into Spain through the Republic of Andorra; then along the wildest Pyrenees into civilization again at Luchon. From Toulouse they took the train to Paris, where Albert Rutherston conducted them on a tour of picture-seeing and James Stephens gave them tea at his pension. They were back in London on October 5, and as on his return from the Mediterranean Marsh went straight to Shawfield Street to relate his adventures to Denis Browne.

Pleasure in the new paint and wallpaper at Raymond Buildings was somewhat tempered by one of the two letters that were awaiting him from Brooke in Vancouver. The later in date of the two was harmless enough. News of the accident to Marsh's ankle had only just reached him. 'Isn't ligature—or is it ligament?—a lovely word?

> Is it prudent? Is it Pure
> To go and break a ligature?
>
> With lissom ligament
> My lovely one she went
> And trod the street
> On quiet feet.

'Torn, like a ligament, his random mind'—Oh it sets one singing. . . . I'm really writing because I'm so charmed by the picture of you in bed and Geoffrey [Keynes] binding you up and Wilfrid [Gibson] smoothing your brow and giving you chloroform that I sat in the bloody lounge and laughed till Sir Gilbert Parker looked askance at me. What a nice lot you are in England! . . . I hate you lavishing all your mad aunt's money on these bloody artists. Don't forget those woodcuts of Gwen's [Raverat] you were going to buy.

He suggested that Marsh should finance a theatrical performance to be given on the lawn at the Old Vicarage, Grantchester, text by Brooke, music by Browne, designs by Stanley Spencer, and the main role for Cathleen Nesbitt. The other letter written two days before (September 6) contained Brooke's ill-concealed irritation at Marsh's having added the word 'boots' to a passage of American dialogue in the past instalment for the *Gazette*. 'You have done me a great wrong. Why the *Devil* weren't you taught American, as well as French and Greek? "You bet your" is a sentence. Your nothing. Neither boots, nor buttons, nor——, nor hopes of beatitude. Just "You bet your". I don't know why. But it's so. And now my reputation is for ever gone. Hell.' Marsh was genuinely upset. The same letter cost him an advance payment of ten pounds. 'Oh Eddie, did you do all I asked about the statuette? I hope so. But there's one thing. I think I never paid Gill. I'm horror-stricken. He may be dead of starvation.' Marsh had complained of his poetic idleness. 'I know I've only sent three [poems] . . . But damn it, what's the good of a friend if he can't sit down and write off a few poems for me at a pinch? That's what I count on your doing if the editors press.' And it should be noted here, for the sake of a chapter to come, that this letter also contained the remark, 'By the way, you seem to be a great comfort to my mamma, as my literary executor. So if it worries you, be sustained by the thought of the good you're doing.'

After the trip to Spain he soon picked up with Gertler and Currie, accompanying them at the Grosvenor Gallery exhibition and buying two Gertlers and Currie's latest painting of consequence entitled *Abishag*. On October 21, having seen *The Song of Honour* in the *Saturday Westminster*, he asked Ralph Hodgson to lunch at Gray's Inn, and next day Edward Garnett called, introduced by Lawrence. A day or two later Gaudier-Brzeska, who had come to see the Girtins he so much admired, walked into the sitting-room with a letter he had picked off the hall table. It was postmarked San Francisco. Brooke wrote that he was due to leave for Fiji in a few days (the first week in October). The plan was Honolulu, Samoa, Fiji, Tahiti, then 'a resting place at the bottom of the Pacific, all among the gay fish and lovely submarine flowers'. Having delivered the six American articles that Miss Royde-Smith had bargained for, he now proposed to continue, so Marsh must persuade the *Gazette* to commission a sequel. He

was delighted to hear that Sargant[1] had been brought up in his
own house at Rugby. 'The only house in any school that has
produced two Georgian Poets. Tra-la!' There was no time for
Marsh to write again until he was once more aboard the Admiralty
yacht at Portsmouth, where he was accompanying Mr. Churchill
on an inspection of the docks. At Raymond Buildings he had left
behind Gibson, Abercrombie, and his wife Catherine, who all
slept the night there on their way out to R. C. Trevelyan's villa
near Florence, where Lawrence and Frieda were to join them for a
Georgian reunion. Brooke's last letter for the *Gazette* was to hand.
'You *do* write good prose. . . . I took one liberty with the sacred
text. You had put "elusive" and "elusively" in the same sentence,
evidently by oversight. I changed the latter to "indefinably"
which I hope you approve—tho' I've been nervous ever since
my downfall over "you bet your" which sometimes wakes me up
in a cold sweat at night.' He wrote of his new acquaintance
Garnett as 'a clumsy, heavy man . . . with a slow moving mind
but I should think an interesting one—however it didn't fit in very
well with mine. He explained to me who "Mrs. Lawrence" was.
She is a German baroness who married a dull professor at Nottingham and ran away with D.H.L. She got divorced last week and I
suppose they will marry. Apparently her people don't mind very
much, which seems odd in a German baronial family. The L.'s go
and stay in her ancestral home. By the way I got a most charming
letter from Lawrence the other day.[2] He has a real genius for
letter-writing. I do hope he will go on. I am to lunch with Garnett
next week and will try to delve into him deeper.' There was news
of *New Numbers*. Marsh had guaranteed the first two issues against
loss (the production costs were estimated at £15 a volume) and
he had started reading fiction again.

> Galsworthy's *Dark Flower* is an odd book—in 3 parts, a different
> woman falling violently in love with the hero in each, at the ages
> (his) of 18, 26, and 47. He always returns it, but every time it's hope-
> less from circumstances. The upshot is as usual, *ce que c'est que de
> nous!* The wreckage inevitably caused by inevitable passion—it's a
> fine book I think, though the 2nd section is very inferior to the other
> two. I wonder what will come of all this new morality of never
> blaming anyone—Dostoeffsky's gospel of the soul of goodness in

---

[1] Edmund Beale Sargant, a contributor to *Georgian Poetry*.
[2] Letter of October 14, 1913, *The Letters of D. H. Lawrence* (Huxley), p. 145.

things repulsive, Bernard Shaw's that all harm in the world comes from people making rules to prevent others and themselves from doing what they want, and Galsworthy's that everything is very terrible but that it can't be helped. I sometimes wish I were safe back with Anthony Trollope. . . . Have you *any* idea when you're coming back, Rupert, it's really very serious. Your letters are very jolly but I do want to see you—and life is very short and quick, I shall be 41 next month—I hope you'll write some poetry in the South Seas.

In the next weeks two first meetings occurred which in the sequel proved of great importance to all concerned, though at the time they were nothing that seemed worth relating to Brooke. On November 10, at the Café Royal with Gertler, Currie, and William Roberts (another new painter whom Marsh was to support) the young Jewish boy whom Gertler had in tow was introduced as Isaac Rosenberg. A week later while Marsh was lunching with George Mallory at Charterhouse a senior boy of literary promise was called in for coffee and Robert Graves walked into this story. By then a letter had already gone off to Brooke with news that Marsh had at last met Stanley Spencer ('Cookham'), the young student friend of Gertler for whom Marsh was already foretelling a great future. He had forgotten his last budget and was at a loss to know where to begin.

For instance, had I met Cookham? I think not—he came up to lunch with me and we got on like houses on fire. I was disappointed and at the same time relieved by his appearance, he has a charming face and his teeth instead of being in three tiers and green, are now quite regular (except for one which sticks out at a right angle) and whiter than any fuller on earth could whiten them (I believe tho' that he has been to a fuller). He writes delicious letters. I gave him *G.P.*—his only comment so far is that he is glad Rupert Brooke appreciates teatime. He says that tho' he has had tea at 4.30 in the same house ever since he was born, each teatime has a novelty, a character and charm of its own. His father aged 67 has just begun to write poetry! which I am to see when I go there.

Your *W.G.* letters have been excellent, I really can't tell you what I think of the Niagara one—a masterpiece! . . . The *Saguenay* was very fine too, but how *could* you bathe without knowing about the current, it was terrifying to think of "What Might Have Been". By the way I nearly got drowned myself last Sunday. Mark Gertler and I went to stay with Jim Barnes at Cambridge and they made me go out in one of those abominable Rob Roy canoes, which fitted like

a glove. I knew I should upset, and of course I did, in the millpool
—I'm a poor swimmer as you know, and found that in clothes I
could hardly swim at all! but luckily I wasn't far from land, and got
near enough for some kind roughs to throw me a life-belt. I wasn't
really in danger for a moment, and I only tell you for the sake of Mrs.
Elgy's comment. Do you know the trait of her mind by which she
sees misfortunes multiplied in past and future, as if in opposite looking-glasses? For instance I had a supper party here in the Summer at
which ½ the people didn't turn up, so when I was having another
3 weeks ago I said, 'I hope they'll come this time.' 'Yes,' she said,
'they always disappoint you.' Similarly, when she unpacked my
clothes last Monday and found them still wet—'Whatever have you
done, Sir?' I explained, and she said, 'You always do that when
you've got a new suit on.' Wouldn't that make a good 'humour' for
a play? I make you a present of it.

Chesterton's new play *Magic*, of which I went to the 1st night (is
that English?) has a delightful 1st act after which it goes off in a
fizzle. The only good plays are *The Witch*, and St. John Ervine's
Jane Clegg, which is magnificent. I haven't seen Cathleen except on
the telephone—and Denis is so terribly merged in choir practices etc.
that I can hardly ever get hold of him. Now I must go to bed. I
stayed in London today for a speech of Winston's at Alexandra
Palace, and a 2nd visit to *The Witch*—tomorrow morning I go to
George [Mallory] at Charterhouse for the night. Next Sunday I go
to Lady Desborough's to meet Rudyard Kipling. I hope I shall get a
letter from the South Seas soon.

On the day of his return from Charterhouse, with some
Carthusian school-magazine verses by the boy Graves in his pocket,
Marsh took Jim Barnes to dine with Mr. Asquith in Downing
Street, and after dinner they had the Prime Minister and J. M.
Barrie to themselves when the ladies retired from table. Later on
in the month there was a breakfast visit by Robert Bridges at
Gray's Inn, charades with Rudyard Kipling at Lady Desborough's party at Taplow, a Yiddish play at Whitechapel in
company with Gertler and Rosenberg, and a mission to Portsmouth with Mr. Churchill. Early in December Cynthia Asquith
brought Henry Tonks to tea ('Gertler says he can't think how I
can have such people in the house,' Marsh complained to Seabrooke); on the 10th Hugh Walpole entertained him to tea with
Henry James, Max Beerbohm, and H. G. Wells, and that evening
Marsh escorted Lady Hamilton to a function at the Savoy to meet

Anatole France. 'What a deep sagacious old bloodhound he looks,' he wrote to Gosse afterwards. 'I thought his French not *quite* so good as Lord Redesdale's.' On the 13th, mindful of Flecker's interests, he arranged to meet Basil Dean at luncheon in the hope of persuading him to produce *Hassan*. Next day he was complaining to Brooke that he had heard tell of a positive rain of postcards from Honolulu, yet none had come to Gray's Inn. 'I'm green with jealousy. Your mother says you start back in December, Cathleen that you are settling down in the South Seas indefinitely. Which *am* I to believe?'

I do miss you. There have been such heaps of events since I wrote last that I don't know where to begin. Wilfrid [Gibson] is spliced, he writes radiant, he slept here three nights on his way to be married in Dublin—the picture of health and happiness, but completely deserted by the Muse, who seems to have yielded her place to Miss T. with the most deplorable tactfulness.

Did anyone give you an account of Marinetti's visit? I only attended one of his manifestations, a lecture at the Bookshop, in a kind of loft which looked as if it was meant to keep apples in, and as if one ought to get into it by a ladder through a trapdoor. It was illuminated by a single nightlight which I thought at first must be a Futurist tenet—but it turned out to be only a fatuity of Monro's. Marinetti began his lecture by asking how he could possibly talk in a penumbra about Futurism, the chief characteristic of which was Light, Light, Light? He did very well all the same, he is beyond doubt an extraordinary man, full of force and fire, with a surprising gift of turgid lucidity, a full and roaring and foaming flood of indubitable half-truths. He gave us two of his 'poems' on the Bulgarian War. The appeal to the sensations was great—to the emotions, nothing. As a piece of art I thought it was about on the level of a very good farmyard imitation, a supreme music hall turn. I could not feel that it detracted in any respect from the position of *Paradise Lost* or the *Grecian Urn*. He has a marvellous sensorium, and a marvellous gift of transmitting its reports—but what it writes is not literature, only an *aide-memoire* for a mimic.

New Numbers is prospering. There are well over 200 subscribers already—only the authors hang back. I *do* hope you are sending them something. England expects from you more than one sonnet.

I have given Flecker's play to Tree, and I'm really hoping that something may come of it. Basil Dean (ex-Liverpool Repertory, now stage-manager to Tree) thinks the world of it, so does Alan Parsons. . . . I have just bought Cookham's great picture of the Apple

Gatherers. I can't bring myself really to acquiesce in the false proportions, tho' in every other respect I think it magnificent—I've made great friends with him. I went down to the place Cookham 2 Sundays ago and spent the afternoon in the pullulating bosom of his family. There are too many of them, 6 out of 9 were there, besides the parent birds; and they are very gregarious so I never got Stanley to myself—but it was an amusing experience. . . . I've been having a vehement correspondence with Lawrence about what I consider the formal deficiencies of his poems. He tells me I am the policeman of poetry—just as Sturge Moore compared me to a schoolmaster— but I am impenitent. . . . This is a very ramshackle letter, I feel I haven't managed my transitions at all well—but I am so doubtful about you ever getting it that I hadn't the heart to make it a master-piece.

ii

The purchase of *The Apple Gatherers* was a big event in Marsh's career as a patron of contemporary art, and it came at the end of a sequence of vicissitudes which warrant a digression on the Georgian painters. He had first seen the painting at a Contemporary Art Society exhibition in October and had written to the artist. 'I am doing a portrait of myself,' wrote Spencer in reply. 'It is just twice the size of my own head. . . . I fight against it but I cannot avoid it. The next one I do I shall commence by painting in the size of a pin's head.' He recommended his brother Gilbert and also Eric Gill to Marsh's notice. For *The Apple Gatherers* Spencer referred his correspondent to Henry Lamb, who in his turn said the canvas had gone to Leeds for inspection by Michael Sadler, who had already made a firm offer of £50. Lamb, it appeared, had generously bought the painting so as to act as agent and sell it at a profit on the painter's behalf.

During these negotiations an awkward situation arose. Gertler had recommended the work of a youth called Bomberg, saying he was hard up and would sell his drawings cheap. 'They are undoubtedly extremely good drawings and certainly show great power.' Marsh gave the boy £10, and added another drawing to his collection, but when he expressed his thanks to Gertler he found he was at once drawn into a dispute and asked to act as arbiter. Gertler had got it into his head that Spencer had insulted him. As a result he stoutly refused to conduct Marsh on a visit to Cookham to meet Spencer's parents. Being anxious to come amiably to terms for *The Apple Gatherers* Marsh was somewhat at a loss to know where his allegiance should lie. A letter to Sadleir in America, written when Marsh should have been at Cookham, shows that at this stage he was not unduly put out. 'Since we all dined here in my room I've made great friends with Gertler and Currie—especially Gertler whom I see a great deal of and think the greatest genius of the age. . . . I'm afraid artists *are* very quarrelsome, Michael,' he went on after describing Gertler as unaccountable, then gave news of discord in Bloomsbury.

> There's a terrific row about the Omega Workshop. Wyndham Lewis, Etchells, and Wadsworth are sending round a circular accusing Fry of the blackest conduct, intercepting their letters, jockeying them out of commissions, preventing them from exhibiting etc. I hear they are disappointed because Fry hasn't come posting back from the S. of France to meet their murderous attack. I haven't heard his side yet. Of course it must be a misunderstanding, he has probably been very unbusinesslike, but he is certainly quite honest.

Of Gertler he went on: 'Blake and Giotto are about the only people he will let me admire, so I am naturally rather narrow about the New International show—of course I'm allowed Gauguin, Cézanne etc.' It was over Cézanne that Gertler had now quarrelled with Spencer. The Omega trouble was all very well, but this looked like a rift in Marsh's own circle.

Gertler alleged that according to Spencer his recent painting showed he was 'quite incapable of understanding Cézanne'. He demanded an apology, saying that Spencer's own work hardly qualified him to judge. To this Spencer replied that he had no intention of being 'insultingly' critical, he only wished to be critical. 'That makes it worse,' Gertler protested to Marsh, who had prevailed upon Spencer to climb down as far as he could, for then his remarks were 'not insults but *Truths*'. He could not know that at heart Spencer was perhaps the most genuine, as he was certainly among the first, of his admirers. If the vexation it caused at Gray's Inn warrants the record of this petty wrangle, in fairness to Spencer one should note his true estimation of the friend who had fallen out with him.

Currie was now involved. He told Marsh that in his view Spencer was to blame, for his remark not only came first but was 'the more acrimonious of the two', and he argued that even if there were an apology, how could bygones be bygones? 'The memory of

Rupert Brooke

Oh! never fly conceals a hook,
Fish say, in the Eternal Brook,
But more than mundane weeds are there,
And mud celestially fair;
Fat caterpillars drift around,
And Paradisal ~~gudgeons~~ ~~gods~~ ~~celestial~~ are found,
Unfading moths, immortal flies,
And the worm that never dies;
And in that Heaven of all their wish
There shall be no more land, say fish.   Rupert Brooke

(a) End of the original draft of *Heaven* by Rupert Brooke, from the South Seas

It was so old a ship – who knows, who knows?
– And yet so beautiful, I watched in vain
To see the mast burst open with a rose,
And the whole deck put on its leaves again,

James Elroy Flecker

(b) The concluding lines of *The Old Ships* by J. E. Flecker, from Switzerland

I think more of a bird with broad wings flying and lapsing through the air, than anything, when I think of metre. – So I read

◡◡— ◡◡— — ◡— ◡◡ —
◡— , ◡◡— ◡— — ◡◡ —
— — — ◡ — ◡◡ — ◡ —
◡◡ — ◡◡ — ◡◡ —.

I wonder if that is quite unintelligible. I am

(c) D. H. Lawrence explaining his principles of prosody, from Italy such a blow would remain.' Gertler knew of the negotiations over *The Apple Gatherers*, and told his supporter Currie that they supplied the reason for Marsh's irrational bias in favour of the painter at Cookham. Meanwhile a trivial detail seems to have prevented Currie from being entirely won over to the anti-Marsh faction. He had seen an umpire's white coat hanging in Mrs. Elgy's kitchen and hankered after it as an overall for his painting. He was awaiting an auspicious moment to hint that it might be more useful hanging in his studio.

Stanley Spencer remained singularly unruffled, as if unaware of the rumpus he had caused, and on November 7 he was invited to see the collection at Gray's Inn. 'I failed to find the Tate,' he wrote next day, 'so I asked a Policeman and the Policeman said "It is too late" so I walked on to Westminster Bridge, there were no seagulls so I walked all the way back to Gower Street. . . . Is this book of modern poets that you have published expensive? I could afford half-a-crown.' The quarrel had reached a stalemate, and Gertler was growing more and more inflammatory. He stormed out of Marsh's sitting-room, where some Cambridge youths were gathered, and wrote next day to explain his behaviour.

Always there exists that bridge between people and myself. They seem to be clever, very clever. They talk well, argue masterly, and yet there is something—something—that makes me dislike them. . . . I stand alone! But if God will help me put into my work that passion, that Inspiration, that profundity of Soul that I *know* I possess I will triumph over these learned Cambridge youths. One of them argued *down* at me about Painting!

He added that he had even broken off relations with Currie. At this Marsh protested. His agreeable circle of Georgians seemed to be disintegrating. 'There is a grandeur of dignity in solitude,' Gertler replied. 'When I am amongst people of so-called intellect my soul gets torn to bits. . . . I merely wrote and told him that I want to be alone for a while. But do not think that Currie will be put out by my absence. I know him too well for that. . . . He has friends and a woman whom he loves. Remember that I am absolutely alone and that I have loved without the slightest success.' Gertler's recalcitrance endeared him all the more to his patron. Marsh was getting accustomed to it. In answering his first invitation to dine out Gertler had proposed an alternative rendez-vous to the Café Royal. On his last visit there, he said, he had been put under arrest, thrown into a cell for a whole hour, and forbidden the Café for six months.

On November 30 Marsh went alone on a visit to the Spencer family at Cookham. The deal for *The Apple Gatherers* was concluded, Marsh having outbid Sadler by five pounds. 'We are very grateful to you for your kindness to the boy,' wrote the father. He had explained that they were 'only homely folk', so the visitor must not expect too much. Marsh got back to Paddington with the self-portrait he had heard about under one arm and a landscape under the other. 'The family is a little overwhelming,' he wrote to Seabrooke. 'The father is a remarkable old man, still in early middle age at near 70—very clever, but (I beg his pardon, I mean "and") a tremendous talker and frightfully pleased with himself, his paternity, his bicycling, his opinions, his knowledge, his ignorance (due to the limitations imposed by his fatherhood of 9), his Radicalism, and everything that is his. . . . Gilbert is an artist too, but only since 6 months. Stan only had about two things to show, he does work slowly.' Of another artist acquaintance he remarked: 'I'm afraid he has come under the noxious influence of dear Roger Fry whom I love as a man but detest as a movement . . . it seems too wretched that he should spend all his time painting square people because someone tells him to.'

Another new light whom I met today is Wyndham Lewis. (I am going to the Picture Ball, if you please, as a futurist picture designed by him!) He is very magnificent to look at, but I don't think he liked me, and I suspected him of pose, so we shan't make friends. Hoping to strike a chord, I told him I had spent the day with Stanley Spencer and he said, 'I don't know him, is he a painter?' which *must* have been put on.

On December 8, the day *The Apple Gatherers* arrived from Leeds, a letter came from the painter. 'The boy we go bathing with is a Gladiator, only his muscles are not "bumpy" but evenly developed over his whole body. I love to watch the vapour rising from his body when he comes out of the water.' Spencer was becoming the master among the young Georgian painters. In congratulating Marsh on the acquisition of Spencer's great picture Professor Sadler at Leeds did not omit to express his equal hopes of Gertler. He had seen Gertler's *Mother and Child* before Marsh acquired it. 'The pattern is firm. The mother's head and breast vital, but the child's body and other parts of the picture seem to me to fall below the level of the rest. It is a fine work, and with time will get finer.'

Gertler and Spencer were back on speaking terms, but disturbances among the painters were not yet over. It was now Currie who was in difficulties. He had spoken disparagingly of Epstein while in conversation with Augustus John in the Café Royal, and had been overheard. This called for Marsh's diplomatic intervention. At least Currie had made it up with Gertler, which was something, and had been presented with the umpire's coat as a reward. 'I look like Balzac in it,' he wrote after wearing it for a day at home.

iii

During this last quarter of the year the correspondence with Flecker had continued unabated. In November the poet had sent his new version of the National Anthem. 'I can't make up my mind whether it's rather good or a joke or both.' Marsh thought it neither, and suggested many amendments. On December 1 the manuscript of what is perhaps his best poem arrived at Raymond Buildings—*The Old Ships*. 'I thought you might care to see the enclosed which I wrote some months ago. As you suggested my sending you some poems for Jack Squire perhaps you might send this on to him if you think it good enough.' Ten days later he was thanking Marsh for performing this service and for showing the poem to Gosse, but said the guinea fee was too small 'on principle rather than avarice. . . . Please be wicked enough to represent *Hassan* as being rather a better play and more certain of popular success than *Hamlet*'. On the 18th he sent a full synopsis of the play,[1] for

---

[1] There are a few interesting variants from the published edition in this scenario. The list of characters is headed with a note: 'Scenery and costumes should not be vaguely Oriental but strictly Persian. The Persian miniatures reproduced in the illustrated edition of Mardrus' *Arabian Nights* should be the model, with the Mongol element left out.' The action is substantially the same throughout. The scene of Act III runs thus: 'In front of a modest but charming Pavilion in the Caliph's magnificent gardens. A Byzantine silver fountain in the shape of a boy.' And an alternative opening is suggested. 'Before the entry of the Caliph it may be well to show Yasmin entering the Pavilion (which she has discovered will be inhabited by Hassan) helped in her intrigue by the youngest slave and Selim whom she drives away (and out of the play) like a dog the minute he ceases to be useful.' In the following scene the author suggests that 'a little negro eunuch brings him his old beloved carpet . . . It "howls" with the furniture and has to be deposited in the next room.' Of the end of Act IV (Rafi and

Marsh to pass on to Beerbohm Tree at His Majesty's where the full text had already come to the notice of Viola Tree and Basil Dean.

D. H. Lawrence's letter of October 28 brought into the open the conflict on form in verse which had been rankling for some time. With his remarks on Davies, Marsh may have agreed. 'He's really like a linnet that's got just a wee little sweet song, but it only sings when it's wild. And he's made himself a tame bird. . . . I think one ought to be downright cruel to him . . . say to him, Davies, your work is getting like Birmingham tin-ware.' But to the attack on Hodgson's *Song of Honour* Marsh certainly took exception. 'Only here and there is the least touch of personality in the poem,' Lawrence began, and broke off to exclaim, 'I hope to God you won't hate me and think me carping, for this.' He included a sheaf of his own poems copied out in mauve ink. 'Don't put my *Ballad of a Wayward Woman*[1] lightly aside,' he wrote. Marsh's no doubt eloquent defence of Hodgson provoked Lawrence into writing (November 19) what is perhaps the fullest statement of his verse technique.[2] 'You *are* wrong. It makes me open my eyes. . . . I think more of a bird with broad wings flying and lapsing through the air, than anything, when I think of metre.' He complained of being 'a poor, maligned, misunderstood, patronised and misread poet, and soon I shall burst into tears.' He countered some of Marsh's criticisms, and accepted others. 'Your letter was jolly good for me really,' he concluded, having begun very angrily. 'I always thank God when a man will say straight out to me what he has to say.' It was in this letter that he declared, 'You are a bit of a policeman in poetry', and protested against Marsh's admiration of Flecker's *Golden Journey* volume. ' "It satisfies my ear," you say. Well, I don't write for your ear. . . . If your ear has got stiff and a bit mechanical, *don't* blame my poetry.' This letter gave Marsh peculiar pleasure. He had already sent one of Lawrence's new poems to the *New Statesman*, and now, following a pressing invitation from Lawrence at the end of his

---

Pervana in prison, choosing life or death) he explains: 'They are both cowards, both brave in their way. The soul of Rafi, the body of Pervana, is afraid. But such a wave of passion flows over them that they choose death by a sort of moral intuition, for the very honour of life itself.'

[1] This appeared in *Look! We have come through!* under the title *Ballad of a Wilful Woman*.

[2] *The Letters of D. H. Lawrence* (Huxley), p. 153.

long and volcanic letter, he planned to call on him in Italy during
another walking-tour he was going to take with Jim Barnes. In
November Gibson, Abercrombie and his wife, and Trevelyan,
descended upon the Lawrences at Lerici. They found him attending
a peasant wedding in patent-leather boots and a black suit.
Though a little put out at first, Lawrence enjoyed the occasion.

> I loved Gibson still more than Abercrombie—perhaps because I
> knew him better. But I think Gibson is one of the clearest and most
> lovable personalities I know. Abercrombie *is* sharp—he is much
> more *intellectual* than I had imagined: keener, more sharp-minded. I
> shall enjoy talking to him. We both loved Mrs. Abercrombie: she's
> not a bit like a Madonna, neither the Raphael nor Botticelli sort,
> so you're wrong there, Sir.

The whole Georgian party signed a postcard and sent it to
Raymond Buildings to show they had met. 'About metres,' concluded Lawrence, perhaps a little wearied by the controversy, 'I
shall have to pray for Grace from God', and he enclosed an
obscure poem in impeccable iambics called *Grief* and headed:
'To Eddie Marsh, with much affection, this poem for a Christmas
card, which, albeit a trifle lugubrious, pray God may go daintily to
his ear'—(even if not so daintily as the *Golden Journey*, one imagines
him adding in an aside).

While Lawrence was attacking Hodgson, James Stephens was
praising him to the skies, calling his poem *The Bull* 'the most
valuable piece of imaginative psychology that I have ever read.
. . . Whether he is set in life, or whether he can grow in life is the
question.' Stephens' next letter (December 13) was more frivolous.

> Isn't Harold Monro a friend of yours? My heavy curse on him. He
> has just returned me the best poem I've ever written with the state-
> ment that it isn't up to his standard. . . . Do keep an eye on next
> week's *Sphere* and tell me do you agree with Monro's judgement. If
> you don't I beg you to murder that man for me and you can keep
> all the profits from the carcase for yourself. . . . I sometimes am
> afflicted with the idea that poetry is all darn rot (except when it's
> written by me), look at Monro. Imagine that chap turning me down
> and I hitting him with masterpieces. . . . Do agonizing things to
> him. Read him his own poetry, as long as you can stand it, then choke
> him with his own book. Make him eat his words. . . .

While leaving James Stephens to calm down Marsh had second
thoughts on Hodgson and sent him a sheaf of criticisms with a

slight apology. 'I think you no carper,' Hodgson replied, 'but just such a counsellor as I could have wished at my elbow.' Gibson, newly married, was living quietly in his Gloucestershire cottage modestly furnished by a grant of Perceval 'murder money'. Abercrombie in his cottage The Gallows, a mile and a half away, was finishing the second part of *The End of the World*. Robert Frost had taken a room in the house opposite, and Edward Thomas was close by. In December Gibson acknowledged receipt from Marsh of two sonnets which Brooke had sent him from abroad. 'The sonnets[1] have a delicate wistful beauty, but as you say, they don't show much development. That of course may come quite suddenly.' Marsh was still inclined to rate Flecker a little higher than Brooke. He wrote to Sturge Moore, deploring the unenthusiastic reception of *The Golden Journey*. 'A cold reception is the last thing a Parnassian should resent,' wrote Moore, 'and what could the dear creature expect after that tactless, that fond, that foolish preface! . . . There is too much beauty of the foregone-conclusion type and not a little of what the French call *remplissage*.' He disliked the habit of composing lines 'which the poet expects you not only to admire but to be amused at. . . . I fear I have lost my virginity for him. I sent him once an improved version of one of his early poems which he never acknowledged so probably did not appreciate.'

Marsh was keeping in touch with Squire on the editorial staff of the *New Statesman* by acting as agent for J. D. Beresford, Flecker, Brooke, and Lawrence. 'May I keep D. H. Lawrence's poem one or two days more?' Squire wrote. 'I want to see if I can make *a*, Head, or alternatively *b*, Tail, of it.' If Marsh had sent him *Grief* it can be well understood why Squire asked for an extension of the option. Such was his correspondence during this quarter that the theatre was neglected, and many evenings these days were being spent at the Admiralty. But a campaign to convert Lady Randolph Churchill to Ibsen resulted in Marsh's escorting her to *The Wild Duck* at the St. James's, and he took Mark Gertler to *The Doctor's Dilemma*.

Lord Fisher was now frantically urging Marsh to use his influence for the acceptance of an offer from Junkers to build an oil engine. 'I *cannot* exaggerate its importance,' wrote Fisher on

---

[1] 'Somewhile before the dawn' and 'Today I have been happy', both written in October.

December 13. 'If the First Lord does not act promptly we shall lose Junkers as Krupp is offering him a blank cheque. . . . *I do entreat you to get this matter through.* I've been slaving at this matter for months and slobbering and cajoling Junkers till he has arrived at this crisis of being ready to be swallowed!'

Eddie Marsh's last letter of the year to Lawrence must have pleaded pressure of work as excuse for brevity. His life was becoming increasingly complex. Lawrence summed it up perfectly (December 17) and wanted to hear more of the Picture Ball and his friend's costume designed by Wyndham Lewis. 'How did you look, futuristically? Lord, you're a bit of a jig-saw puzzle to start with, mixing poets and pictures, the Admiralty, and what-not, like somebody shuffling cards.'

After Christmas at Knebworth he left England with Jim Barnes and arrived in Rome on new year's day 1914.

iv

Two letters from Brooke awaited him at Rome. The earlier one, written on board ship 'somewhere near Fiji', declared that he was going to imagine his friend in a picture-postcard setting at Christmas 'trotting through crisp snow to a country church, holly decorated, with little robins picking crumbs all round, the church bells playing our brother Tennyson's *In Memoriam* brightly through the clear air. It may not be: it never has been. . . . But I shall think of you so.' As for himself, he must be imagined 'in a loincloth, brown and wild, in the fair chocolate arms of a Tahitian beauty, reclining beneath a bread-fruit tree on white sand, with the breakers roaring against the reefs a mile out, and strange brilliant fish darting through the pellucid hyaline of the sun-saturated sea.' The disappointment to Marsh lay in 'I'm afraid your part as my honorary literary agent, or grass executor, is something of a sinecure. I can't write on the trail.' The other envelope was addressed from Suva, Fiji, and dated late in November. Across the bay from where he sat there loomed a mountain 'forbidding and terrible. The Greeks would have made it the entrance to the underworld . . . when I come back from my cruise I intend to walk among them. Shall I return? If not, spill some blood in a trench—you'll find the recipe in Homer.'

The Italian excursion included a visit to an ancient tower at

Orbetello built near the remains of a canal hewn by the Etruscans out of the solid rock. It was one of Barnes' favourite spots and it meant an arduous walk along a rough track surrounded by the thorny scrub flowering almost head-high. Marsh did not share his friend's taste for this sun-beaten wilderness and made no effort to disguise his unease. It was as if he had a premonition of the appalling experience he was to suffer fourteen years later in just such a place on the island of Corsica. It was not until they mounted the cliff between Ansedonia and the sea that he confessed to at least a partial conversion. More to his taste was the train journey on January 12 from Lucca to Viareggio, where they were met by D. H. Lawrence, and they walked up the slope through the olives to his home by moonlight, and Frieda gave them supper on the veranda overlooking the bay. After the meal they sat looking out over the bay and talking about 'words'. One minute fragment of the conversation has survived. 'Isn't "Farfalla" a beautiful word?' said Frieda. 'If I have a daughter I will call her Farfalla'; whereupon Eddie Marsh interposed, 'They'd only call her Fanny', and Lawrence laughed.[1]

Lawrence remembered feeling rather guilty that he let Marsh carry his own bag to the door. Next day the Lawrences walked with their guests as far as Bocco di Magno. It was the first stage of the journey home, which took in a call on James Stephens in Paris. Within a few days Marsh was with the Blunts at Crabbet Park while George Mallory slept in his bed at Gray's Inn. On the 22nd the visit of John Nash to Raymond Buildings was the start of a lifelong friendship (his brother Paul was yet to appear on the scene) and he was in the room chatting with Gertler as Marsh wrote his first letter to Brooke for some weeks.

> I've just been to tea with Davies, who as I have told you decided to leave Sevenoaks because of the uncertainty of his social position. He said he had parted on bad terms with his landlady. She said that he 'rotted the blinds' by keeping his window open. He said he would buy her new blinds when he left, and went on opening the window. She then said that he rotted not only the blinds but the window-frames.

---

[1] Recollected by Frieda in a letter to E.M. (1939) after reading his Memoir. The only reference to this occasion in Marsh's correspondence occurs in a letter (July 26, 1914) to Bottomley. 'He [Lawrence] always looks as white as an apple dumpling, but he seemed extremely well for him, came for a long walk without seeming in the least tired—in good spirits. He was just finishing a novel which he and Frieda thought his best so far.'

Also a lady, for some reason, used to send a little boy to knock at the door as hard as he could, and the landlady wouldn't interfere—and the lady turned out to be a niece of Wordsworth, which seemed to Davies a strange irony, that the niece of one poet should send a little boy to knock at another poet's door. He is now in very squalid little lodgings near Regent's Park. I nearly laughed out loud when he said he was leading a simple life, 'for instance the milkman only calls once a day'. He's a dear creature, but very funny.

Currie's unhappiness in love was becoming serious. One night recently he had rushed into the Moulin d'Or almost out of his mind. Marsh was waiting for him with tickets for *Hullo Tango* in his pocket. The show did nothing to dispel Currie's gloom. In the first interval he asked if he might go back to Gray's Inn, and there he enjoyed what he said was the first night's sleep for a week. 'Oh, Eddie, it is such peace to be here,' he had exclaimed as he entered the sitting-room. The emotional vagaries of Dolly Henry were driving him to distraction. 'I think he will be done for if he doesn't get Dolly out of his head,' Marsh wrote to Gertler. The sequel showed how well justified was his concern. But at the moment there was yet another vexatious problem to cope with, the future of *Hassan*.

More worries, this time from Flecker. I'd been working quite hard for his play, and interested Basil Dean in it. B.D. really believes in the play but thinks it wants a great deal of doing-to, compression, rearrangement, etc.—*not* re-writing, and he offered to do all this work on it (with a very good prospect of getting it taken, either by Tree, or by a friend of his who is going to have an autumn season) on condition of a percentage, say 25% of profits, and calling it 'By J.E.F., arranged for the stage by B.D.' Now I think *the* thing is to get the play produced, in good conditions—and this seems to me an excellent arrangement for F. I wrote to propose it to him, and he replied (Saturday) 'accepting unreservedly'. Today I get a letter saying he is suddenly feeling much stronger (!) and that I am to tell Dean he doesn't mean what he said at all and that he reserves his complete liberty of negotiation as if he had never written the first letter! I've written very strongly to him, pointing out the advantage of the plan, and also the extreme bad appearance of his writing one thing one day and another the next. I do hope he will be sensible, he is really a most difficult person to be agent for! Poor dear, he has been ill ever since Christmas with fever every night. I'm glad he's better but I wish it didn't have just that effect on the workings of his mind! By the way he sends his love to 'Rupert Brooke, our Donne Redivivus'. He has had 2 lovely poems in the *Statesman* lately, and has a novel just coming out which he thinks a lot of.[1] He also tells me that by dint of translating the 6th *Aeneid* he has just discovered how to write really fine blank verse.

During the renewed exchanges on the subject of *Hassan* Flecker explained that he was still worried about Dean's insistence on the importance of stage effect. 'He imagines there is a difference between dramatic and literary criticism. Now don't you maintain, my dear Marsh, with me that there is *none*?—that if a thing's a Play everything that makes it a better play makes it better literature?' About the same time, Flecker had sent a revised version of his National Anthem 'with your suggestion adopted and a verse added', and he was in half a mind to send a copy to the King. 'Tell me, O you from whom all good advice flows, whether I shall try on some game with it, or send it mildly to the *Sphere?*' (After getting Marsh's opinion he sent it mildly to the *Sphere.*) He was not impressed by *Sons and Lovers*, which Marsh had recommended to him, finding it 'unreal as a dream'. He had bought a zither with his Georgian royalties which he practised in bed, like 'a romantic lady' except that he had grown a vandyke beard. In March, cheered by the reviews of his novel, he was in better spirits. 'If I write my projected Futurist poem beginning "I slobber on the Parthenon" I will send you a copy.'

Marsh's letter to Brooke of January 22 ended with news of Gibson's marriage.

Wilfrid writes still in the 7th heaven. I am to go to him for Sunday week in his new cottage near the Gallows. *New Numbers* is waiting for Lascelles to finish his poem,[2] I hope it comes out soon. Did I tell you how much I like *Aeterna Corpora* now it's finished? I do hope you are writing something longer—and do try something more objective. I think each of the Poems you have sent home is lovely in itself, but when one looks back on them as a group they all have 'Dear' and 'Love' in them, nothing like the variety of your first book. I long for something to take the place, in your new work, of *Fish, Dining-room Tea, Human Shape*, etc.—perhaps you are incubating such things all the time. All the same, the sonnets are beautiful—there are exquisite things in *Psychical Research*—and I like the cloud one in P and D [*Poetry and Drama*] enormously.

---

[1] *The King of Alsander*, Max Goschen, 1914. [2] *The Olympians*.

The plea for 'something more objective' was to strike home to good effect. It prompted Brooke to write *The Great Lover*. Meanwhile James Stephens had sent the manuscript of his new poems to Raymond Buildings and there was a plan for Ralph Hodgson and Marsh to weed them out and send their joint criticisms to Paris, but there was yet another literary task in the offing. 'Davies is also going to send me the proofs of his new book[1] in order that I may point out mistakes in grammar etc. Ain't I becoming an Arbiter Elegantiarum?'

He had spent so much on paintings by Gertler, Currie, and Stanley Spencer that money was now in seriously short supply.

The plays here seem quite terrible, I've only been, or wanted to—be? or go? to one since I came back, *Quality Street*, it is really charming! and Cathleen the *most* perfect angel in it, a lovely piece of acting. Barker's *Midsummer Night's Dream* is Friday week, I'm going with Basil Dean. I'm in hourly dread of Barker coming down on me for £25, which I've rashly promised to subscribe to his Repertory Theatre. Every announcement that the scheme is prospering and that he hopes before long, shortly, soon, in a month, in a week, to lay the details before the public, strikes a chill down my marrow.

Brooke was toying with the idea of joining the Savile Club but Marsh was in favour of the National, 'only you would have to swear allegiance to the Protestant succession and the teaching of the Bible in schools—could you swallow that? Of course it's quite terribly dull—but you could dress as you liked.' He ended his budget with a story he had heard while on holiday in Italy with Barnes.

I must end up with the one good anecdote I have heard. A man [Carmichael, Consul at Leghorn] I met in Italy told me he had once met James Thomson (author of *City of Dreadful Night*), he was quite speechless, and everyone was very shy. My friend summoned up courage to ask, 'Whereabouts do you live in London, Mr. Thomson?' The answer was—in a cockney accent—' 'Ackney. Nice family. Bit o' meat most days. Bit o' pudding on Sundays.' And that was the only thing he said.

[1] *The Bird of Paradise*. In February (undated) Davies acknowledged the criticism 'which has quite bowled me over', and introduced Marsh to the work of John Freeman by enclosing the poem *November Skies* (published later in *Georgian Poetry*, third series).

The letter was enclosed with a parcel of books,[1] 'there's terribly little that a Rip Van Winkle need mind having missed'. Early in February he went down to Gibson's cottage, Greenway. He brought news of William Poel's *Hamlet*, a visit to T. E. Hulme, Drinkwater reading his new poems at Raymond Buildings, a session with Hodgson on Stephens' manuscript, and a letter from Brooke enclosing a poem, probably *Heaven*, worthy of the South Seas. 'I fire this off, as I've finished it. Store it away with the rest. It's even worse. I'll send something real soon.' He was stranded in New Zealand with no money. 'How shall I ever stand England? You'll have to pretend you're very savage, and grow your food, growling on the floor, and dance strangely for me by night, and moan rhythmic chants, or else I shall return to the South Seas again.' A second letter, from Tahiti, was just to hand with the news of 'three fair-sized poems nearly done. I live in a loincloth and an old vest of yours.' Marsh replied after his week-end at Greenway, where a second volume of *Georgian Poetry* had been the question of the hour.

I'm enraptured by the fish's heaven, it is brilliantly amusing, and also beautiful. It certainly mustn't come out in *New Numbers* as all the clergymen would at once withdraw their subscriptions! so I've sent it to Jack Squire. I hope you approve. I've told Naomi to expect the letters.

I had a charming Sunday with the Wilfrids who seem flawlessly happy. She is a very nice woman—without physical charm, but very intelligent and as good as gold, evidently a supreme housekeeper, their cottage is very nice, all with a perfect sense of style—he couldn't possibly have done better for himself. The Lascelles dined with us on Sat. and we with them on Sunday—there is another delightful marriage! with the added charm of children. I don't think you know the 2 little boys, you will adore them. L. read out his *End of the World*, now finished, and to appear in the 2nd *N.N.* It's a sublime work, in its fusion of poetry and comedy there has been nothing like it. I didn't see his thing for the 1st number (which may come out any day now) as it was at the printer. Wilfrid says it is very fine. W. hasn't really begun writing again yet, but he soon will, he feels the stirrings. We had a lovely walk, it's beautiful country—by the way I made rather a good quotation—we passed an odd-looking house, with a leggy colonnade and pink whitewash, comfortable and old-fashioned,

[1] Gilbert Cannan's *Old Mole*, Lawrence's *Sons and Lovers*, Drinkwater's *Cromwell*, Abercrombie's *Speculative Dialogues*, and Flecker's poems.

but new. Lascelles said it had just been built by a Colonel, an Early Victorian house born out of due time. My quotation was

> Oh latest born and ugliest vision far
> Of all Victoria's faded squirearchy.

which you must admit was apt. . . .

The next *G.P.* by the way is going to be a very fine book, better than the first! that is one reason why I'm so *very* glad to hear you are writing poetry. Your sonnets are lovely, but I want something else from you—it is imperative that you should cut as rich and brave a figure in the 2nd book as in the first.

By the way it's lucky I saw the proofs of *N.N.*, they were making you talk of *griping* hands (instead of groping) in the SPR sonnet. It's flattering that Lascelles and Wilfrid should have been quite prepared to take that from you!

Have you seen the notices of Barker's *Midsummer N. D.*? I went to the first night. It's *lovely*, my dear. The fairies all gold, from top to toe (the only failure was their faces, which are gold too and the gilt hadn't 'taken', except on the noses, which gleamed in what looked like puddles of putty, but perhaps they've found out how to do it better now). The scenery very beautiful—the first scene is simply a low green mound rising gradually from each side of the stage to the centre—and the background tall green streamers, suggesting the trunks of trees. The grouping is so fine that I longed to be a painter and immortalize every pose. There is one long folk-dance in the wood, the golden fairies against the green—it made me cry! and the acting is mostly excellent, making the story thrilling—the clowns extraordinarily amusing. Of course most of the papers are stupid about it.

I hear Masefield's new Japanese play is very disappointing. I hope my informant misjudged it—but I'm rather afraid M. is having a bad period, it's most unfortunate as there's a strong reaction against him. It's awfully difficult to live up to a boom, and so fatal not to! I'm unhappy about Stephens too, the book of poetry that I think I told you he was sending me turned out to be very poor, and we felt obliged to advise him against publishing it—don't mention this!

I've just got such a gloomy letter from poor Beresford, there was a perfectly exquisite little story of his in the *Westminster* last Saturday. I read it in the train, and then aloud to Wilfrid, who also admired it enormously, so I couldn't resist writing to B. and I said I hoped he would publish a collection of short things. He says he can't get anyone even to print them in papers, except by accident. 'Pretty beastly, isn't it?' he says. I really think if I were rich the very first thing I would do is to become a publisher.

I think I told you I was wanting to buy a Gill statue. Well, I have! it's a lovely thing. I shall trust to luck to be able to pay for it.

It's splendid to think that you're really on the way back, Rupert dear. I do long sometimes to see you. Every now and then it comes over me, how much more I should be enjoying everything if you were here.

On February 14 Stephens sent from Paris a joint letter to Ralph Hodgson and Marsh after getting their criticisms.

That was the devil of a letter. Behold me ever since squatting with my chin on my knees in a cold silence . . . I disagree with some of your accursed little crosses (I will never like the Christian emblem again) . . . I'm going to write a big, gorgeous, gigantic, magnificent, and truly inspired poem this almighty present minute. I will surround myself with lightning and fury. I will call in the gods and the devils, but that collection is going to have a big poem in it for which those other bubbles will make a pretty background. If I fail then I allow the two of you to eat each other's hats. Now (as the Americans say) watch me smoke.

He had been hard at work, 'twelve poems in two days is my average', and now he wanted advice. 'When you are putting a book together do you work on any plan or do you pray to God and then go forward?'[1] Marsh was also criticizing Monro's new poems at this time and in reply Monro described Marinetti in the Bookshop giving a private performance for Yeats and making 'the whole room shake'. And D. H. Lawrence sent work for critical comment (March 14). 'You must remain my poetic adviser. When you do tell me what you want for your 1914-15 edition tell me the faults you find and I will try and put them right.' Marsh's critical exertions at this time were not confined to verse. He was corresponding with Hugh Walpole, who had shown him the manuscript of his new novel, *The Duchess of Wrexe*.

You certainly have a great power of keeping up the interest. The Duchess is a fine conception and admirably carried out in everything except her speech. The more she is wrought up the more one would expect her to be tense, packed, and weighty—but when she lets herself go she pours herself out in a style which is indistinguishable from Francis or Rachel. . . . You know my morbid eye for detail. . . . Programmes at balls had gone out of fashion well before 1898, and

[1] He was compiling *Songs from the Clay*.

'extra dances' along with them. I'm not sure of the exact year when Bridge came in, but I *think* not before 1900 and I am *quite certain* that even if a few people were playing it in '98 the Duchess wasn't one of them.

Middleton Murry was keeping in touch from Paris, where he was at work on a study of Stendhal and struggling to make ends meet by reviewing. By March he was back in London and Katherine Mansfield had found a room in Chelsea for a few shillings a week. 'Katherine is trying to get on the stage,' wrote Murry, 'but it's a damnable sordid business without influence.' Meanwhile Marsh had acquired a new neighbour. In response to Sassoon's request to keep an eye out for somewhere to live, Marsh had found the top flat vacant in 1 Raymond Buildings, and Mrs. Elgy had sent round a woman to do the housework. By May Sassoon was installed in the 'peacock-blue sitting room' and wrote to say he had engaged Mrs. Elgy's protégé—'in spite of our first tremulous electric interview'.

The main event before the next letter to Brooke (March 9) was the visit to Iver Heath in the company of John Nash, who introduced his brother Paul. On March 4 Paul came for the first time to see the pictures at Gray's Inn, and thus yet another Slade student joined the circle of young painters who were making Marsh's rooms their frequent rendezvous for discussion and association with the poets. Marsh's patronage of the arts was becoming useful to him in his official life. In February he introduced Eric Gill to Mr. Churchill at the Admiralty and the artist undertook to design the Flying Corps Badge. The First Lord's proposal for the design was in keeping with his ambition for this newly formed and pioneer unit. 'I'm not the least bit confident that I can perpetrate such a badge as Mr. Churchill desires and suggests,' wrote Gill after the interview. 'He seems to me to want a blooming picture.' But none of this was considered as news for Brooke; nor was the Sunday at Cambridge with Maynard Keynes and Lowes Dickinson; E. M. Forster's stay at Raymond Buildings; Nijinsky's first night at the Palace in the company of Viola Tree; nor Gaudier-Brzeska and Currie quarrelling over Mrs. Elgy's coffee. On March 9 Marsh acknowledged receipt of two poems from the South Seas.

What fun to be stranded in Tahiti, but you must make up for lost time on the rest of the journey. You shouldn't give your poems prejudicial titles such as Bilge and B—s. I don't care much for B—s, but Bilge is quite good (the longer one) tho' not so good as *Heaven*. I've sent them to Wilfrid, as he was cross with me for not giving *N.N.* first chance of *Heaven*. If he doesn't want them for *N.N.* I will send them to Jack Squire. *N.N.* is out! it's *very* good, the shape, print and appearance quite excellent.

I was at Cambridge for Sunday, and for the Marlowe performance of *The Alchemist* on Sat. which was supreme—I confess I hadn't the smallest conception from reading it of the acting merits of the play. It went with a roar. Frankie Birch (Face) is one of the best living actors, he has practically three parts to do, the Captain, Lump, and Jeremy—he was a different creature in each, yet subtly the same and marvellously funny, and accomplished in all. Denis Robertson, made up as the Master of Trinity, was good as the Alchemist.

Quiller-Couch came to dine at Downing yesterday, he's a jolly man—he asked if it was likely you would care to come and help him at Cambridge, he's very keen that you should. I smiled on the idea, but didn't commit you! I've got another job in my eye for you—a very nice man called Rooker has just been here, to discuss a 'series' he wants to bring out, of 2*s*. 6*d*. books, on modern development of foreign thought, he wants me to get Gosse as general editor. Is there any Modern Foreign Thinker you would care to do? about 40,000 words. Strindberg? Think about it. Rooker would like very much to have you. He was impressed with your Donne.[1]

The English Association is bringing out an anthology of modern poetry for use in secondary schools—and Frank Sidgwick wrote to ask if they might have *Grantchester*. I said yes, I didn't know what to say about a fee. I told F.S. that you had strong views about not giving poetry for nothing, so I asked for £1—but added weakly that perhaps you might think as this is 'educational' and not for private profit you might consider it a special case.

In the days that followed there was a dinner at Downing Street and 7*s*. lost to Mr. Asquith at Bridge; a piano recital by Scriabine at the Queen's Hall; Abercrombie staying the night and Davies joining them for breakfast; Mr. Churchill speaking on the Naval Estimates in the House of Commons followed by an evening at T. E. Hulme's flat with F. S. Flint, Davies, and Epstein; and a luncheon with Henry James. On the 22nd, having heard no more from Brooke, Marsh wrote describing Abercrombie's introduction to London life.

---

[1] Review of *Poems of John Donne*, edited by H. J. C. Grierson, in *Poetry and Drama*, Vol. I, No. 2, June 1913.

I had a delightful visit last Sat. to Wed. from Lascelles, I tried to show him as many aspects of London as could be got into the time, here is the programme, do you think it was good? Sat., Denis and Clive Carey to tea, then *Midsummer N.D.* with a visit to Lillah between the acts. Sunday, Davies and Michael [Sadleir] to break-fast, luncheon with the Dunsanys—a beauty party at tea here, Cathleen, Diana [Manners], Katherine [Horner], Ruby Peto, all looking their very best (Lascelles almost speechless with admiration, he didn't know there *were* such people!), dinner with Gosse and Henry James who was *magnificent*, with adjournment to Cathleen's rooms (to meet Sally Allgood and Maire O'Neill but they didn't turn up). Monday, the Ihlee show at Carfax which is very good, Hodgson and Basil Dean to luncheon, the Palace in the evening to see Nijinsky but alas he was suddenly ill so we had only Wilkie Bard, then Café Royal with Mark Gertler and Jack Squire and a distant view of Epstein. Tuesday I was no good as it was the Naval Estimates. I got L. into the House to hear Winston's speech which was rather dull and technical, and L. had to go, before the end part which was better, to read the *End of the World* at the Bookshop, and we only met at T. E. Hulme's after 11—and L. had to go next morning. I've made a good thing out of it all, as L. is rewarding me with the dedication of the *End of the World*, which will in itself assure me of immortality. My next 'week-end visitor' is to be Cookham!

The most interesting new book is one by Austin Smyth on the Composition of the Iliad, he has discovered that in order to make it easier for the rhapsodists to remember, or rather to make sure that they didn't forget it, the poem was written in 45 cantos of exactly 300 lines each—this necessitates getting rid of over 2,000 lines, and making a few transpositions, in the course of which he maintains that all the immemorial Homer difficulties disappear. I've read the book with a good deal of care, though not of course with either care or knowledge enough to come to a certain conclusion—but the argument is marvellously ingenious and convincing in every detail. If it isn't upset, it will be the most important Homeric study since the Question began! as of course it would be conclusive on the side of single authorship. I forgot to mention that I had Smyth to meet Lascelles at breakfast on Wednesday in order that they might fire off their respective classical novelties at each other. L. has been doing wonders with Empedocles and proving that he was the first Nietzschean—and much besides.

The Times has a very fine review of *New Numbers*, it quotes your *Psychical Research* in full—it says nice things about everybody, and ends with a tremendous eulogy of Lascelles. The 'venture' is now well 'launched', the only thing is that the power to send, as distinguished from promising, a subscription of 7s. 6d. seems denied to all but a few specially gifted persons. I am doing what I can as a collector, but I'm terribly afraid lots of people will never pay up. Wilfrid asks *me* to remember that *you* have to contribute at least 20 pages to No. 4, so please pity my poor conscience. He's sent me a proof of *Heaven* for No. 2, it looks very well in print.

I've read most of George Moore's *Vale* today, the 3rd volume of his Irish trilogy. It's frightfully caddish and there is one indescribably filthy paragraph—but it's most extraordinarily amusing almost all through. I actually had to leave the National Club because I got a *fou rire* over his description of the proceedings of Horace Plunkett and Gill, his colleague in the Dept. of Agriculture, in the character of Bouvard and Pecuchet.

Talking of Ireland, I'm really in a great state of depression and anxiety about the 'situation'. It is clear that the Tories are simply determined to use it at all costs to break the Parliament Act—using first Ulster and now the Army as their instruments. It seems to me impossible for the Govt. to give way. Asquith's proposal of exclusion for 6 years, with 2 general elections before anything could be done to Ulster, seems perfectly fair and generous—to be bullied into a referendum, which would be merely a general election in disguise, would be fatal to all they have achieved in 8 years against the oligarchy. Yet the consequences of civil war, and the disruption of the Army, are appalling. It's no use writing this at such a distance, it will all be stale when you get it, but it's such a thick black cloud over everything that I can't write without a word about it.

'I seem to have been in the visions of God,' wrote Abercrombie after his excursion to London, 'on a Miltonic mount of speculation, viewing the whole of modern life in an amazing succession of dazzling instants, from Henry James to Austin Harrison, from Lovely Ladies to Cubists. Henceforth you stand for London to me.'

By the time Marsh wrote to Brooke again (April 15) there had been a painters' evening at Raymond Buildings with Spencer, Gertler, Currie and his mistress Dolly Henry, and Gaudier-Brzeska. He had also left for Spain with Mr. and Mrs. Churchill and seen two bullfights. Before leaving he had news from Brooke that he had been laid up for nine days with what he called coral-poisoning. The sores on his legs had been made worse by bathing, and they had caused a high fever. This was the second time in his life that his blood had been infected; the third attack, in fourteen

months' time, was to prove fatal. Marsh addressed his reply from
a hotel in Madrid.

Here's an unexpected place to write from—Winston and Mrs. W.
suddenly made up their minds to come here, and I was ordered to
accompany. . . . We left London a week ago today—just before that
I got your letter about the coral poisoning, which wrung my heart
—it was no use writing at once as your Mother told m'e she had no
address from you—but perhaps she has one now. I hope you were
really all right again—but it's painful to think that you don't take
better care of yourself. The Ranee[1] mentioned that your money had
come just before you posted your letter to her, so that was an anxiety
the less! Your 2 *Westminster* letters, Outside and the Rockies I think
they were called, were splendid, you will be the best living prose
writer. I liked the two poems[2]—it's rather a pity one of them is so
like *Mutability*, Plato would be much flattered at your not being able
to get away from the Ideas. I thought the surprise-poem didn't quite
play the game, there are bits in the beginning that don't fit in when
one reads it again knowing the point. I sent them both to Wilfrid
but haven't heard from him since.

I'm rather depressed by this place, to begin with I can't stand
living in this sort of hotel, with its standardized unpleasurable luxury,
among people who don't deserve money squandering it on things
nobody would possibly want. The latest improvement (at any rate,
thank goodness I never met with it before, but perhaps it's all over
America) is bells that go on ringing till they are answered—it's all
very well if it's you that rings the bell, but everyone else does it too,
and at certain times the air is one large long buzz. Compared with
this I hardly mind the band playing ragtime whenever I want to
read or write. There's *nothing whatever* in Madrid except the Prado,
which is of course magnificent, and I'm jolly glad to have seen the
Velasquez and some other things, especially El Greco, whose fame I
never understood before—but there isn't a building in Madrid that
looks more than 20 years old (except the Palace, which is quite handsome). I went today to the Tate Gallery of the place, it's really
incredible, far worse than ours—just as if all the *biggest* pictures at the
Academy had been bought and assembled together for the last forty
years, altogether I shall be glad to *have been* here, but it hardly makes
up for having missed the country this spring.

I saw Cathleen several times before I left, she has moved to some
rather nice rooms in Westbourne Square. Cookham, no less, came to

[1] Mrs. Brooke.
[2] Probably *Retrospect* and another piece since cancelled.

stay with me for a Sunday and I took him to tea there, he was much interested in the people—Harry [Ainley] and Donald Calthrop etc. He is a delightful creature, he came without a hat of any kind, he seemed not to know of the existence of any sort except bowlers, which he rightly dislikes, but was much pleased and interested when I showed him a felt one, and promised to get one like it. . . . Your box of 'curios' arrived (costing £1 17s. 10d.). I unpacked it as you told me, and found everything in good condition except a pair of tiny shoes which were ½ eaten away.

I remember when I last wrote I was desperately unhappy about politics. Things took a better turn afterwards, and I feel much easier in my mind! I don't think there *can* be a 'civil war' now. Winston expects the Govt. to go on till this time next year. This letter is getting duller and duller so it shall stop. Oh I'm reading Cornford's book on Aristophanes, it's very interesting. Who would have thought there was so much left to find out about the Classics? Rose Macaulay's new novel is very clever and amusing, and I've just read *Lord Jim* for the 1st time, it's a magnificent book. How did you get on with Miss Austen when you took her into the wilds?

A week after his return on the 22nd another rather disquieting letter from Tahiti came to hand. Brooke's mail was accumulating at San Francisco, so having heard nothing since October he could only speculate on the news he *might* have received—'your letter of November announcing your marriage with Cathleen; your kindly Christmas information about the disastrous fire in Bilton Road and the disposal of the Ranee's and Alfred's cinders; your New Year Epistle announcing your, Wilfrid's and Albert's Knighthoods; . . . the later letters that recorded your series of conversations with Shaw, the earthquake, the war with Germany, the Chinese ballet, Stravinsky's comic opera, the new El Greco, Mrs. Elgy's illegitimate twins, Gilbert's trial, Masefield's latest knockabout farce, Arthur Benson's duel, all these I have not yet had.' Then he went on: 'The game is up, Eddie. If I've gained facts through knocking about with Conrad characters in a Gauguin entourage—I've lost a dream or two. I tried to be a poet. And because I was a clever writer and because I was forty times as sensitive as anyone else—I succeeded a little. I am what I came out here to be—hard, quite hard. I have become merely a minor character in a Kipling story. I'll never be able to write anything more, I think. Or perhaps I can do plays of a sort. . . . I want to talk, talk, talk, and in the intervals have extraordinary adventures.' On reflection he thought he would become a theatre manager.

After going to *Die Meistersinger* with Lady Gwendeline Churchill, Marsh sat down to write.

I've just got your I suppose last letter from Tahiti announcing your complete change of character and our consequent probable incompatibility. God forbid, but I'm not much alarmed, from Gauguinland what Avatar? I think I'm prepared to love you under whatever transformation. I'm more concerned about your Farewell to Poesy. That sharp-eyed little Francis Birrell! I remember his telling me, as long ago as when I barely knew you and he took upon himself to explain you to me, that your public form was the Youthful Poet, but the real basis of your character was a hard business capacity. But even here I shall cling to hope. You have achieved your instrument, and I expect a time will come when you will want to play on it again. It will be the bitterest disappointment of my life if you aren't 'among the English poets when you die' as Keats said. By the way when I made my impertinent remark about your running Love to death, or whatever I said, I didn't mean love as a subject, but Love with a capital L as an abstraction, it seemed to be becoming a mannerism of style.

I'm only afraid you will find *me* changed beyond bearing. I seem to myself to have grown terribly dull and unattractive lately, let's hope it's only a phase—but certainly the contrast between anything I have to tell you, and the alluring picture you draw of my letters that have missed you, brings home to me the dismal character of the life I've been leading. There is only one really great literary event— Gordon Bottomley's play *King Lear's Wife* of which he sent me the MS last week. I don't want to dethrone Lascelles but I must say that I think this thing is at least *as* good as anything of his—the poetic drama is born again, of that there is no doubt. It is short, but the action, the character drawing, and the verses are all the work of a master. There are lines that are like nothing but the famous things in Webster. Harry Ainley is to read it here next Monday to Cathleen and I hope Maire O'Neill and 7 or 8 others of the profession, it ought to be a great occasion! I wish you could be here.

When you get this, will you be near home enough to be starting an interest in home politics again? or will you be thinking of nothing but Mexico! I am still hopeful about the Ulster settlement, but it's tremendously touch and go—Asquith must simply *make* Redmond or rather the Irish (for I think R. himself is prepared for the pill) accept Winston's proposal made yesterday for 'excluding' Ulster till a federal solution can be reached in which Ireland should be a unit. I've been in the House the last two afternoons, Winston's speech yesterday was very good, and Arthur Balfour's and Carson's today really great things to have heard—tho' A.J.B. ought not to have described Winston as an 'agent provocateur'! Carson is a glorious man really—the only possible Tory P.M. Bonar Law becomes more hopeless every day. Winston had a fine thing to say about him, tho' I'm very glad he didn't actually say it. 'The raw and rowdy Under-Secretary, whom the nakedness of the land, and the jealousies of his betters, have promoted to the leadership of the Tory party!'

King Lear's Wife is important to the history of Georgian poetry. Bottomley had enclosed the manuscript with a letter of April 16 addressed from R. C. Trevelyan's house, where he had finished the play. 'I promised Bob it should be finished for you by Easter. Revision has all the strain and none of the delight of composition . . . but I kept my word and finished two days before Good Friday.' He had just bought a house, The Sheiling, near Carnforth, which was to be the scene of his life's work.

> We are absolutely on a sunny hill-top, and our joy is a petite drawing-room among the tree-tops, with windows larger than itself whence we see Everything—sea and wood and Turnerian estuary and all the lake mountains. It is an amazing outlook, of the utmost value to me with my restrictions. I sit with my back to it, for fear I might grow too accustomed to it. . . . We are delighted that you have seen our debonair and amusing Paul [Nash] and that you too find him charming. I should like to know what you think of his work, for I believe I was responsible for persuading his father to let him follow art. His first step in art was the embellishment, in his extreme youth, of a copy of my 'Crier' with naive but impressive drawings.

For the present Marsh could give but little thought to Nash's work. He was reading the enclosure. On April 22 he sent a telegram, 'It is a masterpiece.' The poet's acknowledgement was dictated to his wife. 'I pirouetted on velvet-pile for several hours after your telegram came.' Then he received the inevitable list of critical notes, but Marsh had lost none of his enthusiasm. 'I expected a great deal—but it surpassed all that I had hoped or imagined—it is one of the great things. . . . It seemed hardly possible beforehand that a play about Lear should not find itself in a slightly false position! but yours can hold up its head against any such thought', and he had read the whole manuscript aloud to Paul Nash, who happened to be staying when it arrived. The only criticism of substance concerned Bottomley's choice of names. 'What is the eye or ear to make of Hygd? Your Queen's name ought to become a sacred and familiar thing to everyone who cares for poetry—you must not make us gerk it up like a cough.' Bottomley wrote again, April 30. 'I put all into it I could command, both of resource and energy; perhaps I am happiest of all to feel that my work has not suffered from the adverse conditions under which I have had to do it.' (For much of life Bottomley lived under the threat of recurrent haemorrhage brought on by the slightest physical exertion. Since July 1913, when *King Lear's Wife* was begun, he had been constantly stricken and unable to hold a pen.) Concerning the Queen's name (pronounced 'Higg' by him) he was unmoved by Marsh's complaint, saying that the name had 'a kind of gaunt monolithic dignity which rather satisfies me'. On May 4 Ainley gave the reading at Raymond Buildings to members of Granville Barker's company, and next day Marsh left for Birmingham to see the opening performance of Drinkwater's *Rebellion*; 'the subject raised moral problems which are treated superficially', he reported to Bottomley. He was a fellow-guest of Gibson and Abercrombie under Drinkwater's roof and he wrote again on the 5th with news of Ainley's performance and apologizing for the delay. 'There was only one pen in the house, John Drinkwater's fountain, and it was so much in demand by the 3 poets that I never got a chance.' In his reply Bottomley promised to wait three years before publishing his play, so that the forthcoming *Georgian Poetry* (planned for publication in December) could derive full benefit from its presence. In return he was to receive a double share of the royalties. 'I have loved the theatre all my life,' he wrote on hearing of Ainley's reading, 'and the drama more than any other art-form, so you could not have done anything that would have made me happier and more your debtor than just what you did on Monday night in letting Mrs. Lear share your hospitality.' And later, on hearing the manuscript was being sent to Granville Barker, he declared: 'I can only sit on my mountain top and praise the gods that I am in the world at the same time as you. . . . I have always been at a disadvantage in having to live so far withdrawn from my fellows; but you more than make up for that to me.'

On the 8th Isaac Rosenberg came to Gray's Inn for the first time, bringing samples of his paintings and his poems, and next day at an exhibition in Whitechapel Marsh made the acquaintance of Edward Wadsworth, whose curiously vivid and precise delineations on a seashore had caught his eye as being the work of a man to watch. Since February, when the idea was first put forward by Stanley Spencer, Marsh had been consulting his young painters from the Slade on the possibility of compiling a volume of reproductions, a companion to *Georgian Poetry*, to be called *Georgian Drawings*. Paul Nash and Gertler had already agreed to keep an eye out for contributors. Professor Sadler was interested as also was Lord Henry Bentinck, whose collection of contemporary works at Underley Hall was becoming a rival to Marsh's own. The book was being planned to consist of fifty drawings by about twenty unknown artists, of whom the leaders would be Marsh's circle of friends—Gertler, Currie, John and Paul Nash, Seabrooke, William Roberts, Rosenberg, Stanley and Gilbert Spencer, Nevinson, Ihlee, Tryon, and Gaudier-Brzeska. It was to be launched by subscription, and it was considered unwise to proceed until four hundred promises of half a guinea had been collected. For several months the project developed. Paul Nash and Professor Sadler's son Michael being particularly active in its support, and though it was not immediately destroyed by the outbreak of war, it was the lack of finances that finally caused it to peter out. Marsh himself could only have carried it through at the expense of the painters themselves, whose work it was his main object to buy from time to time. He was now administering his funds with the utmost tactical precision, for there was no margin and the objects of his patronage were mounting in number with bewildering rapidity.

On May 10 a letter from San Francisco told of Brooke's return to civilization. 'Oh I am as old as death,' he ended. He was twenty-six. On the same day Marsh wrote from home.

Just got your letter from Frisco (or is it very amateurish to say Frisco, like calling New College 'New'?). I do feel for you in your return to civility, but how right La Rochefoucauld was, there is something that pleases us in the misfortunes of our friends—in this case the diminution of the distance between us. I hope your next letter will say something definite about when you will be back, as it may affect my plans for Whitsuntide. Parliament is only going to rise for a fortnight, so I don't think we shall be able to go for the cruise and in that case I should like to arrange for being here when you come—it seems much more than a year that you have been away. I shall be dreadfully shy and afraid of comparisons with cowboys and beach-combers, so you must make allowances at first.

I enjoyed my visit to the Drinkwaters—Lascelles and Wilfrid were both very delighted—W. has written a quite excellent poem, *Hoops*, a dialogue between a camel-keeper and a clown at a circus, one of his best. John's play went off quite well—it isn't really good, I'm afraid, and his company is only so-so, the heroine quite charming. Mrs. Drinkwater is a cheery hoyden, I rather liked her. Catherine Abercrombie fainted at breakfast on Sunday, and kept her bed, which cast a slight gloom. She is going to have a 3rd child, poor Lascelles will have to review more than ever. . . .

I've just been with Cathleen to a Tchekow play at the Stage Society—*Uncle Vanya*—the first of his I have seen. I was terribly disappointed. It was vilely produced and acted, but even allowing for that I couldn't see that it was good. For one thing I don't really like a play in which one wants to shake all the characters all the time. And I thought it was a vindication of the well-made play! The 3rd act was full of explanations of points which in any sensible system of play writing ought obviously to have been made clear before the action began. I've made up my mind to be a Philistine about Tchekow.

In the last week of April Brooke wrote in the train travelling to New York, having only just picked up the parcel of books Marsh had sent him. He was half-way through *Sons and Lovers*. 'It's so extraordinarily vivid in its conception of scenes. He's always *hectic*, isn't he, a little? But I must proceed. He's a big man.' Since his last letter abroad Marsh had entertained Rosenberg at breakfast, bought the painting he had come to show, and hung it at the foot of the bed in the spare room over a drawing of Irish peasant women by Currie. The new acquisition, entitled *Sacred Love*, was a small oil-painting of curiously dry texture and pallid tone, like a pastel. In the foreground, a green clearing in a wood, a youth was kneeling by a girl who sat on a rock, and in an attitude of adoration he gathered her hands to his lips. In the background naked figures seemed to be scattering in alarm through the tilted trees. It glowed with a strange, dream-like intensity, reminiscent of Blake—a lovely vision which for the next quarter of a century confronted on their waking all the guests in this little room.

Marsh had lunched with Countess Benckendorff at the Russian Embassy when for the last time he directed a letter to Brooke across the Atlantic.

I'm glad you liked the books. I felt rather hot about them. You are perfectly right about them all—Gilbert's fumbling with things and not going on with them is *exactly* my crab of him—it's all such an improvisation—just as one is beginning to get interested, hey presto and where are you? it's so slapdash—nothing really *done*. I go to him for next Sunday and what I shall say about *Old Mole* I can't imagine. The Speculative Dialogues are simply over my head, I can't even pretend they aren't. I'm glad you feel the greatness of Lawrence—if he could arrive at 'form' he would be splendid—but he doesn't seem even to try. It's wonderful to get a letter from you posted 9 days ago!

Cathleen tells me you sail at the beginning of June but that you mean to arrive like a thief in the night—make an exception for me. I won't tell anyone else—but it would be so disastrous if you came and I wasn't here, or couldn't give you a bed! and I've got tickets for 18 Beecham operas and ballets. There's no time for a Mediterranean cruise this year so I can quite well be here to receive you if you give me notice.

I never got much further with Garnett—he is so melancholy and so tentative. I feel there is a sort of drab beauty in his mind and character but that I should have to give more than I have quite handy, to get at it. I admire conscientiousness, which he has, but I love lightness of touch, which he hasn't. His tendency is to like things because he thinks them right, and mine is to think things right because I like them; and this difference prevents a merging in the warmer feeling!

This and a number of other letters were awaiting Brooke at his hotel in New York. His reply of May 24 talked of 'hundreds and hundreds of letters, most of them from you. Yours were all very nice to read (some of the others weren't).' He picked on the account of Abercrombie's day in London. 'Even the best of the best people in Ryton—nay, Dymock itself—must have seemed to him a little tame after that.' He warned Marsh that he would arrive in the company of two new friends, Maurice Browne and his wife, who ran the Little Theatre, Chicago, 'acting nothing but Gibson, Abercrombie, and Euripides'. He was due to sail on the *Philadelphia*. 'I'm infinitely vigorous and excited. I can't sleep for thinking of England.' After sealing the letter he heard details of his voyage and despatched a cable, 'Will you be in London Friday night June fifth I shall', to which the prompt reply came, 'Yes. Eddie.' On the fourth he wired again, this time to the Admiralty, 'Arriving midnight alone will wire. Rupert.'

On June 5 Denis Browne was rung up at Shawfield Street and invited to dine with Marsh and Miss Nesbitt at the Queen's restaurant, Sloane Square. After the meal Marsh took them to the Royal Court Theatre, then to Raymond Buildings to fill in the time with talk and a 'tour of the improvements', then to Paddington where the train, much delayed, pulled in at 2.45 A.M. Brooke was extremely brown and the sun had slightly bleached his hair. They all went back to Gray's Inn, where Mrs. Elgy had left a sumptuous cold supper. Brooke stayed the night in the new spare room and on finding Spencer's *Apple Gatherers* hanging over the bed at once christened them 'The Bogeys' which was thought a disappointing reaction. Such was the talk that night, there was hardly any sleep.

Chapter Twelve

TOWARDS GALLIPOLI
(June 6, 1914–February 27, 1915)

NEXT day Brooke left for Rugby, leaving Mrs. Elgy to pack his luggage and put it on a later train. The friends had parted on the understanding that there was to be a reunion supper in Raymond Buildings a week later. From home Brooke wrote: 'Do get hold of whatever poets, actresses, or lovely people there are.' Abercrombie must stay the night so that they could talk at breakfast. He couldn't sleep. 'England is *too* wonderful.' Marsh began the week with Denis Browne at the first night of Chaliapin's *Prince Igor* at Drury Lane. On the Tuesday he dined with the Churchills before escorting Lady Plymouth to a ball at Buckingham Palace. He had answered Brooke's suggestion 'Let us be bourgeois, I think' with 'I shan't invite the smart set', and ended: 'This reminds me of an official letter that someone here drafted once and Winston made me rewrite because "it seemed to proceed by a succession of afterthoughts".' Next day he had supper with Granville Barker and was introduced to Arnold Bennett.

Brooke, who was now a fellow-guest with André Gide at Royston, where the Raverats lived, then wrote: 'I'm glad Jim Barnes is coming. You can't think of another gentleman to balance the actors and artists?' To which Marsh replied: 'I'm sorry the party is going to be so horrible; you are the last person I should have expected to complain of the absence of the Oligarchy at my entertainments—but I'm afraid the male gentry are too stupid and the female too clever for the occasion.' On the great day (June 11) Brooke arrived in London for luncheon with Marsh and Drinkwater; dinner at Simpson's followed and Brooke introduced Maurice Browne and his wife, the friends from Chicago; then all went on to see Fokine and Karsavina at Covent Garden in a programme which included the first performance of *Papillons*. By the time the late-night party at Gray's Inn began Marsh and

Brooke had exchanged eight letters in five days (three of Brooke's afterthoughts arrived in one day). Mrs. Elgy, who stayed on to serve the supper, had never seen so many guests.[1] Abercrombie came the following night, and Brooke slept on the sofa, then Marsh left for Portsmouth, where he boarded the *Enchantress* for the visit of the French Fleet. From there he discharged a shower of circulars in search of subscriptions for his new venture, *Georgian Drawings*, then ascended into the air for the first time, in a Sopwith seaplane, an experiment 'not wholly reassuring' he decided, but he was anxious not to seem less intrepid than his Chief, whom he was assisting in the pioneer task of founding a combat unit equipped to discharge torpedoes from the air.

A week later he was met at Princes Risborough by Brooke, Miss Nesbitt, and Dudley Ward, and they all stayed at the Pink and Lily tavern. Next morning they walked to Wendover, Marsh read aloud 'Mrs. Lear', and material for the new *Georgian Poetry* volume was spread out on the grass and discussed. Perhaps the chief problem was Ford Madox Hueffer's poem *On Heaven*, which Marsh rather admired, Gibson disliked, and Abercrombie abhorred. The last was more in favour of Gibson's American neighbour, as his report on Hueffer showed:

> The poem is what I call slop, but it's certainly by far the best specimen of the slop-pail school that I have come across. . . . However repulsive, it is an interesting experiment. . . . But may I say this? which of course you must rule in or out of order according to your position as master of the feast. If you do put Hueffer in, I think (looking at both men from my own point of view only) that you certainly ought to put Frost in too. . . . Frost, at his best, is far more genuinely and deeply original, much more beautiful and interesting, and however experimental, is firm, finely proportioned and intellectually constructed—the very opposite of slop. . . . Wilfrid is doing some magnificent things, quite in his top manner, which is the top of all today.

Hueffer solved the problem by refusing permission, and since the editor wanted to keep his collection of poets as exclusively British as his painters Frost was reluctantly pronounced ineligible.

[1] Among those present were Granville Barker, Lillah McCarthy, Duff Cooper, Laura Cowie, Norman Wilkinson, Hugh Walpole, John Drinkwater, Wilfrid Gibson, Harold Monro, Donald Calthrop, Basil Dean, Cathleen Nesbitt, Maurice Browne, Denis Browne, Albert Rutherston, Mark Gertler, Henry Ainley, Jim Barnes, Duncan Grant, and Desmond MacCarthy.

On the 27th he succeeded in bringing Frieda and D. H. Lawrence and Brooke together at the Moulin d'Or. At Charter-house on the morrow it was Robert Graves who listened to Marsh's performance of excerpts from Bottomley's play, and the boy was told that his contributions to *The Carthusian*, the school magazine, showed high promise of a future Georgian. From this time until the end of July the spare room at Raymond Buildings was Brooke's home, and the July 'London season' that Marsh conducted for their mutual delight was the principal feature in both their lives.

The season began with Gaudier-Brzeska coming to dinner and going on with them to the ballet at Drury Lane, then to supper with Lady Ottoline Morrell, where they picked up both Browne and Barnes, who came back and slept on sofas at Gray's Inn. Next day they attended a meeting with Monro at the Poetry Bookshop and in the evening were the guests of J. M. Barrie and Granville Barker at the Savoy with Marie Tempest and Gerald du Maurier at their table. The breakfast-party on the 9th provided one of its guests with the material for what is the most vivid description of a Georgian occasion at this time. Mrs. Elgy had dropped a note from Marsh in Sassoon's door on her way home the night before—'Come to breakfast tomorrow and meet Rupert and W. H. Davies.' Paul Nash, who had slept on the sofa, was also there. Brooke came in after the meal had begun. He was wearing a blue shirt open at the neck and flannel trousers, and he hadn't had time to brush his hair, which Sassoon observed was brown-gold and 'just a shade longer than it need have been'. He had blue eyes, a Cambridge accent, sunburned skin, and bare feet in sandals. Davies did most of the talking during the main dish of kidneys and bacon, animatedly relating an adventure of his on the banks of the Mississippi which was not quite as enthralling as he thought it was.

Soon after the host's departure for the Admiralty, Sassoon found himself alone with Brooke.

> We agreed that Davies was an excellent poet and a most likeable man. I then asked him a few clumsy questions about his travels. His replies were reserved and unilluminating. One fragment of our talk which I remember clearly was—as such recoveries often are—wholly to my disadvantage.
>
> 'What were the white people like in the places you stayed at in the tropics?' I had asked. ('The tropics' sounded somehow inept, but it was too late to correct myself now!)

'Some of them,' he said, 'were rather like composite characters out of Conrad and Kipling.'

Hoping that it would go down well, I made a disparaging remark about Kipling's poetry being terribly tub-thumping stuff.

'But not always, surely,' he answered; and then let me off easily by adding, 'I used to think rather the same myself until Eddie made me read *Cities and Thrones and Powers*. There aren't many better modern poems than that, you know.'

I could only admit that I had never read it.[1]

On the 10th Marsh and Brooke lunched with Henry James, having received precise instructions from their host at Carlyle Mansions. 'Will you please mount in the lift to *me*, at the said 1.45 . . . when I will conduct you to the immediately adjacent scene.'[2] Later that day Stanley Spencer joined Marsh and Brooke at a Debussy concert and slept on the settee at home. In the days that follow they lunch with Henry Festing Jones; on the 21st lunch apart, Marsh being guest with Lord Morley and Kitchener at 10 Downing Street, then meet again for dinner with the Duchess of Leeds and talk with Maurice Baring; on the 24th (the day on which Marsh scrawls WAR CLOUD in his engagement-book) Conrad Aiken drops in to breakfast; Denis Browne takes them to Shawfield Street and Brooke climbs a drainpipe to the first floor and breaks in, his host having lost the key; Frieda and D. H. Lawrence join them again (July 30) for luncheon at the Ship[3]; and in the evening, to end the season, they dine with the Prime Minister at Downing Street, where at last Marsh is able to present Brooke to Mr. Churchill. Next day Brooke leaves to stay with Gibson in his country cottage. 'He *has* grown up!' Gibson exclaimed on a postcard.

During these last weeks of peace Marsh had been in constant touch with Isaac Rosenberg and had used his influence at the Emigration Office to help the poet's arrangements for a visit to a sister-in-law in South Africa. Rosenberg had also consulted Marsh about his scheme for a new pamphlet of his poems to be

---

[1] *The Weald of Youth*, by Siegfried Sassoon (Faber), pp. 223-232.

[2] The letters of Henry James, from which extracts are quoted in the following pages, appear, with the exception of those marked †, in *The Letters of Henry James*, edited by Percy Lubbock (Macmillan, 1920).

[3] In a letter to the author (March 18, 1954) Frieda Lawrence recalled this occasion. 'Eddie was late and excited and told us, "I believe Sir Edward Grey has just prevented war with Germany."' Of Brooke she commented, 'He was so good-looking, he took your breath away.'

called *Youth*. This was Rosenberg's second publication and it was privately printed for a modest sum which Marsh provided.

> I've given my things to the printer—he's doing 16 pages, for £2 10s. I know for certain I can get rid of ten. . . . If you like you can have my three life drawings for the money if you think they're worth it. You don't know how happy you have made me by giving me this chance to print.[1]

Marsh put in a lot of work on the manuscript of *Youth* and soon Rosenberg wrote again. He was amazed that anyone should take his work so seriously. 'You don't know how encouraging that is. . . . I am not going to refute your criticisms; in literature I have no judgement—at least for style.' He left for Cape Town in June and wrote asking for a book of reproductions for a lecture on art he was preparing. When he wrote acknowledging the parcel he realized that his patron's thoughts would be fixed on other things.

> By the time you get this things will only have just begun, I'm afraid. Europe will have just stepped into its bath of blood. I will be waiting with beautiful drying towels of painted canvas and precious ointments to smear and heal the soul, and lovely music and poems.

Lawrence reappeared by letter in May, delivering a diatribe against Abercrombie's contribution to the second issue of *New Numbers*. He had admired *The Sale of St. Thomas*, but *The End of the World* (which Marsh was to defend against all comers in the following years) upset him. 'Why, why, in God's name, is Abercrombie messing about with Yokels and Cider and runaway wives? . . . And you encourage it—it is too bad.' Marsh's riposte was not so furious that it prevented Lawrence from inviting him to be a witness at his marriage, which took place in Kensington on July 13. A heavy day at the Admiralty prevented Marsh from attending, but to make up for it he acted on a hint of Lawrence's that he was contemplating a critical study of Hardy and sent him the complete works. Lawrence was dumbfounded when the parcel arrived.

> I began to yell—'but I didn't *ask* for them'—and I rushed round the room almost cracked. . . . Frieda was getting in my way crying:

[1] This and subsequent quotations are from *The Collected Works*, ed. Bottomley and Harding. *Youth* did not appear until 1915, but these editors have placed this undated correspondence before the visit to South Africa, so it has seemed best to follow their example.

'Never mind—never mind—take them—how lovely—oh, how I shall revel—let him give them you—' I still feel shaken. I've never had such a lot of books in my life.

And he promised Marsh the dedication 'with a fanfare of trumpets'. On July 27 Michael Sadleir wrote asking Marsh to bring together his friend Lawrence and the American poetess Amy Lowell. So it was Marsh who sent Lawrence to the literary luncheon at the Berkeley where the poet was invited to support the Imagist group of poets which was soon to be actively anti-Georgian. The difference between the progressive and traditional styles in verse was not yet clearly defined. For the present to be Georgian was, oddly enough, to be thought obscure. Flecker wrote complaining that the critics were calling him a minor poet 'because I'm not obscure. But it's true enough, I'm horribly un-Georgian.' He was now revising *Hassan* for the last time, and reading the books that Marsh had sent to his sanatorium at Davos, among them *Les Copains* of Jules Romains. 'Honestly I don't expect to trouble the face of the earth much longer—and as long as *Hassan* comes off I shall expire contentedly.' His bouts of fever were becoming more frequent and even the slight effort of reading exhausted him.

The painters were still dropping in and out of Raymond Buildings, and on July 20, while Marsh called on Gaudier-Brzeska at his studio in Putney, Stanley Spencer was in the bathroom opposite Mrs. Elgy's kitchen with his *Self-portrait* balanced over a bowl of hot water. He left a note to say he had scrubbed the painting with the half of a potato, then wiped it with a hot towel, then stood it over the bath and varnished it 'beginning at the top downwards. I think it has improved the picture'. He hoped he had not overstepped the mark. 'I shall get so odious and familiar that you will regret having allowed "that boy Spencer" such freedom!'

Paul Nash was given the money to travel north to his friend Bottomley's new home.

I came away I believe a humbler and wiser man. The house is a treasure-box of books and pictures within and surrounded by an enchanted jungle without. Its windows command the silver bay and grey green country to the mountains. You can't think with what awe and apprehension I regarded those distant mountains—I who had never yet met a mountain. . . . Some lakes were terrific with their guardian hills—my aunt, you should have seen them at night! My pictures are promising for future development but individually rather nice and gentlemanly. Still, I feel I have given a jump right away from 'Nash trees'.

On the way home he had called on William Rothenstein and considered his painting *The Doll's House* a 'knockout. . . . Yes, I'm a man come home with some revised opinions and a more catholic taste'. This was an improvement on his earlier letter of the year, written while Gertler was staying with him, 'I intensely dislike all the work I have ever done.'

The day after Brooke had left the spare room empty, Marsh wrote in his engagement-book, 'Germany declares war on Russia', and orders went out to the Fleet at Portland not to disperse, although the naval manœuvres were concluded. 'The crisis is terrible,' he wrote to de la Mare. 'Isn't it strange what an air of unreality there is about very real things!' Next day (August 2) he acted as messenger between the Government and the Conservative ex-Ministers who had been convened by Lord Lansdowne at Brooks's in St. James's Street. In the small hours of the morning Edward Horner walked home with him. There was a letter on the table from Brooke at Rugby. He was on the way to stay with the Cornfords in Norfolk. 'I give you my address because I feel you're the one link I have with the heart of things in this bloody time. Send me a card, once, to say how things are.' Mrs. Elgy had packed the wrong books, and if Eddie was missing a green trunk he had pinched it, having first asked for another of his, only to find it had already been walked off with by Shaw-Stewart. Then he went on:

> Mrs. Elgy said, 'Ar, Mr. Marsh, 'e *thinks* Mr. Shaw-Stewart sent that bag back. But he ain't. But Mr. Marsh *thinks* 'e 'as.' She spoke with gloom, as if it was a well-known monomania of yours. . . . Now this thing has really happened I feel as if I *can't* sit still. . . . Tell me if you hear of any jobs. Tomorrow I'm twenty-seven!

He ended on a note of foreboding: 'Do you have a Brussels-before-Waterloo feeling that we'll all—or some—meet with other eyes in 1915?'

On Brooke's birthday, the only entry in the engagement-book was: 'Henceforward at Admiralty from 9.30 to any time between 12 and 1.30 A.M.' Next day, after dining with Denis Browne at the Ship restaurant he arrived at the Admiralty shortly before the hour (11 P.M.) when the ultimatum to Germany was due to expire. He was present when his colleague Masterton-Smith, the Naval Secretary, issued the First Lord's order to the Fleet to begin hostilities. The *Goeben*, a powerful German cruiser, escorted by the *Breslau*, was in the Mediterranean and making for Turkey, whose vacillating Government only needed a demonstration on Germany's part to determine her future policy. The *Goeben* was already being shadowed by British ships. Meanwhile Marsh escorted Mr. Churchill as far as the door of the midnight Cabinet meeting in Downing Street. Some hours later as he was walking the First Lord back to the Admiralty, he happened to remark that he had noticed how the crisis had drawn all the Ministers into a united brotherhood. 'But you'll see,' said Mr. Churchill, 'it won't last long.'

A week went by before Marsh answered Brooke's plea for a postcard.

> My dear, I should think that what has most brought home to you 'what war really is' is my not writing to you when you asked me. . . . I shall be a wretched host, as I *must* go to bed directly I get home. But I shall what is nowadays called 'glimpse' you every now and then. You are in the upstairs room with the bogeys in it.

Though Brooke was back in the spare room from the 10th to the 22nd Marsh lived an independent existence. From now on the engagement-book, once packed with references to ballet, plays, and the names of acquaintances encountered at balls or in the intervals at the theatre, carries little more than abrupt official entries—(August 24) 'To Kitchener's house to get Lord French's telegram'—(August 31) 'To Kitchener's. Home at 3 A.M.'—(October 5) 'Agitating evening at the Admiralty'. The few leisure hours he managed to snatch in the evenings were divided between the agreeable company of Mr. Churchill's mother and the solace of Denis Browne playing the Bach preludes and fugues in Shawfield Street. On August 12 he received the last of Fisher's emphatic communications. (Fisher had not yet been recalled to serve as First Sea Lord.) The *Goeben* was still at large.

> It *was* kind of you when SO overwhelmed with work to write and tell me that the *Indomitable* and *Inflexible* were outside Messina waiting for the *Goeben* to come out! but why was not Sir —— there with the *Inflexible* also? and Troubridge and all his fine armoured cruisers as

well and all other vessels also? Nelson said that an admiral was a
dam fool to fight 10 to 1 if he could fight 100 to 1! ——— ought to be
shot. Surely he is going to be superseded at once! Surely he is not
going to be allowed to hoist his flag at the Nore after such utterly
effete incapacity! The Nore should be kept for Jellicoe when he
comes back with one arm!

But days went by, no decisive engagement occurred in the North
Sea; the *Goeben* finally eluded its pursuers, and the enemy gained
considerable advantage. Before many days Turkey was allied
with Germany. The North Sea Fleet carried out the dual function
of island defence and the shipment of the Expeditionary Force
across the Channel, but those who watched and waited at home
grew more and more impatient for the great encounter which the
enemy would not risk. The Fleet was already at its war station in
Scapa Flow when hostilities began. Von Tirpitz could not take
it at a disadvantage, and after the engagement in the Heligoland
Bight at the end of August he was all the more inclined to stay in
port.

At the special request of Kitchener the First Lord also undertook the responsibility of aerial defence. Since 1911 Marsh had
witnessed and assisted in the formation of the Royal Flying Corps.
Before the end of 1914 its Naval Wing had become the Royal
Naval Air Service and a movement was afoot to re-establish the
air arm under an independent Ministry. In these months Mr.
Churchill and his staff were also in consultation on the problem
of inventing an armoured car equipped with a portable bridge
for crossing a trench, a device which contributed to the evolution
of the tank.

In his private life, which at this time must have seemed curiously
small and remote, the first and most obvious necessity was the
cancellation of *Georgian Poetry 1913-1914*. In giving the news to
Bottomley he made no complaint of his present circumstances.
'It's marvellously interesting and in a way exhilarating in spite
of the awfulness of what it's all about.' For Bottomley this postponement meant that his play would have to remain in manuscript for at least another year, but he replied that he was 'happy
in a hope that after all this vast unreason is over there may be a
chance of making a wiser and more fruitful world for us to grow
old in'. Harold Monro commented, 'I realize of course that all
idea of the second *G.P.* is absurd at present', and expressed the

hope that by December the Prussians would be cooped up in Berlin. To him the cancellation was something of a relief since there had already been three muddles in succession over the accounts of the first volume, which was now in its ninth edition, and he had only just reduced the chaos to order. 'I have often thought of you during the last three weeks,' he wrote, 'and marvelled at all the splendid secrets you must have known, while we have been helplessly aching with curiosity. Everything else has sunk into silly insignificance. I am holding on somehow and must pull through of course, but "business" has absolutely stopped. From the day war was declared scarcely anyone has entered the shop.' Gibson was alone in contending that the anthology should appear. 'I think it essential to do all we can to keep our flag flying during the triumph of barbarism.' A week later he was gravely concerned for his neighbour Abercrombie, who, his reviewing for the *Manchester Guardian* having come to an end just when his wife was expecting another baby, was in desperate straits. De la Mare had consulted Edward Thomas, who knew vaguely of some relief fund for men of letters. Meanwhile Catherine Abercrombie was urging her husband 'to go harvesting in the hopes of earning something, but he simply hasn't the strength for that kind of work. . . . I'm much relieved to hear Rupert is still in England. Don't let him leave.' Marsh found time to enlist the support of Gosse and Bridges and eased the situation for Abercrombie. The last letter from the Poet Laureate (March 31) had exclaimed: 'If your political friends go on as they do, shall I be expected to write war songs?' It is curious to realize the poet was referring to the troubles over Home Rule for Ireland, so suddenly and so totally had everything been overshadowed by the invasion of Belgium. Lawrence wrote (August 25) from his cottage near Chesham, his letter coinciding with a brief note from Maurice Hewlett, 'D. H. Lawrence, one of your poets, is in great distress.' Lawrence himself wrote to say he was finding the war 'like one of those nightmares when you can't move. . . . I'm glad to hear you're enjoying yourself slogging at work. I've whitewashed the house.' The remark thrown in that he and Frieda were 'sitting here on our last sixpence, holding our breath', prompted Marsh to send him a cheque for £10 with a note reaffirming his unshaken confidence in his young friend's genius. 'I am moved almost to tears by the letter and the money this morning,' Lawrence replied. 'Why should I have thought you a bad friend? I know from Mark Gertler how busy you are. It really touches me very close, when you write so warmly. After all, there is no reason why you should take thought for me. . . . Gertler says all your work makes you happy. . . . I cannot get any sense of an enemy—only of a disaster.'

A letter from Rosenberg in Cape Town enclosed the text of his illustrated lecture on art.

> I know my poor essay stands no chance by the side of the bristling legions of war-scented documents on your desk; but know that I despise war and hate war and hope that the Kaiser William will have his bottom smacked. . . . Are we going to have Tennyson's 'Battle in the Air' and the nations deluging the nations with blood from the air?

The month of August passed with much momentous work and little sleep. On the 16th while dining with Lady Randolph Churchill Marsh sat next Madame de Polignac, who offered to lend him the book she had been reading. It was by a friend of hers and called *Du Côté de chez Swann*. Thus Proust came into his life. It was the only book he read during these months and his minute study of it was to be of help years afterwards to its translator Scott-Moncrieff. Brooke wrote from Rugby on the 24th enclosing his poem 'When colour goes home into the eyes', which he entitled '*Unpacking* or *Contemplation* or *The Store* or whatever'. In his covering note he added 'two bad sonnets yesterday'—the first hint of his war poems. On September 1 he came back to Raymond Buildings. After an evening at the theatre watching Gerald du Maurier in *Outcast* Marsh came out with a proposition. Mr. Churchill was about to form a new force for special service, the Royal Naval Division, and if Brooke wished to join he would almost certainly be given a commission. Brooke was greatly relieved to find something to do, but he tried to make the condition that Denis Browne should be offered a commission as well. The secretary of the selection committee was due to start work on the 10th. Not till then could Marsh obtain the two application forms, and in a letter of the 9th he promised to recommend them both 'for all I'm worth', but he warned Brooke that if Browne were not accepted he could hardly back out.

Browne had been so constantly in Marsh's company of late that there had been no need to communicate by post. The last postcard from him looked as if it had been dated before the Flood, though it was only July, when he was on holiday in Buxton. 'The hills here are so charged with significant form that they are all the same shape, and a large bird flew over me for an hour this morning singing in 5/4 time.' Now he had sterner business to perform. To his well-timed request to join up with Brooke the answer came. 'I'll do my best, tho' I *hate* you both going, as this force is sure to be put in the field pretty soon and I'd *so* much rather you were "just behind the battle, mother".' Soon Marsh was sending Browne a form of enlistment to fill in, saying he would 'pass it on with my panegyric'. Brooke signed his at Raymond Buildings. By the 14th both forms were back in Marsh's hands. He wrote to Browne.

> Col. Ollivant and Winston took my word for you without form or interview or anything! I'm glad I could do it for you since you wanted it, but I feel I'm 'giving of my dearest' as the newspapers say. I arranged for you and Rupert to be in the same Brigade. . . . Don't tell a soul that I did it all on my own or I shall be plagued to death.

On September 9 Marsh and the First Lord left the Admiralty for an unrecorded destination. They were away for three days, probably at Soissons, discussing with Sir John French the project to be known as the Dunkirk 'Circus'. This was the demonstration of comparatively small forces on the French coast (behind the German front line) which was to bring about a diversion of enemy strength of crucial value to the Allied cause during the weeks to come. The plan had been conceived by Marshal Joffre, and Kitchener entrusted its execution to the First Lord, since the Navy was in possession of the only forces available. When Marsh dined with the Prime Minister, Mr. Churchill, and Kitchener, at Downing Street on the 15th, the 'Circus' was no doubt the dominating topic. Six days later, September 21, Dunkirk was without any doubt the destination of the First Lord and his secretary. They travelled first to Liverpool with F. E. Smith. That same night they left for Dover by special train and in the morning reached Dunkirk. The Germans had been halted on the Marne and were now advancing on the Scheldt with Antwerp and the Channel ports as their objective. Later that day, while he was still on the other side of the Channel, alarming news reached the First Lord that three cruisers had been torpedoed in the

North Sea. He returned at once to London. Back at Gray's Inn that night Marsh discovered the pale and disconsolate figure of John Currie awaiting him. He begged for the use of the spare bed. The furies of sexual jealousy were in hot pursuit. Dolly Henry was driving him out of his mind.

Somehow it was possible to arrange a luncheon meeting between Robert Bridges and Brooke on the 25th and that same night Marsh called at Shawfield Street to say goodbye to Browne. Orders had been issued for the men to report at Betteshanger, the estate of Lord Northbourne, where the Second Naval Brigade Headquarters had been set up. The force known as the Royal Naval Volunteer Reserve was being mustered in haste for the defence of Antwerp. For Brooke and Browne it was a false alarm. Their departure was postponed until Sunday the 27th, when Marsh, for the first time setting eyes on them in uniform, saw them off at the station then motored to Knebworth, where he confided his anxieties to Victor and Pamela Lytton, and his old friend Lady Gladstone whom he found staying there.

The First Lord crossed over to Antwerp on October 2nd to make a personal reconnaissance and persuade the Belgian Government to hold Antwerp for a few more days. The hitch in the German plans caused by this prolonged resistance appreciably affected the situation on the main front. At Dunkirk three days later Mr. Churchill was hailed on the jetty by Shaw-Stewart, who was acting military embarkation officer and managed to get a pencil scrawl off to Marsh reporting the extraordinary *sang froid* of his Chief under fire. The R.N.D., with Brooke and Browne as junior subalterns of the Anson Battalion, had embarked on the 5th at dawn. While in camp Brooke had drafted two more sonnets. These may have included the first draft of 'If I should die, think only this of me', but he was rash enough to take over with him these and other manuscripts in his kitbag, which was subsequently jettisoned in the retreat and never heard of again.

Much of the First Naval Division had been taken prisoner and the Second was marching twenty-five miles under fire back to the coast, their retreat delayed by swarming refugees, when Marsh was rung up at Admiralty House by Albert Rutherston. John Currie had shot Dolly Henry dead and then turned the gun upon himself. He was in a critical condition. Marsh at once went round to Chelsea Infirmary. Currie was conscious, but hardly knew him.

He died next morning, the day Antwerp fell. A letter was in the post from Rutherston. His visit to the Infirmary had coincided with Mark Gertler's, who had broken down completely. Marsh wrote to Michael Sadler in Leeds.

He was in a dreadful state of exhaustion—but very peaceful and gentle, not seeming quite to realize what he had done. I had hoped that his unhappy passion was dying away. There was no great harm in her, but she was extremely vain and empty-headed—and jealous of his work.

Currie made several attempts to break away, but he really seems to have been unable to live without her, and she loved him too in a way. . . . Isn't it a dreadful wasteful business? I did think his love for his work would keep him from what he has done. I am sure he would have become a fine painter if he could have freed himself from that disease of heart and will.[1]

Currie's last letter accompanied a sketch by a young artist he was anxious to bring to Marsh's notice. 'This drawing is the work of a friend named Dobson. The whole character of his work shows a remarkable development for a fellow working alone.' He hoped Frank Dobson would be included in the Georgian anthology of reproductions, a project which was still not finally abandoned. In fact Marsh had forgotten about it. Currie, one of the youngest of this brotherhood, passionately believed in the advantage of artists working in association. Through him Marsh had first met other students from the Slade, who accepted him as one of their group and determined his attitude to modern art.

Meanwhile Marsh had heard that the troops were under orders to withdraw. He wrote jointly to Brooke and Browne: 'I do trust you are coming back unscathed. I've been racked with anxiety all this week as you may imagine, and I haven't yet got any definite news of you two. . . . I think we should have heard if you had been hurt. You must have had the most thrilling time of your lives, however horrible. I only just missed coming out, through not having my bag ready! I could have hardly arrived in evening clothes and not a stitch to change into.' The order to go had reached him in the interval of a play which he was seeing with Paul Nash.

As Mr. Churchill did not return until October 7 this meant

[1] From *Michael Ernest Sadler, a Memoir by his Son* (Constable, 1949).

that for five days Marsh and Masterton-Smith were in charge at the Admiralty.

What remained of the Second Naval Division was put ashore at Dover on the 12th after a week of gallant and, as it seemed at the time, unavailing active service. Browne had managed to send a picture-postcard from Bruges. 'So this is what happened. We're back and nothing done. Very footsore and sleepy, but otherwise fit.'

Brooke and 'Oc' (Arthur) Asquith, the Prime Minister's son, who was also a subaltern in the battalion, went straight from Dover to Whitehall, where they called on Marsh, who admitted them to the First Lord. Mr. Churchill listened to their accounts of the Antwerp expedition. They had been granted a week's leave before rejoining their unit at Chatham, so Brooke went back to Raymond Buildings, where during a bath which lasted over an hour he gave Eddie Marsh a fuller account of his adventure.

Brooke was still on leave at Gray's Inn when a letter from Gaudier-Brzeska arrived from the Western Front. He had enlisted in the French Army, and this was to be the last word Marsh had from him before he was killed. 'Here I am face to the foe,' he began, and went on:

> We crept through a wood as dark as pitch, fixed bayonets, and pushed some 500 yards amid fields until we came to a wood. There we opened fire and in a bound we were along the bank of the road where the Prussians stood. We shot at each other for some $\frac{1}{4}$ of an hour at distance of 12/15 yards and the work was deadly. I brought down two great giants who stood against a burning heap of straw, my corporal accounted for four more—and so on all along the line. They had as much luck unhappily, for out of 12 of my squad that went we found ourselves 5 after the engagement. . . . We have had three days rest. Now we are again very near the lines and we are expecting a sharp encounter for tomorrow as the Germans seem to like Saturday nights for their prowess. Confident in ultimate success I remain yours ever Henri Gaudier.

Gaudier had been among the first of Currie's acquaintance to be put in touch with the patron at Gray's Inn. As early as September 1912 he had written, 'Your envelope bearing the Admiralty seal gave me a sort of fright—I had a vague idea I was going to be arrested for some reason or other', but he benefited less than the others from Marsh's friendship. He was too proud to let him know of his grievous poverty, and only showed him work that was priced far above Marsh's means.

For Brooke on leave there was more news of his friends. Marsh had sent Lawrence to call on Seabrooke at Ambleside, and the painter had just written to say that his guest had spent 'the whole of one evening describing his home life with sudden lapses into broad Derbyshire'. Flecker, still worse in health, had written on October 2 enclosing his poem *The Burial in England*. 'I've written this in short fits; it has cost me a lot physically.' When Squire received the poem for his journal he took the opportunity of delivering a gentle reproof to the poet for troubling Marsh at such a time. 'Horrors,' he wrote to Squire, 'he must be wroth with me, worrying him to hawk my verses!' Marsh would no doubt have shown Brooke a letter just received from Gosse, who had admired his work in the recent issue of *New Numbers*. It ended on a grim note: 'I suppose Rheims is only the prelude to Westminster. We are entering the Twilight of the Gods.'

After Mr. Churchill's return from Antwerp on October 7 Marsh had slept the night at the Admiralty, and shortly after midnight, being at last off duty, he tried to catch up with his private correspondence. Prominent in his mind was de la Mare, whose modest income, according to report, was seriously depleted by the times. Last thing before bed, with no great hope of success, Marsh addressed himself to the poet.

I am here all day and a good deal of the night, cut off from all my usual sources of expenditure, and unable to get rid of more than at the most 5*s*. a day for food and taxis. . . . The wish of my heart is to do anything I can to help my own personal friends, whose work is work that I care about—whose proper sources of income are suddenly cut off by no fault of theirs—and who are not catered for by the [war-time] Funds that everyone else is quite rightly helping. You have never had any material reward for work that will profit the world for generations. Will you not let those who are blessed in knowing its value make up for the indifference of the others?

I haven't much to dispose of, but already two or three men whose character and talents you respect have let me help them. Painters are easy, because one can buy their pictures—but no one can buy poetry! Yet that is no reason why those who like it should not pay for it.

The truth is that I know (alas only from hearsay) about your enchanting family and simply can't bear to think that just because

Bloody William has chosen to fight us they must go without things they are accustomed to have. You tell Miss R.S. [Royde-Smith] you are all right, but forgive me for saying that I always knew you had a hard struggle, and it stands to reason that it is now twice, if not three times, as hard as it was before. It is 2 A.M. and I feel my powers of persuasion are flagging, so I will only say that I shall love you even more than I do already if you will let me send you £10, as a loan, if you like, till your tide turns. Don't be angry with me anyhow, and believe that I am, whether you give me my wish or not, your affectionate friend.

Two days before Brooke had come to London on leave Marsh heard from de la Mare that the difficulty of his position had been exaggerated. He promised not to conceal the truth, he said, if things should ever become as bad as Marsh supposed. This recent correspondence would certainly have been discussed with Brooke during his sojourn at Gray's Inn, for Marsh was not entirely placated by de la Mare's reassurance, and he remained worried. It is safe to assume that this conversation with Brooke was recalled a few months later when the poet made his informal will in favour of three of his fellow Georgians of whom de la Mare was one. The elder poet was apparently incapable of regarding himself as worthy the notice of a good Samaritan. It may have been at this time that he glanced casually at a letter which had been sent to him in error, saw that it was a charitable appeal on behalf of some literary personage, overlooked the fact that it referred to himself, and sent it back with a pound note and an apology for the smallness of his contribution.

Meanwhile Brooke and Marsh continued their determined efforts to be gay whenever duties at the Admiralty allowed. They managed to get a play in during the week, Laurette Taylor in *Peg o' my Heart*. At luncheon with Mr. Churchill on the 17th Marsh was introduced to Bernard Freyberg of the R.N.D., and on the last evening of Brooke's leave (October 18) Mrs. Lionel Guest, the mother of 'Johnny' Dodge, another subaltern in the Anson battalion, entertained Brooke, Marsh, and his new acquaintance, Freyberg, to dinner.

At Chatham, Browne, Brooke, and Shaw-Stewart were finding themselves in an unpleasant situation. It was their firm belief that a certain officer who had served with them at Antwerp would be the cause of a mutiny if he remained in the unit. Either he or they should be transferred. Brooke's letters from Chatham mounted in exasperation, and the other two wrote in ardent support. On top of everything else Brooke's trained men were being drafted away. It was 'like trying to build a statue out of sand'. On November 7 Brooke and 'Oc' Asquith dined with Marsh and the Prime Minister at Downing Street. A plan for transfer was agreed on. From 13th to 18th Brooke and Browne were back at Raymond Buildings on short leave. Two days after they left Brooke got a letter. 'All is changed again, and you are all to go to Hood [battalion of the First Naval Division] which is splendid. It will be done a little gradually, but all will come right in the end. Have *you* got the latchkey or has Denis?' Gibson was bringing his wife to stay and Abercrombie too was expected. Marsh's letter of reassurance to Browne (November 22) ended with an anecdote.

I had a very interesting dinner tonight with Winston and Garvin. Winston said some very good things, among others that the Germans had prepared for the war by setting themselves a sum, which they did quite right, only they went on the principle that 2 and 2 make 4, and that 4 and 4 make 8, *which in real life they hardly ever do.*

A few days later there arrived an unexpected note from Raymond Asquith.

I find myself hovering round 'Winston's Army' like a moth round a candle (or rather perhaps like a kitten round the bucket in which the rest of the litter are already engulfed). Could you, d'you think, procure me a commission in R.N.V.R.—not *instanter* but at some time within the next month? I have a few cases which I want to finish off in the courts before this term ends. . . . Either just before or just after Xmas I ought to be ready to take the Sword, if you could 'nick a nook' for me as George Moore calls it.

Marsh was no doubt feeling relieved at his solution of Brooke's problem when a prickly communication arrived. 'Well, my dear, here I am, and very angry.' Brooke was in Portsmouth with the Nelson battalion; Browne was at Portland with the Howe, and Asquith in yet another battalion. 'I can only wish things may get bad enough for the affair to disintegrate and we'll all get shifted into the Army.' By December 1, however, he was at Blandford Camp, Dorset, with the Hood, and in a company under the command of Freyberg. Asquith, Shaw-Stewart, and Dodge were there already, and Browne's arrival from the Howe was expected, so Brooke despatched to the Admiralty a telegram in jubilant Latin.

On December 5 Marsh attended the christening of his godchild Sarah Churchill, then his Chief left on a secret visit to the Front. It was rumoured in Blandford that the First Lord was coming to inspect the unit, so Brooke at once wrote: '*Insist* on coming with him. Don't be caught in your dress clothes this time.' He wanted to talk to Abercrombie. 'Couldn't he come as an Assistant Clerk or Admiralty Bard or something?' When this arrived Abercrombie happened to be staying in the spare room so as to be taken first to dinner with Gosse, then on to Downing Street to meet Mr. Asquith. Marsh evaded the enquiry about the First Lord's visit. 'It's wretched to think of you down with *deliberate* typhoid [Brooke had just been inoculated]. I hope you've got Denis by now. He was too conscientious [reluctant to leave a C.O. who had just promoted him]. I was terribly disappointed when I thought that all my machinations were foiled and that my happy band of brothers was to lack one of its best jewels.' Mark Gertler and Frank Dobson had just come to breakfast, but he only gave one item of news from among his painters. 'My little Paul [Nash] is to get married on the 17th. Did you know he was engaged to a very nice and rather remarkable young woman called Margaret Odeh? I think it is all very happy.'

Marsh had just bought a drawing of an elm by Paul Nash for eight guineas, a special reduction, the artist explained, so as to leave more of the fund available for others. 'You are one of the very few men who collects honestly,' he wrote, 'and about the only one who is going on collecting during the war. You are a valuable man, but at the moment your money is more valuable —since you can't keep artists going by any other means.' From early December Nash was possessor of the key to Raymond Buildings. He described years afterwards how the block of buildings seemed to him like 'a drifting Ark or a black iceberg afloat, and the many plane-trees looked down on from the back windows were more like pythons and boa-constrictors than trees'. Looking at leisure at the walls he was struck by a collection of paintings that was exclusively English and yet contained nothing of the Pre-Raphaelites. He noticed that Mrs. Elgy seemed to be bravely competing in the kitchen by hanging a proliferation of picture calendars round the stove. 'I decided there was something equine about Eddie in a mettlesome sort of way . . . he had a certain way of rearing his handsome head, up and across to one side, that was reminiscent.' And in the morning he was awakened by the sound of his host reciting *Kubla Khan* in his bath.[1] The other painter of this time was Gertler. From December 1 he was the subject of a new experiment in the expenditure of the Perceval grant. The rent of his studio was paid and he received £5 a month pocket-money for an indefinite period. With the promise of the first refusal of Gertler's work, a Frank Dobson for five guineas, and three John Nash sketches for a guinea apiece, the collector's ardour was but little affected by the war which had suppressed Georgian poetry.

It was early in this month that a lucky instinct urged Marsh to send some books to Flecker in Switzerland with a letter as unreserved in its encouragement as his note to Lawrence of about three months before. Flecker's reply of the 12th marked the end of a correspondence which had lasted for two years. Flecker, now gravely ill, was obviously much moved. 'The last sentence of your letter is the sort of thing a fellow doesn't forget—or write about on a postcard. Oh why didn't poor Middleton have such luck as mine?'

The First Lord's visit to Blandford was postponed. Browne and Brooke, on short leave, were buying each other Christmas presents in Bournemouth while Marsh and William Rothenstein were doing likewise in Bond Street. A few days before, Marsh had taken his first day off for weeks. It was like old times, with Rothenstein to breakfast, Michael Sadler to tea, and dinner with Gosse and George Moore. On Christmas Day he gave a dinner at Admiralty House with Lady Horner, Raymond Asquith, Lord Haldane, and Patrick Shaw-Stewart as his guests. Meanwhile a forthcoming week's leave was being organized by post. Brooke planned to see the new year in at Rugby and come up for a London theatre on January 4. 'Denis wants to give the Admiralty a treat,' he explained, so Mr. and Mrs. Churchill must be induced to join the party. More instructions followed. 'Desideration in regard to companions at the Ambassadors [Theatre] is divided into three parts. (1) People one *likes* to be with. . . . (2) Amusing People (very important after camp). . . . If for instance Maurice Baring

[1] *Outline, an autobiography*, by Paul Nash (Faber, 1949).

were back from the Front. You and Denis aren't excluded from your natural place under (2) by the fact that you are under (1) . . . as you *are* excluded from (3) WOMEN. . . . Supper afterwards? Is there still any place where one can drink alcohol out of tea-cups?'

Two days after the date of Brooke's excited letter an urgent appeal for help from the Grand Duke Nicholas of Russia was received in Whitehall. There was now no question that somehow the Russians must be relieved in their grave discomfiture at the hands of the enemy. The Allies had already sustained more than a million casualties in France. There was a shortage of men. If the Navy could force the straits of the Dardanelles by bombardment from the sea Russia could have access to British munitions and in return the Allies could draw upon her reserves of wheat.

Thoughts at Whitehall were turning towards Gallipoli as Brooke came up from Rugby on the 4th, when the convivial plans were complete. The final addition to the party was Violet Asquith, who, as Marsh explained, 'came under both (1) and (2) and (3)', and her brother Arthur, and the scene for the supper was the Carlton Grill. They did not know that Flecker, aged thirty, had died at Davos the day before. The news was in the paper next morning. Three days later Gosse wrote to Gray's Inn: 'He owed more to your generous kindness than to the help of any other person. If he had lived he might have done you credit—or he might not. There always seemed to me to be a worm slumbering at the root of his talent.' Brooke did not write from Blandford (having again gone off with the latchkey) until January 8. 'London's a lovely Dream. It was fun that night, wasn't it?'

I spent, forwent, a lovely hour of the afternoon with Cathleen penning some absurd phrases about Flecker. I was grotesque and ornate: not having time to be simple. What a miserable task, writing a friend's obituary in *The Times*. At the same table as he wrote *Yasmin* in your book, the last time I saw him, I jotted notes and *The Times* interwove their gems. 'Educated at Balliol (then me) *his Muse was stertorous with lush slumbers of the East. His father is the* Rev. W. Flecker. *Apollo yielded to Marsyas and fled crying strangely . . .*' what a bloody jest and a bloody world.

Browne's letter of thanks for the London jaunt described how he was teaching the band to play *The Magic Flute*. They would soon be so proficient that Eddie must 'bring Winston down to dine and hear them'. But the First Lord was too busy drawing up his plan for the naval forcing of the straits. On the 13th Marsh prepared his papers and walked with him as far as the door of the War Council, where the scheme was approved by Kitchener and at least not obstructed by Fisher. Marsh left for a week-end with the Prime Minister at Walmer Castle, then wrote to Browne. 'Henry James was there, very delightful, and I liked seeing the rooms in which the D. of Wellington died and Q. Victoria spread her nuptial couch, *in statu quo*, or rather *in statibus quibus*. . . . Is it true that as Oc tells Violet you have all been turned on to breaking stones for the roadmakers? By the way, I never cautioned you against X who is well-meaning but deadly—as I expect you have found out by now. . . . Bless you, my dearly beloved Denis, and the same to Rupert.'

Within a fortnight Fisher was beginning to feel less sanguine about the Dardanelles plan. It was at this stage regarded as a purely naval operation. He was anxious to prevent a reduction of our resources in the North Sea, and as is well known he was not reconciled to his own position subordinate to Kitchener and reliant upon the First Lord. On the 28th he aired his view in the presence of the Prime Minister and Mr. Churchill, and was afterwards in discussion with the First Lord, Masterton-Smith, and Marsh, at Admiralty House. The reconciliation which followed was precarious.

At the end of January Brooke tried to enlist Marsh in a campaign for getting an increase in pay for the lower ranks, and Shaw-Stewart on short leave put the case in person. The men were getting restive. 'Do tell everyone not to be in too much of a hurry,' Marsh replied. 'Winston is very ambitious for the R.N.D. and especially for the 2nd Brigade.' Some of the R.N.V.R. officers, frustrated by their too brief taste of action at Antwerp, were infecting others with their ill-concealed impatience. Browne was busy enough with his band, but Brooke could not deny that time was hanging very heavy on his hands. The ground surrounding the huts was mud and slush, and a cold looked like developing into influenza. Fumes from the coke stoves had given almost everyone a sore throat. On top of everything else there was a feeling that the much needed military instruction was ridiculously inadequate. Browne could not resist sending Marsh his impression of a senior officer who 'has shown himself so far as a kind nice old

thing, but otherwise seems to be a goop. After some night operations he said: "Yes, very nice . . . but all these new . . . developments. . . . Now . . . yes . . . suppose now an armoured motor car
came along the road our column was marching on . . . what
would we do? . . . I'm sure I don't know what we *could* do."
And so on. But I tell them all he's as great as he is good, which I
hope is true.' So day followed day, and there was no news of a
move.

During these early weeks of the year there was no time for the
criticism of poetry, but Marsh was glad to accept the dedication
of Drinkwater's new volume *Swords and Ploughshares*, and another
poet, the youngest of them all, seemed so worth while taking
trouble over that he could not resist agreeing to look over the
sheaf of poems which had been left behind at Gray's Inn. His
first piece of advice to Robert Graves was that he should properly
acquaint himself with the 'modern' style and in particular study
the work of Brooke. 'I think he is really good,' Graves wrote after
a few days. 'What a torture his sensitiveness must always be for
him, poor fellow!' The boy Graves was growing up. He could
take frank criticism, and was promising enough to deserve it.
Marsh only hoped he would take it in the proper spirit. Graves
replied that he might have acquired a backward-looking conception of verse technique owing to the amiable but reactionary
influence of a 'father who has memories of Wordsworth'.

> No, I'm not annoyed, why should I be? I always try to look at myself
> objectively and dispassionately because this helps me to get the full
> flavour of romance out of life, so now I can see that it would be most
> extraordinary if my technique wasn't obsolete. . . . However, I am
> still in my teens and when this ridiculous war is over I will write
> Chapter II at the top of the new sheet and with the help of other
> young Georgians to whom I trust you will introduce me, will try to
> root out more effectively the obnoxious survivals of Victorianism.

Shortly after this letter arrived, in the first week of February,
Brooke turned up at Gray's Inn with a high temperature. He
grew rapidly worse, and as there was no one to nurse him Violet
Asquith suggested that he be moved to 10 Downing Street.
Having announced his approach by wire, it seems that instead of
going to bed on arrival in London he had looked in at a music-
hall. 'Beloved but monstrous R.,' Marsh complained in a note
left on the breakfast-table next morning, 'to make me drag myself

away from my delicious dinner-party only to find your dimity bed flickering in the firelight.' He was due to dine that evening with a friend who claimed to have 'a marvellous gift of healing. She is simply longing to come and rub your back, and guarantees a cure in ¼ of an hour . . . she is famous for it throughout Canada, and I really advise you to ring her up in the morning . . . *Do* take this seriously.'

From Downing Street Brooke was moved to Walmer Castle for three days' convalescence, and soon wrote from there, wanting to spend a night in London on his way back to Blandford. 'Here's the key,' came the answer. 'Your room is ready if you want to sleep there, even to your pyjamas which are in attitude of expectancy on your bed.' February 9 was the last night he spent in his London *pied-à-terre*, lingering late in the cot-bed pushed against the wall under Stanley Spencer's 'Bogeys', and with Mrs. Elgy beaming over his breakfast as she brought it in on a tray. Marsh took him to dine at Admiralty House but had to go back to his work immediately afterwards, so that Brooke was left to finish the evening alone with Mr. Churchill. It was their first and last conversation *à deux*.

On February 17 Mr. Churchill inspected the troops at Blandford in torrential rain, and Marsh sat between Brooke and Browne at dinner in the Mess. Within a day or two came the news that they were going to embark. The effect was electrifying. The King was expected to come for a march past of the Division on Thursday, February 25. Marsh wrote to say he was travelling down with the First Lord, who would sleep at Canford, but was there a bed available for himself in the 'A' Company huts? 'It's a great thought that you are all going out at last. I hope everyone is pleased.' Brooke wired, 'Yes rather we will stow you somewhere.' A telegram from Gray's Inn followed almost at once. 'Can Clemmie [Mrs. Churchill], Goonie [Lady Gwendeline Churchill], Violet [Asquith], and I lunch with Hood on Thursday. Do please arrange.' The problem was whether the meal could be arranged in the Mess, so Brooke consulted his C.O. and wired again. 'Yes rather what fun Quilter says prepare Ladies for hardships will you bring me Eliot's Turkey in Europe and any other thinkable useful books for voyage.' Two days later the naval bombardment of the straits began. The results were indecisive, but already it was foreseen that the task might not be carried to a successful conclusion without the assistance of land forces under the direction of the Admiralty.

On the 25th Marsh saw his boon companions for the last time. 'With you putting all the eggs in one basket we're quite a jolly party,' Browne had written on Christmas Day. If Paul Nash had not preferred the Artists' Rifles to Marsh's offer of a place in the Hood the basket would have carried even more human treasure than it did. When he got back to London next day there awaited him a letter from one of the great ladies of London society to whom Brooke was almost a stranger.

> I am so unhappy that Mr. Brooke is going off to fight. I think he is the most perfect human being I have ever met. I never knew that human beings could be like that, and I think it would be so terrible if anything should happen to him that I want to send him anonymously a charm that will keep off evil.

It was an amulet with 'all sorts of facts attached to it which make it charmed'. If Eddie Marsh would make his friend promise to wear it she would arrange for a special messenger to convey it to the ship at the port of embarkation.

The day after the royal inspection the Hoods and Ansons struck camp and marched to Shillingstone, where they entrained for the docks at Avonmouth. There they boarded a Union Castle liner which had been converted into a transport. The last mail was in. It had fallen to Marsh himself to despatch the Admiralty order to strike camp at Blandford. He then wrote three letters. To Shaw-Stewart he sent a wrist-watch and Herodotus, and to Browne a folding mirror and a pocket edition of the *Iliad*. 'I've written to ask R. to take care of you,' he wrote, 'I told him that it's only where you and he are involved that I feel the personal terrors of war—so do both come back safe and sound. You're very precious and dear to me, Denis, as you know. . . . I'm so glad I saw you all yesterday in your glory.' His letter to Brooke accompanied a pocket Shakespeare in two little volumes, the book on Turkey he had asked for, and the amulet.

> My dear, this is from a beautiful lady who wants you to come back safe—her name is not to be divulged. I have promised that you shall wear it—and I beseech you to make my word good. It's a very potent charm, she says; and even if you don't believe, it's a sign of the sort of way people care for you, even if they don't know you very well.

I hope all the love and wishes that go with you may be in some way an armour to you.

Denis promised to take care of you, and you must take care of him—I shall live in a shadow, Rupert, till I see you and him safe and well again—you know I'm glad and proud that you are going, and I don't think it's particularly dangerous as such things go—but it's where you and he come in that I feel what the war can do to me as a person.

I expect you know what you are to me—certainly the thing I'm most proud of.

Send me a nice message for the lady of the charm, and say you will wear it. I've just telegraphed to Quilter that the band is to go.

After one night in port the *Grantully Castle* set sail for the Mediterranean.

Chapter Thirteen

THE END OF AN EPOCH
(March–November, 1915)

ROM now on, although the spacious wall-map behind
Mr. Churchill's desk showed the scope of his official concerns,
the private hopes and fears of Eddie Marsh's life were
inevitably bound up with a single vessel, the overloaded transport
which on March 5 passed through the straits of Gibraltar and
three days later anchored off the Fish Quay at Malta. There
Browne posted a letter saying he found it difficult to believe the
wireless news which reported the penetration of the Dardanelles
by eighteen miles. F. S. 'Cleg' Kelly, another musician on board,
was disappointed to find the men reluctant to sing folk-songs. 'Of
course it never comes off—and they would never sing them, as
you and I might easily see. But he goes on hoping.' Brooke
acknowledged the amulet. 'I'm sure it will bring me Luck. But
what "Luck" is we'll all wait and see. At least we'll all wait, and
you'll see perhaps. . . . War seems infinitely remote, and even the
Reason, foreseeing Gallipoli, yet admits that there are many blue
days to come—and the Cyclades.' He had been studying military
manuals, and he had something to say of each of his fellow-
Argonauts. 'Patrick is the life and soul of the party—the life,
anyhow. Denis is competent, Johnny [Dodge] inquisitive and
simple-hearted, Oc Oc-like, while Freyberg (whose comment on
you is that you're a "white man"—a great compliment) often
rushes across the room to say, "I say, do you think this is going to
be a bloody good show? *I* do."'

They went ashore at Malta, where they found Charles Lister
who had come out earlier on the *Franconia*, and Shaw-Stewart
persuaded him to get himself cross-posted to the Hood. With
Lister of their number (as he was, once they reached Port Said)
'A' Company was led by as legendary a band of young men as ever
sailed to war. Three days later the *Grantully Castle* was one of a
huge assembly of ships anchored in Mudros Bay off Lemnos.

'The island where Philoctetes, the archer, was left wounded with a snake bite,' wrote Lister, forbidden by the censor to be more explicit.[1] The classics were very useful to all the officers of 'A' Company as material for circumlocution. 'We are now on an island not unconnected with the education of Neoptolemus,' Shaw-Stewart was to write from Skyros. 'I am going to take my Herodotus as a guide book,' he said in a letter home.[2] At Lemnos they remained a week, then after sailing down the coast of Gallipoli thinking they were going to be put ashore (though in fact it was a feint attack to make the enemy reveal the strength and disposition of his defences) they returned to Lemnos, only to weigh anchor again almost at once. On March 27 they reached Port Said. There Browne despatched a letter written during an equinoctial gale. The men on board were afflicted with campaign lice, otherwise all was well. 'Rupert is splendid, Pat deliciously gay—Oc is a calculated and measured delight, Johnny a dear unconscious funny, and Freyberg a fine big jolly thing. Cleg is a problem but I'm clearing him up.'

Awaiting Browne at Port Said was a letter from Raymond Buildings (March 20) written two days after the naval assault on the straits in which the Allies had lost three battleships. 'We are disappointed but cheerful and resolute after Thursday's operations, which I hope will be ancient history before you get this.' On the 16th he had accompanied Mr. Churchill to a meeting with Sir John French.

I have had great times this week, as at 4.15 on Tuesday Winston suddenly ordered a special train for the Front to be ready at 4.45—I tore round to Raymond Buildings, jammed some things into a bag, and got back just in time to start—we flew across the Channel in a destroyer and got to Headquarters in time for a late dinner—next day we motored about all over the place—there was very little fighting going on as it was the middle of the lull after Neuve Chapelle —we got to a place called Laventie, half in ruins, from which we could see a good deal of the battlefield from the top of a tower, and we saw 4 6″ shell put into Auber from a naval armoured train. One of the new 15″ naval howitzers was thereabouts, a formidable creature, called Granny—but we did not see her fire. She has had a great success. We lunched with Sir James Willcocks among the Indians

[1] *Charles Lister, Letters and Recollections*, with a Memoir by his father Lord Ribblesdale (Fisher Unwin, 1917).

[2] *Patrick Shaw-Stewart*, by Ronald Knox (Collins, 1920).

who are tremendously bucked by their success in the battle and looked as pleased as Buddha. Then we motored into Belgium and went up a considerable hill at Kemmel, all the top of which is pitted by shell exactly as if it had had smallpox, and nearly all the trees in half—and primroses ironically coming up among the débris as if nothing had happened. We lay behind a parapet at the top and listened to the shells shunting through the air. Next day we went to Ypres, a most harrowing sight, the Cloth Hall and Cathedral both exquisitely beautiful in their ruin, but quite beyond repair. Then we went on to Nieuport les Bains on the coast, where there isn't a house that is complete. Here I was allowed to go into the French trenches at the extreme end of the line, and got to within about 50 yards of the Germans, who sniped at me unsuccessfully. I saw about 20 German corpses which had lain in the sand about 4 months, neither side being able to get at them and bury them. They looked like old umbrellas with their spokes sticking out anyhow (the spokes were their rifles). Then we came home—you'll laugh at me for giving this long account of my non-combatant experiences to a fighting man—but you can imagine how intensely interesting it all was to *me*, and I suppose it was the nearest I shall ever get to the real thing.

The most encouraging tale I heard was of one of the Neuve Chapelle prisoners, a barber in Dresden, who said that 3 *days before the battle* he was suddenly snatched out of his shop, put into a uniform and a train, and taken straight to the trenches. Before he had been there ½ hour he suddenly found he was surrounded by Indians. His first thought was 'I'm a German, and mustn't surrender'—but he looked round and saw all his Kameraden throwing down their rifles, and 'not wishing to be peculiar' did the same. . . . I have nothing to fill up this page with except anecdotes, here is an interesting one that Ld. George Hamilton told me last night of the quarrel between the Kaiser and Bismarck. They both described the scene afterwards to Ld. Odo Russell, and Bismarck said, 'To give you an idea of the temper he was in, there was a large glass ink-stand on the table between us, and I had to keep my eye on it because I thought he was going to throw it at me'—then Ld. Odo R. saw the Kaiser, who said, 'Do you know he was in such a rage that I had to keep my eye on a large glass ink-stand there was on the table between us because I thought every moment he was going to throw it at me.'

I haven't any private news—except that Mark [Gertler] has painted *the* most lovely picture that I ever saw, of 2 bunches of daffodils against a blue background—it's a real inspiration I think, and convinces me of his genius more than anything he has done—

and it's wonderfully painted—It will be nice to show it you after the war—(it's mine).

By the same messenger he asked Brooke if he had agreed to join Sir Ian Hamilton's Staff. 'It was entirely his own idea to ask you, so don't think that I put it into his head. Winston was all for it.' Marsh had written to Mrs. Brooke to say that Rupert was going to have the offer, and he was anxious to have news of the appointment. He enclosed a cutting from *The Times Literary Supplement* of March 11. It was a review, probably by Gosse, of the fourth and last issue of *New Numbers* in which the 'Soldier Sonnets' made their first appearance. 'These sonnets are personal—never were sonnets more personal since Sidney died—and yet the very blood and youth of England seem to find expression in them.'

'I do hope he won't be foolish enough to refuse, but surely he daren't!' wrote Mrs. Brooke, when she heard of Sir Ian's proposal. (She was to acknowledge the cutting rather belatedly, saying she had seen it already. 'The Clergy are all in raptures. A Dean quoted him the other day! But those sonnets are remarkably good; I think we shall hear more of them.') About a week later Marsh wired Mrs. Brooke that the Staff job had been accepted. Her acknowledgement expressed her 'enormous relief'. A letter from her was already on its way to Gray's Inn. She had just heard from her son. 'He seemed afraid that they would find the work all done, he needn't be. Will they land the Naval Brigade before the infantry? Are there good hospitals?' Meanwhile Marsh discovered that he had been misled. Thinking it best to explain the awkward position to Brooke himself he wrote on March 27. Lady Hamilton had written to him expressing her pleasure in Brooke's new appointment. Naturally assuming that she had been given the news officially by her husband, Marsh passed it on by telegram to Mrs. Brooke only to discover that the C.-in-C.'s wife had not heard from her husband. Her only source of information was Lady Lytton, to whom Marsh himself had spoken a day or two earlier saying no more than that Sir Ian had suggested making the proposal. Doubtless it never occurred to Lady Hamilton that Brooke would decline. On discovering the mistake Marsh thought it wiser for the time being not to undeceive Mrs. Brooke, for he was expecting to hear the official confirmation any day. Before long he found himself obliged to confess that his news was both premature and incorrect—a trifling matter, but one of a succession of unlucky circumstances which, taken together, were profoundly to affect his private life in the years to come. For the present he could only make his leaving Mrs. Brooke with the wrong impression an added inducement for her son to accept the offer when it came. He ended his report to the poet by saying he had seen Henry James, 'who was thrilled about you going out, and I said I would send him your sonnets'.

Henry James was prompt to answer (March 28). 'Dear admirable Eddie!' he began, then launched into a rolling period: 'The circumstances (so to call the unspeakable matter) that have conduced to them, and that, taken together, seem to make a sort of huge brazen lap for their congruous beauty, have caused me to read them with an emotion that somehow precludes the critical measure . . .' and then 'this evening, alone by my lamp, I have been reading them over and over to myself aloud, as if fondly to test and truly to try them'. Marsh particularly enjoyed the sentence, 'Splendid Rupert to be the soldier that could beget them on the Muse! and lucky Muse, not less, which could have an affair with a soldier and yet feel herself not guilty of the least deviation!' James made one or two critical points and ended a long letter with, 'I think of him quite inordinately, and not less so of you, my dear Eddie.' Marsh at once reciprocated this warmth of friendship. In the months to come they were to be drawn even closer together. 'Praise of one's friends,' Marsh wrote, 'is always more unmixed pleasure than of oneself, because there isn't the slightest discomfort of doubting inwardly whether it is deserved!' which prompted James to write again: 'Splendid R., indeed, and splendid *you*, in the generosity of your emotion.'

While James was writing his panegyric on the sonnets the troops were disembarking at Port Said and on the same day Sir Ian Hamilton dictated a letter (March 28) as he was dressing for dinner with the Consul-General. He had not yet been able to speak to Brooke, but a cipher officer had given him news of another writer.

He tells me Compton Mackenzie, the man who wrote *Sinister Street*, is frightfully anxious to see some military service. I am all for encouraging the best writers to come and gain some martial experience, for I think they are usually thereafter more manly fellows, and a better influence on their generation. I told Williams to write to Compton Mackenzie (upon my word I am not sure if that is his right name, but the author of *Sinister Street*) to tell him that if, through you, he can get out as a Naval Brigade private soldier, or anything of that sort, I will fish him out and make him something on my staff even if only a sergeant in the Office.

I have just come back from lunching with the Sultan. He did his best to terrify me by his descriptions of how all the finest veterans of Constantinople had been rushed out to meet us at the Straits. I am puzzled a bit how to get through the masses of barbed wire, and I have just been looking at a trench mortar which will throw a really big bomb for about a couple of hundred yards. . . .

All the Navy think de Robeck[1] is the man of all others for the job now in hand. They like him, if possible, better than ever since they saw how he stood the successive incidents of the 18th. I do wish with all my heart the First Lord could have seen that self-same impressive spectacle of the 18th. I would never forget it were I to live to a hundred years.

Mackenzie was at Capri, writing the last pages of *Guy and Pauline*. Hugh Walpole had brought him round to Gray's Inn two years before. It so happened that Mackenzie had already written to Marsh on the cipher officer's advice. Within a few days he was posted to Hamilton's headquarters.

While Hamilton dictated his letter, Shaw-Stewart was still on board writing Eddie Marsh a letter of thanks. 'Really, when I am particularly pleased with my dinner or the view or any of those little amenities which have made this good ship our Capua, I often say to myself, "Remember that under God all these things come from Eddie."'

It really is a most diverting campaign, and though I suppose we shall all be killed sooner or later, I am (as I think I said before) almost soppily grateful for being sent on it. It is difficult to say how much I love Rupert and Denis (I have been sharing a cabin with him)— they have made me remould all my concepts of Cambridge men of my Oxford generation.

In the evening of the following day, leaving Browne on duty, Brooke, Shaw-Stewart, and Asquith decided to spend their short leave together in Cairo, where they stayed at Shepheard's Hotel.

[1] Admiral de Robeck had recently taken over the command at the Dardanelles after the illness and retirement of Vice-Admiral Carden.

On the next afternoon they motored to the Pyramids and spent about an hour riding round them on camels. The heat was as mild as an English summer afternoon. The morning of the following day they spent in the Bazaars and the afternoon on the Citadel, then returned to Port Said. Brooke showed no sign of illness. Asquith remembered his reading aloud Shakespeare's description of Cleopatra's barge on the Cydnus, and recalled that he bought a little glass tear-bottle for his mother and an amber necklace for Cathleen Nesbitt. Next morning, April 1, Shaw-Stewart was feeling bad and did not want to get up, so Charles Lister took him from the sandy tents to the Casino Palace, an hotel overlooking the sea. Brooke meanwhile was having a strenuous morning on a field-firing exercise with his company on the shore, 'running backward and forward between his men and the target in the full blaze of the sun'. It was hot, but he had not omitted to wear his helmet. That evening he went with Asquith to call on Shaw-Stewart at the hotel, where they stayed for dinner. 'He did not seem very gay,' wrote Asquith, 'but he did not complain of feeling ill.' But during the night he was sick twice, complained of headache, and was too ill to take part in the march past and the inspection by the C.-in-C.

'The sun was brilliant and the bayonets flashed like magnesium when it is burnt,' wrote Charles Lister to his father. Shortly before noon Sir Ian Hamilton took the opportunity of having a word with Brooke. 'I have just had a great day inspecting the Naval Division,' Hamilton began his letter that evening. He had found Brooke lying on a camp-bed under an awning of green canvas, 'rather off colour for the day, poor boy. . . . It was nothing, and essentially he was looking in first-class physical condition. . . . Rupert Brooke very naturally would like to see this first adventure through with his own men. After that I think he would like to come to me. It was very natural and I quite understand it—I should have answered the same in his case had I been offered a Staff billet. . . .' Before returning to Cairo Sir Ian spoke to Colonel Quilter. 'Mind you take care of him,' he said. 'His loss would be a national loss.' Next day while Lister fished for prawns the men of 'A' Company were building a little boat 'like the ship of Odysseus on a Greek vase'. A hot wind was scooping up the sand, and Brooke was only one of thousands who began to suffer from dysentery.

The camp was situated in an exposed area just outside the docks and about three minutes' walk from the Arab quarter of the town. Browne described it to Mrs. Brooke. 'The tents were pitched on the sand, and the whole camp might have been in the middle of the desert, except for the ships and the town behind us. If you stood with your back to them, there was nothing in sight beyond the camp but desert. The salt lagoons of the Delta and the Canal were there, but they lay below the level we were on and could hardly be seen. Everything was yellow with sand. . . . Rupert's tent was next to mine.'

Shaw-Stewart was in bed at his hotel, sorry to have missed the grand parade and wondering how it went, when Cleg Kelly looked in with the news. He said Brooke was ill too, and the C.-in-C. had sat on his bed 'talking poetry'. Brooke had said nothing of Sir Ian's Staff proposal. Shaw-Stewart attached no importance to the illness, so he was rather surprised when that same afternoon orderlies put up an extra bed facing his own, and Brooke entered, feverish, having been almost unable to walk up the stairs. His temperature was 103, and a civilian doctor suggested moving him to a fever hospital next morning, but Brooke was strongly opposed to exchanging Shaw-Stewart's company for 'tiresome brother officers'.

A week of hilarious discomfort followed, for the humiliations attendant upon their complaint became an inexhaustible source of crude amusement to them in their enfeebled condition. First Shaw-Stewart thought he was recovering and began eating salads, then both of them were confined to arrowroot for two days, after which they began subsisting on little Mediterranean soles. Brooke even worked out a short poem for Denis Browne to set to music.[1] For their frequent departures down the corridor they shared Brooke's British-warm overcoat until Shaw-Stewart received his dressing-gown from the ship; and they both grew beards, one red, one golden brown, and in their vacuity of mind went into paroxysms of laughter at the Italian waiter's effort to understand their requests. Shaw-Stewart was vexed to observe that his elementary Italian proved to be a less communicative medium than his companion's 'gesticulated English'. Browne called on them and seeing them under their mosquito nets remarked that it was like entering a harem. He brought the letter (March 20) from

[1] *The Dance.*

Marsh which he handed round, and later described its effect. 'Rupert and Patrick, both suffering from acute diarrhoea, read it with gurgles and fled to the rear. How wonderful of you to go to the Front. I needn't tell you how thrilled we all were.'

During these days Marsh's private correspondence had dwindled almost to nothing; but on April Fool's Day he was surprised to receive a communication from the Poet Laureate. 'This you may think a very good date for my letter,' wrote Bridges, 'but I can't help writing it. Of course I know that your people are up to everything, but it seems to me that what would destroy submarine warfare would be fast small "submarine" rams. They would be imperceptible to the enemies' torpedoing submarines and could lie in wait for them alongside the bait.' The suggestion was duly passed on to the experts.

Another letter now in Browne's hands at Port Said was scribbled when the news came that *Grantully Castle* had reached Egypt.

> Violet[1] says you were all packed into it like soldiers in a box of soldiers, 1,000 mules at the bottom, then a layer of stokers, then Rupert, Oc, Denis etc. and then the tents on the top—and that if once you were unpacked and the Authorities forgot exactly how you went they would never be able to get you back again . . . anyhow you will be much more comfortable at Alexandria . . . will you be able to get leave to see the Pyramids? I hope so—do you remember what Mr. Micawber said when they got to Maidstone on the way to Canterbury—'having got so far, it would be rash not to see the Cathedral'.

On the morning of April 9 Colonel Quilter looked in at the Casino Palace Hotel to say his two subalterns should now go aboard if they were up to it. Shaw-Stewart certainly was, but Brooke, who had been troubled by a slight swelling on the right side of his upper lip, was hardly strong enough. Quilter encouraged him to stay ashore but he would have none of it, saying he would look pretty silly, convalescing on shore, if *Grantully Castle* proceeded to do nothing but hang about for three weeks in radiant sunshine off Lemnos. He went aboard, slightly worrying Browne by the spectacle of his thinness, and retired to bed.

[1] Violet Asquith had seen them off at Avonmouth.

Grantully Castle sailed at 6 A.M. on April 10, and steamed very slowly, at about four knots per hour, because they were towing a lighter to be used for embarking the troops. Brooke spent a few hours on his legs each afternoon, and on the fourth day resumed light duties. He told Asquith he was quite sorry the last few peaceful mornings were over. He had been lying in his cabin 'composing an ode', but there was no excuse any more. The sore lip was quite healed and the dysentery gone.

There was now more space, since they had left the Anson battalion behind, but the mules were still on board and they were to be met with on the lower deck, hanging their noses out of their boxes. The Argonauts sat together at meals at what came to be known as the Latin table, because their talk was spiced with classical quotation. They were all deeply conscious of 'battles long ago'. The sea under the setting sun 'is really wine-dark', wrote Lister. 'I shall take Constantinople and avenge the Byzantine empire,' remarked Shaw-Stewart, and explaining a later stage in the voyage to his friend Ronald Knox he declared, 'Then we came almost straight to the edge of the tyranny of Miltiades—in sight of Samothrace, in imaginary sight of windy Ilios itself and not so very far from Aegospotomi.' Between meals, which were enormous and noisy (though Brooke was observed to be listless and uninterested in the food), there were Swedish exercises, machine-gun drill, and practice in sending messages in semaphore. They sailed slowly back to Lemnos, towing the lighter (which broke loose near Cos and a whole day was spent trying to recover it), only to find the harbour congested, so they were ordered to make for an anchorage off Skyros.

Two days before they arrived at Skyros there was a fancy-dress ball, with Kelly and Browne taking turns at the piano. Brooke went to bed early. For some reason most of the men attended as Negroes, but one stoker, declaring himself to be Queen Elizabeth, wore Denis Browne's cabin curtains and an antiseptic blue bandage as a veil. 'Here we are at the end of another delightful voyage,' wrote Browne that same evening (April 15), 'and I haven't thanked you for it.' He couldn't get over the excursion to the Western Front. 'It must have been most extraordinary for you to be suddenly sitting with Winston within a few yards of the Boches. Fancy their rage if they ever heard it. . . . The Colonel [Quilter] was greatly excited about it and admired you hugely and said he'd no idea you were so intrepid.' Charles Lister had set the table aroar with an impersonation of Eddie Marsh. 'Were you responsible for our Divisional Notes about the character of the Turks? We laughed a good deal over them, particularly at one which said they didn't like night attacks because they hated the dark and invariably slept with a nightlight! *Surely* there's your hand? Charles parodied them inimitably.'

On the 17th they anchored in Trebuki Bay, off Skyros, arriving on a mild, pellucid evening, and Shaw-Stewart, Lister, Brooke, and Browne strolled together round the deck, sniffing the sage and thyme that came surging off the shore. 'It's divine here,' wrote Browne on the 18th, not naming the place out of respect for the censor, 'the valleys are full of crocus and thyme and underfoot there's nothing but the most gleaming marble. We found Theseus's bones too yesterday and the racecourse where all the tortoises practise running against Achilles. We brought back three of them, incredibly large and kicking violently.'

For the first day in port Brooke was on watch, so he could not accompany Lister and Shaw-Stewart, who went ashore to spy out the land. This meant he was the first to get the mail which came aboard that day bringing no less than five letters from Marsh, two for Browne, and three for himself. He had only just sent off one of his own to Gray's Inn with a slight reproach. 'I saw a lovely letter of yours to Denis—the only breath of England I've felt. You seemed to have been in very perilous places: far more, certainly, than me.' He said he was well, though notably thinner, and he had managed to do some writing during his convalescence, 'a sonnet or two almost done; and the very respectable and stately skeleton of an ode-threnody. All of which shall travel to you, if and when they are done.' He told of Sir Ian's proposal, 'which for the time, I didn't accept'. He preferred to be with his friends. 'My long poem is to be about the existence—and non-locality— of England. And it contains the line "In Avons of the heart her rivers run". Lovely isn't it? Freiberg [*sic*] sends his chin-chin.'

The earliest in date of Marsh's letters was his account of the mistaken message to Rugby about the Staff appointment. He had not yet felt obliged to contradict it 'as I hope so much that you *are* on the Staff.' The second letter to hand was written at the Admiralty on March 31 and enclosed a copy of the heartening eulogy from Henry James about the sonnets.

My dear, you will be pleased with this lovely letter from the dear old boy—do write to him, it would please him so much.

I took up the cudgels for the rhyme of given and Heaven,[1] by saying that I didn't think a rhyme being hackneyed mattered if the words containing it were the ones required by the sense, and that in this case I hardly saw how you could have avoided given and heaven even if you had been writing in blank verse. This seems to me commonsense, if commonplace—but it has drawn forth the following delightful sentence: 'I think, if you won't feel me over-contentious for it, that your reasoning rather halts as to the matter of rhyme and sense—or in other words of sense and poetic expression. Note well that, poetically speaking, it's not the sense that's the expression, the "rhyme" or whatever, but those things that are the sense, and that they so far betray it when they find for the "only" words any but the ideally right or the (so to speak!) quietly proud.' This lovely rigmarole seems only to mean the old truth that you can't split up a poem into meaning and expression. I agree, but I can't see that it affects my argument which only deals with the conditions in which a purely accidental and extraneous circumstance, such as that a rhyme has often been used before, ought to affect one's feeling as to its fitness to play its part in any particular compound.

I hope you won't get this in the trenches or at any time when you are feeling specially warlike! I *do* wish I knew whether you were on the staff or not, if only for convenience of addressing letters—I daren't send them to Headquarters without knowing.

Martin Harvey has just telegraphed to ask Winston whether it would be safe to send his company to Dublin a fortnight hence. Masterton-Smith said we had better ask what he meant by 'safe', so I suggested we should telegraph Bishop Westcott's answer to the Salvation Army lass who asked if he was saved—'Do you mean σωθεὶς or σωζόμενος or σεσωσμένος?' but I'm afraid it would be wasted on Martin Harvey.[2]

I went to see about half the Palace revue. Elsie Janis very wonderful (but you don't like her, do you?) with a magnificent imitation of Ethel Levey. There are some very good puns in the songs, for instance—

'You forgot she dropt her h's when you saw her raise her eyes.'

[1] In the sestet of No. 5, *The Soldier*.
[2] The three Greek words convey subtle distinctions between three states or conditions of safety, which, if used interrogatively would make the Bishop's question to the young woman amount, roughly, to—'Do you mean (1) Was I (once) saved but am not necessarily so now? or (2) Am I at this present in process of being saved? or (3) Am I one who *has* been saved and is still in a state of safety?' The passage is worth quoting as an example of the extremely recondite sort of joke with which Marsh, Brooke, and Shaw-Stewart were in the habit of entertaining each other.

The third letter that Brooke found while the others were on shore leave had been written on Easter Monday (April 5) after an event which to a great extent was to be the foundation of his immediate fame. Dean Inge had seen the sonnet 'If I should die' in the recent *Times Literary Supplement* review of *New Numbers*. He had quoted it in full during the course of his Easter sermon in St. Paul's, and *The Times* had reprinted it next morning in their report on the Dean's address. His text was from Isaiah.[1] 'He had just read a beautiful little poem on this subject,' *The Times* reported, 'a sonnet by a young writer who would, he ventured to think, take rank with our great poets.' The Dean then spoke the lines and praised them highly. 'And yet it fell somewhat short of Isaiah's vision,' he said, 'and still more of the Christian hope.' Marsh's letter began: 'My dear—you will be pleased to have been recited in St. Paul's Cathedral on Easter Sunday, and the Dean is a fine scholar and critic, though a Dean. I suppose in his position he could hardly do otherwise than say that the sonnet would have been better if it had been written by Isaiah!' Marsh had been to Cambridge to see his father, who had been seriously ill and suddenly become a really old man (he was seventy-six). The familiar streets were packed with men in khaki. 'Virginia's book is very good,' he concluded.[2] '*When* shall I know if you are on the Staff or not?' Such tributes from Dean Inge and Henry James in one post must have given Brooke a lot to think about while he was alone on duty—but he said nothing to his friends. They would never have heard of the quotation in St. Paul's had not Denis Browne also received a copy of *The Times* report from Eddie Marsh.

Marsh's letter to Browne was dated April 7.

I'm consumed with curiosity to know whether Rupert is on the Staff or not. I hear he has been to Cairo.

You will have been in action I suppose before you get this. You can imagine the suspense we are in—and my own private anxieties. The war has been very monotonous lately—but the stress will soon begin again—how we shall hang on the telegraph. Nothing seems worth mentioning. . . .

You know we are trembling on the verge of 'Prohibition'. I don't

---

[1] *Isaiah 26, v. 19. 'Awake and sing, ye that dwell in dust: for thy dew is as the dew of herbs, and the earth shall cast out the dead.'*

[2] *The Voyage Out*, by Virginia Woolf (1915).

suppose it will come to that, but I have an uneasy feeling that every
bottle of champagne will be my last. The typical song of the moment
is

> Swallow your whiskey while you may,
> Old Time is still a-flying.

I hear Oc has been telegraphing to his father to keep the flag
flying. . . . With all my power of wishing I wish you all glory and
honour and a whole skin for a week hence and onwards—and all
my love.

The day after Brooke and Browne had got their mail there was
a battalion field-day during which Browne, who was parted from
the others, made a small discovery. About a mile from the shore
in a dried-up river bed, overlooked by the highest point of the
island, he came upon a secluded olive-grove bare of scrub and sheltered by about a dozen olive-trees. On the following day, April 20,
during a lull in an exhausting divisional field-exercise in which
they had all done a great deal of clambering among loose rocks
and torn their boots, he conducted his friends Lister, Shaw-
Stewart, and Brooke to this place. There they rested, and Brooke
remarked on the pleasantness of the shade.

They had begun the exercise at 8 A.M. and it was now 4 P.M.
They had invited some officers on the *Franconia* to dine at the
Latin table, and the day's work being over they took their
stumbling way down to the shore and swam for about a mile out
to the ship, all but Brooke who was dog-tired so took charge of their
clothes and hired a peasant to ferry him across. Lister had found
the island 'made of pink marble out of which sage and balsam
grew'. It hummed with bees, he said, and in the ravines that sloped
to the sea were thorn-trees and groves of olive; the shadows
between the rocks were cobalt blue and the water was 'utterly
blue and cold'. In England Mrs. Brooke had heard by now of her
son's decision. 'I think he was right to refuse,' she was writing to
Marsh on this evening of the 20th. 'I do wish there would be a
move on. I fear I am somewhat pessimistic.'

Only two of their guests turned up, but the meal was none the
less convivial. The two men from the *Franconia* sat with Asquith,
Kelly, Shaw-Stewart, Lister, Browne, and Brooke. The Latin
table was met in full strength for the last social occasion of Brooke's
life. They drank copious draughts of hock, and the dishes had been
cleared away when Brooke, who had grown very quiet, turned to

Shaw-Stewart and remarked, 'I believe it's making my lip swell.' It was certainly swelling again, but this time on the left side. Browne thought him 'very quiet (for him) all the evening', and Asquith wrote to his sister, 'R. was very silent at this rather noisy party; he said he felt tired, and went to bed immediately after dinner.'

Next morning he was not at breakfast. Shaw-Stewart looked in on him soon after midday and found his batman applying a hot towel to his face. The doctor, McCracken, who had attended him in Cairo, told Asquith in the morning that the temperature was 101. He considered the lip a case of local septic poisoning, unconnected with the slight temperature and the aches in the back which the patient had complained of. However, McCracken made two small incisions in the lip and prescribed hot fomentations. Shaw-Stewart did not stay long, for it looked as though it might hurt him to speak, but in reply to his enquiry Brooke admitted that he was feeling 'damnably ill'. In the evening Shaw-Stewart paid a second visit, this time so as to pass on to him the general plans for the next few days which Quilter had just been detailing to his staff. It looked as though there was to be another fèint attack or demonstration off the Gallipoli coast. (As it turned out this proved to be the long-awaited landing itself.) Shaw-Stewart, however, assured Brooke that he needn't bother to stir from his cabin. He could demonstrate equally well, he said, simply by 'looking frightful' through his port-hole. He considered that the patient was at least no worse than before, and left after about ten minutes. Later that evening Denis Browne called to show him the cutting from *The Times* reporting the Dean's Easter sermon. Brooke said he felt very bad and asked Browne not to switch on the light. As to the newspaper cutting, he said he had seen it already and, adopting a pleasantry from Eddie Marsh's last letter, said he was sorry to hear the Dean didn't think him quite as good as Isaiah! He did not show Browne Marsh's letter or even trouble to say it was he who had sent the paper. He wanted to sleep. Neither Browne nor anyone else ever heard him speak coherently again. His temperature was now 103, and the doctor admitted to Shaw-Stewart that he was anxious. The patient did not seem to him to be in a condition to withstand septicaemia. To Browne he spoke less frankly, quoting a similar case which had cleared up after three days.

Early next morning (April 22) Kelly looked in and found him 'dazed' as also did Shaw-Stewart, who used the word 'comatose' in his account, and for the first time he was really worried. Kelly had no idea his condition was critical until about tea-time, when he spoke with the doctors who had just been in consultation. 'The pneumococcus germ has poisoned his blood through a bad lip,' they told him, and added there was little they could do for him. 'I have had a foreboding,' Kelly wrote in his Journal, 'that he is one of those, like Keats, Shelley, and Schubert, who are not suffered to deliver their full message, but there seems just the slenderest chance he may live.' At midday the battalion surgeon had sent for three of his colleagues from the ships near by, including the Senior Medical Officer of the Brigade. These were A.D.M.S. Fleet Surgeon Gaskell; his assistant, Captain Casement (2nd Staff Medical Officer of the Division); and Dr. Schlesinger (Staff Medical Officer of the Brigade), known to Browne as an able man from Guy's. They came over at 3 o'clock, diagnosed 'acute blood poisoning', and after some disagreement proposed making an incision in an abscess which had formed on the left side of the neck. They could not conceal from Browne their serious view of the case. It was their opinion that the place on the lip was an accidental scratch or perhaps a bite infected with pneumococci, which were multiplying and passing into the blood-stream. The nearest British hospital ship was in Lemnos, but the French *Duguay-Trouin* was anchored fairly close by. Built in 1878, she had been a training ship in Brest harbour, and was converted to her present function at the outbreak of war. Within half an hour a steam pinnace from H.M.S. *Canopus* was alongside, and Kelly and Shaw-Stewart leaned over the rail to watch the patient lowered aboard. Brooke had said 'Hullo' to Browne as he stooped to lift him into the pinnace, but he soon lapsed into unconsciousness. From the rail Shaw-Stewart could only see a tuft of hair, and a hand come up from under the wrappings to draw them free of one side of his face so that he could breathe more freely. Oc Asquith and Browne were in attendance. By 5 P.M. Brooke was safely bestowed in one of the two cool and airy cabins that were situated back to back on the sun deck aft of the French vessel. On board there were twelve French surgeons and no other patients. 'I explained that R. was our best young poet,' wrote Asquith, 'and the apple of Winston's and Sir Ian's eye.' Soon after 6 P.M. Browne and his companion said they must return to their ship but would be back early on the morrow. Asquith asked Brooke if he wanted anything. He was in so deep a coma that it seemed idle to enquire, so the visitor was surprised to get an answer—'Water.'

They took the pinnace to the divisional transport ship and asked General Paris to sign marconigrams, one for despatch to Mr. Churchill, the other to Sir Ian Hamilton at Lemnos, whom they asked to send one of the two English hospital ships from Mudros Bay.

Next day, April 23, Asquith and Browne, this time with Dr. McCracken, were back shortly after 9 A.M. They found the French surgeons about to operate. They hung about, unable to do anything. Apparently about noon Brooke spoke to Dr. Schlesinger, saying he had suffered some pain earlier in the morning, but he was aware that the French were doing all they could for him, and now he was comfortable. His temperature was 106. Sir Ian at Lemnos was aboard S.S. *Arcadian*. It was some twelve hours before he transferred to the battleship *Queen Elizabeth*, the newest vessel of the Fleet equipped with 15-inch guns. She was to follow the transports in the approach to Gallipoli. The C.-in-C. was in the act of writing to Marsh as the troopships set off. 'This moment,' he wrote, 'at 12.30 P.M. just as the mail is going, I have got a most alarming wireless from Naval Division telling me, for the first time, Rupert Brooke was ill, and dangerously ill. The wording of the message terrifies me. Alas, what a misfortune! I have kept his A.D.C.-ship open for him all the time. . . . I have his last poems on my table. . . . Ah, well—I pray fervently that he may yet pull through. We are off!!! Unless the weather plays us a scurvy trick we shall be at it on Sunday next, and may the best cause win.'

After luncheon an enquiry from Sir Ian reached the French vessel. The chief French surgeon instructed Asquith to reply '*État désespéré*'.

In London that morning Mr. Churchill was first to arrive at Admiralty House, where he found the message from Lemnos. Marsh was still at Gray's Inn, having an early breakfast with Currie's widow, the girl he had deserted for Dolly Henry, when the telephone rang. It was Mr. Churchill reading the marconigram. The visitor left without a proper goodbye, and an hour

later ran into Gertler's studio at Hampstead. Something dreadful
had happened, she said. She didn't know what. It was something
to do with the Dardanelles. Having sent a wire to Rugby, Marsh's
first impulse was to confide in Henry James. 'I must turn to you
in my anxiety,' he began, and added what little he knew.

By now Browne was going off to fetch the Chaplain from the
Franconia. He then fetched the Brigade S.M.O. from H.M.S.
Royal George, and got back as Asquith stepped aboard from the
Grantully Castle. The English doctor confirmed that it was only a
matter of hours, and the Chaplain remained but a few minutes.
Asquith left with him in order to make arrangements for the last
honours, for the flotilla was now under orders to sail for Gallipoli
at 6 A.M. the next morning. Browne had only left the cabin for
a few minutes while the orderlies tidied it up when the Chief
Surgeon called him back, thinking the end was come. It was then
4 P.M. Denis Browne was sitting alone at the bedside when at
4.46 P.M., still unconscious, Rupert Brooke died.

Asquith and Browne decided to bury him in the olive-grove
a mile from shore which had served as a rendezvous during the
divisional field-day and where he had rested with his friends.
Charles Lister commanded the burial party, which consisted of
Browne, Freyberg, and a few men of Brooke's platoon. They went
ahead and prepared the grave, lining it with flowers and sprigs
of olive. At 8.15, Kelly, Shaw-Stewart, Quilter, Myburgh
(second-in-command), and eight officers of the battalion got into
a life-boat and were joined by a steam pinnace from H.M.S.
Dartmouth (containing General Paris and officers of his staff)
which took them in tow to the *Duguay-Trouin*. There they picked
up Asquith and the coffin, on which he had branded the name and
date with a surgeon's cauterizing iron. It took two hours for the
eight petty officers of Brooke's 'A' Company who carried the
coffin to negotiate the rough ground of the dried-up watercourse
which led to the rendezvous overlooked by Mount Komaro.
They had gone about half-way when at 10 P.M. a second telegram
reached the Admiralty. Marsh was in the lobby waiting for news.
He wired Mrs. Brooke in Rugby and ran round to the Asquiths at
Downing Street.

At 10.45 Browne saw the procession approaching, led by
Brooke's platoon sergeant Saunders, who carried an improvised
cross of white wood bearing the poet's name in black paint.

There was a clouded half-moon. Shaw-Stewart was in command of the firing party. 'It is strange,' he wrote next day to Marsh, 'to think I had been wondering if I should ever use my sword!' and he enclosed a Greek epigram he had composed while walking up the ravine, hoping Marsh would correct it. Kelly wrote in his diary, 'The small olive-grove in the narrow valley and the scent of the wild sage gave a strong classical tone which was so in harmony with the poet we were burying that to some of us the Christian ceremony seemed out of keeping'; and in his letter to Marsh (for they all wrote next day as they steamed towards the Gallipoli peninsula) he said, 'It was as though one were involved in the origin of some classic myth.' Shaw-Stewart, always more fatalist than the others, was dimly aware, even then, before ever they marched away from the grave, that he had assisted at the burial of one who had become the symbol of his generation.

The Chaplain, Mr. Failes, read the service. On the coffin they had laid his helmet, belt, and pistol (he had no sword) and on these Colonel Quilter placed a wreath of olive. 'The moon thinly veiled,' wrote Asquith to his sister, 'a man carrying a plain wooden cross, and a lantern leading the way; some other lanterns glimmering, the scent of wild thyme, a dim group of French and English officers, the three volleys: the Last Post.'

'I don't (as you know) set much store by what happens to me or anyone else after death,' wrote Shaw-Stewart as he watched the bombardment next day, 'but even I am fired by the extraordinary beauty and aptitude of his grave.' After the short ceremony they all retraced their steps down the ravine, all but the five companions of the Latin table. These gathered around and raised a low cairn over the grave. At the head they set up the platoon sergeant's white cross, on which the Greek interpreter had inscribed an epitaph with his pencil, and at the foot a smaller cross, roughly put together with two odd bits of wood, a tribute from his platoon.

When Kelly got back to the ship he copied out of Brooke's little black notebook everything that was legible, in case the package that Browne was hurriedly doing up for Gray's Inn should fail to arrive.

The escorting cruisers were under orders to open fire on the enemy coast at 5 A.M. As *Grantully Castle* steamed out of Trebuki Bay, soon after dawn, they wrote their letters to England. Browne

apologized to Mrs. Brooke at the end of his long story. 'It is hard
to think things out clearly, when one is just going into action.'
Before he reached the end of his nine-page letter to Marsh they
were barely 600 yards from the enemy coast. The first bombardment was over. It was night and Freyberg was swimming ashore,
alone, on a flare-lighting expedition, and Browne was anxious
for his safety.

Marsh got back to Gray's Inn very late on the night the news
came through. A telegram from Mrs. Brooke was lying on his
table. 'If message of love can be sent send it please at once waiting
anxiously for the news Brooke.' He had already written again to
Henry James, and to Rugby.

MY DEAR MRS. BROOKE,

There is nothing more to tell than the message I had the in-
expressible grief of sending you tonight.

It is the greatest sorrow I could have, and I dare not think what
it must be to you—I have never known or heard of anyone like him
—his genius and his beauty, his wisdom, honour, gentleness and
humour made him such a man as has seldom lived. Everybody
loved him, there was no one who had so many devoted friends and
so many charmed acquaintances.

Most things in my life depended on him for a great part of their
interest and worth. It is your glory to be his mother—and mine to
be his friend—the loss to the future cannot be guessed.

Next morning he wrote to Browne of the loss which had become
an additional bond between them. 'We shall both feel it to the
end of our lives. . . . I feel that my whole plan of life has broken
down.' Mr. Churchill had already written his noble valediction
which was to appear in *The Times* on April 26 appended to the
obituary which Marsh was now about to compose. 'His mother is
very brave—my heart bleeds for her—Winston is deeply moved.'
Browne was to send all papers, etc., to Gray's Inn. 'You will I
know rack your brains to tell me *everything* there is to be told of the
time since you went away.'

He was determined imaginatively to relive as much as possible
of those last days. He knew they would constitute the central
event of his life, and, if humanly possible, nothing must remain a
mystery outside his experience. The foregoing account is the
composite story which he must have pieced together in his mind

from the five accounts[1] which came to hand in the course of the following weeks. At this juncture, April 24, news of the landing on Gallipoli was imminent. So much had already happened, and yet these were hours of mounting anxiety. Almost as if nothing had occurred so far, he ended his hurried note to Denis Browne— 'I am in great suspense for the news.'

ii

After the bombardment of the narrows on March 18 a situation arose at Whitehall which did nothing to improve relations between the First Lord and Fisher. It was the opinion of de Robeck, the Admiral in command, that operations should not be resumed without the assistance of the Army, and Fisher was in full accord with this point of view, in opposition to Mr. Churchill, who maintained that delay for any purpose would only be to the enemy's advantage. The Prime Minister agreed with the First Lord but would not consent that orders which overruled the Board of Admiralty should be transmitted to the Mediterranean. Unfortunately it was not known until long after that the Turkish gunners were desperate for want of ammunition. If the First Lord was advocating a gamble, our losses in ships having become serious owing to an undetected minefield, his appreciation of the position seems to have been absolutely sound, and the discomfited enemy were astonished as first hours then whole days of respite went by while they made good their losses. With the absence of any decisive action in the North Sea, the U-boats increasing their baleful manœuvres, a naval deadlock in the Dardanelles, and a general misconception of the value to the Allies of the delaying action at Antwerp, the pre-war differences were again coming to the surface, and the First Lord was at once an inevitable and a convenient focal point for Tory criticism. The Conservatives were determined to make the best of this opportunity, and it was hardly in Fisher's interest to do anything to discourage them.

After the first landing on Gallipoli (April 25) the First Sea Lord concentrated his disapproval on the presence of the brand-new battleship *Queen Elizabeth* which Sir Ian Hamilton had made his headquarters. He argued that the great vessel was an extrava-

---

[1] Denis Browne to E.M. (April 25); Shaw-Stewart to E.M. (April 24); F. S. Kelly to E.M. (July 25); Denis Browne to Mrs. Brooke (April 24); Arthur Asquith to his sister Violet (April 23).

gance in the Dardanelles, exposed as it was to submarine attack when it could be doing more valuable service elsewhere. In this Mr. Churchill supported him, but the concession did little substantially to alter Fisher's growing inclination to resign as a gesture of protest against the whole campaign and the limitations of his influence in the War Council. At its meeting on May 14 he openly stated his disapproval of the operations in the Dardanelles. That evening a private conversation between Churchill and Fisher in the First Sea Lord's office ended in what to the former at least seemed to be a reconciliation; but late that night Mr. Churchill authorized the despatch of four light cruisers to the Italian fleet in the Adriatic. (It could safely be calculated that their prompt arrival would influence Italy's choice of alliance, just as the *Goeben* had tipped the balance in Turkey.) He then requested more reinforcements for the Dardanelles. On the 15th Fisher resigned. He could neither be persuaded nor cajoled to revoke his decision. Mr. Churchill's own appeal was couched in the most conciliatory terms, and as a personal friend of the First Sea Lord Marsh did his utmost to act as intermediary. Late on the 15th (a Saturday) Marsh left London for a short week-end at Rugby while Mr. Churchill stayed with the Prime Minister in his country home. Mr. Asquith was not unduly alarmed. 'Fisher is always resigning,' he remarked, and was ready to receive the First Sea Lord's withdrawal of his letter of resignation without any surprise. But this time Fisher meant it.

Meanwhile alternative plans had to be proposed. Sir Arthur Wilson consented to fill Fisher's post (granted Mr. Churchill was retained in office) if called upon, and the details of a new Board of Admiralty were drawn up during the week-end for presentation to the House of Commons on the Monday. On the same day Lord Fisher was energetic in enlisting the support of certain members of the Opposition. It was not difficult to find Tory members who would be only too ready to justify a course of action which was injurious to one who, as it seemed to them, was a deserter who had gone over to the Liberals.

A major crisis was developing in Mr. Churchill's career, and Marsh was closely involved. His loyalty as a Civil Servant was backed by his opinions as an individual. There was no doubt in his mind that, having committed themselves to the forcing of the Straits, if de Robeck and Hamilton advised the co-operation of land forces they should have them, together with a fleet off-shore adequate for their protection and supply. In his private capacity he had had several conversations with both Fisher and the Prime Minister. The pressure of events was accumulating, and Mr. Asquith could not indefinitely hold the balance between the First Lord and the mounting number of his critics.

While this dispute was coming to a head the first landing was made on the peninsula and a precarious foothold was gained. Four days later the R.N.D. were still waiting in readiness on their transports, and Denis Browne addressed his next letter from 'The End of the World'.

> I wonder if you can guess what we feel like. Freyberg—who sends you all his love—is wild with joy. He wants frightfully to make a big thing out of it, and I hope he will. Patrick has been writing letters which he describes as 'almost perfect in tone, whimsical, but striking a deeper note' . . . Oc is his patient steadfast self; Cleg, wild with rapture or kindred emotions, makes curious bestial noises everywhere. I wonder who made him.
>
> Oh Eddie, I feel I don't care one way or the other. But I want you to know how often we all of us think of you and shall—as long as we can. This battle is the most wonderful thing there ever was, as heroic by land as it is wonderful by sea. We watch with bated breath from the deck until our eyes drop out. The coast looks so peaceful and sunny until suddenly a shell goes biff and up goes a huge column of smoke.

He took part in the second push forward on May 6 when the Hoods gained some ground which they later had to abandon. For several hours Browne, Shaw-Stewart, and eight others, sheltering behind a 'little bean-shaped hill', were in the foremost position of the whole force on the bridgehead. Eighty men, dashing across exposed ground in twos and threes, joined them to hold the position before they were obliged to retire. Quilter was killed, Lister and Asquith hit. Browne was unscathed that day. But on the following afternoon a sniper's bullet passed through his coat-collar and injured his neck. 'There's much of this I'm glad Rupert did not see,' he wrote, 'and yet if only he could have seen it all! It is wonderful when you are away; when you are in it war is hateful and utterly horrible!' He was describing Freyberg's gallant flare-lighting exploit when the doctor interrupted him and declared he was to be sent to hospital in Cairo. A letter of the 3rd was on its way to him from Gray's Inn. Lists of casualties were pouring in and Marsh was weighed down with anxiety. 'I feel as if I could never be light-hearted again.' Six days later it was 'This is Sunday night, and for all I know you are still safe and sound— that is almost the only good thing in my life! . . . but really it has been hard to live through these last few days . . . What a band of heroes. I'm very proud of you all, Denis, through all my fears and miseries—and the whole thing seems to be going well tho' slowish.' He could not conceal his other worries. Catherine Abercrombie was having a serious operation. (He did not add, as he might have done, that Mrs. Brooke had given him to pay for it the £25 instalment of Rupert's usual allowance which would have been due in June.) Edward Horner was dangerously wounded. Two days before the letter was written, the *Lusitania* had been sunk by a submarine. 'But really,' he concluded, 'I seem to have got almost to the end of my powers of feeling things.'

In the peace of his billet in Pyramid Road, Cairo, Browne tried to recall the epic events which he had witnessed on the 25th, the day of the first landing.

> Eddie, I wonder if people know or realize at all the extraordinary heroism of the actual landing. The 29th Div. have immortalized them-selves. Imagine the conditions: endless barbed wire down to and under the sea and a rain of rifle and machine-gun fire. The Dublins and Munsters and Lancashires found it impossible to get ashore at the actual level landing place, so they simply swarmed up the cliffs on either side. Their getting and holding a footing there is marvellous. No troops ought to have been able to land, and our men, at any rate, could have made it impossible for an invader. They stuck to the top of the cliff all that Sunday, the Turks gave way in the evening, and Tuesday they were 2 miles inland.

From Cairo Browne was moved to Alexandria, where he re-mained until the end of May. In the meantime Marsh's dealings with the tragic woman in Rugby were destined to exert an influence on his life for years to come.

On getting his telegram of April 23, which left her in little doubt of the news that would follow, Mrs. Brooke wrote saying she hadn't been happy in her mind ever since Rupert's last letter. 'I have no hope. All the same I know all has been done that was possible. I have no complaint for anything except the war. Indeed

I am thankful and grateful to all. I can write no more. You will understand and forgive.' It was the next day when she received Marsh's letter of confirmation that she wrote, 'You were indeed a friend in whom he trusted and who never failed him, but you have other and important interests.' She asked that he should use his influence with the War Office and get special leave for her surviving son Alfred, who was a subaltern with the Post Office Rifles at Le Havre. She was lost without Rupert. 'A few days ago I got a little Egyptian tear-bottle from him sent from his sick-bed [at Port Said].' She then started surveying Rupert's life and next day wrote to say that 'the many painful attacks of illness which he had as a young boy would fill a book. . . . All my life and sur-roundings are so bound up in him, my sitting-room full of his books and things waiting for his return as my heart is.' She wondered whether Marsh knew of any will or last wishes, a parcel of papers had come from Blandford, she had never dared to look at them. 'It's likely that he left nothing, he seemed so sure of coming back. He spoke of it as "when this job's done" I'll do so-and-so. Of course he may have done this simply to put me off, for never was there a 'more considerate son', and she again pleaded to have Alfred recalled from France. She was writing every day, asking this one favour—the return of Alfred—which Marsh was powerless to perform. In his next letter, in which he expressed admiration of her courage (which prompted the reply, 'I'm only brave because I can't be anything else'), he irritated her a little by remarking that he had got the impression that her son expected to die. 'He was right to conceal it from me!' she exclaimed, 'but I wonder why he expected it, he oughtn't to have done so, but as you say it can't have made any difference to what has hap-pened, but he never was a fatalist.' In the same letter she asked, 'Do you know who Cathleen Nesbitt is?' First the disclosure of a confidence that Mrs. Brooke had not shared, and now the dis-covery of an intimate friend, unknown to herself, whom Marsh had brought into her son's life—it was galling, but as yet she kept her vexation to herself. 'I know how he regarded you,' she wrote, 'amongst his many friends he certainly placed you first, almost his Second Self. . . . Before the war when he was going to London a good deal I suggested he had better take some rooms, he said, "No, Eddie wouldn't like it at all. I am really not much trouble." He said the housekeeper and he got on well together.'

On May 2 Marsh went down to Rugby for the week-end. He was not to bring evening clothes, Mrs. Brooke said. 'My boys never dress when with me.' He took with him a letter from Henry James which began, 'If there was a stupid and hideous disfigurement of life and outrage to beauty left for our awful conditions to perpetrate those things have now been supremely achieved, and no other brutal blow in the private sphere can better them for making one just stare through one's tears.' He probably read aloud the passage where James declared that the war sonnets would 'enrich our whole collective consciousness', but he must have kept to himself the difficult wisdom which followed '. . . meanwhile all my impulse is to tell you to entertain the pang and taste the bitterness for all they are "worth"—to know to the fullest extent what has happened to you and not miss one of the hard ways in which it will come home'.

Gilbert Murray had boldly asserted in the *Cambridge Magazine*: 'I cannot help thinking that Rupert Brooke will probably live in fame as an almost mythical figure'; Mrs. Asquith in conversation had suggested a memorial in the Henry VII Chapel at Westminster; Festing Jones was reminded of the death of Samuel Butler—'I went through something of this kind when Butler died. . . . Life consists of things that one never gets over.' Marsh would also have produced a letter from Bridges, who was compiling an anthology which 'promises to be unlike any other book, which makes it difficult to describe. . . . My book is very severe, in that lighter things (unless quite "ideal") are incompatible.' He left it to Marsh to decide how Brooke was to be represented in this collection, which was eventually entitled *The Spirit of Man*. Gibson was more personal: 'When I was with him I used to wonder and wonder—is it possible that this radiant creature can really care for me? . . . I always thought of him as one of the Sons of the Morning.' Bottomley was conscious of the broken circle. 'It grieves me to think that that Georgian fellowship which we all owe to you should have been broken (now twice broken) ere it was completed.' But among Marsh's letters of condolence none seemed to him more beautifully expressed than a scrawl from the Duchess of Sutherland, who was running a hospital in France. 'Beautiful last sentence,' he wrote at the top of the page. 'Don't you think,' it ran, 'this war is a greater "heart-searcher" than the coming of Christ? the most terrible "Revivalist Meeting" of all time. Everything has lost its value—except the exulting soul of man, and whither, whither, rich with life, does it fly? . . . The wind is in the N.E. and the guns go on and on. I shall be very, very old soon, like a grey moth that has lived in dust and darkness too long to remember that its underwings were orange.'

Marsh and Mrs. Brooke still had only a vague idea of what had happened, and believed that the burial had taken place on Lemnos. Meanwhile their relationship was continually sustaining petty but cumulative injuries. While Marsh was at Rugby on May 2 Brooke's trusted friend Dudley Ward went down to the Old Vicarage, Grantchester, and spent the day sorting papers and books with Mrs. Neeves the housekeeper. He was accompanied by Jacques Raverat, whom Mrs. Brooke did not consider a person qualified to handle her son's belongings. A day later Raverat called again, took away some half-dozen books, and left more bundles of papers addressed to Marsh at Gray's Inn. At this Mrs. Neeves felt uneasy and wrote to Rugby asking for instructions. As far as she could gather Mr. Ward was all for sending everything to Raymond Buildings, where they could be sorted at leisure, but she did not want to let anything go out of the house without the permission of the 'executors'. Mrs. Brooke replied that Mrs. Neeves could certainly send any manuscripts to Mr. Marsh, 'a very great friend of my son's, who wished him to be his literary executor', but the correspondence must all go to her at Rugby. She then wrote at once to Marsh, for she must have felt she was interfering with his plans. 'As you know I feel very strongly about Rupert's private correspondence.' Her anxieties were less for her son's sake, she explained, than for the people who had written to him, pouring out their hearts because of his 'very great power of inspiring love and confidence'. On his father's death Rupert himself had suggested that all the correspondence should be destroyed unread. Mrs. Brooke now proposed to make that a precedent. 'No power on earth would make me look through those letters; my own can be burnt with them. Now, my dear Eddie, you won't be vexed with me will you? If I have said too much put it down to a somewhat distraught woman, but one who feels *sure* that her *ideas* are right.' She added that Marsh himself could come to Rugby to retrieve his own letters but 'don't let anyone else have a hand in it'. She suspected that it was Marsh who had arranged the visit to Grantchester while he called on her at Rugby. Of course he knew of it, or Dudley Ward would not have given Mrs. Neeves the Gray's Inn address for the papers, but he never imagined there could be the slightest objection to Brooke's good friend Raverat lending a hand. To Marsh it was all part of the work of a literary executor, who must have sight of family documents before they are dispersed or ignorantly destroyed. Mrs. Brooke was so overwhelmed with trouble he naturally thought she would be only too grateful for this work to go ahead without her being bothered with it. He would see to everything. While at Rugby he did not even think it necessary at this stage to say that he was contemplating a Memoir of her son. He was going to do it without causing her a moment's extra grief by asking her to revive old memories. Her last letter had ended: 'Now there is nothing between suicide and setting my teeth; I daren't choose the first with his face before me. Forgive me, I had to say this.'

She had found no testamentary papers in the bank at Rugby, so that as yet they had nothing from which to deduce Brooke's last wishes. However, 'You are indeed good, arranging about R.'s things being well taken care of', she wrote (May 8), so he went ahead with his editorial plans. Being responsible to Frank Sidgwick the publisher, it was necessary for him to get his position authorized by a formal letter signed by both the next of kin, Mrs. Brooke and her surviving son. She agreed to write to Alfred. 'I think I told him about your being R.'s literary executor,' she remarked in her letter consenting to this plan. So as yet there was no disagreement.[1] But on the same day (May 8) the *Cambridge Review* published an article by E. J. Dent, quoting some of Brooke's letters to him which Mrs. Brooke would never have allowed to appear had she been consulted. They showed him making fun of schoolmasters. Dent was not impressed by the war sonnets and maintained that with maturity Brooke would have outgrown them. The observation was just and the letters harmless, but Mrs. Brooke developed a horror of biographical writers of any kind. 'It has torn me to bits,' she complained bitterly to Marsh, who knew nothing of the

[1] Mrs. Brooke's letter was dated May 8 and endorsed by Alfred on May 18. The operative sentences were: 'I am only too glad to think that you are making arrangements about Rupert's works being published and as one of his legal heirs I empower you to deal with the copyrights on the assumption that he died intestate. I know very well that is just what he would have wished himself from what he said to me before he went to the South Sea Islands.' Her letter of May 21 (see below) carries this a stage further.

article and saw no harm when at last he read it. However, he
offered to send a protest to the author. This he assured her he
would do at once, and at the same time copied out for her a
tribute to her son just received from Sir Ian Hamilton. Her
answer of May 11 was reassuring. 'You are indeed a good friend
to me. When our dear R. first joined the Naval Division I said
that I knew I should always get every help possible from you if
trouble came and this has proved that I was right. *The* great
sorrow you couldn't prevent, but you have done everything possible to ameliorate it. If it be possible, may R. be watching you.'
Dent argued in reply to Marsh that his article was written 'because
the papers had been saying such damnable nonsense and tending
to create a legend with all that silly talk about the young soldier
poet. It was important to say the truth.' But nobody now could
destroy the legend. The suffering time had found an emblem of its
agony.

Henry James was told of these distressing circumstances and
on May 11 he agreed to write a special contribution for the
Memoir of Brooke that Marsh was now resolved to compose and
publish at the earliest possible date together with the collected
poems. 'I rejoice at hearing from you what you have soundly
elected to do for the present hour ·about the presentation of
Rupert's *reliquiae*. . . . I will do what I said to the best of my
embarrassed possibility. . . . Meanwhile I feel I can hardly tell
you what afflictions I gather from the sight of other appreciations
—almost as if in presence of intrusive fumbling profaning hands.'†
The great man, afflicted in spirit by 'the awful perpetrations of the
Enemy, amid the liveliest sense of which you must be living', was
obviously happy that Marsh should be turning to him more and
more. He welcomed the chance to be of service. 'I do so rejoice
in our admirable community of grasp.' 'Heaven help you with
his mother!' he had written on hearing of a forthcoming visit to
Rugby, 'of which occasion, however, I shall be deeply interested
to hear.'† On Sunday, May 16, Marsh was again with Mrs.
Brooke, but with Fisher's resignation the centre of interest in his
life had suddenly shifted to Whitehall.

On the Monday Marsh left Rugby very early in the morning
while Mr. Churchill travelled up from the country. The names of
the new Board of Admiralty were to be put forward in the House

of Commons. Neither the First Lord nor his Private Secretary had any inkling of the forces which were gathering around Bonar Law, Leader of the Opposition, as a result of Fisher's resignation. On arrival at Downing Street Mr. Churchill learned that his revised Board would not be called for. A Coalition Government was being discussed, and the Conservative element would not tolerate him in office. It was just then that news came in that the German High Seas Fleet had put to sea. With the extraordinary possibility of a sudden and complete reversal of his fortunes resulting from a second Trafalgar, Mr. Churchill went back to his place of office and waited. Masterton-Smith and Marsh were in attendance. There was no First Sea Lord. Fisher had declined the invitation to return to his place and share the credit. By 10 A.M. next morning there was a sense of desolating anticlimax and a return to the drab realities of home politics which had been temporarily put aside. The German Fleet was steaming back to port.

During these past days and in those which followed (until Mr. Asquith announced his newly constituted Government on May 25) the figure of Edward Marsh seems to dwindle in the imagination at the very time when he was doubtless performing a major service, but it was done in private and in confidence. While trying to watch him at this stage one must picture him with the First Lord, whose side he never left, drafting letters, discussing their substance, arguing around and about the situation, giving what good counsel he could. The value of what he said or did can only be inferred from the unswerving friendship that Mr. Churchill bestowed on him throughout the vicissitudes of private and public life in the years to come. Fisher gained no personal advantage from his ostentatious gesture. His hopes of full control at the Admiralty were dashed when A. J. Balfour, an ardent supporter of the Gallipoli operations, whom Mr. Churchill himself had recommended, was appointed the new First Lord. Soon more ships were earmarked for the Mediterranean than ever Mr. Churchill had requested of Fisher, and every effort by land and sea was reinforced and redoubled.

Marsh soon found himself Private Secretary to the Chancellor of the Duchy of Lancaster, a sinecure which at least left Mr. Churchill free to devote himself to the deliberations of the War Council, on which he still sat. For some while Marsh continued to work in Admiralty House in the lobby adjoining Mr. Churchill's room, and he was to remain in close touch with Gallipoli affairs to their bitter and abortive end. It was never in his nature to be detached where the fortunes of his friends were concerned, and by now his official association with his Chief was as much a collaboration between friends as was his literary life with Rupert Brooke. Mr. Churchill's long and impressive letter of May 21 to Bonar Law, asking to be judged by the true facts, which the Opposition leader had not hitherto been acquainted with, was unavailing. The First Lord was sacrificed to national unity. The blow was hard, the prospect of comparative inactivity almost intolerable, and Marsh shared the bitterness to the full. The day after the news was made public Mr. and Mrs. Churchill and Lady Gwendeline Churchill motored down to their farm in the neighbourhood of Godalming, and took Marsh with them. On May 25 he wrote to Violet Asquith, who more than anyone else in the past few weeks had stood by him in his private troubles. Before the drive to Hoe Farm he had paid a flying visit to Cambridge.

It was very sad and sweet to see the places he [Brooke] had loved so much. This morning was almost harder to bear. Winston had taken me down to their farm, which is the most exquisitely lovely place, and the real English country (the first time I have seen it since April 23) in all its glorious and to me cruel beauty of the first day of perfect early summer. Nothing in the world could bring home to one so vividly the feeling of what Rupert was—every ray and every leaf and flower seemed to cry out for him—the elm-clumps greatly standing, the mayfields all golden showing, the sleepy grass and the cool lapse of hours—all his lovely phrases came back to me, and most of all 'Her sights and sounds, dreams happy as her day'. Clemmie and Goonie seemed to feel what I was feeling—they had both planned for him to come and stay there! and dear old Winston, at dinner last night, had suddenly broken out, *à propos* of nothing, in the midst of discussing his own troubles, that nothing had grieved him, or went on grieving him, so much as Rupert's death, and went on to abuse me quite angrily, as he has done several times, for not bringing them together sooner.

I am miserably sorry for Winston. You can imagine what a horrible wound and mutilation it is for him to be torn away from his work there—it's like Beethoven deaf. . . . However he has recovered his serenity since the moment he was convinced it was irrevocable and he has now set his face to the future with his own courage.

I'm not very pleased about myself either—isn't it strange, Violet, how my whole life has suddenly come crumbling round my ears. There were two things I cared for supremely, Rupert and 'doing my bit'—now Rupert is gone, and the day after tomorrow my bit will have eluded me—for how on earth I am to persuade myself that I am serving my country as Pte. Secy to the Chancellor of the Duchy is more than I can imagine.

The alternatives he had in mind were going to join the Red Cross in Serbia or offering himself as 'bottle-washer' to a philanthropic scheme being run by Masefield. And now he had just heard that Denis Browne had sailed from Alexandria to rejoin his unit on Gallipoli. 'I had hoped for a longer respite from anxiety about him.' Within a day or two he came to the conclusion that doing his 'bit' lay in serving Mr. Churchill, whatever his position. In the office Marsh picked up a photograph of Admiral Fisher, in one corner of which the First Sea Lord had genially inscribed 'Yours till Hell freezes', tore it into pieces, folded them neatly, and dropped them in the wastepaper basket.

While he was travelling up from Rugby on the 17th to play his part in the political crisis which came to a head later that day, Mrs. Brooke broke down completely, so that the following morning, when he was already bewildered by the sudden turn in public events, Marsh received a letter which plumbed the utmost depths of sorrow. After he had left the house she re-read Arthur Asquith's account of her son's death and burial, and brooded over it with morbid intensity. Beside this picture of grief the only bright spot in the day's post was utterly ineffectual as a consolation. It was trivial by comparison, the news that he had at last effected a reconciliation between W. H. Davies and Gosse, who had taken offence at an ill-judged letter of the poet's. 'You are the Angel of Conciliation whose coming was announced by the prophet Zephaniah,' Gosse wrote, and asked his correspondent to bring Davies to luncheon. At Whitehall, a few days later, the Angel of Conciliation was being less successful in larger affairs when Mrs. Brooke at Rugby received a message from her son written only to be despatched in the event of his death. Eddie Marsh also received one, and with it arrived Browne's account of the last days and burial. Soon after leaving Malta, in the second week of March, several of the officers aboard the *Grantully Castle* had written to the same purpose. The note to Marsh which now came to hand (May 19) with the package of papers done up by Browne was dated March 9.

MY DEAR,

This is very odd. But I suppose I must imagine my non-existence, and make a few arrangements.

You are to be my literary executor. But I'd like mother to have my MSS till she dies—the actual paper and ink, I mean,—then you —save one or two you might let Alfred and Katharine Cox have, if they care.

If you want to go through my papers, Dudley Ward'll give you a hand. But you won't find much there. There may be some odd stuff at Grantchester.

You must decide everything about publication. Don't print much bad stuff.

Give my love to the *New Numbers* folk, and Violet and Masefield and a few who'd like it. I've tried to arrange that some money should go to Wilfrid and Lascelles and de la Mare (John is childless) to help them write good stuff, instead of me.

There's nothing much to say. You'll be able to help the Ranee with one or two arrangements.

You've been very good to me. I wish I'd written more. I've been such a failure.

Best love and goodbye.   RUPERT

Get Cathleen anything she wants.

Fortunately the bequests to the three poets (which were to make such a difference to their lives) were duplicated in the farewell note to Rugby, but the references to Marsh's functions as literary executor, and the exact distinction between his responsibility and Mrs. Brooke's, showed just enough discrepancy to cause trouble. On May 21 Mrs. Brooke interpreted her instructions as to the literary remains quite clearly. 'He wishes you to look after the publication or be literary executor, to decide which of his writings, including, if necessary, letters, are to be included. Rupert asks that you will consult me in the matter.' All went smoothly enough at first. On the 23rd she expressed satisfaction with Marsh's obituary article in the *Meteor*, the Rugby School magazine, and this encouraged him to believe that he enjoyed her confidence in biographical affairs. She sent him a copy of her son's juvenile poem *The Pyramids* and left him in charge of the negotiations with our

Ambassador in Athens for the maintenance of the grave on Skyros.
She had just seen the Admiralty announcement.

> I am very sorry for Winston and for you too; the only blessing is
> that I believe neither of you could have gone on at the present high
> pitch, but he has been treated in a most ungrateful manner. At the
> beginning of the war he was a public hero, the Saviour of England
> etc., everyone has his faults and perhaps his Successor will have too.

To which he replied, 'It is tragic! and the only ray of light is
that I expect I shall have more time now to work at the Edition,[1]
and shan't have to sit up till 3 o'clock if I am to do anything at it!'
Two days before, Dudley Ward had gone to Grantchester again
and instructed the housekeeper to send all the printed books to
Gray's Inn. 'It is important for me, I think,' Marsh explained, 'to
see what books he had and if there are any literary notes in them,
as I do so want to steep myself in all that kind of knowledge about
him before I edit his prose works and write anything about him.'
Mrs. Brooke saw no objection to this, 'as you ought to look over
them for the literary work you are thinking about; I don't know
definitely what you contemplate, but I dare say we shall talk it
over some day'. He was of course contemplating the short Memoir
for publication in the autumn. There was no need to bother Mrs.
Brooke with it as yet. She had already consulted two lawyers as
to the validity in law of her son's last letter and had been told that
it was a private communication of no legal substance. Her official
letter of May 8 was still valid. It was up to her to interpret her
son's wishes as best she could. She was particularly anxious to
protect Alfred's interests, and began to complain that Marsh was
trying to rush her into decisions. He was buying the copyright of
the last photographs so as to reserve their exclusive use for the
forthcoming editions of the poems. This riled her, though she let it
pass for the present, and Marsh went on with the negotiations,
misunderstanding the grounds for her objections. She did not regard
it as editorial foresight. To her it was the purchase, without
consultation, of something which should belong to no one but
herself. 'I feel as if you and I had been doing something rather like
fighting over these matters, but this mustn't be,' she wrote agreeably on May 28, 'our interests are exactly the same.' Her letter of
May 31 must have dispelled any anxiety from Marsh's thoughts.

[1] *1914 and Other Poems.*

'I shall be only too glad for you to take the whole thing off my hands. . . . I do know that people often get more kicks than halfpence in return for this trouble. . . . I will sign anything on earth you like.' Marsh was now anxious to give his friend Frank Sidgwick confirmation that he was legally entitled to handle the poet's affairs. This was necessary since throughout May he had been editing *1914 and Other Poems*, which was due to come out in three weeks' time.

At the end of May he claimed the first reward of his regular allowance to Mark Gertler. He had carefully watched his health, sent him to an optician, and successfully combated the deleterious effects of what Gertler called 'excessive tea and smoke'. His *Daffodils* was an important acquisition to the collection, and after Marsh had carried it away from the studio the artist wrote him a letter.

I must tell you that I feel that what you are doing for me is *far* more valuable to me than anybody else has ever done. The only thing is that you shall have to have patience with my work. Although I get such little done, you must always know that I am working *extremely* hard and that I never stop working. It being the only thing I have to care for now. You see I am terribly secretive about my work, and I cannot leave a picture unless I feel that I have got it as near to my conception as possible. With your present help I am able to carry this out. . . . In painting nothing can be hurried. . . . There is just one more thing I want to say, and that is, that if you find that you are hard up or that you don't feel inclined to continue your help during the war you must *immediately* tell me, I mean supposing my work disappoints you or you get hard up or supposing the war lasts too long!

Marsh replied on May 26.

Of course I can't expect to like everything you do equally—I know your work is very original, and it is natural that I should want time to take in anything that is very new. Sometimes I take to your things at once and am fascinated and enchanted, as I was by the daffodils—but that can't happen every time, and the only thing I ask is that you should not be hurt or depressed if I don't rise to everything immediately as I did to that! Another thing is that my great sorrow has so completely absorbed all my power of feeling for the present that I really have nothing left over, even for the greatest masterpiece. . . . . All I want is that you should go ahead on your own lines, and that I should be able to help you to make things easier for you.

Most of the Georgian artists were by now engulfed in the war, though Stanley Spencer was still at work. He had written in early April, 'Something has gone out of me, something I had two years ago that I shall never have again', but he gave news of the first of his Resurrection pictures. 'The picture of good and bad people coming out of graves is not quite done.' Among the poets Graves had joined the Royal Welch Fusiliers and his first letter from the Front (May 22) arrived at the height of the political crisis.

My Father (dear old man!) said that this was a fitting end for Rupert killed by the arrows of jealous Musagetes in his own Greek islands; but fine words won't help. . . . I feel exactly like a man who has watched the 'movies' for a long evening and then suddenly finds himself thrown on the screen in the middle of scalp-hunting Sioux and runaway motorcars; and rather surprised that I am not at all frightened. . . . You may disbelieve the following, but I swear to you, Eddie, it's a true bill, that a violent artillery duel going on above my dug-out two nights ago simply failed to wake me at all . . . but when this had ceased I was wakened by a very persistent lark which hung for some minutes over my platoon trench swearing at the Germans. . . . I know it is very rude and inconsiderate of me, inflicting my verses on you, but last January you told me to bring my technique up to date and try to do a bit better than what I showed you so I send a thing I wrote at Wrexham with your advice still ringing in my ears . . .

The work he enclosed was to become part of *Over the Brazier*, his first publication, issued by the Poetry Bookshop in 1916. Rosenberg, back from South Africa, turned up at the Admiralty with a parcel of drawings. He was feeling hard up, and was quite unaware that he had walked into the arena of a national crisis.

I am very sorry to have had to disturb you at such a time with pictures. But when one's only choice is between horrible things you choose the least horrible. First I think of enlisting and trying to get my head blown off, then of getting manual labour to do—anything —but it seems I'm not fit for anything. Then I took these things to you. You would forgive me if you knew how wretched I was. I am sorry I can give you no more comfort in your own trial . . . . Thank you for your cheque, it will do for paints . . .

'Forgive my weak and selfish letter,' he wrote next day '. . . but one gets so bewildered in this terrible struggle.' Within a few weeks he enlisted in the Suffolk Regiment and confided in Marsh that fearing his mother's distress he had left home without any-one knowing where he was going. Before long he was in hospital, having tripped and cut his hands as he ran past his Colonel. 'If you could send me some novel or chocolates you would make me very happy.' After rejoining his unit in Bury St. Edmunds he wrote: 'My feet now are the trouble. Do you know what private's military boots are? . . . Could you send me a pound to buy boots with and to get to London for Xmas. . . . You can have the pick of any drawing I do after this. . . .' He enclosed the manu-script of his play *Moses* and added, after an account of his cook-house fatigues, 'All this must seem to you like a blur on the window, or hearing sounds without listening while you are think-ing.' One after another the Georgian artists were joining up. It was at the end of May that Gibson wrote to say the elms around his cottage, The Old Nailshop, and at Ryton Dymock near by, where Abercrombie lived, were being hewn down. He considered it symbolic. Even the Georgian countryside was being stripped to furnish a war. An age was coming to an end.

It was now the beginning of June and Browne was at sea on his way back to Gallipoli. He had read of the change of Govern-ment. 'I feel quite certain that Winston and his wife (sweet almond-eyed gazelle) would never consent to face life without you.' On June 4 Marsh wrote to him. 'I gather there is to be a great battle tomorrow. I won't say any more about my anxiety for you. I envy believers who can pray for people.'

I can't remember if I've written to you since our awful catastrophe —Winston's I mean, which is in white satin, and mine in white cotton—(you remember—'Enter Tilburina stark mad in white satin, and her confidante stark mad in white cotton). I hope the R.N.D. mind. . . . I have hardly realized it all yet—partly I suppose because my other grief is so much more final and so much more serious. But it really is awful, Denis, and so cruelly senseless and meaningless. No one pretends that it is because he was running the show badly. . . . The 'Duchy' is of course a farce so far as work is concerned—the last two days he has been busy with the speech he is going to make at Dundee tonight. After that I really don't know how he will occupy himself, he has been so entirely absorbed in work for the last four years that unlike Mrs. Elton he has no resources in himself. He puts a very good face on it, as one would expect, but oh dear oh dear, it is a dreadful blow. And you can imagine how I hate not having a war job. I feel it's my clear duty to stick to him—otherwise I should try and go out to Clive [Carey] and help him to scrub floors or something, anywhere where I could take my chance with other people—it's really almost unbearable to be a' gentleman of England at home at ease and in safety when the real gentlemen of England are doing the exact opposite.

He reminded him that tomorrow would be the anniversary of their going to Paddington to meet Brooke on his return from America. 'Forgive me,' he ended, 'I've lost all my bearings.'

The battle that Marsh was dreading occurred on the very day he wrote his letter. Browne was on the left of the line of 250 men advancing on a front of 200 yards. The objective was the farther of two enemy trenches about 350 yards ahead. Browne jumped into the first trench, bayoneted a Turk, and was almost instantly shot in the left shoulder; turning to one side he bayoneted a second Turk as another bullet drove the iron buckle of his belt into his body. As a petty officer bound up his wounds he fainted. On regaining consciousness he offered the man his watch and some money. They were refused, but the man accepted his pocket-book, then had to retreat in haste. The ground was at once retaken by the enemy, and not until almost a week later was Browne reported 'wounded and missing'. His body was never recovered. But there was soon to be more news of him. His last letter to Gray's Inn was on its way.

On the day after the assault Marsh travelled to Leamington to meet Browne's mother and sisters for the first time. He sat at an open window overlooking the garden. 'I simply must write to you on this note-paper,' he began. 'I'm writing in your own bedroom—the first thing I noticed was a photograph of Brahms, which gave me a momentary triumph till calm Reason pointed out that no doubt it's a relic of the same period at which you bought the head by Greuze.' The Spirit of Irony must have looked on with rare satisfaction while Marsh spent the week-end meeting relations, looking through the family album, and exchanging happy reminiscences of Denis Browne who was already dead.

Of course all the pleasure of this Sunday here has been shadowed by the knowledge that you have been fighting—and *I* know, what I didn't tell them, that the Naval Division had been in a tight place on Friday. . . . Your Mother is marvellously brave and it's my nature to hope for the best—but oh Denis it's an awful time for those who love you.

P.S. Your Mother is firmly convinced that I have had a 'good influence' on you and persisted in this in spite of all I could say! Never mind.

The news was received on the 8th, coinciding with a letter from Henry James, who had been sent an advance copy of *1914 and Other Poems*. 'His [Brooke's] place,' wrote James, 'is now very high and very safe—even though one walks round and round it with the aching soreness of having to take the monument for the man. . . . And he isn't tragic now—he has only stopped. It's we who are tragic—you and his mother especially . . . for we can't stop, and I wish we could!' But Marsh could think of nothing but this new and almost intolerable grief. He at once confided in Henry James.

There is no reason why I should bring my sorrows to you thus, but I must tell you to explain why today I have no heart to think or write even about the poems. I shall return again and again to your letter. Last night I copied it for Rupert's mother, who will love it tho' she will not understand it.

James replied asking his young friend to spend an evening with him alone. 'I unspeakably feel with you and for you. . . . I long to talk to you.'† As the days went by and no further news came in, Marsh realized that he would never see Browne again. On June 12 he spent a long evening with Henry James at Carlyle Mansions, and told him the whole story of the Georgian enterprise which has filled these last few chapters. A powerful bond of sympathy was drawing them closer together. To Marsh it was as if for the first time he were confiding in a father who loved and understood him.

During that long session in Chelsea Marsh read aloud Browne's account of Brooke's last hours. Next morning Henry James wrote to say he had been grieving for the young musician, 'the reading by you of whose letter last night, under the pang of *his* extinction, the ghost telling of the ghost, moved me more than I could find words for. He brothered you in it as he had brothered Rupert— and I could almost feel that he practically a little brothered poor old *me*, for which I do thank his spirit!' At the same time Marsh was writing to say he had just received a letter from Browne dated June 1.

> It is wonderful how understandingly you enter into my sorrow for a man whom you have never seen, and make it your own. The morning after I had been with you I got a long letter from Denis, written on the Transport that took him to his death—the last I shall get I suppose. By some compunction of the gods he had been inspired to say nice things about me—which was unusual, it was his custom to laugh at me.

He ended by quoting the passage in which Browne described his feelings on passing within sight of the island of Skyros. With those words Marsh was to conclude his Memoir of Brooke.[1] Henry James in his acknowledgement referred to that paragraph of noble prose 'which makes me almost sick, or almost ready to howl, with its unspeakable intensity of pathos'.

> Under what piled-up weight of tragedy do we not live, with dead exquisite Rupert exquisitely commemorated to you by D.B., dead almost in the act of commemoration, and the beauty of the setting of the whole thing so strangely mixed up with the misery! Well can I see you blinded by your tears. . . . I thank my strange stars that I can't *not* feel these things. . . . But it is all beyond words, all ache within ache—and all making me, dearest Eddie, quite infinitely yours.†

On the same date as Marsh's letter to James Mr. Churchill decided to quit his temporary apartment in Admiralty House and move to Arlington Street. When Marsh walked out of Admiralty House for the last time there came to an end the most eventful period of his official career.

iii

For the next five months of this catastrophic year there were two main elements in his life, the gradual deterioration of his relationship with Mrs. Brooke and the consolation of a growing intimacy with Henry James. It is impossible to follow the story of his dealings with Mrs. Brooke without being infected to

---

[1] 'Coming from Alexandria yesterday, we passed Rupert's island at sunset. The sea and sky in the East were grey and misty; but it stood out in the West, black and immense, with a crimson glowing halo round it. Every colour had come into the sea and sky to do him honour; and it seemed that the island must ever be shining with his glory that we buried there.'

some extent with the vexation which they caused each other. It would be so much easier for the chronicler if they could be shown in frank and open opposition, but they were not. Each clung to what was regarded as a 'sacred trust'. Barely a day went by without a letter from Rugby. Alfred had captured three prisoners. 'He's quite sure Rupert would have hated it. I think he's right.' She had consulted a lawyer who said E. J. Dent's article was a breach of copyright. 'I should love to frighten him, but you needn't be afraid, I shan't. . . . I should hope no one else would need to be warned.' She was annoyed that eight packing-cases of books from the Old Vicarage had not yet arrived, and had to be reminded that she had previously agreed that Marsh should see them first. Early in June she got her advance copy of *1914 and Other Poems* and was 'much distressed' to see that the poem *Mary and Gabriel* had been reprinted from the *Poetry Review*. It had already wounded the susceptibilities of some of her friends owing to its attitude to the sacred theme. She had been shown the proofs, she admitted, but somehow she had overlooked this piece. Then came the first hint that she was going to go back on her past willingness to leave all literary problems in Marsh's hands. 'I think in joining you and me in this business Rupert meant me to choose both in poems and letters.' In her footnote she exclaimed, 'I heard of you in the *Westminster Gazette* office searching for Rupert's anonymous contributions!!' as if she had caught Eddie Marsh trespassing. However, next day she was making suggestions to further the research, but 'I still regret *Mary and Gabriel*. I can't be too proud to mind. Just now I am very thin-skinned about any criticisms of him. . . . I greatly fear for a change from the whole-hearted praise I have heard of him lately. It wouldn't matter if he were here to defend himself. . . . I agree with E. Gosse in dreading the appearance of R.'s poems.' But Gosse's 'dread' was of a different order from Mrs. Brooke's. He feared that the appearance of the work as a whole might induce some people to modify their admiration of the war sonnets. The disillusion *she* feared was not of a literary kind. The sonnets were good in her view because they revealed a good state of mind. Certain other of the poems were less happy because they revealed a side of their author's character which was not in keeping with her idea of civic virtue. She regarded the composition of a poem as a form of social behaviour to be approved or censured by the austere standards of Dr. Arnold.

For her there could be no such thing as literary merit outside this code of values. There was no hope of her ever seeing eye to eye with Marsh when the issue was one of literature or ethics. Meanwhile she was being elevated into a sublime region of sorrow where no ordinary mortal could converse with her on equal terms.

A week later (June 18) her letter was no more than three sentences. 'Alfred is killed. I don't see how I can live. Tell everyone.' He had been hit on the 14th at Vermelles when acting as Reserve Machine-gun Officer. Taking cover in a shell-hole, he had dropped asleep when the mortar bomb which left his companion quite untouched killed him outright. Henry James was so appalled that for three days he refrained from putting pen to paper.

> I have literally been afraid to write to you since reading of the new bolt that has fallen on that Mater Dolorosa of whom we have talked, and that makes me simply and pusillanimously wash my face with horror. Even the sense that she drank deep of the cup weeks ago, so much so that she may perhaps taste less this new bitterness, doesn't make the thought of her bearable or one's compassion anything but woe. I feel that it all comes on *you*—as if you hadn't enough to deal with. . . . I am only the more tenderly yours.†

'I nearly wrote to you about that too,' Marsh replied, 'but I got almost ashamed of my accumulated calamities.'

> I now hear from Rupert's godfather, the fine old scholar Robert Whitelaw, that her courage has reasserted itself and that she has renewed her brave fight for—what? she has nothing to fight for, except her dignity under the bludgeon—but I am proud to think that Rupert's mother will not lose that. I feel so powerless to help her. . . . Next Sunday I go to Denis's mother—she is of a far softer temper and more accessible to sympathy. And she believes in meeting her boy in the next world as she believes in the sun rising tomorrow.

Having despatched this he received a summons to go at once to Cambridge, where his father, aged seventy-five, was ill with pneumonia. On the following day the Master of Downing died and Marsh's first thought was to spare Henry James the burden of yet further commiseration. 'This time it is really for once to ask you *not* to grieve for me. . . . We were very good, but not very close, friends. . . . After those deaths of the "fair and living" youth which have broken my heart, this ending in the fulness of time, of a prosperous and useful life, seems merely serene and fitting.' James' further reflections on the loss of Alfred were already in the post.

> This is just to acknowledge what you so responsively write me and what so unspeakably lacerates me! One's soreness of soul for that poor tortured woman is beyond all speech—and I feel the vision of her as a nightmare within the nightmare. I am also more moved than I can say by the courage with which you face going to see her. I think of you as an absolute ministering angel.†

Of the news from Cambridge James wrote: 'You are finding already, probably, that it has made you, at a kind of jump, feel older. . . . I desire soon to put my hand on you again, and am entirely yours.'† For these last few months of his life Henry James himself was to fill the parental place.

Early in July Shaw-Stewart's and Kelly's accounts of the loss of Denis Browne reached Gray's Inn. In the very act of conveying his sympathy Shaw-Stewart inadvertently occasioned his friend what was almost the bitterest pang of all. There was one thought —one of many sombre reflections—that Marsh had never let stay in his conscious mind for more than a moment. So far he had always managed to suppress it, but here it was at last in black and white. 'I feel very much for you in this additional shock,' wrote the young man in all innocence. 'You will feel you have put your friends into the Hood to be killed—but indeed this is a bloody campaign. . . . That fourth of June was a fearful day—I don't suppose I ought to write it, but there is very little of us left, only 4 now.' The notion that but for him all those brilliant young men would be alive today was intolerable. In an agony of doubt he put the whole matter candidly to Browne's mother, and at the same time confided in Cynthia Asquith.

> I think Nemesis must suddenly have noticed that I was 42 and had never had anything very bad happen to me—and decided to down me once for all. . . . It's a melancholy thing for someone who has always lived very much in the present, as I have, to realize that I've had the best of life and that the old lighthearted time has gone for always.

He had barely finished this, lamenting 'my young, splendid friends who should have had all life before them and could have used it greatly,' when Mrs. Browne wrote from Leamington. She assured him that she was conscious only of the happiness which he must have brought into the lives of Denis and his companions, and she adapted to her purpose Hamlet's affirmation of the divinity that 'shapes our ends', saying there was no need to look beyond that primary and divine ordinance in search of second causes. So far from reproaching him, she found it in her heart to thank him for being the means of her son's enlistment in the R.N.D.; and as for Marsh's tormenting suspicion that perhaps she might not wish to set eyes on him or even hear from him again, he must forbid any such thought to enter his head. His recent letter had revealed a perceptive and most unusual understanding of the relationship between mothers and sons, and he must never cease to look on her as his devoted friend.

He had awaited her answer with more desperate longing than any other communication of his life, and the relief, with its revelation of Christian charity, was almost overwhelming.

The loss of her last surviving son only interrupted Mrs. Brooke's activities for ten days or so. With extraordinary courage and pertinacity she continued to keep in touch with the endless little matters connected with Rupert which Marsh was trying to cope with on his own in London. Three days after the death of Howard Marsh her letter contained the first touch of undisguised asperity. Marsh had now paid for the copyright of the latest photographs. Mrs. Brooke regarded this as presumption, and before he had a chance to say that he would be only too happy for her to pay him back if she wished, and that he had only gone ahead with negotiations to save her the nuisance, she wrote insisting firmly on settling the account. 'It is my right and privilege as Rupert's mother.' Then on July 17 the clothes and papers from Gallipoli arrived at Raymond Buildings and he took them down, unopened, to Rugby. What followed was recorded for Henry James in the small hours on the Monday morning.

I brought with me all that came from the Dardanelles, and put them in a room at the top of the house, rather hoping that she would put off seeing them till I had gone. Last night and today passed well— she was marvellously collected and composed and cheerful, and talked much, both of the two boys and of other things and people, with a calm and interest which made me think that she had become mistress of her agony.

But when she said goodnight she asked me to come up with her and show her the things, and when we got upstairs and I opened the boxes she broke down—I have never seen such suffering. It was very terrible, as of course there was *nothing* I could say or do—after a while I persuaded her that she had better leave everything as it was, and let me come back again in a few weeks . . . it is dreadful to leave her in such misery.

Henry James was once more ready with his compassion.

How endlessly, how heroically, you are bearing the brunt—and how no inch of the dreadful pressure of the whole misery seems to be spared you. Beautiful and dismal your generous last letter from Rugby—sinister name now! . . . The vision of that lacerated mother is almost to me as the imagination of a physically tortured and smashed state going on before one's eyes. Before *your* eyes it *has* gone on, and it's you who have paid for all of us. You'll continue to pay.†

Mrs. Brooke herself was not ungrateful 'all the more because you said so little; that was because you had the strength of a man and could keep your feelings under. . . . You must indeed have loved R. very much to do so much for him.'

Marsh went straight from Rugby to Wilfrid Gibson's cottage, The Old Nailshop, within a short walk of the Abercrombies at Ryton. He was given the attic room away from the household noises, and for eight days he worked solidly on the Memoir of Brooke, which he finished at 2 A.M. on July 27. Next day he congratulated Henry James on the announcement that he had become a British citizen, addressing him as 'Dear Master and beloved friend. . . . First I must tell you of the thrill of joy with which I read this morning's announcement. It means much to me, and I am sure to countless others, that you should at this moment so beautifully "come over and help us".' He went on to suggest that instead of writing something for the Memoir, Henry James might prefer to supply a Preface to a collection of Brooke's articles from abroad which Marsh had begun to prepare for publication. His other enterprise was going well. 'I have just roughed out the draft of the Memoir, and I think I may say without vanity that it will be delightful reading.' It consisted chiefly of Brooke's letters, he said, 'not much more than strung together by my clumsy parentheses. . . . It still has dragons in its path—for I *cannot* publish anything to which I might fail to win Mrs. Brooke.' A note from her had come this morning. Mr. Whitelaw had conceived the idea of a memorial medallion in Rugby Chapel. She had misgivings about the project. 'I am so *very* anxious for it to succeed that I don't want it to start wrong. . . . The only objection that occurs to me is that the portrait of R.B., if it is at all like him, will make Matthew Arnold and Clough look even older and uglier than they do at present.' A more serious matter was her objection to an article in the *Academy* which reprinted with approval Brooke's criticisms of his father's funeral, first published by Dent in the *Cambridge Review*. 'I hope Dent will see the mischief he has set going.' This smouldering condition of mind boded no good for the Memoir.

Marsh planned to visit her the following week-end. His script was not typed in time for him to bring it with him, so he sent it on the Monday; but before leaving Bilton Road in the early hours, Mrs. Brooke being still asleep, he placed on the dining-room table a letter to her which he had written the night before. 'I am very anxious that you should *in the main* like the way I've written about Rupert,' he began, and went on to mention certain things he wanted her to bear in mind while she read it. 'What I've tried to do, tho' goodness knows I must have fallen short, is to draw him as I see him. . . . And you know I'd far rather shoot myself than bring a shadow of shame on his memory. So I *mean* right, anyhow.' He didn't anticipate any damaging criticism, 'especially if the edition is published fairly soon before the glamour has had time to wear off and before the inevitable jealousies have begun'.

> But we must remember that *if* anyone wants to criticize, there is no way of preventing them. If any little faults or absurdities are admitted, they can criticize those; if none, they would say I was a slavish admirer making my hero into a prig or a plaster saint. . . . R. would have *wanted* the truth told about him, and had no wish to be disguised or decorated into anything but what he was.

His next point was that a Memoir should be addressed to the young, rather than to an older generation—'so I think it would be a pity to leave out things which make him vivid and human because of the fear that aunts or schoolmasters might shake their heads'. Next he hoped she wouldn't think he had written in too lighthearted a vein, and if in future he didn't at once accept an objection of hers she mustn't 'think I do it for the sake of argument and opposition! I *did* think you were a little hard on me once or twice today. I'm sure you know really that I have literally two objects in what I've written (1) to do justice and honour to Rupert and (2) to write what you would approve.' He then tried to show that he had not neglected what was perhaps her strongest prejudice of all. 'I was forgetting to say that I've made scarcely any reference to love affairs. I've just hinted, in guarded language, at the fact that one was part cause of his illness in 1911 (this is so obvious from his poems that I think it would be absurd to pass it over altogether). . . .' In the letters to Cathleen Nesbitt he had left out 'practically everything that couldn't be written to a man friend' and had referred to her as X. 'I don't think I've left in any clue that would show the general public who she is.' To someone like Mrs. Brooke this awareness of all the things she *might* object to could only reveal a guilty conscience. As if he hadn't done himself enough harm already he concluded in a vein that was no more tactful than the rest.

> Remember that my work on this has been very near to my heart, and don't think severely of anything that may not please you in it. I feel very diffident about it, and of course it's quite impossible for one person to do anything that another person will think exactly right. I'm more than sorry *now* that I didn't bring it to show you in its untidy form, but I didn't realize that you would wish me to be here when you read it, and my only idea was to let you have it in a presentable shape.

The whole thing might have been calculated to cause trouble. Her reply did nothing to put Marsh on his guard. He had indeed lost his bearings. 'The letter I found when you had gone has certainly frightened me,' she wrote; 'it is evident that you feel pretty sure that I shan't like the Memoir.' If Rupert wanted the truth told, she argued, that didn't necessarily mean such 'truth' as might hurt her. She thought there was no need for a memoir at all. She had told many neighbours that it was her son's wish that she should share the responsibility of his posthumous publications, and now it was her *own* criticism of Marsh's work, not that of the professional critics, that she feared. 'I am sorry if you thought me hard on you, but remember you are the person who has made me fear the Memoir.' Marsh replied: 'You frightened me, and now I've frightened you! . . . my letter was only *meant* to reassure you. I'm afraid it was a sad failure.' He was writing on Brooke's birthday. 'I know what a sad day this is for you. and I shall think much of you.' On the same day he sent off the typescript and enclosed a second letter in which he was so unwise as to compare the relevant passages in Brooke's last messages to his mother and himself, and while acknowledging the duty laid upon him in the phrase 'of course he will consult you and you will tell him what you want' he drew the conclusion that this 'makes it clear that he wished the *responsibility* to be mine'. Although his inference was obviously correct, and only proper in any normal instance of a literary executor, this was hardly the moment to point out that anyone other than Mrs. Brooke herself was entitled to the last word.

The result was that next day, before she had read a word of the manuscript, she was feeling thoroughly impatient and wrote of it in downright repudiation. Any memoir when the country was suffering so fearfully seemed to her, 'to say the least of it, bad taste. . . . I say this as Rupert's mother who hates the idea of her son's name being almost derided.' The *entire* responsibility would be hers. The work should be undertaken by several hands. Anyway, what had already appeared in the newspapers was quite enough. In the light of this Marsh must be prepared for her refusal to allow any of her son's letters to be quoted and, if need be, she would not hesitate to write to Mr. Sidgwick, the publisher, informing him that what remained of narrative or comment would be issued without her consent. In this benevolent spirit she sat down at last to read the Memoir.

Meanwhile Marsh heard from Henry James. Of his new nationality James observed, 'Though it didn't seem that I *could* come much nearer to you in general community of feeling, I take comfort in having taken whatever formal step that remained',† and he generously undertook the work that had been proposed to him. Another letter by that same post was less welcome. Mrs. Brooke's reaction was a blunt refusal. The Memoir must be postponed for at least a year and remodelled in the meantime. 'It doesn't represent Rupert as he really was at all. It is too evidently written by someone who knew him for a comparatively short time and even for that time quite a small part of him.' No one would believe from this account 'that he was a happy natural schoolboy full of life and fun and influencing others for good'. She was especially annoyed that Dent's views had been treated with respect. '. . . I couldn't possibly admit the letters referring to schoolmasters as his do. Remember my husband, his father, was a schoolmaster.' It now appeared that Marsh had given permission for a letter to be quoted in the school magazine 'for which you asked no permission from me nor will you ever get it. . . . I know quite well that by writing like this I risk losing your friendship and hurting you considerably, but I can't help it.' She returned the manuscript. It was at once passed on to Henry James.

Unfortunately Marsh did not let the matter rest. He found this communication written 'more in the spirit of a friend than the one that came yesterday; though I don't think you need have said that I didn't know Rupert well.' He gave assurance that he would publish nothing without her consent, then proceeded to counter her objections one by one, urging her to consult Whitelaw and Frances Cornford, fair-minded representatives of the older and younger generations, and giving three reasons for his persisting in the matter. There were many people who wanted, and deserved, to know what Brooke was like. 'I am personally anxious that his fame should be *immediately* established and therefore I want to take advantage of the special interest that is now felt in him before it dies away.' And thirdly, he wanted to correct certain wrong impressions which he knew to be current. 'I hope you will remember that Rupert trusted me, and that trust is sacred to me.'

She felt somewhat mollified on hearing later that the British Museum had accepted the holograph of the sonnet 'If I should die', but she soon returned to the charge. 'I really don't think we ought to think that Rupert's fame rests on us bringing out a Memoir, people will be bored by it. . . . I feel sure it will not be widely circulated.' Whitelaw was a schoolmaster and would be offended by parts of the text, so he must not see it or be consulted. Moreover, many people at Rugby believed that Brooke as a boy 'was either posing or somewhat "decadent" and naturally masters dread that sort of idea spreading'. She then asked for this correspondence to stop 'after your next letter'. Marsh's answer was very brief and subdued. For the first time Mrs. Brooke was sufficiently touched to catch at least a glimpse of his point of view.

During these weeks he was often at Godalming sitting for his portrait to Mr. Churchill, who had begun practising the art of painting with characteristic zeal and rapidly increasing skill. About this time Marsh must have chosen his moment to pass on a message from Freyberg on Gallipoli . . . 'tell him that we feel he is our father and we will always look to him for help as we always have'. It so happened that Mr. Churchill was expecting his wife home any minute when Frances Cornford (wanting a last-minute talk before her visit to Rugby) rang the bell and, the door being suddenly flung open, found herself gathered into the embraces of the Chancellor. 'Eddie, there's a lady to see you!' called a disgruntled voice from the door.

Frances Cornford and her small daughter Helena went on to stay at Bilton Road. At the first opportunity Mrs. Cornford did what she could to represent Marsh's attitude. 'Eddie always seems to be thinking of Rupert's *fame* and I can't stand it,' was Mrs. Brooke's retort, but later that day she softened under the influence of her guest. She described how Marsh helped her when she had at last steeled herself to open Rupert's box which had come back from the Dardanelles. 'There were all his books,' she said, 'his clothes, and a lock of his hair. It was like seeing Rupert's body stretched out dead on the floor. I must say Eddie was good to me then. If he'd been my own son, he couldn't have been more good to me.' In the course of time she was to develop a less charitable view of this episode, but for the present, on August 11, she did her best to put things right. She withdrew her wounding remarks. 'You and I who knew very little of each other before Rupert's death were suddenly placed in somewhat intimate relations towards each other as regards his affairs; perhaps both of us have been more or less used to having our own way. . . . You must write and say that you forgive me and then we will dismiss the Memoir.'

The first round of this distressing conflict had come to an end, with courtesies exchanged and not one inch of ground ceded on either side. Although Marsh was accepting the deadlock, he had no intention of abandoning the Memoir, and at no juncture was he going to modify his standards of what he thought fit. Mrs. Brooke, for her part, would sit in her drawing-room at Bilton Road, lying back in her chair, her feet drawn together and thrust straight out, her hands clasped tightly on her long black dress, her lips set firm, her face strongly resembling the poet's though crisscrossed with numberless little lines and furrows. On either side of her chair stood two easels, each holding an almost life-size enlargement of one of her soldier sons, as with tireless watchfulness and flashes of bitter humour she fostered her pride as Rupert's mother in the eyes of local society. Her utterance was loud and rapid, and consisted of whatever came first into her head. For years she had resented with a kind of inverted snobbery the distinguished and cosmopolitan people who had made so much of her son, presuming to direct his life as if he were more their property than hers. Marsh might go on doing the so-called 'right thing' by her till kingdom come but in her eyes he would still be in the wrong. Rupert would be hers dead if not alive, and he would be presented to the world by the standards of the world which had produced him, or not at all.

It was not long before there arrived at Gray's Inn the anxiously awaited opinions of Henry James.

> I found the Memoir and all its contents in the highest degree interesting and vivid and for the most part very *right*, in the degree in which your materials impose rightness. But to express the matter thus crudely, hastily and provisionally, the perusal of it all has had a signal effect—and a rather unexpected one—that of making me understand better poor Mrs. Brooke's actual wincings and waverings. It's an account of her son which must make in her the impression of taking him totally away from her and breaking her links with him, taking him altogether out of her world of association of thought and credibility, the moral of which is that you must give her time *to get used* to that. She *will*, probably, but there are meanwhile too many notes of paradox and 'sophistication' that must simply bewilder and scare her. Those notes probably played no part in *their* intercourse (there were others for mother and son). Coming at her in the brilliant onset of your pages all at once they make her repudiate connection with them. Some graceful bridge could be constructed with art—though I can't tell you how to construct it. It's a rather curious but to *me* comprehensible case—but then I'm a battered old novelist and it's my business to comprehend. This isn't *half* all, dearest Eddie, and we must talk as soon as I am fitter. The great thing to my mind is that waiting a while does seem indicated.†

By this time Marsh was able to tell him of a lull in the storm 'though I'm afraid our relations are altered . . . and my nerves haven't quite recovered tone from the buffeting she gave me!'

> Your letter has already contributed much in the ¼ hour since I read it to put me in sympathy with her—and will do more as it sinks in. There is great virtue in being a 'battered old novelist whose business

it is to comprehend'. Not many men have such a father-confessor as you are to me! . . . . I have a vague dread—not from anything you *say*—that I have ever so slightly disappointed *you* about Rupert. If so, my thing must be like Alice's recitation 'wrong from beginning to end'. . . . You wouldn't need the 'correction' which I sometimes almost thought of putting in, if it wouldn't have been so boring, for the sake of the un-understanding:—'Of course he didn't *mean* that.' But we must talk of all this.

So they met and talked and for a while Eddie Marsh was prevailed upon to turn his thoughts to other things.

Harold Monro succeeded in persuading him to resuscitate the *Georgian Poetry* volume which was abandoned a year before, and by the early autumn an effort was being made to bring the selection up to date while Monro announced the forthcoming book in his publications. 'A woman in the shop,' he wrote, 'asked if the same poets were going to be "incarcerated"—she looked unhappy after she'd said it.' He enclosed some of his own work and expressed some misgiving because 'you told me you found it difficult to like a man whose poetry you didn't like'. The envelope enclosed *Overheard on a Saltmarsh*, so he was promptly reassured. Five of the previous contributors (Chesterton, Sturge Moore, Ross, Sargant, Trevelyan) were dropped on grounds of seniority, and two new names first appeared on the list, Hodgson, and Francis Ledwidge who had been recommended by Lord Dunsany. Concerning the latter, a young Irishman, Marsh naturally consulted James Stephens, who answered by return:

He is only a beginner and must digest his ancestors before we know what he really is like. Meanwhile he has a true singing faculty, and his promise is, I think, greater than that of any young poet now writing. I do not believe, however, that he will ratify this promise by any almighty performance. I don't believe that his thought will equal his faculty for utterance. . . . A man is a mind, and so is a poet, and they are man and poet only to the extent of that. This is the croaking of the crow. . . . I do not know Ledwidge at all well. . . . He is what we call here 'a lump of a lad' and he was panoplied in all those devices, or disguises, which a countryman puts on when he meets the men of the town. Country people and children are all play actors.

He had been sent the new list of Contents. 'I am glad you are including Hodgson's *Bull* and *Song of Honour*. . . . I think if

Hodgson can stick it he will produce a book at last of which Englishmen may be proud and which Irishmen may envy.'

The script that was eventually sent to Monro began with *King Lear's Wife* and ended with Abercrombie's *The End of the World*. Between these appeared the best poems (excluding *Retrospect*) from the posthumous volume of Brooke which Marsh had brought out in mid-June; *The Bird of Paradise* of Davies; the six best poems from de la Mare's *Peacock Pie*; *The Old Ships, Santorin*, and the serenade from *Hassan*, by Flecker; *The Snare* and *Deirdre* of Stephens; Masefield's *The Wanderer*; and three poems (including *Cruelty and Love*) by D. H. Lawrence. It was a better volume than the first, and it was to sell over thirteen thousand copies. A slight hitch had been caused by de la Mare's reluctance to have *Off the Ground* included in his selection. Marsh badgered him with praise of it. 'I feel sure it's a masterpiece,' he wrote, and won his point, but did not let it rest. After the book came out in December he sent a brief postcard. 'Mrs. Verrall writes about *G.P.* "W. de la M.'s dancing farmers alone are worth the 3*s*. 6*d*." So there!'

With Brooke's *Westminster* Letters as well as the new anthology to edit there was not much time for attention to the painters. But Gertler was the exception. The object of Marsh's especial fostering was at this time in Leeds painting a portrait of Michael Sadler. He could hardly have had a more sympathetic sitter, but by the middle of August, having decided that commissioned work was beyond his capacity, he was beginning to despair.

> Since I have been here I have appreciated even more your help to me. You just let me paint that which I want to paint. But the future looks very black to me because the more I go on the less I can paint that which does not very forcibly move me to paint. It is the *Idea*, the *Idea* that matters to me. It is torture to me now to touch a canvas without a definite Idea or conception. And my ideas are becoming more and more mystical. . . . Ideas for future pictures come to me very often. And these Ideas are so mysterious and wonderful that when they come over me they come in waves. I get so excited and feel so physically weak that I can scarcely stand. It is almost too much to bear.

Marsh did what he could to sustain him.

> Your birth-pains over your pictures are quite torture enough for you —don't worry yourself additionally about how you are to live—so

long as you can manage on what I can do for you and the extras that are bound to come in. Since the war, and still more since my friends died, I don't care to spend money on myself beyond just keeping up my life here. You know I believe you were born to be a great painter, and if that is true it will have been a grand thing in my life to have been able to help you and leave you more or less free to develop yourself unhampered. . . . I should be ashamed of being comparatively well-off, if I couldn't take advantage of it to help my friends who are younger and poorer and cleverer and better than I am.

I'm glad to hear what you say about the way ideas crowd you and turn you inside-out—fertility, if it doesn't water-down intensity, is a fine promising thing in a young artist. You should take courage and not alarm when you find yourself tormented by inspiration. All great artists have a hell of a bad time like that now and then. 'I am glad you say every man of great views is at times tormented as I am,' says Keats in a letter to Haydon that I read this morning.

Since May he had been making the acquaintance of Lance Sieveking, who had been introduced by Paul Nash. Sieveking, who was soon to be a Flight Sub-Lieutenant, R.N., has recorded his impression of Marsh at the Admiralty. 'I saw a dapper man of about forty in an elegant grey suit and grey silk tie. He held himself upright, making quick movements like a bird.' The voice was bird-like too, he observed, and his discourse was pointed by the removal or replacement of his monocle on its black thread. While being shown round the picture-gallery at home Sieveking was amused by his host's manner of leaving sentences in mid-air. '"This little Sickert . . . You like it? . . . I've always thought it rather . . ." And a moment later: "Stanley Spencer. I bought it at the Carfax Gallery. Do you think I was wrong?" And then, letting his monocle fall, "I thought it rather gay and . . ." But the height of eloquent omission was reached when we peeped into Mrs. Elgy's room. This too was completely hung with paintings, but she had hung her dresses over some of them. Eddie pursed his lips in vexation. "I do *wish* . . ." he said.'[1]

To Sieveking Marsh sent an account of his first ride in what was called 'a fast motor'. He was accompanying Mr. Churchill on a visit to Detling, where there was to be a demonstration of bomb-throwing. The chauffeur was a Jehu. 'My appendix came into

[1] *The Eye of the Beholder*, by Lance Sieveking (Hulton Press, 1957).

my throat several times, tho' I preserved an outward calm. His principle is not to make allowance for people being fools, and we met several who were—but all escaped with their lives. . . . If you put "Secretary to Winston Churchill" on my envelopes I shall put "Narrator of Dirty Stories to Commander Sitwell" on yours.'

In September Gosse came back into the picture. A few weeks before he had acknowledged the gift of *1914 and Other Poems*. 'Compare his large virility of tone with the sexless falsetto of Francis Thompson. . . . You will be remembered with Rupert as Severn is with Keats.' He had now received the Memoir while staying at Airlie Castle. He complained that the end was too abrupt. At his suggestion Mr. Churchill's tribute in *The Times* was incorporated. The picture was too one-sided. 'He was vastly more than a local Apollo among undergraduates and flappers.' But a week later there followed the most wholehearted panegyric that Marsh could ever have seen from the pen of a major critic. By unlucky coincidence this wholly unexpected tribute from Gosse was eclipsed by a scrap of paper from Gallipoli which came by the very same post. The petty officer who took Denis Browne's wallet had handed it over to Shaw-Stewart. Inside was a message for Marsh.

I've gone now too; not too badly I hope. I'm luckier than Rupert, because I've fought. But there's no one to bury me as I buried him, so perhaps he's best off in the long run.

I got a little image from a tomb for you in Cairo; will you ask my mother for it? it is with the rest of my things, packed in a cigarette box. Dent is looking after my MS. music.

It ended: 'Goodbye . . . bless you always for all your goodness to me. W.D.B.' After this even the praise of Edmund Gosse must have seemed irrelevant and hollow.

Gosse had read the whole Memoir aloud and had completely changed his mind. All he had said before was cancelled. 'I shall never feel quite the same after this,' he concluded. 'It has made *you* seem so much more precious to me than before; I cannot explain this.' No one must persuade him to change a word. 'Nothing more touching, more lovely, was ever produced.' There was, however, one slight flaw. The sudden change to 'goodness' was unexplained. 'The reader expects that he is going to be "converted" or to be-

come a missionary, or to preach. I know it is merely our wretched
conventional treatment of the word "good".' Marsh tried to
explain.

> Suffering, bodily and spiritual, turned him in on himself, and what
> had been an instinct became a principle. There wasn't room for
> very much outward change—what there was, was in the direction
> of simplicity, seriousness, and above all *gentleness*. .'. . But this grow-
> ing gentleness was counterbalanced by a new burning indignation
> against anything or any person that he thought 'bad'—and I some-
> times thought him a little arbitrary in the selection of his victims.
> There were several of his old 'intellectual' friends whom he came to
> think evil and unwholesome (with exactly how much reason I
> didn't always know) and for whom he came to feel an uncompromis-
> ing hatred.

Mrs. Brooke didn't think the emergence of this Puritan trait
needed to be explained away. To her it was nothing remarkable
in a normal young person, and since Eddie Marsh believed it was
due to a period of 'unhappiness' (the reality of which she would
never admit) the reference to 'goodness', he argued, must remain
obscure, if obscure it was. A cut passage which Gosse urged the
author to restore should remain cut, Marsh insisted, because he
must have something to bargain with. The same applied to the
brief reference to the actual cause of Brooke's last illness which had
left Gosse rather puzzled. Medical details were considered distressing by the next of kin. For Gosse's enlightenment, however, he
filled in the picture a little. 'I have always understood that there
were millions of lethal germs everywhere in the air and in the
earth. . . .'

> It seems to me such a pathos and such irony that these infinitesimal
> fellow creatures, merely doing their duty (*viz.* to keep themselves
> alive in that state of life to which it pleased God to call them) should
> inflict such an incalculable injury on the world. Acting up to their
> lights, they killed a man whose like is not born twice in a hundred
> years.

After this he could not resist passing on Gosse's encomium to
Henry James, who was impelled to rejoice with his young friend
in these 'splendid superlatives. . . . They are more exuberant than
I, with my poor old pondering and comparing habit, felt myself
moved to, as you will remember; but I quite see what he means

by them.'† At this moment when Marsh's relations with Edmund Gosse were almost fully restored, they were subjected to the strain of a difference of opinion concerning W. H. Davies. It was Marsh's custom to enquire of his poets from time to time whether their heads were above water. He had found Davies in serious difficulties. His private income of a few shillings a week had been stopped for over a year. The rent coming in from a few rather ramshackle houses was now negligible and even that could never be relied on. Moreover he was under an obligation to help his mother and a brother who lived with her and was unable to work.

Marsh called on him, listened to his story, and sent his impressions to Gosse. By reviewing for a certain magazine, he began, Davies could count on earning £8 a year, 'and that, he tells me, is big money'.

> He's a dear little man, and rather comical. He has a high idea of his vocation as a poet, to which he considered he has sacrificed the last 8 years of his life (he's 46) which he might have spent in the ordinary pleasures and excitements of the clan from which he sprang. He thinks he'd have had much more fun as a tramp—and now he feels disconsolate and hopeless because after all his efforts he finds himself without the means to live the 'higher life' in moderate decency and comfort. He *wants* very much to marry and settle down in the country (he says there's a very nice girl of his own clan in Wales who he thinks would have him) and he doesn't like London, where, being a ductile and amenable creature, he finds himself slipping into the society of second-rate journalists whom he's too goodnatured to resist, but thinks unworthy of him as indeed they are. He told me he thought he had a dozen good lyrics left in him, and that he could get them out if he could afford to settle in the country. . . . He's proud and absolutely refuses help from friends. Of course if one thinks his poetry worthless there's no reason why he should have public money any more than any other tramp. If on the other hand he is allowed to have any talent at all it seems to me the clearest of possible cases for a pension which would enable him to live in the modest and decent way he wishes—a man from almost the lowest class who has (as I think) a genuine poetic gift and has sacrificed everything to it and raised himself into a clean and self-respecting way of life. . . . Forgive me, but he is such a dear little tragi-comic man, and I shall always think he has written some delicious things which will live.

Gosse was, for once, uncompromising. He did not consider the poetry worthless but he was bound to repeat that he thought it thin and poor and without durable character. The languor and poverty of the technique were reprehensible.

No, I cannot think that Davies, either in his prose or his verse, either in his sentiments or his fancy, ever gets beyond the purely amateur stage of the loose 'poetic' person who has dreams and aspirations but has never learned the business of the art of writing. He strikes me as having never done an hour's strenuous thinking in his life, he is just a moral and an intellectual tramp, willing to wander in rags if he may be spared taking trouble. I know you will be very angry with me for saying this, but you can take comfort by telling yourself that I am a stupid old ass incapable of appreciating the Higher Uselessness.

Marsh replied on September 26.

You didn't really think your letter would make me angry! Davies' poetical merits are a subject on which we can well afford to differ. I happen to rate them higher than you do (and so do many of our friends—Rupert loved his work, and so do Lascelles and Gibson, and I think de la Mare) but as Stevenson said of Walt Whitman they aren't a *casus belli* as the choruses in *Samson Agonistes* would be! All I hope is that you won't actively oppose a grant if the question comes before you, for though I think he is a clear case as a poet, I do think that on any wide view he is one as an object for public help. It's incredible to me that there are not a large number of babies born among the quite poor who have the makings of poets in them but circumstances keep them mute and inglorious. Here is one of the *very* rare cases in which the talent comes—as you don't deny— at any rate to *something*. The man discovers his gift too late to perfect it (for I believe that if he'd had 'advantages' he would have avoided the faults you find in him—there'd have been rhymes enough in his poems if he'd had 'access to the best models' in his youth)—but from that time forward he gives up his life to it, and strictly meditates oh such a thankless Muse, and the result is, as I don't think you'd deny, that it would be difficult to make a list of, say, the thirty best people now writing poetry without including him? Think how rich he'd be if he were among the best thirty people doing *anything* else! but here he is, finding it impossible to make £50 a year! I'm afraid I may run up against a feeling which I believe you have, that it would be a pity if there were too many good poets. I see the force of that view though I don't consider it practically important because I think the danger is chimerical—I think the gift is too rare—and when it *does* appear, I hate that it should be handicapped by inequality of circumstances.

During this exchange *King Lear's Wife*, produced by John Drinkwater, with Ion Swinley as Lear, received its first performance on September 25 in Birmingham. Marsh had made a last appeal to the author for the name of the leading female character to be changed, but Bottomley was not going to be deprived of his Hygd. 'Truly I don't want it to be mellifluous,' he argued. 'I want it to be gaunt and Stonehengey and hard, with a hint that if she had lived to be an old woman she would have been something eager and terrible, bony and fangy.' Abercrombie and Gibson turned up for what was considered the birth of Georgian drama (Marsh had promised to call on Mrs. Brooke and dared not alter the plan) and Bottomley was carried upstairs, planted in a box, supported by bolsters with his feet resting on a purple cushion, and everyone was impressed except the critics. 'A Gifted Mistake' was the headline of one article, which complained of Shakespeare being dragged into the divorce court. 'I suppose there hasn't been such an outburst since Rossetti's 1870 poems,' wrote Bottomley, undismayed. Drinkwater's report to Gray's Inn that the piece 'acted admirably generally, a little doubtfully in one or two places, and superbly at the great moments', showed that the management was also refusing to acknowledge defeat. He went on:

That Gordon and Wilfrid were delighted there is, I think, no doubt, and in work of this kind it is the opinion of the two or three that outweighs the world. But the world took it well and applauded loud and long. When, however, the world turns from its quiet feelings to its blind brain for expression about these things there is always smother and foolishness. The papers today are brutal and obscure to poet and play and players and instigator of this event alike. No one escapes, though the hardest fury falls on Gordon and Kathleen[1]. . . . Gordon himself laughs at them out of his great beard and I console myself by blaspheming in my loudest voice. The Censor added to our gaiety by sending horrified protests on Saturday about the louse and the lady's shift,[2] in a letter which I have given as an heirloom for ever to the clan Bottomley.

By the end of the limited run of a week Drinkwater was lamenting the small audiences. 'This is all the poets can hope to do in the

[1] The first Mrs. Drinkwater, who played the part of Goneril.
[2] The theme of a lyric which opened the play.

theatre, but it doesn't matter. Those who do come care very much.' Marsh referred to all this as 'the slings and arrows of outrageous Birmingham' and drew reassurance from Abercrombie's opinion that 'its power came out in an amazing way. It seemed to me the high watermark of modern drama. . . .' Undeterred by apparent failure Marsh was already in negotiation with Viola Tree for a charity performance at His Majesty's, her father's theatre in the Haymarket.

In September D. H. Lawrence moved from Greatham, where he had been a guest of the Meynells, to a little red brick villa in the Vale of Health on the edge of Hampstead Heath. With the aid of a loan from Marsh he bought a blue Persian rug for the flat, but his friend's official connection with Whitehall and the administration of the war created a barrier in Lawrence's mind. 'We must not cease to be friends,' he wrote soon after arrival, 'though all this misery separates everybody like a darkness.' Marsh combined his request for poems to include in his new volume with praise of *The Rainbow*, which had just come out. 'I'm glad you like the Rainbow. . . . Do as you like about the poetry. I cannot get the hang of verses again, after I've left them for a long time.' He wanted the work of Anna Wickham represented, but a month later he was too indignant over the suppression of his new novel to care about other people's affairs, and even Marsh's view of the book seemed less palatable in retrospect. 'You rather jeered at the Rainbow, but notwithstanding, it is a big book, and one of the important novels in the language. . . .' He was sick and tired of England, 'so sick, body and soul, that if I don't go away I shall die. . . . I want you, if you can, to give me a little money to go with: if you can, easily, that is, God knows I don't want to mulct you. . . . I owe you £10 already. And I will give you full and final possession of some poems, when I have any you like.' Marsh's anxious enquiry into his wellbeing found him staying with the Morrells at Garsington. 'I feel as if the whole thing were coming to an end—the whole of England, of the Christian era. . . . It almost makes one die. . . . It isn't my novel that hurts me—it's this hopelessness of the World.' At the same time Marsh heard from Ottoline Morrell herself. Lawrence wanted to take himself off to Florida, she explained. 'Poor fellow, he is miserably depressed and hopeless and he feels that there is *no* opening for his work here. . . . It seems an awful pity that we should lose him, as he is a real genius, isn't he? but I don't think he would live through the winter if he remained. He has £40 altogether to start forth on his voyage. . . .' Marsh sent him half as much again from his Perceval fund.

Throughout October Henry James was working on his Preface to the volume of Brooke's articles which was eventually called *Letters from America*. He was battling against ill-health, and some confusion of mind. In the first week of October he wrote to say he was returning the Memoir 'to Raymond's Inn (you know what I mean!)'.

> My disorder, though waning, still gives me kicks, and I am having today a beastly interruption. . . . I must ask you a little more patience still (the thing will have been done under inauspicious stars!) but the worst of the difficulty is over.†

In the middle of this month Marsh received another blow from an entirely unexpected quarter. Up to the end of August the bills from the optician and the regular maintenance payments to Mark Gertler had come to over a hundred pounds, two of his paintings had been bought, *Daffodils* and *Agapanthus*, and for several months the painter had enjoyed possession of the key to Raymond Buildings. He had, however, come under the influence of Gilbert Cannan, D. H. Lawrence, and others of the Georgian circle who were growing more and more violently opposed to the war. On the 19th Marsh found a note on his table.

> I have come to the conclusion that we two are too fundamentally different to continue to be friends. Since the war you have gone in one direction and I in another. All the time I have been stifling my feelings. Firstly because of your kindness to me and secondly I do not want to hurt you. I am I believe what you call a 'passivist' [*sic*]. I don't know exactly what that means, but I just hate the War and should really loth [*sic*] to help in it. . . . Of course from this you will understand that we had not better meet any more and that I cannot any longer accept your help. Forgive me for having been dishonest with you and for having under such conditions accepted your money. I have been punished enough for it and have suffered terribly. I stuck it so long because it seemed hard to have to give up this studio which I love. . . . Your kindness has been an extraordinary help to me. Since your help I have done work far far better than before. I shall therefore never cease to be thankful to you. Also if ever I earn any money by painting I shall return you what I owe you. I shall

send you the latchkey and please would you get Mrs. Elgy to send me my pyjamas and slippers.

Gertler found a lodging elsewhere, and now another of the poets was about to be exposed to the hazards of war. Sassoon was under orders for France. Although he had enlisted at the outbreak of war, an injury sustained when his horse rolled over him had so far precluded him from active service. In the first week of November he crossed the Channel as an officer of the First Battalion, Royal Welch Fusiliers, reported at Battalion H.Q., Béthune, where his unit was being reorganized after the fighting round Loos, and was added to the strength of 'C' Company situated close by at Locon, just north of Cambrin. From the front, fostering his literary hopes, he wrote to Gray's Inn.

About my poems, I suppose it's no good doing things in a hurry, but I should like to see them in print—the ones you like best—it is a sort of link with reasonable existence which seems lopped right off out here. I can't get the new ones finished properly; either too tired, or else someone there to distract ideas. . . . I go blundering on, and hope some day to get quiet weeks to finish and remould the new impressions, so sharp and exciting. I wonder if you will get a typed copy of the poems you liked best sent out to me, so that I can get an idea of the effect they make when collected. Going up a hill behind our reserve lines in the evenings I see a most wonderful and tenebrous picture—not one tree—only bare rolling slopes and folds of hills, and a disused road setting out from nowhere along the ridge; a bank with some blackthorn blossom in the gloom, and the grey skies meeting the distant country which seems to go on and on for ever. And the booming of guns all round and the wind piping in the dead grass. O yes, this is some life—and the men almost make me weep sometimes, so patient and cheery and altogether dear.

At the same time as Sassoon had joined his unit, Robert Graves, who had been in France since May, was posted to 'A' Company of the same battalion. One day during his first week at Locon he walked over to call on a friend in the officers' mess of 'C' Company. Intrigued at the sight of so unlikely a book as the *Essays of Lionel Johnson* lying on the table, he turned up the fly-leaf and saw the name of the owner. It was the first book other than a military manual that he had set eyes on for many weeks (his own volumes of Keats and Blake excepted) so it was with special curiosity that he glanced around the room in hope of tracing 'S. Sassoon'. Making a guess, which turned out to be a shrewd one, he introduced himself. Sassoon, he learned, had only just come out from England, and before long, being off duty, they were walking to Béthune and exchanging such poems as they happened to have in their pockets over a plate of cream buns in a cake-shop. Friendship between such men was inevitable, but neither at this early stage was exactly bowled over by the other's poetical performance. The verses that Graves had with him were shortly to appear in his first book, *Over the Brazier*, while Sassoon's poems were to wait until the appearance of *The Old Huntsman* (1917), which came out along with Graves' second and more ambitious collection, *Fairies and Fusiliers*. The progress of all three books was to be encouraged and watched over by Marsh during the months to come, but for the present, the first week of November 1915, when the two youngest of his poets were making each other's acquaintance in the front line, grave developments in the political scene at Whitehall must have driven from his mind all thought of his scattered family whether at home or abroad.

The War Council was reconstructed without Mr. Churchill. Gallipoli was to be evacuated. The Chancellor of the Duchy resolved to try his fortunes on active service at the Front, tendered his resignation, and on November 11 handed Marsh the rough draft of his personal note of farewell to the Prime Minister. On the 15th he took his seat in the House of Commons as a private Member. Free at last from the restraints and responsibilities of office he rose to deliver the speech which surveyed the whole panorama of his administration at the Admiralty. No doubt Marsh, who had witnessed the unfolding drama at every stage, was helpful in the assemblage of this formidable apologia which was to fill twenty-two columns of *Hansard*. To Marsh it was the climax of the most terrible year of his life. That his official career should seem to have evaporated overnight was nothing to the realization that he was now left with no one for whom he could work with that ardour of personal attachment which alone enabled him to live and serve at his full bent. By coincidence, on the same day as the delivery of Mr. Churchill's farewell address to the House, *Georgian Poetry 1913-1915*, dedicated to the memory of Flecker and Brooke, was published from the Poetry Bookshop.

The departure of Winston Churchill into the sphere of those same perils which had already destroyed his younger friends seemed to Eddie Marsh symbolic of the calamities which had overtaken him during the year. He spent the day with Lady Randolph Churchill, doing what he could to fetch and carry as Mr. Churchill got ready to cross the Channel and join a battalion of the Grenadier Guards. He had managed to bear so much with equanimity, but these làst few hours of preparation seemed intolerable. At this juncture he makes a tragi-comic appearance in the public chronicles of his time. His emotion, which can only now be fully understood, since so much of his private history lay behind it, was not unobserved. It has furnished a detail in a description of Churchill's departure by one of his biographers.

> The household was upside down as he completed his preparations. Downstairs his faithful secretary, Eddie (later Sir Edward) Marsh, was in tears, upstairs Lady Randolph was in despair at the thought of her brilliant son leaving for the trenches. . . . Mrs. Churchill alone remained calm.[1]

Mr. Churchill had not overlooked the small detail of his secretary's future. He drew Mr. Asquith's attention to the secretary who was being abandoned, and the Prime Minister invited him to join his staff at 10 Downing Street as an extra secretary in charge of Civil List pensions. This was an act of rescue on the part of Mr. Asquith. Marsh knew that something bigger than his private world had collapsed. All round there was evidence of worlds disintegrating. Mrs. Brooke at Rugby, with those life-size photographs in place of her living sons, had become a figure hardly less symbolic than Rupert himself. Acknowledging the cheque for twenty pounds D. H. Lawrence wrote, 'I feel as if some hope were broken in my chest that has never been broken before', and two months earlier Shaw-Stewart had expressed the feeling in Gallipoli which Eddie must have applied to himself as 1915 neared its end: 'I continue to believe that the luck of my generation must change. . . . Nowadays we who are alive have the sense of being old, old survivors.'

[1] *Winston Churchill*, by Lewis Broad (Hutchinson), p. 140.

Chapter Fourteen

INTERLUDE
(December 1915–July 1917)

O N December 5 Henry James's secretary sent news that he had suffered a stroke. Ten days later the proofs of his Preface arrived, but he was too ill to look at them or have them read aloud. 'It will distress him to know he can't attend to them himself,' the secretary wrote. Marsh must keep in touch by telephone. 'The 'phone does not seem to disturb him.' He had dictated the whole work twice, so there could be no faults of carelessness. To Marsh this news meant so much more than the imminent loss of a great man of letters, and he cast about in his mind for something he could do. First he sent a copy of the proofs to Mrs. Brooke. 'His tribute to Rupert will almost certainly be the last thing he will write—if so, it makes a beautiful end to his work.' He then spoke to the Prime Minister and won his consent to raise the question of the Order of Merit. On the 18th he put his case in writing.

PRIME MINISTER

May I write a few words in the hope that the question of the O.M. for Mr. Henry James has not been irrevocably set aside?

I think there should be little doubt of his right to stand beside George Meredith and Thomas Hardy—the only novelists yet admitted to the Order. If they have qualities which he has not, the converse is also true. It has been said that the great French novelists are conscious artists, the English inspired amateurs. Henry James is the exception. No writer of his time gives the same impression of knowledge and mastery in the architectural structure of his works, and in the gradual building up of atmosphere, character, and situation.

This was I think what was meant by the words used in the letter (signed among many others, by Arthur Balfour, Granville Barker, J. M. Barrie, Arnold Bennett, Edmund Gosse, Sidney Colvin, Austin Dobson, John Galsworthy, Ld. Rosebery, J. S. Sargent, H. G. Wells, and George Wyndham) which accompanied a presentation made to him on his 70th birthday: 'You are the writer, the master of rare and beautiful art, in whose work creation and criticism meet as they have never before met in our language.'

He's sometimes blamed for dealing only with characters drawn from the hothouse life of the leisured classes, hypertrophied in intellect and emotion; but an artist should be judged not by his choice of material but by his treatment. It would be equally fair to rule out Thomas Hardy for his complete failure to represent any educated person.

Henry James' shorter stories are certainly not inferior to those of any English writer. His style may be criticized as mannered, and sometimes obscure; on the other hand it is one of the most individual that has ever been evolved; it is infinitely expressive, except when it defeats itself by trying to express too much; and it rises at times to the height of beauty.

Apart from fiction, his critical work is of the highest order; and his introductions to his own novels in the Library Edition are I think a uniquely illuminating account of an artist's creative processes.

He has had a determining influence on several of the most distinguished novelists of the generation succeeding his own, such as Edith Wharton and Ann Douglas Sedgwick; and many others, such as Arnold Bennett and H. G. Wells, would recognize him as their master, as R. L. Stevenson would if he were alive. I am sure the profession of letters as a whole would warmly welcome the appointment; and I am positive that Edmund Gosse (tho' I have of course not mentioned the matter to him) would be enthusiastically in its favour.

There are two extraneous considerations. His recent naturalization was a generous and impressive gesture of adherence to our national cause, and deserves some grace of recognition. And the compliment would no doubt be appreciated in America.

I understand Lord Morley is against the proposal; but with the greatest respect for him I could wish that some opinion might be taken which would be representative of a later epoch in taste.

Two days later a message from Lord Stamfordham gave the news that the King approved the award. Henry James was at once informed.

On December 1 Mr. Churchill had written his first letter from the Front. Marsh suspected he had inadvertently run off with one of the office keys. 'Eddie dear,' came the reply from G.H.Q. in

France, 'I have no split key—nor any key—except the key to heaven. . . .'

> *Tout va bien ici.* I am now 'resting' after 10 days in the line. I had a lot to live down with the Grenadiers, having been so long in the Government: but I parted from them this morning for two or three days as if from home.
>
> The return of K [Kitchener] fills me with delight.[1] It is the most enlivening item in the public prints.
>
> You would enjoy yourself out here, if I could find you a coign. Raymond [Asquith] does well with the Guards.
>
> Best love. Write sometimes.
Yours always,
W.

Meanwhile negotiations with Viola Tree about the Georgian matinée were progressing. She did not favour His Majesty's 'because there I should be haunted by terror of Daddy [Beerbohm Tree] and be unable to get any of the modern fearlessness into the performance'. She was going to borrow the scenery of *Die Walküre* from Covent Garden for *King Lear's Wife*. On the coming Friday Marsh was going alone to see Lily Elsie in *Mavourneen* at His Majesty's theatre. Viola's letter ended, 'I may be going too but with a young man whom I have on my hands and who I must take alone because I promised I would.' On the 11th Marsh visited her in her box during the first interval and her young escort was introduced as the composer of a new song that was very popular with the troops. He didn't quite catch the title. 'Keep the what?' he asked. 'Home fires burning,' said Miss Tree, and she hummed a few bars. 'Oh *that*!' Eddie Marsh exclaimed, reassuringly, and was invited to watch the rest of the show from the box. David Davies, the youth from Cardiff, who had begun calling himself 'Ivor Novello', was trying to get into the Royal Naval Air Service. A letter next day from Viola Tree tried to enlist Marsh's help with the application form. 'He liked you so much and felt you would help him.' Later Novello asked if he could bring the papers in person. 'I've only been fit for six weeks and have been agitating ever since. . . . I *am* the right age.' So he called at Gray's Inn and was invited to compose the music for the performance of *King Lear's Wife*, a most improbable début for the future master of musical comedy. He seemed unusually gifted, however, another

[1] Lord Kitchener had visited the Gallipoli Peninsula.

young artist in search of his niche (if rather lacking as yet in drive
and education), so Marsh began to take an interest in his welfare.
First he took charge of the papers which were to turn the musician
into an airman.

By the middle of the month Mr. Churchill's hopes of being
appointed to the command of a brigade had been dashed, and
now Marsh had told him of Kitchener's final advocacy of complete
evacuation in Gallipoli; he must also have talked of his feelings of
listlessness at this time when all his friends were so usefully and
dangerously employed. Major Churchill wrote on the 15th.

> My information is only good in parts: but distressing letters from
> various quarters had already apprised me of the decisions which have
> at last been reached. You know only too well what I think about
> them. I was glad to be able to occupy my mind with the practical
> trifles of trench warfare and the bickering of the rival artilleries.
>
> I do not know what effect the unhappy recall of my friends[1] will
> have on my local fortunes—but I feel superior to them. A Brigade
> or a company in the Guards is the same or almost the same to me—
> during the present interlude. I have fallen back reposefully into the
> arms of Fate; but with an underlying instinct that all will be well
> and that my greatest work is ahead.
>
> I should like to set you free from your present surroundings, and
> if it were in my power to find you a little island here I should not
> hesitate to prepare it for you.
>
> Brigades have an 'interpreter' who has a jolly time. Let me know
> what you feel. I am glad you found a cigarette case among those
> which Clemmie produced which appealed to you. 'Tis but the poor
> symbol of a deep affection. Yours always, W.

During these weeks the new anthology was being received by
the critics with qualified enthusiasm, and Bottomley's play was
the focal point of their attention. The dramatist had carried too
far the Georgian reaction from the notion that 'beauty' was interesting in itself; his King Lear was no more interesting, no more
alive and growing, than Tennyson's King Arthur; the character
was 'as rigid and unreal in his own conventional baseness as King
Arthur in his conventional loftiness'. The same anonymous critic
(probably Gosse) foreshadowed what was to become the main
objection to the Georgians in their last phase. Davies and

[1] Sir John French was recalled, and Haig, his successor, had not endorsed the
promotion for Major Churchill which French had approved.

Stephens seemed to affect simplicity for the purpose of their art, as if they had 'warned off the intellect' like a mischievous child. 'They are charming, no doubt, but simpler, one feels, than anyone has a right to be nowadays.' In the *New Statesman* 'Solomon Eagle' (J. C. Squire) preferred Bottomley's play to Abercrombie's, but complained that there was no lifelike complexity in any of the characters, and he too regarded the movement as a group of poets who were 'sick of stale beauties and clutching at the ugly and grotesque'. This prompted Marsh to send Squire a long screed on the character of Goneril. It left the critic unconvinced. 'It is not safe,' Squire replied, 'to make people inhuman and try to escape the consequences by calling them Ancient Britons.' Marsh then argued that he was criticizing art by ethical standards, to which Squire replied: 'Really great art can't help being morally useful, but certainly the notion of teaching is the wrong one to start with. A poet must start from a deep emotion in himself. . . . Bottomley I don't feel started from anything of this sort. I feel he merely wanted to write a play, and invented some puppets to write it round, disguising the bareness of this conception with the beauties of his execution and the incidental riches of a penetrating mind.'

Bottomley created a bleak, megalithic world of his own. It is consistent and it exists imaginatively in its own right. Not all the work of the early Georgians enjoyed this kind of advantage. Squire had done more than point out the limitations of the Georgian drama. By criticizing the emphasis given to expressiveness over the general conception and the substance of the thing said, he had detected the cause of that thinness of texture which later became a characteristic of much Georgian verse. It was decorative art. *King Lear's Wife* was never intended, one feels, as a comment on reality but as a grandiloquent decoration of it. De la Mare also created his own world, but it was fashioned out of the dreams and nightmares of common humanity, not of Bronze Age monoliths. Yet Bottomley's ornamental world does exist as a reality on a plane larger than life, and must have its place among things of lasting value. In retrospect the virtues and lurking weaknesses of this Georgian movement look rather like reflections of certain qualities in the editor's own character. Both the man and the poetry were products of an age.

By Christmas Frank Sidgwick had read the Memoir and welcomed it as an 'emplacement from which base we shall go on

firing his works off into the welkin. . . . I sweat with pride at the
official connexion of a printed title page. . . . I spoke with him but
briefly a dozen times. And now it is mine to pull a trigger that
lets off his spirit and essence into a naughty world!' Working in
closest collaboration with the editor, Frank Sidgwick was being
prodigiously successful in this function, and his personal enthusiasm was contributing a great deal to the establishment of Brooke's
reputation.

On new year's day 1916 Eddie Marsh paid his first visit to the
top floor flat above the Strand Theatre where Mr. Davies and his
wife, the singing-teacher Clara Novello Davies, lived their far from
placid existence, and their son occupied a small room of his own
plastered with photographs of Lily Elsie in *The Merry Widow*. In
the ensuing years these rooms were to become as familiar to
Marsh as his own home at Raymond Buildings, and it was now
that he began the custom of walking to Whitehall in the mornings
so that he could look in on the Aldwych flat on the way, a habit
which was to be almost unbroken for the next twenty years. His
first move in Novello's education was to give him Brooke's *Letters
from America*, and he began a commonplace book in which from time
to time he copied out some passage of contemporary prose or verse
that qualified for inclusion in the private anthology. He supervised
his reading and had an upright piano installed at Raymond
Buildings so that Novello could practise or compose away from
the distracting shindy of his mother's pupils. Since the father, who
had retired from the rates department of Cardiff municipal
council, seldom did much more than amiably stare into space ('the
laziest man I've ever known,' Marsh described him), and the
dominating mother had little time to spare from the pursuit of her
tempestuous but distinguished career, there was something of a
parental vacuum at 11 Aldwych which Marsh unobtrusively took
it upon himself to fill.

The rest of his circle were scattered. Abercrombie was an
inspector of shells at Liverpool; Bottomley was all but bedridden
by the Northern lakes; Sassoon, at the battle front, had been
making up his mind about Robert Graves. 'He is a strange
person,' wrote Sassoon of his new acquaintance, 'full of ideas and
originality. I am rather disappointed with his poems. Do you
think it wise for him to publish them? I am sure he will do some
much better work before long when he has recovered his balance.

I enjoyed reading *King Lear's Wife* and thought many times of your reading it to me at R.B.'

> How I long to be a painter, everything out here is simply asking to be painted or etched: it is wildly picturesque. Soldiers in barns with one candle burning, and wintry evening landscapes with guns flashing and thudding. I put '*angry* guns that *boom* and *flash*' in my poem, but really they flash and *thud*—the flash comes first, and they only boom when very near and in some valley.

In reply Marsh was rather more sanguine about Graves' chances as a poet.

> I've been a good deal interested in some that I've seen before— things with a turn of thought or vision, and a happy easy flow of expression—no quintessence about them, but they are fresh, pleasant things (some I don't like at all) I shouldn't be at all sorry to see him publish them.

Criticizing Sassoon's new poems he objected to the irregular rhyme schemes, and told how Gosse found the same fault with Davies. 'I always defend W.H.D. to Gosse, and cite Blake—but at heart I agree. I haven't seen Davies for some time, he's rather on my conscience, as he ought to have *respectable* friends like me.' A letter from Graves showed that he too was in favour of the controversial *King Lear's Wife*.

> It's very fine. But besides admiring a play or poem I like to feel in absolute sympathy with the writer, to the point of wishing I could pirate his work as my own. I can't feel that about Bottomley or D. H. Lawrence. I can in the cases of Hodgson and Flecker—and especially Brooke. I hadn't read the fish's Heaven before, it is an exquisite thing. *The Great Lover* is so bantering yet so serious. . . . I feel in reading him that his is exactly the language I'm floundering to catch—musical, restrained, refined, yet not crabbed or conventionally antique, reading almost like ordinary speech.

Marsh was helping Graves put in order his first small collection for publication by the Poetry Bookshop. Graves wrote again to say he sometimes forgot that his parents were apt to take him a little too seriously 'and last month I had an absolute *snorter* from Father about some verses giving a point of view he regarded as immoral'. So the enclosed poems were being sent in strict confidence. Since last November Mr. A. P. Graves, the young poet's father, had been trying to pin Marsh down to a discussion on the young man's literary future.

Rosenberg was now at Farnborough, doing coal fatigues and feeling grateful to Marsh for sorting out his pay and seeing that his mother got her allowance of 3s. 6d. a week. 'I added some lines to that Marching poem which you will think vague but I like them.' He was having his play *Moses* privately printed. 'I want you to make allowances for the play as I had to write it in a very scrappy manner and even got into trouble thro' it. It made me a bit absent-minded and you know what that means in the army.' He arranged to bring the proofs to Gray's Inn on his next leave, saying they offered a special attraction. 'The printer is superb. He's made quite an original thing of it, and given me a million hints for new things.' (The piece was original enough without the aid of printer's errors.) 'The plot is droll,' said Rosenberg. 'There is a famine in Egypt caused by the superabundance of slaves who eat up all the food meant for the masters. To prevent this all the back molars of the slaves are drawn, so they eat less. The plot works round this.' So Marsh corrected the proofs and did what he could to distribute copies. They were not easy to dispose of, although there were three or four among the Georgians whose talents together could not equal the natural genius of unassuming little Rosenberg. In late spring the King's inspection of the 'Bantam' Regiment[1] inspired one of his characteristic asides. 'At a distance we look like soldiers sitting down, you know, legs so short.'

There had been a long silence from Lawrence, but Cynthia Asquith wrote to him in Cornwall (the Florida plan had collapsed) to the effect that Eddie Marsh was hurt. She said he had heard he was being laughed at. At any other time he would have welcomed the news as a sign of popularity, but he was sensitive these days. There had been too many knocks of late. 'We have *often* laughed at you,' Lawrence confessed, 'because you are one of those special figures one can laugh at; just as I am, only I'm ten times more ridiculous. . . . I always feel a real gratitude to you, and a kindness, and an esteem of the genuine man. . . . I did feel rather bitter about the way you took the war—"What splendid times we live in."' Lawrence had feared his continued friendship might prove an embarrassment to Eddie Marsh. By now Marsh had broken with Bertrand Russell, Gertler had taken himself off, and Gilbert Cannan was to be the next. The coolness towards Lawrence was

[1] A unit recruited from men (*e.g.*, miners) who were below the standard height.

due solely to the feeling that he was no longer needed. He did not resent it any more than in other similar cases. But when he felt no longer 'necessary' a kind of spell broke and he fell out of love.

Cannan was the only pacifist of his circle with whom Marsh ever allowed himself to be drawn into controversy. It is probable that Marsh reinforced his own ideas with those of T. E. Hulme, who had told him of his friendly dispute with Russell. Hulme had set out to show that the pacifist point of view was based on 'a romantic conception of progress and an over-valuation of "life" as against the absolute ethical values that make life worth while.'[1] In July, 1917, while with the siege guns in France, he was to send Marsh a long and impassioned appeal on behalf of Jacob Epstein, for whom Marsh had already obtained a period of exemption from service. To Hulme's disgust there had been adverse comment in the Press. Epstein was now called up again and Hulme was determined he should not be wasted like Gaudier.

> I'd willingly give a year's pay and undergo an extra day's shelling in order to be able to beat those beastly people. Of course Chesterton is quite right on the general principle that the artist has no more claim to immunity than anybody else. We're all equal in that sense, I suppose. But that isn't the point. Is the State making an economic use of its material? and ought it not to preserve a sculptor like E. in exactly the same way that it would preserve the only man who was capable of making some particular kind of instrument—not because instrument-makers were, as men, more valuable than anyone else.

Hulme's ideas on the position of the artist in war were shown to Mr. Churchill, but before Hulme could be apprised of the result he was himself killed and his critical essay on Epstein destroyed with him.

While Eddie Marsh was still coping with the impoverished little Rosenberg's literary affairs another soldier on active service sent him a document. It was a report on the Western offensive written at the request of Sir John French by Major Churchill, who now wanted it typed and passed on. 'I expect to go to the Royal Scots Fusiliers tomorrow [January 4]. It is a good battalion—but it was torn to pieces in the big battle. The Divisional General Furse and his Chief of Staff seem to be anxious to have me and the project originated with them. We go back into the line in about a fortnight.' On the 10th he wrote again. He was puzzled to learn that

[1] *T. E. Hulme*, by Michael Roberts (Faber, 1938).

his report had not reached either Lloyd George or Bonar Law. 'Is there any reason against its being circulated to the members of the War Council? If not pray at least let these ministers have a copy each.'

> Tell me again the name of your young friend who wants 'to bask in the sunshine of my smile'. Such characters are rare. We have just finished 6 days in the trenches, and now 'rest' for a like period before beginning again. Write to me, I like letters. They are the only literature which hold me here. You may not always have the opportunity.
>
> Yours ever,
W.

At the same time Marsh heard from Delhi, where Lutyens was at work on his great architectural enterprise. He was anxious to know who would be the next Viceroy. 'Will you, or can't you, appoint him? Won't *you* come? as a man who has some standard of Taste and would not leave decisions to stand for centuries—in the hands of accountants.' Marsh was nervously exhausted, jaded by public affairs, rather disillusioned, and in no vein to be amused by Lutyens' problem or stirred to do much about it. But he was beginning to go about again on the social round.[1] He attended a rehearsal of a new play by Yeats in Lady Cunard's drawing-room and described it for Cathleen Nesbitt.

> I had to go away in the middle, which was wretched, as I was getting quite worked up and impressed. It's the beginning of an attempt to give poetic plays in such an inexpensive way that they can be done for quite small audiences—many of the conventions are taken from the traditional dramas—rather unluckily for us called the No-drama, of the Japanese nobility (when is a play not a play? when it's a No-drama). I find I can manage quite well without *any* scenery at all—but they had been a little too careful not to disturb the room, and I couldn't help being disconcerted, just when I had persuaded myself that I had before me a wild mountain tract of semi-historic Ireland, to notice the characters skirting round a Louis XV table covered with French novels. The actors wore masks made by Dulac,

[1] He was rather pleased with his acceptance of an invitation from Lady Guendolen Osborne, on the Prime Minister's notepaper (January 31)—'Stern Daughter of the Duke of Leeds! As you know, I am the slave of Duty—the word has only to be mentioned, and I am up and ready—so the light in which you have put your invitation leaves me no alternative but to accept it, at whatever cost of personal inconvenience. Yours ever, E.'

awfully good, and I found it quite easy to accept the convention. But I had an odd sensation just before the play began. Harry Ainley had a mask very like his own face, and I didn't know it wasn't his own self till he came up to me roaring with laughter and not a *muscle* of his mouth moving, it was quite uncanny. The play began with very atmospheric 'keening' behind the screen and a man in black solemnly pacing to the front—he got there, made an impressive bow to the audience, then started, and said 'Oh we've forgotten to light the lanterns!'—lighted them, retired, paced solemnly forward again, and began his speech.

He had been for too long without that element of light relief—or what his mother with a slightly pained expression used to call 'pleasure'—and the growing acquaintance with Novello brought a timely and brilliant solution. Novello's papers had been approved, but for several weeks there was no vacancy at Naval Air Service headquarters, then situated at the Crystal Palace, so he was at large in London, 'looking remarkable and practising saluting' with a capacity for frivolous amusement which seemed almost inexhaustible. Viola Tree, Eddie Marsh, and Novello became a trio which met every evening for supper in Soho, then adjourned to the Aldwych flat and sang songs at the piano. They called this informal brand of recreation 'having a jolly', a species of loud and somewhat hectic gaiety which was to become a national characteristic in the early 'twenties. They were soon joined by Lady Juliet Duff. For weeks they were rarely seen apart in the West End. On one occasion de la Mare was with them at their sing-song. At this time Marsh became a regular theatre-goer, and developed an unexpected penchant for musical comedies. The first night of *The Bing Boys* at the Alhambra, for which Novello had composed a march, provided the occasion for a late-night 'jolly' with everyone acclaiming Violet Loraine as a genius of the first order and finding each other extraordinarily witty and daring. The laughter, while it lasted, did something to palliate the grief and lingering sense of frustration which he had brought with him into the new year.

On February 5 he submitted the Memoir to Mrs. Brooke for the second time.

ii

He had been encouraged by Frank Sidgwick to persevere. 'Mrs. B.'s view is a mystery of mysteries to me,' Marsh had written to him. 'How Rupert could be produced by a woman without sense of humour or beauty, and narrow to that degree, I shall never understand.' When the script came again into Mrs. Brooke's hands she found the school and Cambridge sections revised, and a covering note drew her attention to certain new 'pages of generalization in which I tried to bring out or rather to emphasize some sides which you might like to have dwelt upon'. Otherwise it was much the same. She was distinctly pleased, and asked that A. C. Benson, Robert Whitelaw, and two of her son's oldest friends, Dudley Ward and Geoffrey Keynes, should be invited to contribute to the Cambridge section. Marsh welcomed these suggestions, but he made bold to draw the line at Benson. 'He is a great friend of mine, and I am very fond of him as a man; but he has overwritten himself so terribly that he has come to be looked upon as almost a comic figure in literature, always popping up everywhere.' Sidgwick had laid up a great stock of paper in confident anticipation, and since the war-time difficulties of publishing were increasing every day 'the sooner the collected poems with the Memoir can come out the better it will be'. On February 10 Marsh was able to send Sidgwick good news. 'Mrs. B. now writes that she agrees to publication in June—so far so good. There will be one or two corners to turn still—*e.g.* she is sticking to her wish that Arthur Benson should be asked to contribute, which I am determined to resist if possible to the end. He is a relation of yours? Sorry. I love him as a man, very much, but I don't want him in the Memoir.' The situation was eased. If necessary, Marsh was prepared to play the role of the stubborn negotiator, but by the end of the month Whitelaw, Ward and Keynes had all declined the offer to contribute, and Marsh was still standing out against Benson. 'I have made every other concession that you have asked for,' he contended. To his surprise she actually gave way, but after more reflection she withdrew her consent to publication on the ground that there would be no contribution by Keynes. She complained that she had never before been given to understand that the Memoir was to accompany the poems. She did not like the idea, and she was annoyed with Henry James for giving the reader of his Preface the impression that a Memoir would soon appear. She felt she was being tricked and stampeded into submission.

It was no use now Marsh reminding her that he had sent her

the proofs of the James Preface. Instead he protested against her whole attitude. 'You have more than once given me to understand that you do not think my feelings need weigh with you. I must say this seems strange to me. I do not like to claim any merit, but you know what endless trouble I have taken over Rupert's affairs and yours.' He thought it 'very hard' that he should be made to suffer 'because someone else, over whom I have no control, refuses to write'. As to Sidgwick who was helping to make Brooke's name, 'I know you do not allow him any importance in the matter but to me he is a friend and a man of business.'

When the blow fell he had only just got back from Rugby, where he had introduced to her Havard Thomas, the artist engaged to design the chapel memorial. He also gave her the news that he had engaged Eric Gill to execute the lettering. In the course of the afternoon he had tried to persuade Mrs. Brooke to let stand in his text an extract from E. J. Dent's article of last year. It was this article, though not this part of it, which had caused offence. Marsh's approval of Dent's work, whether it were good or bad as biographical material, seemed to her tactless and disloyal. So she now made the failure to obtain anything from Keynes her pretext for quashing the entire project. A secondary reason was that the undergraduate section was too sketchy compared with the subsequent career in London, which she seems to have regarded as a period less creditable and less interesting. It is clear that she was now clutching at any straw to make Marsh throw up his executorship. *Letters from America* came out on March 8. She had already condemned the Preface for its reference to the Memoir. There was now an opportunity of embarrassing the relations between editor and publisher. This might do something towards making Marsh realize that he had taken upon himself more than he could manage. 'Mrs. B. seems to be in rather a stuffy mood again,' Marsh told Sidgwick. 'She wrote to complain of the American book being sold at 7s. 6d. without her being consulted! If it were anyone but Rupert I should have hurled back my executorship at her long ago.'

That he should once more try to make out that he had been unfairly treated prompted her to discharge the most tremendous broadside. She was surprised in the first place to hear he had written a Memoir within three months of Rupert's death and had shown it to people. Such haste was indecent. 'This was your initial, and as regards the Memoir your worst, mistake.' How could he have failed to realize that her consent of a few weeks ago was strictly conditional? As to Sidgwick, the matter was too important to her 'to feel bound by a publisher's convenience'. The Preface by James had reached her in 'printed form'. 'I knew it was your fault for misleading him [Henry James] and I suspected you of wishing to corner me.' Anyway, now that James had had his say there was less excuse than ever for a Memoir. Marsh had flouted her wishes from the first. 'You couldn't bear me taking my stand as his mother.' Every time he had been to Rugby he had disconcerted her by acting as if he had more right than she to deal with Rupert's affairs. When he went through the papers 'I should have locked the study door, forbidden you to take them, but I was bewildered with trouble. . . . You have never recognized my position at all.' The worst instance was when the boxes were opened at Rugby (on July 21 the year before) and she got the impression that they had been examined before she saw them. This tirade was only half written when there arrived from Gray's Inn a letter in which Marsh was so ill-advised as to quote a few laudatory sentences about the Memoir by Gosse and Lord Lytton, two representatives of that cultivated society which Marsh, as it seemed to her, had shared so exclusively with Rupert and his London acquaintance. She was of course only confirmed in her antagonism and withdrew none of the barbed shafts from her protest, which she at once despatched.

Somewhat shaken, Marsh turned to Gosse, who suggested bringing out a private edition, citing the precedent of Shorthouse's *John Inglesant*. 'You have met Mrs. Brooke with patience and generosity, but there comes a limit and she has crossed it.' Such championship was welcome, but he could not find it in his heart deliberately to oppose Mrs. Brooke's wishes. Gosse was ready to write to the *Edinburgh Review* and *The Times* when, a few days later, the death of Henry James sent Gosse's thoughts back to the great novelist's 'last words', his Preface. 'He came, the oldest to the youngest writer that England has, with this splendid stirrup cup of gold in his hand. It touches me to tears,' Gosse wrote to Gray's Inn. 'I always adored him. But now that he is gone he seems to me almost supernatural in the beauty of his sympathy and intelligence.' Perhaps Eddie Marsh was put in mind of the gentler methods that James would have advocated in this new crisis at Rugby. At any rate he declined Gosse's generous offer to champion him in public, rejected the idea of a private edition, and at last got down to answering Mrs. Brooke's latest budget of resentment and recrimination. 'I am very glad to have your frank letter,' he began, 'and sincerely sorry that my conduct last year should have been such as to make your view of it possible. It all shows how differently two people can see the same set of circumstances.' He had honestly inferred from all she said that she wanted as much as possible taken off her hands. 'You seemed to lean on me a good deal, and it was very hard to know how much to take on myself. You misunderstood me, of course, entirely, if you thought that I had such an absurd and horrible idea as to rate my claims to Rupert above yours. I ask you to forgive me for all that you thought wrong in my conduct, and to believe—as I think you do —that I always meant well.' This contrition and restraint must have come as a surprise, and perhaps almost a disappointment, to the unhappy woman at Rugby.

Possibly because he had concluded by asking her whether she had any more suggestions to make, showing by this that he was still not regarding the withdrawal of her consent as her last word, he received no answer, but a month later he wrote again to condole with her on the first anniversary of that fatal April 23rd. 'I must send you a line to tell you how I am feeling with you in these days. . . . Your courage will carry you I hope in peace.' It was only a few days after this that Mrs. Brooke's bookseller at Rugby happened to tell her in all innocence that he was looking forward to doing his best for the forthcoming Memoir. On being asked how on earth he knew about it he explained that he had been told of the publication scheduled for June by the publisher's traveller. One can imagine in what an access of rage Mrs. Brooke began to suspect that Marsh had authorized Sidgwick to go ahead regardless. It is hardly credible that she really believed Marsh would do anything so naively unprincipled. She wrote at once, forbidding the appearance of a Memoir until after the war, when it would be placed in the hands of a committee of friends. As before, she seized on this as a pretext for putting Marsh out of countenance with the publisher. If Mr. Sidgwick could be induced to lose interest in bringing out these books for the promotion of Rupert's 'fame' she might get her way after all. 'She believes you stand for something Wrong,' Frances Cornford explained, after a new and less successful attempt at mediation. 'Eddie is always thinking about his "fame"' was still her complaint. She was fighting for her boy, she had said, 'And I *will* fight'. She also maintained that the Memoir was 'idolatrous'. Since four-fifths of the text was now the composition of other hands than the author's this was not easy to substantiate; but she had forbidden any reference to romantic attachments, political socialism, or private unhappiness, and it was true that an idealized, sub-human lay figure was beginning to emerge with its features worn smooth almost beyond recognition. The 'idolatry' objection was never brought up even in the most inflammatory of her letters to Marsh. If the text did reveal something of that tendency between the lines, she was quite unconscious of her own share of the blame. It certainly suited her as a means of discrediting Marsh in the eyes of Brooke's other friends. A story became current that on a certain page of the Memoir there was the phrase 'Rupert returned from the South Seas in a blaze of glory' and that Mrs. Brooke had deleted 'blaze of glory' and substituted 'June' in the margin. It was quite apocryphal and, judging by the brand of humour, may even have been invented by Marsh himself. What was certainly true, however, was the story that alongside the only passage in which Marsh had ventured a literary opinion of his own Mrs. Brooke had scribbled '*applepie . . . applepie*'. Such was the unhappy pass this association of strangers had arrived at in May 1916. Both parties acting self-righteously for the best as they saw it, the possessive jealousy of the one well matched by the vicarious literary ambition of the other. A peculiarly rigid sense of duty was almost the only thing they had in common. It was also their only defence against each other's relentless opposition.

On May 10 Marsh enclosed a letter from Sidgwick which proved that no one had authorized the traveller to make any such announcement as that which had angered Mrs. Brooke. He was genuinely bewildered by what now seemed undisguised hostility. 'I should never have imagined that you would treat me with what of course seems to me such great unfairness. . . . I have agreed to make all the alterations you asked for, and there is nothing in the M. to which you object.' In the course of a long and un-availing letter he made it clear that his concessions would stop short the moment they showed signs of compromising his literary judgement.

I must go back to what I have discussed with you before—your saying once that you 'did not care about the literary merit of my work'. What you mean by this, I suppose, is that you do not care whether I get any credit for it—and neither do I, except in the sense in which anyone who does a piece of work, especially in such a cause, must hope that it will be thought well done. But there is another meaning which the expression cannot help bearing, and that is that you do not care whether the memoir is well- or ill-written, shapely or formless, readable or unreadable. . . . And there is no possible doubt that if I followed your plan of swelling it out with a number of contributions, uncontrolled by me, with the object of making it a composite portrait rather than the work of a single hand, it *would* become an ill-constructed, uninteresting, bad piece of work. . . . You really ought not to brush aside my opinion on literary questions, or to dismiss such questions as unimportant. Their importance is quite practical. 'Literary merit', in the humble sense in which I am using the words, is not a scholar's fetish, or a mere inessential ornament; it is the quality which makes the difference between a book that will do, and a book that won't.

In her answer written next day Mrs. Brooke denied having ever given her consent. Without stating her motive explicitly, she made an all-out effort to discourage him from any further memorial exertions. Three posthumous books had already appeared, impeccably arranged and edited, and three more were in preparation.[1] There had been no plausible excuse for obstructing these, although—the war sonnets (1914) excepted—she greeted each volume with frigid disinterest. But biography was another matter:

I don't consider you knew Rupert well enough to write his Memoir; you didn't really understand him nor would you have had much sympathy with a good deal in him had you known him better. I could name several of his friends who are much better fitted for the work from this standpoint. . . . This to my mind is the one necessary qualification. I have no doubt whatever of your literary ability to

[1] The main publications edited by Edward Marsh and published by Sidgwick & Jackson are as follows:

1914 and Other Poems (June 1915)
'1914' Five Sonnets (November 1915)
Letters from America (March 1916)
John Webster and the Elizabethans (November 1916)
The Old Vicarage, Grantchester (December 1916)
Selected Poems (March 1917)
Collected Poems, With a Memoir (July 1918, revised 1928)
The Complete Poems (October 1932)

do the work, but I must put that a long way behind the other. . . .
It seems to me quite impossible that anyone who had so little opportunity of knowing anyone as you had of knowing Rupert could write
at all an adequate account of him and if I speak the honest truth I
was much surprised that you ever attempted it.

I am not trying to force you into any course which you think
mistaken, as you say, but to give up a course which *I* think mistaken.

I cannot take any blame to myself for any loss that the publishers
may fear. You most certainly ought to have waited till all my conditions were fulfilled before you gave him leave to proceed, for they
were very important conditions, and I said most decidedly that they
must be fulfilled. I cannot reopen this matter, so it is quite useless to
try to persuade me.

This was at once passed on to Sidgwick. 'I got the enclosed
disgraceful letter yesterday.' A reply, he added, 'will take time and
temper'. Fortunately there was now material of a fairly pressing
nature to hand which might serve to ease the tension by causing a
diversion.

Mrs. Brooke had recently heard that her son had been posthumously awarded the Howland Prize in the gift of Yale University, and had been deeply touched by the letters notifying her of
this new honour to her son's memory. It was a condition of the
award that the winner should give a lecture at Yale, and Marsh
was now in search of a spokesman. Gibson and Abercrombie
were unable to go. He had now written to the President proposing a visit from de la Mare. His reply to the particularly hurtful
letter from Rugby began by making no reference to its contents.
Instead he discussed the question of the envoy to Yale as if there
were nothing more on his mind. At the end he briefly acknowledged her letter with its final ban. 'I deplore it for many reasons
which it would be useless to mention.' There was no further
comment. Gosse was now alarmed lest Marsh should altogether
lose heart. 'I am afraid only that you in the face of so much ingratitude and aspersion may throw up the thing and give way.
This I entreat you not to do.' Her ingratitude was 'almost
ludicrous. . . . It is your energy which has fostered and even
founded his reputation.' But Marsh had already sent a draft
announcement of postponement to Frank Sidgwick. '"Owing to
wishes of the family"—I should like to insert the word "bloody"
before "family", but I don't insist on this.' It was May 17. The
vexed question was in abeyance for the next thirteen months.

To Gosse he sent an admirably objective summary of the affair. 'Anyhow, there it is, and no doubt there were faults on my side. . . . I think it is quite intelligible how this frame of mind in a narrow, obstinate and extremely masterful woman, loving her son tigerishly, had led up to this unhappy situation . . . on her premises she is right in thinking that any consideration of fairness or graciousness to me must take second place. The fact that she is wrong from beginning to end cannot be brought home to her.' At least he now knew where he was. 'There's nothing she'd stick at to dish me!'

iii

The Georgïan matinée at His Majesty's, the culmination of endless discussions on casting and designs, went into rehearsal at the end of April under the direction of John Drinkwater. Viola Tree, manager of the enterprise, playing Goneril, was often Novello's companion at the play during these weeks, and her rehearsals were still in progress when she appealed to Eddie Marsh to arbitrate in a quarrel which had grown to embarrassing proportions. Novello, by her own report, had said she was 'too vibrant' and professionally detached so that she 'blighted his enthusiasm' in the theatre, and when she was moved to tears she 'cried too loud!' Her complaint of *him* was on rather similar grounds. She had been brought up never to 'edit' when at a play, she said, not even to the deaf or imbecile. 'Ivor, as you know, gives you a concise résumé of exactly what the people will say, not only that but a little private eulogy just anticipating their action by three minutes—the same with the safety curtain which though I agree is always a pleasing sight, needs no italics. Supposing before my entrance as Goneril someone said, "Viola Tree comes on soon. She's 6 ft. high but not so slim as she was—her boots will be green." . . . I hate to be a blight on his greatest pleasure and I want you to stick up for me.' Later it was the senior member of the trio who had taken umbrage. 'Curious man Eddie Marsh,' wrote Novello, 'must I with great ceremony *ask* you to join us at our frugal meal of macaroni-cheese and strawberries?' But the show must go on, and all differences were forgotten when on May 19 *King Lear's Wife* was the main item in the grand matinée at His Majesty's. Lady Tree played the title role and Viola sang the two settings by Novello. Gibson's *Hoops*, and Martin Harvey in Brooke's *Lithuania*,[1] completed the bill. Debutantes sold Monro's Poetry Bookshop Chapbooks in the auditorium (among them the first poems by Graves, which had come out on May 1); Marsh sat in a box with Novello and Bottomley, and all declared the occasion a success, though Gosse was unimpressed by *Lithuania*, regretting that Brooke in searching for a subject for melodrama should have chosen, as he declared, one of the most hackneyed in all dramatic literature. 'Lillo's *Fatal Discovery* should have warned him off.' This short play was the only work of Brooke's that Marsh considered unworthy of publication. Sidgwick was anxious to bring it out between the same covers as the thesis on John Webster and the Elizabethans that Marsh was now editing, but it was certainly to the advantage of the poet's reputation to keep this grotesque one-acter out of the canon. In recent years the theme has again emerged as *Le Matelot*, the one-act opera by Milhaud, where music serves better than Brooke's prose to make interesting a crude and improbable episode.

On June 25 Novello reported as Probationary Flight Sub-Lieutenant D. Davies, R.N., at the Crystal Palace Training Depot, found himself in a barrack-room with four others, and, as he reported, 'much to my surprise I understand the lectures'. At the same time Juliet Duff went over to France on war-duty, so the 'jollies' came to an end, and Marsh found himself obliged to continue the gossip by letter. 'I feel like the Last Rose of S., all my lovely companions, tho' happily not faded, are gone.'

I had an absurd evening yesterday—dined with Maud [Cunard] and met the celebrated Mrs. Gough. She's *very* lovely—a white face and cloudy black hair, and had a wonderful electric blue gown. 'Do you like my gown?' she said to the company, in a deep rich soft lustrous languid Andalusian tenor voice. 'I thought perhaps it was too *jeune fille*. It's the youngest gown I've had for five years' (she's 22). Nancy appeared in a man's black evening waistcoat with a white

---

[1] *Lithuania* was first produced by Maurice Browne at the Little Theatre, Chicago, in November 1915, and Marsh treasured among his papers a report by a local critic which ended: 'It thrilled openly, and the atmospheric effects achieved, combined with the very typhoid of utterance and action, made the Brooke play memorable not only for its shocking integrals but because the players sank keen fangs in the heart of it and pierced its human preachment.' The same critic referred to the chief character as 'the gnarly daughter'. One is reminded of Bottomley's Goneril (a much superior creation) and given to wonder why 'the gnarly daughter' should have been a characteristic figure in Georgian drama.

'slip', and buckle behind, and fluffy white stuff instead of a shirt, very becoming, but it enraged Maud who thought she meant to go to Mrs. Keppel's ball in it. . . . We sat round the lovely lapis lazuli table, miles apart, I could just hear Nancy twitter across it.

He was making the acquaintance of Novello's mother. 'She accounts for a good deal of Ivor but he's still a freak of heredity. She has a bracelet with a photograph of him on each arm.' The father he described as a 'dear pathetic old thing, but not much of an asset to the vortex'. Nothing ever stimulated him to write a second time so much as the absence of a reply, so he persisted.

There are two possibilities (1) that you've been torpedoed, (2) that you forgot, and I prefer the latter, though less flattering, and have persuaded myself it's on the whole more probable. The luxury of grief at your departure was broken in upon by Léonie [Leslie] carrying me off to dine on, or off (which do you think the more elegant preposition?), some excellent cold beef at the Italian restaurant—such a funny *bonne fortune* for me. I hoped someone we knew would see us, it would have been so extremely compromising —like the people in Henry James who were found at the Soane Museum—but no such luck. She told me a story about Spy Mania in Paris, a wife says to her husband, 'You remember that horrid old fat Alsatian cook we had for two months before the war? Well, she was General von Kluck in disguise.' *'Oh, quelle, horreur! et moi qui t'ai trompé avec lui!'*

In mid-July Novello was posted to the airport at Chingford, taken up for his first flight, and for some minutes hovered precariously over Sydenham. 'It was a reward,' Marsh wrote to Juliet Duff, 'for making a senior officer's wife laugh by playing *Onward Christian Soldiers* as ragtime. He found he had a perfect nerve and simply loved it and as the Senior Officer couldn't hear for the noise he could give vent to his feelings by screaming Jesus! and kissing his hand to God.' Novello's first report to Marsh was, 'Words fail me! I've got *marvellous* nerve—not a tremor—although he tried to put the wind up me by making a spiral descent.' A few days later Marsh gave news of a dinner where Munthe was among the guests.

Axel Munthe arrived at 7.30, just as we were sitting down (we were going to the Opera) to pay an afternoon call, and was persuaded to eat his mutton with us. I didn't know him, but Léonie whispered to me that he was rather a poseur (in fact the greatest she knew) and with this light I was enabled to enjoy the conversation. He had been asked to the notorious luncheon at Grosvenor House tomorrow, and he was very anxious to be told about it and advised whether to go or not. I rather cruelly threw all my weight into the adverse scale, expatiating on how unworthy of him it would all be—only the Stage and Society etc.—meanwhile there had been a lot of talk about people and L. suddenly said to him, 'This conversation is too frivolous for you, Munthe.' 'To tell you truth,' he said, 'I wasn't attending.' I compared him to Dr. Johnson who said in similar circumstances, 'I withdrew my mind from the conversation.'

George Moore was always a slightly grotesque figure in Marsh's eyes. At the Opera that night a lady of the party 'found it in her heart to compare G.M. to a white swan, but there was a phrase in the libretto', Marsh commented, 'that described him much better—"You libidinous old gargoyle".' He capped this with another story.

George Moore is ill in bed from a nightmare in which he thought the Germans had invaded England and were storming his bedroom —he jumped out of bed with the intention of resisting to the last, and slipped right along the floor to the other end of the room, cutting himself all to bits. He wants Maud [Cunard] to get him the V.C. on the ground that anybody can be brave when they're awake, but to be brave in one's sleep is the *real thing*.

After the Opera he called on Violet Bonham Carter (formerly Asquith), 'who had Bernard Shaw to dinner—it was rather against my principle as I don't like meeting people who are too fair about the war, but I was quite conquered, he's a singularly charming man. Maud [Cunard] was there at the top of her form. "I never know what 'obscene' means—is it the same as salacious? or Elizabethan, or pornographic?"' At a party the next day he was presented to an illustrious guest 'who *looks* as if she had a sense of humour which is half the battle'. The end of this letter to Lady Juliet Duff is characteristic in its gentle compliment.

I hope you get my letters before they're quite dried up and have to be put in water like anemones from the Riviera. I shall look forward immensely to the two hats. It will be great fun to see you looking a fright (but I'm not building *too* much on it).

In August he stayed a few days at Trent, the country house of the wealthy Mrs. Duggan.

Everything quite pre-war, 4 footmen in the hall when I arrived and dinner beginning with caviare; conversation on 'the fantastic way in which actors and actresses are admitted into English Society'; it was chiefly remarkable for eliciting from Lady Paget a tribute to Art —'Personally,' she said, 'I admire Art very much.'

Lord Curzon was there. There *would* have been George Moore, but he had left the house suddenly before breakfast—no one knew why—but Mrs. D. told me after dinner that it was because after (1) blaspheming the Sacrament of Mass before her two little boys who are Roman Catholics, (2) abusing Lord Curzon to her, he had finished up (3) telling her on Saturday night that she was a 'dainty little morsel'.

A week later Marsh was again at Trent, with Curzon, Balfour, and Maud Cunard. He was somewhat put out by the attendance of a fellow-guest 'who really has an abnormally commonplace mind and looks upon me as a kindred spirit. . . . Lord Kitchener came but was routed by Maud who said she took no interest in him.' After dinner some of the party played table-turning, which was 'interrupted by the hostess's late husband'.

What was rather pathetic was that 'Mr. Duggan' kept chipping in, and *tried* to tell us all about the war, but in a much more confused and less convincing way than the others, till at last Mrs. D. said, 'Alfred, I wish you'd get away and let the others tell us'—She said it quite nicely, but I did feel it was a bit rough on him, what?

The more intelligible 'voice' informed the party that the Hohenzollerns were destined to lose their throne and the English statesmen at the Peace Conference would be Bonar Law—'and —who? Lord Curzon'.

It was amusing to hear him [Curzon] lead up to this by enquiring about other possibilities—'Will it be Lord Lansdowne?' 4 raps (no). 'Will it be Lloyd George?' 4 raps (no). 'Will it be Mr. Balfour?' and so on, and at last, 'Will it be Lord Curzon?' 3 raps (yes) and dark as it was I fancied I could detect a little bridling movement. By the way, the King is to be assassinated within a month from now, but Lord C. said we weren't to put this about, so don't let it go any further.

He then embarked on a story he had just heard from Mrs. Churchill. It illustrated the charmingly eccentric zeal of his friend Lady Islington after a summons on the telephone.

Nancy Astor rang her up and said, as she was the *only* woman she knew who went on buying clothes, would she lend her a hat to go to a wedding? Anne said yes, and spent the whole morning routing out all the old hats in the house—about 60—including the servant's, and Jack's, which she trimmed with feathers and artificial flowers, and arranged them in the dining-room with labels, such as 'Jack's last present to me'—'my Favourite Hat'—and 'As worn by Gaby des Lys'. Jack wanted to go out in the morning and couldn't find his hat. The butler said, 'Her Ladyship's got it in the dining-room, me Lord; she's trimming it with feathers'. Anne wouldn't give, it up and made him send to a shop for another. Finally she went out, leaving word that Mrs. Astor was to be shown the hats when she came.

Then he gave news of a ducal residence in Arlington Street which was being turned into a hospital. 'The Duchess's bedroom is to be the operating theatre, and as she's the world's greatest Molly Corker[1] you can imagine the collection of odds and ends, the accumulation of years, that has come to light, behind the looking-glasses etc. The room must be a regular jackdaw's nest. Sounds *terribly* insanitary.' He had dropped into a bookshop to buy Juliet Duff a present. 'I nearly bought a book called "How When and Where to Catch Fish off the East Coast of Florida", as it seemed so stupid not to know—but I didn't dare.'

iv

As the summer went by Marsh was amazed by the speed of his recovery from the stresses of only a few months before, and this was brought home to him afresh while acknowledging a letter in which Lance Sieveking had described how he was often sustained by the thought of his pre-war pleasures.

I do envy you your new-found power of enjoying your past. I haven't got it a bit. So long as I'm on the same page in the book, I love thinking back the earlier lines of it—but once the leaf is turned, the previous pages bore me a little—partly because I'm ashamed, *both* of what I was *and* of having changed (which is a bit inconsistent!). I sometimes say to myself in bed, 'Now before I go to sleep I'll go through such-and-such a walking tour', but I soon weary of it and fall to thinking of last week, or next Sunday, instead. It's very wasteful, and I do hope I shall get the gift by the time I'm old.

The young poets were in constant touch with him. There was enough in the present to prevent him from dwelling too much

[1] Baring expression for one who tidies up by merely pushing things out of sight, derived from an Irish maid of this name.

on the past. De la Mare had agreed to go to America to receive Brooke's award: 'The prospect does not fill me with unadulterated joy, principally because I'm a stupidly shy bird that prefers its own small cage.' The Brooke royalties that Marsh was distributing among the three legatees had begun to make a big difference to their lives. 'If only Rupert could know what his thought of me was to mean,' wrote de la Mare, 'more rest of mind.'

Robert Graves was now putting his affairs in Marsh's hands. 'If anything happens you're the only person I can trust as literary executor of my poor Remains. I want you to have absolute free hand to chop and change anything. . . . I hope to God Siegfried is all right. I saw a man in hospital in Rouen who was hit with the 1st Bn. just as they had gone over the top on the 1st of July.' A similar request had come from Sassoon himself. 'O Eddie, you *must* get my poems printed soon, it will be such fun to think of them when everything becomes horrid and people begin to get sent away hurt.' Soon he was able to give news of Graves.

> I've just seen Robert, his Batn. came along and bivouacked 300 yards away [outside Mametz Wood, on the Somme]. And we sat among the thistles under the cloudy night sky lit with flashes and the hidden moon . . . and talked of how we'd go to the Caucasus, or any old place, *après la guerre*, while his men snored under their piled rifles a little way off. And there he sleeps now. And tomorrow I suppose we'll both be up in the show.

In July Sassoon was awarded the Military Cross and wrote to Gray's Inn: 'Eddie, I chased 40 Boches out of a trench by Mametz Wood all by myself. Wasn't that a joyous moment for me? They ran like hell and I chucked bombs and made hunting noises. I wonder if I shall ever be able to take soldiering seriously.' A note followed: 'Two poems enclosed. The usual drivel I suppose.' Concerning this intrepid exploit Marsh commented: 'Never take it more seriously than that. . . . I'm proud that you're in it. Bless you—come through.' It's curious that he should have made these remarks to the one soldier who was shortly to take it more 'seriously' than any other man in the Army, even to the point of public protest. 'I'm sorry to hear Robert is unhappy, he hasn't got the art of being all things to all men,' Marsh was writing to Sassoon when the news came that Graves had been killed on July 20. 'All my military virtues seem to have gone fut,' wrote Sassoon in anguish. 'Robert died of wounds yesterday. . . . Won't they leave anyone we are fond of?' He can barely have posted this when a wire reached him from Whitehall. Marsh was telling him that the report was untrue. Meanwhile Graves' father had received two letters by the same post—one from the C.O. in France condoling on the tragic loss of his son, and one from the youth himself, who was lying prostrate in hospital. Sassoon described his relief. 'I felt a sort of glow spreading all over me; or rather like an air-cushion being blown up.' Marsh must have felt much the same. 'I don't think I could have borne those poems if he'd been dead, as it was they moved me deeply. . . . The Dead Boche is very powerful, it nearly made me sick.' At length Graves himself wrote, like a voice from the tomb. A shell splinter had passed through his chest into his back. He was in hospital at Rouen.

> This afternoon I had a sort of waking dream about meeting and making friends with Rupert; it was absolutely vivid and I feel I know him ten times better than before. We talked poetry most of the time and he said amongst other things that it wasn't so bad being dead as you got such splendid opportunities of watching what was happening. The thing ended by your Gray's Inn housekeeper appearing, whereupon Rupert went up and had a bath and I saw him no more. I wonder what suggested it? . . . I came of age on the 24th, think of that!

On August 7 he wrote again from a bed in Highgate. 'As a matter of fact, he began, 'I *did* die on my way down to the Field Ambulance.'

> To cut short a long story old Rhadamanthus introduced himself as my judge but I refused to accept his jurisdiction—I wanted a court-martial of British officers, he was only a rotten old Greek. He shouted out 'Contempt of Court' but I chucked a Mills bomb at him which scattered the millions of mouthless dead in about two seconds and wounded old R. in the leg and broke his sceptre. Then I strode away, held a revolver to Charon's head, climbed into the boat and so home. I gave him a Rouen note for 50 *cm*. which I didn't want particularly. . . . The Doctor was saying 'Hopeless case' (and this part of the tale is true, truer even than the rest) and I winked at him and said 'Dear old doctor' and went off again to sleep.
>
> My sense of humour may have been enfeebled but I laughed till I was nearly ill yesterday over 100 copy lines which a Charterhouse master told my brother to write the other day, to the effect that he must not be a baby. I can't reproduce the original exactly but the

result was written in the very choicest copperplate handwriting. It went something like this for eight pages:

'I must endeavour to emerge from my present phase of infantility—The symptoms of babyhood must be eradicated from my composition—It behoves me to comport myself in a manner less typical of extreme juvenility—I am bound by a moral obligation to rid myself of the characteristics of a youthful and childish baby—I must not be a baby—O God, save me from shrinking smaller and smaller from boyhood to babydom and finally from vanishing completely away etc.'

Don't you love the 'youthful and childish baby'? It has a wonderful naiveté about it. Is the thing so funny because it was shown up to a master or what?

I'm longing to see you on Sat. Try to bring Ivor Novello with you. I'd love to meet him if he wouldn't be bored, and you, busy man, could kill two birds with one stone.

As part of a campaign for 'better lyrics' Marsh had got Novello to try his hand at English *Lieder* by setting a selection of short pieces by Graves, and in a ward at Highgate author and composer were brought together.

It was now that an appeal reached Gray's Inn concerning a writer about whom Marsh knew very little. The only solution was to consult two of the man's compatriots. George Moore's reply opened with a tribute to the manner of Marsh's enquiry 'clear and fluent, and always to the point, expressing everything you had in mind to say. Nothing seems to have got lost between the brain and the pen.'

The only book of Joyce's that I have read is a collection of stories called *Dubliners*, some of them are trivial and disagreeable, but all are written by a clever man, and the book contains one story, the longest in the book and the last story, which seemed to me perfection whilst I read it: I regretted that I was not the author of it. But this story, which I am sure you would appreciate as much as I did, does not prove that Joyce will go on writing and will end by writing something like a masterpiece. A talent, musical, literary or pictorial, is a pale fluttering thing that a breath will extinguish. I will get *Dubliners* from Heinemann to whom I lent the book and you will see for yourself. Of the novel I know nothing. Joyce left a disagreeable reputation behind him in Dublin, but he came back after some years a different man and everything I heard of him is to his credit. Of his political views I know nothing. He was not in Ireland during the sowing of the Sinn Fein seed and I hope he is not even a Home Ruler. Democratic principles are unsuited to Ireland. . . . I am an admirer of Mr. Asquith and regret that he cannot bring himself to believe that there can be no settlement, and that all attempts at settlement will fail. The Irish like discipline, and if Mr. Asquith would treat the Irish as the Pope does he would be the most popular man in Ireland. I am sure that from a literary point of view Joyce is deserving of help.

The opinion of W. B. Yeats was more decided:

His work has a curious brooding intensity. I think one of his poems at any rate a thing of great beauty and great technical accomplishment. If I compiled an anthology of English or Irish Poetry I would include it. *Dubliners* is like a first novel by a great novelist. The background is too consciously studied perhaps. The *Portrait of the Artist* I have only seen in fragments but I saw enough to know that it has great intensity and sincerity. I think him a possible man of genius.

Marsh read the works, thought fit to help the author in his official capacity as adviser to the Prime Minister on Civil List pensions, and asked Ezra Pound for Joyce's address. 'I should like to express my appreciation of the official action in this matter,' wrote Pound. 'I think it would be hard to find anyone more deserving than Joyce, both by reason of his ability and from the way he has stuck to his ideals under most trying circumstances.' James Joyce wrote from Switzerland on September 13.

Mr. Ezra Pound has written to me telling me that you were so kind as to bring my books to the notice of the Prime Minister, on whose recommendation a Treasury grant was made to me last month. Allow me to assure you that I am deeply grateful to you for having used your influence so generously and so effectively on my behalf and to thank you also for the favourable opinion which you have expressed of my meagre writings. I hope too that the difficulties which have made me, much to my regret, a burden to others will now be removed and if so I feel that I shall owe it in great measure to your friendly and benevolent intervention.

'I am simply *thrilled* about you and Joyce,' wrote Lady Cunard, who had initiated the enquiry. 'It is all *you* and I know it and bless you.'

On hearing that Bottomley had been encouraging Rosenberg (whose *Moses* was now in print), Marsh intervened to make quite sure the senior Georgian was taking the right line with the boy.

I wrote him a piece of my mind about *Moses*, which seems to me really magnificent in parts, especially the speech beginning 'Ah Koelue'[1] which I think absolutely one of the finest things ever written—but as a whole it's surely quite ridiculously bad. I hope you mix plenty of powder with your jam. I do want him to renounce the lawless and grotesque manner in which he usually writes and to pay a little attention to form and tradition.

He had also been lecturing Novello. 'He has a dangerous facility of turning out catchy tunes which are very pretty and great fun, but not so good as he ought to do.' Fortunately, perhaps, for British light music this advice fell on stony ground. Novello was artist enough to know his limitations. Concerning Rosenberg Bottomley showed there was no difference of opinion.

I told him I thought it was worth his while to be intelligible and that an especial obligation is on a dramatic poet to meet his audience at least half-way. He interests me because in *Moses* I felt some assurance that in him, at last, has turned up a poet *de longue haleine* among the youngsters; he has paid the customary allegiance to Poundisme, Unanisme, and the rest with an energy and vividness which distinguishes him from the others.

He believed that Rosenberg had shown enough imaginative power to be able to deal with his ancestral mythology in his own way without yielding to fashion. And he had sent him *Joseph and his Brethren*,[2] drawing special attention to Act II 'in the hope that it may help to make him swerve toward the Centre'. Marsh was more uncompromising:

I wrote to him with the utmost brutality, telling him it was an outrage on humanity that the man who could write the Koelue speech should imbed it in such a farrago. I wouldn't have been such a beast but that I wanted to counteract the praise he'd had from you! . . . he seems to me entirely without architectonics—both the shaping instinct and the reserve of power that carries a thing through. It's the same in his painting, he does a good sketch of a design and leaves it there. However, let's hope for the best. No one can write a Koelue by accident.

Bottomley fully agreed. 'I am depressed by the school that emits a Gasp of Beauty and then sinks in exhaustion, like the bee after its sting.'

---

[1] This refers to the last section of a monologue by Moses at the end of Scene One. It was to appear in the next *Georgian Poetry* volume.

[2] The dramatic poem by C. J. Wells (1800-1879) written under the pseudonym H. L. Howerd.

In June Rosenberg had crossed over to France. He was undeterred by Marsh's strictures, and enclosed another poem. 'You
might object to the second line as vague, but that was the best
way I could express the sense of dawn. . . . If I could get a few
months after the war to work and absorb myself completely into
the thing, I'd write a great thing.' Bottomley had sent him *King
Lear's Wife*. 'There are few men living who could whack that as a
play,' wrote Rosenberg. He said he was forbidden to send any
more poems to England 'as the censor won't be bothered with
going through such rubbish'.

It was in October that Marsh, in desperation for something to write about, told Rosenberg that he had discovered
in himself a new talent. 'I was amused to hear of your gardening experiment,' said the poet of what was henceforth to
be his patron's favourite recreation. 'I think I must have
been *born* to be an under-gardener,' Marsh wrote to Juliet Duff,
at whose country home in Wales he had so suddenly seen the
light; and he told Cathleen Nesbitt that he had made the discovery
while trying to plant 'about a thousand wallflowers . . . and I dug
bindweed roots out from almost the Antipodes'. Within a few
days he was regarding his new hobby with mixed feelings. He was
advising de la Mare on the preparation of his lecture to Yale
University and on how to address his American host. 'I call him
"Dear Mr. President" when I write and he doesn't seem to mind,'
he wrote from 10 Downing Street, then lodged a complaint.

> I've got a grievance against you. I spent a Sunday in Wales and was
> made to work in the garden—the chief part of my work was the
> destruction of convolvuluses or bindweed which were strangling
> everything. I rooted them up and tore away their tendrils and cast
> them on a heap for burning and generally made myself as beastly to
> them as possible, and in the process conceived a bloody-minded
> hatred for them. Now in today's *Mirror* there is a poem about them by
> you, most lovely, representing them in a thoroughly sympathetic
> light, and I'm filled with remorse, and when I go back as I'm going
> next week it will be impossible to get up any animus against them.
> See what you've done—ruined my gardening.

By early October de la Mare had arrived in America and was
on his way to Yale.

> Dear Eddie—if I may make so bold and be Jack in return (you have

been absolutely the first in this mortal life to burst into the cold seas of Walter) here I am.

'Rupert must be amused,' de la Mare wrote of his comparative affluence, 'though when I think of that generous careless letter I have misgivings.' Throughout September he had been preparing his lecture on Brooke. Gibson, whom Marsh had managed to dislodge from the Army on account of his defective sight, followed de la Mare on a reading-tour to America a month later. 'You really must send me a letter some time without a cheque in it,' was his parting word, and he committed all his manuscripts into Marsh's safe keeping. Graves and Sassoon had spent September together convalescing in Harlech; the one preparing *Fairies and Fusiliers* and the other putting *The Old Huntsman* in order for publication. They corrected each other's verses, discussed Marsh's copious critical notes, and Graves even enjoyed the unique privilege of suggesting an emendation in Sassoon's elegiac lines written to his own memory. In mid-October Graves, whom Marsh had taken to dine with Henry Festing Jones, where he had been allowed to look through the Samuel Butler papers, wrote to say that Butler 'overshadows all life for me just as Handel did his'.

Siegfried's verses are getting infinitely better than the first crop I saw, much free-er and more Georgian. What a pity he did not start earlier! I suspect Gosse of being his retarding influence 'keeping me to my moons and nightingales and things' as S.S. put it himself yesterday. . . . S.S. and I have great difficulty in talking about poetry as the other officers of the Btn. are terribly curious and suspicious. If I go into the mess and he wants to show me some verses he says, 'Afternoon, Graves! have a drink. . . . by the way I want you to see my latest recipe for rum punch.' The trenches are worse than billets for privacy. Why should the Germans get Verdun? Why this pessimism?

By the early autumn Mr. Churchill had become a civilian. It was still impossible for Mr. Asquith to give him office without alienating the Tories and splitting a Government which was already the target of criticism. It suited Mr. Churchill, however, when a Commission was set up to investigate the failure at Gallipoli; but many months, perhaps years, might pass before its findings were made public. Mr. Churchill himself gave evidence. A brief note (September 13), addressed from the Cromwell Road, expressed his feelings.

My dear Eddie, What is the use of my tormenting myself with these painful enquiries? *Vae victis.* Yours ever, W.

It was at this time that Lady Randolph Churchill invited Marsh to bring Sub-Lieutenant Davies to dinner, for *The Home Fires* (or 'Keep the What?' as Novello now called it) had become a national asset and her son was interested to meet its young composer. He was apparently well versed in the music-hall songs of his Sandhurst days, and though they were of a vintage before Novello's time the composer was able to keep his end up by singing over the port the ditties whose titles came to Mr. Churchill's mind. At one point there came a mutual pause for wonderment. 'Do you know,' said Mr. Churchill, 'you'd be far better off in a home?' Marsh and his protégé exchanged glances. Had the young airman been showing signs of insanity? *You'd be Far Better Off in a Home*, it transpired, was the only title so far that Novello had not come across before. During this autumn Marsh also arranged, through Elizabeth Asquith, a meeting between Novello and Lily Elsie, the object of his admiration, whom they had watched together in *Mavourneen* at their first meeting a year before, and a tea-party was given for the purpose in the drawing-room at Downing Street. The aim was to interest the actress in an operetta Novello had written, but at the critical moment when he had launched into his theme-song at the piano, not only did a military band strike up in the street outside, but Mrs. Asquith made her entrance in time to the music and waltzed round the furniture. The occasion was not an unqualified success, but Marsh was able to applaud the slow advance of Novello's career with the production of *Theodore & Co.* on September 9, the day after they had both paid a first visit to *Chu Chin Chow*. Society had found it at last. The Duchess of Marlborough and Mrs. Asquith, both with their families, were there, though they arrived an hour late. 'The play is terrible trash,' Juliet Duff was informed. 'One's mind refuses to attend to it, but the *spectacle* the most gorgeous you can imagine.'

For some time Robert Ross had been in consultation with Marsh over Sassoon's latest poems, and he was now agitating for a public exhibition of the pictures at Raymond Buildings. 'You stand for the sober side of the future in questions of art and literature,' he wrote, 'as distinct from the "futurist".' Not only Ross but Professor Michael Sadler was urging him to give the public the benefit of his collection. At the head of a pre-war letter from Sadler Marsh had written, 'The most wonderful dewdrop I ever got about my collection.' In it Sadler had declared : 'You have that rarest thing, a love for the great past and a faith in the future. This, I suppose, left me with the strongest feeling of all—intense satisfaction that these great things have come into the keeping and intimacy of one who has discernment and "the divining mind". To have brought these together, out of so many things seen, is itself a creative act like painting a great picture.' This was encouragement indeed, but when the exhibition took place under the auspices of the Burlington Fine Arts Club it was not the modern painters who were brought to the public notice. It was the Horne collection, and it established the reputation of the early English water-colour school outside a small circle of specialists. Alexander Cozens in particular was at last recognized as a master. Meanwhile the contemporaries were not forgotten by their patron. By now Spencer was drilling in the ranks; Paul Nash was a lieutenant in the 3rd Hampshires; Gertler, who had cut himself off from the evil times, had reappeared in April, destitute, and had his Perceval subsidy restored. But of all the artists of one kind or another Brooke was still the cause of all the serious work.

Throughout the last quarter of 1916 Frank Sidgwick was corresponding with Gray's Inn on the subject of the first Selection. The poet's reputation was being planned between them with all the meticulous forethought of a military campaign. *Lithuania* was finally abandoned, and the size, arrangement and typography of the new volume were discussed in almost daily letters. In the absence of a Memoir this would be the most important publication to date. Sidgwick was afraid it would kill the two earlier volumes (the *Poems* of 1911 were being reprinted), while Marsh argued that, even so, it didn't matter. 'I'm really anxious to do the truest honour to Rupert by this publication,' he wrote, pointing out that the poet's commercial success up to now warranted a slight risk being taken on his behalf. The plans were developing when Marsh's official career was transformed overnight and, as it seemed at first, ruined. The fall of Mr. Asquith came as a terrible shock. Criticized by Lloyd George from within and by Edward Carson (who was largely responsible for Mr. Churchill's return to public affairs) from among the unofficial Opposition, the Prime Minister was obliged to resign. For a while there were hopes that

Mr. Churchill would be recalled to office, but nothing had happened to alter the views of Bonar Law and his associates. Once again the necessity for harmony in an administration composed of different party allegiances led to the omission of what might have been its strongest member. When Lloyd George submitted to the King the names of his new Coalition on December 7 Winston Churchill was not among them.

Almost exactly a year before, when the Prime Minister had taken Marsh under his wing, his position was rendered unhappy enough by concern for the safety of his former Chief. Now there was no second patron to fall back on, and this time there was no vacant place commensurate with Eddie Marsh's prestige in the Civil Service. He had staked his official career on the fortunes of one man, who had become the victim of mistrust and prejudice. With all his experience, he dropped back almost to where he was at the turn of the century. In a basement of the Colonial Office, ingloriously remote from the centre of affairs to which he had grown accustomed during the last eleven years, he took his place as a clerk in the West African Department. Unhappy and perplexed, as much on Churchill's behalf as on his own, he wrote to Juliet Duff. Her answer reflects his frame of mind and the gravity of this crisis in the eyes of his friends.

> I have always admired in you that with your splendid brain, intuition, and grasp, you should have had no personal ambition, and it *is* hard that that very quality should have let you down now.
>
> You have got so many interests and abilities that I am quite certain you will be able to make a wonderful life for yourself. Perhaps you won't quite see *how* for some time, but I *know* it will come. . . .
>
> The things that matter in *your* life are your unselfishness to Winston, your countless kindnesses to and sacrifices for struggling people; your encouragement of Art; your marvellous gift of friendship and never failing sympathy, never 'put on' but coming straight from your heart.
>
> I *know*, dear Eddie, that those are the things which count; in fact they are the only ones that matter at all. All the rest is dross.

v

After the Christmas celebrations at Knebworth he returned to his basement in Whitehall, where his prospects for 1917 must have looked peculiarly bleak and humiliating. Turning to his personal affairs, however, there were signs that Georgianism still flourished.

Lord Basil Blackwood was leaving copies of the last anthology lying around in the trenches for anyone to claim; in the Sudan a captain of the Dorsets, so Bottomley reported, had sung the Corpse Washer's song from *King Lear's Wife* to the Pirate's tune in *Peter Pan*; young Ledwidge at the Front was still alive and proud of the association. '*Georgian Poetry* (with my three excluded) contains, I think, the best poems of the century.' But Sassoon and Graves were,causing anxiety. They had left their depot at Litherland and were once more in the line. There was much to be anxious about whichever way he looked, and nothing to lighten the spirits beyond the unexpected return into the picture of Maurice Baring. The intrepid Lord Lucas had been shot down over the enemy lines and Baring had written an elegy which he had sent to Gray's Inn. 'Why are the great elegies so impersonal?' he asked in the course of a general review of elegiac verse. Not only was Marsh's old Cambridge friend proving himself to be a poet, but after all his exploits in Turkey and Russia and France he had lost none of his zest. 'Years ago, when you were a pale young curate and I was a slave in Babylon you tried to instil into my breast a passion for the novels of Henry James.' He had been translating certain of James's sentences into French in the hope of understanding them better in a language other than the original. While wrestling with James's meaning he heard of the impasse with Mrs. Brooke. Her objections were trifling, Baring protested. What about Gosse's dealings with the family of Swinburne? 'He was forbidden to mention ginger beer or warm affection between a man and a woman or the execution of Charles the First.' He asked for a copy of Wordsworth's poems, then wrote in acknowledgement. 'I have just received the works of W. My last copy was taken away, presumably by a leech-gatherer.' More significant in the light of after events was their brief exchange on the subject of translation. 'I think Horace, like La Fontaine,' wrote Baring, inadvertently foreshadowing the two great projects of Marsh's latter years, 'cannot be properly appreciated till one is forty—which is equivalent to saying that lyricism is in abeyance. Youth has not much patience with the Golden Mean.' Baring's letter of a few weeks later gives a clue to Marsh's views on translation at this time: 'I accept your creed *in toto*: that the best poetry should be incommunicable, and that the charm of a thing being said in one particular way should make it necessary for you to learn the language.' The immediate outcome of this correspondence was the acquisition of Baring's *In Memoriam A.H.* as a centrepiece for the next instalment of Georgian verse.

In the middle of January there was trouble over Rosenberg's health. He had been in the trenches for eight months almost without a break, and although he was now an orderly in the back areas he was continually sick. 'The continual damp and exposure is whispering to my old friend consumption.' His sister Annie (who had begun Isaac's career by walking into the public library at Stepney and handing a sheaf of manuscript poems over the counter) called at Gray's Inn and begged Eddie Marsh to intervene at the War Office. He wrote to Rosenberg's C.O., who had the boy medically examined. He was pronounced fit for active service. A confidential note from the War Office tried to allay Marsh's anxieties. 'If the doctors out there say he is fit for trench work we shall have to accept their verdict. Oddly enough the men do not perish of lung trouble as much as one would imagine.' Of this episode Rosenberg remarked with dry good humour: 'He had me examined, but it appears I'm quite fit.' He had made a sketch he was pleased with, called 'The louse hunt', and in a cheery, if inaccurate, effort to be sociable, 'How do you find the Colonial Office after the Treasury?' By April the unseasonal harsh weather and the heavy stiffness of his boots had added to his afflictions but not subdued his spirits. His Muse, he said, had gone off with luckier rivals, 'but surely I shall hunt her and chase her somewhere into the summer and sweeter times'. Marsh was writing to him every week, enclosing small comforts, reporting on the conflict of opinions occasioned by the poems which he was carrying about in his pocket. Rosenberg was grateful.

> My sister wrote me you have been getting more of my *Moses*. It is hardy of you, indeed, to spread it about; and I certainly would be distressed if I were the cause of a war in England, seeing what warfare means here. But it greatly pleases me, none the less, that this child of my brain should be seen and perhaps his beauties be discovered.

At the turn of the year, exasperated by his failure to find a publisher for *Women in Love*, 'which I know is a masterpiece', Lawrence begged Marsh for advice on ways of getting to New York. 'I know it is no good writing for England any more,

England wants soothing pap, and nothing else, for its literature: sweet innocent babe of a Britannia! Therefore I have got to get out some way or other.' His ultimate objective now was to live on a Pacific Island with his 'back to mankind . . . I don't want to have anything to do whatever with quarrelling nations'. In return for information about passports he offered to send the manuscript of his novel. 'It is not that it is "improper" but that it is too directly in antagonism with the existing state of squilch. . . . If you like, I will lend it you for a while—the duplicate MS. . . . I am afraid, to use your phrase, you wouldn't be able to follow it— which means, I know, that you feel entirely out of sympathy with it. . . . Whether it is *unsympatisch* or not, whether it finds a publisher over here or whether it doesn't, it is a masterpiece and a great book, and I care no more. I have written it, and that is enough for me.' As a signatory of his application to leave the country Marsh had to enquire whether he had taken any overt action as a pacifist. Lawrence's denial was accompanied by a cry of bitter isolation and disillusion. 'I have come to the conclusion that mankind is not one web and fabric, with one common being. That veil is rent for me. I know that for those who make war, war is undeniably right, it is even their vindication of their being. . . . One's old great belief in the oneness and wholeness of humanity is torn clean across, for ever.' Then Marsh discovered that the Lawrences would only be allowed to leave the country for some purpose in the 'national interest'. This did nothing of course to sweeten Lawrence's mood, but he gave news of a new book of poems. 'My last and best.[1] Perhaps I shall never have another book of poems to publish. . . . Would you like to see this MS. when I have done it? Then, if there should be anything you would like for *Georgian Poetry*, ever, you can take it.' This probably occasioned the undated note from Frieda, who was aggrieved at Marsh's critical attitude to the poems.

> I want you to like L.'s poetry more than you do—I do believe that in human feelings nobody has gone as deeply in understanding as he has, also in his poetry I think he is so true, and the imperfection of the form seems to me to be born with the worrying emotion. . . . But you prefer rather generalised sentiments in poetry. It grieves me bitterly that you don't appreciate his poetry . . . genuine feeling, straight pouring forth seems to me the chief point.

[1] *Look! We Have Come Through!*

But it was not until *New Poems* appeared (1918) that Marsh believed Lawrence had properly digested the influence of Whitman. Meanwhile Marsh had to admit failure. Lawrence's passport was not endorsed and he had to remain where he was, at Zennor in Cornwall.

In May Ottoline Morrell wrote from Garsington to introduce an undergraduate of promise who needed befriending in the metropolis and was at present staying with his father in Hampstead. 'He is perfectly charming and witty and enormously clever and learned!' began her description of Aldous Huxley. 'He is very delicate and has very bad eyesight. He has lost the sight of one eye. He has published a little vol. of poems which I expect you have seen. I don't think he has many friends in London. He only left Balliol last year.' So another poet came into Marsh's life, and the first to decline a place among the Georgians out of loyalty to *Wheels*, the anthology of the opposition supported by the Sitwells.

Rosenberg now sent off to England his powerful poem *Dead Man's Dump*, which so impressed Marsh that he copied it out before returning it, lest it should be lost. However, he complained that the piece was marred by the poet's having written on two verse principles at once, by which he must have meant that the virtues of measured and freely cadenced verse were in awkward juxtaposition. Rosenberg agreed that this 'spoiled the unity of a poem' but pleaded 'the absolute necessity of fixing an idea before it is lost, because of the situation it's conceived in'. He put forward the odd notion that if Marvell had 'broken up his rhythms' he would have been considered 'a terrific poet'. 'As it is I like his poem urging his mistress to love because they have not a thousand years to love in and he can't afford to wait. (I forget the name of the poem.) Well, I like it more than *Lycydas* [*sic*].' One can understand why Marsh found him so endearing, quite apart from his gifts. He was now working with the Engineers, going up to the line every night and unloading rolls of barbed wire. 'So I have the morning to sleep in unless I happen to be doing some punishment for my forgetfulness.' Bottomley had sent Rosenberg his new poem *Atlantis*. 'It came to me as the news of a great victory might come.' Of all the Georgians who went to war Rosenberg was the least equipped by nature to withstand the stresses of the time. It was a pity that Marsh, who ministered to his creature comforts, never considered him more than a genius in the making. If *Dead*

Man's Dump had appeared in his next anthology, or a selection from *Look! We Have Come Through!*, the third issue might have fared better with some of the critics.

During these months Harold Monro was quietly working out for himself a new technique. 'I am aiming at and experimenting in a rhythm that may change as often as necessary,' he told Marsh in May, 'less formally yet as naturally as Wordsworth's great Ode.' Although he was in a military camp in Kent he still managed to keep an eye on the Bookshop, where his wife, Alida, had been conducting the business single-handed since his joining an anti-aircraft unit in 1916. She had inherited among other problems the extraordinary tangle of *Georgian Poetry* finances which she was now trying to sort out; she was also keeping the weekly Readings going, and soon she was to find herself solely responsible for the publication and distribution of a third Georgian anthology. Without clerical assistance she invoiced and dispatched the orders and, helped by a friend who shared her enthusiasm, hired handbarrows and pushed her parcels to the carriers in the Goswell Road. These days the shop was open from 10.30 in the morning to 4.30 P.M. except on Thursdays, when the Readings were given, and the doors were not closed until 7 o'clock. And so it went on until Monro's release from military service in March 1919. Meanwhile all important decisions concerning the shop's policy were being arrived at in correspondence between Alida Monro and her husband, and now her custodianship of the Georgian continuity was about to undergo its most severe test.

At the end of June Monro wrote to Marsh declaring himself eager to bring out a third instalment of the Georgian series. 'If the war could be over then it would come out most opportunely.' The second volume had done well. Already the authors had shared £130 between them. He planned to publish a first edition of five thousand. 'Our object and triumph should no doubt be to pursue a clear and level course through all tribulations and show as clearly as possible that English poetry does not allow itself to be distracted by such a passing event as a war.' He enclosed a cheque to be divided among the contributors. Nearly eight pounds went to Lawrence in Cornwall. 'It is a nice sum,' Lawrence remarked, 'and *Georgian Poetry* is a good goose.' He had just been examined and rejected for military service. 'As for flourishing,' he went on in answer to Marsh's enquiry, 'I should like to flourish a pistol under the nose of the fools that govern us. They make one spit with disgust.' Marsh let it pass and started the usual round of requests and enquiries. James Stephens had struck a fertile patch. 'One night I wrote nine poems. If I keep on I will get back to my old form of 15 poems between dusk and dawn.' Such facility was a little disquieting.

More hopeful was a little book called *Invocation* sent in by a certain Robert Nichols. Marsh wrote encouragingly to the author, who replied on June 26. He was glad to hear Mr. Marsh appreciated his sense of rhythm, even if he couldn't scan the lines. 'I never scan,' wrote Nichols, 'literally don't know how to. Nothing to do with short or long syllables . . . only waves of phrases. . . . If you have observed waves you will see that first there are little cups all over the water, then there are bigger bumps which are waves proper . . . the binding thing is the paragraph, the waves are the lines . . . and the little cups the varieties in the line.' Dare he send one of his poems to Hardy? he asked, and then began a series of introspective analyses which in the course of some twenty years were often to leave his correspondent nonplussed. . . . 'The poet side of me is quite distinct from my ordinary, slack, rather second-rate self and my quick critical self.' A few days later he was 'stricken with *nostalgie de la lune*', and was saying he could meet his correspondent during his next leave. Nichols was boyish, desperately earnest, self-dramatizing—a little humourless—eager in the pursuit of art; his handwriting (a nervously tense and almost illegible scribble) was to become a familiar and welcome sight on the breakfast table at Gray's Inn. They met, and Marsh prepared for the press his volume *Ardours and Endurances*, which came out in July and enjoyed extraordinary success. Until the last moment the poet would send second thoughts and new suggestions at the rate of two and even three postcards a day, wanting commas and hyphens put in or deleted, new words substituted, copies sent here and there, and one especially to Arthur Symons because for some reason Nichols was convinced that the artists of the 'nineties and their theories were being vindicated in the current standards of aesthetics, 'the poor, fantastic and exasperating heroes!' Quite suddenly Nichols leaps into the small circle of Marsh's close friends with a fervent, occasionally tiresome, but obviously quite irresistible charm.

Paul Nash was invalided home in June, and now his exhibition entitled the 'Ypres Salient' had opened in London. In April John Buchan, then at the Foreign Office, had sought Marsh's opinion on some of the work which had come his way. He was in two minds. Either they were little more than 'curious and interesting as having been made under fire,' or they were the crude work of a man of genius, with a long way to go. Through Buchan and Marsh the July exhibition led to Nash's appointment as an official war artist. The painters were finding their place. Stanley Spencer was training for the R.A.M.C. In June he had given news of himself and his brother.

I feel when I am drawing heads that I am a chronicler. Gilbert described in a letter his idea for a picture: Cookham Regatta—You remember Cookham churchyard as you look at it from the village, that is the scene of the picture and there will be a long line of people walking down to the river in the winding pathway. Among the people will be the man who sings and plays the banjo and he will have a large pole in his hand to the end of which pole is attached the net into which is dropped the 'remuneration' he receives for his labours. Appearing above the hedge which separates the meadow and the river from the churchyard are the marquees and the little wedge-shaped flags from the tops of them.

There was a storm last night at about 5.30. I looked to the top of the hill and I could see that behind it there was a small cloud below another big cloud, which was travelling at a great speed while the big cloud was practically motionless. This small cloud came climbing up the side of the world and I could hear a distant hissing sound which as the cloud got nearer to the hill became louder and louder, and then quite suddenly as I watched this cloud it seemed to hit the back of the hill and it shot straight up into the air and fanned out and the edge of the cloud which had hitherto been rounded and compact became broken and dissipated into wonderful airy fragments. And then the wind came, a mighty rushing wind and one of my mates (who was a sailor) gave us orders in proper nautical style 'Heel to the Por-r-rt!'

Spencer had been absent-minded on parade and had formed fours in front, instead of to the rear, of his next man. The Sergeant was 'like a flash of lightning and yet quite gentle'. The same letter reveals the painter again.

We go along a road arcaded with beech trees, the sun pouring its rays through the young transparent leaves making a green light.

The shadows of the leaves dart aslant down the men's backs in jerks as they march along bearing their heavy packs. The oak trees are fine down here, they are smothered in large puffy apples. I disliked places like Clifton and Plymouth Hoe for very good reasons, there was something so horribly 'tidy' about them. . . . The only thing it is possible to think of when you are there is which is the best way to part your hair and what is the best stuff to use when waxing your marstouche (never *shall* spell that word).

Meanwhile Novello had made two solo flights and two crash landings, climbing out of the wreckage with a curious air of detachment as if it were no strange thing to suffer a grave mishap and survive. After the second occasion Marsh recommended him for transfer to an Air Ministry office at the Hotel Cecil. There he found himself confronted with a typewriter, which he proceeded to master. His first exercise was a letter (July 4) to Gray's Inn, addressed from Room 113.

Dear Sir, Re your post-card asking for information regarding entering the R.N.A.S. (presumably as a Mochanic [*sic*]) I beg to inform you that if you care to call and secrete yourself behind the chair of General Novello between eighteen minutes past and twenty-to and cough gently but firmly until the sun sets and attract his attention by throwing ink at him, he will *not* be able to give you any *trace* of information!! In other words, the matter is receiving our furthest attention. Believe us, Yours most conscientiously, Gravsgane and Brue.

The ludicrous *alias* always fascinated him. Later this year Mrs. Elgy was to leave a note by the telephone, 'Mr. Cardboard rang up to wish you happy returns.' At this time Novello was a mercurial being of whim and impulse, unorganized, as indolent as his father, gentle in his ways, absolutely lacking in affectation. Marsh received a letter from a friend of the family explaining that the youth found little guidance or understanding at home where there was seldom much domestic harmony beyond what came out of the piano. 'It's times like these when one wishes he had a family life in the usual sense of the word—to be properly taken care of.' He was often feverish with over-excitement and was obliged to go to a doctor for treatment of the heart. In all Marsh's acquaintance no one changed with the years so much as this playboy with the delicate chiselled features, wistful in repose, who became a man of taste in painting and literature, himself a patron, alive to his responsibility as a leading figure in the world of the theatre.

Early in July Robert Graves drew attention to the next member of the Georgian brotherhood who was destined to cause a crisis. 'I hear you've been converted to S.S.'s new poetry: the later stuff is very curious and vigorous. I don't know if you realize that you are responsible for giving me advice which I passed on to him. But the earlier sort he wrote, though I suppose perfect technically, meant nothing at all to me.' It was on July 7 that Marsh heard from Sassoon himself and at once all other concerns were eclipsed. 'I feel I must send you the enclosed document,' he wrote, 'although you will not approve of my action. So I won't say any more; except that I have sent it to my Commanding Officer at Litherland and shall proceed thither in a day or two. It's a bloody performance altogether. But I could do nothing else.' And then, as if nothing had happened—'It *was* jolly getting that message of Masefield's via Nichols and R.G.' Enclosed was the formal statement in typescript by 2nd Lieutenant Siegfried Lorraine Sassoon, M.C., which began by flatly asserting that it was made in 'wilful defiance of military authority'. The substance of this protest was a humanitarian appeal to end the slaughter. Earlier in the year Sassoon had been hit in the shoulder while engaged on another of his improvised bombing sorties on the Hindenburg Line, and had spent several weeks in hospital, ending with a visit to the Morrells at Garsington, where Bertrand Russell was staying. Robert Graves was now at Oxford, convalescing from an acute attack of bronchitis, when he too received the Statement from Sassoon, but his copy was in the form of a newspaper cutting. He at once got leave to meet Sassoon at Liverpool. From there he wrote to Marsh on the 12th.

It's an awful thing—completely mad—that he has done (Sassons won't let anyone hush it up). I don't know what on earth to do now. I'm not going to quarrel with Sassons. I'm so glad you realize he's not a criminal which was the line I was afraid you'd take. Personally I think he's quite right in his views but absolutely wrong in his action. . . . In theory the war ought to stop tomorrow. Actually we'll have to go on while a rat or a dog remains to be enlisted. . . . Better no world than a world ruled by a Prussia (there speaks my old Danish grandmother).

Marsh had so often consulted the War Office for one reason or

Rupert Brooke is dead. A telegram from the Admiral at the island of Lemnos tells us that this life has closed at the moment when it seemed to have reached its springtime. A voice had become audible, a note had been struck more true, more able to do justice to the nobility of our youth in arms engaged in this present war, than any that has been noticed other... more able to express their thoughts of self surrender with a power to carry comfort to those who watch them so militantly from afar. The voice has been swiftly stilled. Only the echoes & the memory remain;

First draft of Winston Churchill's valedictory tribute to
Rupert Brooke, which appeared in *The Times*

Winston Churchill and Edward Marsh (*in bowler hat*) at the ceremonial march past of British troops in Lille, October 28, 1918. In left foreground, Field-Marshal Montgomery, then a Lieutenant-Colonel

another connected with his artists that he knew exactly what step he should take, but unfortunately he was no longer in a position of influence with a Chief of ministerial rank to give him support. The obvious policy was to get assurance from the War Office that there would be no court-martial but a medical board to examine the officer's mental condition. With Sassoon's outstanding war record to refer to it should not be very difficult to point out the inconsistency of his behaviour. In answer to Graves' urgent enquiry from Liverpool as to what he should do next one can assume that Marsh's advice was to impress upon Sassoon that if he refused to be medically boarded—as he certainly would, his mood being one of resolute self-immolation—he would certainly be shut up in a lunatic asylum. In his own account Sassoon says Graves 'swore on an imaginary Bible that nothing would induce them to court-martial me and that I should be treated as insane'. Without a court-martial, and the publicity of a scandal, Sassoon saw himself deprived of the means of martyrdom in the cause of humanity. So he called off his campaign, enabling Graves to ask for a medical board. Graves had saved the situation, but with a lie, assured that Sassoon's condition was such that he could not go through the ordeal of court-martial and prison without complete breakdown. Such indeed was the impression which Sassoon made upon Graves, but when W. H. R. Rivers in Scotland came to make his diagnosis of the case a week or two later he drew a different conclusion. 'There are no physical signs of any disorder of the nervous system,' he wrote. 'He [Sassoon] discusses his recent actions and their motives in a perfectly intelligent and rational way, and there is no evidence of any excitement or depression. . . . His view differs from that of the ordinary pacifist in that he would no longer object to the continuance of the war if he saw any reasonable prospect of a rapid decision.'[1] Sassoon had in fact made his gesture on an entirely emotional impulse, and having once committed himself to his action and its consequences, was calm and resolute at heart, whatever impression to the contrary he may have given to the outward view. Graves formed an honest opinion, and Marsh naturally accepted it. This was fortunate for Sassoon, if not for his cause. At this juncture the War Office had no grounds whatever for not proceeding with disciplinary action.

[1] *Siegfried's Journey* (Faber & Faber), p. 64.

The C.O. at Litherland depot rang the General commanding the Mersey defences, who in turn telephoned Whitehall. When Marsh walked in to put his case the authorities knew one side of the affair already. Feeling handicapped by the insignificance of his official status Marsh was anxiously awaiting the War Office decision when on the morning of July 16 the telephone rang in his basement office. It was Mr. Churchill. Lloyd George had offered him the Ministry of Munitions.

Chapter Fifteen

THE MINISTRY OF MUNITIONS
(July 1917–March 1919)

THE country's war industries were controlled from the Hotel Metropole, Northumberland Avenue. Its fifty sub-departments which the new Minister found in operation on his taking office were at once reduced to twelve, a small advisory committee of experts was constituted, and the main departments of the new administrative machine were redesignated on the alphabetical system which obtained at the Admiralty: P for projectiles, G for guns, etc. The Italian armed forces had to be re-equipped as well as the American expeditionary force and the British. Within a year Marsh was working night and day at the right hand of a Minister who controlled over five million workers in an industrial empire that was still expanding. When at last the cease-fire was ordered a demand had been issued for the immediate construction of ten thousand tanks.

Meanwhile there was a by-election and, high on Marsh's personal agenda, the relatively small matter of a subaltern at Liverpool who had made a solitary protest on behalf of humanity. The medical examination was authorized and under great emotional stress Graves gave evidence. He wrote on July 19.

> After an awful struggle with everybody (I arrived at 59 minutes past the eleventh hour) I've smoothed it all down and he's going away cheerfully to a home at Edinburgh. . . . He's written to the pacifist supporters. I'm quite knocked up.

Sassoon was pronounced a case of shell-shock, and directed to journey under escort to a convalescent home at Craiglockhart (he called it 'Dottyville') near Edinburgh. These instructions he carried out, although Graves, who was detailed as the escort, missed the train, and arrived at the destination long after his charge. Within a fortnight Wilfred Owen was to walk into

Sassoon's room with copies of *The Old Huntsman* for the author's signature, and Sassoon himself was to begin the composition of *Counter-Attack*. The Georgian fellowship had survived a crisis, and through it, as will be seen, the influence of Freud began to affect the younger poets of Marsh's circle.

The election was uneventful. While he learned the workings of the vast organization which it was now his duty to serve, Marsh had to finish the compilation of his new Georgian volume which Monro had already announced. J. C. Squire put the editor in touch with W. J. Turner, who was doing service in an A.A. Training Depot, and Squire declared himself happy to be represented for the first time with his poem *The Lily of Malud*.

> You say that this is one of the few things which make you contemplate a third Georgian book. I do hope this doesn't mean that you had thought of stopping the series. It seems to me your bounden duty to literature. Readers 200 years hence will be hunting up the Georgian books as we do the old song books and miscellanies, only more so. I think there is a good deal of stuff going.

He was right. The last volume had featured only two new names. Now there were to be nine. Sassoon had at last qualified for inclusion, and his eight poems from *The Old Huntsman*, foreshadowing the candour and intensity of his next book, *Counter-Attack*, showed more than anything else that the editor could move with the times. This was a very different kind of war poetry from the Brooke sonnets. An acrid and Dantesque wilderness of cratered mud lay between the present age and the crusade of 1914. Georgian poetry was entering its second phase with a new and vital element which made it once more contemporary. Poems in the early manner of Robert Graves—another old acquaintance who now qualified for the first time—also strengthened the collection. Other new arrivals of note were Squire, Turner, Freeman, and Nichols. Discussion on poetics with Rosenberg had continued sporadically. The poet's comments give a clue to Marsh's side of the argument. In granting permission to quote the speech from his play *Moses* he remarked: 'I think with you that poetry should be definite thought and clear expression, however subtle; I don't think there should be any vagueness at all, but a Sense of something hidden and felt to be there.' This was to be his first and last appearance in the series, and his contribution was too short to make the impact he deserved. For the only time in the series there was nothing by Lawrence. Baring's elegy succeeded *King Lear's Wife* as the bone of contention. On getting the first draft Harold Monro was not entirely happy. He welcomed Nichols, Freeman, and Sassoon, but Baring's piece was another matter. 'If I may be quite frank I am absolutely positive that you are wrong to include it.' In his view it would create a wrong impression with its 'Victorian language and images, its forced or obvious rhymes. It is not only not Georgian poetry to my mind, but it's definitely bad poetry'. He reserved judgement on Squire. 'Yes, there is a certain kind of power under the surface in Rosenberg—but I can't believe you would have included him on your standard of two years ago. I am afraid I agree with you that Lawrence and Stephens[1] should be dropped.' He wanted Masefield in again, and strongly recommended Charlotte Mew.

> I do hope you will agree with this, but if you don't, there—it's your anthology and its value depends to a great extent on your being true to your own judgement. . . . Are you a little more inclined nowadays to be influenced by other people's views or by general opinion?—I don't see you nowadays, but I expect you are really just as strong-minded as you were about the other two volumes—which is the only way.

A later stage in their discussion brought home to them poignantly one of the difficulties in maintaining a strictly objective standard of taste in time of war. On July 1 Ledwidge had written to Marsh from the front line in France, thanking him for representing his work in an anthology 'that will live'.

> Just now a big strafe is worrying our dugouts and putting out our candles, but my soul is by the Boyne cutting new meadows under a thousand wings and listening to the cuckoos at Crocknahara. They say there will be peace soon. If you visit the Front don't forget to come up the line at night to watch the German rockets. They have white crests which throw a pale flame across No-man's-land and white bursting into green and green changing into blue and blue bursting and dropping down in purple torrents. It is like the end of a beautiful world.

In the first week of August Monro wrote again to Gray's Inn.

---

[1] He changed his mind later and recommended five pieces for children from *The Adventures of Seumas Beg* which Marsh accepted. Their lightweight pleasantries were hardly in keeping with the prevailing gravity of the volume.

I'm afraid I want to quarrel mildly with your point of view as Editor! Should you not be, as far as possible, a stern and remote figure judging merit or qualification quite apart from personal relation? *G.P.* seems to me to have become quite a big responsibility—though that would be a horrible way to think of it. But when you express great concern for Ledwidge's feelings I can't help thinking *that* a consideration apart, and the fate of *G.P.* is much involved in its being kept so; also that it is to the direct advantage of a poet to be——

While writing he happened to glance at the newspaper. The letter breaks off with a dash, and then goes on:

——foolish my last sentence seems. I was beginning to discuss Ledwidge as someone alive with a career before him, while all the time he was dead. Lord! how ugly it is. The whole world is a kind of corpse factory. It surely wasn't worth while to kill him. We wanted to know what he would do. He might have been so much use—real use. Well, after this blow I think I'd better shut up laying down the law on the duties of an Editor! But I do feel really you should be able to do just what you like, and if people are offended may one not consider it their own silly fault that they are? . . . In short, provided we can raise a good *G.P.* damn all people!

Turner, Freeman, and de la Mare recommended Edward Thomas. De la Mare even offered to stand down so as to make room for him. On de la Mare's initiative Marsh had secured a maintenance grant for Thomas in the previous June, but he was largely ignorant of him as a poet, and never appreciated his quality until it was too late. So many hundreds of bereaved parents had begged Marsh to include unacceptable poems in memory of their sons that he made a strict rule never to represent any writer for the first time posthumously. Thomas had died in April. Had he made this fine poet an exception he would have been embarrassed with protests. 'I didn't know before the principle which restricted your choice,' wrote Freeman. 'I've had the privilege of seeing probably the whole of his verse and I only made the suggestion because so far as my own opinion might stretch or be worth anything it would be splendid if the next *G.P.* book included any other new poetry of comparable individuality and power.' Working single-handed at night Marsh could not afford to weaken the simple and ready-to-hand excuse, which saved his anthology from becoming a literary memorial without literary standards. In two years' time the same exclusive principle was to contribute decisively to the growing conviction among critical readers that Georgian Poetry was a thing of the past.

While Marsh was writing pages of critical notes for Drinkwater on the poems he had submitted, Gibson was feeling dispirited by the criticisms which came his way.

> I cannot help hoping you are wrong about the songs. I haven't shown them to Lascelles yet. I didn't show them to de la Mare because they weren't finished when he was here, and anyhow he is quite out of sympathy with my work at any time. . . . But it is better to have a friend than to write the loveliest song in the world.

By August the compilation was complete, but the other concern of his leisure hours was still lying heavy on his hands. Mrs. Brooke had launched what he called her 'autumn offensive'.

ii

Almost simultaneously with the summons from Mr. Churchill a letter arrived from Rugby, where a silence on the vexed topic of the Memoir had lasted for several months. So many memorial volumes were coming out that she would like to reconsider the manuscript again. She thought it might be possible to contemplate issuing the work with a short preface by herself to the effect that she considered the portrait 'somewhat incomplete'. So on July 17 the manuscript was sent off for the third time. He had done no work on it, after laying it aside with only negligible emendations, 'only a "damn" or two', he explained, 'and a remark here and there. And most of the mentions of Cathleen were to go.' There was also a contribution about schooldays by Mr. X, a friend of Mrs. Brooke, which came in after they had stopped corresponding. This he ruled out as an outrageously poor bit of work. 'I'm afraid that, especially coming so early,' he wrote with admirable restraint, 'it would produce an impression of unreadability.' He suggested that her prefatory note might be more telling if quoted in the course of a preface of his own. 'Mrs. Brooke asks me to say that etc. . . . but of course this is only a suggestion, and I will do just as you like about it.' He said he had just started official work again. 'It is evidently going to be very hard, and I can't tell yet when I am likely to be able to come to Rugby.' As he knew of no outstanding revisions which had to be made, he suggested publishing the work as it now stood with a note to say it was composed 'soon after R.'s death and that altho' there has been delay in publication I have thought it best not to attempt to recast it.'

She must have suspected that this note was intended as an oblique way of airing his grievance, for she answered by return in scathing terms which took him completely by surprise. He was almost a stranger to herself and Alfred, not even a name to the rest of the family, yet he contemplated writing a Memoir! He had chosen the material himself and when she objected he actually fancied himself injured! 'It never seemed to strike you for an instant that *I* was the person to choose letters and other material. . . .'

> No amount of good literary style will make up for the want of reality your writing has . . . in some ways it is almost absurdly inaccurate. What it needs in order to make it really good is the hand of a contemporary who was 22 when he was 25. You must remember that you were all the time 14 or 15 years older than he was and he knew it.

In spite of this she ended with the assumption that he had promised to let her add or subtract material as she thought fit. She may have been hoping that he would let this pass for the sake of peace, for the end of this onslaught took an abrupt turn by stating that she now believed everything would be quite all right in the future.

There was nothing to do but point out gently that she had got a mistaken impression.

> I can assure you that I have every desire to carry out your wishes. . . . I am sure you cannot expect me now to give you an unconditional promise. You have your responsibility, but I also have mine, and I also look upon mine as a sacred trust. . . . I feel it is my duty not to pledge myself blindly at this stage to put in absolutely anything that you would like to include. . . . You speak of the memoir of X as if it were a parallel case, but surely it is nothing of the kind. That will probably be seen only by a small circle of his friends. . . . Rupert is a famous poet and his life will be read critically by all sorts of people all the world over, both now and long afterwards. Heaven knows that I don't think what I have written worthy of him, but I *know* that from the very fact of my being so much less close to him than you I am more able to form an unbiassed view. . . . Rupert trusted my judgement and I appeal to you, with all sincerity and with all respect, not lightly to brush it aside.

She waited a day or two until the anniversary of her son's birthday when she could take up her pen 'with full sense of my responsibility to his memory'. It now emerged that her main objection all along was his showing her a more or less finished article before she had consented to his embarking on any such project. 'I believe that you honestly thought you ought to write it, though I don't know how or why you did; but it's quite unbelievable that you thought it right to leave me out entirely. It was nothing less than an insult.' She had heard that he had told certain people of their quarrel. But did they know the facts? Were they told that she had been ignored? He has never breathed a word of apology, but has persistently defended himself against her charges. The contribution by Mr. X which he is so presumptuous as to disapprove of must *certainly* be included, and some of the letters to himself and 'Cathleen' omitted. Does he really imagine that he knows any more about her son than his other friends? 'I am sure you don't and I am sure they *know* you don't', and so on, without mincing matters, to the bitter end.

Marsh's reply must be given in full, especially since, in justice to Mrs. Brooke, it is necessary to show that if she was bigoted and intransigent she was not altogether without grounds for complaint.

I must try once again to remove some of the misunderstanding between us. You still write as if I had ever intended to publish the memoir without your approval, and I really must ask you to get such an idea out of your head. It is difficult to be sure of every detail so long afterwards, but my recollection is that I came to Rugby one Sunday when I had just finished writing the memoir, but when the whole of it had not yet been typed. (I had shown it to Dudley and Ka [Cox][1] and I cannot see why I should not. One of my objects was to find out from them whether there was anything in it they thought you would dislike, so that I might alter it before showing it to you.)

On the Sunday I told you I had written it, and that I would send it as soon as it was ready for you to see. I certainly hoped that you would like it! But there was nothing to prevent you either from forbidding its appearance, as indeed you did, or from making any number of suggestions for altering it. At that time I imagined that we were on terms of affectionate intimacy. It never occurred to me for a moment that you would expect to be formally *asked* to make

---

[1] Dudley Ward and Katherine Cox (later Mrs. Arnold Forster) were among Brooke's most intimate friends.

suggestions. Your attitude of utter dislike and rejection of the whole thing came to me as a complete surprise. As for my not having asked for any of R.'s letters to you, I thought it decidedly more decent to leave it to you to offer them.

I cannot see that there was any 'insult' in all this. I am extremely sorry that you should think I have ever insulted you; but to apologize for having done so would be to accuse myself of what I have never intended, and so far as I can see, have never done.

You speak of my writing as if the memoir were as important to me as it is to you. It is of course important to me, but I don't think I have ever dwelt much on that. The only importance I have insisted upon is the importance of whatever is published being, as I said in my last letter, reasonably presentable from a literary point of view. You never seem to see that this is of any consequence; but it is—not for my sake, but for R.'s credit—and it is my duty to safeguard it.

Tho' I can't with any honesty write as penitently as you would wish, I hope you will accept my assurance that I never meant to offend or disregard you.

Yours affectionately,

EDDIE.

Dudley Ward, equally trusted by both sides, went down to Rugby the following weekend. Work at the Hotel Metropole was so intensive that there was no possible chance for Marsh to go himself. On the Monday Ward brought back the manuscript and gave an account of his talks with Mrs. Brooke, but Marsh let several days go by before he wrote again. It was the most crucial moment so far in the course of this dispute. Ward delivered a list of directions, 'for a drastic revision', as Marsh described it, 'altering and omitting a great deal that you had previously acquiesced in'. Marsh was bound to state frankly and roundly that he could not be responsible for the work in the condition which would result, nor was it possible for him to be reconciled to a version in which 'my own point of view, my standards of judgement, and my beliefs, were entirely or almost entirely eliminated as you seem to wish'. Either the work must carry his initials and the responsibility they imply, together with a prefatory note 'in which you could say anything that you wished to correct the wrong impression which you think I convey', or the whole question, which she had herself brought up, must again be dropped.

He may have been so astonished by the mildness of her response to this ultimatum that he sent it in triumph to a friend who lost it, for it is missing from the series. If our sympathies are drawn towards the tragic woman whose struggle to nurse her maternal pride was only prolonging the bitterness of her bereavement—in her eyes it must have seemed as if mere literary and professional acquaintance were presuming to claim precedence over the ties of blood, forcing her to part with her son as it were all over again —there is much to claim our respect on the other side. The opening passage of Eddie Marsh's reply before resuming work on the Memoir under more taxing conditions than ever before, is tender in its reproach, and firm as a rock.

> I hope you will not mind my saying that if you would always write in that spirit we should get on much better. It is not my place to criticize you—but I have often wished to say (and I think I ought to say it) that you sometimes write with what seems like asperity and peremptoriness, even hostility—which inevitably puts me on the defensive. I felt this particularly in our most recent correspondence, when after your first nice letter (which I certainly thought I had answered in the same tone) you suddenly, for no reason that I could see, began reviving all our old differences, which I thought might be treated as bygones, and scolding me in a way which, to put it bluntly, I could not stand.
>
> Tonight, for the first time almost, you write as if you recognized that I have a right to a point of view of my own—and this makes a great difference!
>
> I write this entirely with a view to the future—So long as you are dictatorial, and I resentful of it, we shall never come to an agreement. If we do our best to meet each other half way, it isn't of course *certain* that we shall manage, but I think it's more than likely.

It now transpired that she was still outraged by his suggestion that she should not even have a preface to herself. 'My sole idea was,' he explained, 'that if I quoted you it would be clearer that I agreed completely to your saying what you wished to say, even if it was against me, and that it would look less as if we were at variance.' So under the illusion that the conflict was over for good he made the Memoir his midnight task. On August 21 he reported from Walton-on-Naze that he had begun looking through the new material.

During these weeks an unpleasant incident occurred on the home front. He described it in a letter to Juliet Duff as the narrowest shave 'since the Rhinoceros'. He was accompanying Mr. and Mrs. Churchill on a visit to a munitions factory outside London, and they had begun the drive back to town.

Clemmie and I were inside, Winston in front—the other car (containing a convalescent out for her first airing) charged us broadside on, and over we went. There was I with Clemmie sitting on me, in what struck me at the time as a remarkably becoming attitude—I felt inclined to ask her, as a man in one of Gilbert's plays asks the lady who has fainted in his arms by arrangement, Is that comfortable? hoping she would reply, as the lady does in the play—It is luxurious! We were neither of us frightened till Winston began banging in the glass over our heads. Don't do that, we said, irritably —but he explained that he wanted us to get out before the car caught fire (which it didn't) so we forgave him.

Two of Mr. Churchill's fingers were bleeding. What happened to the unlucky convalescent is not on record. Marsh wound up the anecdote by envisioning an unlikely imbroglio.

Last night Winston, Clemmie, and I dined out with X and his new wife, widow of his Private Secretary. If I were married, I should have green-eyed visions of me and Clemmie dying and Winston marrying my widow before the year was out—but luckily I'm not.

On September 13 he crossed the Channel on a destroyer with Mr. Churchill and began a journal-letter which he sent to Novello on his return.

iii

They disembarked at Calais and lunched with Sir Arthur Duckham.

I wish I were writing for someone like Alice, who 'always took a great interest in questions of eating and drinking', and would care to hear of the delicious crust in which the French contrive to envelope their war-bread, and of how nice it was once more to taste Gruyère cheese. The waiter came up to Winston and said, '*Cela fait du plaisir. Je vous revois de temps en temps*', and this set Winston off on previous visits. He reminded me of one on August 19, 1914, when we came over with the Governor of Dunkirk to discuss with the Governor of Calais the possibility of defending the town against a German attack, which then seemed probable. (On that day the station was choc-a-bloc with Belgian locomotives which had taken refuge there.)

The Governor of Calais told us he had two redoubts, which he was confident of holding against any force the Huns could send—'*Mais mon pauvre ami* . . .' the Governor of Dunkirk began, in a tone of pitying contempt.

Winston went on with reminiscences of the scale on which we thought at that time that the war could be carried on. Lord Kitchener planned to provide 600 guns—and a Cabinet Committee of which Winston was a member raised the number to 4,000. Lord Kitchener proposed to provide each regiment with 4 machine-guns instead of 2—'more than 4,' he said, 'would be a luxury'. They now have 32 each. Winston confessed that he himself at one time (but some time before the war) had visions of putting as many as 100 aeroplanes in the field!

After the meal Mr. Churchill and his secretary loitered about on a bridge watching the passers-by, a squad of native troops 'everything from black Mumbo-jumbos to little pale gold coloured men—mostly very cheerful, laughing, jumping about, catching hold of each other', then a group of German prisoners, then British Marines, 'dirty, cheerful, and alert'. As they drove to Cassel Mr. Churchill told a story about a French Canadian sentry and his compatriot. 'Halt! who it is?' 'I am.' 'Pass, she goes well.' At Cassel they picked up an artillery officer who directed the driver to Wytschaete Ridge in the battle area, where they got out and put on steel helmets.

We had been told that Messines was 'unhealthy' so we didn't go there, and preferred Wytschaete which was reported 'quiet'. But no sooner did we begin to walk along the Ridge than 6″ shells began to burst around us. One of our batteries must have been firing at the Huns yesterday or this morning, and they were trying for their revenge. Columns of smoke rose from the ground, 60-100 yards from us, and bits of shell fell quite close—5 or 6 yards off—while all the time our own shells were whistling and shrieking over our heads. I was rather surprised at not feeling the least frightened—the only thing was that I was a tiny bit self-conscious, and perhaps a little unnecessarily anxious to keep up the conversation, for fear the others should think I was rattled! The landscape was extraordinary. There was a sudden line of demarcation between the fertile wooded country we had been driving through, and a tract of land where there was nothing but the black naked trunks of trees, with all their branches broken off short. The ground was practically all shell-holes, filled with water, and their edges all grown over already with vegetation, mostly a vigorous plant with flowers composed of masses of pink buds, which I happen to know is called persicaria. We found a fairly sheltered place, a few yards from a heap of red bricks, all that is left of Wytschaete Church, which I saw in March 1915, from the top of Kemmel Hill, when it was still recognizable as a church. Winston lent me his excellent field-glasses, through which I could see the emplacement of the Boche lines, about 3000 yards off in the plain —and several towns, including the utter ruin of Ypres. Winston soon began to think it was silly to stay there, and we began picking our way back through the stumps and round the shell-holes of Wytschaete wood. The shells were still falling, all in a radius of about 150 yards —we saw one burst about 30 yards in front of a huge lorry packed with troops which went on as if nothing had happened.

They then drove to St. Omer for the night, where they were Haig's guests at G.H.Q. 'Sir Douglas doesn't "do himself" so well as Lord French did when we stayed with him at St. Omer. There is no champagne here, the house is very cold, and the rear doesn't lock!'

There is nothing externally remarkable in Sir Douglas—nothing in his presence or countenance to make one think he is anything beyond the usual; and he is very quiet—not a talking animal. Winston didn't get going, and dinner was dull, especially at first. Later on there was a rather interesting discussion, about tanks, and the possibilities of a huge aerial offensive next year. Haig thinks highly of tanks, in their proper place. He told us of a little enterprise of Gen. Maxse's which would normally have cost 600-1000 casualties —but owing to the tanks there were only 15. Curious news came from Paris by telephone after dinner. Painlevé, after refusing to join Ribot's Ministry because there were no Socialists, has himself formed a Government without a single Socialist in it! and Ribot is his Minister of Foreign Affairs. We shall get more light on this at Paris.

The new French Minister of Munitions would have to spend most of his third day of office 'discussing these knotty points with his English opposite number, and *such* an opposite number!' Next day they left in the afternoon with F. E. Smith and Lord Castlerosse and drove to the H.Q. of an Anzac unit near Poperinghe where John Churchill was the Camp Commandant. They arrived as General Birdwood was being presented with 'an enormous crimson satin banner with white stars representing the Southern Cross (looking quite as groggy as the original). . . .

Everybody was perfectly solemn about it.' After a not very brilliant tea ('Jack is an extraordinary fellow,' said Mr. Churchill in an aside to Marsh, 'quite un-borable') they started back, passing masses of troops on the march. 'Many of them recognized Winston and cheered and waved their hands. He was as pleased as Punch.' At dinner that evening Marsh sat between General Botha's son and Philip Sassoon. The next day (September 15) was uneventful. Mr. Churchill was in conference until they left for Amiens in the late evening.

> I was much struck by the ease and serenity with which Haig carries his burden. I am sure he is quite imperturbable. He and Winston seemed to warm to one another as the visit went on, and at our last luncheon Haig was quite genial and cracked several jokes. Philip says the passion of his life is for being talked to, but that he combines this with a fatal propensity to nip topics in the bud. The tone of G.H.Q. is tremendously optimistic—so much so that I found other people were quite irritated.

In the evening they were joined by Neville Lytton, who was superintending the foreign Press correspondents, and next morning Marsh walked with him to look at the cathedral. 'I had only 5 minutes there, but in a sense it was enough. I hadn't for a long time seen anything of that kind—of that majestic and over-whelming beauty—and it was a bit much.' Later the whole party drove through Arras to Albert, where stood or hung the famous statue of the Virgin in her arrested fall.

> The Virgin is curiously moving. She's nothing in herself, the battered church is a hideous and vulgar building, and she gives the tower the shape of a fool's cockscomb. Yet her position is so evidently a miracle —the edge of her pedestal has somehow just caught in the parapet, and there she stays month in month out in the very act of her head-long dive; one feels it *must* be an omen. For a few minutes beyond Albert the country is still country—I saw an untouched bend of the Ancre flowing through grass meadows among poplars and willows. Then comes a sudden change—the land becomes featureless and unmeaning, like the face of a leper (a leper with small-pox as well, for it's all pitted with shell holes). Coarse grass and weeds have sprung up everywhere, so the unimaginable desolation one used to read about has passed off—but there are still the lines of bare tree trunks with their stumps of boughs, and *everywhere* the tiny nameless white crosses, single or in clusters, 'like snowdrops' as Winston said.

From there they proceeded to Bapaume—'It looks as if some-one had crumpled it up and torn it into little bits, meaning to throw it in the wastepaper basket'; and from there to Arras where Mr. Churchill had a conference with two gas experts while Marsh and Lytton went on to look at Vimy Ridge. They set off again at 4.15, 'so we were already about 2 hours late. And we hadn't gone far before Winston was attracted by the sight of shells burst-ing in the distance—irresistible!'

> Out we got, put on our steel helmets, hung our gas-masks round our necks, and walked for half-an-hour towards the firing, there was a great noise, shells whistling over our heads, and some fine bursts in the distance—but we seemed to get no nearer, and the firing died down, so we went back after another hour's delay. Winston's dis-regard of time, when there's anything he wants to do, is sublime— he firmly believes that it waits for him.

They proceeded on their way to Péronne. 'The sunset light, when we got there soon after 6, was the loveliest I've ever seen— and the ruins, softened and glowing in its warmth and sweetness, were unutterably pathetic. Here Neville left us, and at last we got away from what had seemed the endless battlefield of the Somme.' They entered Paris late at night. On the 16th Mr. Churchill had talks with General Foch and M. Painlevé. Still in Paris on the 17th they started work at 9 A.M. with a visit to M. Loucheur, *Ministre de l'Armement*.

> He is a brisk little man with a spaniel's button nose, very business-like and capable. Winston lunched with Painlevé, Lord Derby and my brother-in-law Fred Maurice turned up from the Italian front and had long talks with him. Fred gave us great accounts of the Italians. We dined with Drexel, and two crimson-faced Americans, at his house in the Avenue du Bois. Most entertaining—he told us of an old letter he had found today, from King X, thanking him for lending him 20,000 francs to pay off an awful old woman he had been living with in Paris. Winston very eloquent on the necessity of bringing every possible American soldier over to France as soon as possible, and training them here or in England instead of in America —so as not to waste transport during the time of training. Drexel much impressed, and promised to pass it all on to Pershing. He told me that Nijinsky had been released from internment in Austria and allowed to go and dance in America by the good offices of the Pope! the best thing he has done in the war.

After luncheon they drove out of Paris for Mr. Churchill to meet General Buat and go into the problem of heavy artillery on railways, 'I meanwhile having a more than sticky conversation with a French colonel in French on the same topic'. At Amiens that evening they were joined again by Lytton, who entertained Marsh with what would pass anywhere as a highly improper story.

I told this afterwards to Winston, he was much shocked, and in order to lead the conversation gradually back to more decorous lines, he told me a tale of two lady farm-workers in the course of whose duties they had to take a bull to a cow. The farmer thought it a rather delicate matter—also perhaps rather difficult for them, but they were so confident that he let them try. They came back looking very discomfited and with an air of failure, excusing themselves by saying that they could *not* get the wretched cow to lie on her back.

Neville said he had told some of his foreign correspondents that I had wept at seeing the ruins of Péronne—and they said '*Nous avons malcompris les Anglais*', so my bad habit of facile tears has contributed to the Entente!

On September 18 a destroyer brought them back to Dover.

At Gray's Inn Marsh found an urgent appeal from Harriet Weaver, editor of *The Egoist*, on behalf of James Joyce. For the last seven months he had been suffering from a serious disease of the eyes and was now in a Zürich hospital having undergone an operation. 'Mr. Joyce is again in distressing financial difficulties. We have done what we could for him by turning publishers in order to produce his novel [*A Portrait of the Artist as a Young Man*] which no ordinary publisher would touch. . . . It seems lamentable that a writer of such power and talent should be so handicapped by constant financial worry added to the burden of ill health.' The operation was paid for, the Perceval 'murder money' coming to the rescue of yet another artist. An appeal was also received from Lady Cynthia Asquith. D. H. Lawrence and his German wife had been ordered out of Cornwall after their house had been searched by the police. 'He came to see me yesterday, very thin and harried. I have promised to try and help him, but what is the channel? . . . I think he ought either to be left in peace or interned at the country's expense. . . . He has no money beyond the *prospect* of £18. . . .' Frieda's being obviously German had given rise to suspicion in what was a prohibited area. There was little that Marsh could do, beyond getting Mrs. Elgy to give the Lawrences a round meal at Raymond Buildings, and 'lending' them something to tide them over the difficult patch. Marsh noticed that Lawrence seemed both physically and spiritually ill. He was angry and on edge. He regarded the intrusion of the police as an outrage on his privacy. Easier to deal with was the request for information from Edmund Gosse. Mrs. Colefax was arranging a public reading for charity by the poets. Gosse was going to supply Nichols, Sassoon, and Graves, 'but the protagonists are Edith and Osbert Sitwell, of whom I know nothing. I pray Apollo they be not Pacifists'. *Georgian Poetry 1916-1917* came out in the middle of the month.

Gosse disapproved of Stephens. 'His buttermilk is getting very sour. . . . Who is Rosenberg? I feel sure he is a Dane, his verses are so like those which come to me in Danish from young bards in Copenhagen. Your selection of S.S. [Sassoon] is admirable. . . . It will be impossible for future historians to write, even superficially, of the literature of this age without doing honour to its Maecenas.'

In September *Arlette*, with some interpolated numbers by Novello, had opened at the Shaftesbury. He was managing to organize his life a little better as a result of Marsh's supervision, and he had got it into his head that he might stand some chance as a film actor. In August Marsh had accompanied him to a film studio at Twickenham, 'a huge sort of barn,' he wrote to Juliet Duff, 'partitioned off into little rooms furnished for different scenes. It was a trial to see if he was promising—I'm afraid he was!' Though nothing came of it, Marsh thought there might be a future in this medium for artists of serious purpose. On his return from France he wrote to J. M. Barrie (having just been with Novello to *Dear Brutus*) suggesting that he devise a scenario for a possible new star. Barrie replied on October 29.

It is a form of drama that I am at sea with, at present it is entirely in the hands of the mechanical expert, and to mix an author's way of doing things with his way would probably spoil his results. The cinema is a wonderful thing and in its infancy like the flying machine, like which I believe it will some day astonish the world, but that will be when it is no longer in the hands of the 'trade', and when authors understand it and write their plays for it as elaborately as for the spoken drama, and then themselves produce them. Thank you for what you say of *Dear Brutus*. I am glad you cared for it.

The Munitions work at the Metropole left little time nowadays for correspondence or even playgoing. On a clear night shortly before the new year 1918 he got home to find a group of Anzacs at the lodge gate of Gray's Inn, clamouring for food, and cursing loudly because the restaurants were shut. It was past midnight, so Marsh asked them up to his rooms, raided Mrs. Elgy's larder, and produced the decanter. When they had gone he sat down to write to Juliet Duff. He had enjoyed the incident, but conversation had been an uphill job. One of them began:

> You'll have done a lot of horse racing?
> N-no, I'm ashamed to say I never have.
> You'll have done a bit of boxing?
> Well, not *very* VERY much.

but when it came to partridge shooting I couldn't help myself and embarked on the full tide of deception and said yes I was a nailer at partridge shooting. They'll never know, as I doubt very much whether it will be mine to fulfil my promise of visiting him in Victoria, but it's nice to have an invitation.

He had recently spent a night or two at Sutton Courtenay near Abingdon where Lister, the Grenfell brothers, and their circle used to forgather in halcyon pre-war days. A few weeks before Edward Horner had been shot dead by a sniper, and this very week Patrick Shaw-Stewart, who had survived Gallipoli, was killed in France by a piece of shrapnel. Marsh had wandered alone through the garden at Sutton Courtenay, the one-time playground of Balliol. It was 'tremendously haunted', he said. 'Every inch of the garden is full of them still.'

It was unusual for him to be so quietly reflective. Back at Raymond Buildings he wrote: 'It's such a wonderful moonlit night, so bright and soft that the pavement of Gray's Inn, with the shadows of the leaves on it, looks like striped velvet, black on silver, and one is surprised to find it as hard as usual underfoot.' But his levity soon reasserted itself. 'Winston is having me made a C.B., a Companion of the Bath (I hope a hot one). I asked him not to, it's a terrible waste.'

iv

During the first weeks of 1918 the new volume of *Georgian Poetry* was being treated in the newspapers with the respect due to a national institution, while contributors sent in their opinions of each other's latest work. Bottomley, impressed by Sassoon and Graves, believed that the newcomers would make this issue historically important so that 'your fortunate Georgian adjective will there take on a new and full significance, and the earlier confraternity will appear to be transitionists'. After Marsh himself, he was the first to recognize the promise of Robert Graves 'for his nimbleness and variety and the promise implicit in the vivid contrasts of his reactions. But if little Rosenberg can ever write twelve consecutive pages as fine as this one page, he will swamp us all except Lascelles.' Bottomley was conscious that the movement which had meant so much to him had survived into what already seemed to be a new world.

> But 'the merry days are gone', and I feel I want to found a high, exclusive Society of Original Georgians, with the power to add Ralph Hodgson to their number. We should dine in state once a year: the alphabetical first among those present would sit at the head of the table, while on the wall above his head would hang a portrait of E.M. by the first artist of our time. The oldest member present would deliver an oration on Rupert and Flecker, the youngest member one on the last Georgian who had absented himself for ever from the muster. As the years passed the dwindling group would call to mind the similar gathering of the Balaclava Veterans, the memory of achievement would cause the sunken eye to flash and life to glow again; empty places at the board would consecrate vanished companions and renew their presence: the Last Toast 'E.M.' would make the aged voices resonate and thrill once again as the glasses were lifted and the old wine caught the light.

An attack on the new volume had been delivered by Edward Shanks in the pages of the *New Statesman*, and on December 29 Graves wrote to commiserate with Marsh. 'I don't suppose you mind; sufficient it is to know yourself the Father of Modern English Poetry. . . . Eddie, I am just beginning to feel that I know what I'm getting at and in this next year of 1918 if I'm spared I hope to satisfy the expectation you've had of me since I was a sixteen-year-old at Charterhouse.' Then he gave what must have been the first news to reach the metropolis of a new star in the literary firmament.

... I have a new poet for you, just discovered, one Wilfred Owen: this is a real find, not a sudden lo here! or lo there! which unearths an Edward Eastaway or a Vernède, but the real thing, when we've educated him a trifle more. R.N. [Nichols] and S.S. and myself are doing it.

Owen had walked into Sassoon's room at Craiglockhart a few months before. In January he was with the three Georgian war poets at Rhyl, when Graves wrote again.

I send you the few poems of Owen I can find, not his best but they show his powers and deficiencies. Too Sassonish in places. Sassons is to him a god of the highest rank. Isn't it good that Bob N. and Sass get on so well; nice for me to have introduced two such great men. ... I'm beginning to understand more clearly what Georgian Poetry means, and what it's going to mean by God's Grace.

These few pieces by Owen were all that Marsh saw before his next anthology came out. The London introduction which Sassoon gave Owen was to Robert Ross, so he never mounted the stairs to the picture-gallery at Gray's Inn. Since the previous August Sassoon had been writing the poems of *Counter-Attack* and for the time being he was regarding the Secretary at the Ministry of Munitions as hardly a fit person to foster the writings of such rebels as Owen and himself. Inviting Marsh to his wedding, at which George Mallory was to be best man, Graves added: 'Owen, I told you, is fearfully uncertain, but he can see and feel and the rest will be added unto him in time.' With the example of Sassoon's war poems before him to release his own genius, and Graves and Nichols also at his side, Owen's mature work was the fruit of progressive neo-Georgian influence. And yet, as will be seen, his verse was to be the direct cause of the beginning of the end in the history of Georgian Poetry.

Rosenberg was now back in the forward trenches. 'We spend most of our time pulling each other out of the mud.' He said he felt more in the way than of any use, while to his other friends he confided that overtiredness was affecting his memory, and he was constantly having to do pack-drill for minor offences. Sitting in a quagmire he read the new Georgian poems. 'Turner's are very beautiful and Sassoon has power,' he wrote in pencil on lavatory paper. His devoted sister Annie had begun urging Marsh either to get him transferred to a Jewish battalion in

Mesopotamia or brought home on sick leave. Marsh put the former scheme in train, but for once was too busy to write to Rosenberg himself. The problem of the moment was again Sassoon. He had decided after all to consult Eddie Marsh about his war poems.

Early in February the manuscript of *Counter-Attack* arrived at Gray's Inn. Enclosed was a letter to Sassoon from William Heinemann in which the publisher had asked for the inclusion of some 'amiable stuff to mitigate the horrors'. Sassoon was quite prepared for Marsh to advise against publication. Here was a small book in which the anti-war element of *The Old Huntsman* was developed and concentrated without relief so as to add up to a terrible indictment of man's inhumanity to man. The poet harboured no very sanguine hopes of its reception at the Ministry of Munitions. Marsh's comments came as a surprise.

I think H. [Heinemann] is quite wrong in wanting the book stuffed up with things foreign to its present character. It's of its essence that it should produce its own effect, which it can only do by keeping homogeneous. And I think it is *better* short. I want you to add 'Repression of War Experience' but if you added *many* poems in the same key there might be an effect of monotony which would be as weakening as an effect of contrast.

I have no doubt whatever that it would sell as a short half-crown book—and I don't believe for a moment that it would kill *The Old Huntsman*.

I think *The Dressing Station* quite worth putting in, but not really important—you might quite well leave it out to please him . . . as you know I have grave doubts whether it is right from the national point of view to publish the book at all, but I have assumed all along that you've made up your mind about that.

I am as convinced as ever that we are in the right, and that we ought to carry on at whatever sacrifice so long as there is any chance of our achieving, say, President Wilson's or the Labour Party's war aims—whereas the tendency of your book is to make people think peace necessary at almost any price to stop the horrors. So that in advising you on points like the length of the book, I am leaving that main question aside altogether and considering the matter from your point of view.

Sassoon, at Litherland again, was 'greatly inflated' by this verdict, and agreed to make certain amendments. 'I don't think the tone of the poems will affect my position as a soldier. Maybe

I'll be posthumous before long. (But everyone thinks that when they're going out.) . . .'

I hope you'll keep an eye on Bob Nichols. He is very wayward and easily says things he doesn't mean, but gets misjudged by them. *Don't* take anything seriously (except his good poems). He is so different from R.G. who can look after himself. But R.N. is at the mercy of his moods.

Luckily Marsh found time in March to send Rosenberg one of his encouraging budgets of news. The reply (March 28) came from the front line almost by return. 'It's really my being lucky enough to bag an inch of candle that incites me to this pitch of punctual epistolary. I must measure my letter by the light.' There was a lot going on and 'poetry is right out of our scheme. . . . I wanted to write a battle song for the Judains but can think of nothing strong and wonderful enough yet. Here's just a slight thing.[1]' He ended his letter (his inch of candle having guttered to the stump) with an apology for his enclosure. 'My vocabulary small enough before is impoverished and bare.'

These were his last words. Within a few hours he was over the top and shot dead. So sudden was the sequel that his letter bore the postmark April 2 when he was already buried.

'I never joined the army from patriotic reasons,' he had written. 'Nothing can justify war. I suppose we must all fight and get the trouble over.' He also thought that if he joined up his mother would benefit from the separation allowance. If Brooke was a symbolic figure of the last of the Old Wars, here was another sacrificial victim, a symbol of War new style. 'The light is gone out of our home,' wrote Annie, and on behalf of her mother begged Marsh that he should bring back the other son on compassionate leave. On about the same day an acquaintance who had been reading the new Georgian book encountered its editor in the street. 'Well, Eddie,' he exclaimed genially, 'your Georgians certainly know how to write!' For once Eddie Marsh was unsmiling. 'And how to die,' he said, and walked on.

For some weeks Frank Sidgwick had been pressing for the final text of the Memoir, so on March 18 the manuscript travelled to Rugby for the fourth time. As before, Marsh gave an account of

---

[1] *Through These Pale Cold Days.*

his revisions, but now he allowed himself the luxury of appearing a little less amenable to Mrs. Brooke's criticism. He had come to the end of his concessions. He was ready enough to beg, if he could not persuade or convince. He would do anything, in fact, except give way. The contribution by Mr. X which she had insisted on last year he finally condemned as 'hopelessly commonplace and uninteresting', but he wisely appealed to her sense of power instead of merely asserting his superior judgement. 'I implore you to acquiesce in my leaving it out.' He had made excisions, but only when 'I found that I could in any way enter into your reasons'. His own reason for letting stand various passages in Brooke's own letters which she had objected to was less tactful. He had not touched, he said, these passages of slight extravagance

> very characteristic of R., which would delight and amuse hundreds of people and which I think it would be a great pity to sacrifice merely because a few people with no imagination or sense of humour and with no power of distinguishing playful exaggeration from solemn statements of fact, might possibly think them silly.

Moreover he declared that she must have crossed out certain passages for no ostensible reason other than that they were his own composition. His belief was that he had met her more than half-way. To his astonishment her reply was amiable. She wondered what could have put the idea into his head that it might be otherwise. 'I was certainly afraid you might not like the Memoir,' he replied. 'You never had before!!'

> As to the part about the illness. I think it's common ground between us that R. did at that time go through something which might be called a serious crisis, moral, mental, and spiritual. He had, as we both know, had a time of great trouble and unhappiness, about which the Memoir cannot give full explanations. Luckily it was very short—but it seems to me to have been important in his life, and I do think it essential to give some indication that he *had* a period of suffering. If that is unduly slurred over, the picture has practically no shadows anywhere and becomes false . . . to make out that he had *none*, would, I feel, be to diminish his stature, and to confirm the idea of him which some people have, and which I am more anxious than anything to knock on the head, as a charming young poet of roses and lilies and boyish chivalry, not to be taken very seriously, in spite of a crude penchant for meddling with ugly and painful subjects which he didn't know much about.

Later in the month Dudley Ward, once more the mediator, took notes of Mrs. Brooke's comments, then spent an evening passing them on to the author at Gray's Inn. She had at last agreed in principle, so it was only a matter of coping with a few trifles. She had given way over Mr. X. But Marsh was now wanting to quote a letter of Brooke's that was 'certainly amusing and poetical', as he explained, 'and only very mildly blasphemous'. Within a day or two she sent off her prefatory note. 'I would rather you didn't "apologize" to me,' he asked in his acknowledgement, 'though it's very nice of you to wish to.'

> I'm very glad you agree to Cathleen being mentioned. I will certainly camouflage 'bloody' if you wish, though really the word has become so common lately that I don't think anyone would notice it!

She had asked for the omission of a reference to her son's flippant views on cremation, and Marsh explained that readers of 'the poem' later in the book might need this page of the Memoir for a full understanding of it. When she wrote again it had seemed to her that in asking for a few slight alterations to improve her English in the wording of her ten-line preface Marsh was only trying to get his own back. Meanwhile on April 25 he submitted the typescript for the fifth time. Their letters crossed. In Mrs. Brooke's she wanted him to understand that if she 'approved' she did not necessarily 'like' the Memoir. But what was this he said about 'a poem'? Were there to be any 'poems' in or together with the Memoir? Surely she had realized all along, Marsh protested, that the whole point of the thing was its introduction of the Collected Poems. She wrote at once saying this would be a 'swindle'. Most people possessed the poems already. She knew of many people at Rugby and elsewhere who would not dream of paying half a guinea for a volume the bulk of which they already possessed. To prevent this she suggested an announcement that the Memoir would shortly be appearing by itself. Marsh was now desperate, less for his own sake than for Frank Sidgwick, who for more than three years now had shared his devotion to Brooke's reputation and had taken risks. It had been a model association of publisher and executor. The perils of book production were now 'eight times greater than in 1914'. The strain that Marsh had been undergoing now threatened to become a nervous breakdown. He tried to explain his case, how he would be 'in a terribly awkward position if you were to repudiate me ... it does seem to me *impossible* now to go back on such an old understanding; I must therefore really implore you to agree to the proposal which I sent you yesterday'. Her reply is missing, but one may imagine a note of frigid consent accompanied by an assurance that her final approval must not be misconstrued as a change of heart as to her poor opinion of the work. On May 31 Marsh brought to a close the most vexatious episode of his life.

Thank you for your letter—which I do not think ungracious in the circumstances.

I believe I understand your feeling about the Memoir—and though I know that, so far as it is *feeling*, nothing that I could ever say would change it, yet I should be much happier if I could persuade your *reason* of what I am myself convinced of—that while the kind of book you would have liked would have been very delightful to have, for Rupert's friends, yet it would have been less suited for publication abroad than even mine. I don't know of a single instance of a book consisting of independent contributions by a man's friends and miscellaneous companions that has been successful or even readable, except by those who have a strong personal interest in the man. You might have got a few good bits, but nothing could have prevented repetitions and well-meant dullness. It takes a born writer to make copious details of undergraduate days interesting, unless they are made far more intimate than you would have liked. Rupert himself could have written an account for instance of the Dorsetshire tour which everybody would have loved, but I very much doubt if Dudley could have. And when you say that a book on your lines would have been 'him', I very much doubt it— because the mere fact of having known a man, and wishing to convey an idea of him, doesn't give the power to do it. . . . So I do honestly believe that in the absence of a genius for writing, my plan of telling the story by stringing together interesting bits of R.'s own letters, with a minimum of narrative, and a selection of such bits of other people's accounts as could be woven together into a fairly consistent and coherent whole, was the only way in which anything worthy to be called a book could have been written. No doubt it could have been done better, though in all the circumstances I don't know by whom.

I also think privately, though I can't expect you to admit this, that difficult though you have found *me*, you would have had greater difficulties still with Rupert's more unconventional friends. I think I have taken far more pains to avoid the sort of criticism which you wouldn't like, than either you recognize, or than would have been taken by many of the friends whom you now would have preferred to write.

I say all this, not in the least to praise or even to defend myself—but because, now that the book *is* coming out, it is so distressing, and such a pity, that you should look so exclusively on the aspects that you dislike.

One other thing—it grieves me that you should have such a wholly disapproving view of R.'s 'London seasons'—because of course I was largely responsible for them. It would have been quite impossible for a man like him to have confined himself for ever to a small set of school and Cambridge friends, however delightful—and if he *was* to enlarge his circle, I really cannot see anything to deplore in his having done so in the direction of people like the Asquiths, Wyndhams, Churchills etc, to say nothing of all the artists and writers whom he was meeting and making friends with. It isn't in the least as if he had given up, or would ever have given up, the older friends who meant anything to him—no one was more loyal and faithful—it was a real case of widening a circumference, and not merely shifting it. When the time came for them, he was every bit as ready as ever for the untidiness and barefootedness (which I wickedly remember you were not always so keen on as you are now!). And don't think me impertinent for saying what I know—that the more he saw of other people the fonder he got of you.

However I don't in the least expect to convince you—but I don't like to leave any stone unturned in trying to make you take a *tiny* bit of pleasure in the Memoir instead of your present whole-hearted dislike of it.

This doesn't expect an answer, in fact I'd much rather not have one, unless by any chance I have succeeded in bringing you round a little! which is most unlikely.

As the Memoir went to press, almost twice the size it was in 1915, the first rumours of iconoclasm were heard in literary circles. 'How wrong about Rupert,' Graves wrote. 'We all look up to him as to our elder brother and have immense admiration for his work from any standpoint, especially his technique, on which we all build. I know it is fashionable to pretend to dislike him: but no one does really, least of all R.N., S.S., or R.G.' The Memoir would put everything right, or so Eddie Marsh believed.

And now more manuscripts came under his critical eye, the first essays in criticism shortly to appear in the *Eton Review*, from the pen of Lord David Cecil, who was still at school. Meanwhile, along the Hindenburg Line the fighting had flared up, and

Sassoon, restored to health, wrote to say he was once more with his men in the thick of it.

> But you chose the right moment for your letter. Think of a frowsty bed in a dingy, fly-buzzing room, with a brick floor; a midden-smelling yard full of whistling soldiers outside the window. A mule brays uncouthly—afternoon sunshine, and busy noises of boots walking to and fro, the clatter of a pail, voices raucous or shrill . . . rustle of wind in leaves, drone of aeroplanes above the whole lot. On the bed someone dozing, resentfully, wondering whether it's influenza or war-weariness—head full of jumbled snatches of daily worries—fitful dreams where everything connected with the 'company' goes hideously awry—body full of aches falling, falling through the bed with heavy tiredness.
>
> Five o'clock—been lying here since noon, when I came in from a morning of company training, and suddenly decided that I couldn't walk about the military earth any more. Funny that I never heard anyone come in, but there's a mug of tea on the floor—and a letter!
>
> Not a re-addressed bill, or an anxious note from a female relative who hasn't heard from me for weeks—a letter from the real world where exciting events take place and people suddenly write a poem. The wind must have flicked it through the window—that letter.
>
> > Far are those tranquil hills, Dyed with fair evening's rose,
> > On urgent, secret errand bent, A traveller goes.
>
> That's *me*; hurrying back to Gray's Inn to tell you I'm still alive—portentous tidings indeed! But I wish you'd tell Fortnum and Mason's to send me some potted Bach, tinned Delius, and preserved Russian opera—I was reading *Sea Drift* and it made me feel famished for music. . . . Robert won't show me his new poems. Robert N. writes me long haunted letters about his feelings, poor dear. Wonderful things in them too. I don't mind being at the damned war, but I do want to see my friends again.

By July Sassoon was back in England with a bullet wound in the head, lying in a hospital at Lancaster Gate where Lady Randolph Churchill worked as 'a sort of Olympian head matron'. There Marsh, Nichols, and Robert Ross were his first visitors. Marsh left with him an advance copy of the Memoir, and the horrors of war began slowly to fade from his mind.

> . . . One by one or all in a bunch, I forget which, the furies flapped out of the window; they sat on the top bars of Lancaster Gate for a few hours; it was quite dark, but not raining, and I could hear them making arrangements about coming back next evening; they tried

imitating dying men sobbing, then they flapped away over the grass, it was getting light by then, so I fell asleep. I dare say they won't come back. And I've been reading your Memoir all the evening, half sad and half happy over it, and wishing I'd more to remember of Rupert than looking into his eyes as he shut your door one morning after breakfast and I went clopping downstairs.

On July 24 was published the *Collected Poems of Rupert Brooke, with a Memoir*. Owing to the additional letters by the poet which had been collected since 1915, chiefly by Mrs. Brooke herself, the long delay turned out to have been of great benefit to the text, and in that respect she achieved her aim of doing her best for the memory of her son. But her narrow outlook which had exerted a restraint upon the author, resulted in a somewhat idealized portrait. For this Eddie Marsh has been held to blame. The Memoir was not untrue as far as it went, no skeleton-in-the-cupboard had been left concealed, but by ignoring certain qualities common to human behaviour it presented something less than the whole truth, and owing to Mrs. Brooke's ban on Marsh's own opinions it was also uncritical of its subject as a man of literature. The extraordinary thing is that in spite of everything the Memoir hangs together as a work of biographical art and will always be a model of its kind.

As a subject for critical study Brooke became an object of slight embarrassment to anyone wishing to forget the legend and assess the value of his work in a responsible frame of mind. It is easy to blame Mrs. Brooke for this, or Marsh himself for his over-anxiety to honour a friend about whom it was impossible for him not to feel a little sentimental. Rupert had become an emblem of his own pre-war youth and of the world they had been happy in which was now a smouldering ruin. The truth is that something incalculably more powerful than the literary fastidiousness of an individual at Gray's Inn or the watchfulness of a mother's injured pride was responsible for the portrait which was now enchanting the public and annoying some of the poet's old friends. Brooke did not live to achieve greatness. Greatness was thrust upon him by the circumstances of his death. Regarded in the perspective of history there is nothing false in his legend. Within a few days of his burial he had entered the racial consciousness as a symbol of a nation's agony of sacrifice and pride. Both Marsh and Mrs. Brooke were of the generation which had unconsciously created that image. Both accepted it. How could they do otherwise? There it was, a ready-made myth, without any assistance from either of them. If Marsh had been left to his own devices the Memoir would have been 'truer', but it might never have been 'true enough'. To him, no less than to so many others, Rupert was far more than a promising young poet. To later generations which have had their own hells to endure, the *mystique* which surrounded Brooke may seem false and sentimental, merely because those agonies and exaltations, whose emblem he was, have long since burned to ash, and they were never theirs. Concerning the poems the issue is simpler. By his choice and arrangement, strictly excluding the inferior pieces such as any young poet must inevitably perpetrate, Marsh produced an authoritative edition which cannot be superseded. The juvenilia, some of them surprisingly inept for so self-critical a writer, which have been added to the canon since 1932, are of value to students concerned with tracing an artist's development, but they add nothing. The edition of 1918 (as revised in 1928) with its Memoir will remain the basis of Brooke's reputation.

Many readers would have endorsed the comment made by Robert Graves on reading the Memoir in 1918.

> How impossibly these days such enjoyment of life and featherheartedness reads: I am much more of an optimist than any of my friends (indeed I expect the war to finish within a few months) but my capacity for such prehistoric happiness as Rupert had is nothing. . . .

W. H. Davies found it 'more real than anything I have ever read before, because it holds a part of our life as it does yours'. Gibson was reminded of that bygone week at the Old Nailshop when every evening Marsh would read aloud what he had written during the day. Stanley Spencer wrote from Salonika.

> He used to inspire me. There are men who when you see them excite in you a desire to do some great work—which after all is the simple desire to live. As St. Augustine says (or something like it) 'One flaming heart sets the other on fire.' I think that friendship is a wonderful thing . . . the exact purpose of which is to cause one another and encourage one another to bring forth the joy of Heaven. I think King David when he desires to build an Altar is the true Artist. As I think I said to you before—the joy of giving perfect praise. I have the feeling in me now of praise but I can't 'give' it.

I often wish I could write or do something *solid* like David's altar. I love those words, 'And David danced before the Lord with all his might, and David was girded with a linen ephod.'

Spencer was longing to get back to his proper task. 'It's awful, Eddie, I have everything ready in my mind, all aching to become "flesh" . . . I am a complete stranger in this world without a brush, and it makes me feel terribly lonely and empty and meaningless.'

Marsh was now distributing the royalties of his last anthology. Nichols, the newcomer, was astonished to receive as much as eight guineas, and argued that E.M. ought to keep it; 'after all, you invented us and gave us a status!'

Georgian P. must have sold like blazes—I like to think of the little houses where Robert N. was a name unknown until the eldest daughter (d'you know it's always the eldest daughter who buys Georgian?) bought the Great Green Book (not without an air of challenge toward her father who is fond of saying 'Poetry?—Now when I was a boy—yes, Isle of Wight—Putney Hill'). Georgian is the best possible advertisement in the world. When I learned I was to be in it I assure you my stature increased by an inch. I walked as Anna Wickham so naively remarks 'with a new rhythm from the hips', a bad poetess on the whole, but she promises . . . I do wish people would write with more gusto. Brooke had gusto all right— gusto is half the battle.

The neo-Georgians were at the height of their confidence and success. 'Turner is having Squire as best man,' wrote Graves. 'I love to see the affection that is between us Georgians. Good sign, don't you think?'

The Memoir came into Drinkwater's hands on August 7, the day after he had written the last words of *Abraham Lincoln*, the only Georgian drama which was to hold its own in the commercial theatre. Some days later he read his new play to Edmund Gosse at Lichfield. Gosse had thought the subject unpromising for a play 'but he has produced what seems to me a political tragedy of extraordinary merit'. Meanwhile Novello, the young man of the theatre in the Gray's Inn circle, had been sent to Stockholm on a goodwill mission. To this end Marsh had applied on his behalf to Mr. Churchill, who granted leave of absence for three months. 'Has a coalmine been discovered in the drawing-room?' asked Novello, trying to forestall a sensational letter from London. 'Or have you included me in *Georgian Poetry*?' Through the good offices of Marsh's friend at the Legation, Sir Coleridge Kennard, he spent an afternoon in the royal palace having tea and singing his songs to the Crown Princess. At her request he sang her the *Home Fires*, and followed it with *The Page's Road Song*, his setting of the poem by Whitman. His report went on to say he was having recourse to a money-box. 'Being able to see it in my hand has given me a much clearer idea of money. . . . I hope it doesn't mean that I'm reforming.' He had £7 a week to spend. Apart from the glamour and charm of Royalty in informal circumstances (which he was frequently to reproduce on the English stage in Ruritanian disguise) he was also much influenced by making the acquaintance of the young ballerina Jenny Hesselquist. He detected in her a special quality—'I think it's a *humility*, and she gives one the impression of each utterly beautiful movement being just for that moment only—and created *then* and never to be repeated. It makes one hardly dare to breathe for fear one second of her should be lost.'

In August one of the newcomers to the Georgian pages begged a favour on the exchange system. Squire offered to introduce Marsh to W. J. Turner if he could persuade Mr. Churchill to meet him for a drink. The encounter took place in the lounge of the Savoy. Squire was not disappointed.

Ten thousand thanks, he was fascinating—and I didn't entirely expect it, although I had heard him a hundred times. One couldn't get far with him at first meeting. He has enormous qualities, especially the primary quality of courage; one defect—the defect of romanticism—or rather, since romanticism may be good, of *sentimentalism*. You don't sum up Russia by calling Lenin a traitor, or by calling munition workers well-fed malcontents. That is melodrama. I have met many politicians; this is the first one who was *alive*.

Mr. Churchill's next poetical encounter, which occurred within a few days, was at his own request. 'Winston knows several of the *Counter-Attack* poems by heart,' Marsh wrote to Sassoon at a convalescent home in the country. The offer of a job in the Ministry of Munitions was hardly consistent with the theme of his latest publication, but such a compliment was not to be brushed aside, so he came up and occupied the spare room at Gray's Inn, was taken to meals with Lytton Strachey, Edith Sitwell, and Baring, and on the third morning put in an appearance at the

Mrs. Elgy

1917

IVOR NOVELLO

1951

Hotel Metropole. An informal and leisurely talk of upwards of an hour with Mr. Churchill 'was making me feel that I should like to have him as my company commander in the front line',[1] when it developed into an eloquent monologue in vindication of militarism, only broken into by Eddie Marsh announcing the arrival of Lord Fisher. A second interruption some minutes later to the effect that Fisher was growing restive brought the interview to a close. Eddie Marsh weaving the strands of his life, putting his head round the door, standing aside, at work in the wings, arranging, watching (off stage even in his own life story)—it is characteristic of the man.

Mr. Churchill was about to leave on a tour of munition factories in the North, where there had been growing rumours of a strike. He was accompanied by his secretary, and on their return they left almost at once for France.

Another journal letter, handed to Novello after his return from Sweden, continues the story for the next five days.

v

October 25 was too misty for flying, so they went by special train to Folkestone.

Winston invited Gen. Dawnay to lunch with us in our coupé, and there was a lot of War talk and speculation. Winston quoted one of the best and truest German remarks I have heard, from one of their newspapers, that 'The British believe in victory as a cow believes in grass'—and I amused them with Laurence Binyon's remark that when we enter Berlin as conquerors, 'we must be just before we are merciful, and leave it intact'.

They were met at Boulogne by a 'magnificent 1914 Rolls-Royce' and driven to the Château at Verchocq 'near Fouquien-bergue which I am sorry to say Winston has christened F— and b—', which the French Government had specially reserved for the British Minister of Munitions. They were a long time getting there.

First a tyre burst with one of those loud reports which make one think one has been assassinated—and then, in the village itself, Winston gave the chauffeur a wrong direction, left instead of right, at a cross-road. The chauffeur (an admirable man called Patterson

[1] *Siegfried's Journey*, by Siegfried Sassoon.

who has been driving at the front since August 1914) preferred not to back, but to go on till he could turn the car—and on we went in the dark, on and on literally for kilometres, between the close hedges of the roadside, it must be the original 'long lane that has no turning'. It's impossible to imagine anything alternately more comical and provoking. The climax of Winston's cursings was, 'Well, it's the most absolutely f—ing thing in the whole of my bloody life.' At *last* we came to a possible spot, turned, and got to the château about ½ an hour later than we otherwise should. Archie Sinclair, who is to be appointed liaison officer between Munitions Inventions and the front, turned up to dinner, luckily late himself—I went to bed early, leaving him and Winston to gossip.

Saturday Oct. 26. I went out before breakfast in the lovely early sunlight to see the avenue which is the glory of Verchocq. It is the best I can remember, except the one at Savernake—a mile and a half long, running parallel to the front of the house and some way from it, leading, like most French avenues, to *nothing*, except a wooden gate at one end and a round of blue sky at the other. For a short distance, at the end nearest the house, it is of tall black pine trees— all the rest is magnificent birch trees, 150 ft high at a guess, with pale smooth glistering stems, and the tawny and golden foliage far overhead—between the stems, glimpses of lovely undulating wooded country, all the colours of autumn. I went in to breakfast feeling quite uplifted.

After breakfast they motored through St. Pol to Arras, where they were amused by a Canadian sentry who challenged them at the frontier of the battle area.

He took first Winston's 'white pass' and then mine, and copied all the particulars into his note book, very slowly. Then he asked for Winston's again. 'Again?' said Winston, who was getting very impatient. 'Yes,' he replied, with a sweet smile and his soft drowsy vowels, 'I forgot to take the number. I'm very rattle-headed.' The part of Arras we passed through looked much the same as when I was there a year ago, still with the semblance of a town, but not a house undamaged. On the ruined boulevard I was struck by a pre-war notice board saying '*Habitants d'Arras! les arbres font la beauté de vos promenades. Protégez-les!*' It was all very well to say '*Protégez-les*'. They would if they could.

They left by the Cambrai road and saw 'thick bands of rusty brown shattered wire wriggling from end to end of the landscape'. They stopped at le Cateau and lunched on 'eggs, sardines, cheese,

Beaune, and brandy', sitting in the car, then got out to have a look
at a field at the top of a slope near by.

Débris of all kinds, water bottles, German boxes beautifully packed
with unused belts of machine-gun bullets, a dead horse, and most
touching of all the kit of a dead British private, left there when he
was taken away to bury, his toothbrush, shaving brush, cap, socks,
etc, and a printed page of prayers and a torn New Testament. We
motored down into le Cateau, and on by the Bazuel road, which
would soon have taken us close up to the Front, but we were stopped
by a railway bridge which had been blown up by the Germans and
fallen clean across the road—a large repairing party were at work
on it, but it was quite impassable. This settled a quarrel which had
been raging all day between Winston and Archie. Archie had
promised his Colonel to be back before luncheon, and was determined not to be very late. Winston on the other hand wanted to
go on with the joy-ride indefinitely. The broken bridge put Archie
in a strong position, and he positively refused to be taken any further
afield. Winston yielded very sulkily, and we turned for a south-
easterly round, parallel to our latest advance, through Busigny and
Bohain, dropping Archie at Brancourt. He and Winston parted
quite coldly, and when I tried to defend him by saying it was
because he was so terribly honourable, Winston snapped, 'It isn't
honourable, it's asinine, I shall take no more interest in him.'

Seeing a car approaching which might be Lord Weir's Marsh
jumped to the side of the road to stop it but was mistaken for a
refugee thumbing a lift and the vehicle passed on, only to turn
back after a while because the driver fancied he had recognized
Churchill. With Lord Weir they went on to Bapaume, 'the ruins
were ghostly and majestic in the twilight, lost our way in Arras,
punctured another tyre' and got back to Verchocq very late for a
conference of senior gas officers. 'There was good talk between the
Arch-Poisoners.' Next morning they picked up John Churchill
and drove to Lille through Béthune.

We passed the celebrated brick-heaps (the brick-kiln has totally
disappeared) and the railway triangle, where there is still a goods
train which was cut off in August 1914, with coal still in the trucks.
La Bassée is an utter wreck, and looked specially dismal on this grey
rainy day. We got out to look at an elaborate Boche cemetery with
stone graves, some of which had been knocked endways by shell. In
the middle was a huge dumpy and extremely solid grey cross, with
sketchy *art-nouveau* women's figures weeping up against the sides. I

thought it clumsy and ugly, but this may have been prejudice, as Winston and Jack were rather impressed with its sternness and simplicity.

Lille had been liberated only ten days before. 'I was a little disappointed that no pretty girls flung themselves on the motor and suffocated us with kisses.' They lunched at Divisional H.Q. with General (Reggie) Barnes, a brother of Irene Vanbrugh.

Reggie is one of the best soldiers in the Army—rather worn and tired by the war, as determined as anyone to make a clean job of it, but very anxious that we should not prolong it unnecessarily by making the terms of the armistice stiffer than the minimum required to make it impossible for the Boche to begin again. This point of view is pretty general among the sensible fighting men, and it makes me furious with the journalists, shop-stewards etc. at home who scream about this being the moment to give the Hun bloody socks etc.

John Churchill had booked rooms for them at the Hôtel de l'Europe, 'to which we were guided by a bourgeois who got on the box of the motor. When Winston thanked him he said, "*C'est bien peu pour ce que vous avez fait pour nous.*" . . . It was odd to creep up the broad staircase with only a candle-end to light me.' Then Marsh's interest in creature comforts reasserted itself—'dinner at 10 francs a head, a bottle of Clicquot (alas not dry!) for 75 fr. Brandy was 6 fr. for the *petit verre* (we got some at Bruges next day for 1 fr. 50!) so we contented ourselves with Kümmel at 5 fr.'

He then gave a lurid account of German atrocities which they learned during dinner, culminating with the least credible. 'Before they went the Germans turned 300 syphilitic women loose from the hospital to infect the Tommies.' Next morning (October 28) the Duchess of Sutherland turned up to breakfast, then they all walked to the *Grande Place*, where seats had been reserved for the ceremonial entry of the British troops into the city.[1]

The *Grande Place* is a fine open square, with a crowned statue of a woman, representing the City of Lille, on a column in the middle. I wonder why the Huns hadn't melted it down. There are no remarkable buildings, except the sober old Town Hall in front of which our stand was, and one very beautiful 17th-century house, taking up half one side of the square, built of grey stone, and covered with fine slightly rococo carvings. Festooned with flowers and fluttering with Allied flags, and with every window from the gables downward

1 See illustration facing p. 417.

crowded with people, it had all the glittering gaiety of a Venetian palace in a Guardi picture of a festa. Of course there were Allied flags everywhere, not only in the *Place*, but in every house in the town—some say that the Germans had them all ready and sold them to the inhabitants when they cleared out—but I do not vouch for this!

At 10.30 General Birdwood rode into the Square with his staff, dismounted and exchanged greetings with a group of French officials, *Maire*, *Préfet*, etc., some in frock coats and toppers, others in municipal uniforms with lace and cocked hats. He made a short speech in French, which he doesn't know a word of, but he had learnt the pronunciation by rote. The *Maire* answered—the General presented him with the flag of the 5th Army, and was given the flag of Lille. Then the march past began—all London troops—a little under strength, but every component represented—infantry, pontoons on huge waggons, field kitchens complete with cooks, artillery, signallers, etc., thoroughly business-like, and with something majestic in their serious and serene faces and regular marching —their uniforms splendidly brushed up for the occasion—the old ones they had been fighting in all the time. There wasn't a smiling face, or a self-conscious one. And the crowd was serious too— interested, admiring, and sympathetic (half the soldiers were carrying little bunches of chrysanthemums etc. that had been given them). It jarred rather, tho' it was extremely funny, when the cinema operators chose out a section of the crowd to look excited and wave pocket handkerchiefs. The only real fuss was over a detachment of Irish pipers who played *Cock of the North*, and were mistaken no doubt for Highlanders.

They were obliged to leave before the end and drive to General Tudor's H.Q. for luncheon.

The house belongs to the Burgomaster, who had gone off with the Huns, to the great disgust of his son, a flying officer in the Belgian Army, who thinks he must have been over-persuaded by his wife and daughter, ill and terrified. In the dining-room the last German officer left in the town had been killed a week before. The floor was stained with his blood, and his last two revolver shots had made a hole in the cornice and cracked a looking-glass in the hall.

General Tudor then drove them in his car towards the Front, but *en route* Mr. Churchill's eye was caught by a village church with 'a most alluring steeple'.

The General didn't at all want to take us up it, but Winston coaxed him, and we climbed up the broken staircase to the belfry, where we got a wonderful view into the German lines, running through a village ½ a mile away. While we were looking, the sound of guns began, and we saw shell bursting in the German village. Evidently the Huns would retaliate, so we began a dignified retreat. It was only the beginning of a tremendous strafe (quite unexpected by the General, who would certainly not have let us go there if he had known) and as we walked back to the motor shells whizzed over our heads every second—and sure enough German shell began dropping in the village we had just left. Suddenly the General smelt mustard gas, and made us stuff our handkerchiefs into our mouths till we got back to the motor.

They managed to return unscathed to General Tudor's H.Q., where they spent the night. As it turned out the congratulations on their escape were premature.

Oct. 29th. We started for Bruges after breakfast, and had the surprise of our lives. After the usual difficulty in finding an unexploded road out of the town, we struck one which seemed all right, and were just entering a village when I saw a smoke-burst in the street in front of us—a woman with her hands to her face, swaying, other figures starting up round her and falling into a frightened group. We turned to the left, men and boys jumped up and began to run, or fling themselves on their faces in ditches, it was like a Bible picture of the inhabitants of Gomorrha, fleeing from the wrath to come. Shells began to burst in the fields (gas, I expect), at one moment I looked back and saw one fall on the road where we had been less than a minute before. At first we thought it might be an aeroplane dropping bombs and pursuing our car—I felt rather excited and quickened with the idea that 'every moment might be the next'—the car pushed forward across the fields till we came to the river Lys—bridge broken! and only a narrow improvised wooden one which would not take the car. We got out and consulted peasants and a Belgian soldier. At first there seemed nothing for it but to go back into the village! but luckily we found a road branching out to another bridge which was intact. We bowled along discussing the event, thinking that every minute we were getting further from danger, when the shells began again in the fields on both sides, evidently aimed at the road, but not getting very near it. The fact was, we hadn't realized where the front line lay. It bulged westward where we thought it was straight, also the speed of the motor had carried us eastward faster than we knew, and at one point, when we thought the line was 10,000 yards away, it was more like 1,000. After this emotion we had a peaceful run into Bruges through beautiful autumnal avenues, and drew up in the central *Place*, where it was delightful to see with my own eyes that the beautiful watch tower is still standing unhurt.

They were conducted to the Docks by a Belgian Boy Scout who walked with Marsh ahead of the others while he told of thirty young women of the town 'who were known to have couchéd with Germans without the formality of an engagement. . . . Their fellow citizens had sacked their houses, cut off their hair, painted their heads green, and flung them into prison.' After luncheon they motored to Ypres across the battlefield of Passchendaele, 'which of all the desolate battlefields I have seen is the most abominable'.

It was a gorgeous autumn afternoon, with bright sun, a light golden haze which didn't prevent one seeing to the horizon. Miles and miles of undulating country, with nothing in sight that had existed before the war, and nothing that could have had a name or meaning apart from war—an expanse of coarse ragged rusty unsightly grass and weeds, drab earth, reddened here and there where the bricks of a village had crumbled into it, ruined sand-bag shelters, here and there a forsaken tank, everywhere the little wooden crosses, and a universal litter of papers, boots, water bottles, cigarette tins, scraps of metal and nameless rubbish. We looked into one shelter which had evidently been a field dressing-station. I found in or round it an instrument case with a German name on it, a scrap of an English comic paper, a typewritten letter in Flemish, and the fragments of a mathematical book in French. We took a turn down the Ypres-Menin road as far as Hellfire Corner, and then drove into Ypres. When I saw it in March 1915 it was still a town—now there is nothing left but here and there a shapeless mass of bricks—except that the tower of the Cloth Hall is still recognizable, and still beautiful in its pale greys and yellows; and the lovely west door of the Cathedral has even some of its carvings left. Winston wants to turn that group of buildings into a cemetery, with lawns and flowers among the ruins, and the names of innumerable dead.

They were again at Verchocq for that night, and flew back to England the following afternoon (October 30); Marsh travelled separately from Mr. Churchill, in a DH.4. 'I had no idea how neat the world is, or how like it toys are.'

The day after his return he wrote to Cathleen Nesbitt and recorded a fine Churchillian remark.

It was yesterday that Turkey gave in and it will be Austria tomorrow —'a drizzle of empires', Winston calls it, 'falling through the air'.

On November 4 a messenger brought a pass into Marsh's office at the Metropole which he duly signed, and Lieutenant-Colonel T. E. Lawrence, newly come from his campaign in the Hejaz, entered for an appointment with Mr. Churchill. It is probable that the instantaneous friendship with Marsh was largely due to Lawrence's request to meet the author of *Counter-Attack*, for the very next evening Marsh brought Sassoon and Lawrence together at the Savoy and 'directed the conversation towards Arabia'. Lawrence began to warm to Sassoon after he had exclaimed— 'What I can't understand is how you come to be a Colonel!' Next day Sassoon called again at the Hotel Metropole, found Mr. Churchill as friendly and forthcoming as ever, then went on to Dorset for his first meeting with Hardy at Max Gate. He took a message from Marsh which offered Hardy the dedication of the next Georgian volume, and he also brought with him the Little Book. Since 1912 all the poets had copied their poems into it. But all had avoided the first page. This was now allotted to Hardy. He hesitated, telling Sassoon that he feared it might look conceited. 'I hardly liked to write my poem[1] on the first page of your book,' he wrote to Marsh on the 17th, 'but as there was absolutely no other place I had to do it.' (There was plenty of room.)

On the morning of November 11 Marsh was standing beside Mr. Churchill, looking from the window towards Trafalgar Square, when the jubilant bells rang out, Mrs. Churchill ran in, radiant, to share this moment with her husband, and the pigeons rose in a gyre around and above the Column.

Next day, late in the evening, Sassoon arrived at Gray's Inn. He found John Drinkwater reading from a sheaf of new poems with rather more persistence than the staying power of his host. Sassoon stayed the night and was taken next evening to a supper-party given by Lady Randolph Churchill. The riotous celebrations were still in full swing, and as they made their way down the Strand through the singing crowds some rowdies climbed

---

[1] *In Time of the 'Breaking of Nations.'*

on to the roof of their taxi and yelled and whistled. Later that evening they were listening to a string quartet, and Marsh introduced Sassoon to Sir Ian Hamilton. Perhaps the last poet that Hamilton had met was the victim of 'a touch of the sun' stretched at ease under an awning of green canvas at Port Said. If he happened to recall the occasion, it must have seemed a very, very long while ago.

In the weeks that followed, the immense task of bringing the war machine to a standstill, supervising the disposal of surplus goods, reconverting the factories to their normal use, and all the problems attendant upon the redistribution of labour, meant no relaxation of effort at the Hotel Metropole, and no earlier return in the evenings to Gray's Inn for the Minister's secretary. Graves was in good heart—'Wait till I have the leisure and peace to write away from these ruddy soldiers'; so also was Sassoon, preparing a selection of his war poems—'What shall I call it? I thought of "In the Pink". . . . I went to tea with Ronald Firbank—a most fantastic creature. He has seen almost no one for three years and lives in Hill Street with the blinds down and a bowl of orchids from Blenheim.' Among the Georgians there was but one problem.

After the enormous success of his *Ardours and Endurances* Robert Nichols had left on a lecture-tour of America. Work and a dire spiritual malaise had brought him to the depths of melancholy. He had begun to doubt the reality of his success, and to question whether he had ever encountered reality of any kind except while in the trenches. 'Everything since has tasted like dry bran.' He had once aspired to become a major figure, 'not quite a Keats but something a good deal more than Tom Moore and a Lord de Tabley'. But now he believed there was little hope. 'I see the things but can't get 'em down. . . . I simply go wandering around chronicling hole and corner moods.' Alfred de Vigny had forestalled him. 'Blast him, he's not even translatable.' Then there was Hardy, 'the type of genius whose *idea* is poetic, not execution . . . to read him is like looking at a night landscape'. As for America, in his present mood it seemed like a Blue Point oyster 'very large and very insipid', although he had seen a railway-station more beautiful than any cathedral in Britain. He wrote again to say he felt his heart would break. Marsh was doing what he could to prop the morale of this passionate and suddenly disillusioned youth when the new year of 1919 came in, heralding an age of what 'for want of a better word is called Peace'. The slightly cynical phrase was to appear in the Preface of the next Georgian anthology.

Sassoon's volume of war poems had certainly caused a stir, but several readers in high position, whose reaction Marsh had awaited with some misgiving, proved to be its foremost advocates. Among these was Lord Esher.

> There is a rough splendour about your friend Siegfried. It is good for the character of our people that a picture of War should be presented by a man so close up against it in the crude manner of El Greco. I am astonished that the mollycoddling Censor permitted the publication of these poems.
>
> Literary censorship seems to have been based on the assumption that the British high-strung imaginative nature required truth to be carefully whitewashed with sugar and that Britain had been subjected by the Greeks and not by Caesar. These poems are bitter aloes.

On January 15 (1919) Mr. Churchill took office as Secretary of State for War. Once more he invited Marsh to accompany him, and Lord Esher wrote again, 'Good luck to Winston and you. Here is an extract I put in my Journal after reading the Antwerp papers lent me by Winston. I hope he will not temporize or compromise with the failures and failings of the W.O.' The extract from Macaulay's essay on Chatham that the Secretary showed his Chief must have struck a peculiarly sympathetic chord.[1] Mr. Churchill was taking office at a time when discipline was rapidly deteriorating throughout the armed forces as a result of the unsatisfactory system of demobilization, and Marsh had barely settled in when from the window in Whitehall he witnessed the Household Cavalry gaining control over a mob of three thousand demonstrators. New Army orders on demobilization were issued before the end of the month and general mutiny was averted. In the months to come the most urgent problems centred in the presence of British troops on service at Archangel in support of the White Russians, many of whom had played their part against Germany in the early stages of the war, and whose

---

[1] 'The Minister, before he had been long in office, had imparted to the commanders whom he employed his own impetuous, adventurous, and defying character. They, like him, were disposed to risk everything, to play double or quits to the last, to think nothing done while anything remained undone, to fail rather than not to attempt. For the errors of rashness there might be indulgence. For over caution . . . there was no mercy.'

society was now in liquidation owing, at least in part, to Britain's failure to sustain the Czarist armies by forcing the Dardanelles in 1915.

There was also the tangled problem of our commitments in Mesopotamia. Marsh's rapidly developing friendship with T. E. Lawrence gave him a special knowledge of those territories which were soon to become the kingdom of Iraq. His more regular association with Lawrence began with an embarrassment. Having accepted an invitation to dinner at Claridge's and a party afterwards, Lawrence ignored the former and graced the latter in Arab dress. He wrote afterwards to apologize. 'I behaved like a lunatic yesterday. But I have been trying for three years to think like an Arab. . . . ' In Eddie Marsh he found not only a link with Whitehall but a source of information about the world of poets and painters from which he had been divorced for so long. At Raymond Buildings he was shown *The Cornfield*, the first picture painted by John Nash after his return to civil life, and in March there was news of Stanley Spencer, who had written to describe his picture of the wounded arriving at an advanced dressing-station.

> Along the bottom of the picture and in the immediate foreground are great thistles. The leaves are large and have great spikes. They have milky lines all over them like variegated holly leaves have. The flowers are mauve and look like great maces. Whichever way the flower goes the leaves form a kind of halo round it. . . . The 4 wounded I think of as being separate groups of nebulae. Each group is the same density but each has a different kind of density. For the feeling they will give one, they might be 4 saints enthroned, the stretcher handles being so to speak ornaments. . . . Above the wounded will show the great buttocks of mules and above the buttocks their firm solid necks. These mules will be black and will look like great vases.

C. R. W. Nevinson, heartened by Marsh's praise of his new development, also sent an account of himself.

> It needed a little moral courage to come out of what I now consider the *cul-de-sac* of pure abstract painting and the mere consideration of pure plastic form for its own sake, though I admit I have learned more from this *cul-de-sac* than from any other school. But, quite simply, at the front I suddenly felt a desire to express something more than a picture . . . and I began to argue why should it be a sin for a picture to be literary or a virtue for it to be musical? pictorially they

are both equally impure. Now I am convinced any work of art (poem or picture or building or symphony) should be plastic, musical and architectural *simultaneously*. Hence the Vere de Veres of Art flatter me by dismissing me as a 'mere journalist', and only now keep to a geometrical formula as the *simplest* conceivable architectural form . . .

At the end of March the Abercrombies came to stay at Gray's Inn so as to travel down with Marsh for the unveiling of the medallion of Brooke in Rugby Chapel on March 28. Mrs. Brooke had been making elaborate preparations for a tea-party in her drawing-room after the ceremony and for another next day after the concert, which consisted chiefly of an elegy for strings by Cleg Kelly. He had begun the composition the day after the burial on Skyros. He too was dead now along with all the other companions of the Latin table, excepting only Oc Asquith. Kelly's sister was there, and Denis Browne's mother and, sole representative of the Argonauts, Bernard Freyberg, who captivated the ladies and set them speculating on his age. Mrs. Brooke had to write to Gray's Inn to settle the question. The three legatees, Abercrombie, Gibson, and de la Mare (who were now enjoying quite considerable annuities)[1] were present, as was General Sir Ian Hamilton himself, who made a speech and unveiled the medallion—the profile of an ambrosial youth, straining forward as if awaiting his turn to throw the discus at some Olympic event in the playing-fields of Elysium, an image almost perfectly conforming to the figure portrayed in the Memoir, which by now, of course, everyone had read. The young man who had stepped out of the railway carriage at Paddington in the small hours of the morning on a June day in 1914, sunburned, hungry, over-excited, human, was now irrevocably frozen into the bas-relief of a beautiful myth.

The little ceremony in the chapel was itself symbolic. Almost from that day the Georgian movement began to decline.

---

[1] Three impressions of *1914 and Other Poems* were sold within seven days of publication. In June 1915 each beneficiary received £58 19s. 9d., and on the same day a year later each received £267 2s. 6d. This was increased after 1918, and in the ten years up to 1926 altogether just under three hundred thousand copies of Brooke's poems were disposed of by the publisher.

Chapter Sixteen

GEORGIAN IN DECLINE
(April 1919–August 1924)

*G*EORGIAN was the 'proud, ambiguous adjective' whose validity as a term, signifying a brand of art peculiar to the age, declined during the next five years. Certain of the poets themselves were to mature in a later decade and look back on Georgianism as their cradle. But in the early months of 1919 there were no serious signs of change and decay. A dinner was given at Raymond Buildings in the last week of May to re-establish the fraternity in an atmosphere of peace and to celebrate the phenomenal success of Brooke's *Collected Poems*. Mrs. Elgy, who as usual refused assistance, was set a task as cook and butler which she accomplished with the perfection of culinary skill and punctuality. Eight sat down to dinner: Abercrombie, de la Mare, Hodgson, Davies, Nichols, Freeman, Drinkwater, and their host. They were joined for coffee by Squire, Turner, Shanks, Monro, and Sassoon. Abercrombie read aloud his *Witchcraft, New Style*, and Shanks a few pages of his newly published *The Queen of China*. One of the main topics was a fourth volume of the Georgian series.

When Bottomley received an account of this occasion he also became the first of a great number of artists to benefit from a new fund which Marsh had decided to administer as a memorial to Brooke and a supplement to his 'murder money'. The first royalty statement for the Memoir was more than £500. He offered half to Mrs. Brooke for her own charitable purposes, but she declined, insisting that Marsh should keep it and buy a picture for his collection. So he bought Augustus John's portrait of Davies and presented it to the National Portrait Gallery as yet another memorial to Brooke, and distributed the rest between four writers. The plaque in Rugby Chapel had been paid for by subscription for which a committee had been formed early in 1916. The balance was now given to W. H. Davies. '£30 is more than I ever made out of a single book—with the exception of the Autobiography,' he wrote. One of the beneficiaries from the Memoir was D. H. Lawrence.

> Queer, to receive money from the dead: as it were out of the dark sky. I have a great belief in the dead—in Rupert dead. He fights with one, I know. That is why I hate the Oliver Lodge spiritualism— hotel bills and collar studs. The passionate dead act within and with us, not like messenger boys and hotel porters. Of the dead who really live, whose presence we know, we hardly care to speak—we know their hush. Is it not so?

Nichols had sent from Pittsburgh the manuscript (with many alternative readings) of his poem *The Sprig of Lime*, and was still philosophizing on American architecture. The same spirit of melancholy and majestic Will, he said, that jointed the towering arches of Notre Dame, 'most sinister of cathedrals', rejoices today in 'the nine Satanic resources of steel, glass, and ferro-concrete'. Intellectual Pride had replaced the Intellectual Humility which built Chartres, 'the spirit is dead in a coffin provided by the Renaissance, and fastened with nails driven home by the pistons of the first steam-engine as hammer'. He inveighed against Christianity and declared that God, for him, was either 'the Sun or Fire glowing in iron upon the Anvil of Prometheus'. It was not very clear what he meant. From Bottomley two plays arrived. *Gruach* won Marsh's praise, but he complained of '4 anticlimaxes' in the last pages. *Britain's Daughter* revived an old problem.

> You know I was a staunch upholder of all that was attacked by the critics as 'brutality' and 'coarseness' in *K.L.W.*, so you will not accuse me of squeamishness, and I hope you will bear with me when I say that the Soldier's opening song about the shining white bellies and the brown rats on the plague ship strikes a note of horror and disgust which is unrelated to anything that follows and is therefore an unnecessary and injudicious challenge.

In the new play he perceived no clue as to its moral content or guide for the spectators' sympathy, and Bottomley quoted in defence Flaubert's axiom that 'the artist must not take sides'. Marsh was not satisfied.

> I have been trying to think about Flaubert's axiom. I think it wants a little expanding and guarding and must not be swallowed whole like a chemist's prescription. Of course it is obvious that the artist

must not appear in his own person and urge the merits of one side or the other. But is it true that the artist should disinterest himself in rights and wrongs? Shakespeare takes sides for Lear against Regan and Goneril: he does not take sides either for Lear against Cordelia, or for Cordelia against Lear, but by the end of the play Cordelia is seen to have been right and Lear wrong but pardonable. Must not the artist stand at an angle from which he can control the moral aspects as much as any other of the aspects of his work? It seems to me this must be so, if he is to get unity and harmony of impression. In the dramatic form I think it is specially necessary. The audience must not be left floundering, it must have some indication of the direction in which the truth is to be found. Flaubert's canon seems to me to be satisfied if both sides are treated with the sympathy that is due to them (and even this does not preclude the artist from dealing 'faithfully' with sides—such as Regan and Goneril—to which no sympathy is *due*). It is not necessary that the Truth itself should be left an open question. Of course a play may be written of which the object is to send the audience away, asking 'What is Truth?'—in that case I almost think the old-fashioned expedient of a '*raisonneur*' is desirable to make this object clear.

Marsh's preference for *Gruach* (produced at the Old Vic in 1922) prompted the author to relate the peculiar circumstances of its origin. After the Georgian matinée three years before, Marsh had beckoned him 'into a rococo withdrawing room opening from the vestibule', filled with people, where the poet's attention was drawn to a woman 'little and not quite young and dressed in misleadingly modest black. And she asked me in a gentle undertone whether I contemplated any more plays on Shakespearian subjects. And oh Eddie, I fell. Remember I was full of elation and glory at just having seen my very own play on a stage, and think indulgently of me.' So the poet said that he did indeed (though in fact he was contemplating no such thing) but he added facetiously that he feared his example might encourage some young men at Oxford to commit such a sacrilege as, for instance, to write a play about Macbeth's mother-in-law. 'I had never thought of it before, and I should never have thought of it again, if I hadn't learned later from you that I had been speaking to the Duchess of Rutland.'

Compilation of the fourth anthology which began in July led to an interesting controversy with John Freeman, whose *Memories of Childhood* was now in preparation. Marsh's selection of his work made the poet uneasy because the pieces chosen did not seem to stand on their own. 'Perhaps I'm simply getting tired of little lyrical gasps, but on looking back at my last batch in *G.P.* . . . they don't seem to be or do what they should.' Monro had told him he was writing too much and too fluently, and he had come to believe that his lyrics only made their point when met with in the course of a sequence. Marsh, however, was never without good reason for his choice.

Nearness for instance impresses me most deeply as a formally perfect and emotionally poignant rendering of the universal human consciousness that the individual is alone, even when in the most utter communion with someone else. To say that this is of value only as 'part of a mind' seems to me to cut lyric poetry down at the root. And when you call it 'trifling' I couldn't say what I think without frightful rudeness. *The Alde* again is certainly a most lovely little poem, not depending in the least on a context for interest, charm or beauty. . . . I don't think you can want *only* to have the very small audience of people who have the insight, sympathy, and patience to study as a whole a series of poems which is not ostensibly or at all obviously a sequence and to do for themselves the elaborate work of piecing together. There must be a hundred who would appreciate and enjoy the best of the poems as units, to one of the more strenuous kind of reader, and they are well worth appealing to. *Georgian Poetry* is meant for this general public.

Only Posterity can decide which of us is right! Meanwhile I am bold or perhaps you will think impudent enough to set my judgement against yours. . . . I have often known people to get momentarily sick of their recent work when they are off on a new tack and quite wrongly to despise what they have done because they are more interested in what they are now doing.

Freeman had a good argument ready (one feels that Lawrence would have made precisely the same defence of his *Look! We Have Come Through!*):

It seems to me that modern poetry must, if it live an hour, express personality and a view of the whole that's outside personality and time: must express them both and cannot indeed express them independently or singly; and so inevitably one tends to the longer (not always the very long) poem—the lyric prolonged into steady reflectiveness, the brook becoming a lake fed with unnoticed springs and holding at least the image of unsurveyed hills and moving clouds.[1]

[1] *John Freeman's Letters*, edited by Gertrude Freeman and J. C. Squire (Macmillan, 1936). When Marsh was shown this collection in manuscript by de la Mare, who wrote

To this, impressed but not convinced, the editor replied (August 2) by return:

> I was thrilled by your letter, with the beautiful image of the lake, you certainly ought to make a poem of it. I never meant that 'throwing over the brief lyric was suicide'. . . . It doesn't seem to me likely that at the beginning of the 20th century the short lyric should become obsolete, and that Sappho and Herrick, if living now, would find their occupation gone.
>
> I do hope you're not going to concentrate exclusively on content, and give form the go by. I have no reason to think that you will, except this depreciation of these lyrics, in which it seemed to me that you had so much more mastery of form than ever before. . . . Except for a few odd people like Donne, I'm convinced that it is by form (not alone but as a *sine qua non*) that poets live.

Freeman's answer was reassuring. 'Content is the root—not fixed in a pretty crystal bowl but growing in the earth and sending up at length some flower which is neither form alone nor subject alone, but truly the *flower*—the poem.'

In April Marsh had greeted the appearance of a new poem by de la Mare. 'I'm on my knees before your "Veil" in the *Athenaeum*—what exquisite grace, charm, and sheer perfection. It's as immortal as a Herrick poem to Julia—and the two loveliest and highest-soaring lines of all are the last two[1]—you wise old thrush.' By August de la Mare was in Cornwall. 'I wish the old thrush had a mouthful of tune in his throat,' he complained to his friend. 'But it can't be helped, and [one] only wants to shut the mouth in joy of these cliffs and meadows.' Of his reappearance in the next anthology he had some misgiving. 'I am rather a stale old bird to be chirping in the new nest.' He knew that Masefield had been superannuated, but perhaps he did not realize that good work in the old tradition was not so easy to come by in these days. He was preparing his first collected edition, and wanted Marsh's advice.

> My own difficulty is if once I attempt to amend to know where to stop. My experiments over the second edition of *Songs of Childhood*

the preface, he remarked: 'Letters such as these are one of those queer encouraging counter-currents which impede the modern trend towards barbarism.'

[1] Why in that little night disguise
   A daybreak face, those starry eyes?
                    (*The Veil*)

were for the most part a sorry failure. Even if the patch *is* better material it's a patch. . . . But if in the event there is far too much of the worse and worser included in the new edition, it will be in order to keep some kind of peace with Constable's! Freeman suggested that the whole collection should be rearranged. . . . It's a depressing task, rather like that of trying to re-light the fire when one had much better go to bed. Ideas are mildly sizzling in my head, but it's difficult to find time and quiet for it.

Marsh welcomed the chance to help him in the revision of his previous work.

You may depend upon it that if I am lucky enough to find any atrocities I shall bring them to your notice with gusto and malice. The only one I can remember off hand is one which I told you of years ago, the monosyllable 'mockdst' in one of the *Listeners* poems. I remember the contortions I went through in trying to pronounce it, and I shall think I have deserved well of future generations if I can save them from the strain.

In February Sassoon had gone on a lecture-reading tour to America, where he found his trail had been effectively blazed by Nichols. He was temporarily antagonized by Mr. Churchill's views as expressed in a recent election campaign at Dundee, and was causing Marsh a certain amount of exasperation. 'It would be humbug for me to go about with you when I feel as I do about it,' wrote Sassoon. 'You know perfectly well that I liked him when I met him and he was very kind to me. He may well talk about "the hush before the storm" when he thinks that "peace but not friendship with Germany" is the right game. It's simply an appeal to mob sentiment. . . . What the hell does it matter what I think? I refuse to take the narrow (or patriotic) views which are so easy and comfortable.' Marsh suggested that he read Churchill's recent speeches, but he declined. He was too much disillusioned by Mr. Churchill's apparent opposition to President Wilson's attitude to Germany. 'Wilson may be a pedantic old bore but that doesn't matter,' he wrote again. 'After all your kindness to me it seems a rotten way to write, but I can't help feeling as I do.' The new anthology was to contain several of his latest war poems. Among them *Everyone Sang* was to start its career as an anthology piece, but Sassoon was by no means happy about the collection as a whole.

I think it is very important that the selection should contain nothing half-baked. The danger with *G.P.* is that it will become too tidy. I hear you are putting in Mrs. Shove. I would suggest that Edith Sitwell ought to be asked, as her work is far stronger and quite as original. But when you've got people like Drinkwater in the thing it's bound to be more or less an academic hotch-potch. The same thing applies to Shanks—delightful as his verse is—it doesn't excite and is all based on echoes from the past. Turner's stuff (unequal as it is) is on a different plane, he has *real* creative imagination.

Shanks himself had recommended Edith Sitwell as having 'a definite, solid, and individual talent, limited though it may be', and he had advised against Fredegond Shove, who was 'like a house in which all the fittings for electric light are in position, but which is not yet connected with the main'. In the autumn Shanks fell out with Nichols, who had resented his criticism. 'A creature,' wrote Nichols, 'who's a poet and nowt else, like Monro, makes me mad.' The contributors were beginning to fall out with each other and the editor, a hitherto undreamt-of thing in the annals of the fraternity.

Nichols and Sassoon did not meet in America. Before leaving New York Nichols wrote to Gray's Inn describing his friend and patron as 'a man with a voice as high as his heart is deep'. Everywhere he went he had found a letter from Marsh awaiting him. In one of them Marsh had confessed he was quite incapable of following him into the rarefied heights of philosophical speculation. 'Give me a man,' wrote Nichols, 'whose thoughts on Life and the Soul are stained with the colours of the sunset outside his window and not with the cold light of reason.' Although he now perceived that the World had 'the illogicality and evil of a dream' he had in one important respect arrived at a state of wisdom.

I begin to see that fame, celebrity, all that sort of thing, is vanity: one should as quietly as possible do the job for which one is fitted and then with indifference towards one's self, with love towards others, turn our faces to the wall and yield up this engine of life—of which one has tried to make something practical, harmonious, and resolute.

Marsh's hopes that Nichols would now do anything 'as quietly as possible' were not very sanguine. On his return to England and being shown the details of the next anthology he joined the Georgian Opposition and contended, with justice, that there was no such thing as sitting down and writing poetry. 'That is I think where my quarrel with the orderly Georgians comes in. Lawrence, thank the Lord, is not one of them—they have a loathsome trick, or so it seems to me, of doing this. One can, by giving one's mind to it, parallelize the appearances in nature by rhythm and sound ... but the real thing is to be able first to see into the heart of things. ... You will find *au fond* that the really big effects come from the rhythm being affected by the beating of your heart and not by an imitation of nature ... a certain extreme sensibility accompanied by a native vehemence of spirit is what is needed.' After this perceptive expression of the post-war attitude to poetry he went off into the empyrean with 'I love the extreme and have a taste for the infinite'. He was however in full accord with Sassoon and his latest product.

> By the brushes of all foxes that ever left scent and by the quills of all poets that ever left couplets I am a rogue and a filthy scoundrel and a lying bastard of an equivocating knave if I do not summon all good followers of Phoebus (who is said to have been both a poet and a fox-hunter) to go, hustle, fly, pillage the bookshops for this poem.

Nichols' habit of over-emphasis was making him the Lord Fisher of the poetical brotherhood. During the autumn he submitted a new poem for Marsh's critical scrutiny. 'Say what must be said but even more gently than usual.' When a damning report was returned 'How could I be furious?' he wrote. 'It's a bloody bad poem and I wanted you to say so—it was just to see. ... As it is I have roared with laughter over your growls.' Shortly before this Marsh had received from him the peremptory request: 'I want a word for not eating muffins, sleeping in a night-cap, and reading the *Daily Telegraph*. Find it!' Another letter exclaimed: 'Chaos! I love that expressive American journalistic word. ... When they open my book I want them to feel the letters kicking. ... I'd rather be the Muse's prize-fighter than her lackey!' On another occasion he was anxious to make it clear that he had been luxuriating in no foolish Byronic pose, for the *furor scribendi* was apt to seize upon him with such intensity that 'I feel as if I could walk through a brick wall'.

> Last night I saw my face in the glass when the 'storm' part seized me, and I was afraid my head would turn I had such a strange frantic look—the cheeks faintly flushed, the lips firm and turned

down, the nostrils expanded in an extraordinary effect like a tiger of Blake's, and the eyes, with huge purple blots under them, enormous in the pupils, burning, and black as the grave, and oddly large.

The climate of literature was undergoing a change. Marsh had fostered the central tradition which was now being challenged by writers whose work he could not in honesty admire. There seemed to be no new young writer appearing to take the place of those who had either been killed or grown too old for representation among the men of the moment. Not only were there stirrings of discontent within the circle, but the movement might well soon peter out for want of new blood. The fourth selection had already gone to press when a diminutive book called *The Harbingers* arrived by post. The covering letter was dated September 11 and addressed from a village near Newmarket.

DEAR MR. MARSH,

Siegfried Sassoon has written me saying that you would like a copy of some schoolboy (and just after) poems of mine. Hence the enclosed, and this letter.

Whatever my qualms as to putting before you such decorative attempts, I feel sure that you will forgive the follies of youth!

This book was printed by my brother then aged 14—and put on sale locally. Result: 1 copy sold!

Perhaps that was one too many.

Yours very truly,

E. BLUNDEN.

Marsh wrote from Mells, where he was staying with the Horners. He had read the little book 'with real interest'.

I take it from you that they are really a boy's work, and as that they give me great hopes of your later attempts. What strikes me most is the determined way in which you kept up your mastery of the sometimes really complicated forms in which you wrote—it shows such a genuine love of technique, which is a very promising sign in a young writer. However intent you were on telling your story you could not be content without hammering it out into the exact form you had chosen for it. I like also your love of exact words. Of course the poems are childish in their main content and outlook, but your descriptions are so competent and so well-studied that they would almost stand in grown-up work, and every now and then there is a touch of real poetry that I expect you will save up and use again, such as 'The shallows are sullying to a haze'—the rocks 'like satyrs

danced to stone'. . . . And *The Silver Bird* is very near being a good
poem I think. Let me know if ever there's a chance of seeing you in
London.

'I must thank you, not *sotto voce* either,' wrote Blunden 'for the
kindness and carefulness with which you tackled my purple
work. . . . The glibness with which I as a youth scribbled out
those poems is an astonishment to me now. Poetry is now to me
a most difficult and laborious affair, and I begin to wonder whether
I have any poetry in me since I write so little. . . . If I lived in
Kent I should write good poems in bundles of ten. As it is I'm
now going on for the 50th time with some doggerel about an old
varlet who keeps bees.'[1] Marsh suspected that the boy was short
of means.

> I think perhaps that if you will forgive me for asking you to take me
> into your confidence I might be able to help you in a small way. I
> have a little fund to dispose of, arising from the profits of my Memoir
> of Rupert Brooke, which I try to lay out in the way I think he would
> have liked best by helping young poets and painters, and only this
> morning I got a cheque from the publishers, which has put it into
> my head that I might be able to smooth your path to a certain
> extent—so if the idea is not distasteful to you, perhaps you would
> let me know the sort of sum that you would want to give you the
> necessary start, and I would then tell you quite frankly if it came
> within my limits. I should want you to look upon the help as coming
> from R.B. and not from me personally, and needless to say it would be
> quite between ourselves.

He then sent double the very modest sum which the poet
diffidently quoted, and followed it up with a copy of the Memoir
on the grounds that the young man ought to know something of
his benefactor.

> You will read in it that he left the profits of his poetry to be distri-
> buted among three poets he admired. 'If I can set them free to any
> extent,' he said, 'to write the poems and plays and books they want
> to, my death will be more gain than loss.' I don't agree with him.
> But I hope the thought of him will encourage you and stimulate you
> to do your best in poetry.

Blunden was set on his feet by the Memoir. 'My dear Edward
Marsh—if I may address you so; fame long since bereft you of the
Mr.—' he began his letter of amazement and thanks.

[1] This refers to *The Veteran*, a poem that was to appear in *The Waggoner* (1920).

And now I am going to read your life of that splendid Benefactor of mine, having till now known little of him but that mental beauty and power that burn in *Grantchester* for example. I feel sure from my first glances through the book that there are a thousand things in his life and letters which will indeed encourage my poetry.

Graves had taken a cottage on Boar's Hill at the end of Masefield's garden, and his home became a centre for the young post-war poets, comparable with Abercrombie's Ryton Dymock before the war. 'Thanks for looking after Blunden,' Graves wrote. 'You'll have a lot of interceders for your halidom (right word?) at the Final Trump chiefly from the Poets' Corner.' Graves' education grant being held up, he also benefited from the Brooke fund. 'Blunden is beginning to write in a magnificently competent way. You should see his *Almswomen*. It makes me cry every time,' he wrote, and again later, 'He is on the whole the best fellow I've met since I left school (Siegfried excluded) and is going to beat the lot of us as a poet if he goes on at the present rate and if he learns to let himself go "all out" a lot more. A million paternosters for the repose of R.B.'s soul.' Graves had given half his Brooke money to Blunden, and it was *Almswomen*, copied out in the author's lovely script, which finally convinced Eddie Marsh that another poet of consequence had come into his life. Although his judgement no longer went unchallenged, Graves was still trying out his work on him.

I feel that this is one of the many occasions on which I've finished a poem decently, and then moralized on for another verse unnecessarily. I am so terrified of being didactic. What did S.S. say to the intelligentsia of Balliol when he lectured there last term? He said: 'Gentlemen, the golden rule of writing poetry can be summed up in six words' (the men of Balliol pricked up their ears for something terribly earnest and brilliant, and Sassoon went on)—'when in doubt cut it out.'

Production of the fourth anthology was well advanced when de la Mare received a suggested emendation.

May I print, in *The Tryst*, 'twixt the sleep and wake of Helen's dream' instead of 'a Helen's dream'? To me, the sound is better, but that isn't the reason. In the rest of the poem all the people are mentioned as persons, not as types—Noah, Elijah, Leviathan—not a Noah, an Elijah, etc.—and this makes it so much more vivid—a real Paradise, not a Platonic or Hegelian abstraction. I would so much rather imagine an actual Helen dreaming than a type.

De la Mare saw the point.

Please take the 'a' out. It's horrible after a moment's thought. . . . This reminds me of the very moment when you and I and Rupert went back to your rooms and talked about Coleridge, and I told him—I believe he hadn't heard it before—of the most wonderful revision in English verse: when he altered 'alone on the wide, wide sea' to 'a sea'.

The new anthology was to contain two new names which did not occur again, Thomas Moult and Fredegond Shove. Shanks and J. D. C. Pellow were also newcomers, as was the author of a small book of poems published by Collins, a young doctor, Francis Brett Young, destined to become one of Marsh's especial friends. There was talk of D. H. Lawrence's plan to take a cottage near Brett Young. 'D.H. is a most interesting and in many ways delightful man,' Marsh wrote to Brett Young, 'with a sense of humour one wouldn't guess from his books. . . . But I do feel that even the thought of the proceedings described in *Look, We Have Come Through* going on next door would be a discomfort, and to be dragged into them, as would no doubt happen to you, would make life unendurable.'

Three days before the publication of *Georgian Poetry 1918–1919* Marsh stood with Mr. Churchill in Whitehall for the two minutes' silence on the first anniversary of the Armistice. He described his emotions for Juliet Duff.

I was rather ribald about it beforehand. *The Times*, which has been going in for misprints lately (did you see a delicious one yesterday in the index, 'Parish Fashions'?) declared that 'People in the streets will stand at attention, *man* removing their hats', which called up a delightful picture of someone running down the streets with a stick and knocking hats off. . . . And I was touched by the official list of exceptions—trains in tunnels, and ships navigating dangerous narrow channels, being allowed not to stop. But once the maroons sounded ('causing Ethel to jump') it was really solemn and impressive —everyone standing like statues, and the dead silence. The only thing was I was far too much occupied with the spectacle to cast a single thought to the Perils from which we had been delivered.

It was a day of spectacles. In the evening he went to a theatrical first night with Novello. 'Suddenly Viola [Tree] appeared, 9 foot high, in white satin, leading Arnold Bennett, looking 5 foot high, with his hair elaborately done to look like a golliwog.'

The new anthology had sold five thousand copies by December. 'I'm not sure how much I like this popularity!' wrote Monro. 'I *am* sure that I think it the worst *G.P.*—but that's in confidence. The second one set such a very high standard.' He was right, although de la Mare was well represented, including his *Fare Well*, and there was Turner's fine *Talking with Soldiers*, and Sassoon's *Concert Party* and *Repression of War Experience*. Graves had not yet come into his own; Lawrence was meagerly represented; and Drinkwater's *Moonlit Apples*, which deserved its place here—if not in all the subsequent anthologies—seemed representative of a rather too conscious charm which recurred in different guises on several pages of the volume. It was as if, flattered by his popularity with the general reader, the anthologist was now setting out deliberately to flatter him in return.

The views of the Opposition were voiced by Graves, the youngest of the contributors. He admired Sassoon, Nichols, and Abercrombie, but welcomed only Shanks among the new arrivals. '"It's a very arboreal book," said Bob Nichols to me, and I remarked on the apparent instability of all the elms as contrasted with the enormous vitality of the nightingales.' He felt that there was a tendency among the poets to be infected with each other's style.

I really think that when they do that it's a signal for someone with a personal style to take over the torch. (This craving for exotic colour is the sign of anaemic old age: university dons always love red robes and their wives purple hats. And in the vacation they revel in fine red sunsets on Brighton esplanade. Compris?) If the tendency increases you'll have to go and publish in British North Borneo or Brett-Young's E. Africa on bamboo paper using ape-blood for printer's ink and crocodile for the binding. Blunden is getting into his stride finely here, and is—don't you think?—just the sort of thing for next time: after all, he does write Blunden. At present I admit he's a bit of a gamble (and even a year younger than Robert Graves the Georgian infant). I'll get him to send you some new stuff.

It was more serious when Gosse himself took rather the same view. Then on December 5, 1919, the *Athenaeum* published a long article on the new Georgian book and *Wheels*, the anthology founded by the Sitwells in 1916, both anthologies being in their fourth issue. From this moment E.M.'s anthologies ceased to hold their position as the acknowledged vehicle for the best in contemporary verse, and the spokesman of the new trend in literature was John Middleton Murry.[1]

'Shall we, or should we not, be serious?' Murry began, and went on to affirm that 'this question of modern English poetry has become important to us, as important as the war, important in the same way as the war.' He likened *Georgian Poetry* to the Coalition Government and *Wheels* to the Radical Opposition. 'Out of the one there issues an indefinable odour of complacent sanctity, an unctuous redolence of *union sacrée*; out of the other, some acidulation of perversity.' His argument was all the more cogent for its justice to both sides. *Wheels* up to now had been a curious farrago of experimental misfires—some of them more archaic in style than the Georgians themselves—intermixed with a few positive achievements that reached towards the realization of a new technique. 'On both sides we have these individuals-by-courtesy whose flavour is almost wholly corporate; on both sides the corporate flavour is one that we find intensely dis-agreeable . . . they are still more remarkable as an index of the complete confusion of aesthetic values that prevails today.'

Murry exempted de la Mare, Davies, and Lawrence from his censure, and to a lesser degree Abercrombie, Sassoon, and Nichols. For the rest he diagnosed the corporate flavour as 'false simplicity' and characterized it as 'a strange blend of technical skill and an emotional void' which invited the reader to hunt for reminiscences. Against all this of good and bad in the Georgian book he set what he considered the only good poem in *Wheels* (*Strange Meeting*) which, he said, was obviously influenced by the revised Introduction to *Hyperion*, and yet 'touches greatness by more than the fringe'. It is ironical that Owen, the author of *Strange Meeting*, should have come into his kingdom through the example and personal influence of Sassoon, and with the encourage-

---

[1] Adverse comments had also appeared in *The Egoist*, iv, 8 (September 1917), and v, 3 (March 1918). The former issue recognized the effort to recover the accents of direct speech but deplored the lack of philosophical substance—'The vague is a more dangerous path for poetry than the arid'; in the latter, Mr. T. S. Eliot, writing under the pseudonym 'Apteryx', described the prevailing tone as 'minor-Keatsian' and detected a pervading quality of 'pleasantness' which was either insidiously didactic or merely decorative, whether playful or solemn '. . . the Georgians caress everything they touch.'

ment of Graves and Nichols, all Georgian. 'We appeal to the documents,' continued Murry.

Read *Georgian Poetry* and read *Strange Meeting*. Compare Wilfred Owen's poems with the very finest things in the Georgian book, Mr. Davies's *Lovely Dames* or Mr. de la Mare's *The Tryst* or *Fare Well*, or the twenty opening lines of Abercrombie's disappointing poem. You will not find those beautiful poems less beautiful than they are; but you will find in *Strange Meeting* an awe, an immensity, an adequacy to that which has been most profound in the experience of a generation. . . . You will remember three forgotten things— that poetry is rooted in emotion, and that its significance finally depends upon the quality, and comprehensiveness of the emotion. You will recognize that the tricks of the trade have never been and never will be discovered by which ability can conjure emptiness into meaning.

He summed up the characteristic flavour of the *Wheels* opposition as 'false sophistication'. He maintained that 'false sophistication' was nothing worse than irritating, while 'false simplicity' was 'positively noxious'. But to Marsh, who was first and foremost a scholar with an abhorrence of pretentiousness in any form, it was decidedly the other way round.

Marsh never quarrelled with Murry's estimation of *Strange Meeting*, but one can hardly be surprised that he was annoyed by this article. He was indignant on behalf of his friends.[1] Murry replied:

Now, Eddie, I want you to believe this of me. Nothing in my literary career has given me greater pain than being compelled to fight against you. I want you to believe that I hold you one of the kindest friends I ever had; that it is an agony (no less) to me to be driven to fight one of whom all personal memories are fragrant with generosity and loving-kindness. . . . I don't mind how mistaken you think me; but that you should think me base is intolerable.

Your devoted friend,

JACK MURRY.

The last section of Murry's letter to the author (which has already been given in part) glances at certain incidents that the reader will be acquainted with, then carries the story of Katherine

[1] Owing to the royalty system the poets who had featured in more than one issue stood to make annually what in those days was almost enough for subsistence. Marsh was afraid such opposition might reduce sales and take the bread from their mouths.

Mansfield, Lawrence, and himself up to the juncture when the first major assault on the Georgian position had been delivered in the *Athenaeum*.

When the *Blue Review* had finally expired, Katherine and I migrated to Paris. Not long after we returned, the war broke out; and we went into the country with the Lawrences. Just before that Eddie, hearing that Lawrence contemplated a book on Hardy, sent him a complete set of Hardy's books. 'Just like Eddie!' we chorused when they arrived at Gordon Campbell's little house in Selwood Terrace. Then came the war. And that put a sort of barrier between us: partly physical because Eddie was fully occupied at the Admiralty, and we were in the country; partly spiritual, because we could not share Eddie's view of the war. Like the Lawrences, we felt it as the beginning of the end of Western civilization, and not at all as a glorious manifestation of English vitality and patriotism. Lawrence's letter to Eddie, of February 12, 1916, repudiating the report that he abused Eddie, quite rightly included us, though we were then in the South of France. 'I'm sure we laughed kindly and affectionately: I know the Murrys and us, we've always laughed affectionately'; and what he said of himself was equally true of us.

'I have thought it best to keep no constant connection, because of your position in the Government, and of my feelings about the war. But that I do out of respect for your position.' Thus we drifted apart.

Nor do I remember actually seeing Eddie again—save once. My memory tells me this was at the War Office, not at the Admiralty (but I may be wrong). Anyway, I think it was after the war had ended and I suppose he invited me to call. It was a very brief meeting: for suddenly T. E. Lawrence, then at the height of his glory, entered. Eddie introduced us, but I seized the opportunity to escape from company so august. Nor, during the brief period when I edited the *Athenaeum* did I meet him; for by that time Katherine and I were definitely opposed to much of what appeared in *Georgian Poetry*, and I wrote a rather scathing review of the new volume, exalting the poetry of Wilfred Owen in comparison. But that intellectual opposition did not interfere with our affection for Eddie, nor, I believe, with his for us. Shortly after, when Katherine died, he wrote to me from Raymond Buildings:

'Though it is so long since I had seen Katherine I have never forgotten old days here and in Chancery Lane, and her courage, gaiety and lovableness made me so very fond of her, and admiring of her even before I knew what a wonderful writer she was to become.'

It ended: 'Ever your affectionate friend'. And I knew it was true.

It was significant that three years elapsed before the fifth and last anthology of the series, a gap of time as big as that enforced on the series by the outbreak of war. The centre of creative work was shifting, but by the opening of the new decade, a few weeks later, the dust had settled, and Graves sent reassurance from Boar's Hill.

> I don't think you need worry any more about the Georgians falling out with one another. It's quite superficial and they all love you still in spite of individual political consciences and swelled heads.

ii

During the month of December, while Murry's article in the *Athenaeum* was doing so much to clarify the post-war change in literary taste, Marsh gave a good deal of his leisure to a somewhat unusual piece of home-work which drew his thoughts to literary problems of a very different kind. It had been wished on him by Novello. The task was to bring his theatre-going experience to bear on the manuscript of a play by a young friend of Novello's who was determined to be a dramatist. Noel Coward was aged nineteen. He had first met Novello in Manchester during the summer of 1917 when the musical comedy *Arlette* was being tried out before its appearance in London, and soon afterwards he had come upon Marsh among the other friends, plentiful cups of tea, and hilarious anecdotes, in the Aldwych flat. The script which arrived at Gray's Inn was probably *The Rat Trap*, its author's first experiment in a play of psychological conflict. Reacting at last, and perhaps with excessive zeal, against what he has described as a 'somewhat elfin and whimsical phase' in his development, Coward had recently plunged into realism, and lurid types such as 'tarts, pimps, sinister courtesans and cynical adulterers whirled across my pages in great profusion'. Writing from his flat in Ebury Street shortly before Christmas, he was grateful to Marsh for his '*brilliant* criticism of my play, you've pointed out a lot of very important faults which I hadn't noticed—I *know* I'm too deliberately epigrammatical'. A few years later, after the first night of *Hay Fever*, Marsh met with one of the rare occasions when his critical faculties let him down. 'Not *this* time, Noel,' he sighed, shaking his head in disappointment on meeting the author back-stage.

Within a few weeks of his return from Sweden, shortly after the Armistice, Novello had sailed with his mother for New York where she had rented a studio for giving lessons in singing. He was still a rather desultory composer of light music, and no more. Coward, although his junior by seven years, had already made some headway as an actor, if inconspicuously, and soon there were three plays in his drawer—at least one of which contained some promising scenes—awaiting their opportunity. By comparison Novello's gifts were only latent, and even as a composer, not really helped by his easy success, he was still lacking in a sense of purpose and drive. With his arrival in New York for his twenty-sixth birthday in January 1919 he entered a new and more promising phase of his life. He seemed to be infected with the air of restless vitality around him and, unconsciously learning his business at every turn, neglected none of the theatrical experience which New York could afford. In April he wrote to Marsh, saying he had seen '26 plays, 6 operas, and been to 18 parties'. Within a few weeks he was trying out his hand as an actor and finding it as effortless a pastime as extemporizing popular melodies at the piano.

An unexpected cable received in mid-Atlantic on his way home led to his playing a part in his first film *The Call of the Blood*. Most of the work was done in Sicily, where he caught sun-stroke, and afterwards had the good fortune to be held up by bandits of positively Ruritanian aspect such as he was one day to present on the stage of Drury Lane. Impressions of Sweden and Sicily were combining in the back of his mind to form a romantic never-never land, not wholly divorced from reality, which one day in various theatrical guises would furnish him with a stage-setting for his music. And now through filming he discovered the value of his profile to his rapidly expanding career. His physical presence, always unassuming and unselfconscious, yet always dominating, became his greatest asset. It served eventually to lead his other gifts to their fulfilment in popular entertainment. While in Sicily he wrote to Gray's Inn. 'Apparently I'm thought to have a marvellous flair, and a great future and fortune, and really, Eddie, it does seem to come so easy.'

From Sicily he went to Rome, where, as in Sweden before, Eddie Marsh had prepared the Embassy for his arrival. He was royally entertained. 'I can't tell you what fun I'm having—the

best for ages—to start with there's a cinema strike which entirely
prevents me from working. . . . We're all going to *The Merry
Widow* tonight. . . .'

> But what I know you will think is the best news of all is—I am *working*
> oh terrifically hard and have entirely finished the libretto of *The
> Argentine Widow*! I have done the 2nd act and the 3rd, all the
> dialogue! . . . the audience by the way are kept well in suspense
> right up to the end—and so shall *you* be until I come home!

Marsh had been anxious for him to develop what seemed to be
a talent for writing. He started by suggesting exercises in self-
expression such as describing his feelings on sitting in his office at
the Hotel Cecil. This quaint relic has survived. 'My office at 3.30
is mud colour . . . the paint on the walls was put there by the
people before and they didn't care, the glue pot has one dead fly
in it and it hated dying. I have drawn faces on the blotting-pad
until their smirks madden me . . .' but at 6.30 the place is transformed, the fly comes back to life, the doodled faces grin with glee,
and so on. Another literary exercise was on the emotions occasioned
by opening a parcel. To encourage him Marsh had got his short
story *Red Buttons* published in the *Westminster Gazette* (September 27, 1919). He was by no means convinced that Novello's
future lay solely in music. Novello's frequently over-stimulated
heart and aversion to work were, of course, a worry, for Marsh was
absolutely convinced that the young man had some sort of genius
beyond the facility to write simple ragtime for revues. Either he
should try his hand at operetta of the Viennese variety, and write
the dialogue himself, or he should become a writer of drawing-
room ballads. With the latter aim in view Marsh had given him
poems by Graves, Turner, and Sassoon to set, and Novello even
undertook the far more ambitious task of setting Hodgson's
Song of Honour. The news from Rome about an operetta was
hopeful, but once again the problem of suitable lyrics was holding
it up. For the present, and for want of a better solution, Marsh
himself was writing the lyrics in his spare moments.

The Argentine Widow never came to anything, but one evening
in the Aldwych flat this January (1920), Novello was extemporizing at the piano when he happened upon an idea and asked Eddie
Marsh to listen. To this melody Marsh then wrote words, and the
song was published under the title *The Land of Might Have Been* by

Ivor Novello and 'Edward Moore'. In March it was recorded by Maggie Teyte, a little later it was sung in the Albert Hall by Clara Butt (who requested Marsh to 'rewrite the second verse on a note of optimism') and before long it had settled down as a popular classic. It is still heard occasionally, and its admirers may well speculate on the identity of the lyrical and nostalgic Mr. Moore.

Meanwhile Novello's commonplace book was constantly being added to, and so it continued over the next twenty years. In the hands of Logan Pearsall Smith for a few days it occasioned the composition of *Jeunesse*, an item in his volume *More Trivia*. Also for Novello's enlightenment Marsh was making a collection of autograph letters, which eventually filled six volumes, beginning with an authenticated fragment of the handwriting of Michelangelo. Marsh enjoyed such employment for its own sake, but his ultimate purpose was to stimulate Novello's imagination and widen his experience of life and literature. In May Marsh joined him in Avignon, where he was filming, and they had talks on the French theatre with Réjane. Later in the summer Novello took charge of the entertainments at a soirée of Lady Ribblesdale's attended by the Prince of Wales, to whom he was presented. A year later, while staying at Charlwood, Marsh was to enjoy the unusual spectacle of Novello and the Prince of Wales trying to recapture a flock of parakeets which had escaped into the garden.

In November there was a concert in the Aldwych flat: Heifetz and Novello at the piano played duets, Violet Loraine sang numbers from *The Bing Boys*, Noel Coward sang excerpts from *Chu Chin Chow*, Olga Lynn sang *The Land of Might Have Been*, and in the parlance of the day everything was pronounced 'too wonderful'. From now on the Aldwych replaced Knebworth House as the scene of Marsh's Christmas and New Year celebrations. Since his return from New York Novello seemed imbued with vitality and even something like a purpose in life. Marsh confided in his diary that he was still not accustomed to his young friend's peculiarly gay and eccentric ways. He would be found asleep at odd hours, or when not asleep nothing could tempt him away from the piano, or he would ask Marsh to luncheon and dress by stages between the courses, or go out of the room and come back pretending to be a Sultan with a purple cushion balanced on his head. After Christmas Novello left for Italy, which gave Marsh the opportunity to play one of the most elaborate epistolary tricks of his life. Dated December 29, it was headed, '2000th night of *Chu Chin Chow*. Midnight'.

Such an evening! I'm so excited that I can hardly write, yet I *can't* go to bed without trying to describe it.

There was such a crowd at the door of His Majesty's, both audience and curious, that Lloyd [Williams] and I were afraid the curtain would be up before we could get into our seats. However it began a few minutes late, so we had time to see who was there. In one box, Queen Alexandra, the Queen of Norway and that dear little Prince Olaf—opposite Mrs. Lloyd George and Megan (the P.M. came in later, for just the third Act). In the boxes above, Ellen Terry on one side and the Bishop of London, whom I have never seen at a play before, on the other. 'Scattered among the stalls' (which always sounds so untidy) were the Duchess of Portland, Maud [Cunard], Lady Ancaster, Lady Maidstone, Pamela [Lytton], Mrs. Kendal, Genevieve Ward, Marion Terry, Irene Vanbrugh, Winifred Emery, Bancroft, Hazel [Lavery], Arnold Bennett, Sargent, Lord Lonsdale, the Curzons, Mrs. Gubbay and Lady Rocksavage, and all the usual Gilbert Millers of life—and really everyone you can think of. There was a marvellous souvenir programme, the cover designed by John, and sketches of the new dresses in the new 'Joseph's Coat' process, which has superseded the 'three colour' one. (I'll send it to you tomorrow.) All the principals, especially those in the original cast, had tremendous receptions—Asche, L. Brayton and Courtice Pounds stopped the play! Frederic Norton 'wielded the conductor's baton', the audience tried to encore all the favourite numbers, and actually succeeded with *Kissing* twice!

After the 2nd act Lily Brayton conducted an auction for the Theatrical Orphanage (I'm beginning to wish I were a Theatrical Orphan, what a time they are having!) and sold the pots which the potter had made in the Mean Street scene. The biggest was knocked down to Jimmy White for £250, the underbidder being Horatio Bottomley!

I won't attempt to describe the new clothes, both the Slave scenes have been entirely redressed, and I really think they're more amazing than ever.

At the end, by the time the curtain had risen for the 15th time, the stage presented the appearance of a vast herbaceous border. Lily B. and Aileen both nearly fainted from the scents of their bouquets—even the comic negress had a gold basket full of arum lilies, and there was a garland of stephanotis for the little donkey!

Oscar Asche tried to make a speech, but he broke down after one or two sentences.

I nearly forgot to say that for this occasion only he doubled the parts of Chu C. C. and the Desert Botanist—which I thought a little inartistic, as tho' his voice and singing were much better than one expected, they *couldn't* be as good as the real man's—and he *is* too fat! Besides which he gagged a good deal, for instance when Lily B. says 'Are my eyes less bright, from the tearrrs I have shed?' he answered, 'It isn't so much your tears that are wrong, as your nose.' I saw his point, but it was going a little far don't you think?

That was the sort of evening I had expected! now for the truth. We arrived at 2 minutes to 8, and there was not a soul at the entrance—I thought it must have begun at 7.30, like the Pantomime. When we got in, the theatre was about ½ full—entirely of pew-openers and clergymen's wives, including several of those women with growths on their faces, like the ones at the Devonshire House Ball. The *only* people I knew were Viola [Tree] and Alan [Parsons] in the stage box—Wolkoff, who was the only other person in London who had had the idea that the 2000th night might be worth going to—and Jimmy Reynolds, who didn't know it *was* the 2000th night! The theatre filled up all right, but entirely with dowdies—and there was no sort of difference in the performance from what it must have been yesterday, and will be tomorrow and the next day and so far as one can see for ever. To think that I'd half a thought of putting on a white waistcoat! *How* wise you were to go to Venice! Really one would think the London public had no historic sense. We dined at the flat, on boiled eggs and Stilton.

With the end of the war Marsh had begun that phase of unmitigated theatre-going which lasted for a quarter of a century and earned him the popular title of 'The first-nighter'. His stern refusal ever to breathe a word concerning his official relations with Mr. Churchill had already won him the title 'The perfect Private Secretary'. He never relaxed that discipline, so that much that would now be an interesting gloss to history was to die with him. He began the first-night habit the more fully to enter into Novello's world, and so as to keep him informed of the latest events when he was out of town, and he came at length to rely on it as one of the main features of his social life. He liked to watch acting rather than see plays, and often enjoyed himself enormously when the quality of the play itself was far beneath the notice of a man of his intelligence. 'Eddie's a terrible fellow', growled Arnold Bennett. 'He enjoys *everything*.' This was almost true. There was often somebody's acting performance to take his fancy, if nothing more. 'Heavens!' whispered James Agate one evening when Marsh had clapped a player's exit soon after the rise of the curtain, 'you *can't* be enjoying it *already*!'

Stanley Spencer was the one artist who never lost touch with Gray's Inn. At the close of 1920 he reported that he had finished 'The Last Supper' and was now engaged on 'The Moment after the betrayal when the Apostle takes hold of the High Priest's servant's ear and the man rushes away naked'. He was looking for a studio, preferably a disused stable, built with bricks. 'I want to feel that the wall that is round me is worthy of the name of Wall.' During the summer Abercrombie had been staying in the North with Bottomley, writing his *Theory of Poetics*; Shanks wrote from Portofino: 'I am as usual at Ethel Smyth's chariot wheels, helpless. She looked at me once, with that expression of a West Highland terrier into which has entered the soul of Frederick the Great—and I am writing a libretto for her!' In July the Hawthornden Prize for imaginative literature was awarded to John Freeman at a public ceremony in the Wigmore Hall. W. J. Turner was present in the audience, and Marsh sat on the platform as one of the judges. The proceedings were somewhat under-rehearsed and the occasion thinly attended. It was another indication that the Georgians were losing their hold on the public. Some months afterwards Turner sent Marsh the typescript of an article on the affair. He began by pointing out that the event came at the tail-end of the season.

Mr. Marsh with a subtle smile and that misleading air of the fashionable idler sat as if he were just thinking of giving his button-hole to a child and had a whole year in which to do it. Beside him sat Mr. Laurence Binyon looking as if he had just murdered a Chinese mandarin to create a feeling of liveliness in the British Museum, and that it had failed. Next to him in a bright grey suit was Mr. Squire with the air of a man who was going straight down to Goodwood and was on a sure thing. Gilbert Murray made a speech, but hadn't been told who was the winner. Chopin's *Funeral March* was practised in a room near by. Darkness fell on the empty hall. No one had provided steps. Standing on tip-toe Mr. Freeman received the cheque. . . .

If someone had to look ridiculous that afternoon, one is sorry it was Freeman. Marsh's comment to Turner was brief. 'I'm sure this is very funny, but it calls up too painful memories—you have given a terribly true picture of that nightmare afternoon.' He did not know until over a year later that, where the Georgians were concerned, Turner was disenchanted for good.

iii

Eddie Marsh was for a second time sitting to Mr. Churchill for his portrait when on February 15, 1921, the painter became Colonial Secretary with special problems for solution in Ireland and the Middle East. Marsh was now back where he belonged, and glad of the change. An undated sheet of Colonial Office paper probably belongs to this time as witness that the gravity of world affairs was not such as altogether to preclude the lighter moment in the working life of the Colonial Secretary and his right-hand man. Pinned to the sheet is a paragraph from an evening newspaper with the headline: 'WELL-CONNECTED MAN WHO WANTED TO GIVE TROUBLE.' One imagines that it was left on Mr. Churchill's desk for his urgent attention. The brief news item runs as follows:

> *When Edward Marsh (33) of no home was charged on remand at Tower Bridge Police Court today with stealing a suit case . . . he made a statement virtually accusing himself of the murder of Miss Wilkins at Bournemouth.*

Below this in Marsh's hand we read:

> Secretary of State
>   In view of the above I have no alternative but to place my resignation in your hands. E.M.

Under which there is an endorsement in red ink.

> *Accepted with great regret. W.S.C.*

Another slip of paper is presumably the record of a remark which had amused him. They must have been talking of America's contribution to the victory in Europe.

> E.M.: I'm in favour of kissing him [Uncle Sam] on both cheeks.
> W.S.C.: But not on all four.

Almost their last visitor at the War Office was T. E. Lawrence, bringing the Little Book in which he had persuaded Doughty to copy out a passage from *The Dawn in Britain*. No doubt he had come to discuss his new post as adviser to the Colonial Secretary.

This brought Lawrence into almost daily touch with Eddie Marsh. It was in February that Lawrence left on Marsh's desk a small section of the rough draft of *The Seven Pillars of Wisdom*.

> I don't know that you read prose, except on official subjects: this is unofficial. They are objective extracts from a MS. story I wrote of Feisal's campaign. . . . I was short of cash. . . . They may make you laugh: and after all it's not like a telephone call. You needn't unhook them: they can be minuted back to me saying 'have seen' or 'good' or 'most amusing' or 'I really think you ought to publish them' . . . I don't ever want to see them again: but they would be difficult to destroy; so perhaps you might return them next year or so.

These fragments of a monumental work[1] were a less exacting task for the critical reader than the complete text of de la Mare's *Memoirs of a Midget* on which Marsh was to write many pages of notes before its publication in December. To the first batch of his comments on the *Midget* he attached a postscript which announced with pride that Graves was gaining in stature as a poet. 'I hope you like R.G.'s little book *The Pier-glass*—I'm immensely struck with it. A good deal of it is rather odd, but I think there can be no two opinions about the excellence of the writing, and much of it is sheer beauty.' He was now also engaged in correspondence with Ronald Storrs, then Governor of Jerusalem, who was tackling problems of which he felt the Minister should be kept informed.

In May there was disturbing news from Brett Young. The sales of his recent novel *The Black Diamond* were negligible, and he was seriously wondering whether he should not go back to his profession of medicine. Marsh was certain this novel held promise of better things. He wrote on June 2.

> I am sure popularity is only a question of time—such work must tell in the long run—meanwhile I feel most deeply for you in your disappointment. I can well imagine the temptation to shrug your shoulders and turn to some job in which you would get a sure reward. But of course you *mustn't*. You are a born writer, and it would be a sin to chuck it—and I think a folly too.
>
> I had a talk with Jack Squire about *The B.D.* and it may interest you to hear his point of view. He admires it immensely and considers

[1] They were fragments of the second draft, which were first published in *The World's Work* (New York, 1921) and the proceeds given to Robert Graves.

it almost perfect except for one thing—that it lacks *salient* beauties at the critical moments. Everything, he says, is done to perfection— but if Thomas Hardy or Shakespeare had done it there would be every here and there an extra turn of the screw which you just miss giving and which would have brought the entire public, as well as the critical few who know consciously what good writing is, to your feet. Coming as this does from a real admirer, I'm sure you won't resent it, and it may interest you . . . to my mind the least improbable explanation of its really unaccountable failure is that it doesn't really come to an end. I should have been very much dissatisfied with the conclusion myself if I hadn't supposed there was to be a sequel, and my advice to you would be to pay enormous attention to the end of your future books. . . . It's very easy to advise you not to despond, and you mustn't think that I don't entirely sympathize with you in your indignation and disgust, because I do. But I feel so certain that there's a good time coming for you, if you will persevere, that I have no misgivings about my being too facile in imploring you to keep a good heart and stick to your guns.

Another writer was saved. 'The mere fact,' wrote Brett Young, 'that a man like yourself knows and sympathizes when an artist is putting the last ounce of his heart and his intelligence into something that he believes to be beautiful, without a hint of response from the public, helps to make him feel that he isn't working altogether in vain. Of course I shall keep on.' As the Georgians waned, prose bulked more and more in Eddie Marsh's life. A chance remark to Hugh Walpole in the previous October[1] had led to the novel whose chapters Marsh was now going through. 'I've changed all the lunches,' wrote Walpole, 'into luncheons most meticulously.' Marsh was agreeably surprised.

I may say that it's admirable of you not to be faintly annoyed (or to conceal it if you are) at my shoals of little carps, which I should have thought would be like having one's hairs pulled out one by one, pleasant at first, one is told, but then maddening. As like Lady Catherine de Burgh I love to be of use, I shall be delighted to repeat the treatment if you will honour me again.

The younger poets meanwhile were profitably at work near Islip. 'Edmund writes magnificently,' wrote Graves, 'but too much—he points out that I write more, I point out that I write

---

[1] He had accompanied Marie Belloc Lowndes to a lecture by Walpole, to whom Marsh remarked afterwards, 'I wish you would write a comic lighthearted novel in that improvisatore vein.' The book which resulted was *The Young Enchanted*.

in a more varied way, and so we wrangle.' Graves was anxious
to reimburse the Memoir fund. 'That fund would be a finer
memorial (kept up thro' the centuries) than marble busts and a
slab in Poets' Corner.' Monro, sending upwards of £90 for distribution among the contributors, gave news that the Indian Army
had ordered a hundred copies of each of the four issues, and there
was now a growing demand for a fifth. Marsh advised another
interval of three years before the next issue of *Georgian Poetry*, not
only because he wanted to give time for the appearance of good
work, but because a situation had arisen in his official life which
fully engaged his leisure and his working hours. He allowed himself but few distractions, the opening night of Novello's *The
Golden Moth* on October 5, and the composer's first appearance
as an actor on the legitimate stage on November 3 (he had a small
part in a play called *Deburau*), and one other evening when
Novello was acting as master of ceremonies at a soirée at Devonshire House, but no more, for at this time Marsh was engrossed
in the question of Home Rule for Ireland which had been in
abeyance since the outbreak of war.

Early in 1921 Mr. Churchill was in Cairo, presiding at the
conference which led to the creation of the kingdom of
Iraq. Meanwhile Ireland began to suffer the horrors of civil
violence. In July an Irish delegation under Mr. de Valera arrived
in London. Among the chief negotiators on the Irish side was
Erskine Childers, the undergraduate who had taught Eddie
Marsh fly-fishing on one of the summer vacations some thirty
years before. Seeing Marsh again for the first time after so long,
seated on the opposite side of the table, he showed no flicker of
recognition. The terms eventually arrived at were rejected by
the Dail, and another conference opened at Downing Street on
October 11. This time Mr. de Valera was not present, but an
addition to the Irish delegation was Michael Collins, an agitator
who had been outlawed with a price on his head, but whose
political convictions were combined with singular charm of
personality. Soon after their first difficult and frigid encounter,
Collins and Marsh recognized in each other a quality of integrity
which enabled them to hold informal talks that served a valuable
purpose. Not only could Marsh convey to Collins at leisure and
in his own way the Colonial Secretary's point of view, but he was
able in return to enlarge on the arguments put forward by Collins

for the benefit of Mr. Churchill. The negotiations were continued in an atmosphere of fluctuating tension until December 5. Next day the agreement was signed which offered to an Irish 'Free State' the status of a Dominion within the British Commonwealth.

How the Dail ratified this treaty, Mr. de Valera resigned, and civil strife broke out, is familiar history. Griffith and Collins were now leaders of the new State, but their position was insecure owing to the armed extremists. What brought Marsh into the foreground of the picture was his friendship with Sir John and Lady Lavery, who were closely associated with the new Irish leaders, especially Kevin O'Higgins and Collins himself. It was at Lady Lavery's house in London that Marsh had his talks with Collins, found himself in an advantageous position to act as intermediary, and realized the matter was too vitally important to let his usual modesty hold him back from playing an active part in the affair.

After the Treaty Lady Lavery wrote from her home in Ireland while Collins and Bernard Shaw were talking in the same room.

> I am trying to write this with a babel of conversation which I dare not miss, going on around me. G.B.S. is reading aloud to Michael Collins his article for the *Irish Times* on Ireland, it is very funny but quite futile. . . . I'm enclosing a cutting to show you that I am in the thick of the fight! The car that was ambushed had just been left by Michael as something had gone wrong with the clutch and he had jumped into a Ford car standing near, so his lucky life was spared again. He had been dining with us at an hotel near Dublin and it happened on the way home—he rang us up from H.Q. at three in the morning to assure us of his safety because we had heard the ambush which wasn't far from the hotel.

Throughout the first half of 1922 the lawlessness continued, and there were protests or threats or appeals from Belfast and Dublin, while the Colonial Office maintained contact with Collins. Griffith and he were handicapped in their dealings with the opposition by their shortage of arms. There came a point when the 'wild men' sallied from the Four Courts, their stronghold in Dublin, and kidnapped the C.-in-C. of the Free State Army, almost simultaneously with the assassination of Sir Henry Wilson at the hands of two Irishmen on the steps of his house in Eaton Place, London. Collins restored the situation and was

proceeding to stabilize his Government, when in mid-August
Griffith died of heart failure, and ten days later Michael Collins
himself fell victim to an ambush. Writing from Cromwell Place
(undated) Hazel Lavery described to Marsh his elevation as a
national hero—'At the Memorial Mass the Cathedral was
crowded right out into the street, people kneeling on the steps.
There is a constant and daily pilgrimage to his grave at Glasnevin,
and so many wreaths you cannot get within twenty feet of it.' In
the same letter, after making allowance for the writer's tendency
to dramatize, one may note a passage which shows that Collins
himself was not unaware that as Private Secretary, with free
access to the attention of both parties, Marsh had made his
contribution to Mr. Churchill's achievement in Eire. 'Kevin
O'Higgins said the other night at dinner when they were all
saying who made the Free State etc. that there wouldn't have been
any Treaty or Free State without *you* . . . he was full of praise for
the way you were always helping quietly and without recognition,
Michael felt that too, and told me so.' Beside which one should
place the Irish patriot's last message to the Colonial Office—
'Tell Winston we could never have done anything without him.'
In his own Memoir, after confessing his admiration for the
personal qualities of both Sir James Craig and Collins, Marsh
wrote: 'Winston, who at the start was instinct with the spirit of
"not shaking hands with murder", was cross with me at first for
being thus beguiled; but in daily contact he came to recognize
Collins's quality. . . .' It would be pleasant for the biographer of
an unassuming scholar to be able to throw in among his accomplishments the mere matter of having brought into being a new
Dominion. It must be enough to note in passing that his happy
gift of identifying himself sympathetically with the feelings and
opinions of people very different from himself enabled him to
smooth the way a little for the great statesman he served.

The Treaty with the new State was not ratified by Parliament
until December 1922, when a new British Government was in
office. Before then the Colonial Secretary had been confronted
with a different problem, which was potentially of even more
alarming proportions. For the Colonial Office it was a year of
mounting crisis. But first one must turn to the private life at
Gray's Inn before glancing again at the world events in which
Eddie Marsh was once more involved.

iv

Through the last days of 1921 he was reading the manuscript of W. J. Turner's play *The Man who Ate the Popomack*. It is not necessary to know the play to appreciate the style of Marsh's dramatic criticism.

I feel, as I expected to feel, that the choice of subject is a mistake—it seems to me grotesque rather than fantastic, repellent rather than troubling.' Morally, the sufferings of a stinker (once one believes in him!) are as painful a spectacle and as little suited to farce, as a cripple's—and there is added the physical disgust.

But you will say, it is not altogether farce, there is an element of tragedy. Yes, but directly you get away from farce a new requirement comes in—sympathy. (You may think me old-fashioned, but I do believe that in the acted drama some lodgement for the audience's sympathy is a prime necessity.) And how can one feel the smallest sympathy for a man with a blue face stinking like a skunk who first browbeats his acquaintance for not treating him on the same footing as when he was white and sweet, and then revenges himself by trying to reduce them all to his own condition?

You know what Aristotle says about probable impossibilities—let us call them for the purpose credible incredibilities. To the degree in which a playwright calls on his audience to turn their backs on verisimilitude and to start from credible premises, he is bound to smooth their path, once they have entered on it with him, by rigid logic and flawless plausibility in his working out. I do not feel you have been careful enough about this, and I will give you two instances. (1) I continually asked myself how the prestige of the popomack's flavour could have supported itself for centuries in the East against the disgrace of its odour. (2) I could find no hint of an explanation why the smell was (apparently) not noticed either by the cook who prepared or the guests who consumed the soup in the last act. (Don't say because it is a Vision—the vision is the product of Belvoir's mind, which must be governed by the hypothesis of the play.) The first act is a beautiful piece of literature. I was quite charmed by it. But it has the fault that it doesn't even approach the fringe of the subject of the play. This seems to me flying in the face of every structural principle. . . . It is quite certain that if you are to have discussions in drama they must be dramatic on the lines on which discussion can be dramatic, i.e. the arguments must take the place of personages, each distinct from the other, and must have their own little vicissitudes of well-marked advantage and repulse, victory and defeat.

Turner was grateful, but unpersuaded. 'I have had no illusions about the likelihood of its appealing to any theatrical business man, yet I am foolhardy enough to believe that with the right production it would make a tremendous effect. This may be the illusion of conceit but I doubt it. . . . The play is symbolical. Belvoir's affliction is only a fantastic abstraction of some disability which every man suffers from.' Eddie Marsh's failure to see eye to eye with him over his play did nothing to reinstate the Georgians in Turner's esteem. Later in the year Turner was to give the sign which more than anything else opened Marsh's eyes to the truth that the Georgian days were numbered.

A tragic episode began in the new year when he received an appeal from de la Mare on behalf of Ivor Gurney, the composer and poet, who was then unemployed and slowly going out of his mind. He was sent some 'Rupert money' and with this he made himself presentable enough to apply for the job of playing the piano 'effects' in a picture-palace at Bude. 'This morning,' wrote Gurney, 'I have been walking reading the *Iliad* shortly after dawn. . . . It is the noblest stuff and went with thunder and the streaked north-east.' He particularly wanted an appointment in the Income Tax office at Gloucester. 'Cinema posts are hard to get, fearful to retain, easy to lose.' He was apparently dismissed from the cinema, and somehow Marsh got him his job at Gloucester. By October his shell-shocked condition was growing worse. A friend wrote to say that he kept begging his doctor for poison and going to the police for a pistol to end his misery. 'He seemed like a man running a high temperature and could only follow conversation with effort.' Gurney came to Gray's Inn, tried to explain why Ben Jonson and Socrates could manage without sleep, and brought some poems by his friend William Kerr (which rather to Marsh's surprise turned out to be good enough for inclusion in his next anthology), and presented Marsh with his musical settings of two sonnets by Brooke as a thank-offering for his help. It was not long before Kerr had to assist his friend to an asylum, where the genius whom some have described as the 'English Schubert' lingered on the fringe of existence for several years, discovered in himself a vein of real poetry, then died insane.

On March 2 there appeared in the *London Mercury* a letter to the editor entitled *The New Byron Letters*, the first of several in the next few years which established Marsh as something of a latter-day Verrall. He pointed out nine possible misreadings in Sir John Murray's recent edition of Byron's correspondence, especially in the letters to Lady Melbourne. Finding yet more, Marsh wrote to Mary Lady Lovelace (the widow of Byron's grandson, the author of *Astarte*), who possessed her husband's copies from the originals as against those copied by Lady Dorchester which, Marsh suspected, had been the source of Murray's text. At Wentworth House, Chelsea, Marsh worked with Lady Lovelace. They detected seventy-seven alternative readings, almost all Marsh's emendations were endorsed, and the findings were sent on to Murray in instalments. At the same time he was corresponding with Ethel Colburn Mayne, whose *Life and Letters of Anne Isabella, Lady Noel Byron*, was in the early stages of preparation. July found him spending a short holiday with the Poet Laureate, who wished to discuss with him the principles governing the 'loose alexandrine' measure which he had already used and had decided to employ in his new philosophical poem, *The Testament of Beauty*. 'He has had a marvellous St. Martin's Summer,' Marsh wrote to Gosse from Boar's Hill. There followed a slight awkwardness. With Graves in support, Bridges wrote recommending the work of a poet who was in 'a queer desperate condition and recognition would soothe him'. Marsh thought the proffered examples not only poor but ridiculous. 'Your letter is amusing enough to be in some sort a reward to me for my charitable effort,' wrote Bridges. 'Still Graves and I would say that you do not recognize the *sort* of excellence that this man has. You could have pulled Blake to pieces in the same way—and Palgrave refused Blake a place in *The Golden Treasury*.' Bridges had been reading Clutton-Brock on Shelley. 'I agree with the general tone of it; but who would imagine from it that the greater part of Shelley must fairly be called bosh?' This gave Marsh his opportunity. Coupling Shelley and the Laureate's candidate, he remarked, 'I remember Vernon Lee's brother making me laugh by saying his trouble was that in reading the works of the *very* greatest poets one had to keep one's standard extremely low!'

In June Marsh brought Davies and Blunden together at Gray's Inn. Blunden produced his most recent work and afterwards wrote: 'I should have liked to have convinced you with one of my war poems, but alas, your silence towards them shows me I didn't. Then must I wait for another war? I am at present waiting for breakfast. Thomas Hardy with whom I've been staying (thanks, I am sure, to Siegfried's commendations) says imaginative work is impossible before that meal.' Blunden was beginning his work in belles-lettres with an essay on Shelley in the *Nation* and now considered embarking on a translation of Horace. 'There wouldn't be a penny in it,' was Marsh's comment, 'and if you are to work for love it ought to be at something of your own.'

The selection from Blunden for the next anthology, headed by *Almswomen*, was easily agreed on. Monro was less amenable. 'The absence of Charlotte Mew is of course again a conspicuous flaw,' he complained (with some justice, though Marsh was being supported in his opinion by de la Mare) and observed of one of his own pieces, 'I feel somehow that *Unknown Country* is almost too Georgian even for *G.P.*!' which was possibly the first instance of that epithet's use in the now familiar, derogatory sense. But for better or worse, no one, not even the Laureate, was going to make Marsh distrust his own judgement. Monro's poem was included, Mew and the Laureate's candidate rejected, Aldous Huxley was asked for a poem, but his appearance in *Wheels*, he said, had 'become a habit'. De la Mare tried very gently to disengage himself.

> Books slip so quickly into the past, yet one still wants to write on—like those tedious old bores who insist on finishing their remarks. If only the tap were a real index of the cistern! There's my heart, and now steps in commonsense—which bids me once more declare, asseverate, and vow that I am far too old a bird for this new nest. You *must* shed as you go, if you decide to continue, and my hour arrived with No. 3 really. To be in 5 would be monstrous—not only because our friend Walter is a Victorian, but because of all these young things clamouring for admittance. . . . I am quite certain the critics would welcome such removals. 'Old ruts'—can't you hear the echoes?

Marsh was seriously alarmed. A few days before, he had written to de la Mare: 'With most of my poets the difficulty is to find enough that I want to put in—with you it is the opposite, I should like at least ¼ of the book to be you.' He now wrote again in the form of an appeal.

> You *can't* really mean it. All I can say is that half my pleasure and nearly all my pride in the new book will be gone if I mayn't have

your poems. I can't quite say that I should give up bringing it out, because I've invited too many people—but that would certainly be my wish. Your things are almost the only ones of the last 3 years that I am *sure* are *really* good; and without them the book would be a wilderness.

You needn't be afraid of crowding anybody out—several of the old stagers are dropping out anyhow, and there is heaps of room for quite a lot of new people; and my great difficulty, even with them to my rescue, is to get enough stuff that I really like to fill a respectable-sized book. It would really break my heart if you persisted.

De la Mare gave way. Monro and he had acted individually. The Boar's Hill group found a candid spokesman in Robert Graves. He suggested compiling the new anthology in two parts, one representing the senior writers, the other with an age limit of thirty-three, confined to those 'whose characters are entirely moulded by war experience', and continued:

> This grouping will make the book more sensible and will account for the breaking of the excellent Abercrombie—Hodgson—de la Mare—Brooke tradition of early Georgianism. It will be kinder both to old and young to put 'em in separate cages if the murmurings I hear are to be trusted. At present you are ploughing with a Bull and a young Camel. By that token the Bull has begotten a rather ineffective Ox which disgraces its very excellent Sire and annoys the Camel. Its name is not Georgianism but Georgianismatism, and it is against the inclusion of this occasional ox that the real hostility to recent volumes lies. Tortures wouldn't drag from me the names of this sham-Georgian school, but it is recognized by its infernal cleverness and its damnable dulness. Remember the end of the Yellow Books and forgive my impertinence, and don't trouble to answer, but take this view (about the Ox) as expressing the secret opinions of that group—Turner, Blunden, Nichols, Sassoon, Graves, etc., the Camel which thrust its nose into the Arab's tent in 1916 (see the Fable).

Among his recommendations Marsh was glad to discover Peter Quennell, and he also took some work by Frank Prewett. He rejected other suggestions, including the dual structure. At this time Graves was introducing Marsh to a new element in poetics. From a letter asking him to accept the dedication of his book *Whipperginny* one gathers that Marsh had expressed himself sceptical of Psychology as a factor in art on the grounds that the human race was fundamentally the same now as it was before the

new science began to be formulated. ' "The New Psychology",
did I say that?' Graves answered: 'I hope not. It sounds awful....'

> The psychology of the human race is the same as it ever was, but
> the proved research by capable scientists is getting on paper now,
> and the Poet may take advantage of it surely. Freud is unattractive
> but his self-analyses are the more likely to be fairly true to Truth
> if they show him in an unattractive light. Dr. Rivers is my mentor
> in these matters and I am inclined to believe in his theories because
> they are all tested practically by the treatment of war-neurosis
> cases—including Sassoon, Owen, and Frank Prewett.

Both Graves and Sassoon had first met Dr. Rivers at Craiglockhart. Sassoon himself did not include this kind of influence in
his great debt to Rivers. 'R.G. interprets his poems most elaborately
in accordance with scientific theories of analysis—psychic and
otherwise,' he wrote, 'but surely poems should be comprehensible
to ordinary intellects without any scientific jargonry about dreams,
etc., being dragged in by the lunar complex?'

The literary climate was growing a little too variable for Marsh's
comfort. Then came the moment in early July when he wrote to
Turner for permission to quote his poem *Search for the Nightingale*.
The poet courteously declined and was moved to question the
genuineness of his admiration. Marsh was candid in return.

> It's quite true that I don't like the last book so much as your other
> two, but I like the *Nightingale* poem *very* much. I think there are
> obscurities in it which prevent it from being perfect, but it is full of
> beauty, and your refusal is too severe a punishment for not being
> worthy of the rest of the book! I should *hate* not to have you in, and
> it would make a sad gap in the book, so do please reconsider.

In his reply Turner was anxious lest Marsh should think him
'foolishly perverse. No one appreciates more than I do all you
have done for living poets. In fact the personal appeal is so strong
that it is with the greatest difficulty, believe me, that I can resist
it. But sometimes a devil rises up in us that will not be denied.
I cannot properly explain . . . it is merely a blind instinct . . . so
I do hope you will be indulgent to my caprice with your characteristic generosity.'

This was something new. Huxley or Pound might well stand out
if they wished, but for an acknowledged contributor to secede! . . .
This, and D. H. Lawrence (now 'Lorenzo' in Taos, New Mexico)

sufficiently well off to be returning a gift of £20 for the benefit of some more needy writer—these were new times indeed. And as nothing had happened to shake his faith in his own judgement— it was post-war literature which had gone awry, he believed, not his powers of discrimination—he sat down to write a preface to the new volume. The majority of readers still had no idea who 'E.M.' was, but the series had a reputation to protect, and the time was forcing the anonymous editor to declare his hand.

As much by the manner as in the matter of his preface E.M. endeavoured—inevitably in vain—to disclaim any pretensions to being a professional arbiter of taste. His critics, he said, were on the wrong tack altogether.

> Not only did they very properly disapprove my choice of poems; they went on to write as if the Editor of *Georgian Poetry* were a kind of public functionary, like the President of the Royal Academy; and they asked—again on this assumption, very properly—who was E.M. that he should bestow and withhold crowns and sceptres, and decide that this or that poet was or was not to count.

Such a disclaimer was all very well, but what else in effect had he been doing all these years than acting as an arbiter? 'I have neither the sure taste,' he went on, 'nor the exhaustive reading, nor the ample leisure which would be necessary in any such role.' What authority could he hope the series to exert after this modest apologia? He provided the answer himself. 'If they have won for themselves any position, there is no possible reason except the pleasure they have given.' The setting of a critical standard was no part of his aim. He had overlooked or was unwilling to admit that the work of an anthologist was itself an act of criticism and that over a period of ten years a position of authority and a standard of taste had been established whether he intended it or not.

He categorically denied the accusation of 'sameness' in his pages. 'To my fond eye those who have graced these collections look as diverse as sheep to their shepherd, or the members of a Chinese family to their uncle.' The ideal anthology could only be achieved, if at all, he said, by setting up a Royal Commission. Finally he gave an oblique answer to Graves and his friends, as well as his critics in public, who had agitated for the inclusion of work of a kind which he had persisted in regarding as inadmissible.

Much admired work seems to me, in its lack of inspiration and its disregard of form, like gravy imitating lava. Its upholders may retort that much of the work which I prefer seems to them, in its lack of inspiration, and its comparative finish, like tapioca imitating pearls. Either view—possibly both—may be right. I will only say that with an occasional exception for some piece of rebelliousness or even levity which may have taken my fancy, I have tried to choose no verse but such as in Wordsworth's phrase

> The high and tender Muses shall accept
> With gracious smile, deliberately pleased.

Watchful attendance and reliance on that gracious smile, without whose favour no poet of the eighteenth century could have thrived for long (but which might perhaps be dispensed with on occasion in an age of heartbreak which had begun sinking shafts in the unconscious) set those limitations which had caused *Georgian Poetry* to yield its ground since the Armistice.

His new selection was now complete, and there were seven new names—Blunden, Richard Hughes, Vita Sackville-West, Peter Quennell, Frank Prewett, William Kerr, and Martin Armstrong. Bottomley had dropped out. Sassoon too was absent. In spite of this it was undoubtedly a better book than last time, but not even Lawrence's *Snake*, a great poem, nor *Almswomen*, nor de la Mare's *The Moth*, nor *The Pier-glass* by Graves, and a few other outstanding pieces were enough to offset the prevailing sameness of tone. Rather were they themselves toned down, almost absorbed in the air of emotional low tension. As usual there was nothing incompetent or slapdash, nothing incongruous. It was now July, and, confident that his tribute was not unworthy, Marsh decided to offer the dedication to Alice Meynell. She had grown old and infirm, and her husband, himself a patron with a secure place in the chronicles, answered on her behalf. 'You seem to have a double mission, which I hope is also a double delight, to show the young that they are appreciated, and the old that they are not forgotten.'

From August 10 to 23 Marsh was with the Churchills at Biarritz. Mr. Churchill had probably been working on *The World Crisis*, for on his return to London began the exchange of memoranda on facts, syntax, and punctuation which continued from now on for many years.

Colonial Office,
Downing Street,
*S.W.*1

Eddie

You are very free with your commas.

I always reduce them to a minimum: and use 'and' or an 'or' as a substitute not as an addition. Let us argue it out.

W.

31.8.22

I look on myself as a bitter enemy of *superfluous commas*, and I think I could make a good case for any I have put in—but I won't do it any more!

E.

No do continue. I am adopting provisionally. But I want to argue with you.

W.

3.9.22

These discussions were interrupted a few weeks later by a crisis of such magnitude that it eventually brought the Lloyd George Coalition to an end.

v

The Turks, who had precipitated the war-time operations in the Dardanelles, were now threatening a small occupation force of Allied troops stationed in a place called Chanak, a fortified base whose defences overlooked the narrows facing the Gallipoli peninsula. Since the Armistice in Europe the new Turkey under Mustapha Kemal had enjoyed little or no peace. After repudiating the treaty of 1920 the Turks resumed hostilities and were met by the Greeks acting in the Allied interests of keeping Turkish nationalism out of Europe. By September 15 the Turks had recovered from their initial losses at the hands of the Greeks, and now looked as if they were going to overrun the neutral zone of Chanak as a preliminary to crossing the straits of the Dardanelles. Marsh's engagement book shows that he stayed late at the office on Friday the 15th 'detained by telegrams to the Dominions on N. East question'. The Dominions were being asked if they were willing to associate themselves with an armed effort to compel the Turks to a negotiated peace. Mr. Churchill drew up a communiqué on the situation which was published on the following

Sunday. Its threatening terms, which showed that Britain was ready to use force immediately the Kemalists set foot in the neutral zone, alarmed public opinion at home with sombre visions of the clock put back to 1915, disconcerted the French Premier who was not so ready to commit his country to armed intervention, and bewildered the Dominions where the explanatory telegrams of the previous Friday were not yet fully decoded. It is not surprising that Mustapha Kemal himself was pulled up short, and began to withdraw from Chanak. The bombshell from the Colonial Office had restrained the Turks in Asia Minor with spectacular success, but the crisis at home continued unabated while the Opposition accused the Colonial Secretary of trying to 'dragoon the Empire into war'. During the second week of October the Coalition was attacked from all sides. A note to Marsh from Lord Trenchard at the Air Ministry shows that T. E. Lawrence was consulted. 'I understand Mr. Churchill wants to see Lawrence. In order to avoid publicity in this I would like you to let me know at least 48 hours beforehand when you want him. . . . I think Mr. Churchill will agree that it is inadvisable for anything to be put on paper disclosing Lawrence's address.'

Lloyd George fell, Bonar Law formed a Government, and a general election followed, but Mr. Churchill was handicapped. On October 16 he complained to Marsh of pains in his side. When Marsh called at Sussex Square next day he found that the doctors had already decided to operate for appendicitis, and Mr. Churchill was on the point of leaving the house for a nursing-home in Dorset Square. Marsh did not see him again until he visited his bedside on the 31st. The election campaign in Dundee would have to start without the candidate. With the fall of Lloyd George, Mr. Churchill had ceased to be Secretary of State for the Dominions and Colonies, and Marsh was left as it were in mid-air. If the new Minister had secretarial plans of his own Marsh would drop back into the obscurity where he was after the fall of Mr. Asquith in 1916; but on October 25 the Duke of Devonshire took over the office and with it, as Marsh said, 'the livestock on the premises'. As an old friend of Lord Richard Cavendish, the Duke's brother, this was for him a most agreeable solution and a profound relief, but it had its drawback. Marsh was powerless to assist Mrs. Churchill in her campaign at Dundee, which was gallantly fought by her husband's supporters and herself. Mr. Churchill arrived two days before the poll. His side was still unhealed and he was unable to stand to answer the hecklers who persisted in raising the dreary spectre of the Dardanelles. Marsh was at ease with his new Chief among the Holbeins and Van Dycks at Chatsworth when the defeat at Dundee left Mr. Churchill 'without office', as he said, 'without a seat, without a party, and without an appendix'.

As November 18 approached Marsh began to wonder whether he was going to feel a sobering difference after his fiftieth birthday. He celebrated the occasion at Harlech with Peter Quennell, the youngest of his new poets. Quennell was a friend of Richard Hughes, whose first book *Gipsy-Night* (1922) had impressed Marsh as the work of a born writer. 'The Quennell family when I was there were gradually working themselves into a state of terror at the prospect of your visit,' wrote Hughes; 'Peter must have painted you very fiercely.' His pretext for writing was a rumour that his beard had somehow given Marsh offence when last he lunched at Gray's Inn. 'I thought you were a little distrait but didn't really know the reason. . . . By all the laws of logic, working on the best architectonic principles, it is essential that I should wear a beard, in order that the large spaces under the eyes as well as the detail and scroll-work above them should be properly supported.' Hughes, just down from Oxford, had grown his beard in a doss-house in Trieste, after wandering about the Balkans. 'That beard seemed to upset Eddie,' he recalled long afterwards. 'I lunched with him when I got back and he made me sit beside him instead of opposite him so that he needn't look at it.'

Hughes and Quennell had become the pride of their first patron, but they had leanings towards the Georgian Opposition. After looking through the latest anthology Quennell thought that most of the older contributors suffered from having read too much of each other's work. 'I shall write an essay tracing the decadence of English Poetry to the system of presentation copies.' Like so many of his contemporaries he could not agree with Marsh's constant objections to obscurity in verse. 'So many of the best things of existence are cloudy-ish.' One may imagine that such topics as these were uppermost in Eddie Marsh's mind as he reached the climacteric of his fiftieth year among his youngest friends in Wales.

On November 27 he received a note from Francis Meynell.

'Mother is dying', it began. *Georgian Poetry 1920-1922*, in boards of assertive scarlet, was due out in the second week of December. An advance copy was laid in the hands of the poetess before she died, and on December 7 the last of the Georgian series appeared on the market. The Irish Free State had been inaugurated the day before, but the Sinn Fein dangers were by no means passed. On the 8th Marsh found a note on his desk.

> Will you do your best to get the Secretary of State to take reasonable care of himself for the next 10 days? The dangerous period is until our evacuation of Dublin is completed, and the danger points are the doors of his house, Club, office, and Parliament. Last night I happened to quit this office as he was going out. There may have been a safety man, but I saw none . . . and to my consternation he stood just outside the door talking.

In this atmosphere of tension the notices of the fifth anthology began to appear. The *Spectator* (December 22) regarded it as 'the epitome of the methods of the English with institutions'.

> A private citizen comes along, he observes a want or an abuse in a sphere which is entirely outside his professional interests. He supplies the want or remedies the abuse unobtrusively but with success. In a moment he finds himself a public institution with definite obligations. He is freely abused if he does not fulfil them.

One reviewer described Lawrence's *Snake* as 'laboured realism that quite misses fire', another considered it a 'diffuse and whimsical soliloquy'. Marsh's judgement was not in all respects behind the times. Writing in July[1] Edmund Gosse had brought the Georgian venture back to public notice.

> The Georgians ought to be a happy clan. No other body of writers, since English first began to be written, has received so much composite attention or has had its way so comfortably smoothed for it . . . they have swept along the road together in a comfortable charabanc with E.M. as their beribboned driver.

After the new book was out Gosse became critical, and sent Marsh a copy of his article before it was published. He put forward the notion that these poets, in their rejection of general ideas in favour of a pictorial representation of the physical phenomena of life, came very close to the method of the cinematograph. Moreover as a result of their 'almost crazy fear' of being

[1] *The Sunday Times*, July 2, 1922.

rhetorical they could not always escape bathos. 'They are so determined to be simple that they succeed in being silly. . . . They listen to their own inner feelings, and the daisy at their feet doth the same tale repeat. The result is that they lack in some degree the sense of proportion.' They were restricted by an obsession with the charm of nervous sensibility cultivated for its own sake. 'They are exquisite, but poetry should not always be "breathing through silver".' This was a perceptive analysis of Georgianism in its last phase—but in the minds of Monro and Marsh there was as yet nothing to prevent the series going on for another decade.

In the back of the editor's thoughts, however, there was a distinct waning of interest which he was reluctant to admit even to himself. The poets were going their own ways, and with his blessing, but he could not in honesty follow, and there was little more he could do for them. Blunden was heartening about the preface, calling it an 'act of vengeance which leaves you in possession. The enemy lies strewn about you, and all done with a rapier.' Of the rest he was gently critical. '*G.P.*, I see, sells like scandalous revelations—though surely this time it is the mirror of all innocence.' Glad to be rid of his new book, Marsh went off to Cannes (his holiday task was making notes on Harold Nicolson's *Byron, the Last Journey*) and saw the new year in with the Churchills. The plaudits at the performance of *Treasure Island* were ringing in his ears. He had written a long critique to J. B. Fagan with suggested improvements and Arnold Bennett had taunted him in the interval for 'leading the encores'.

Mr. Churchill was seriously pulled down by his exertions in Dundee, and by turns he was painting, or revising the last pages of the first volume of *The World Crisis*, or discussing plans for his new country home. By coincidence Marsh's stepmother used to buy her vegetables from Chartwell garden and knew the little place which the Churchills were converting into a suitable residence. 'I wonder what your Chief will do with the double lot of cellars. A fearful place. . . . Mariner's Cottage is rather lonesome in the winter.'

The year 1923 was one of art and scholarship. Marsh's election by the Contemporary Art Society as its 'buyer of the year' gave stimulus to his interest in the visual arts just when he was beginning to realize that his work among the poets must soon draw to a close. It brought him into collaboration with an old friend, Lord Henry

Bentinck, Chairman of the Society, whose home at Underley near the Lakes with its fine collection of contemporary drawings was from now on one of his favourite places of call in the country-house tours which always constituted his Easter or late summer holiday. From Underley, the low grey house by its lake, he might go to Lady Moyra and Lord Richard Cavendish at Holker, not far away, with the great Poussin, in the dining-room, of ancient Tiber tilting his urn among the nymphs of the glade; from there to Escrick or Skipwith near Selby, then Pixton, St. Fagan's, Bowood, Breccles, or to the home of Lady Wemyss at Stanway with its gateway by Inigo Jones, the long refectory table beneath the oriel window, the eighteenth-century obelisk on its hillock beyond the stables, and the display of parlour accomplishments after dinner. It would generally be a three-week tour meticulously worked out by letter beforehand, every stage of the itinerary timed to a nicety, and the car was always standing at the wayside station. His cumbersome bag, well packed and strapped by Mrs. Elgy (the evening shoes and somebody's galley proofs—the inevitable holiday task—arranged at the bottom among the latest publications), would be lugged from pillar to post, and up and down back stairs by the manservant who loosened the straps and laid out the evening clothes in readiness. The footman would be taking for granted the green prospect from the window, never pausing to look out and muse 'Girtin would have sketched those trees' as did Mr. Marsh, putting down his watch and a fistful of small change on the dressing-table. 'I wonder who's here *this* time,' he would ponder, glancing round to see if there was a pen and ink on the writing-table, and a quotation would come into his head. '*Diffugere nives, redeunt jam gramina campis Arboribusque comae . . .*', he might start, and continue aloud, very loud, declaiming as he undressed for a leisurely bath before dinner.

Early in March he addressed a long letter to the editor of the *London Mercury* on the subject of the corrupt text of Proust. He appealed to the editors of the *Nouvelle Revue Française* 'to take a nail out of the coffin of the Entente by presenting English readers (if they will not do it for their own countrymen) with a tolerable text of the masterpieces which the death of this enchanting writer has left to their mercies'. He gave a list of maimed or distorted words, and drew attention to the special importance of punctuation.

The fascinating Saint-Simonian syntax of Proust's more elaborate passages makes the same kind of demand on an English reader's attention as that of the speeches in Thucydides or the later autobiographical writings of Henry James; and the strain is wantonly increased when the comma, which can be such a useful little creature under control, is allowed to gambol among the long paragraphs like an *ignis fatuus.*

He then showed how the compositors had printed sentences and even whole paragraphs the wrong way round, or had given in sequence what was both the original and the revised draft of the same passage. 'Upon my word, we ought to be thankful that the actual titles of the books have been kept from coalescing, and that there is no volume labelled *A la Recherche des Jeunes Filles Perdues.*'

Within a few days he heard from Charles Scott-Moncrieff, whose translation of *Swann's Way* had come out in the previous September. The translator welcomed the exposure of these errors in the original. 'You are the only person I have yet come across who is enough interested in the text of Proust to have noticed them.' His second letter was unduly modest. 'My trouble is that I know comparatively few French words and no grammar—so when I come to the most frightful howler, like the German musician on whose score a fly alighted, I "play him".' By the first week of August he had discovered three alternative positions for an interpolated passage. 'I have done one-third of Guermantes,' he wrote. 'I am brought up by a crux which you must solve at once.' By then Scott-Moncrieff had met his fellow enthusiast. On April 7 he dined at Gray's Inn and stayed until 2 A.M. discussing the problems of the Proustian text, and a correspondence followed in which Marsh was able to be of considerable help in the enormous work of translation which Scott-Moncrieff had so well begun. A few days after his entry into the sphere of Proustian scholarship Marsh met with a new experience while a guest in the country. He 'listened in' to a crystal set. 'Curious' he noted in his engagement-book, 'but very tiresome'.

Official visits to painting exhibitions on behalf of the Contemporary Art Society were enabling him to widen his acquaintance among the new artists and revive old friendships. 'I'm sorry not to come,' wrote Stanley Spencer on May 1, 'but I am trying to settle to this new picture of mine and I want a long spell of silent contemplation. I have been on too much of a buzz of recent years and it has got into my works.' Three days later he wrote from Poole, Dorset.

I do badly want some subject that I can build my Resurrection idea on to in the same way that Giotto based his ideas on Dante or Protovangelium or New Testament. This idea is like a creeping plant that has no wall to creep on. I am thinking I would like to write the whole 'vision' myself: it might be rather inferior, but then Giotto often used to do marvellous pictures from 'inferior writings'. . . .

There is nothing I more enjoy than a prolonged stay in one place (provided there are present with me ivy-covered walls, dust-bins, clothes-lines, etc.; even when I was in Salonica I used to find myself gravitating towards incinerators: out there they used to remind me of sacrificial altars). Last summer when I was in Jugoslavia the places were so different one from another that I used to shut myself in my hotel bedroom and every wardrobe was the same, it didn't matter where you were, so I felt at home.

At the end of May he wrote again.

My present ambition as far as pictures are concerned is to do a picture of the Resurrection. Already several incidents have occurred but the fault is they are only incidents, and there is such a pack of them and they are proving to be rather a Cup Final crowd and are getting crushed and muddled. Already I have had to split the picture up into 4 pictures and hardly anything is on paper. What I really want is a central idea. So far the time and place seem more or less settled: time 2.45 on a Tuesday afternoon in May. Place Cookham, containing view of hedges all white with may; fields, grass in the middle, nice and green skirted with cow-parsley. On the right a buttress showing, belonging to Cookham church. This will be mostly covered with ivy. Everything will be just the same as it is now only with faint differences.

By November Spencer was in lodgings near D. H. Lawrence's villa in the Vale of Health, Hampstead. 'I have got a composition that I badly want you to see, as it is going to be my next opus and somehow I feel I have made a great leap, no not forward, backward, in it. This is my final idea of the Resurrection which began in 1915.' And he was asking advice on the precise purpose to which he should put the chapel that Mr. and Mrs. Louis Behrend were erecting for him at Burghclere in Berkshire. He suggested 'a sort of Odyssey of my war experiences'. Gilbert Spencer, too, was giving news of himself. 'If you remember,' he wrote, 'you were the first person to have a picture of mine; you bought a little wash drawing called *Feeding Pigs* and you rightly reprimanded me for not mounting it properly.' Marsh had lost touch with Gertler; Paul Nash and his wife were at Dymchurch, where the dream quality—a dream of primitive existence strangely resembling the stark and spacious images conjured in the mind by the plays of his friend Gordon Bottomley—was reappearing in his work with renewed force, as in *Nostalgic Landscape*, which was painted about this time.

The latest Georgian book had reached Nichols in Japan (which he described as 'a thunderstorm which never breaks'), where he was teaching English at Tokyo University and making friends with Paul Claudel at the French Embassy. They had discussed the anthology.

> Paul Claudel said to me not long ago, 'I don't like your—how shall I put eet?—no, I cannot like your daffodeel poetry—there is too much daffodeel round your English Helicon', and he rated Wordsworth pretty roundly.... 'Daffodeels, Mr. Nichols, and what you call them, ugh! (elaborately) butt-er-cups—eet is not a pretty word—I cannot—how d'you say?—stomach them.' And I see what my adored Claudel means, so much of our pastoral poetry is namby-pamby.

Blunden's *Almswomen* was the only piece entirely exempt from his censure. Nichols maintained that the 'daffodeels' invalidated both Abercrombie and Armstrong, author of *Miss Thompson Goes Shopping*. '*Miss Thompson* is too easy—the curse of Georgian easiness. Why, damn it—I could write such in my sleep.' He earnestly wished young poets wouldn't write like 'dons, Rosicrucians, journalists at play, jazz-band performers who have got St. Vitus's dance after prolonged sexual orgy.... But it's vain to wish. D.H.L. isn't bad, but why *will* he stand with arms akimbo so ostentatiously taking his ease? ... "Lords of life" indeed.'[1]

> Reading the volume I feel once more that what Hazlitt said a hundred years ago is true today. I had meant to send you this after the last Georgian.... 'The great fault of the modern (read Georgian) school of poetry is that it is an experiment' (alas, I wish it were more experimental) 'to reduce poetry to a mere effusion of sensibility, or, what is worse, to divest it both of imaginary splendour and human

[1] A reference to the last section of *Snake*.

passion' (think how little intellectual passion there is in the Georgians —why, even sexual is lacking) 'to surround the meanest objects with the morbid feelings and devouring egotism of the writers' own minds. . . . Shakespeare and Milton owe their power over the human mind to their having had a deeper sense than others of what was grand in the objects of nature or affecting in the events of human life' (i.e. no caterpillars[1] and no interviews with snakes etc.). . . . Of course it applies with even more force to Pound, Sitwell and Co. That is why I adore Siegfried. He seems to have a great spirit. The rest don't.

On May 26 Marsh began his answer to what he called this 'magniferocious' document from Japan.

Of course I agree with a good many of your strictures on 'Georgian'. I am far from thinking every poem a masterpiece. But one of the many differences between us is that my first love has always been and always will be what you stigmatize as literature and poetizing, whereas you care first and foremost for 'idea'. You may very likely be right for here and now, because there must be times when the old kaleidoscope gets worn out, or at any rate when it has to be filled up with new bits of glass—still, in the long run I believe it is the 'literary' side which is the important one. The 'ideas' become common property, and unless they are beautifully arranged and expressed there is no reason why their first embodiment should continue to be sought after—whereas if they *are* beautifully arranged and expressed the work which contains them will keep its value long after they become not only common property but *exploded*.

You say you could have written *Miss Thompson* in your sleep, but I take leave to doubt it. The work is exquisite, and must have taken an enormous effort of thought and skill—and what you call senti-mentality I call wonderful imaginative sympathy—so there!

Also I beg you not to believe all that the adored Claudel says about *English* poetry. If you accept his *ipse dixit* that 'buttercup' is an ugly word, you are renouncing your heritage as an Englishman. A Frenchman is not to blame for not seeing that it is beautiful but you know better. I remember Prof. Tyrrell saying in print that French was a contemptible language because it calls a sword an *épée*! not seeing the flash of the word or hearing it whizz through the air.

As for flower-poetry in general, no doubt it can be abused and overdone, but we must distinguish. You and Claudel would, it seems to me, rule out Perdita's catalogue, the daffodils that come before the swallow dares and the violets dim but sweeter than the

[1] A reference to the poem *Caterpillars* by John Freeman.

lids of Juno's eyes. Is that to be condemned as botanizing and put lower than the Lesser Celandine because it contains no 'idea'? I say let us be thankful for beauty where we find it, and not put it into categories some of which are to be rejected *a priori*.

Nichols had enclosed one of his own manuscripts. A brief example of Marsh's comments is enough to reveal both his methods and the deep, quarrelsome affection in which these two held each other. He had no scruples about being outspoken 'because I always feel in my bones that you don't care a twopenny damn *what* I think'.

If only like Phocion you could have considered how you could shorten what you were about to say to the Athenians![1] Of course it is more than possible that it is simply over my head—but the impression it gives me is that in the old phrase you were intoxicated with the exuberance of your verbosity and let your pen run away with you. . . . There is only one thing about which I am certain I am right—you are a Professor and I am merely a male Governess, and I expect you will think my criticisms carping and insignificant to the last degree—but I *know* they are important and I do beg you to give them your attention before you dismiss them. What I want to bring home to you is this: when you describe, you are a master of English . . . but when you get on to your 'ideas' you treat the language *like dirt*! . . . What kind of flowers of speech are 'sepulchritude' and 'peripatatious'? And what about 'the gardenia which decorated his buttonhole with an air of satisfaction'? (I know this isn't what you mean, but it is what you *say*.) . . . I could multiply my instances but I have annoyed you enough. I know you will think it all terribly pedantic, but after all the first business of a writer is to *write*. I remember how Rupert used to go over everything, test every sentence for what could be left out and what could be put with more verve and force. . . . It is only because I am one of the most devout believers in your genius that I make these little representations about what are really such easily avoidable blemishes—so don't brush them aside.

This concern with abstract theories among certain of his youngest writers was becoming rather a trial. No sooner had he made his point with Nichols than Quennell came to the fore with Hughes in support. In no vein for further controversy Marsh

[1] This refers to an ancedote in Plutarch that Marsh often quoted for the benefit of a writer whose work was diffuse.

must have had to confess to Quennell that the long and the short
of it was he was growing 'old and fossilized'. 'Oh, but you're not,'
Quennell protested.

> You'll be a gay green brilliant young epicurean when all your poor
> old Georgian protégés have leapt under the wheels of trams or got
> married or done something else final and disastrous and dreadful.
> Dikkon [Hughes] and I will grow very old, our theories will get
> funnier and funnier, but you'll go on enjoying yourself properly till
> in about 500 years you'll go up like the Phoenix in your own glory
> and God will give you a C.B.E. and pension you off in a block of
> flats on the other side of the Elysian fields—and your bathroom
> windows will look out (not in Raymond Buildings fashion over a
> mews) but on to the myrtle grove where unhappy lovers and minor
> poets are kept—like cats in a shrubbery—Pasiphae, and Phaedra,
> and Procris, and Nichols and Graves and Dikkon and perhaps—if I
> haven't repented soon enough—me.

Conscious that the post-war generation was reaching out towards
areas of experience where he had no inclination to follow, but
anxious not to discourage their philosophical explorations, Marsh
gave a dinner at Gray's Inn so that he could listen to some of his
own contemporaries discussing this very theme—the guidance in
aesthetics and ethics of this newly arrived generation which was
so eager for enlightenment. Mrs. Elgy devised a special con-
coction and brought out the best silver. This was always such a
pleasure to her that every so often Marsh felt it his duty to provide
an outlet for her love of Edwardian display. There were six guests
on this occasion—Roger Fry, Goldsworthy Lowes Dickinson,
Maynard Keynes, Bertrand Russell, Desmond MacCarthy, and
E. M. Forster. Russell—whose ideas, except on pacifism, were in
accord with Marsh's own—undertook to cope with the philosophical enquiries, which were apt to find Eddie Marsh rather
disinterested and at a loss. It was principally Nichols whom
he was concerned not to let down. On two occasions in the
future Marsh invoked Russell, and the statements which
resulted did much to provide Nichols and some of the other young
men with the answers they were seeking. The first of these letters
to Nichols, dated June 17, was written in response to a request
for a survey of philosophy in English. Erdmann's *History*, translated by Bosanquet, and Alexander's *Space, Time, and Deity* were
recommended. Russell went on:

Yes, I regard metaphysics as dead. It is true that without meta-physics there can be no certainty; but as there is no certain metaphysics, that doesn't help much. As to whether we 'know' any-thing, it is necessary to define 'knowing', which is a difficult matter (see my *Analysis of Mind*, Chap. XIII). Our knowledge is all vague and approximate; the more vague, the less likely to be mistaken.

I hesitate to advise you about reading, or about the kind of abstract ideas to which, as an artist, you should give life. . . . I think Man, in our day, is too proud, but men (in relation to the mass of other men) are too humble. Both effects come from science via industrialism. Blake says 'humble to God, haughty to Man', but nowadays we are the other way round.

As to the functions of the artist and the scientist: the scientist is concerned only with knowledge, which is valuable chiefly as a means. As an end, it has some value, but only as one among ends. As ends, the artist's ends seem to me better. Blake, of course, is a moralist as well as an artist, which complicates matters. It is clear that to commend an ethic successfully, artistic gifts are required; but that is outside the value of art as such. In literature, Shakespeare is almost the best instance. Why was it worth while to write 'Come unto these yellow sands' or 'A great while ago the world begun with heigh-ho the wind and the rain' or 'Still through the hawthorn blows the cold wind'? I don't know; but I find a quality of magic or enchantment which seems to flood the world with golden sunlight, and 'gild pale streams with heavenly alchemy'. I think delight in life and the world is the ultimate good for man, or at least part of it, but that as our mental powers develop delight has to have more and more mental content if it is to be satisfying and not very evanescent. It seems to me that the artist supplies the means of continuing to feel delight in spite of expanding mental power. Mental power seems also good in itself, and is the business of the scientist. The moralist has a different function, dependent upon the existence of evil, and there-fore not concerned directly with ends, but with means. I doubt whether the moralist ever does good unless he quickens people's sense of the value of ends; but to do this a man must be an artist.

Russell's second letter to Nichols (November 5, 1925) concluded with a paragraph which should be quoted here not only for its own sake but as a view of man's place in the universe to which Marsh himself subscribed.

I do not believe there is any 'why', or that the world 'means' any-thing at all. I agree with Satan in the Tentation de Saint Antoine. But I do not find that I lose capacity for happiness or for feeling life worth while. The point is this: Human life may have significance, through human desires, though Nature at large has none. When you suggest that the artist creates significance, I agree: he creates human significance, even when he thinks he discovers cosmic significance. I want man to be more lordly, and less afraid of asserting himself against an indifferent universe. I think all values are human, but none the less important on that account. Your letter deserves a longer answer.

Certain strands of Marsh's life were apt to recur like the threads of a carpet. During these months Basil Dean had again been striving for a chance to present *Hassan* on the stage. Mrs. Flecker reported a conversation with Dean in Paris, saying that she had asked for 'stylized scenery in the Persian miniature style', giving news that Frank (as she called him) Delius was at work on the score, and asking Marsh if he would get Dean's permission to keep an eye on the rehearsals. The first performance was given on September 20, 1923, at His Majesty's, with Henry Ainley in the title role and Cathleen Nesbitt as Yasmin. Marsh's companion was his old friend Gerald Wellesley (later Duke of Wellington) and he gave a supper afterwards at the Carlton where the guests were Maurice Baring, Sargent, Somerset Maugham, J. C. Squire, Wellesley, Mrs. Flecker, Edward Shanks, Fokine, Harold Nicolson, and Vita Sackville-West. *Hassan* was at last public property and a success ten years after its composition.

Another letter to the *London Mercury*, this time on emendations in Spenser's *Prothalamion*, private correspondence with Roger Ingpen on the corrupt texts of Shelley's letters, and with Olwen Campbell on Shelley's relations with Mary Godwin, kept him occupied throughout his autumn holiday.[1] His studies in Shelley were now of use to Blunden, who had begun writing his book on Leigh Hunt, and he arranged a meeting for Blunden with Harold Nicolson, who was then going through the Murray papers. Having failed to convince Blunden that Leigh Hunt hardly warranted his critical attention, Marsh devoted almost all his leisure to re-reading Hunt's works and sending his comments. He admired an observation on Coleridge which seemed to have 'a curiously modern

---

[1] Among his other emendations perhaps the most ingenious concerned a passage in Trollope's *Dr. Thorne* where he was able to prove that the first two words in the phrase 'lacking more sympathy' were a misreading of the single word 'lachrymose', and that the printer had added a comma beforehand so as to give the sentence a 'phantom of meaning and grammar'.

ring'—'It is a mighty intellect put upon a sensual body, and the reason why he does little more with it than talk and dream is that it is *agreeable to such a body* to do little else.' But in the main he was unimpressed. 'There are one or two pages which are "written", but most of it is so loose and vague that one can hardly tell what he means, and *how* vulgar it is when one can!' Blunden was undeterred. 'Hunt's vulgarity seems to me by no means a besetting sin. Lamb could not have remained his friend, nor Shelley, had it been so. Here I am preaching already, putting you off my book.' It was Marsh who preached instead, and despatched a pile of notes on the first batch of manuscript, ending with a postscript:

> And dear Edmund, do let me try to undermine in your affections the insidious locution 'in the case of'. My attention was first awoken to its dangers in early days at Cambridge when I read a telegram at the Union about a shipwreck in which the crew had been washed overboard 'and drowned in two cases' which sounded so uncomfortable.

H. G. Wells had recently brought out a satirical work entitled *Men Like Gods* in which both Mr. Churchill and his Private Secretary were caricatured under transparent disguises. Marsh featured as Mr. Freddie Mush whose chief characteristics were 'Taste, Good Taste. . . . He's dreadfully critical and sarcastic. . . . Mr. Mush with his preposterous eyeglass and love of good food . . . spoke in a kind of impotent falsetto.' With these crude observations in mind, and others, less warranted, directed against himself, Mr. Churchill wrote from Sussex Square on September 27.

> You are always so kind in looking over my stuff and I have such confidence in your English and punctuation, that I should be very grateful to you if you would look through the proofs of one or two articles I have written lately. The first is about my escape from the Boers which I have written for the *Strand Magazine*. I will send the second portion of it in a few days, if you will let me. I have also written an article answering Wells and giving him one or two wipes in the eye. I particularly want you to look through this for me, and I think you will like it in view of the impudent references to you in his book.

That he was capable of giving the superficial impression described by Wells was no new discovery for Marsh. He was only sorry that so distinguished a writer as Wells should have shown himself in the light of so superficial an observer. For the next twelve years the caricaturist and his subject forwent the pleasure of being on speaking terms, which was hard on so sociable a being as 'Mr. Mush' who would always much rather say something than nothing, but he had neither experience nor skill in the art of conducting a quarrel.

His new poet this autumn was Vita Sackville-West, who had shown him her poem *The Beemaster*.

My dear Vita, I woke up at 5 o'clock this morning and read *The Beemaster*. I now know about ½ of it by heart, and I can't let the *undern* pass without telling you that I think you've really done it this time! You know I've admired a great deal of your poetry, but this is in a different class from anything before; you've attained the great manner of English poetry and produce the sort of lines that make one think they have long been buried in the recesses of the language, like statues in a mountain of marble, and have at last been set free in all their clear and polished beauty by the blessed skill of the artist. The lovely passage about Syrian Queens—and

—hear the bee about his amorous trade
Brown in the gypsy crimson of the rose

and the frilled spires of cottage hollyhocks which Matthew Arnold strangely overlooked when he was digging for the stanza about the high midsummer pomps of *Thyrsis*.

Her reply outlined her scheme for 'a more or less consecutive poem about country subjects—a sort of English *Georgics* is the only way I can describe it, while fully realizing the pretentiousness of such a description'. Meanwhile Marsh was writing again, enclosing the usual bundle of notes. He gave his principles on the use of the 'short line' as in *Lycidas*, the use and nature of the alexandrine, punctuation in verse, and he picked on phrases here and there.

I'm not very fond of 'Having regard to bushes all ablaze'—it takes a moment to see that what you mean is 'having an eye to', and I'm not sure that the phrases are synonymous. 'Having regard to' has a slightly official ring, it's the sort of thing you say in a letter to the Treasury.

He wished a line cut, finding himself instinctively leaving it out when he spoke the passage from memory and 'in my pardonable vanity about my subliminal self' he felt this was a sure indication that it could be spared. 'I'm extremely glad to hear of your Georgic plan, Georgian Georgics the book will be! It's just what is wanted nowadays—some real enterprise of pith and moment instead of this succession of short detached lyric cries which are all that most people can manage.' The author was heartened.

> Above all I liked your phrase about the 'short lyric cries' of modern poets, which exactly expresses the irritation that is driving me into trying the experiment of a volume of *connected* verse. . . . I'm glad you think the idea a good one, and I'm simply mad with energy to carry it out.

Just when traditional verse was in act of yielding its central place to a new orthodoxy it was to produce a major work —*The Land*.

Novello, meanwhile, had been making his mark as a film actor in America. In August he had come back to England and fared less successfully in a stage play, which put into his head the idea of writing his own scripts in future and running his own management. In collaboration with Constance Collier he adapted a film scenario of his own and on November 1 he read aloud the stage version to Marsh. In case it should fail Marsh undertook to make a translation of Bernstein's play *Israel* as something to fall back on if need be, for although Novello had made money, he had also spent it. A loan of 'murder money' went towards the small cost of production, to which Novello added what little resources he still had. So while Novello worked on *The Rat* Marsh spent his late nights translating Bernstein's play from the French and found no time for correspondence until a 'diatribe against Swinburne' from Nichols in Japan recalled him to poetical affairs. He replied:

> I think there's an enormous amount of truth in what you say, except about his 'horrible and barbarous rhythms' which I don't understand at all—and he's at the opposite pole to you in everything, you couldn't like him if we both tried till we were blue in the face. I don't think I should ever read him 'for the sense' except in a few pieces most of which you name (and I would add the prologue to the *Songs before Sunrise*) and enormous tracts of him are as you say ground out, maddeningly or superficially mechanical, a bloody flux of words. But my inclination always is to think that a poet is no weaker than his strongest link—and surely he has written a lot of things that are absolutely marvellous and exquisite in music and diction? The first I ever read was *The Triumph of Time*, when I was about 15, and perhaps it's a rum compliment but I was so intoxicated with its

beauty that I read it three times without having the vaguest idea
what it was about. . . . I'm glad you have a good word to say for
Baudelaire.[1] Only the other day I learnt it by heart again (having
rather forgotten it) and I was rather disappointed, as a good deal
of it seemed to me terribly over-elaborated, but I still think parts of
it are supreme. . . . But you don't like 'jewelled' poetry and I do.
It takes all sorts to make a world.

Summing up his views on Nichols' last manuscript he remarked
with severity, 'The Thinker and the Artist in you had simply not
fused, and the result was an abortion'; moreover Nichols had been
unjust, he thought, to a new novel which everyone was discussing.
Marsh could not let it pass.

Lady into Fox [by David Garnett] is a thing which exists and which I
can't imagine not continuing to exist, it's a most original conception
worked out to a nicety and written to perfection. I think one is
bound to consider *how* a thing is done as well as what it *is* or rather
might have been. I feel perfectly certain that Posterity will read
L. into F. Now I've given you as good as you gave, or better. I won't
apologize or pretend to think you'll be hurt, as I know that in your
heart of hearts you quite rightly give only a few damns for my
opinion.

Nichols had announced his plan to leave Tokyo and accept
an invitation to visit Hollywood as a script-writer. Marsh was not
sure it was a good idea.

I *cannot* make out what to think of America. From such a book as
Babbitt you would gather that practically the whole country was
given up to the most petty and paltry form of materialism. From
other sources one gets a picture of soppy, silly, or superstitious
idealism founded on a wholly derivative and half-understood culture
—and now you make out that it's the only hope of the world. I hope
you are right.

The books have been terrible. Arnold Bennett's *Riceyman Steps*
is very much admired by good judges but I'm afraid I rather failed
to rise to it—I can see that it's good work, but I couldn't work up
enough interest in whether the servant lit the gas ring too often or
stole cheese out of the cage. Aldous Huxley's *Antic Hay* is having a
bad press. I must say the first six chapters or so amused me quite
enormously, but it tails off into a rather nauseating caricature of X
and her surroundings which I think he might have left to Michael

[1] Swinburne's *Ave atque Vale*.

Arlen. . . . I've read very few books as I had a great fit of reading about Shelley which lasted two or three months and now I think I'm going to embark on Wordsworth.

I've also had a return of the lust for pictures. . . . There's a superb show of van Gogh just begun at the Leicester Galleries, he really was a swell! There's a picture of a little brooding sturdy squat wooden kitchen chair with a straw seat which has more character and soul than most human beings.

It was finally arranged that Blunden should take Nichols's place in Tokyo. Marsh was not at all sure this was the best thing for Blunden: 'My feelings are mixed, so please sort them out and take whichever you please'; but when in February (1924) the decision was made he helped with the passport and visa, and arranged for him to be supplied regularly with literary magazines. The passport arrived with a note.

When you are away remember I am a real true friend. I find you are one of the people who inspire a steadily growing affection, and I hope you like me pretty well, so if ever you want anything done on this side please realize I would always love to take any amount of trouble for you. I really mean this—and it may be nice to think you have someone here steady and willing.

Blunden wrote from the ship:

Your telegram did much to cheer me, though in the words of Samuel Rogers—

> The sailor sighs as sinks his native land
> And all its lessening turrets bluely fade.

Isn't it curious, what poetry one chances to remember?

By now Novello's play, on which he had staked his all, had provided Marsh on January 14 at Brighton with one of the most anxious nights of his life, but all went well. So great was the success that his translation of *Israel* was forgotten and subsequently lost.

The year ended with a domestic revelation recorded in the engagement book. 'Spent the whole day without seeing a soul except Mrs. Elgy, who recited a long religious poem which she had learnt as a girl (about 200 lines!).' In national affairs those last weeks saw the fall of Stanley Baldwin (who had taken over from Bonar Law in May) and the emergence of the first Labour Government. At the end of January 1924 J. H. Thomas was appointed Colonial Secretary. Eddie Marsh's new Chief, to whom he soon became warmly attached, was the son of an engine-driver. An evening newspaper published a cartoon in which the new Minister was shown in immaculate evening clothes while his Private Secretary stood by in corduroy trousers tied under the knee with string.

vi

Marsh's one misgiving, that his new Chief might harbour class-feeling, was quickly dispelled, and before long he was happy to be welcomed by Mrs. Thomas as an addition to her family circle. 'Human,' wrote Marsh in his Memoir, 'is an unscientific term of praise, for we are all human; but everybody knows what it means, and it hits off J.H. to perfection.' Marsh was never quite sure how to pick his way between the deliberate and the unconsciously humorous traits in Mr. Thomas's nature. Of the erratic *h*'s he came round to the belief that they were misplaced with conscious art. The mixed household phrases, however, were certainly accidental. '*He* doesn't carry much ice,' said Mr. Thomas of a member who had criticized him in the House. 'No,' said Marsh, 'and he doesn't cut many guns either.'

Mr. Thomas's exertions to fire his secretary with an enthusiasm for horse-racing met with only partial success. Indeed one afternoon they sustained a definite setback. Marsh had just returned to the office after luncheon when he overheard his Chief on the telephone in the next room, putting money on a horse. The sum was of disquieting magnitude, but that was nothing. Enunciating with unwonted clarity, the backer gave his name as 'Heddie Marsh'.

While growing accustomed to these altered circumstances he sent an article to the *London Mercury* entitled 'Notes on the Text of Miss Austen's Novels'. These were occasioned by R. W. Chapman's new edition, and they resulted in Chapman inviting Marsh to bring his critical acumen to bear on the text of the Letters, which he was then about to edit. 'A little on the Verrall-ish side', remarked A. B. Walkley after studying the new emendations, 'in assuming in J.A. a subtlety and ingenuity where perhaps she was only slack.' The reference to Verrall was shrewd. On March 3 Logan Pearsall Smith told Marsh that he would 'go down to posterity with Bentley and Theobald and the other great emendators. . . . I was inordinately solaced to find that you had detected a misprint of Chapman's own. We are all human, and those of us whose pasts are spotted and pimpled with misprints delight in derelictions of this kind in the supposedly impeccable. But you point out his slip with great kindness and I do not think that it is on this account that he has taken to his bed.'

At the same time Marsh was trying not to quarrel with Gordon Bottomley over Abercrombie's verse drama *Phoenix*, which had just been presented in London. The previous autumn he had refused to include in the anthology Abercrombie's *Witchcraft, Old Style*, which Bottomley had strongly pressed upon him, and now, in flat contradiction of Bottomley, he was saying of the new play that he 'couldn't see that it had any artistic merits sufficient to counterbalance the disgusting squalor of the situations'. His disappointment in Abercrombie's later work, combined with its championship by Bottomley, only created another weak spot in the Georgian circle which was already rifted elsewhere. And then there landed on his breakfast-table what had the effect of a great bombshell from Hollywood. Nichols stated in his usual forthright way that the works of Fanny Burney were preferable to those of Jane Austen. What Nichols may have intended was no more than a mildly provocative contribution to friendly controversy, but it succeeded in making Eddie Marsh for once extremely angry.

I got this morning your perfectly outrageous letter about Miss Austen. I'm sure I've often told you she's my 'favourite author', so I suppose that from some obscure reason you are trying to bait me or pull my leg (you always seem to look upon me as a bourgeois to be *épaté* as often as possible). If so you have certainly succeeded— but at what a cost to your own figure!

Miss Austen is one of the small number of writers (such as Sophocles, Plato, Horace, Catullus, Racine, La Fontaine, Milton, and Lewis Carroll) whom I not only believe but *know* to be first-rate. It is conceivable, though it is certainly rare, that a competent critic should not like or enjoy her novels; and it is of course common to prefer other kinds—Middleton Murry for instance would not name her on the same day with Emily Brontë or Dostoieffsky. But to deny her merit is to be oblivious of all that constitutes literary or artistic merit. A cheese-fancier may like Stilton less than Gruyère or even

Petit Suisse, but he would recognize that it was cheese and not chalk.

I should be the last person to wish to discourage a liking for the naive and charming amateur novelist Miss Burney. *Cecilia* I doubt if I shall read again, but *Evelina* I re-read two years ago with much pleasure and amusement, tho' without any great degree of admiration; and the Journal has been my delight, and I hope will be again. But to put her above Miss Austen is like putting Heywood or Dekker above Shakespeare—it puts you out of court! Hitherto when we have disagreed about books I have always been willing to believe that you had perceptions which were denied to me (for instance, the other day about Swinburne) but never again! What a good thing for everyone concerned that you have ceased to be a Professor of Literature!

There, that is my Philippic—and I hope I've pulled *your* leg for once. An elegant couplet came into my head the other day while shaving.

> If second thoughts are good, third thoughts are better.
> Post not until next day your angry letter.

I shall now act on this maxim, but not because I have any idea of not posting my letter, but because it is midnight.

I shall now devote a day or two to meditation on your many fine qualities, hoping afterwards to continue in a better temper. Goodnight. [No signature.]

He had barely recovered from this emotion when he read a book which convinced him, at least for the time being, that Branwell Brontë was the author of *Wuthering Heights*. 'What a περιπέτεια if that poor despised wastrel is recognized to have written one of the great books in the language,' he wrote to Blunden, who was now settled in Tokyo.

Miss Low's only weak argument is from the use of the delightful word 'penetralium' to describe the innermost house in the first chapter. Such learning, she thinks, was entirely beyond Emily's range, whereas it was only to be expected in a classic scholar of Branwell's attainments! Of course 'penetralium' is *typical* Woman's Latin.

After confessing to Blunden that he had just been impelled to write a 'stinker' to Nichols he broached another topic—*Measure for Measure*.

I've been having rather bad luck with Shakespeare lately. For the first third of the play I was thrilled. I thought to myself here is the S. one is told about, what a dramatist, what a humourist! Then it all goes to pieces; the end seemed simply lamentable. Why, oh why didn't S. have an artistic conscience? He is ready at any moment to sacrifice character and probability to some cheap dramatic effect which in the end doesn't come off. Two instances to show the sort of thing I mean: When Edgar finds Gloucester with his eyes out, and hears him saying the one thing that could comfort him would be to see his misjudged son again and make it up to him, there can't be a sympathetic soul in the audience that doesn't cry out to see Edgar throw himself into Gloucester's arms and reveal himself—but does he? No, he pulls himself together with an effort and begins his tiresome 'poor Tom's a-cold' again—Why? for no reason that I can see except to save up an anagnorisis for the end of the play, when it makes no effect at all. And again, in *Measure for Measure*, is it possible to forgive the Duke for not telling Isabella that Claudio has *not* been executed, when he sees her writhing on the ground in grief for him? The Duke *says* it's for the sake of giving her a still greater joy later on—but really, again, it's because S. won't let the pot boil over till the last scene, when nobody cares whether it does nor not. . . . Last night I came round to the Shakespearean clown—isn't Pompey about the best of them? the scene between him and the constable Elbow when they are brought up for trial before Escalus was quite new to me, and made me laugh till I was sick—it's so extraordinarily modern and George Graves-like.

The counterblast to Nichols had now been lying on his table for nineteen days. It was time to send it off with an added page by way of antidote.

Your letter about Miss Austen got my goat more than anything for years, and I wrote you a perfect stinker—which I now enclose because you deserved it, but I thought I'd wait till I recovered my temper and could accompany it with something in a more honeyed strain to show there was no ill-feeling.

To oblige both Nichols and Novello he had been trying to make up his mind about the art of the film.

Sometimes they are wonderfully interesting in a sort of historical way, for instance the trek to the West in *The Covered Wagon*—and there is really beautiful acting, for instance Lillian Gish in *The White Sister*—but there is always a dose of sensationalism or sentimentality that spoils them from a rational point of view. In *The Ten Commandments* the history of the Children of Israel in Egypt and the Wilderness is colossal and overwhelming—tho' even that is spoilt by the Personal Appearance of the Ten Commandments which bolt at one out of the blue, one after another, and then stand twinkling foolishly, like Many Happy Returns of the Day in frosted sugar on a birthday cake. And the modern part of the story which follows to show what happens in the 20th century when people don't keep the 10 commandments was too puerile. . . . Charlie Chaplin is the best producer, in *A Woman of Paris* he has discovered a substantive and consistent film technique and the comedy is first-rate. I've also seen one or two German and Austrian films, such as the celebrated *Dr. Caligari* with its Cabinet setting—but they seem to me too childishly stuntish and quite dull. Do tell me something about your ideas. I'm sure there are marvels in store. The film is a prodigious medium, but there are only hints so far of what it will become.

He went on to say he had resisted the temptation to take an extra holiday. 'I flatter myself I'm indispensible to the Labour Government—which isn't a position I had ever mapped out for myself in my speculations about my future! . . . Now you can read my Philippic. Remember Stevenson's dialogue illustrating the difficulty of answering questions—"Is it still the same between us?" "Why, how can it be? It is eternally different—and you are still the friend of my heart."'

Correspondence with Blunden was less prone to sudden and disquieting changes of temperature. 'I'm having a solitary Sunday morning,' Marsh wrote on May 6, 'which is a time I generally use to do odd jobs about my mind, such as looking up quotations that have tantalized me during the week.' By now he was suitably ashamed of having attached any significance to the Brontë heresy, and his present reading was so unsatisfactory it had made him a little light in the head.

As a specimen of the writing: I was reading with a quarter of my attention as one does when one has taken a dislike to a book but thinks that having got so far one may as well finish it—when my mind was suddenly arrested by the following sentence—'Her eyes were riveted on his; and he realized that unless he desisted they would fall out.' The lovers were in a tree-top cabin.

When I said I had no odd jobs to do this morning it wasn't quite true. I ought to be reading a new book of poems by Alfred Noyes which he has just sent me as a present, called *The Songs of Shadow-of-a-Leaf*, a pretty title, but it is difficult to think of him as the Shadow of a Leaf, as he is so corporeal, don't you think? . . . I am not one of those who ask themselves 'What noise annoys an oyster?' and reply 'An Alfred Noyes annoys him.' I prefer to think of him as the

Noyes of a hidden brook in the leafy month of June, and I go further, I am pleased to know that whereas in the Ancient Mariner 'still the sails made on their pleasant noise till noon' it is now Noyes who still makes on his pleasant sales till closing time. If you are inclined to resent my puns and to think them unworthy of us both, pray remember that Charles Lamb's letters to Manning contained several. . . . Jack Squire has agreed to stand for Parlt as a Liberal candidate for whichever division of London Chiswick is in! He stood at Cambridge for Labour, and why become a Liberal *now*, when the party is in a hopeless position and Labour is booming? It comes of not being able to say NO. . . . Well, this is a very silly letter to send so far. I hope my next will be more cosmic.

It was some while since he had allowed himself to be *quite* so silly. It was a cheerful sign. Recovery from the disasters of 1915 was now almost complete. Within two months he was to come upon the means of overcoming the last vestige of bitterness. A new interest was to be the decisive factor in the Georgian decline so far as he was concerned. On June 29 he asked Blunden for more personal news. 'All that Robert ever told me about the University was the depressing effect of lecturing for a whole morning on half a page of *John Halifax, Gentleman*—so please don't keep back your impressions under the idea of having been forestalled.' Quennell had shown him a new poem called *Leviathan*. 'Has not this boy of 19 washed his loosened hair in the pure dew of Castalia?' He had been reading Baring's new novel *C*, and Forster's *Passage to India*, 'which is certainly a masterpiece, tho' rather spoilt for me by my being completely mystified about the main incident in the story, and there has been a strain of occultism in his books which has baffled me—but he's a great and charming artist . . . but everything else that I have read has seemed to me tosh.'

> There's a movement to make out that Powys who wrote *The Left Leg* is a good writer, but I've never been able to see it, and I threw his new book away when I read on p. 75 that the hero had never learnt to read and p. 85 that he had found out something important by reading a scrap of newspaper that he picked up in the street. I do think an author ought to remember as much about his characters as his readers do!

A new interpretation of Horace had beguiled a few leisure hours, which prompted him to report on a lecture by Mr. Churchill.

I come now (Edmund, have you ever in your life got a letter in which the transitions were so carefully managed as this one?) to a lecture on classical education which Winston gave last week at the School of Economics—he complained of the confusing new pronunciation forced on learners by pedantic dons since his time—according to which we are obliged to pronounce our old friend the well-known verb *audire* as 'ow-dearie'!

I will now throw my transitions to the winds, as I want to apologize to Shakespeare for what I said about him in my last letter, which is a complete jump from my Latin topics. I went to see *Romeo and Juliet* at the Regent, and I've *never* had a more rapturous evening. When one gets a performance like this all doubts of Shakespeare's supremacy vanish away.

Through J. H. Thomas he had been widening his scope by going to race-meetings, 'where we are now known as Our Betters. . . . I spend all my evenings just now going to balls, dinners, and plays—and it's just as well that I have a distinguished literary correspondent in Japan to recall me from time to time to higher things.'

Then on the night of August 1 he was lying in bed, saying over to himself one of La Fontaine's Fables, *Les Obsèques de la Lionne*. The first to bear witness to his extraordinarily retentive memory was J. S. Barnes in his account of the pre-war walking-tours in Spain and Italy. 'Books were superfluous. I had only to ask for a recital and I got it free, anything I wanted. Milton's *Ode on the Nativity*, Dryden's *Ode to St. Cecilia*, Keats's *Ode to a Grecian Urn*, or Victor Hugo, Verlaine, La Fontaine, or Musset.'[1] On this August night Eddie Marsh found himself automatically transposing the Fable into English verse. He had translated and committed to memory twelve lines before turning over to sleep. In a week's time he was due to leave with the Colonial Secretary on an official visit to South Africa. He had completed three Fables in English and sent them off to J. C. Squire for the *London Mercury* by the time the ship sailed on the 8th. 'I'm not lost,' he wrote to Blunden from on board, 'but gone before, or behind, or beyond (it depends on how you visualize the Equator).' He did not realize that he had embarked on the biggest literary operation of his life.

[1] *Half a Life*, by James Strachey Barnes (Eyre & Spottiswoode, 1933).

Chapter Seventeen

LA FONTAINE
(September 1924–November 1933)

WITHIN thirteen days the South African visitors had called at Cape Town, Durban, and Bloemfontein, and they had entered Zululand when J. H. Thomas received a message to return at once for a special session of Parliament on the question of the Irish Boundary. So the rest of the party went on with the itinerary while the Colonial Secretary, Sir Douglas Hogg (Lord Hailsham), and Eddie Marsh took the boat home and arrived back on September 29. He now had forty-two translations in his bag. By October 12 he was at Rushbrooke Hall, Suffolk, where he wrote to Blunden. His translations had become his chief recreation 'for the moment in bed when after dismissing the events of the day one sets one's face towards sleep'. His tone to de la Mare was almost apologetic. 'Prepare yourself for a shock,' he began, and broke the news of his translations 'into English (verse if you please). I never expected to blossom out as a Poet.' To Nichols he was more casual in his confession of authorship.

> I've often had to complain of the inhuman character of your correspondence which consists entirely of panegyrics or diatribes on third persons—and makes me feel immodest and irrelevant if I tell you my own news in my replies. . . . The terrible thing is that I contracted deplorable habits of drinking cocktails at all hours and smoking incessantly, and throve on them so conspicuously that everyone who has seen me since my return has been almost uncivilly emphatic about the improvement which has been effected in my personality—and this has shaken my fundamentally Puritanical nature to its foundations, stultifying as it does the resolution which I had formed on board to return to my former correctitude. Another unexpected consequence of my journey was that I became an author!

Marie Belloc Lowndes had already taken a sheaf of his translations to the office of Messrs. Heinemann. They were accepted at once and two editions were planned for November, one limited, the other 'I hope unlimited', he remarked to Nichols, 'except by the number of those who will be curious to see what sort of a donkey the Editor of *Georgian Poetry* makes of himself when he enters the field of composition in person. . . . But I have a sort of idea you probably class La Fontaine with Miss Austen as a more or less elegant but entirely insignificant trifler.'

The panegyric from Nichols this time was on Leopardi and for his diatribe he chose the unexpected target of the Dean of Westminster, who had declined to erect a monument to Byron in Poets' Corner. Marsh could not find it in himself to take a very grave view of this issue.

> I must admit, tho' it will damn me deeper than ever in your eyes, that if I were a Christian I'm not sure I shouldn't boggle at putting up a monument in a Christian church to a man who lay with his sister. Did I ever tell you the story of Alfred Douglas in Italy when the conversation turned on Incest, and when it came to his turn to *placer son mot* he said, 'I'm afraid I can't speak of incest from personal experience. My sisters are protected by their sex and my brothers by their looks.'

He was correcting the proofs of his Fables when a legal action brought by the Attorney-General against the editor of a Communist newspaper occasioned a vote of censure in the House which led to a General Election and the establishment on November 7 of Mr. Baldwin's second Government. Winston Churchill returned to office as Chancellor of the Exchequer, and Marsh was once more recalled to his right hand, where he remained, well content but conscious of his shortcomings as an economist, for nearly five years.

The Chancellor's first undertaking, his measures to restore the value of the £, which had dropped 2s. in the course of the war, the embarrassing consequences to the coal-exporters, the industrial upheavals which followed, and the five Budgets presented over the period April 1925-29, did not touch Marsh as closely as the previous events which he had shared in Mr. Churchill's service. There was a financial secretary and staff (whose presence and efficiency he never ceased to be thankful for) who could assist their Chief in the sphere where Eddie Marsh was frankly out of his depth, leaving their senior colleague free to supervise the personal and literary affairs with which he was more at home.

He had been parted from J. H. Thomas for about a week when

Forty-two Fables of La Fontaine appeared on the market. Following the precedent of John Gay each poem was dedicated to one of the author's friends, and for a time there was some speculation as to why Mrs. Patrick Campbell should grace a poem about a monkey, or Viola Tree another concerning a 'large elephant', or the Duke of Devonshire be awarded a rhyme about a singing cobbler. The search for clues of subtly malicious innuendo led to slight awkwardness in one or two instances, although Eddie Marsh, missing or perhaps ignoring the opportunity, had innocently intended nothing but compliment. The graceful artifice of La Fontaine, his wit, humour, and worldly wisdom, put into the mouths of lowly beasts of the field and the beaks of birds, was well suited to Marsh's temperament and love of anecdote. Within the next ten years the book was almost entirely rewritten. Some of the modern allusions were retained, but the rendering of '*Je suis Gros-Jean comme devant*', for example, translated at first by way of a reference to *The Diary of a Nobody* as 'I'm still plain Mr. Pooter, as before!' became in the last edition 'I'm still the same old Gaffer John'. Also the liberties forced upon him by the necessities of rhyme were all ironed out in the second attempt. In 1924 'The Dairymaid and the Jar of Milk' contained a couplet whose second line was an interpolation.

> *I shout defiance to the Sophy*
> *And bring his head home as a trophy.*

Ten years later this became:

> *When I'm alone, I brave the least afeared,*
> *I stride and strut, I pull the Sophy's beard.*

He was equally painstaking in his efforts to reproduce his author's Arcadian grace without losing the economy and precision of the original. In 1924 Thyrsis addressed 'the little fishes':

> '*O citizens of this pure wave,*' sang he,
> '*Come, leave your Naiad in her watery chamber,*
> *And swimming up through green and amber*
> *Behold a goddess lovelier far than she.*
> *Fear not to enter her captivity;*
> *Towards men alone her heart is hard;*
> *You will be nourished tenderly,*
> *And not one silver scale be marred.*'

By 1933 Thyrsis, like Phocion, had considered 'how he could shorten what he was about to say to the Athenians', and the same passage became:

> *'O citizens of this pure wave,' sang he,*
> *'Come, leave your Naiad in her watery grot,*
> *And hail a goddess lovelier far than she.*
> *Fear not within her prisons to be barred,*
> *Towards men alone her heart is hard;*
> *Her gentle care shall be your lot.'*

J. C. Squire's review in the *Observer* (November 23) was responsible for encouraging Marsh to start work on a sequel. But it was Edmund Gosse, a month later, who first put before him the monumental task of a complete translation. It was certain, he wrote, that Marsh had

> at last found the secret, so long denied, of reproducing for the English reader the charm, the irony, the natural freshness of the most illusive of French authors. . . . I should like him to continue his labours, to translate all the Fables, and so to display the architecture of La Fontaine's mansion from its imperfect foundation in 1668 to its coping-stone of 1692. This would involve a strenuous effort, but the result might be a permanent addition to English literature.[1]

Moved by this encouragement, Marsh at once embarked on a new series, this time of forty-eight pieces, which were to appear under the title *More Fables of La Fontaine*. As yet he could not positively commit himself to the undertaking as it had been envisaged by Gosse in its full magnitude. Meanwhile he was drawing up a list of critical notes for Charles Whibley on his edition of the collected essays of W. P. Ker. Before Christmas he sent a progress report to Japan.

> I have neglected my correspondence shamefully, and the only thing to do is to carry this war into your camp and say that I shall be very much aggrieved if I don't get a letter from you in a day or two complaining of my silence. It's all the worse because I have at last achieved an easy way of remembering your rather baffling direction:
>
> > Blunden does his lyric tricks
> > Down at No. 26
> > Kitayamabushi-cho
> > Ushigamé, Tokyo.

[1] *Sunday Times*, December 21, 1924.

But the fact is (quite truly, in spite of the Admirable Crichton saying that statements introduced in those words are always lies) I've been extremely busy—I should like to leave it at that, but my fatal candour forces me to add 'except at my work' . . . I am as bad at arithmetic as a Higher Mathematician without his compensating insight into deeper problems. Luckily there are two trained Treasury men who do all that is necessary. . . . However, I say to myself, every man has the right to have his declining years solaced by a sinecure—but it did make me laugh when I read in one of my press-cuttings that 'Eddie is a typical Treasury Clerk'.

He confessed he was in trouble about his dedications. People were saying things like 'I wonder how X likes being called an Old Rat', and the Fables were on their way to becoming a *succès de scandale*, 'which is good for sales'. The most charming compliment so far was from Augustine Birrell, who, so Marsh had been told, picked up the book at a friend's house, read it aloud for about an hour, and put it down at last with the exclamation 'Cheeky Devil!' Drinkwater was less encouraging at first. 'I told him some weeks ago what I was doing, and he received the announcement with the sort of smirk a grown-up gives to a little boy who says, "Look at my boots, I did them up myself." . . .'

I had a Sunday at Oxford lately, and went to see Robert Graves whom I found radiantly happy at a teatable with five or six bread-and-buttery children and the village postmaster and wife. His combined jobs as Poet and maid-of-all-work suit him curiously well —and I was greatly struck with his beauty. Something has happened to his face which makes it, in spite of his crooked nose, one of the finest I've ever seen, and I transgressed the bounds of good breeding so far as to write and urge him to be either photographed or painted by his father-in-law—to which he has made no reply.

His latest enthusiasm was for an epigram by Cecil Baring on Lady Diana Manners entitled *To the Glasse of a Lady of Quality*.

> *In all the world this Glasse holds pride of place.*
> *Well for thee, Glasse, tho' frail, thou art not tender;*
> *Else how could'st thou endure Diana's face,*
> *Daily possessing, daily to surrender.*

Isn't it lucky he didn't have a paralytic stroke after writing the third line?

By now Nichols had received the gentle reproach that his letters were apt to be marred by philosophical abstractions, and he had shown some signs of reform. Marsh was not ungrateful for his concession.

> You know, Bob, I don't and can't live on your high plane, and sometimes I wonder why you ever bother your head about me at all. I expect you don't realize how much I am one of those persons 'ignorant and unworthy of life' who 'think about pleasure and happiness'. I admire you as a voice and a thinking machine, but that is not why I am fond of you, and I enjoy your writing to me about 'third parties' but a few little details like 'we live in a little bungalow and Norah does all the housework' are essential to make me feel that I am listening to the voice of a friend. Personally I don't feel that the human affections are a poor thing to live for, and the small incidents and humours of daily life make up a great part of my interests—so naturally I persuade myself that if you squeeze all this out of your life for the supposed benefit of some higher part of you, you impoverish yourself, or at any rate cut yourself off from something that might in the end enrich the part of you to which you sacrifice it. However we must take each other as we find each other, and I am glad enough that you take me at all.

The year ended with a heartening note from Blunden:

> La Fontaine comes over in all his lucidity and eternal ease; you are a Vanbrugh at the art of Fable, with the short lines beautifully companioning the long, and the double rhymes as cool as cucumbers. I don't know, but aren't Fables in general a pleasing kind of literature? Give me a frog, a bumble-bee, and an exciseman holding a conversation on some moral mushroom, and I am happy.

The royalties on the Memoir for the last half-year were so big (£606) that he sent a new-year present to Nichols with another mild remonstrance. 'I don't think you are "conceited" but I do thing you're rather arrogant. You so absolutely condemn the whole human race except two or three people like Goethe and Leopardi and it *can't* be as bad as all that!' Marsh was still unable to sympathize with Graves in his application of psychoanalysis to literary criticism. 'I can't see that his explorations of how a poem came to be written cast the smallest light on whether or why it is a good poem or not.' But he admitted he could not afford altogether to dismiss Graves's critical apparatus—'He'd been reading my Fables again and had come to the conclusion that technically I was much the best of the Georgian Poets. (Who's being conceited now?)'

At the end of March (1925) T. E. Lawrence wrote urging him to do what he could to get him transferred from the Tank Corps back into the R.A.F. by persuading Mr. Churchill to use his influence with Sir Samuel Hoare. He had now, he said, reached the stage of writing begging letters. 'Trenchard has had three . . . and now here is No. 4 to you—but with compunction, since Winston doesn't approve of my hiding in the ranks. He was born for power: whereas I got suddenly afraid of the openness of the world, so that the R.A.F. became a refuge. . . .' He ended by saying he had noticed that Thomas Hardy had a copy of the Fables on his table. On April 12 Lawrence tried to get Hardy to express his opinion of them. 'His memory is getting patchy; and it is no good springing a question on him.' Besides, there had been an untimely interruption.

> He said, 'The Fables . . . oh yes . . . I thought they were excellent reading. Good.' Then he went on to talk of the rat which found oysters upon the sea-shore and thought they were ships. . . . It was going to be quite worth reporting . . . and then this old hen butted in, and when she had stopped, and I asked again, he had forgotten that he had read the Fables. The truth is that a film seems to slip over his mind now, and the present is then obscured by events of his childhood. He talked next of seeing Scots Greys in a public-house in Dorchester drinking strong ale whose fumes made him (*aet.* 6) drunken. . . . Many thanks for seeing Winston for me.

The Fables brought word from Gertler. 'I am interested because Renoir loved them so. He used to say *Tout est là*'; and St. John Lucas, Brooke's friend and editor of the *Oxford Book of French Verse*, had written to say, 'Of course you know this is a classic.' On August 20 Marsh finished the new set of forty-eight for publication in October, and was contemplating the possibility of revising all he had already done, then making translations of the remainder. He reckoned it might take him ten years. He was not so daunted by this prospect as he might have been. The translations had become the regular business of his mind in solitude, and life without them was becoming increasingly difficult to imagine; moreover in June a load was lifted from his mind which removed the last obstacle in the way of the great enterprise which would leave the whole of La Fontaine re-created in English. It was now three years since the appearance of the last Georgian anthology. Another would soon be due, and the compilation had always been started in early summer. Monro was aware that the old system of editorship agreed on thirteen years ago could no longer stand up to post-war criticism, but he was bent on adding a sixth volume to the series. He wrote on June 8: 'There is a suggestion I am so tempted to make that I really can't resist it. The booksellers clamour for a sixth volume of *G.P.*' Marsh had already said that he did not have enough confidence in the available material, so also had Monro himself, but more recently Monro had changed his mind.

> Some of them are volumes for extracts for which I feel certain you would not care to act as sponsor, although you well might not be unconscious of their merits. I mention only the names of Edwin Muir, Sacheverell Sitwell, Roy Campbell, and T. S. Eliot. . . . Far be it from me of course to drag out a 'movement' after it has lost its natural impetus. . . . Even if you had to cavil, or to object, or to question, or to doubt, would you at any rate undertake to introduce such a volume into the world?
>
> I much hope, Eddie, that you will be sympathetic toward my idea, which will not plan out unharmoniously with the original scheme, will not be outrageous to anyone and actually and really will constitute a most fitting and suitable method of adding an appendix to the excellent little period in English poetry which the volumes of *Georgian Poetry*, under your tutelage, have represented.

In his reply Marsh began by saying that he had originally set out with the single object of stimulating public interest in contemporary verse, and he believed he had achieved that aim. Since then there had been 'a pullulation of other anthologies'. Where once it had stood alone the Georgian scheme was now competing with a number of rivals.

> The other point is what you call the new directions. In my own opinion, I have always been catholic to a fault! But everyone must have his preferences, and mine have been for verse which seemed to me to be in the direct line of tradition. I will not say that the new directions are not in that line, *de peur*, as M. Bergeret said, *d'offenser à la beauté inconnue;* but I own that my feeling towards their chief exponents is one of tepid and purblind respect, which would make me quite the wrong person to anthologize them, even if they had any wish to be anthologized by me, which is more than doubtful. And I hope it isn't dog-in-the-mangerish to feel that after being solely responsible for the previous books I should not care to come forward as sponsor for a selection made by somebody else from work with

which I wasn't really in sympathy; still less to make my exit with the gesture of moribund salutation which you seem to suggest. So I hope you won't be vexed if I stick to what we settled.

Georgian Poetry had lasted for twelve years and nine months. The news of its end was made public in one of Monro's Chapbooks issued from his bookshop, and in that form the news reached Bottomley in the Lakes, at a time when the latest Fables had just come to hand. 'Well, it is all over,' he wrote. 'It started my work with the larger public: I do not think I shall ever feel more honoured than I did in your inclusion of me and support of me, and I do not forget it. You chose to enter English Literature that way. I am happy that, as the adventure ends, you have staked out a new claim that so deliciously confirms you in an unassailable place there and gives delicate hopes of continuance.'

The review of the first Georgian volume in *The Times Literary Supplement* had turned out in at least one aspect to be prophetic. It had suggested that E.M.'s venture would establish a new orthodoxy in the place left vacant by the death of Tennyson. For several years now the anthologies had demonstrated the nature of the central tradition in English verse, so that the post-war poets, including some of the younger Georgians themselves, were able to see illustrated clearly and for the most part at its best the conception of poetry which they were impelled to react against. If in 1912 some of the Georgians had reacted too violently against the nebulous moods of the *fin de siècle* poets, so also, inevitably perhaps, the post-war revolution in criticism went too far at first and all work of a traditional kind was lumped together and dismissed as glib and guilty of the 'bogus rustic'. The time had come when the typically *modern* talent would have to be other than 'Georgian' in character. Not only was there now a new conception of form, but psychoanalysis had given access to a vast new territory of experience which could no longer be expressed in traditional technique. The artist traditional by temperament and vision found his potential subject-matter as well as his method no longer of his own age. The last important Georgian discovery, Edmund Blunden, came to the fore as witness that creative work could still be written in what was once the central tradition, even though the rise of a new orthodoxy had shifted it from centre. Both the best and the weakest traditional verse of the early 'twenties was pastoral in character. But by then a new movement, which as long ago as 1909 had begun obscurely enough with Hulme, Eliot, and Pound, had provided a new world with a new poetic method. A kind of tide had gone out, and where critical interest was concerned E.M. was left high and dry. The second anthology, which sold over 19,000 copies, established a record for a book of its kind which may never be surpassed. The fifth volume of 1922 touched the 8,000 mark. The drop was a sign of the times. Such figures are of no consequence to literary history. What matters is the quality of the editor's selection within his own field. It was such that he will always be a reliable guide to the nature and merits of that tradition in English poetry which relies for its effect on a sequence of logical thought combined with the graces of craftsmanship within a given form.

The five volumes represent four generations of writers, several of them introduced to the public at the critical outset of their working lives. That so much of what he stood for was eventually outmoded should do nothing to obscure the value of E.M.'s achievement. With judgement more sensitive and assured than Quiller-Couch, a task demanding quicker response than was ever required of either 'Q' or Palgrave, who could look back over tracts of literature which had already sorted themselves out in the process of time, E.M.'s individual contribution as *choragus*, personal adviser, critic, and friend in need, may never again be met with in the annals of patronage. A Welfare State which does not altogether ignore the welfare of the artist has taken over the functions of that unofficial and single-handed Arts Council which operated at Gray's Inn. Nor should it be overlooked that for many years E.M. himself had the benefit of a critic and encourager in the person of Edmund Gosse. When Monro announced the end of the Georgian anthologies it was from Gosse that E.M. received the compliment that pleased him most, and the fact that its significance would probably be lost on the general reader only added an agreeable piquancy in his eyes. In a valedictory tribute Gosse declared—'He is with Tottel'.[1]

'Now nothing,' Marsh wrote to Bottomley, '*nothing* stands between me and La Fontaine.'

[1] Tottel's *Miscellany*, published in 1557, introduced the poems of Wyatt, Surrey, and other precursors of the Elizabethans.

ii

In far Gray's Inn, what time the frosty Bear
Grinned through a cloud's black fringe of humid hair
And on the roof-ridge fierce Grimalkin sped
And in the panel channering worms proceed,
Alexis smiling sate and tuned the gay Arcadian reed.
This might be Aaron Hill, and yet I meant
In Dryden's style to have you closely pent.
Aid me, Polonius, while I start again. . . .
O thou translator, O thou text-reviver,
Of Epigram, too, almost sole Survivor,
What wouldst thou hear of Tokyo at large?

Blunden had received his fragment of rhymed topography and
was replying in kind. Marsh saw himself in the role of a Maria
Gisborne receiving a verse epistle from Shelley, but his efforts
to compose a suitable reply were foiled. 'I preferred murdering a
dead French poet to supplying a live English one with current
literary gossip.' The best books of the year had been Huxley's
Those Barren Leaves, *The Orissers* by Leo Myers, and a re-reading
of *Middlemarch*, 'a wonderful piece of architecture and very little
of it has lost its savour'. There had been an attack on Brooke.
'His view of the war, for instance, had been superseded by S.S.'s
which is far truer. This may be so, but it has very little to do with
his poetical merits as the exponent of the view which he happened
to take himself.' To Nichols he confessed his sanguine hopes for
the English theatre. Ibsen and Chekov were being supported by
the public, as well as Pirandello, whom he had recently met with
Shaw at Hazel Lavery's house, '—and then there is Noel Coward
who for a boy of 26 is really miraculous—I don't mean to put him
too high, but he has a sense of the theatre and a sense of style
which might carry him anywhere. It is certainly the most hopeful
year of the English stage that there has been in my time.' Then
there was the film *Raskolnikov*. 'As an experiment they gave it
without music, and I must say this added incalculably to its
intensity and impressiveness. I realized that for the first time I was
taking a film quite seriously and not merely as an entertainment.'

On Christmas Eve the Duchess of Sutherland gave the last ball
of the season and Marsh said goodbye to the linkman, a little old
body in a scarlet plush waistcoat and top hat who turned up at
every ball and received sixpence for 'calling the motor'. At the

Sutherland ball Marsh was dancing with Lady Plymouth when a young man came up and asked his partner for the next dance. 'But I haven't got one until Number 16,' came the reply. 'Oh, you *are*—what shall I say?' exclaimed the young man, 'I can't call you a gay *dog*', and Lady Plymouth replied with a look of misgiving, 'Perhaps, on the whole, you'd *better*.' Marsh also Boswellized the same partner as having remarked, 'At my own parties I never know whether or not to talk across the table to the silent one, for fear of being *gratingly* charitable.' The night before he had dined with Princess Mary, and played the now fashionable after-dinner game of mah-jong. A ball at Lady Astor's the previous week provided an anecdote. The Queens of Belgium, Rumania, and Greece were present, and the proceedings were gatecrashed by a drunken sailor who, on being shown the door, remarked loudly, 'I went to a ball last night where there were a lot of queens, but not *this* sort.' On the same unelevated plane (it would be presenting Eddie Marsh in a false light to omit this element entirely) was the story of a bishop who went to stay at a 'fast' country-house. 'He was driven from the dining-room by the drunkenness of the men and out of the drawing-room by the dissoluteness of the women—so he took refuge in his bedroom where he found a flapper lying in his bed. Being a courteous old gentleman he asked if he could be any use to her, and she said, "No, I don't expect you can, but I drew you in the lottery." '

On January 29 (1925) he had brought together some of the principal strands of his life for a brief encounter. Mrs. Churchill called at Gray's Inn and took away fifty of the Horne collection drawings so that her husband could take his pick for the office. He then gave the Churchills luncheon at the Savoy, took them to a matinée of *The Rat*, and conducted them to Novello's dressing-room, where they also found Ellen Terry.

Marsh's social manner in the theatre was apt to give a misleading impression. 'I would not have it thought that I am incapable of misery before the footlights,' wrote Marsh to Cynthia Asquith. He has been blamed for his apparently uncritical enjoyment in the theatre—and his remarks in the intervals were certainly apt to be indulgent to a fault—so that it may do his memory more good than harm to show him in the less agreeable light of his true feelings as revealed in his letters to Novello. 'She is very pink and flaxen,' he wrote of a certain actress, 'and looks like a wax doll which has been repaired after slight injuries from fire but can still say Papa with startling gusto.' Of another actress he remarked: 'She smiles like Malvolio and can hardly finish a sentence in her impatience to get all her teeth on view again.' Yet another actress 'looked like D'Alvarez with the pip and spoke from the boots upwards', and there was another who 'sings like a cow with adenoids, besides which her head is too big for her body, which is saying A LOT'. An astute observation concerned a comedy which was overplayed: 'It was an object lesson in *broadening*, one might have been looking at the play in the bowl of a spoon.' Another comedy failed more seriously: 'I tried all the way home to think of anyone I hate enough to make them see it and I could only think of X who has seen it already. . . . I writhed in my stall the whole evening, too exhausted to sleep. Expecting to laugh and never to move a muscle for three hours ought to have been one of the punishments of Tantalus. At the end there was continuous but slight applause kept alive by the curtain coming down and going up again before you could say knife, let alone Jack Robinson.' He found curtain speeches almost invariably ludicrous.

> The author began by mentioning every single performer by name (applause) including 'my dear sister Amy' (applause), 'then my wonderful producer' (by the way I thought the production shocking) 'who has given my script the same relation to the play you have seen tonight as that of a skeleton to a living body' (applause) 'and I must add that in the audience there is my best friend and critic my dear mother' (loud applause) 'and there is also the memory of my dear brother Tom who was drowned in a submarine in 1914' (beginning of deafening applause which suddenly wilted as the audience realized that one ought not to clap when someone tells you his brother has been drowned). I'm afraid this gave me the giggles which had been coming on for some time.

Another curtain speech moved him to describe the authoress.

> She had a powerful, aquiline, weather-beaten face under matted grey hair, a short square body, huge rough-hewn legs and feet like an unfinished-looking modernist statue, clothed in low black evening dress covered with spangles just down to her knees and an Indian shawl which looked as if she had slept in them for weeks. I really never saw such a what my nurse called 'objick'. She made a rather long and almost entirely inaudible speech of thanks and when the

gallery shouted 'Speak up' said, 'Oh, can't you hear? Thank you *so* much', and disappeared.

'It does seem a pity,' he remarked after seeing a play which other people had admired, 'that "good plays" are always intolerable. You would think Kingsley had said, "Be good, sweet play, and let who will be entertaining." ' He had been taken to task, he said, for his 'celebrated observation that I didn't dare leave London for fear of missing a first night at the Globe'. He was generally less communicative about the musical plays, but it would have been a pity had he not recorded that 'the animals got the biggest receptions. Pedro whatever-his-name-is was very tall and commanding, but with sadly thin legs and when he sings *piano* he puts his lips inside his mouth which begets a primness in his most voluptuous moments.' There was a play this year in which Tallullah Bankhead received no applause at her first appearance.

> The explanation is they mistook her for an antimacassar. The curtain went up and there she was upside down on a sofa, her legs over the back of it and her head nearly touching the ground. The butler came in to draw the blinds and was frozen with horror at the discovery. By this time the audience realized her identity, but, I suppose, thought it would be tactless to applaud her having been strangled before the play began.

He had a better opportunity of appreciating Ethel Irving. 'She got in her usual detonation, but alas I'm no longer so impressionable as I was, or she has lost her power; it was quite good but I knew perfectly well where I was all the time, and never got the feeling of being flattened out by a typhoon which used to be so enjoyable.' Then there was the scene in a comedy where a wife had to placate a jealous husband 'by feeding him, one after another, with the utmost archness, with *every* component of breakfast, from grapefruit which she over-sugared, through *two* eggs which she peeled for him successively, to marmalade and toast— it was one of those scenes in farce which slowly grind one down into an abyss of hypochondria and make one wish to have been born in any epoch but the present.' On this occasion he awarded the male lead 'full marks for want of charm. Even so he was supreme in Act II as a eunuch (spiritual) caught up in a maelstrom of seeming adulteries.'

He was rarely so carried away that he failed to observe what was ridiculous. There was a musical comedy, for instance, in which 'she gets estranged from the hero and they have a *Merry Widow* scene in which he asks if she will dance with him. "Yes," she says, "on the condition that you remember that I am *Miss Stewart*", whereupon they do *the* most bacchanalian dance, in which he throws her up in the air and whirls her round his head (of course remembering all the time that she is Miss Stewart), then both jump through the window.' That week he saw another play, in which the leading actor had become 'alarmingly ugly, all the human components of his face have disappeared, and I can't think what has happened to his mouth. When it is shut it looks as if he had no teeth, but when it opens there are far too many.'

A critic has said that this is a greater play than *Mary Rose*, which is just a ti-iny bit uncritical, don't you think? not to say a blasphemous ineptitude. Poor X looks *literally* 'like nothing on earth' but like a photograph of a mountain on the moon and her voice and delivery are of an unnaturalness that makes incest normal. When the same critic says she is an example to the younger actresses he reminds me of the housemaid who said 'Take example by me, Sally', as she was led away by the police—but there was a three-minute passage that was beautiful.

Whenever Novello was out of town every new play was fully described for him, and an eye kept alert for new talent. 'Ivor, you must freeze on to that woman,' Marsh wrote of Isabel Jeans in *Cobra*; 'grapple her to your management with hoops of steel.' And always the social gossip alternated with the theatrical.

I lunched with Lady Birkenhead today and met whom do you think, Rudolph Valentino. He really is a bit of a shock—just a dago waiter with brown skin and octoroon hair. Upon my word I thought him the ugliest man at table (the others being the Duke of Sutherland and myself!). I didn't talk to him—he seemed quite pleasant and un-assuming but without a particle of charm. The Duchess was *en grande beauté*—and rather amusing about an Indian Prince who offered £500 for a box at the Albert Hall Ball on condition he was introduced to her. They had a very dull conversation, merely, 'Have you been in India?' 'No.' 'When you do you must come to me for your first tiger.' So she introduced him to the Queen of Spain, who had a much better one. 'Are you any relation to the Begum of Bhopal?' 'I'm her son.' 'Oh, that *is* a near relation.'

He had also been amused by report of a set-to between Edith Sitwell and Mrs. Keppel, who took her to task for not living with her people and gave her a long lecture. 'Miss S. explained it was because she could write better if she lived alone. "And do you," asked Mrs. Keppel, "prefer Poetry to Human Love?" "Yes," answered Miss S., "*as a profession.*"'

The illness which was eventually to end his life had already declared itself. On November 10 he marked one paragraph of his budget to Novello '*Private*'.

Do you remember me telling you a year or two ago about my getting out of bed and finding myself flat on the floor, having missed a heartbeat as the doctor told me next day? It happened again this evening. I went to sleep on a sofa at my Club before dinner—woke up and looked at my watch which said a minute to 8—so I jumped up in a hurry and the next I knew was that I was sitting on the floor with my back against the sofa with no recollection of falling down— I looked at my watch again, and it still said a minute to 8. Luckily there was no one in the room. One of these days I suppose I might miss more than one beat and never come to. What a marvellous death it would be! If it happens, don't be sorry for *me* (this is why I tell you the incident).

Shortly after his birthday in November Lawrence's *Seven Pillars* came back to his desk in the form of proofs. The author was asking him to look at the references to Mr. Churchill. In July Lawrence had given news of his forthcoming return to the R.A.F. 'It's wonderful to feel secure, after all,' but it had proved to be a false hope. By now (November) all was well.

The red foot-note on Page 257 is the only reference later than 1919, and the only mention of Winston, in my war-book. I haven't, of intention, said enough: because I feared that people might say that in praising him I was praising myself. And there is a limit to the disclaimers and protestations that a man can make.

Yet I don't think that he'll object to the briefness or the purport of the note. It's only going to you to make sure. . . . A miracle (called Baldwin, I believe, in the directory, but surely a thing with wings and white robe and golden harp) put me back suddenly into the R.A.F., when I had completely lost hope. And now I'm a ludicrously contented airman.

A few days before Christmas Marsh began a journal letter to Blunden with a characteristic pleasantry: 'I like your notepaper with its defiant NO at the top of each page. Sometimes it comes in quite happily, for instance: "Little news comes from England, except that our number is up" (turn over) NO.' At that point he broke off to see in the new year 1926.

iii

Peter Quennell, who frequently occupied the spare room at Gray's Inn during this winter, has given a picture of his host.[1] 'Eddie would return home, coming from a dinner-party, about the hour of midnight. Having removed his collar, but still wearing his decorations, with a long cigarette-holder between his teeth and a tall glass of whisky and soda at his elbow, he would at once sit before his library table to translate La Fontaine.' He was now revising the two previous volumes and, still encouraged by Squire, had made up his mind to translate the whole work, two hundred and forty fables in twelve books, including the preface and the Life of Aesop. This labour was to take him five years.

It was early in January that he received from Nichols another metaphysical bombshell, which fell a little short of its full effect owing to the poet's splenetic handwriting. Marsh's new-year letter to Blunden with its affectionate mockery of Nichols described the latest sensation:

> He is looking forward with uncontrollable excitement and pleasure an early date (the only drawback is that he may die too soon to participate, 'worn out with *seeing*', but he hopes for the best) when 'we shall live greatly again, with the grave staring at us and'—something or other (I'd give anything to make out this word)—'far more enormous and terrifying than Aeschylus ever dreamed of hedging us round'. This delightful state of things we shall apparently owe to the recent undermining of the sinister and pernicious Law of Cause and Effect brought about by Rimbaud, Romer Wilson, Aldous, Stokes (who is Stokes?), Bertie Russell, and, last but not least, Einstein. He admits that it will all be very unpleasant for 'gentle and comfortable and dreamy folks'—of whom I should have thought I was obviously one (except perhaps dreamy) yet he expects me to share his raptures. I am constantly reminding him that I am a contented and humdrum person, quite unworthy to be the recipient of his rainbow and ferocious visions—yet he persists in writing as if my one interest in life were revolutionary metaphysics.

[1] *Eddie Marsh, Sketches for a Composite Portrait* (Lund Humphries, 1953).

It is part of dear Bob's complete want of practical commonsense that he never studies πιθανότης[1]—he never considers what audience he is addressing, in public or private, or what form of presentment is most likely to make his notions acceptable. I suppose his biographers will make out, as Shelley's do, that he was remarkable for his grasp of affairs and powers of dealing with his fellow men. By the way I hope this letter won't be printed in *your* biography, it would show me up as almost as unworthy to be the friend of the Divine Poet as T. T. Hogg—but you know I do *sincerely* admire and love him.

'When you write to me, and I imagine to many others,' wrote Blunden, inspirited by news of his literary friends, 'you in a short time fulfil a long time; it is like the Angel Gabriel practising his resurrection alarum, it is an earnest, eager, and motive sound.' On another occasion it was: 'I should not say no, now, if Satan appeared and said, "If you will write a few well-chosen words recommending me to the British public, I will set you down by my special air-service at Gray's Inn." '

When Marsh wrote to Nichols in May he was trying to make little of the General Strike. 'Perhaps you sympathize with it! So far it has gone off with amazingly little fracas. A party of foreign correspondents started out with cameras on Sunday to photograph it, but to their astonishment couldn't find it anywhere!' The strike would have been less easy for him to dispose of had he written a little later. Mr. Churchill was now personally in charge of the presses of the *Morning Post* and editing a new daily newspaper called the *British Gazette*, and from time to time Marsh was involved in the maelstrom of an editorial office which Mr. Churchill described with relish as 'the combination of a first-class battleship and a first-class general election'. In the evenings the social round continued unabated. Novello was now rich enough to engage a string orchestra for the entertainment of his guests at the Aldwych (where compositions by Ravel and Honegger alternated with the percussion of popping corks) and Marsh escorted Mrs. Patrick Campbell to Lady Colefax's, where Coward and Gershwin played their latest numbers. In July a new experience came his way when he broadcast seven of his Fables from Savoy Hill. 'Does one have to shout?' he asked anxiously when confronted with a microphone. It may have been about this

[1] A sense of the right approach.

time when he entered Mr. Churchill's sanctum with a chill in the throat. 'What's this?' asked the Chancellor, as a barely audible message was delivered. 'Is that resonant organ altogether extinct?' Marsh was now in charge of Churchill's private correspondence, and as certain acknowledgements had not been received, he was asked if he had not forgotten to despatch the Chancellor's mail. Marsh protested that he never forgot things in general, nor had he forgotten those letters in particular. 'On what *grounds* can you say you did not forget them?' asked Mr. Churchill. 'Because I *distinctly* remember the gesture,' came the reply. Their friendly dispute on the use of hyphens must have begun in this year, since in December Marsh consulted Herbert Fowler, author of *Modern English Usage* (which had just come out) in the hope of enlisting support. The academic dispute was to be revived again with ever mounting fervour over the next ten years.

In December the big event was *The Triumph of Neptune*, the ballet by his friend Lord Berners with Lifar 'whom I have always thought the best thing since Nijinsky', and Danilova 'who is a revelation—in dancing and acting I thought she eclipsed Lopokova and equalled Karsavina at her best'. In the same letter to Novello he described a charity dinner at the Café de Paris.

> I ensconced myself on the soft side of the table next the wall, beside the Diamond Queen of Johannesburg, Lady Oppenheimer, with whom I had great fun. She is a very original and humorous woman, with the face of Mary Clare (she must have been lovely) and the body of Margaret Yarde. She was very downright and comical about X's arrangements—the impudence of Y attempting to sing and all the follies of the evening. Lolling in the comfort of her natural proportions, the security of a really beautiful skin, which she told me had never been touched with anything but water and occasionally a little soap—and let me add the invulnerability of immense wealth and real pearls, she poured scorn on the pains which the poor old dears like Y (who really is what Stevenson calls 'a thing to set children screaming') bestow on their old skins and their desperate complexions or the imitation pearls which her eagle eye detected on almost every neck but her own.

Almost his only connection with painters this year was when he was astonished to come upon a coloured reproduction of a painting by Ethelbert White of which he possessed the original. It was posted up in a Tube station as an advertisement bearing by way of inscription the sub-Georgian couplet 'Live in Surrey Free from worry'.

The new year 1927 began with what seemed to him a vindication of his now somewhat discredited conception of poetry. Indeed it was further evidence that what was not strictly contemporary in style could still be as valid poetically—if the writer was true to his own temperament—as work conceived and composed in more progressive technique. Vita Sackville-West sent him *The Land*, and he at once recognized an achievement which made some of the recent Georgians of the pastoral variety look rather like week-end word-spinners. 'I have no doubt,' he wrote, 'you are the best living poet under eighty and it is such a joy to find someone writing the sort of poetry I like so unmistakably and indisputably better than other people write the sort I don't like so much. Nobody in face of such a book could go on making out that the tradition of English poetry is exhausted, and that sense of beauty, rhyme, and metre, must be given up.'

> I read *Winter* with admiration and pleasure, but (perhaps through not being warmed up) without any great excitement, except over the lovely passage beginning 'Here is no colour'—but *Spring* is one long enchantment, especially from the 'ghostly orchard' onward, through my old love the Beemaster with the splendid added passages, to a whole series of various miracles, the list of herbs in *Gardener*, the technical triumph of the *Island* with its 18 rhymes so managed that the cleverness only enhances the beauty of the poetry—the exquisite *Wild Flowers*, the sinister and surprising power of *Fritillaries*—the profound beauty of *Spring* flowering in the little lyric about the moorhen's nest which I couldn't see to read to the end till I had tried about six times. I do say, Vita, with my hand on my heart, that this is one of the perfect things in English poetry. And as if this were not enough you finish with a poem about the Nightingale which is as lovely and as new as if no one had ever written about it before.—(Here comes one of my few cavils, the fourth stanza has not the simplicity and limpidity of the rest, I still can't make out the syntax, and therefore the exact meaning.) I can't go on with this catalogue. . . . I don't know how you dare to write prose as good as your poetry, it's almost too much!

The author wrote from Knole, glad that he had found evidence in her work 'that it is *still* possible to write in the traditional manner, and yet to avoid falling into "pastiche", and that it *is* possible to eschew the fireworks of today without being too

boring. Indeed, you might find a certain symbolism in the title.
. . . You have fired me to go on with various abortive scraps I've
accumulated since last year; hitherto I have been feeling like a
very small breakwater in very heavy seas, trying to stem the tide,
but now I shall take my scribbling book out to Persia with a
bolder heart.'

He hastened to give the good news to Nichols, who was at work
on his play *Wings over Europe* which led him to enquire from
Marsh the official procedure at Downing Street. At the same time
Marsh urged him to write his new piece with more circumspection.
'I dread the lava torrent of your inspiration.' He also passed on a
tip from W. S. Gilbert, who had pointed out that a novelist
might say 'Eliza undressed and stepped into her bath' and no one
would turn a hair, but the incident would not be available to a
dramatist.

T. E. Lawrence wrote from Karachi on February 2, asking
that Mr. Churchill be reminded that he had promised him a copy
of *The World Crisis*, Vol. III.

> The voyage out on a trooper (H.M.T. *Derbyshire*) was something
> vigorous in the way of experience. Your improper department has
> ruled that at sea three airmen can be packed into the air-space of
> two sailors. Kindly meant, no doubt, to keep us warm and companion-
> able. But in the Red Sea and the Gulf we grew sick of each other's
> smell. Try not to forget that book. Half our day is leisure, and I am
> not very good at entertaining myself.

When he wrote again on June 10 he had got the book. 'Winston
wrote me a gorgeous letter. Called his *Crisis* a pot-boiler! Some
pot! . . . I suppose he realizes that he's the only high person since
Thucydides and Clarendon who has put his generation
imaginatively in his debt.' Marsh had commiserated with him
over an inept review of *Seven Pillars*, but in the meantime
Lawrence had come upon an even more vexatious article in the
London Mercury and was particularly riled by the critic calling
him a physical weakling.

> I'm not that yet, despite my extreme age. In fact I passed into the
> Army as a first-class recruit, in 1923. In 1914 I was a pocket Hercules,
> as muscularly strong as people twice my size, and more enduring
> than most. I saw all the other British officers' boots off in Arabia:
> they went to base, or to hospital, while I did two years in the
> fighting areas, and was nine times wounded, and five times crashed

from the air, and had two goes of dysentery, and suffered enough hunger and thirst and heat and cold and exposure, not to mention deliberate maltreatment, to wreck the average constitution. I go so far as to claim that I've been perhaps the toughest traveller who has ever written his true history. 'Mooning about the towns of South Italy.' Gods!

In the same letter Lawrence expressed his belief that Russia would make the next attempt at world domination.

It works from West to East, doesn't it? And England has been the main obstacle each time. Usually there has been about a hundred years between each effort: but the tempo of life has grown so much faster since the age of machines opened, that it's quite on the cards Russia may have her go in our time. It will be a complicated and difficult affair, which we will win, of course, after we have learnt the necessary modification of tactics. The Dardanelles and the Tanks both show how much dead weight has to be moved in favour of a new idea. Do you know, if I'd known as much about the British Government in 1917, as I do now, I could have got enough of them behind me to have radically changed the face of Asia? Russia, to these people, seems the new and growing idea: whereas there is more promise and capacity in our structure than she will contain in the next thousand years.

Marsh had again been appointed buyer for the year by the Contemporary Art Society, and a purchase in April brought him the acquaintance of a new young painter on whose short life he was to exert a considerable influence. 'I feel it will start the ball rolling,' wrote Christopher Wood on April 29, 'and that others who can't make up their minds may have the courage to follow your brave example.' Early in May Wood called to see the collection at Raymond Buildings before paying a visit to Paris. While still in England he heard that Marsh had persuaded Mr. Churchill to commission a portrait from his friend Neville Lewis and that the Private Secretary was putting in some time as a model sitting in the Chancellor's robes. Christopher Wood was in high spirits.

You are the only person who takes true interest in the painters of your own country. . . . We are going to be the best some day quite soon now. I am convinced of it. It's a pity the dealers don't take a leaf from your book. . . . This is beautiful mysterious country, curious little valleys carved out by glaciers, little streams full of trout and big elm trees, all black against buff-coloured downs. Very different from the South of France and I hope to get the hang of it soon and show it to you on canvas. Wish you were here to drive me on.

Later this spring the rooms at Gray's Inn were opened to the public at half-a-crown a head in aid of the Y.W.C.A., and Mrs. Elgy took it upon herself to keep an eye on the silver from noon until 7 P.M. 'You seem to have got hold of all the best painters when they were fourteen,' wrote R. H. Wilenski.

During the preparations G. M. Trevelyan and Mr. Churchill had come to luncheon. 'What would be a suitable dish for my two old friends?' the host asked Mrs. Elgy. 'What are they?' 'They are two great historians.' 'Oh,' said Mrs. Elgy with relief, as if that information had somehow solved the problem at once—'Creamed haddock.' She was justly proud of her function. 'I may not be a *posh* cook,' she once exclaimed, 'but I hope I'm a *cook*'.

Another visitor at this time was Oliver Messel, who 'made himself very agreeable. Instead of being a formidable young modern as one might have thought, he is quite boyish and simple-minded, and did all the things that go to my heart such as adoring Mrs. Elgy and noticing my window-box.' The young dramatist John van Druten called with an introduction from Francis Brett Young, whose new novel *Portrait of Clare* Marsh had just hailed as 'a really big piece of work. You get the effect of Time, which Henry James used to think the most difficult and important thing. The love affair between Clare and Ralph is magically beautiful. . . . I feel about it as I used to about the one in Richard Feverel (which I daren't read again now that I'm off Meredith!).'

Novello being out of town, the comments on the theatre and society began again. Near the end of May a thriller called *The Terror* was produced.

> Luckily I sat next Gordon Selfridge and could clutch him at the worst moments—if I had been next a stranger I should have screamed like the people in the gallery. I am blessed by Heaven with an utter inability ever to fathom in the smallest degree the mystery of a mystery play till the author reveals it in his own good time. On the way home I realized that a baby in arms must have known who the Terror was by the end of Act I, but I give you my word I had been completely bamboozled, and had no theory of any kind, till the last scene. This is a priceless asset, I wouldn't be otherwise for the world.

On May 22 he attended the first performance of D. H. Lawrence's play *David*.

The fun began with a rather tactlessly worded announcement in the programme that 'owing to unavoidable circumstances the part of Saul would be taken at short notice by Mr. A,' as if they had strained every nerve to prevent him from acting but had failed. This would have been believable, for he was extremely bad. Perhaps the funniest scene was when Saul went mad and Jonathan brought David in to see what he could do about it. Saul was raving on a throne at the back of the stage and David sat down on a settee near the footlights and began singing one of his own psalms to the tune we all know so well from Morning Prayer, which seems a very unlikely cure for the jimjams. Saul took no notice, and went on with a rigmarole, the point of which seemed to be (as far as I could hear through the psalm-singing) that God was really an enormous Beetle who had laid the Earth as an egg and a bad one at that. Every now and then he made David jump by throwing a javelin at him, which rattled him a good deal, so that he sang things like 'Thou hast given him dominion over the works of thy Feet, and put all things under his Hands'. Another good bit was near the end, when Saul again went mad on the top of Mt. Gilboa or wherever it was and began abusing David. 'David,' he said, 'is like a—like a—(to *Prompter*) what?' (*Prompter*—'A weasel') Saul: 'Oh yes, a weasel, a virgin weasel which cannot bring forth her young.' I should have thought if there *was* a line that it would be hardly possible to forget it was the one about the Virgin Weasel.

Goliath was killed 'off' after a partly-audible slanging match with David in the wings, which was a pity, as I should like to have seen the fight. When David returned in triumph Saul's daughters and their handmaidens rushed to and fro with their tambourines saying *Tootleoo*, they sang it so often and so distinctly that I can't have been mistaken. I didn't know the expression came from so far back.

It is now midnight and I am at home after a very smart dinner at 11 Downing Street which Clemmie was obliged to give to pacify her very good cook who gave notice because she hadn't enough work. I sat next the lovely Lady Maureen Stanley whom I'd never talked to properly before. Winston had a good story of Nancy Astor. She was making a speech in the House in favour of Prohibition and X the drunken Labour member shouted, 'Why don't you go to America?'— 'Why don't you go and have another?' said Nancy, as quick as lightning.

He then passed on his best anecdote of the week.

Tree and Landon Ronald between them gave the Sicilian actor Grosso a supper in the dome at His Majesty's at which Grosso got very drunk, and when the party broke up kissed everybody goodbye, male and female. Hoping to escape their share of this the two hosts hurried downstairs on pretext of getting him a taxi, and waited for him in the street. However it was all in vain, G. embraced them both on the pavement, and got into the taxi, telling the man 'Garrick Theatre'. 'What can he be doing at the Garrick Theatre at 4 o'c. in the morning?' asked Landon Ronald. Tree replied grimly, 'I expect he forgot to kiss the fireman.'

In August Marsh was staying at Chartwell with the Churchills. Walter Sickert was also there.

He told me that it was he who gave Marie Lowndes the idea of *The Lodger*. His landlady had been Jack the Ripper's—and if he hadn't gone to the dinner party where he sat next her there would have been no novel, no play, no film! . . . One of the *coups de table* was a joke in *Punch*—'The Athenaeum Club is closed for cleaning, but it is intended when it is reopened to replace the members in their original positions.'

It was probably during this stay at Chartwell that Sickert made an observation which Marsh never forgot. At his instigation Mrs. Churchill had bought a picture, only to find on getting it home that her husband did not share her adviser's enthusiasm, 'Look at that picture that Eddie has made Clemmie buy,' Mr. Churchill exclaimed to Sickert. 'Can *you* see anything in it?' The painter peered at the canvas, 'Oh yes,' he said, after a pause. 'Our little friend Eddie is not without a certain idiot flair.'

In September Eddie Marsh travelled to the South of France accompanied by W. J. Locke, 'a charming old gentleman of a much higher mentality than I should have expected from his books', to stay with the Guinnesses. The hospitality began with a hill-top picnic.

We got to the top as night fell and a great bar of blood-orange full moon broke through the clouds—just as we had collected wood, lit a fire, and put on our potatoes to *sauté* them, a thunderstorm broke out, and what with the lightning, the red moon, and the motor headlights turning the rain into bright threads of Venetian glass, it was the most wonderful display of complicated illumination I ever saw—and shall never forget ('You will though,' said the Red Queen, 'unless you make a note of it').

There was much gaiety. Marsh scored a *coup* at the cold-meat stage of luncheon out of doors when one of the guests complained of the light in her eyes and he remarked, 'Oh my dear, it must be the *glare* from the veal!' Lady Carisbrooke, who looked 'extremely elongated and elegant in lilac pyjamas', was taken to meet Christopher Wood in his cottage not far away and she commissioned him to paint her portrait. This inaugurated one of the painter's few really happy spells of work. 'I destroyed most of my summer's work which was done in the wrong atmosphere,' he wrote. 'I feel at last on the right road, less effort, with no striving after originality, it just comes naturally now with a real blast of fire and energy.' Marsh took a few of his canvases back to London, hoping to interest the dealers. 'The picture you liked of the table flowers and lamp', Wood wrote, 'has become beautifully improved out of all recognition from its former self.' By then it was October, and the painter's spirits were once more depressed. 'I want to be amongst my friends for I am not in a fit state to be alone at the moment. . . . Thanks so much for the enormous cheque, it gave me quite a shock, as I really didn't expect to be heavily paid for paintings by you.' He was upset that an example of his new method of deliberately causing the paint under the varnish to crack had been frowned on by a London dealer.

> I was very surprised about it as I thought it was a good one and was quite aware that the background was cracked and the face was not, as I had done this on purpose like all the other things I did during the first month at Cannes. This is what I call Poetry of Paint, for I love cracked paint under varnish. One sees so many cracked pictures in museums don't you? It is easy to make paint crack and that is why I varnish some of my things almost immediately. . . . Picasso and others all thought it pretty good.

Soon after Marsh's return from Cannes some of the 'murder money' was put to an unusual purpose, after Lionel Curtis, writing from Chatham House on October 27, had made a proposal concerning T. E. Lawrence:

> I frequently hear from Lawrence, and am happy to say he is betraying a thorough boredom with his surroundings. It is good news to me that he contemplates a change in 1929. His idea is then to become a night-watchman. Oddly enough, St. John Hornby and I were lunching today. We are both happy possessors of a copy of *Seven Pillars*, which can now be sold for £400. I suggested that some of us

should put a little money together and send out to Lawrence a first-class gramophone with first-class records. Such a gramophone was a joy to him at his cottage at Wool. Of course, his greatest joy was his motor-cycle, but he tells me he has not yet been outside the camp at Karachi, and I doubt whether the thing would be any use to him there. We might get someone to tell us about this as the motor-cycle might be the better alternative. St. John Hornby said he would be only too glad to contribute. I think if the gramophone or motor-cycle just arrived for him that he would not return it or give it away, and we need not let him know who sent it.

Another thing which you in particular might do is to get him reviewing or translating work. He condescends to supplement his pay by such degrading occupations!

Incidentally, I may tell you, Herbert Baker and I raised £1,000 to send him to China to buy pottery, pointing out to him that with his nose for good things we could repay the £1,000 in no time. It really would have been interesting to see what would have happened had we dropped Lawrence into the middle of China; but he just treated us like dirt and defeated us—tragic little being!

On Marsh's fifty-fifth birthday Novello came to Raymond Buildings and chose fourteen pictures to adorn the country house he had just bought at Littlewick Green, near Maidenhead, and he was also allowed to select for his drawing-room 110 volumes from the library. Before the end of the month there occurred the first night of Coward's *Sirocco*, a fiasco well known in theatrical history since the author and Novello, who was playing the lead, were viciously booed for the first and only time. Marsh sat through it in a fever of discomfort and joined in the post-mortem discussions with the author and the leading man at the Aldwych flat, which lasted almost until dawn. On the 26th, accompanied by the actor Robert Andrews, he was driven down to see Novello's home. During the drive it was decided to call the place Redroofs. Novello's father was there to greet them on arrival, and they were up until 3 A.M. arranging furniture. Late next morning a lorry full of books, pictures, and flower-prints arrived from Gray's Inn, and the large painting by Neville Lytton of Arab horses cropping the foliage in a glade was given the place of honour over the drawing-room chimney-piece. It was not long before Marsh was celebrating his tenth Christmas in succession among Novello's friends, but this time it was in the white-washed, two-storeyed house which for the next fifteen years was to be the scene of so many of his leisure hours. When Coward came down after the new year he found Marsh in his shirt-sleeves manhandling the furniture, and the gramophone was roaring all day.

iv

Stephen Gooden had been engaged to do the illustrations for the limited two-volume edition in which the complete Fables were to make their first appearance, but he was already at work on a set of plates for George Moore's *The Brook Kerith* and could not start on La Fontaine until the following December. While Moore was being persuaded to reduce the number of his illustrations Marsh began the year with a stocktaking of his picture collection and a round of enquiries among his painter friends. Among others, these included Richard Eurich, Frank Freeman, John Skeaping, Edward Wolfe, V. Pitchforth, John Armstrong, Richard Wyndham, Rex Whistler, Ivon Hitchens (Marsh had spotted him in 1925 and had been the first to buy one of his paintings), and Tristram Hillier. Barnett Freedman entered his life a year after this, in 1929, then followed Leonard Appelbee, Eric Ravilious, Mervyn Peake, Anthony Devas, Michael Rothenstein, William Coldstream, Robert Buhler, George Berger, and Graham Sutherland. Between the wars he corresponded with eighty-six artists, about thirty of whom knew him as a regular visitor to their studios, and all the while he kept in touch with the development of his older friends, the Spencer and Nash brothers particularly, Matthew Smith, William Roberts, and Edward Wadsworth. These interests, more widespread than in the field of letters, are by comparison thinly documented. Talks by the studio stove were the counterpart of critical correspondence among writers; moreover there was less that he could 'say' about a painting than a book, for perhaps his aesthetic response to the visual arts was purer, as it was certainly wider in scope, than it was among the new forms of literary expression. It was as if the classical basis of his scholarship sharpened his judgement in literature while setting a limit to his sympathies. Confronted with a piece of writing, he probed and tested, made his incision, and staunched the wound, combining in one person the skills of his parents, the professor of surgery and the hospital nurse. But in a picture-gallery his frame of mind was more passive, and there perhaps his sensibilities were more untrammelled and exposed. What he called 'the lust of possession' was an immediate and intuitive response. He described it as 'a curious and very pleasant sensation of tingling, or perhaps gooseflesh'. In no circumstances was he ever uncritical, but with the graphic arts his emotional and intellectual resources worked together in subjection to his instincts. His 'innocent eye' was quick to perceive creative life, and it served as an inward mirror which might reflect nothing for minutes or hours together, then catch the living image in a flash, thrilling him with instantaneous delight. Graham Sutherland observed this quality when he first met Eddie Marsh in Rosenberg's gallery. The patron was then (in 1938) no more to this artist than a name. 'I had heard stories about him as the friend of Churchill, and as a collector whose very bathroom door was covered with paintings.'

> I don't remember who introduced us. I was unaware of much except the high, light, slightly lisping, withdrawn, yet infinitely persuasive voice—those extraordinary upturned eyebrows, the quizzical regard and the tensed elegant body. He appeared as if from nowhere—quite suddenly. One could have believed he had seen no paintings. Yet— 'that's the one I want' he said, and disappeared. I was overwhelmed and delighted (this was my first show of paintings at Paul Rosenberg's). Afterwards, as I met him from time to time— suddenly appearing—always shy and physically tensed—forearms hugged close to the body and parallel with the ground—delicate hands clenched—as if with some suppressed pleasure—(usually he was coming from a private view of paintings)—I came to realize that this was his way. For himself, his mind was quickly and clearly made up. The sharply inquisitive nose and eye seemed to lead him by some invisible course to what he wanted.[1]

It was probably in the early months of 1928 that Christopher Wood, who had sent his latest canvases to a dealer, wrote from his cottage on the coast at St. Ives.

> Do ask him to show them to you and tell me *exactly* what you think of them as I have no critics. The weather here is one fury of storm and spray. The sea knocks down houses now and again and as mine faces the Atlantic ocean I may find myself up against it one day. It has been a wonderful time though, moderately happy and very vigorous. There is so much going on here. The sailors or fishermen

[1] *Eddie Marsh, Sketches for a Composite Portrait* (Lund Humphries, 1953).

are fine fearless-looking people and their boats full of purpose and dash.

By now Novello was away, so the serials of London gossip began again.

The guns are firing for Haig's funeral. I went out on to the Horse Guards parade to see the procession. . . . I couldn't see much for the crowd. I thought the rule Alice objected to, of people falling flat on their faces in a procession, would be so sensible if everyone *else* did it—but I just caught a glimpse of Foch. . . . Winston has got such a good thing to say in his speech at Birmingham tonight, after answering Ramsay MacDonald's statement that by introducing the Betting Tax he showed that he enjoyed tearing the clothes off children's backs—'There I leave Mr. MacDonald where he lies— perhaps to prevent misunderstanding I had better say "I leave him where he fell".'

At a performance of *Macbeth* in modern dress Marsh thought he had detected one of the leading actors of the future.

I had speculated a good deal beforehand as to what was modern dress for witches, and couldn't be sure whether they would be got up as Ladies Tree, Alexander, and Wyndham, or as the Misses X. However, they were only ordinary tatterdemalions. It was a really terrible performance and Jim Agate rushed up to me in the entracte and said, 'I call it obscene buffoonery.' All the poetry deliberately neutralized and Banquo's lovely speech about the temple-haunting martlet delivered as if by a retired colonel making conversation in Cheltenham. . . . There were exceptions. There was also a very good new juvenile—Laurence Olivier as Malcolm or, as it was pronounced throughout, Mawlcom—he acted with great intelligence and made a lot of the part. By the way, Bobbie Harris had asked him what he was going to wear, and he answered quite seriously, 'First a Tartan uniform, then silk pyjamas, then a grey flannel suit, and then a kilt.' Quite a good selection, wasn't it? George Arthur told me Mrs. Kendal had said to him, 'I'm an old woman, but I shall live to see Lady Macbeth play the sleep-walking scene in pyjamas.' She's a mordant old woman. George asked her if she had ever seen Mrs. Langtry act, and her answer was, 'Never—no more did you.'

Marsh had begun to spread the idea that he should be put on the free list for all first nights on the understanding that he would pay *afterwards* if he didn't like the play. He was always at pains to convey the exact nuance of his likes and dislikes. 'Perhaps "dull" isn't quite the word,' he wrote of one production. 'Bobbie Andrews was there. I only saw him for a minute and said, "It's rather good, isn't it?" "Yes," said Bobbie out loud, then "It isn't really", in a whisper. I think he hit off the truth with those two remarks taken together.'

Afterwards to Lady Astor's ball for the Duke and Duchess of York, which I thoroughly enjoyed, except for discovering that I have absolutely forgotten how to dance a waltz! I was attempting it with Pamela Lytton and nearly killed Blandford, so we gave it up. . . . Lady X (who I'm glad to say has gone to pieces) has a daughter whom she dresses as a Gibson Girl with madonna hair ending in a bun on her neck, and a very old-fashioned dress to match. Opinions on this were hotly divided, some thinking it a success and others cruelty to animals. Y was so carried away as to say that the bun was dirty. I wonder she didn't say it looked as if it had been refused by an elephant.

This afternoon there was a scene at a picture-gallery. I went with Clemmie Churchill and Nellie Romilly to a private view at which Walter Sickert's showing a portrait of Winston done from photographs, making him look like Horatio Bottomley in a public-house. Nellie lost her self-control and attacked the manager of the Gallery who told her, he didn't suppose she had ever seen Mr. Churchill, and much fur flew. He appealed to me as someone who knew about pictures—I was very judicious.

At a supper with C. B. Cochran which went on till 3 A.M. he sat with Frederick Lonsdale while Noel Coward sang his songs at the piano.

They are brilliant to the last degree. My only fear is some of them are too good to get across, it took my comparatively nimble mind all its powers of attention to keep pace with them—but others couldn't fail to get across. . . . Lonsdale was deeply impressed and said, 'You're a great boy, Noel.' Noel has got a tremendous contract with Boosey. Lonsdale telephoned it to him, and he was so flabbergasted that he remained speechless for 2 minutes and L. thought he hadn't heard.

A few days later he lunched with Lady Colefax to meet André Maurois. 'The Rudyard Kiplings were there, announced as the the Ruddy Kittens.' On another occasion he sat next Mrs. Patrick Campbell.

She was full of ornithological comparisons, asking me, 'What's the name of that woman with duck's disease—you know—her behind sticks out?' and again, 'Do you admire that girl like a jackdaw?' She had another very good expression. I told her a friend of mine had turned over a new leaf and she said, 'Yes, but leaves sometimes blow back!' I asked her why she hadn't played in a certain piece and she said she was reading the script in bed, and when she came to the line 'I know all about Kings—I've seen them in bed', she was so horrified that she threw the book under the bed 'and it was a very low bed, and it's there still! No one has been able to fish it out.'

He had just lost £9 at 'a disastrous evening with the King of Portugal at mah-jong', so couldn't afford to go to Manchester for Coward's first night. His anecdote of the day was a story of F. E. Smith calling on the German Foreign Minister, Dr. Stresemann. 'He was shown by a handsome parlourmaid into a room where there was a dear little dog which, being very fond of dogs, he played with while she went to announce him. When Dr. S. came in F.E. began the conversation by saying, "What a delightful little bitch you've got!" "Yes," said the statesman, who spoke English perfectly, "we've had her for two years and now she's going to marry our chauffeur." ' Marsh had recently called on de la Mare at Taplow and collected a remark of the poet's when at his worst in a recent grave illness. His daughter had come into his bedroom and asked him, 'Would you care for some fruit, or some flowers?' The poet replied, 'It's too late for fruit and too soon for flowers.'

On April 20 Lance Sieveking, who had become one of the pioneers of sound broadcasting, produced him in a fifteen-minute talk on Brooke. An announcement of the Cup Tie trains to Wembley overran and reduced the talk to eight minutes. 'I had to think all the time what to throw overboard and couldn't concentrate on my vocal chords.'

This afternoon I went to the contemporary exhibition of Albert Dürer at the British Museum. There was a charming drawing of a demure little lady staidly muffled up in walking clothes called 'Woman of Nuremberg going to church', and next it one of a completely naked woman holding a hoop. 'H'm,' I said to myself, 'Woman of Nuremberg *not* going to church', which made myself laugh, and a bystander looked at me with distaste as if I were the sort of person who can't see a nude without sniggering.

The other day at luncheon with Lady Leslie the conversation led me to say, 'But then, I've had a very sheltered life'—'How *can* you say that!' Shane [Leslie] exclaimed, 'when you've been Winston's butler all these years?'—'How do you mean he's been Winston's butler?' everyone asked. It turned out he had meant 'buckler', to shield Winston from the slings and arrows of outrageous fortune. . . . I was glad, yea, *glad*, it had been cleared up.

Lady Cynthia Colville, Lord Crewe's daughter, told me a charming old-world story. She was brought up at Crewe by her great-uncle, a very old Lord Crewe who had no sense of time, and used for instance to come in for luncheon at 5 P.M. After dinner he went to his own room and sat up alone till all hours. One morning he rang his bell at 6.30 A.M.; his valet jumped into his clothes and came down —to be told, 'I shan't want anyone to sit up for me.' Outside the sun was shining brightly and a mower at work on the lawn.

When Evan Charteris was a struggling barrister, he got on to a solicitor who sent him a lot of briefs and as a reward Evan asked him to dinner to meet Harry Cust and Ribblesdale. Harry got rather drunk and very brilliant and ragged the solicitor, making fun of everything he said, and it was so glorious that when they had gone Evan sat down and wrote to Harry, 'You've ruined my life, but it was worth it.' Harry wrote back, 'Your letter was of a kind I am more accustomed to getting from women.'

At this time Robert Graves sent news of his memoir *Goodbye to All That*. 'It will have taken eleven weeks from first to last. . . . You have been very good to me these last 13 years and I could not even tease you in print.' The Brett Young proofs on Marsh's table were of *My Brother Jonathan*. 'For some chapters *before* the very end,' he wrote to the author, 'I felt your writing was getting rather fatigued (and no wonder!). If I had had the book in typescript I would have tried to get you to pull some of your sentences together.' As usual the theatre news went to Novello, and by far the best new production was *Young Woodley*. 'The Lord Chamberlain went to see it last night and I'm told said it could never be licensed because it would put ideas about public schools into the heads of the Labour Party. I needn't tell you why I think this quite absurd, and it's rather unlucky that I should be lunching with him on Wed., as the play will inevitably be discussed and I shan't be able to conceal my opinion.' This was an unfortunate coincidence, since Marsh had just applied for the appointment of Reader of Plays as adviser to the Lord Chamberlain, and did not succeed, so he believed, for this very reason. He was beginning to make plans for his retirement. He would need a small salaried occupation to eke out his pension. It was the first time he had ever lifted a finger to procure a position for himself in public life. He never tried again.

He complained that the bands at balls were getting too raucous, and the dances too rough, then gave news of a 'Charity Pageant of Hyde Park' in which George Grossmith appeared as Beau Brummel, Oliver Messel as Byron, and he himself cut an elegant figure as Thackeray in a curly wig, dark brown coat, stock, frilled shirt, flowered waistcoat, and sugarloaf beaver.' It was his last social appearance before the holiday which provided him with the one terrible misadventure of his life.

v

On August 21 he went to stay with Louis and May Spears at Villefranche on the French Riviera, now in its third year of fashion as a summer resort. After three days he left for Ajaccio on Corsica, where he was met by his niece Nancy Maurice, who had planned a motoring tour of the island. On the 26th they took rooms in the seaside town of Piana half-way up the western coast. Richard Wyndham had urged them not to miss the turquoise bay of Porto, so on the 28th they began the day with a visit to that beauty spot, ate an early midday meal at a fisherman's café, then decided to walk back the three miles or so to the Hôtel des Roches Rouges.

They had covered about half the distance, the way being uphill and the sun scorching, when the road ahead was seen to make a loop, turning back the way they had come in a wide detour. Nancy was still fresh, but her companion's legs were beginning to drag when he noticed on the right what looked like a fairly straight and pleasantly grass-covered track through the scrub. It was obviously a short cut that would join up again with the main road when it eventually curved back at some point nearer their destination. So they both left the road and took the goat-track, which after a short while ended abruptly in a dried-up water-course littered with rocks. Nancy was now in front and clambering over the rocks with agility, but Marsh felt it would be simpler to turn back. Calling to each other, they agreed to make their way home separately. She would go on and join up with the road farther down, he would retrace his steps to where they had left it and trudge the longer but more easily negotiable way

round. Soon after starting back he caught sight of what promised
to be yet another short cut, but this too came to a dead end. He
was confronted with a dense thicket. Still convinced, however,
that the road must lie not many yards ahead, he entered the scrub
and thrust onward, expecting any moment to come out into the
open. He did not realize that he had mistaken his direction and
was only plunging deeper and deeper into the tangles of thorn.

He was growing desperate. For about four hours he battled with
the briars, while shreds were snatched from his sleeves and
trousers. At one stage he noticed that his breath was coming in
irregular gasps. 'Now you mustn't whimper!' he exclaimed aloud,
firmly, and rallied his will enough to control the palpitations in
his chest. At length he had no doubt that he was going to die. 'I
have never had the instinctive belief in a future life from which so
many of the splendours and miseries of the world have sprung,'
he wrote in after times, 'nor have I been able to see anything
objectionable in extinction, of which by the nature of the case one
would be unaware.' Uppermost in his mind was La Fontaine.
Would it occur to Mrs. Elgy to send his last revisions to the
printer? Would she know what they were when she saw them on
his table? If only his Fables could be secured his life would not
have been entirely wasted. And then he began to imagine himself
rescued by some miracle. Would Ivor be able to arrange for a
stretcher-case to attend the first night of his new play *The Truth
Game*? In a box perhaps? Then he could telephone Mrs. Elgy
from the theatre and explain about the La Fontaine papers. No,
that would have happened before, if at all. It was then that an
obsessive thought like a thunder-cloud began to spread over the
whole sky of his mind—the growing conviction that perhaps his
consciousness was the only reality in the universe and everything
else no more than the creation of his own delirium. His last thought
was a recollection of Bertrand Russell at Cambridge expounding
this theory, known to philosophy as solipsism, and seriously
maintaining that it was incapable of disproof. . . . At length he
fell unconscious in a brackish puddle near the sea, at the bottom
of a cliff down which he had torn his way through the maquis.
There he remained for nineteen hours.

Nancy Maurice had rejoined the road, without misadventure,
after ten minutes, but when, after waiting three-quarters of an
hour for Marsh to catch up with her by the longer route, she got

a lift from a passing car and returned to the hotel, there was no uncle awaiting her there. She at once hired another vehicle and drove back along the road to Porto. There was no sign of him. At Porto she organized a search-party. To the Corsicans, who seemed incapable of being galvanized into a state of urgency, there appeared to be various alternatives. Nancy was the Englishman's mistress (or possibly his wife) who had quarrelled with him so that either he had run away from her and was in no haste to be found, or she had murdered him, buried the body, and was now brazenly facing it out with a show of innocence. It was clear that no one really believed the simple and relatively humdrum explanation she supplied. It was already dusk when the search began; and the Corsicans refused to enter the maquis after dark. So Nancy and a French doctor who was on holiday at Porto traced the water-course where the two had parted company, and all the goat tracks round about, while the Corsicans remained on the road, firing off blanks and shouting, but making no other effort to help. And now it was the niece who had to keep iron control of herself. By midnight it was clear that further exploration was useless till dawn, so the people from Porto were thanked, paid, and disbanded, and she went back to Piana and sought the help of the *gendarmerie*. They agreed to meet her at the hotel at 4 A.M. and renew the search. Till then she waited, with no hope of sleep, her thoughts clear but her senses of sight and hearing subject to hallucinations. Eddie was groaning, dying below her window, having come back, or she would suddenly catch sight of his body hanging from a tree in the maquis.

At first light the search began. By 7 A.M. there had been no answering call to the volleys fired as a signal, or the din of klaxon horns, and she was giving up hope. If he could not shout, how could he be alive? The *gendarmes*, three boys all under twenty, were ready to break off the search, but she now conceived the theory that he might have pushed on towards the sea where the scrub was thickest, and she begged them not to give up yet but to prolong their efforts in the direction of the shore. They went, and she waited, seated under a tall tree, dazed, not daring to contemplate what they might still discover.

They penetrated the scrub, and coming down at last to the shore gave up the search as a bad job and pulled off their clothes for a bathe. It was 11.30 A.M. when one of them found that he still had a blank round left in his carbine, so before going into the water he fired it off at the sky for fun. By chance his companions were not talking or laughing, for in the moment of silence which followed the shot they heard a very faint call, and in a ravine close by, where there were no goat tracks, they came across a shallow pool. There lay the man they were looking for. He was naked except for his socks and shoes and shirt collar. His jacket and trousers must have been torn off him or thrown away, his skin was lacerated all over by the clinging thorns and dark with contusions from repeated falls, and his eyes were sunk far back into his head. He could slightly move one hand. His speech was feeble and inarticulate. He was conscious, but evidently dying. They dressed him in a fisherman's butcher-blue trousers and jacket, carried him to a boat, and rowed him to Porto. There he was transferred to the car his niece had hired, and brought along the road to Piana as far as the place where, down in the maquis, Nancy was still keeping her vigil. She scrambled up the cliff and together they returned to the hotel, accompanied by the French doctor who had joined the car at Porto. He told Nancy that if her uncle had not been found within two hours he would have been dead.

The story became a local legend. Over ten years later, the man who had driven Nancy Maurice up and down the road on the day of the search, stopped the car at a certain spot between Porto and Piana, half-way through his anecdote, and rendered dramatically the Englishwoman's cry. 'Edda! Edda!' he called in shrill despair, then allowed his party of tourists to proceed with their excursion.

While he slept unstirring twice round the clock, Nancy realized he was sinking into a coma. She summoned a doctor from Ajaccio, who diagnosed uraemia and nephritis and brought him through the crisis. As soon as he could be moved they went to Ajaccio, where facilities for treatment were available which did not exist in Piana, and not long after their arrival the French doctor who had been the first to treat the patient happened to pass through on his way home to France. He felt bound to give the warning that Eddie Marsh was probably suffering from general paralysis of the insane and should be taken to London immediately to see a mental specialist. For some time he suffered from a complete breakdown of will, but Nancy never left his side, except to sleep on the balcony where she could still watch him at night, and as the days and nights passed she gradually nursed him back to health of mind and body. There were three books at his side, Boswell, *David Copperfield*, and Trollope's *The Claverings*. All three contained at least one masterly description of a round meal. The lamb-cutlets and asparagus tips evoked by Trollope were almost too much to bear for the patient who was on a diet of saltless gruels. It is curious that the only lasting effect of this adventure was that the pleasures of the table, which he had never under-estimated, were from now on to be an obsession which he sometimes had difficulty in concealing behind the façade of his elegant and impeccable manners.

He wrote his first letter in quavering pencil to Novello. 'Do remember to make a little fuss of me when we are together again. I've really had a baddish time. I can't write with any command of my ideas.' He was the victim, he said, of uraemia. 'It seems the opposite number of diabetes, with salt the enemy instead of sugar.' In spite of the heat, the damnable noise, and the flies, he was chiefly concerned for his niece. 'It's so infernally dull for her, poor child, and I've *never* known such sweetness.' He described himself as feeling on the *minus* side of everything—'everything just fails of having a *tang*', and now he must stop because a reporter from a London newspaper had just walked in.[1] This led to two or three wholly unexpected and unwarranted communications of the Poison Pen variety. One ill-wisher in Hammersmith wrote merely for the sake of calling him 'an effeminate fop with an undue fondness for publicity'—which contributed an interval of light relief to the otherwise unbroken tedium of hungry convalescence.

On September 11 Nancy Maurice, who had undoubtedly saved his life and sanity, took him by air to Nice and for two nights to stay with the Spears' at Villefranche. On arrival in London they were met by Mrs. Raymond Asquith, who drove them to Gray's Inn. Mrs. Elgy was weeping and wringing her hands for joy. Novello called after the theatre and stayed until 2 A.M. Next day he sent Marsh and Nancy down to Redroofs in his car and himself followed by train. There the patient snoozed or read Johnson's *Lives of the Poets* until the 27th, when Mrs. Churchill called and drove him to Chartwell. The Chancellor was on his way down from Balmoral and arrived next day. Eddie Marsh

[1] 'London Clubman Lost in Maquis' was the ensuing headline.

wrote in his engagement-book: 'With Clemmie and Winston. If only there were a God I could thank for those who love me.'

There had been a series of crises over the production of Novello's new play, and for a time it looked as if the venture would collapse. This was no slight matter, for the actor-playwright was still his own manager and he had practically no reserves to fall back on. 'Yesterday I was much *unhappier* than at any moment in Corsica,' Marsh wrote to him from Chartwell. 'My only comfort was when I thought of making a list of pictures I could sell, to help if you were forced into cutting your loss. I didn't really get to sleep till 2, and woke up this morning feeling tired and depressed.' But the problems were solved in time and Mrs. Churchill drove her convalescent back to London for the first night of *The Truth Game*, where he sat between Marie Tempest and Lily Elsie. The old life was beginning again, but he was very weak, and would feel unsure of himself when parted from his niece. He was picking up the threads of his literary life. Ronald Storrs, writing from Cyprus where he was now installed as Governor, hastened the process. 'Will you, resuming your intellectual dictatorship over me, tell me what to read?' In the previous May Edmund Gosse had died, and Marsh was collecting his papers and reminiscences for Evan Charteris, who had undertaken the biography, when an invitation from Lord Lloyd gave him the opportunity of completing his convalescence in Cairo. Having sold a valuable edition of *The Faerie Queene* to pay for his ticket, he left England on the last day of the year. But first he gathered together his latest revisions of the Fables and delivered them to the publisher by hand. If anything should go amiss again on his travels, those at least would be safe.

vi

While staying at the Residency in Cairo he recovered the full vigour of his extraordinary health. He played poker with the Aga Khan, who was no less excited by his fortunes in the game for having consented to a sixpenny limit, visited Luxor where Howard Carter showed him the tomb of Tutankhamen, and enjoyed the shock when an Arab footman in scarlet and gold advanced across the lawn with a summons to the telephone— 'Jerusalem wants Mr. Marsh.' Startled, he turned to his host with 'I feel like Habbakuk at *least*.' Mrs. George Keppel, who was his fellow-guest, pleased him with an anecdote which he passed on to Novello. A friend of hers had her portrait painted by Picasso in Spain and set off to take it to Paris. 'At the frontier she was told she couldn't go on, and on her asking indignantly why not, was answered, "How can we let you go to France when you've got a plan of the fortifications of Madrid in your luggage?"'

On his return in February (1929) he started work on the proofs of H. S. Ede's *Savage Messiah*, the study of Gaudier-Brzeska much admired by T. E. Lawrence who was often at Gray's Inn at this time. A meeting between Colonel Lawrence and Charles Morgan at one of Mrs. Elgy's luncheons provided material for another letter to Novello, which opened with news that he had made a new friend, Alan Pryce-Jones, who had recently accompanied him to a theatre.

> He told me he was going to an Ice Carnival got up by his great-aunt, so I asked him if he liked skating, and he said no, he hated it to such an extent that whenever anything unpleasant happened to him he was able to console himself by reflecting how much worse it would be if he were also skating. This was the obverse of what I remember the great philosopher Bertrand Russell once telling me, that he couldn't imagine himself in such a painful position that the un-expected gift of a chocolate-cream would not be to some extent an alleviation.
>
> I had a very good luncheon-party here yesterday. Colonel Lawrence and the Charles Morgans. Mrs. Morgan told us that Osbert Sitwell once came to tea with her, and she injudiciously had her little boy aged 2 brought down. The baby fell instantly in love with Osbert and gazed at him with such fixity as to prevent all conversation for 10 minutes, at the end of which it was sick from sheer adoration. Lawrence said, 'Oh how I wish I could express my feelings by being sick at will—I'd go straight to the Home Office and have an interview with Jix [Joynson-Hicks]!'

Marsh had given Lawrence a copy of the limited edition of *Lady Chatterley's Lover*, which he had been unable to get through himself. 'Surely the sex business isn't worth all this damned fuss?' Lawrence wrote. 'I've met only a handful of people who care a biscuit for it', and in return offered him a private view of his R.A.F. book *The Mint*, which was going the rounds in manuscript. When Marsh at last received it from Maurice Baring he found it in one respect similar to the controversial novel. 'Just as in reading

Lady C.,' he remarked, 'I was battered and oppressed by the monotonous thudding hailstorm of *gros mots*.'

In June occurred the general election which brought the Labour Party back into power. On the day of the poll he was at Wembley Studios watching Novello make his first 'talkie' in *The Return of the Rat*, then he attended the election party given by Gordon Selfridge. At a crucial moment, when a new announcement of results was expected, the tension was eased by Mrs. Patrick Campbell descending upon him with 'Isn't it awful this rabble shouting in the streets? do tell me which is winning, Oxford or Cambridge?' J. H. Thomas, who became Lord Privy Seal and Minister of Employment, took back the Private Secretary who might otherwise have been left in the air. The accommodation of the new office at the Treasury was a come-down. When Marsh and his new Chief entered it for the first time together, 'What a bloody hawful 'ole,' said J.H., 'more Privy than Seal about it.' Marsh echoed the sentiment, and sent his comments to Novello. 'All the days following the election I was saying to myself " My Country, oh my Country!" ' Now since I've been back with J.H. I've been feeling quite calm and certain everything will be all right. I can't make up my mind whether this is a sign of deplorable levity or of admirable philosophic adaptability.'

The new appointment brought him an unusual amount of publicity, and he was disconcerted by the descriptions of himself. 'As for my "impassive face" I always thought the expressions chased each other over it like shadows over a field of barley.' In a good character-study headed 'The Man behind Mr. Churchill' the anonymous author began by describing a dream in which Marsh applied for entry into heaven. He was promptly recognized by St. Peter, who urged him to accept a post as his Secretary. 'Why, that is very kind of you,' Mr. Marsh replied. 'But you must understand that I am to be absolutely free when Winston comes up here to take over control.'[1] It was almost twenty-five years since he had begun his association with Mr. Churchill. He would have been less easily reconciled to this new separation had he realized that they would never again be in office together. For someone with a real understanding of Mr. Churchill's qualities it was not easy in these years to combat the lingering prejudice against him which was to keep him out of office for so long. In March a

[1] *Evening Standard*, June 15, 1929.

literary review by Arthur Ponsonby had given Marsh the impression that Mr. Churchill was being accused of a 'lust for war'. His vigorous protest drew a reply from Ponsonby (March 11) which serves to illustrate the mixed feelings of respect and mistrust which Marsh was constantly having to oppose. Ponsonby explained:

> That a war atmosphere gives him opportunities for exercising his great talents and that he naturally enjoys such opportunities is generally admitted. That he would miss something in the absolute elimination of all such possibilities of threatened or possible conflict is obvious enough. . . . I referred to his 'eloquent indictment' of modern warfare, and I quite admit that with his literary talent and imagination he has done this better than it has been done before. Sam Hoare has not done it badly in the House before now, Baldwin's platitudes on the subject pass muster and even Austen Chamberlain occasionally squeezes out a phrase on the subject. But quite frankly all this makes me rather impatient. Denunciations of war, however eloquent, coming from the leaders of one of the most powerful Governments of modern times speaking for a nation which still has a leading position in the world, ring false and appear as pure hypocrisy. . . . I have been criticized for having buttered up Churchill too much. I have a great admiration for him. He is so far and away the most talented man in political life besides being charming and a 'gentleman' (a rarish bird in these days). But this does not prevent me from feeling politically that he is a great danger, largely because of his love of crises and faulty judgement. He once said to me years ago, 'I like things to happen, and if they don't happen I like to make them happen.'

T. E. Lawrence wrote to commiserate on the parting from Mr Churchill. 'For himself I'm glad. He's a good fighter, and will do better out than in, and will come back in a stronger position than before. I want him to be P.M. somehow.' Marsh shared the hope, but believed the chances were forlorn. When Lawrence reverted to *Lady Chatterley* (which he was later to re-read in a more sympathetic spirit) he was the first of Marsh's correspondents to mention *The Testament of Beauty*. On putting down the novel he had felt depressed that anyone should have gone through life 'and found that it means no more than that in the end. Old Bridges, now, has just finished his longest poem, a philosophic poem, and is happy.' Bridges himself wrote on November 20, glad to report that both the original editions were 'cleaned out on the first day'

> The boom has been useful if not altogether healthy, and the forced utterances of the startled critics (which as Milford supplies them to me in press-cuttings I paste chronologically in an old disused diary) are making a rich pie. I wonder whether if you have read it, whether you felt the poem to justify the versification which alone made it possible. It is certainly not as good as the Grk hexameter proper; but it has the advantage of admitting every possible speech rhythm, and, as far as I see, all manner of diction and subject-matter without bombast or bathos.

Bridges must have been rather perplexed that he had so far heard nothing from his old friend and admirer. By an oversight Marsh's letter was posted late.

> I wonder how many people spent Sunday reading your great poem and blessing your name as I did. . . . I haven't yet tackled Book IV and I don't pretend to have grasped your thought as a whole! but what I am sure of is that no more glorious poetry than this has appeared in my memory. I was overwhelmed by the beauty of many passages.
>
> I think your metre is a wonderful invention for your purpose and 'comes off' almost completely. I believe you mean us to read straight ahead without bothering minutely about the scansion, and I often succeed in doing this. Still, the knowledge that there *are* twelve syllables in each line will sometimes obtrude itself and set one counting too curiously and crabbedly, and then I thought I found an occasional line which called for too much *ménagement*. But there is only one general consideration that I want to put before you. Unless I am mistaken, you do not admit double endings; and all the lines which seem to have them are really to be accounted for by a final trochee instead of the usual iambus. I would rather be allowed to take them at their face value, as an agreeable variation, without the uncomfortable consciousness that their true character is something else. But you know best!

On October 24 Lord Sandwich opened an exhibition of the Marsh collection in Whitechapel: 270 pictures were hung, fetched from every nook and cranny of Raymond Buildings. 'I feel stark naked,' Marsh exclaimed as he gazed round the plundered walls of his rooms. 'Do you good for a change,' said Mrs. Elgy. 'I never saw such a lot of clobber as was took away.' He had relatively few dealings with painters this year, but a remark to Stanley Spencer, that his landscapes were in such demand that he should produce more for the sake of his livelihood, drew from the painter an interesting confession.

What is good in my landscape is simply an excellence acquired through the continual practice of trying to express my feelings. I feel when my landscapes are admired rather like the young man who when he thinks his girl is admiring his thoughts and ideas and feelings finds that it is the way his hair curls that is the real attraction. I feel very nearly that a lock of my hair would be as *representative* of my work as a landscape. If it were not for the fact that I find it a productive and creative diversion (like reading *Paradise Lost*) I would have to regard it as a prostitution of my work. I think the tree landscape you have of mine has a feeling of leading to something I want in it. I know I was reading old English Ballads at the time and feeling a new and personal value in the Englishness of England.

In July of the following year (1930) Mr. Churchill was sending instructions with his proofs.[1] Marsh was to keep an eye on the following points: '1, Punctuation 2, Grammar and style 3, Longueurs 4, Repetitions of words and phrases 5, John Buchan thought the religious and philosophical disquisition either too long or too short, and out of focus. I do not quite feel this. It is of course intended to be a subaltern's outlook. Let me know what you feel about it after having read the book as a whole. There are about 3,000 more words to come at the end about the "Hooligans" and the first threats of tariff reform, ending up with my marrying and living happily ever after.' A month later he wrote again. The question of hyphens was still unresolved.

I have adopted your punctuation although I had been inclined to let 'and' play the part of a comma as well as itself. I am very startled at your hyphens! Parade-ground, riding-school, thorn-bushes, etc. On these lines you would write party politics with a hyphen. Surely nobody does that. Could you let me know what is the rule about hyphens?

Most of the discussions over these proofs were carried on by word of mouth and have no record. A brief entry in the engagement book on a day in March is the sole relic of many meetings. 'My remark to Clemmie as we sat waiting for Winston in the

[1] *My Early Life.*

motor—that he is such a sportsman, he always gives the train a chance of getting away.'

Throughout these years Eddie Marsh had never relaxed his efforts on behalf of Brooke. While at Villefranche after his misadventure he jotted notes for a new edition of the Collected Poems. At the beginning of this year he presented the original drawing for the Rugby medallion to the National Portrait Gallery and persuaded Stanley Baldwin to support a public appeal to raise money for a monument on Skyros. This venture was initiated by a Belgian poet of admirable intentions who wrote round to everyone on specially printed writing-paper of startling pretentiousness. He won the support of Gide, Maurois, and Valéry in France, and used Marsh as the spokesman of his campaign in England. There were many who thought the grave should have been left in its im-provised state, as it was last seen by Browne and his friends in 1915, but already a conventional stone had replaced the loose rocks, and now a Greek sculptor was making a statue of Youth for erection elsewhere in the island. On being sent a photograph of the completed figure Frances Cornford wrote, 'I dare say I ought to think about the compliment to English Poetry and not that it looks like an advertisement for Elliman's embrocation.' Marsh had no alternative but to support this generous but inessential enterprise which culminated a year later when a cruise was organized for the unveiling, and Abercrombie and his wife sailed as representing Brooke's countrymen. Another memorial venture this year, the aim of which was to have the church clock at Grantchester set permanently at ten-to-three, failed altogether to win his support.

It was in connection with one of these projects that Mrs. Brooke wrote in July 1930, having again got the impression that she was being left out: 'I must have misunderstood the paragraph. I thought it meant for the future I was going to be omitted altogether. . . . I suppose in my old age I'm getting touchy', and she ended, 'With apologies and many thanks for all you have done for my boy.' On October 14 the papers announced that Mrs. Brooke had died, leaving property valued at just under £23,000. On the 20th Dudley Ward telephoned Gray's Inn in order to read aloud the terms of the Will concerning her son. He had taken for granted that Marsh's position would be unaffected, so that it was not until he had incredulously read the passage a second time that both learned simultaneously of Mrs. Brooke's Parthian shot. The functions of literary executor were transferred into the hands of four trustees of whom Marsh was not one. The manuscripts which Brooke had given him, now chronologically arranged and bound, and which, as Mrs. Brooke knew, he had long since decided to bequeath to King's, were referred to by her as being her property, her Will permitting him to keep them for his life-time in trust for King's.

On getting confirmation of Mrs. Brooke's wishes from her solicitor in Rugby, who offered to send him the manuscripts at once (they had been in her house when she died), he replied refusing the 'gift' together with the strings attached to it, and gave instructions for the volume to be deposited at King's, because, as he wrote, 'she has now deprived me of the pleasure and pride I should have had in making such a bequest'. He could no longer put the documents to any use without deferring to others, and they would only be 'a constant reminder of the disagreeable way in which Mrs. Brooke has seen fit to treat me. . . . I trouble you with this long explanation of my motives because I wish to have it on record that if I decline the bequest it is from no loss of regard for my friend's memory, or lessened appreciation of his wishes for me, had they been respected. I may add that I feel sure my decision would have been gratifying to Mrs. Brooke and would, in the circumstances, be approved by her son.'

Beyond this he made no comment. 'I could not have believed this possible,' wrote Abercrombie. 'It is a monstrous piece of ingratitude and injustice and from every practical point of view perfectly insane. . . . I know how cruelly you must feel it and I think that as one of Rupert's friends I have the right to resent this bitterly.' St. John Lucas confessed that his own dealings with her had 'removed my few last sad grey hairs and bruised my shrinking soul for ever. I don't know why she disliked me with such glorious fervour; I suppose that really she was jealous of all his friends. But that she should rend you, of all people, post-humously, is sickening beyond a Frenchman's dreams of the Channel.' Fortunately Marsh was of the opinion that she could not have done better in her choice of trustees had he been asked to nominate them himself, but for years he had let himself believe that all trace of the old rancour was dispelled from her mind. On October 28 Dudley Ward wrote on behalf of his colleagues, saying that while they could not alter the legal situation, of course, they looked on Marsh as morally Brooke's executor and hoped that he would continue to regard himself in that light. And so it was, until November 1934 when, tired of his anomalous position, Marsh formally handed over the direction of the poet's affairs to Mrs. Brooke's nominees. He was well content in the knowledge that his work for Rupert Brooke was already accomplished.

vii

The early autumn of 1931 saw the grave financial crisis in which J. H. Thomas won Marsh's admiration by courageously sticking to his principles in the face of criticism from a great many of his associates and allies. Mr. Churchill's letter from Biarritz on August 7, introducing the first rumour of these troubles into Marsh's correspondence, acknowledged a sheaf of critical notes.

> It is astonishing what obvious points one misses when one's eye and mind are stale upon a proof. I am relieved that you take a favourable view of the book. Thank God it is finished. I am longing to get on to Marlborough, and am most interested to hear what you think about the two jumble chapters in which I broke into the subject. I am deeply indebted to you once again for helping me with my proofs. No one is your equal. . . . I am tired of painting low tone pictures (No sun—at Biarritz). Everybody I meet seems vaguely alarmed that something terrible is going to happen financially. I hope we shall hang Montagu Norman if it does. I will certainly turn King's evidence against him.

By September 2, when Mr. Churchill wrote again, events had happened quickly. 'What an extraordinary transformation of the political scene! I am glad I am not to be responsible for it.' Writing to Novello from Haddon Hall on the 16th, Marsh explained the situation in simple terms and gave his own view of it. 'I don't understand it myself,' he began.

> You know that on Sat. Aug. 24 there was only what is known as a few hours between us and national bankruptcy, because for a long time foreign creditors had suspected that we were 'living beyond our means'; then about the end of July the May (Sir George, not the month!) Report of the Economy Committee was published, saying that before next Budget we should be about 100 millions short, and this started a run on the Bank of England which got worse and worse, till in another minute the value of the Pound would have

fallen to God knows what, and we should have gone as Germany and Austria did after the war, when it took millions of marks to buy a box of matches. The Govt had called in the other two parties and concocted an agreed scheme of economies, which was accepted by a majority of the Cabinet; but when it was explained to the Trade Unions they wouldn't hear of it, and the whole Cabinet, except Ramsay, Snowden, and J.H., got the wind up and said they would resign. On that Saturday I went down to stay with Gerald Berners, thinking I might as well have one last week-end in comfort and meditating how I could contrive to live on Pulse, whatever that may be. On the Monday (no, I think Sunday) Ramsay went to see the King and resign, but H.M. (who has come out very strong all through) said no, he must try to form a National Govt., which he did—with the other two sensible and patriotic Labour Ministers, Baldwin for the Tories, and H. Samuel for the Liberals—a small Cabinet of ten. They had got to work when I left London on the following Saturday, and have now passed through Parlt this gigantic new Budget, which is generally accepted as more or less fair all round, makes us solvent for the time being, and has commanded the admiration of the world.

Now comes the next question, how to redress the Balance of Trade, i.e. pay for our imports by our exports, which we have ceased to do. Almost everyone has now come round to a Tariff— only yesterday, in the House, both John Simon and Winston, who used to be convinced Free Traders, declared in favour of Protection, and so far as I understand the situation the present issue is whether this should be done with or without a general election . . . an election would probably be a fatal disturbance to the business of getting things straight. Winston for one pronounced very strongly and weightily last night that the present Govt must carry on, and I'm sure this is right, though I can't see how either Snowden or Samuel could come round to a Tariff. I hope all this is sufficiently correct and not too boring. . . .

The increase in Income Tax is a very serious matter for some people. For instance, I arrived at Henry Bentinck's (my last visit before I came here) on the day the Budget was published. Lady Henry was telephoning to 150 people cancelling a dance she was to have given on Tuesday, and they were getting rid of 2 foresters and 2 gardeners. . . . Talking of dismissing servants, Lady S. who lunched here yesterday, told us she was discharging her 2nd footman —but I had already heard the fuller version, which was that she announced this as her economy at the very moment when this same 2nd footman was bringing her a cup of tea.

Marsh had begun his holiday with the Carlisles at Naworth,

then spent a week at Esthwaite Lake with Francis and Jessica Brett Young, who were now in the circle of his closest friends, and had listened to Brett Young reading aloud from the unfinished manuscript of *Mr. and Mrs. Pennington*. Before joining Hugh Walpole at Derwentwater, he spent some days at Holker with Lord Richard Cavendish and was fetched by Walpole's valet-chauffeur, who apparently came upon the family in informal dress. Walpole could not resist repeating his valet's impressions. 'A great big house with fifty rooms and all the footmen standing about in livery—but the family! I never saw anything so shabby. The old man with his elbows sticking out of his sleeves and the boy with his chest all bare. I suppose they think that as they're great folks it's grand to go about looking like that, but if I saw *you* in such a dirty shirt *I* should have something to say about it!' From the Lakes to the Bentincks at Underley, then to the Rutlands at Haddon Hall, ending with a week at Chatsworth. With slight variations, including visits to Clovelly, Bowood, and Stanway, this was to be the pattern of his annual holidays in the 'thirties. This autumn mah-jong went out as an after-dinner pastime and was replaced by 6-pack bézique, which was never supplanted in Marsh's favour and over the years was to cause a ceaseless fluctuation of his small cash.

Brett Young received an account of the visit to Walpole. 'I liked him very much, and shall never laugh at him again, at least I hope not. Hugh was so busy writing that I only saw him at meals (including after dinner) and a walk after luncheon. . . . He's three-quarters through *The Fortress* and delighting in it.' Brett Young was soon able to report progress on his novel of middle-class life. So deep in it was he that he could 'even smell that awful kind of cooking mixed with linoleum'. Meanwhile the manuscripts of two plays had come from Novello in America, and one of them, *I Lived With You*, seemed to be a comedy at last worthy of his gifts. Novello was asking which play would best serve him for his return to the West End. Marsh had no doubts. 'For the first time a work of art as distinguished from an entertainment! (not that it isn't entertaining—it made me burst with laughing). You have a real subject and you stick to it; the dialogue is unfalteringly amusing and natural without the half-baked passages which you would sometimes let pass, and without any of the irrelevancies which you used to infuriate me with by bringing

them in for a laugh or an effect without regard for keeping.' With
this note of December went the two volumes of La Fontaine
bound in vellum which had come out in a limited edition at eight
guineas the month before. Gooden had completed the last
engraving in March. No copies were sent for review, but Marsh
was relieved to have the hundred and fifty new *Fables* safely added
to the previous ninety which were already in print. He had to wait
two years before the appearance of the first unlimited issue and
the judgement of critical opinion. 'I would like to be among the
great translators after my death,' he remarked to D'Arcy Cresswell,
the young writer from New Zealand whose *Poet's Progress* had
struck him as showing high promise. He was introducing Cresswell
to literary London and as a companion was finding refreshment
in his forthright and unconventional cast of mind.

Early in 1932 the appearance of Morgan's *The Fountain* seemed
to confirm Eddie Marsh's hopes for the English novel. 'It is sure
to live on the lips and in the hearts of men if anything of our time
survives,' he wrote to Charles Morgan. 'Many have praised you
well, but I haven't seen anyone single out the character of the
Baron, which is surely a masterpiece, seldom is a minor personage
shown so much in the round. . . . And so many satirists have spent
pages on what you put in a sentence—"How cleverly the Baroness,
in her attempt to preserve her youth, had preserved everything
but youth itself." ' He took pleasure in Morgan's reply—'I hope
that I'm only at the beginning of things. Anyhow I feel like an
apprentice just beginning, rather excitingly, to start in his craft.
. . . I must learn not to fall in love with words—though I hope I
shall always love them. And I must digest Stendhal—the right
corrective of my faults, I'm sure.' *The Fountain* was passed on to
Brett Young, and added to his recommendation was a new story
which the King was telling at Sandringham.

One of the tenants lost her husband and told the clergyman who
came to condole that standing in her porch she had seen the deceased
walking towards her down the garden path, just as when he was
alive. 'What do you think it can mean?' she asked. The clergyman
was nonplussed and asked what *she* thought it meant. Answer—'I
think it means we shall have rain.' The King tells everyone.

After the provincial opening on March 23 of *I Lived With
You* had proved as successful as Marsh foretold, he suddenly

developed pneumonia and within a few days the newspapers were reporting him on the danger list. Mrs. Elgy was cooking for two nurses at Gray's Inn. His recovery was equally sudden. At Redroofs he convalesced, tried his hand at writing a chapter of his reminiscences, and was touched to hear from J. M. Barrie, who had shared the general anxiety and, making himself the spokesman of English letters, conveyed his sympathy:

> The occasion prompts me to say what I often wanted to say to you, though we have never seen much of each other, that there are few men of letters who in our time have so abundantly earned the affections of our calling. One can trace your helping hand here there everywhere, you never seem to give a thought to self when there are others whom you can encourage along the way. So many know this, and I just want you to understand that I learned it also and have long had a deep regard for you.

And a letter from Chartwell of April 2 extended an invitation which he hastened to accept.

> MY DEAR EDDIE,
>
> I was much concerned to read in a press cutting which coupled our names of your illness, and now there is your letter to Mrs. Pearman. Randolph tells me that you are recovering alright, but that you had to have two nurses. I am indeed sorry for this calamity and wish I had known about it before.
>
> We shall be down here a great deal now and if you like to come and pay us a visit, pray let us know. You could rest comfortably here. Clemmie says you *must* come. Just vegetate—as I do.
>
> Love from
W.

At Chartwell he had a first glimpse of some manuscript pages of the Life of Marlborough, and while resting in the sun wrote a preface to a forthcoming volume of comedies by Novello, who was shortly to have two plays running in London concurrently. Mr. Churchill had been making a selection of his miscellaneous articles of the last ten years. 'I should like you to let me know which parts you think the best and which the worst,' he had written, 'whether you can improve the order . . . whether any are not good enough to be included; whether there are any repetitions (my eye is jaded) and generally your impression of the whole.' In August Mr. Churchill undertook a volume to be called 'Great Stories of the World Retold', and wrote asking Marsh what six he would recommend. At present Mr. Churchill was favouring *Monte Cristo, The Moonstone, She, Ben Hur, Thais, Uncle Tom's Cabin.* 'I have always liked *A Tale of Two Cities*,' he observed, 'and *Faust* is a fine tale to tell.' Marsh was invited to make a *précis* of each plot as a foundation for Mr. Churchill's reconstruction of the story. This was to prove a more elaborate undertaking than at first appeared. He was also being active these days as a critic behind the scenes, watching the work in progress of Walpole, Brett Young, Morgan, David Cecil, Sackville-West, Nicolson, MacCarthy, and Blunden, and in April he sent a message through Derek Patmore to Richard Aldington in Italy. 'Do give Richard my love, also, if you think fit, a modest request that he won't slog quite so hard and, I think, *indiscriminately* at his rotters. To be really disgusted with them it is essential one should believe in their existence, which one can't do if he plasters them with *incompatible* defects.'

In September it was Mr. Churchill whose health was causing anxiety as a result of a motor accident, and on October 2 Marsh called on him in his nursing-home and noted in his diary: 'Found W. cheerful but he had lost 2/3rds of his blood—talked about his books—I am to see *Thoughts and Adventures* through the Press.' Copy was so urgently needed by the publisher that Marsh had to write the short Preface himself. 'Rather a good pastiche!' he scribbled on his copy of the typescript. The opening paragraph was certainly Churchillian in style, and it covered in lightning review much of the history which Marsh had witnessed while in the service of his Chief.[1]

At the Arts Theatre this month Marsh sat with Bernard Shaw at a performance of *Space Time Inn*. 'The best thing since Shakespeare,' Shaw remarked lugubriously at the end. 'Not a good play,' Marsh noted in his diary, 'but it didn't interfere with the acting',

---

[1] 'The reading of my proofs has brought home to me with even more than usual clearness the extreme diversity of event and atmosphere through which a man of my generation, now in its twelfth lustre, has passed and is passing. First the "settled state of order", as we now see it bright and diminished in the *camera obscura* of memory, full of colour and action but on so small a scale that such a trifle as Sidney Street stood out as a peak of adventure and sensation: then the incomparable tragedy of the war: now confusion, uncertainty and peril, the powers of light and darkness perhaps in counterpoise, with Satan and Michael doubtfully reviewing their battalions, and the world, for all we can tell, heading for the crossroads which may lead to the two alternative Infernos I have tried to adumbrate in *Shall We All Commit Suicide?* and *Fifty Years Hence*: has there ever been an epoch of such pith and moment?'

which was in keeping with his dictum that he would rather see the worst play in the world than no play at all. At Redroofs for Christmas Novello read aloud to him his latest play *Pastures New*, which, under the title of *Fresh Fields*, was to prove the most successful of his comedies. Marsh's holiday task was the condensation of *Jane Eyre* and *Adam Bede* for the assistance of Mr. Churchill, and La Fontaine was still on his mind.

The appearance of the Fables between vellum covers had done nothing to bring to an end the process of revision. Not until April 21 of the new year (1933) did he have to admit at last that he could do no more, and the ordinary edition went to press, not a day too soon, for he was about to start work on the proofs of Churchill's *Marlborough*, a task which as the instalments came in was to keep him busy over the next three years. The letter from Chartwell which accompanied the first batch was dated May 16.

I now send you twenty-seven of the twenty-nine or thirty chapters of the first volume of Marlborough. The other three are of general character and require particular revision. But these form a complete narrative and have already undergone two or three revisions. I shall be very grateful if you will read them for me. The points I want you particularly to mark are:—

1. Clumsy sentences where the meaning is obscure or the grammar questionable.

2. Repetitions of words. I have a good many favourites and they may crop up too often, e.g., vast, bleak, immense, formidable, etc.

3. Repetitions of phrase, e.g. where we talk of Marlborough as a great, wise, profound, imperturbable statesman, etc. in several variants.

4. Repetitions of arguments. These seem to be threatened most in the argument against Jacobite papers and in the vindication, perhaps rather laboured, of Marlborough's desertion of James in 1688. My eye is blunted by much re-reading. Do not be particularly on the lookout, but just see if anything strikes you as being repeated.

5. Dull, boring, stodgy passages. You are almost the first person who will have read this book straight off. You might ask yourself the question 'Which ten thousand words would I cut?' (we have plenty of words in hand), and just mark the slips affected with a pencil of separate colour.

6. Cheap, vulgar, undignified references. I hope you will not find

any. My mature view of style is that it should follow the thought and also that I belong to the modern age and write with their knowledge and modes.

7. Hyphens. I see Macaulay writes 'hotheaded' in one word. I am sure we ought not to have too many hyphens.

Capitals, and punctuation throughout. On this I send the publisher's standing instructions. They do not bind us but we must follow some rule. I like 'régime' printed in Roman and not in italics, and this has always been your view. I agree with the standing instructions in most other points. You need not bother about the footnotes unless you notice anything wrong. They will all be checked again by Ashley who is responsible for their accuracy. You need not concern yourself at all with the accuracy of the work on the whole, but of course if you notice anything which you think is wrong, mark it, also any suggestions to improve would be welcome. But we have taken great pains.

8. I hope you will be able to read this continuously and rapidly. I want to get the reaction of your mind on the ensemble, and whether you miss anything or feel upset about anything in the general structure.

I shall be greatly indebted to you if you will do this for me and I dearly hope it will make a tolerable impression on you. Of course the great period is still to come. I may add that the introduction is incomplete and inadequate. Probably two-thousand more words will be required and these will range over the whole field of Marlborough's life.

Marsh was in his element. On May 21 he wrote in his engagement book, 'Stayed at home all day and worked nearly eleven hours on W.'s M. which was thrilling.' By the 27th he had despatched his first sheaf of notes. 'I am hard at work on your corrections,' wrote Mr. Churchill on that day, 'and I find them invaluable. I told Ashley that it was an education in itself to read a proof corrected by you.' He enclosed an extract from Goslinga's *Memoires* 'which I would like you to translate for me straight away into good readable English'. Marsh was still at work on these chapters when Desmond MacCarthy sent him the manuscript of his book *Experience*. 'Dig up the plantains on its lawns, lop off the withered flowers. . . . My own mind slips along at a nervous and imperceptible speed when I attempt to re-read them. . . . Perhaps, if this letter reaches you, you will answer my imploring, unpardonable, urgent request.' Within a few weeks he was declaring himself 'delighted with the way you have increased in some instances the precision, in others the euphony, of a sentence'. Somehow Marsh found time to start a series of articles on the London theatre for *Harper's Bazaar* and to draft a few anecdotes for inclusion in Novello's autobiography, which a newspaper was shortly to publish in instalments. The irresponsible youth of 1915 had matured into an artist of strenuous industry and almost legendary fame, but while acting in the silent films and cultivating the art of the dramatist he had been neglecting his primary gift for music. Marsh was anxious that he should return to it now that he seemed to have mastered the craft of a popular playwright, but Novello was aged forty-one, no longer the novice who was glad to be set exercises in composition. It was almost symbolic in Marsh's eyes when on the stage of the Globe Theatre this August he enjoyed the privilege of presenting his friend to the Queen of Rumania and the King of Greece. This autumn another of his friends had cause to celebrate. When Lady Desborough organized a presentation and a 'signed letter' to Mr. and Mrs. Churchill on the twenty-fifth anniversary of their wedding she invited Eddie Marsh to compose the message. 'You are not among those who are happy in having no history,' he wrote; 'but from all the vicissitudes of your two distinguished lives, in which Fortune has shown you both her faces, you have emerged with unshaken dignity and courage "breathing united force with fixed thought" and have given your countrymen an illustration of faith and happiness in marriage.' Then in November appeared *The Fables of Jean de la Fontaine*.

'It is Mr. Marsh's gaiety which gives him so long a start in translating La Fontaine,' wrote the critic of *The Times*. He only regretted certain instances of excessive colloquialism. 'May bears "swat" flies, even when they are most anxious not to talk eighteenth-century?' In his Preface Marsh had prepared the reader for this kind of shock as well as for his English equivalents —Surbiton for *Vaugirard*, Aberdeen for *Le Mans*, Colney Hatch for *Petites-Maisons*, etc.—by stating that when in doubt his plan had been 'to substitute English and even modern equivalents if I saw a gain in clearness, or in liveliness—the quality which La Fontaine speaks of as his own contribution to Fable'. The same critic not only maintained that the translator had risen to the occasion of the more tender and elevated Fables (such as *Les Deux Pigeons*, which was everywhere regarded as the test piece), but argued that in places the English language had made possible a neater and simpler phrase than the original, such as *Aucun chemin de fleurs ne conduit à la gloire* ('There is no primrose path which leads to glory') or the last line of *The Miller, his Son, and the Ass—Les gens en parleront, n'en doutez nullement* ('There's only one thing certain—folks will talk!'). Desmond MacCarthy noted the translator's wide range of vocabulary, variety of rhythm, and truth to the spirit of the original author who 'enchanted by an exquisite artful simplicity—his naivety was indistinguishable from finesse'. John Hayward drew attention to the French poet's felicitous use of 'archaisms and slang too difficult for the average English reader' and showed how the English version faithfully preserved this variety of diction in an intelligible form; and like all his colleagues he had taken pleasure in the notes, which were sometimes confined to a point of pure scholarship, sometimes to an 'aside' which the translator was unable to resist, such as, 'It is provoking that the English mealtime verbs—lunch, dine, sup—will all rhyme with drinkables—punch, wine, cup—but none really well with any eatable that I can think of.' Other important appreciations by L. P. Hartley and Richard Church were in agreement that La Fontaine's qualities as set out in the translator's Preface—'his unpretentious manner, his dislike of rhetoric and formality, and, above all, his pervasive humour (often so much akin to Chaucer's)' —had all been reproduced with extraordinary perception and liveliness. They might have gone on to discuss the elegance of the versification as shown in *Daphnis and Alcimadura*, for instance, an eclogue of peculiar grace, or noted the delicacy of the translator's ear which led him so often to devise a phrase or period as smoothly turned as the minor poetry of the eighteenth century at its best— 'One poppy-breathing night when all was sleep . . .'

> Leading her maidens that same eve she trod
> A measure round His image in the glade.

To counter any impression that he was embittered by the events of 1930, or had abandoned an old loyalty, the volume was dedicated to the memory of Rupert Brooke. The modest editor of *Georgian Poetry* found himself promoted to the status of a classic author in the sphere of translation.

Chapter Eighteen

HORACE
(January 1934–May 1941)

UCH as he enjoyed acting as midwife to spirits more creative than himself, facing the world as an author in his own right had its effect upon him. He was never moved by anything so professional as a desire for fame, and such was his nature he would always have found more gratifying pleasure in helping someone else to the composition of a good book than in writing one himself—even now his main satisfaction lay in the knowledge that he had been of service to La Fontaine—but there is no doubt he had grown a little tired of sitting by while other versifiers luxuriated in their gift of language. Translation was the ideal field for his exercise. He would always be modest almost to the point of self-extinction, but now, through being able to operate in the shadow of a greater man, something deep in him was boosted with confidence and reassured. When Brett Young offered to dedicate his new novel to him as being the figure-head of the Georgians he was glad of the compliment, but in two minds. 'My only slight doubt,' he wrote, 'is whether Georgian Poetry isn't too ancient history to be raked up. I feel towards it now very much as I should towards having been Captain of Cricket at Westminster.'

All his life he had relied on a diminutive form of engagement book which could fit neatly into his waistcoat pocket on the side opposite his watch, but for the next six years he used a volume as impressive in bulk as a Victorian novel. Glad to be able to spread himself for a change, he opened his diary for 1934 with various quotations. One was from a letter of Sidney Smith's to Lady Holland—'As long as I can possibly avoid it I will never be unhappy.' A longer passage from the same source began: 'Let me warn you against the unlucky effects of temperance. You will do me the justice to remember how often I have entered my protest against it. Depend upon it, the wretchedness of human life

is only to be encountered upon the basis of meat and wine.'
Another sentence was from one of John, Duke of Marlborough's
letters to his wife—'I am of the humour not to believe the
hundredth part of what is said of anybody, so that I may be easily
imposed upon', and Marsh added below this a remark made by
Anna Seward in 1805, about the critics who had attacked Walter
Scott for his latest poems—'Owls love to make a noonday
darkness.'

The new year had hardly begun when a letter to *The Times*
from Bernard Shaw defending the B.B.C. Advisory Committee on
pronunciation which had come in for some criticism led Marsh to
launch an attack on Shaw of a ferocity which startled his friends.
'His attack on the pronunciation of educated people under the
delightfully assorted epithets "pretentious", "superior", and
"cockney", is a mere base appeal to that "inverted snobbishness"
which is the enemy of distinction. . . . "Decaydent" may be
prettier than "dekkadent" but I have never heard anyone say it,
nor "issolate" except the embarrassed actress on whom he imposed
it in *Back to Methusaleh*. . . .' Logan Pearsall Smith joined issue
on behalf of the Committee, so also did St. John Ervine, who
managed to rile Marsh by seeming to regard him as a diehard
traditionalist. This provoked a private letter which began, 'I
protest against your making a cockshy of me as a diehard!' and
went on to argue that his letter against Shaw was, in the main, 'an
attempt to show that in the cases in which he sought to impose his
likes and dislikes, his taste was bad'. St. John Ervine's pacific
reply introduced the question of spelling (which was the logical
development for the next round in the dispute) but Marsh was
not to be drawn, and did little more than express the hope that
he would never live to read, 'We are such *stough* as dreams are
made on.' But meanwhile Shaw had gone so far as to brand Eddie
Marsh as 'a bumptious novice', which pleased him, since it seemed
to indicate that Goliath was roused. He admitted afterwards that
for years he had been awaiting an opportunity of getting his own
back on Shaw, but never until now had the great man made
himself a sitting target. Many years before, in about 1908,
Marsh and Neville Lytton had called on the Shaws in Surrey at
a time when the dramatist had just taken up amateur photo-
graphy. He exhibited his snapshots with pride, and was expatiating
on the merits of his machine when he happened to remark that

the day might soon come when the Camera would supersede the
art of Painting as effectually as the Typewriter had already supplanted Poetry. This was an observation worthy of his genius as
a *provocateur*, since the first clause succeeded in irritating Lytton
and the second annoyed Marsh. In an unguarded moment
Marsh casually put in that he did not think the like of *Paradise
Lost* could ever be written by a typewriter. 'Oh, Milton,' growled
Shaw in disgust, 'that old hombog, that bag of tricks!' It was now
no longer a joke. Marsh was thunderstruck, 'not being of an age',
as he afterwards explained, 'to sit down under blasphemy'. Mrs.
Shaw now tactfully intervened on the poet's behalf. 'Surely,
G.B.S.,' she said, 'some of Milton's *prose* is very good.'

A few weeks after the controversy in *The Times* Marsh was
taking his seat in the theatre at the O'Casey first night of *Within the
Gates* when he discovered that his neighbour was none other than
Shaw. 'Here's the bumptious novice!' he exclaimed, at the very
moment when Shaw was saying the same thing, and in accordance
with the custom whereby the two speakers of identical words link
their little fingers and name a poet, 'Milton!' cried Marsh
defiantly. 'La Fontaine,' said Shaw graciously, and they resumed
their seats.

Late in February a newspaper in Liverpool announced that
Novello had been injured on the thigh by the iron handle which
turned the revolving stage at the local theatre. He was on tour
with his play *Proscenium*, and Marsh, who always followed his
tours in the press-cuttings, was alarmed and took the first opportunity to join him in the provinces. This occurred on March 9 at
Oxford. There was time to visit a private view of Gilbert Spencer's
paintings in London before catching the train. He spent both
intervals in his friend's dressing-room, then was asked to wait up
for a late supper at the Clarendon Hotel, for Novello and some of
his company were going on to an O.U.D.S. 'smoker' concert.
Marsh was aggrieved that he had not been included in the party,
and retired to his bedroom to correct Mr. Churchill's proofs. (He
had heard on February 18 that Mr. Churchill was determined to
write a third volume on Marlborough 'without which I feel I
cannot possibly do justice to the hitherto unpublished documents
and achieve my purpose of making it the standard life'.) When,
near midnight, Novello fetched him down from his room Marsh
was still feeling 'out of it' as well as hungry, and it must

have cost him an effort to put up a show of affability to the young member of the *Proscenium* company who had just been introducing Novello to some of his Oxford friends round the corner and was now brought back to the hotel to meet a 'distinguished Civil Servant' who might be interested to read his poems.

The restaurant was empty at this late hour but for the three or four people at the table where a cold supper was laid. Marsh knew them all but the youngest, a youth of twenty-two, whom he had twice seen on the stage but had never met. This young man (who had first heard of Eddie Marsh a few days before in conversation with Novello) remarked to himself that, compared with the actor-manager of his company, the distinguished Civil Servant looked rather like a Prussian farmer turned statesman. He strode in, dressed in a dinner-jacket, planting his feet with gingerly deliberateness, keeping them close together, not turning out the toes, as if practising some orthopaedic exercise. Being thick-set and broad-shouldered he looked top-heavy, and one wondered how he kept his balance. He had a habit of not lifting his hand for a handshake but of tensely jutting it out from where it hung, only the forearm extended. He gripped one's proffered hand, holding it firmly until he had finished delivering his opening remark, so that one was first pulled into what was almost a collision, then deprived of the means of retreat. His approach to a stranger was eager and flattering, but it was difficult to follow what he was saying. It sounded as though his breath were by-passing his vocal chords, so that the straining ear caught little more than a flow of rapidly articulated air; but the general effect was agreeable, extraordinarily gentle in a fluttering way, which only made it the more tantalizing, since his utterance conveyed all the inflexions of a witty discourse without the substance of a precise meaning. He was at this time sixty-one, but he looked fifty. He was an inch or two under six foot, with fair hair going grey, groomed and brushed flat, thinly covering his head and receding from a broad forehead. His square shoulders looked very strong. Square too was his head. One marked the straight nose, rather thick and assertive, of equal thickness from tip to bridge, thin lips (very tight shut when listening), large brown eyes, and the eyeglass on the end of a black thread, deftly handled to left and right as a 'personal prop', and the eyebrows, which were still brown, swept upward into points at the outmost edges, standing erect, declamatory, the finishing touches to an urbane, patrician, intimidating appearance. In repose he looked severe. Sitting bolt upright, his whole being seemed poised on tip-toe as if awaiting the next moment with critical expectation, confident of epicurean pleasure. He ate a formidable quantity of cold meat, and without ever making a show of drinking was often unobtrusively letting his glass be replenished with red wine. After a somewhat grumbling start he was happy. When coffee arrived he took out his watch and seemed to be making a calculation. Since the Corsican incident his doctor had limited him to one cigarette every forty minutes. This made smoking a conscious ritual which added to its pleasure. Fitting the cigarette thoughtfully into a blunt and insignificant-looking holder he leaned across the table to his host and raised his eyebrows, saying in particularly soft tones, 'Ivor, isn't there any port?'

Marsh spent the following morning in Novello's bedroom trying to help him disentangle his mother's finances. Then he lunched alone with the young man he had met the night before and found that the one topic which struck a spark was eighteenth-century poetry. There was also talk of the need for Novello to get back to his music. The young man was rather irritatingly diffident, and Marsh who liked cards on the table was hard put to it to make much headway; but since Novello had urged him to persevere, for his sake, this he did by asking the youth to dinner at Gray's Inn in a week's time when the company would have reached Hammersmith. That afternoon he left Oxford and went to Bulbridge for the week-end, and next day, mindful of his new acquaintance, entered in his diary, 'Went home and read Thomson's *Winter* to please Chris H. [Hassall].'

On the following Tuesday Marsh's new acquaintance came to Gray's Inn with a small envelope of poems typed by his sister. Sitting at his writing-table after dinner Marsh glanced at the page on the top of the pile. 'Dear boy,' he said, impulsively reaching out to catch his guest by the hand, 'you're a poet.' His curiosity reinforced by Novello's interest, he then put a string of questions, nicely judging how far he could go, drawing back and starting on another tack, or pressing an enquiry, as the other's diffidence or growing assurance came to the fore. By midnight he had learned that his guest was disheartened by unsuccessful efforts to acclimatize himself to the life and work of an actor and was only waiting

for the first opportunity of whatever kind that showed promise
of an alternative means of livelihood; he had literary ambitions,
but of a vague and unmarketable kind, his one dominating
concern being how to live from one week to the next. He told how
for some years his parents had lived in straitened circumstances,
and for that reason he had been obliged to leave Oxford prematurely after studying literature and music, the former with Lord
David Cecil. For two years or so he had scraped a living on the
stage, and was now occupying an attic over a shoe shop in Kensington which cost him 17*s*. 6*d*. a week, sharing it with a young
musician who had proved a good friend. He happened to be the
only member of the *Proscenium* company who was happy at all
hours to talk about music, and this had recently led to a
friendship with Novello, who passed on to him some of his
clothes (a British-warm overcoat, and three shirts of a lurid bottle-
green colour which he had bought in Hollywood and considered
too 'arty' for general use in the provinces) and whenever possible
gave him meals in provincial hotels as they toured the country.

By coincidence next day at luncheon Marsh happened to meet
David Cecil, to whom he had recently been sending critical notes
on the manuscript of his forthcoming book *Early Victorian Novelists*.
From Cecil he was able to learn something more about the one-
time pupil who had unaccountably vanished from Oxford without
sitting for his final examination. Whatever Marsh heard cannot
have made him less well disposed to the young man, for within a
day or two he arranged to meet him at the theatre in Hammersmith. They walked the long way back to the shoe shop in Church
Street and Marsh noted in his diary that he was rather hurt at
not being asked in. It never occurred to him that his companion
might be ashamed to let him see how he lived—which must have
happened more than once in Eddie Marsh's life before the new
friend had perceived his true character.

For Easter he went to Chartwell, where he found Mr. Churchill
in the midst of a 'building mania', extending an outer wall adorned
with a row of stone balls and digging a pit for the central heating.
He delivered the proofs he had been working on at Oxford and
on June 22 these led to Mr. Churchill's bringing the argument on
hyphens to a head.

   (1) I am in revolt about your hyphens. One must regard the
hyphen as a blemish to be avoided wherever possible. Where a
19*

composite word is used it is inevitable, but I notice Macaulay would write 'downstream' one word, and 'panicstricken' one word. On the other hand 'richly embroidered' seems to me to be two words, and it is terrible to commit oneself to linking every adverb to a verb by a hyphen. In 'salt mines' *you* want a hyphen, but who would ever write 'gold-mining shares are good today'? My feeling is that you may run them together or leave them apart, except when nature revolts. I agree to a hyphen in 'hemming-in'. We had a controversy about this last time and arrived at a compromise the principle of which I have forgotten. Would you mind thinking over this again.

(2) 'Judgment' no 'e'. If so there would have to be 'abridgement' and why not 'developement'? Whereas I always write 'development'. The Oxford Dictionary gives it as optional and I am very much inclined to opt.

I sent you last night the chapters which were omitted, together with the last three. You certainly spotted a great many things and I am enormously obliged to you for the trouble you have taken.

Within a day or two Marsh was beginning a letter to Novello in high excitement.

A real event last night, the bursting on the world of Stephen Haggard in *Laughing Woman*. I'm not sure that I'm a fair judge of the play, it interested me so deeply from being about my friend Henri Gaudier-Brzeska (I can't remember if you read the thrilling Life of him, *Savage Messiah*?) but it did seem an extraordinarily good piece of work, bringing those two strange characters to life with easy power and admirable selection of incident and exquisitely natural dialogue —I believe it's tremendously *your* play, you would love it! Veronica T. [Turleigh] is a beautiful piece of casting, her eccentric beauty and simplicity seem to account for everything, and carry off the wild and wilful character as nothing else could—but it was the boy's evening, his spontaneity and his charm and the unity in variety of his mercurial temperament glued every eye and heart upon him. Except in looks, he was a perfect resurrection of Henri. He got an absolute ovation, nobody could talk of anything else in the entractes or afterwards. . . . I feel rather proud of having 'picked him out' in that tiny part, Silvius, in *As You Like It*, but I admit I had no idea *what* an actor he is!

Marsh expressed his concern for the new friend Novello had put in his way and whom he was now calling Chris. 'He has been writing in a very depressed tone. . . . He doesn't seem very happy on the stage, do you think he is cut out for it? Of course his heart is set on writing—but that won't earn him a living, at any rate not for some time. *How* difficult life is, is it not?'

On October 1 his concern for Novello's neglect of music came to an end on hearing, during a visit to the dressing-room at the Globe, that he had been asked to write and compose the next musical play for Drury Lane. For nineteen years he had shared every vicissitude of Novello's career. There would soon be no more scope for his benefactions, and already the roles were somewhat reversed. His protégé of the mid-war years was becoming the most energetic individual power in the British theatre, and it was often only late at night at the Aldwych flat that Novello could spare the time to discuss his plans with anyone who was not actively involved. Eddie Marsh, however, was no person to be left out of anything that was afoot if he could possibly help it. Since he never missed a first night (he attended 109 during this one year) he could often solve a casting problem, but his comments between scenes, on hearing Novello read aloud a new play, were sometimes less happy. He criticized on rational grounds, although he was dealing with an instinctive artist and a showman to whose work the conventional canons of art could not usefully be applied. There were times when he would warn the dramatist against the improbability of a speech or turn of a situation which later in performance he would have to confess was a theatrical stroke which made its effect. 'Really, Ivor, you simply *can't* say that!' he would protest, interrupting the reading. 'But the extraordinary thing is, Eddie, I can,' Novello would retort, smiling, and more often than not it turned out in the event that he was right.

Motoring down to Redroofs on October 12 Marsh was the first to hear read aloud the opening scenes of the new piece for Drury Lane, and since Chris had so far proved capable of writing words suitable to the music it looked as if everything were conspiring to bring about the fruition of his dearest wish for his closest friend— a revival of his gift for popular melody and its marriage with his newly developed craft of the actor-dramatist. That Chris knew nothing whatever about musical comedy was turning out an advantage rather than otherwise. His work was the less likely to be conventional, and now, if the play won favour, it might prove to be the ready-to-hand means of livelihood he was looking for. To Eddie Marsh all the prospects in this quarter seemed bright with promise, and he was justified in feeling entitled to some of the credit for the perceptive man of the theatre that Novello had become. As for the new type of musical spectacle he was now trying to evolve during this winter, as long ago as 1928 Marsh had remarked in a letter to him, 'I suppose England is the only country where it would be possible to be the hero of a musical piece without attempting to sing a note.' And more recently, after attending a rehearsal of *Conversation Piece*—'It's no good saying the story of a musical comedy doesn't matter.' He was continually dropping hints at random with no precise end in mind other than broadly to keep Novello in the picture while he was away. They were trivial enough but over the years they had been cumulative. There is no doubt that they contributed towards the showman's readiness to make the most of the big chance which had now come.

Marsh noted that the new play was finished on October 23, and he left Novello working on the score when Rex Whistler drove him down to Salisbury. He spent the evening teaching Whistler bézique, then went on to Chatsworth where the party included Princess Mary. Writing to Brett Young he complained that he was 'made to play poker', a game he had never mastered, so that he lost sixpence! His approaching retirement was making him more than ever conscious of every penny, and as his income was apt to be judged by the company he kept, he was sometimes in difficulties. 'I should have loved to come,' he wrote in May (confiding in an intimate friend and declining to join a party at Glyndebourne), 'but it would have cost at least £5'; and yet he found it possible this year to make an anonymous benefaction to the poet Charles Dalmon who had fallen on hard times and another to Walter Sickert who was in distress in spite of his current exhibition at the Leicester Galleries. 'He has brought his new manner to almost the same perfection as the old,' Marsh wrote to Brett Young. 'Marvellous at 75 or whatever it is. . . . I'm snowed under with presentation copies. The best are R. Graves's second Claudius book which I delight in—I think the two together are an indubitable masterpiece—and Bob Nichols's *Fisbo*. It's a really magnificent piece of satiric writing, full of poetry and wit, tho' I can't be sure that poor Osbert [Sitwell] has really deserved all that vitriol.' It was now that he at last gave up the administration of the Brooke royalties and heard from de la Mare: 'For years you have been a blessing and with absolutely nothing in return.'

Marsh was trying to simplify his life, a task in which he had little chance of succeeding since he shared with Browning in his last years a constitutional inability to refuse an invitation. His best hope of an effective brake on his activities lay in his native 'penny wisdom', while his chief handicap was his post-Corsican relish of creature comforts. Although the diary contains several despairing entreaties to himself as art collector, such as 'No more pictures, PLEASE', more revealing was the entry on this November 18 when he was at Chatsworth. It was his birthday. 'I meant to keep it dark, but used it as a means of extracting champagne for dinner, which succeeded!'

As the year 1934 drew to a close he rounded off his series of articles on the London theatre. 'Like Tennyson's Ulysses I have enjoyed greatly and (on occasion) suffered greatly.' They had been interspersed with characteristic anecdotes. ' "I love to hear people calling each other cockatrices," a lady said to me in the entracte of *Love for Love*; and she was hinting at the same quality in Congreve's dialogue which caused Edmund Gosse to turn round to me, at a long-ago matinée of *The Way of the World*, and exclaim with tears in his eyes "The *excruciating* beauty of the language!" ' The foremost place among acting performances he gave to Stephen Haggard, 'the most convincing embodiment of creative genius that I have seen on the stage'. Marsh had gone round to the dressing-room on the first night and introduced himself. As in the pre-war years he still believed in the value to young artists of their eating and talking together, so as soon as Chris was in London again Haggard was asked round to meet him at one of Mrs. Elgy's luncheons. Others of Marsh's younger friends followed throughout the year—among them Noel Langley, Michael Rothenstein, and Etienne Amyot—their visits alternating with survivors of the old circle—Bottomley, Abercrombie, de la Mare, and Paul Nash. Once more, and for the last time, Marsh was doing his best to give a newcomer the privilege of a place in his circle.

There was now a movement afoot for 'raising the tone' of films, and Marsh, who had already become a member of the B.B.C. Advisory Committee on pronunciation, found himself attending meetings with the Archbishop of Canterbury, Lady Oxford, and others. On his part the issue was somewhat confused by his generally being of a minority opinion. In a letter to Novello he gave an instance connected with the film *I'm No Angel,* to which Lady Horner had asked him to escort her on her second visit.

> You will *hate* me, but I thought it quite *awful.* I see that Mae West is a tremendous personality with a great gift for getting it across, but I did think it the most vulgar thing I'd ever seen, and the squalor and sordidness of the whole thing revolted me! It was humiliating, to find that Lady Horner, the friend of Ruskin, Burne-Jones Pembroke, Asquith, and Haldane, was so far ahead of me in adaptation to modern conditions. I can't make up my mind whether I'm the last remaining bulwark of taste and refinement or just an old stick-in-the-mud.

Throughout the new year 1935 he was following every stage of the new Novello production, telephoning or calling two or three times a day. On April 29 he was in the stalls of Drury Lane at the dress rehearsal until after midnight and sat up late with the author-composer in his flat round the corner. On May 1, the opening of *Glamorous Night,* he wrote in his diary, 'It was the night of his life', and this time sat up at the Aldwych flat until 4.30 A.M., when someone ran down into the street to buy copies of the newspapers. He saw the play eight times before it came off in December and of his last visit, seated in the middle of the front stalls, noted with proprietory pride 'Ivor and Mary [Ellis] gave of their best for my sake'. Meanwhile on March 15 the first hint of an absorbing new occupation had been recorded. 'Noticing that in Horace Ode 1, Book V, the *puer* is *gracilis* and Pyrrha *facilis* I composed a stanza for a poem on the obsolescence of old favourites in poetry.

> 'No more beside the isle shall Lancelot
> Surprise the Lady with his *Tirra-lirra;*
> No more with perfumes in the rosy grot
> The gracile stripling urge the facile Pyrrha.'

But it was some months before it dawned on him to try his hand at Latin translation.

The extraordinary success of the musical play; the new staircase, oak panelling, and damask curtains at Redroofs—signs of recovered affluence; the request for more pictures to adorn the walls and books to dignify the shelves, were a continual interest and pleasure. His friends were prospering and of enemies he could name but one. In May of this year the initiative of Lady Wemyss was to relieve him of that one exception. She was anxious that he should spend a certain weekend under her roof. It meant his being in company with H. G. Wells. She was writing tentatively to both. 'Do *you* mind meeting Wells?' she asked, describing him as 'a queer but interesting fish (I rather like all sorts). I did ask H. G. Wells about 2 or 3 years ago to meet our Bishop (Headlam of Glos) but it was Wells who was uneasy, *not* the Bishop! Wells asked me anxiously if the Bishop *knew* that he was going to be here.' Marsh thereupon wrote to Wells, saying that judging from the character of 'Freddie Mush' in his offending book he could only infer that the author regarded him as 'a very unpleasant character whom it could give you no satisfaction to know. But it's a very old story now. People say life is too short for quarrels. I would rather say it is too long.' The response from Wells was no less hatchet-burying in tone. 'All quarrels are foolish. We have pretended not to see each other since 1918—a quarter of a century of lost conversation . . . and I've been moved to speak to you on several occasions but you have a forbidding eye.' Their reconciliation is unrecorded, but Lady Wemyss had won her point.

Marsh was making notes on *The Letters of Charles and Mary Lamb* for E. V. Lucas, working on *Don Fernando*, the first of a series of books he read in proof for Somerset Maugham, and giving biographical advice to Lord (Victor) Lytton who was writing a Life of his son to be called *Anthony*. Marsh passed on some lessons learned from the Brooke memoir. 'I see now that in choosing my material I asked myself two questions, (1) Is this essential or helpful to the portrait I am drawing? (2) Should I enjoy reading this if it were about someone I didn't know? If the answer to *either* question (not necessarily both) were Yes, in it went.' He strongly advised omitting the affectionate beginnings of letters 'as my experience is that people get irritated by the repetition of demonstrative expressions not addressed to themselves.'

On November 1 he went to the first night of *Murder in the Cathedral*—'very impressive tho' I had reservations. Chris swallowed it whole and was deeply moved.' It was an important evening in other respects. Marsh had expressed a wish to take me under his wing as an unofficially adopted son, and he had arranged to call after the performance on my parents at the family home down the road from the theatre. It was a strange and touching encounter. The diary only recorded the excellence of my mother's coffee and 'John Hassall's studio has not been dusted for 39 years'. Next day he gave me two drawings by Richard Wilson and a Crome for the new bed-sitting room I had taken in Chelsea, and, telling me about the 'murder money', suggested I bought some evening clothes. There followed a day of picture rearranging at Gray's Inn, 'especially the Meninsky drawing which we put up in a high place, Chris standing on my shoulders, Mrs. Elgy holding the ladder'. On the 26th he heard the first of my Prologues spoken by Godfrey Tearle at Drury Lane. Two days later, wearing the new clothes, I accompanied him to a performance of *Romeo and Juliet*,[1] and then for the first time occupied what was still referred to as Rupert's bed. For the next three years the late-night readings and discussions of books which were Eddie's chief recreation after the play, if there wasn't a party, meant that I occupied the spare room at Raymond Buildings hardly less often than the bachelor apartment in Hasker Street.

ii

A general election in November resulted in Stanley Baldwin retaining power. For Eddie this should have meant no change, but when J. H. Thomas moved over to the Colonial Office, Eddie remained to serve his last two years under Malcolm MacDonald, who took over the administration of affairs connected with the Dominions. Eddie was corresponding with Logan Pearsall Smith, who wanted to recommend to the B.B.C. the substitution of 'halcyon' for 'anti-cyclone'. 'A large halcyon is approaching our shores!' wrote Pearsall Smith. 'What a touch of poetry that would add to the weather broadcasts! What by the way was the excellent word you suggested for Inferiority Complex?' It was 'inflex', but to Eddie's chagrin it failed to carry the vote. More serious was a diary entry made a few weeks later, in February 1936. 'Horrified at hearing that tho' I've been so economical all this week I had only £10 in the bank when I paid in my January salary!'

His literary work for Mr. Churchill was of course not only rewarding to his self-esteem, but also to his pocket. He had barely made his gloomy memorandum when on February 6 Mr. Churchill wrote to say the proofs of *Marlborough*, Vol. III, would follow and 'I have another literary plan which is taking shape in which we

[1] See *Appendix II*.

might perhaps collaborate'. Eddie was looking forward to the new volume, 'and I shall be interested to hear what the new plan is,' he wrote to Mr. Churchill. 'I shall be "retiring" next September on completing 40 years' service, so I shall then be at leisure, but (1) I want to write a book of my own and (2) *quite between ourselves* I have promised Ivor to help him write a sort of autobiography for which he is generous enough to offer me half-profits, which ought to come to quite a lot!' He had been pressing Mr. Churchill to see a play at the Old Vic about Napoleon on St. Helena. 'I will see it if I can have a night,' Mr. Churchill replied, 'but it would pain me to witness the death agony of a figure about whom I have thought so much.' All the same he went, and wrote a letter to *The Times* which prolonged the run. Late in February Eddie was deep in the Churchill proofs 'with great delight. I think your hand gets firmer and firmer. I've just finished Ramillies which is first-rate and most exciting. With what decorum you refrain from even the most demure pun on "Goslinga".'

The autobiographical scheme with Novello came to nothing but the 'book of my own' was to develop into his Memoir *A Number of People*. The retirement was a false alarm. For administrative reasons it was postponed, as reported to Mr. Churchill when acknowledging in October a bound copy of Vol. III. 'I don't feel I've quite pulled my weight in this volume,' he wrote, 'as I only had one reading, and that not quite the whole.'

As you always take a kindly interest in my affairs you will be glad to hear that my pension, which had been tentatively estimated by the Dept. at £700 has now been definitely fixed at £923, which makes a great difference—and I think now I shall be able to manage. My retiring date is Feb. 15. I've very much admired all your recent speeches, and so has everybody.

Eddie had shown me the two chapters of his Memoir which he had abandoned some two years before, and my comments on the pages about his mother had induced him to pick up the threads. This caused a revision of his plans. Horace was more in his mind than I realized at the time. Indeed his translation of the Odes had had its very small beginning on February 17. 'In my bath, invented a new (?) stanza to translate a verse of Hor. Od. III, 16, which I was saying to myself', he noted in his diary.

What tho' to me the loamy fields of Var
Send no fat fleeces, the Calabrian bee
Sucks honey from the flowers, but none for me,
Nor Bacchus languish in the Lestrygonian jar?

He had little time for his own projects since he was proof-reading Maurice Baring's anthology *Have You Anything to Declare?* (for which he translated some lines of Lucretius), Ronald Storrs' *Orientations*, and a volume of Ethel Smyth's autobiography, which prompted her to exclaim querulously, 'I've revised commas till I'm *blue in the face*'. And in the spring he was giving his attention to Charles Morgan's latest novel, which he considered 'grandly conceived and finely written'.

> It doesn't carry me with it as *The Fountain* did. When I read your books I am always filled with shame, they bring home to me my immersion in the world of Appearances, my failure in divine discontent and in the need of reaching out towards Reality. It would have been a perfectly good attitude for the 18th century, but I feel it makes me unworthy of the times we live in. Anyhow the result so far as *Sparkenbroke* is concerned is that I am quite violently revolted by Mary's final betrayal of George (for a betrayal it is, tho' by what I can't help thinking rather arbitrary means you prevent its taking effect). I don't want to burden you with a controversy, so you mustn't answer this—but I felt I had to explain why I'm less enthusiastic than I was about *The Fountain*.

Of Morgan's *Epitaph on George Moore* he had recently made a curious observation, being sceptical of the author's claim that Moore's intelligence was of a kind that could have invented adhesive stamps:

> I had always imagined him incompetent in such things, and I remember being told that till late in life he never succeeded in keeping his drawers up, so that it was a relief and delight when he at last discovered, or rather was told, the purpose of the little bit of tape through which he was meant to put his braces.

Eddie Marsh's praise would be a poor thing if he were not equally capable of condemnation or even disgust. Where 'good writing' was concerned he considered no one's feelings. One example of his censure was a letter sent this winter to a young prose-writer who had submitted to him the galley-proofs of a biography.

I've got a disarming letter from you—but I'm not going to be disarmed! This will be quite bloody, but tho' I hate writing it, I must. Your writing has not improved in the least degree. You will remember how I implored you, when next you wrote anything, to listen to yourself as you went along, and after each sentence to ask yourself questions: What exactly did I mean to convey? Have I conveyed it? Are there words or phrases that add nothing to either the sense or the beauty of the sentence? Have I repeated words unnecessarily?

If you had followed this process, or even grasped in any degree the qualities in writing to which I meant to point out the way, there's hardly a paragraph in the book which you would have left as it is. There are all the old foozling shots at a meaning you haven't thought out, all the old flabby redundancies, and above all the monotonous and tom-tom repetitions of words, as if there were no such things as pronouns or synonyms. Moreover you have allowed your subject to lead you into a sort of salesman's jargon, as if you had learned English from a correspondence course with an Advertiser's college. This has even infected your prepositions. . . .

I don't for one moment expect you to make a tithe of my corrections, the printer's bill would be enormous! they are meant as an object-lesson in hopes that at last you may pull yourself together. . . . It's all very well to write modestly of your 'wretched stuff', but what I deplore, and even in a way resent, is that after all my bloody sweat you haven't so far as I can see taken a single step in the right direction.

In October his services to art were officially recognized when he was persuaded by Lord Sandwich to become Chairman of the Contemporary Art Society. Henceforth he presided at its meetings. Among the many artists who were engaging his personal interest was Tristram Hillier. An undated letter from Hillier illustrates how painters were still confiding their problems to him and explaining their position.

I think you should allow the painter who, after all, is confronted in our period by considerable difficulties, hitherto perceived to a far lesser degree, the liberty to combine, in his attempt at an interpretation of Truth, the abstract with the conventional or realist aspect of things. And this is indeed the Basis of that much abused term 'Surrealism'. Do you not suppose that the elongation of El Greco was considered in its time with the same disquiet as were the almost gross figures of Picasso in the period 1913-1914? . . . I have abandoned, however, my fat nudes for other distortions which I hope will disturb you less—and in general my painting becomes more and more abstract. I am tremendously impressed and influenced at the moment by some German Primitive missal-fronts.

Richard Wyndham was urging Eddie to do more for Edward Wadsworth. 'Apart from being a great artist he is a thorough craftsman who is willing to spend months over one picture and who will go to the trouble of mixing and grinding his own paints.' And Ivon Hitchens was discussing his method: 'I have a horror of a meaningless smear, but I do try to say very clearly and directly by the tone and colour what I feel is the essence of the object, and I see no point in building this up with many little strokes to make a "picture" where *one* will suffice and be more vital.' Eddie must bear with him in his new development 'else in the absence of friends how shall I get through the last and most difficult stages of the battle?'

This was a year of political crisis in which Eddie took no part. It was in a corner of a public lounge at Claridge's that he listened to the Abdication speech on a portable radio which Somerset Maugham had borrowed from one of the porters. Around the little box, husky with history and atmospherics, the circle included Maugham, Graham Greene, and Osbert Sitwell. Within a few days he was at Maidenhead doing Christmas shopping with Novello and myself. Redroofs was crowded, and at one shop so as to save further thought I made a purchase of seventeen cheap ash-trays. 'I wonder what Chris is going to give us for Christmas,' remarked Novello as if thinking aloud, walking out of the shop. '*Dare* we hope it's an ash-tray?' asked Eddie, rather more breathily than usual. 'If we don't look out it will be half a dozen,' came the reply.

On January 25 of the new year (1937) he sat for the last time in the official gallery of the House of Commons to hear his Chief speaking on the second reading of the Empire Settlement Bill. Later in the month he learned that on Will Rothenstein's initiative a committee had been formed, consisting of Abercrombie, Masefield, Sassoon, de la Mare, and Mr. Churchill, with myself as Secretary, to organize a Presentation Dinner to celebrate his retirement. It fell to me to break the first news of this plan to the guest of honour. I brought it out with studied nonchalance at dinner, just as Mrs. Elgy began circling the table to my side with a dish of sprouts. I thought she would like to be in on the big moment, also Eddie would enjoy recapitulating all the gratifying details at the top of his voice, so that she could hear them. 'Just fancy!' she said (rather too casually, I thought), and then for some obscure reason of her own added: 'What's wrong with the food *'ere*?' 'Nothing,' we shouted. 'What?' she snapped. 'Nothing,' we roared, on the verge of getting annoyed. 'There's nothing what-ever wrong with the food here,' Eddie yelled, now on his feet and gesticulating with his napkin. 'But the Mayfair Hotel holds *more people.*' This mollified her. 'Oh,' she said, 'so it's going to be a party.' By this time I had given myself a liberal helping of sprouts, and she made her exit, saying rather petulantly, 'We'll 'ave to make you look your best *some'ow*', as if it were going to be a considerable strain.

On that same day Malcolm MacDonald disclosed his wish that his Secretary should be awarded the K.C.M.G. in the Coronation List. Eddie was in two minds. Since the number holding this honour is limited, he was anxious not to stand in the way of those who were both more deserving, as he maintained, and married. This scruple seemed to me absurd. 'I consulted Ch. under seal of secrecy,' says the diary. 'My own disinclination was already melting' and to distract his mind he proceeded to read aloud from *New Hampshire*, the volume of narrative poems by Robert Frost. The honour eventually awarded was the K.C.V.O., which is un-restricted and is in the personal gift of the King. It was extra-ordinary that when the day came for his accolade he should have missed the appointment. On February 11 he wrote in his diary:

Imagine my horror at being rung up at 12.45 by Tommy Lascelles asking why I hadn't turned up at B. Palace! I had misunderstood his telephone and misread his letter!! too awful, but he said I could come at 4.15 instead.

. . . Changed into morning coat and to the Palace, saw Tommy who advised me to say nothing about my gaffe. Had 10 minutes with the King who was most charming and unshymaking, left him 'Sir Edward', met the Queen by accident in the passage, didn't think she would know me, but she was most gracious. Back to Office. Rang Ivor and Chris.

His comment was 'What would have happened if I had behaved like that to Henry VIII?' On his return to Raymond Buildings

Mrs. Elgy grasped his hand and shouted at the top of her voice: 'I couldn't have been more pleased if it had been meself!'

On the 12th his colleagues of the Dominions Office assembled, Malcolm MacDonald made a speech and presented a piece of silver. 'When we realized the awful congestion in your rooms,' he said, 'we felt that if we gave you anything large you would merely get in a rage whenever you saw it. You would start banging the telephone receiver even more vigorously than you do now.' But what amused Eddie most was the passage in which his Chief confessed that he dared not contemplate the actual day of his Private Secretary's retirement.

> For one thing, on that day I become again an ordinary 'common or garden' Cabinet Minister, instead of the most distinguished member of His Majesty's Government. For that is what I have been for the last twelve months. Not every Cabinet Minister can boast that he had the honour of sitting in the next room to his Private Secretary who was scribbling notes to Bernard Shaw, telephoning Miss Dorothy Dickson, and correcting the proofs of Winston Churchill's *The Life and Times of the Duke of Marlborough*.

Next day Eddie drove to Raymond Buildings in a taxi heaped with pictures and, by an oversight, the office keys still in his pocket. His first 'free' week-end was spent at Redroofs, and on the Monday, knowing something of his tastes, I gave him the most elaborate dinner at Jardin des Gourmets that royalties from Drury Lane could provide. The principal celebration had been fixed for March 17, but the days of waiting were by no means idle. He had a part of Vol. IV of *Marlborough* and a précis of *War and Peace* to finish for Mr. Churchill. 'It's been the most gruelling job I ever did,' he wrote, 'and I've worked like a galley-slave at every spare moment. . . . How you will hate Tolstoi's contempt for Napoleon and his absurd theory that Great Men are flies on the wheel of History! I wonder what he would have said if he had read your *Marlborough*.' And then he referred to the forthcoming event. 'At the thought of my dinner on Wed "At once with joy and fear my heart rebounds". It is splendid of you to be taking the Chair.

In response to the appeal for funds to buy the two drawings by Augustus John which Mr. Churchill was to present, money came pouring in accompanied by an odd assortment of tributes. Novello wrote suggesting that a deluge of leaflets advertising his current

Drury Lane play be loosed from the ceiling just as the guest of
the evening rose to speak, and signed himself 'President of the
S.P.C.E. (Society of the Prevention of Cruelty to Eddie)'; Blunden
advised the Secretary to introduce a poetical element.

We shall read your Ode on the occasion with full stomachs. I urge
the Ben Jonson model.

It is not growing like a Tree
In bulk can make Bards better be,
But when they're known to Sir E.M.
O how that lustre quickens them.

You will do well to have a Chorus. Abercrombie can really make his
voice heard, even in Merton Common Room.

One hundred and forty sat down to dinner at the Mayfair
Hotel. Abercrombie, Drinkwater, Binyon and Squire presided at
the head of the four subsidiary tables. Among those at the top
table G. M. Trevelyan, H. G. Wells, Walter de la Mare, and
Desmond MacCarthy were the only male guests who did not
speak. Mr. Churchill occupied the Chair between Lady Lytton
and Lady Horner, and Eddie himself sat between Pamela Lytton
and her daughter Davina. James Agate spoke on behalf of the
Theatre. 'Even when the theatre is half empty,' he said, 'every
actor feels he has a full house if Eddie's in front.' Masefield spoke
for Poetry, paying tribute to the Memoir of Brooke and the
translations of La Fontaine. Rothenstein spoke for Painting, and
ended by reading out a message from Max Beerbohm: 'Eddie
Marsh is rather a special case. He has done, for so many years, so
much good in so enlightened and so unselfish a way that really I
think he ought to be given a dinner of this kind every night of his
life. When next I am in England I shall attend every one of the
current meals.' Mr. Churchill proposed the toast 'Eddie the Man',
declaring that the guest of honour had 'rendered a solid contribution to the strength and maintenance of our life as a nation . . .
I don't know what I shall do now,' he said. 'I have never been in
office without Eddie Marsh, and now I shall never be in office
with Eddie Marsh!' Mr. Churchill also told the story of his entering the office on the first day of work with his new secretary in
December 1905. Apparently Eddie had anticipated this moment
with some anxiety, and having carefully prepared his opening
remarks he had them ready for whatever conversational gambit

his Chief might choose to make. Unluckily, in his trepidation he
uttered aloud the wrong side of the dialogue, and when at last
Mr. Churchill came in he rose from his chair and in genial tones
exclaimed, 'Aha, so *you're* to be my new secretary!' When the
laughter had subsided, Mr. Churchill presented the two drawings
and a vellum folder containing an illuminated address and the
signatures of all the subscribers.[1] For days the guest of honour had
been rehearsing his reply. 'A little louder next time,' one would
suggest, 'and above all *slower*. And try not to smile except *between*
sentences.' 'But what if I cry?' 'Then all is lost.' When his turn
came on the night he acquitted himself with assurance although
he had never before made a formal speech. 'To talk about myself
would be egotistical,' he began, 'to talk about anything else would
be irrelevant', and he looked up and down the crowded tables.
'It is a sight to make my good angel weep tears of joy, and indeed
I hope that he will do this, vicariously, so as to save me from the
danger of doing anything so un-English myself.' When it was all
over he left with Juliet Duff to tell the story in the star dressing-
room at Drury Lane.

'You and I were born in an age of civilization,' wrote one of the
oldest members of that gathering, 'and have lived into an age of
savagery; it is indeed difficult to look at any newspaper without
perceiving and resenting the tyranny of the fool and the cad. Last
night, however, I felt that some vestal fire of civilization still
existed.' Mr. Churchill too had taken pleasure in the occasion:
'I thought the tributes paid to you very fine because they were so
true and sincere. Do let me know how things go. . . . I am at the
present time on the brink of a trip to the Riviera and indulging all
my customary vacillation where alternative forms of pleasure
are concerned.' Eddie's reply included an acknowledgement of
another batch of proofs: 'I don't see how even you can get a thrill
into those negotiations, yet they are necessary to the story. You

---

[1] '*We who subscribe our names, lovers and practisers of the Arts, welcome this opportunity
of sharing in a tribute to yourself and to your gifts. For many years we have honoured and loved
you as a friend: have profited by your criticism and encouragement: and admired you as a writer.
Few of our time have shown for the Arts so happy a discrimination, for artists so generous a sympathy.
Now that you retire from public life, we wish to express our gratitude for these things, together
with the hope that for many years to come you may delight us with your writings, and may continue
with so assured an insight to recognize genius and to give it, as in the past, your invaluable help
and counsel.*' The Address was followed by 172 signatures headed by Winston Churchill,
and the names of 71 others who subscribed to the presentation but were unable to be
present.

can only fall back on the pianist Schnabel's answer when he was warned that the public would be bored if he played all the repeats in a Beethoven Sonata: "The public has a right to be bored."'

But the celebrations were not yet over. On April 22 he was invited by his colleagues in the Civil Service to a dinner at Brooks's and sat between Mr. Churchill and the last of his Chiefs. Mr. Churchill spoke, but it is Mr. MacDonald's words which have survived. He observed that every Government of the last thirty years was represented round the table.

> Almost since we began as politicians he has been our guide, philosopher and friend. He was to some extent the tutor of us all. The result is that this table contains a company of Statesmen. If when Mr. Baldwin resigns His Majesty were to command that a real Ministry of all the Talents should be formed, this gathering would be the Cabinet, Eddie himself would of course be Prime Minister.

'It was a really wonderful affair,' Eddie wrote to Bottomley, one of the few of his old friends who could not be with him during these days of festival. 'The rest of my life will be one long anti-climax. I ought to have jumped into the Thames.'

iii

On the wall to the right of the open entrance to each stone staircase at Raymond Buildings the names of the residents were painted one above the other. At Number Five several of the names were grimed with soot, but on a closer look at Eddie's one could still decipher, shadowy under the dust, the pencil marks where Brooke had scrawled his name in letters about three inches high, a relic of the days when this was his London address. At the top of fifty-nine spiral steps a heavy dark green door would be opened by Mrs. Elgy, a comfortable cottage-loaf of a woman in bedroom slippers, with a plump, colourless, sweetly beaming face and wispy white hair. She had a strident, gap-toothed laugh, and a talent for sweeping statements. 'All your old friends are dying,' she once exclaimed when her employer came back from a memorial service, '*all* the gentry.' Her deafness caused her to speak too loud, which gave her pronouncements a force disquietingly like the authority of truth. She had worked here single-handed for nearly forty years, carefully watching the expenditure of every penny in grubby little notebooks which she never threw away in case she should be challenged by a tradesman, and she radiated a sense of rural simplicity and wellbeing. She wore a white apron over thick and rather drab woollen clothes, and when 'Mr. Marsh' was having visitors the apron reappeared severely laundered and starched so that it crackled as she moved around the table serving the vegetables, stooping at the guest's elbow, watching with the suspicion of a frown to see one didn't take too much. One of her specialities was sprouts done under a coat of grated cheese. Knowing they deserved to be appreciated, she served them with head tilted to one side beaming down at her handiwork as if she had brought in an infant for admiration by a godparent. And there was always a white wine (La Joyeuse) which she called 'Joycey' looking a pale greenish-yellow through the thick green glass of a decanter pranked with tiny ornamental flowers.

'Mr. Brooke would be squatting in front of the fire when I brought him his tea,' she once said as she brought in the scones on a heavy copper tray. '"Let's have it down here," he would say, and put the tea-pot in the grate. Now the grate's *no* place for a tea-pot!'—'I suppose it isn't, Mrs. Elgy.'—'He was a writer too, you know.'—'Oh, yes.' She used to tell what she had always treasured as a shocking story, about how she was coming down the stairs one day to open the door when Mr. Brooke got there first and a young woman burst in and flung her arms round his neck exclaiming, 'Oh you gorgeous piece of flesh!' Then she went on: 'Fancy greeting a young gentleman like that, and in Mr. Marsh's hall!' Then she would go all over the ground again, just in case one had missed some of it the first time, and reiterating 'piece of flesh' with gusto break into peals of laughter in which it would have been heartless not to join. Another of her stories was of how she had once asked her employer why he was having a bigger lock put on the outside door. 'So that I can get my key in quicker when I'm chased by the police', was the reply. Then she would add, shaking with amusement, 'Fancy 'im being chased by a police-man—up all our stairs!' Eddie was particularly fond of her remark as she was putting away a set of valuable brandy glasses —'We won't want to break many of THOSE, at seven-and-six-pence apiece!' 'But why,' he asked, curious, 'should we want to break *any*?' It turned out she had been surreptitiously replacing the breakages out of her wages. After the Corsican adventure it was some time before he could bring himself to confess that it was his best grey flannel suit which had been torn to shreds. 'Never mind,' she declared, when at last it was broken to her. 'You can buy yourself a new suit, but good men are scarce.'

She was followed about by a small rough-haired terrier which was often to be found snoozing close up against Micky, a tabby cat, in a vegetable-basket under her table. She did not live in. The sound of her little dog's claws clicking animatedly on the oil-cloth of the kitchen floor when she arrived in the morning was the first sound of the day. Soon after there would come through the bedroom wall intermittent sounds of watery floundering and recitation as Eddie took his bath. He would be somewhat jarringly spry at breakfast, then frown at his watch and leave abruptly for Whitehall. The dining-room was on the upper floor, its window looking out on the tops of the plane-trees. Over the chimney-piece hung Girtin's monochrome *Harlech Castle* and on the opposite wall Blake's *Har and Heva* and Beerbohm's caricature of Mr. Churchill at the Admiralty with his Secretary obsequious at the door, and over a ponderous sideboard hung Roger Fry's *Christ Church Library*. It was a room of water-colours, and in the corner farthest from the door stood a small table with the red Visitor's Book, a blotter, *Pope's Own Miscellany* bound in green leather, and a stone figure of a native girl by Eric Gill. The walls were compacted tight with drawings which somehow made a harmony. Everywhere pictures, even on the doors. As Mrs. Elgy said, 'Mr. Marsh is *always* nailing pictures to the doors', nor was the bathroom immune, with its paintings blurred behind perspiring glass, nor the kitchen itself, where there was hardly room for the Christmas cards and photographs of the housekeeper's relations, none of whom apparently had sat for their portraits after about 1890. On the same floor was a boxroom; Eddie's bedroom, which overlooked the front entrance and the roofs of Holborn, and the spare room where Stanley Spencer's *Apple Gatherers* still hung over the bed which Eddie had used at Trinity. Waking, the guest opened his eyes on the subdued colours and poignant attitudes of Rosenberg's *Sacred Love* and a sketch by Currie depicting a brawl in an Irish village. The paintings in oils crowded the green-carpeted steps and spilled into the hall and the sitting-room. After mounting the stairs, it was like entering a spacious cavern whose walls were dimly aglow with colours. Here and there were small tables piled with books at all angles like assorted bricks, a few pieces of Second Empire furniture, and a William Morris writing-table by the sitting-room fire dominated by Maurice Lambert's head of a girl in red sandstone which jutted half concealed, like a figure from Easter Island, from among the mounded papers, envelopes, more books, and learned opuscula. On an upright chair by this table Eddie would sit—sideways, if he had company, one arm on the table, the other over the back of the chair, the monocle dangling on its thread. Here he did his proof-correcting, reading, writing, as well as talking. The armchair was reserved solely for visitors. He could not sit back in it or relax. He must be erect and poised, or prone and asleep in bed, one or the other.

He loved to make what he called 'plans'. This tended to make life more orderly but not more easy for friends whose nature it was to extemporize. He used to say he was 'born punctual'. After one's arrival Mrs. Elgy always went ahead, opened the door, and stood aside. 'It's yer dear friend,' she announced raucously, as if stating a rather disagreeable fact. On my entering the room he was invariably in the act of replacing his watch in his waistcoat pocket, having fetched it out when he heard the doorbell. I never saw him run or even hasten. Nor did he ever saunter. His life was a sustained movement *andante ma non troppo*, and for him the best things were those that were cut and dried. An unexpected was never an unmixed pleasure. For years he recorded in his diary the least deviation of mine from the appointed hour. There would be entries such as 'C. ¼ hr late owing to tube ignorance', or with an incredulous note, 'C. arrived from Drury Lane about 11.50 having lost his way!!' It is just as easy to be too early as too late, and when the more improbable thing occurred he was torn between the conflicting emotions of being delighted to see me and put out by a minor pleasure he hadn't bargained for. But he was never auto-cratic, always ready to adjust his wishes, never made it seem as if he were suffering fools gladly, nor would he ever risk the slightest hurt unless it were to drive home a lesson in syntax, and then he would appear to make light of it, so that one either laughed aloud and saw his critical point or stopped in one's mental tracks, feeling the barb of ridicule.

It was soon evident to a newcomer that he was a born spectator, never so carried away that he could not at once give an analysis of his feelings, the scholar and aesthete nicely counterpoised, each watching the other so that neither ever carried him to an extreme.

The result was an attitude to life and letters of hair-fine eclecticism and delicacy. With the detachment of a sympathetic eye-witness he regarded the realities of life around him. No wonder his rooms had for so long been looked on as a refuge for artists tormented by ambition, poverty, or the miseries of sex. Infected by his imperturbable good sense, the harassed spirit could enjoy a truce with life, see itself objectively as in a mirror, and take its ease while the bloody field of common existence went on rumbling very far away.

Black coffee in particularly small cups was the last phase of an evening meal, and at sight of the rotund brown pot with its precarious lid he reached for the silver box which contained the special brand of diminutive cigarettes insisted on by the doctor after the Corsican adventure. Then out came the watch again. 'Only seventeen minutes. No time for another canto of *Don Juan*. Shall we walk to the theatre?' On our return we would resume the reading aloud. Over the years we covered tracts of Landor, de Quincey, Hazlitt, Jeremy Taylor; and in verse Byron, Pope, Dryden, Browning, Donne, and there were several abortive attempts to convert me to Swinburne. In modern prose we read Sassoon's autobiographies, Churchill's *World Crisis* and especially Lowes Dickinson's *A Modern Symposium*, which was introduced as being one of the 'most civilized, though not the most beautiful' books of our time. In fiction there was *Villette*, much of Jane Austen; no contemporary verse, but a good deal of Latin poetry, mostly Virgil, Horace, and Catullus. The custom was to have a cold supper upstairs after the theatre, retire to the room below, take it in turns to read aloud for an hour or so, and have a whisky and soda before retiring for the night.

He was without 'mystery', which is not to say that he was in no respect mysterious. The retentiveness of his associative mind, for instance, was extraordinary. Nothing could be said in his presence but it called up an apt quotation or anecdote, so that sometimes it was difficult for the topic to make headway against such a colourful stream of red herrings. The secret of his retentiveness lay partly in his refusal to let sleeping poems lie. He would always be going over the old ground so as to keep it fresh, and he never went for a holiday nor slept a night at home without his dog-eared Milton at his bedside. I remember driving through the Lake District while Pope's *Epistle to Arbuthnot* provided an undersong to the purring wheels, and walking away from the theatre in Regent's Park, jostled by the dispersing audience and for a while even parted from my companion, only to find on regaining his side that *Andrea del Sarto* was still in process of performance. No time or place seemed to be unsuitable for quotation, and Shelley was breathed into my ear in buses or while being seen off at railway stations, when it became a matter of moment whether the last stanza would be ended before the whistle was blown.

When reciting he would never stress a word to point the meaning, for fear of breaking the smooth *legato* incantation which to him was the essential beauty of metrical verse. On occasion he would frown and lower his head in a momentary effort to recapture a word, then jerk up his chin and rivet his eyes again on an object somewhere behind the listener's left shoulder, and proceed softly, tremulously, savouring every phrase with a slightly pained look, as if the keenness of such relish were a kind of ordeal. He wore his sensibility on his sleeve. The time soon came when one was not only no longer embarrassed, but convinced that the rest of the world must by comparison be peculiarly insensitive. The ear had to become attuned.

There was a luncheon-party one day at Gray's Inn. Alan Dent and James Agate were there, and Agate expressed some doubt that Brooke was a real poet. Eddie rose to it, put down his knife and fork, and by way of answer repeated from memory the sonnet called *Clouds*. 'Fetch the book, Eddie,' said Agate, amiably rallying him, and unconverted. 'I couldn't follow a word.' Thanks to a long accustomed ear I realized I had been able to appreciate a speaking of a poem such as one could hope for only once or twice in a lifetime. *Lycidas* (his favourite poem in the language) was often performed, at least in part, but there was also *Alcmaeon and Eriphyle*, the parody of a Greek tragedy by A. E. Housman, in which he played all the parts himself, and which he reserved as his *encore* for the party games after dinner at country-houses. He would start in manner stately, then, just as the climax was approaching, duck behind a sofa, and after emitting high-pitched squeals as of death by hatchet, emerge, his flushed face twisted into a grimace of classic woe, exclaiming shrilly:

> O I am smitten with a hatchet's jaw.
> In *deed*, I mean, and not in words alone.

then, swivelling round to adopt a new role, he would be the
Chorus wide-eyed with its comment:

> Methinks I hear a sound within the house
> Unlike the voice of one who jumps for joy.

Good as this was by way of comic relief, the monocle swinging
as he turned round and about and clinking back against his stiff
evening shirt, the graver items in his repertoire were the best.
He used to say that a poem only came alive when it was spoken,
and he considered this the ultimate test of its merit.

One of his diaries at this time begins with a list of the poems he
held in his head at the turn of the year. It deserves to be put on
record: 'The complete Odes of Horace, *Paradise Lost* Books I-IV,
the Athens bit of *Paradise Regained*, *Lycidas*, *L'Allegro*, *Il Penseroso*,
Epistle to Dr. Arbuthnot, *The Ancient Mariner*, *Kubla Khan*, *Thyrsis*, *Ave
atque Vale*, *Garden of Proserpine*, *Alexander's Feast*, Gray's *Elegy*, *The
Bard*, *Ode to Evening*, *The Immortality Ode*, the Odes of Keats, *Ode to a
Skylark*, *Ode to the West Wind*, *Adonais*, *The Lotos Eaters*, *Ulysses*,
Tithonus, *Thalusia and the Cyclops* (Theocritus), *Andrea del Sarto*,
Si je vous le disais (Musset)', and the list concluded with ninety-two
Fables of La Fontaine.

Rarely can there have been such a mental filing-system. The
wonder was that so crowded a memory should never be the
melting-pot of nightmare; but his dreams were rarely so strange
that they could not furnish an amusing story at breakfast, and they
always savoured of an engaging Alice-through-the-looking-glass
world where words and objects were turned topsy-turvy, not so
much by a distempered fancy as by a sense of wit that had gone
awry. He took great interest in his dreams, and there was always
method in their madness, as when he woke up having invented a
quotation from an imaginary Elizabethan play:

> Who knows
> What grief behind those arid-seeming eyes
> Stands pricking at the lids?

and then there was the character in his dream who advised him
in future to 'work out his jokes on paper so as to make quite sure
they were really *practical* jokes'. Under a date in 1937 he wrote in
his diary—'Dreamt that I was turned out of a country-house
because my host was jealous (I had no idea who the couple were).

The wife came in tears and a peignoir to my bedroom when I was dressing and said how sorry she was about it all, and she would send me a cheque for my fare home and my TEA!' Then there was his dream parody of Keats:

> Earned increments are sweet but those unearned
> Are sweeter.

which he had given Mr. Churchill for a statement on the Budget. The diary also records one of the oddest and most characteristic of his dreams. Between the celebration dinners in the month of his retirement he attended a concert at the Aeolian Hall. 'I was only sleepy for a minute, during which I appeared to be reading an analytical programme which said, "This piece not only deals with the actual killing of the pig, but also glances at various incidents in the life of the animal."'

The trick of deliberate misquotation that he sometimes performed in sleep was a speciality of his waking hours. I forget what report in the newspaper prompted the remark:

> The old order changeth, yielding place to new
> And God fulfils Himself in many ways;
> *Some of them most regrettable.*

'I've just invented a motto for a modern poet,' he once said, greeting me as he rose from the table (and put away his watch) then stepped back so as to get the full value of my expression as he said quaveringly, 'Absent thee from "felicity" a while.' On hearing that a young friend had married unwisely he brought down a clenched fist on his knee and with the pouting emphasis he generally reserved for his impersonation of Henry James declared, 'Where the Heart is there let the Brain be also!'; and once, when I showed slight concern that his interest in my private life might one day degenerate into something rather too much like possessiveness, he retorted, smiling:

> Chameleons live on light and air,
> Why not I on thee?

One day he was talking of Browning and I said I wondered whether his personal manner was as bluff and hearty as his poetry at its worst, which prompted the interruption:

> And did you once see Browning plain,
> And did he stop and shout at you?

A good Browning distortion occurred one evening after the war when we had begun to wonder whether the daily help had left anything to follow the cold meat, and he came back from the kitchen with a livid jelly asway under a sprig of holly, exclaiming, 'The sweet's in the frig, all's right with the world!' And there was the Wordsworthian occasion when I had to confess that I had forgotten to post one of his letters. 'I see,' he said, 'one of your little, nameless, *unperforméd* acts of kindness and of love.' He was never quite reconciled to the limitations he had discovered in my sense of humour. 'Really!' he would sigh, 'I cannot *conceive* why you don't find that as funny as I do!'

'Went home and suddenly started reading the *Iliad*.' Such trifles in the diary interspersed with the catalogues of names and places are clues to the man as I knew him and the home life which he let me share. 'Went home where we put the finishing touches to the proofs and read a little Stevenson's *Child's Garden* that C. had never heard of! His comparison of himself to a flower whose head comes off and lies on the floor when one is arranging a vase!' —'To describe the people I expect would come to my memorial service: the rag, the riff, the tag, the raff, the bobtail.'—'I suggest going to see C. at 4 P.M. but he said that would be just when he was shaving.'—'Went home and by a stroke of genius hung the Cornfield under the new Bergen portrait, they have exactly the same blue in both!'

iv

In June 1937 he was coping with more problems among the artists. This time it was a wood-engraver and an Edwardian illustrator, a pioneer in poster art. During a week-end at Stanway where my sister Joan was of the party it came to light that prolonged worry had brought on a nervous condition which was giving her seriously to suspect that she was losing her sight. Her first public appearance as a wood-engraver the year before (a full and elaborate title-page to *Devil's Dyke*, a volume of my poems) had raised high expectation, and now, on discovery of her situation, Eddie proposed that his 'murder' fund should share with my own resources the expense of enabling her to set up house away from the family home where she would be subject to fewer emotional stresses and distractions. She found a room over a fish-shop near the Cromwell Road, and, managing on two pounds a week, finished the illustrations for Brett Young's *Portrait of a Village*, her first opportunity of importance which Eddie Marsh had put in her way. It was soon after, with the support of such friends as Will Rothenstein, Max Beerbohm, and others, that he was instrumental in securing a pension on the Civil List for John Hassall, my father, who by his irrepressible spirits and Bohemian gusto had for years succeeded in disguising his position. Here was another instance of that brand of patronage which touched the intimate affairs of those he cared for. Eddie had acquired the reputation of a Maecenas, but few realized how modest were his resources. Small sums were administered with such tactical nicety that they gave the impression of opulence, yet they were often enough to tip the balance. In both these instances an artist's mode of life was transformed by the subsidy of a little more than a pound a week.

A production of *Devil's Dyke* in the quadrangle of St. Edward's Hall took him in July to Oxford, where he revived old memories with Masefield and Will Rothenstein and made the acquaintance of W. H. Auden, some of whose work was sharing the bill in Masefield's annual Festival of Spoken Verse. In the early autumn we flew to Paris for the Exhibition of French Art, shared a rapture at sight of Poussin's *Tancred and Erminia* (a painting which had been sent from Leningrad), visited a musical play as guests of Pierre Fresnay, and by resisting the fashionable restaurants managed the whole trip on only nine pounds a head, a feat that Eddie was justly proud of after entering every bus ticket and coffee in a notebook which he consulted wherever he went. On our return we went to Petworth, where after dinner one evening he performed the Housman parody which he had once tried out at Stanway on J. M. Barrie when he was ill in bed with bronchitis, ducking below the foot of the bed, and reappearing, while the patient alternately wheezed and chuckled. It was during this autumn that he was elected to the Council of the Royal Society of Literature, the executive committee of the Old Vic Theatre, and the Board of Trustees of the Tate Gallery. An after-dinner speech by Duff Cooper at a meeting of the Horatian Society so much impressed him that he was brought a stage further towards his decision to translate the Odes. His own speech on this occasion was notable for its opening phrase, 'Gentlemen, you may sleep.'

In January 1938, at Julian Trevelyan's studio at Chiswick, a farewell party was given for Wystan Auden and Christopher Isherwood on their departure for China. There E. M. Forster, Rose Macaulay, and other old friends were gathered, and he made new ones, sitting on the floor while Benjamin Britten, a composer hitherto unknown to him, played the accompaniment to his settings of Auden's verses. There was a shadow in Eddie's mind. Maurice Baring's illness was now chronic. 'It is like having an angry wasp inside one's chest,' he had written. 'I cannot hold a book in my hands and only at times can I bear being read to.' Ethel Smyth was reading aloud to him when he was up to it, and it was largely in the hope of providing him with some light amusement that Eddie was now pressing on with his memoirs. He resumed them with the chapter describing his sojourn with Baring long ago in Hildesheim, and was deeply moved to be still at work on these early reminiscences when he received a triolet from the friend whose youth he was recalling: 'My body is a broken toy.' Later that month he experienced two mental black-outs at the Apollo Theatre, the second overtaking him as he entered the stage door, so that the acquaintance he had come to congratulate was shocked when an unconscious figure was carried into his dressing-room. Eddie took no interest in his physiological make-up. 'If it breaks down it breaks down,' he would say petulantly. 'Never mind *why*.' One had to make clandestine appointments with his doctor an hour or so before his own interview, so as to enlarge on the symptoms he would be too bored to describe himself. There was an alarming occasion when he dropped his cigarette, slumped across the table, his face distorted, and was to all appearances dying; suddenly he stooped, picked up the unfinished cigarette, and continued the sentence exactly where it had broken off, quite unaware that he had been interrupted.

He had recently finished the proofs of Clemence Dane's *The Moon is Feminine* and was working on some poems in manuscript by Mervyn Peake, also Laurence Whistler's *Sir John Vanbrugh*, when he went to stay in Canterbury for the Festival production of my play *Christ's Comet*. My having to preside at the Hammond organ behind the spectators occasioned the diary comment—'C. said I had the most intelligent back-view of anyone in the audience —which included the Archbishop!' His holiday tour included Clovelly, Mells, Pixton, Mottisfont, and Bowood, where for much of the afternoon he would be alone in the garden, silent among the rhododendrons, a venerable scalp just visible above the shrubbery in attitude slightly inclined. On closer view he would be found equipped with gardening gloves and a pair of secateurs actively dead-heading the stalks within the circumference of his reach, snatching out the shrivelled blooms like split infinitives, a process he called 'destrigulating the rhododendrons', a coinage, he explained, of Mr. Churchill's. 'Could one ever be said to destrigulate redundant epithets?' someone asked him. 'Certainly *not*,' came the reply, in the peremptory tone he reserved for etymological pronouncements, 'the word is *strictly* horticultural.'

After a visit to Berkeley Castle he came back to Gray's Inn for a few hours and read aloud to me Mr. Churchill's description of the Armistice at the end of *The World Crisis* before travelling to Chartwell, where he was alone with his host and hostess for the evening. 'Both in very good mood,' says the diary for August 22. 'Winston very apprehensive, thinks Hitler means to attack Czecho-S. without ultimatum in Sept., but he *may* be stopped. Bézique with Clemmie. Long talk with Winston on way to bed.' Sending back the last proofs of *Marlborough* on February 25, he had written: 'My warmest congratulations on the accomplishment of this great task. The end is fully worthy of the whole—I can't say handsomer than that. It is certainly one of the great biographies.' Churchill wrote next day:

> There is hardly one of your comments that I have not accepted, and I could easily explain the two or three exceptions to you. I am now beginning my own final reading, and should be very glad if you would let me know whether there is any part which seems to drag unduly. This book is not to be commended by its purple patches, but by its structure, which I hope will bring home to modern readers the life and drama of that great age. How like their forerunners the modern Tories are!

Eddie was now to check all the French translations. 'I have translated them for the most part myself and rather freely, so perhaps I have not brought out the full strength of the passages.' Eddie wrote on March 7. 'It's very generous of you to send me a further reward!' He had no more general criticisms. 'As I said before, I think the subject-matter of the first (say) quarter of the book is less engaging than most of what had gone before, but that isn't your fault and I don't see how you could have done it better. ... It is frightening to hear that you think the modern Tories are like Abigail's gang. I hope there's no one quite as bad as Bolingbroke.'

At the end of August he was driving back from the country with Novello, who was shortly to play Henry V at Drury Lane. 'In the motor he recited a great deal of *Henry V*, I was quite delighted— made a few small criticisms but he has really come on tremendously and I shan't be anxious till the night.' Meanwhile the world situation was rapidly deteriorating and being reflected in the current jokes. The diary notes a remark of Coward's—'We don't want to fight but by Jingo if we DON'T', and there was someone who had planned a special Christmas card for despatch to his least favourite friends—'Wishing you a merry crisis and a happy new war.' On September 14 at the first night of *Dear Octopus* Charles Morgan came up to him in the second interval. He said he had just heard that Mr. Chamberlain was flying to see Hitler. Eddie turned to me. 'You'll remember that remark for the rest of your life.' On the 30th he was working on the autobiographical chapter to be called 'Private Secretary III' when Mr. MacDonald telephoned, asking him to go to the Colonial Office for the Prime Minister's return from Germany.

> Got there at 6.15, talk with B. who showed me a map from which it appeared that Hitler's terms were really modified from Godesberg. Waited in Creasy's rooms with the Shakespeares and John Rothensteins etc. (Eddie [Hartington] now Devonshire came in) till the P.M. arrived about 7.20—tremendous scene of enthusiasm— got home a little before 8 too late to go to *Mr. Chips* so I went on writing.

Now that the crisis was over, as it seemed, and the world appeared to have some semblance of a future, Eddie and those nearest to him resumed their normal occasions. He sent his Memoirs to the publisher, began sitting to Frank Dobson for his portrait bust, and started his critical notes on the proofs of Maugham's *Christmas Holiday*. Before the year was out we had celebrated my last bachelor evening by drinking Mrs. Elgy dry of 'Joycey', and next day he took his place between my parents at the ceremony conducted by the poet Andrew Young, and signed the register as witness. It must have been the only wedding service he had ever gone to (in company with the groom and best man) by tram. After the ceremony Stephen Haggard was his chauffeur for the day and he saw us off to Barbados. He turned back to Novello and his circle, where there was much to engage his interest. *Henry V* had succumbed to the crisis, but already, after a late-night visit to the Aldwych flat on November 28, the diary had recorded the start of a new venture, 'Ivor incubating a new musical, *The Dancing Years*'.

On March 13 the diary struck the key-note of the year— 'Beginning of anxiety about Hitler, Slovakia, etc.' A week later his reminiscences were published under the title *A Number of People*, and on the 23rd the opening of *The Dancing Years* at Drury Lane once more occasioned his sitting up all night at Aldwych to await the verdict of the newspapers.

When he stayed with Sassoon at Heytesbury and at Berkeley Castle in late spring he was working every day on the first proofs of Mr. Churchill's *History of the English-Speaking Peoples*. One batch of comments had already been delivered and acknowledged. 'Winston rang up and said my notes were an education in writing!' the diary recorded in pride. Meantime the letters about his autobiography began to come in. Frieda Lawrence was touched by his candid references to her husband. 'You had felt his greatness. I feel often bitter on his account, the lies they tell about him, the lies! *He* never had disciples, he was never morbid, only unhappy sometimes and angry, a genuine human being always—and how English he was, and how he loved his English—I know. Still he had his life and he did what he wanted to do.' 'Did you ever suffer in the least from being temporarily word-bound?' asked de la Mare, 'a fairly frequent affliction with me—except in talk! I haven't seen a sentence that suggests it. The unceasing edge, energy and precision, are astonishing. . . . P.S. Will you write me a poem—when I have made up my mind whether it shall be Sanskrit or Chinese?' Gibson recalled a tribute of Abercrombie's. 'Eddie has a mind like a razor, and when he cuts anyone in two with it they never notice it until they tumble over in surprise!' Brett Young detected a limitation. 'I think I miss—not malice, for that is not in you—but the *saeva* (and righteous) *indignatio* of which I know you are capable.' MacCarthy did not think he had done justice to the 'beautiful integrity of G. E. Moore', adding a vain entreaty, 'Please, please turn to criticism in your leisured age: the defence of high and rational literature and art which remoulds experience

in forms delightful and intelligible to man.' In connection with the
Baring chapter Eddie took pleasure in G. M. Young's definition
of the expression 'floater', more commonly known as a 'gaffe'. 'If
I were doing it for *O.E.D.* I should say Floater (noun), a social or
intellectual solecism, committed in company, which causes all
present, by a common impulse, to gaze abstractedly at an invisible
focus.' Charles Morgan, who had first suggested the idea of a
memoir, was in the event not disappointed, and suggested a
sequel, a 'portrait of our times' to be published after the author's
death. Perhaps the most entertaining reaction was Somerset
Maugham's. If anyone detected an error, even a misplaced colon,
they wrote to Gray's Inn in frigid triumph, happy to have caught
the grammatical Homer nodding. The book was not flawless, but
most of the challenges were 'returned to sender' in the form of a
critical boomerang. Maugham, however, scored by means of
parody, hitting off exactly the style of the emendator of his proofs
and applying it to his own work.

I found it very interesting and most entertaining. *You* will say, if a
book is interesting it must be entertaining and if it's entertaining it
must be interesting. Not at all, *Crime and Punishment* is interesting
without being entertaining and any one of the works of P. G.
Wodehouse is entertaining without being interesting. And this
brought me to the word intriguing which you have twice used in
inverted commas. This is sheer pusillanimity. The time has surely
come to admit that commonplace usage has given the word a
serviceable meaning. Down with your god-mammon-serving
commas!

Suppose Mr. M[augham] had written *A Number of People*, this is
what he might have expected to find:

p. 38, l. 16, he had come across who etc.[1]: it is no good trying to
pretend that 'whom' is not understood between 'Englander' and
'he'; why then should you hesitate to write 'and who'? The moral
obliquity which you thus hesitate to face could be avoided by leaving
out 'he had come across', which does not seem important to the
story.

It was in the street while he was walking back from a Cézanne
exhibition on July 26 that Horace once more jumped to the forefront of his mind and he began translating *Nullus argento*, which he

---

[1] He delighted also in the name of a New Englander he had come across, who was
descended from a long line of Bible Christians—Preserved Fish (*A Number of People*).

finished by 1 A.M.; but two days later the chapter of Churchill's History on Henry VIII arrived on his table, and further operations had to be deferred. That evening he was with the Churchills at Stoke D'Abernon. 'I played a new game Chinese Chequers which Winston is wild about. He thinks war *can't* be avoided.' Exactly a month later Horace was again postponed by the arrival of the William III and Queen Anne chapters, and the death of Arthur Asquith occasioned a noteworthy entry in the diary.

Winston rang up asking me to represent him at Oc's memorial service. He said Hitler was evidently rattled, but he didn't see how he could climb down, which would cost him his life.

Next day (August 30) he was up late at the Aldwych flat listening to the reading aloud of a new play. He left at 2.30 A.M. and before he reached home there was matter for another memorandum.

A man shouted from a lorry in Kingsway, 'Hi! Started marching!' which was alarming, but I didn't take it seriously.

Two days later he was sorting pictures for removal to the vaults of the Tate when Mrs. Elgy's 'help' rushed in with news that the Germans were bombing Poland. So as to avoid any more of these Greek messenger entrances he resolved on the purchase of his first wireless set. Late in the evening he went round to the dressing-room at Drury Lane. There had been only 200 in the house, and Novello had invited them to come down and fill up the stalls. Many of them were in tears. 'Ch. wants me to leave R.B.', says the diary, 'but how *can* I?' He preferred to be away from home when ninety of his pictures were moved, so he took refuge at Redroofs and hung on the wireless. 'Winston back at the Admiralty', he noted. The proofs of Churchill's History were to keep him occupied until the end of October, when Maugham's *The Mixture as Before* arrived on his table, but meanwhile he had rung up his bookseller and ordered a new publication, *A Map of Love*. On September 14 its author, Dylan Thomas, had written to him out of the blue.

I am writing to you, a patron of letters, to ask for any help that you may be able to give me. You may have read some of my work, or heard it spoken of. If not, I can refer you to Miss Edith Sitwell and Mr. T. S. Eliot, who will tell you that I am a poet of some worth and deserving help. I have a wife and a child and am without private means. For the last few years I have been earning just enough money to keep my family and myself alive by selling poems and short stories to magazines. These sources of income are now almost entirely dried up. It has occurred to me that you, with your connections with the Government, might be able to obtain some employment for me, either in the Ministry of Information—though that, I am told, is overrun with applicants, stampeded by almost every young man in London who has ever held a pencil or slapped a back —or elsewhere, any other place at all. I have been a journalist and an actor in a repertory theatre; I have broadcast, and lectured. I am 25 years old.

I suspect that this letter is one of many similar that you are receiving, and must apologise for giving you this additional trouble.

I have never, even in my most desperate moments, begged or attempted to seek any employment outside my own limited and underpaid profession. But now I must have work—I want to be able to go on writing, and conscription will stop that, perhaps for ever— and I beg you to help me.

I would very much like to give you, if you wanted it, any information about me and my work. Or I could, again if it was needed, attempt to come to London.

When *A Map of Love* arrived Eddie was puzzled by the verse, but the prose impressed him. He marked two passages in the margin[1] and read the whole book aloud to me. The Perceval 'murder money' came in useful almost for the last time. On the 19th Thomas wrote again.

I know you'll forgive me for not replying at once to your very kind letter and for not thanking you, very sincerely, for your gift. A friend called here and drove me to see my father: I don't often have the chance of seeing him, as he lives fifty miles away and we're both too poor to move much, and I stayed with him until yesterday. Your letter was waiting for me. It was most generous of you to assist me. I had, as you know and said, no thought at all of asking anything other than advice, but I am very grateful and your gift was welcome indeed and will help us *considerably* over a bad time.

I was afraid that the Ministry of Information would be crowded with staff and that it would be useless for me to apply, but I must thank you for mentioning my name there. I do hope that, if anything does come to your notice, you will let me know. For the present I can only wait. . . .

[1] He underlined Callaghan's remark concerning the blind birds in *The Visitor*. 'Do not be frightened. There are bright eyes under the shells of their eggs.'

Eddie was writing critical notes for Maugham—a task he enjoyed —but his interests were divided. On October 16 he noted: 'Spent most of the rest of the day translating *Inclusam Danaen* of which I did 3 stanzas yesterday to join on to a version of stanza 9 which I made 3 years ago. I think it came very well!'

Unfortunately there was yet another distraction. The diary gives a brief reference to what had become a matter of importance to us both. 'Ch. rang up and talked about the books on modern Poetry that he is reading, he has finished Leavis.' After a discussion on a recent work of criticism by Herbert Read we had discovered that there was a divergence of opinion between us on the nature of poetry. I had begun collecting ammunition from various sources, for we had decided to collaborate on a book in the form of a duologue to be called 'Permission to Quote' rather on the lines of Dryden's essay *Of Dramatick Poesie*. Eddie interested Michael Roberts in my problem, and from him I borrowed certain American works of criticism and studied them while Eddie wrote speeches for his 'character'. He wrote on the distinction between *Animus* and *Anima*, the conscious and subconscious principles used by the Abbé Brémond in his *Prayer and Poetry* to represent the complementary aspects of the creative mind. As a recreation from Horace this occupied his thoughts for several months. There is a paragraph in Robert Bridges' memoir of Digby Mackworth Dolben which incidentally sums up Eddie's point of view. He would have endorsed every word of the author's own account of his attitude to poetical form, as against Dolben's.

Our instinctive attitudes towards poetry were very dissimilar, he regarded it from the emotional, and I from the artistic side; and he was thus of a much intenser poetic temperament than I, for when he began to write poetry he would never have written on any subject that did not deeply move him, nor would he attend to poetry unless it expressed his own emotions, and I should say that he liked poetry on account of this power that it had of exciting his valued emotions. . . . What had led me to poetry was the inexhaustible fascination of form, the magic of speech, lying as it seemed to me in the masterly control of the material: it was an art that I hoped to learn. An instinctive rightness was essential, but, given that, I did not suppose that the poet's emotions were in any way better than mine, nor mine than another's; and though I should not at the time have put it in these words, I think that Dolben imagined poetic form to be that naive outcome of peculiar personal emotion, just as one imagines in nature the universal mind conquering matter by the urgence of life.[1]

Somewhere between these two attitudes, represented by Bridges and Dolben, everyone's conception of poetic form must lie. On the same day as Eddie took note of my researches in contemporary criticism, he made another entry. 'Tried to read poems in Dylan Thomas' *Map of Love*, and rewrote the beginning of the first one in other words, meaning to give both in MS to Ch. and see if he could guess which was the real one.' Then on the following day: 'Showed my Horace and my Dylan Thomas, both went well, also discussed W. H. Davies's *Loneliest Mountain*. Walked him to Café Royal. He did guess which was the real D.T. but couldn't understand it.'

'Interesting little talk with Winston who told me a Secret.' The diary entry is tantalizing, and the reticence, even in his private journal, characteristic. Before devoting himself to the great task there was one more entry. 'Nov. 26: Ch.'s dream of helping Winston on with his greatcoat and finding that he had six arms and the coat buttoned at the back.' Next day he started translating *Diffugere nives*. Horace had begun in earnest. And now he could think of nothing else.

v

As the first drafts were finished they were sent off to Ronald Fuller, a young critic and man of letters, who was working day and night in an underground A.R.P. station at the Adelphi. Somehow Fuller found time to despatch his comments by return post; then the counter-comment would follow from Gray's Inn, 'The London Committee gratefully accepts' (or declines as the case might be) 'your suggestion.' By the 'committee' he meant himself and me, though I was hardly qualified to give much practical assistance beyond acting as referee between the translator and his Latin advisers. Being a scholar in harshly uncongenial circumstances Fuller welcomed the task of watching every word and checking it with the original. On his part Eddie was touched by his mental resilience under alien conditions. 'I thought the iron had entered into your soul, but you are treating it as a tonic, as if

---

[1] *The Poems of Digby Mackworth Dolben, edited with a Memoir*, by Robert Bridges (Oxford University Press, 1911).

it came from a Chalybeate spring.' His remarks accompanying the new Ode were sometimes peculiarly subtle, 'In *Cor me quaeretis* I had to cut "si resurgat"—which seems to me just the sort of thing that *I* might have to put in if *I* were Horace translating *me* into Latin'; or on the defensive, 'Of course stake is obviously there "simply and solely to rhyme with" snake, as Calverley said—and I could only be thankful that it *did!*' or, again a problem in rhyme —'I expect I shall keep "jade" partly because I think the rhyme "jade—escapade" is more pointful than "heart—tart", also I don't think my generation *could* make Horace say "tart"'; or grateful for renewed encouragement—'You are a most worthwhile person to send verses to when I hear that I've written Milton. I feel like M. Jourdain when he was told that what he had written was prose.' Before Christmas Eddie sent a progress report on the London Committee's latest session which serves to illustrate its procedure. 'I ought to have told you that "tock" was Ch.'s. I had written "from tick to tick". In the "dura" line I had put "toils by land and sea". He said toils was tame and both simultaneously suggested "throes".' The adjective in the penultimate line of *Parcus deorum* (the final version was 'While Fortune to and fro on clangorous wings') caused endless trouble. 'I had first written "on rattling wings" in memory of Ruskin's description of Tintoretto's Annunciation—"Not in meek adoration of the heavenly messenger, but startled by the rush of his horizontal and rattling wings", but Ch. simply *won't* have a present participle in that line, as he thinks it spoils the *last* line. He suggested "plangent" which I don't think is quite right, and I thought of "strepitant", but I believe I prefer "clattered"—but there must be a really right word if only I could get it! I may have to fall back on "strident" tho' it's rather unenterprising. Is it possible "vibrant" would give the effect?' Meanwhile from the darts and shove-ha'penny boards, the smell of lint, fag-ends, and stewing tea, would come the messages of good cheer: 'Is it really *Eheu fugaces* next? I shall pour a libation for you', or of timely wisdom —'Poetry is a symbol of a spiritual state, and you are exchanging one set of symbols for another—and your exchange depends much more on *your* spiritual state than on the dictionary.'

In the new year 1940 he began showing his new translations to Sir Ronald Storrs and Monsignor Ronald Knox, with whom he corresponded at length on *minutiae* of the text. Though Maurice

Baring was not up to lending a hand he was still capable of the sort of remark which gave Eddie such pleasure. 'I am afraid that reading translations of Horace is to me what Miss Prism thought the chapter on the Fall of the Rupee would be for her pupil: too sensational.' De la Mare was given a preview. He thought the translator 'suicidally bold', and doubted the value in his making practical suggestions because 'a thing once written is apt to crystallize and hinder emendation from within. Don't you agree?'

Since the outbreak of war the way of life at Raymond Buildings had anticipated by many months the general austerity. About three times a week the London Committee would meet for a midday meal called 'Commons'. It consisted of a potato baked in its jacket, split open, and a wedge of mouse-trap cheese inserted with margarine and pepper to taste. But 'Joycey' from the green decanter was never abandoned. 'A little wine with your potato?' Eddie would say ceremoniously. Mrs. Elgy saw no virtue in this revolution. Her office was becoming a sinecure. 'Mr. 'Assall's not an old man like you, 'e wants buildin' up.' 'No, really, Mrs. Elgy dear,' I would protest, adding quite truthfully, 'This is plenty.' Then Eddie would interpose in a loud voice, 'He likes it. Now do go away!' then much louder, for in her deafness she had supposed, or deluded herself with the hope, that he was ordering a substantial dish, 'I said he LIKES it!'

Having practically no social distractions, and feeling that he must do *something* with all his might (he was hoping against hope that any moment the telephone would ring and it would be Mr. Churchill summoning him back into his service) he was giving himself to his scholarly undertakings with peculiar intensity. There were no Churchill proofs, but *Jane Fairfax*, a novel by Naomi Royde-Smith, was sharing his table with the rough drafts of Horace. Now that he had bought a wireless, the news bulletins, which he would never miss, provided the only intermission. 'I think that when we've won Winston will come out as the greatest name in English history', he wrote on July 17 to R. W. Chapman, the authority on Jane Austen. 'The best thing said about the French collapse was by a publican—"Anyhow, we've got the b——s to ourselves now."'

By then the London Committee could only transact its business by letter. It made the strangest counterpoint of thought and feeling to be on the alert in an anti-aircraft gunpit, watching a bursting sky and turning over in one's mind whether the change of tone in the last eight lines of *Diffugere nives* (revised version) which arrived that morning really did make the same lovely effect as the change from anapaests to iambs at the end of Shelley's *The Sensitive Plant* and was justified by that precedent—as Eddie was hotly maintaining. The Horatian problems were sent off every day, and since 'mobile ack-ack' was particularly mobile during the early months of the Battle of Britain, diverted accumulations of mail would catch up with my unit as it arrived at some airfield or other in Kent or Sussex, and almost the only time when the absent Committee member could give a thought to the latest Ode was in the peace of an improvised lavatory or during the fly-blown afternoon rest. Fuller was in a worse case, pulling victims from the rubble, administering first aid, disposing of the dead and comforting the bereaved, and still the rough drafts were being sent off from Gray's Inn as if nothing in the slightest degree unusual were going on in the neighbourhood.

> O Ronald, in my hours of ease
> Stern critic of my q's and p's,
> When pain and anguish wring my brow
> A reassuring angel thou.

I *was* rather pleased with that batch, and it's bliss to be 'corroborated by a competent judge' as Ko-Ko says. I called the Naiads 'soft' to contrast them with the viragos who tore up the trees. Why don't you like 'petty'? I think it's racier than 'trivial'—'Tomorrow and tomorrow and tomorrow Creeps on his *trivial* pace' . . . No?

By the end of August Fuller was even more actively engaged in rescue operations. At one time it seemed as if Gray's Inn were surrounded by fire, but Eddie had made up his mind that his contribution to the national effort would be to prevent Hitler from depriving the world of the Odes of Horace. Raymond Buildings shook. At the end of the month he was at work on *Pindarum Quisquis* (IV.2).

I'm rather pleased with the Pindar part—especially my ingenious circumvention in the final verse of the absurdity that one only has to imitate Pindar unsuccessfully to have a Sea named after one. And I think the last two verses are not too bad—on the supposition that Horace felt a pleasurable relaxation in describing his poor little calf after all that fustian about Augustus.

Ch. rang up asking me to meet him on Thurs. when he got two hours 'bath-leave'. You will be amused to hear that the *first* part of my *Intermisso Venus* was a masterpiece but he didn't care so much for the *second*. When I told him that your opinion was exactly the opposite he said in that case I *must* be right! He upholds the 'blushing floor' which shall now be maintained against all comers.

We had a typical 1940 conversation on Saturday. He had said he would ring me up about 9 P.M. but he didn't get on till 10.30.

Ch.: I'm sorry to be late but there's been an air-raid.

Ed.: Oh that's *quite* all right. Your poem arrived this morning.

Ch. was rather doubtful about my 'nincompoops', but really it's such a heaven-sent rhyme for hoops. I don't think I *can* give it up!

He now heard from de la Mare, who had been sent a package of translations about a month before. Several of his suggestions were adopted; others furnished the translator with material for a letter of what he called counter-diabolization. 'No, I had no idea what "honey-dew" really meant', he confessed in connection with his version of *Septimi Gades*. 'But I think S.T.C. is authority enough for using the word wrong—I'm sure he didn't mean that the man at the end of *Kubla Khan* had fed on green-fly secretions and drunk the milk of Paradise.' De la Mare was dissatisfied with the un-rhymed stanza used for *Persicos odi*. 'I would rhyme, *strictly* for your sake, if I could,' Eddie replied, 'but I don't see how—and for *my* sake, I don't want to!'

By September 9 Fuller had learned that the Horatian opposition was making some headway.

Mrs. Elgy has just been telling me how she saw an 'incidentary' bomb fall and be put out, also a 'parashot' descending from the sky. The southern and western gates of Gray's Inn are closed, and there's still a fire in Holborn not far off, so I send you my new Ode for two reasons, partly because it may give you a brighter moment, partly so that it may be in two places at once.

Not until the end of the month did he deign to take shelter in the basement. Mrs. Elgy had been visited by a time-bomb almost exactly on her door-step round the corner, so she came and slept with her dog in 'Rupert's bed'. Eddie told Fuller that six hours' sleep was now a record for one night, but he was getting on swimmingly and would send another Ode any moment. One visual image of him at this time has impressed itself indelibly upon my mind. The setting was wildly inappropriate—a refuse dump about a mile square near a poison gas factory on the Thames bank near Rainham. I was standing with a companion in a gun-emplacement, when we saw approaching an immaculate figure with precise feet and Whitehall poise, picking his way towards us over the rubbish which, being slightly on fire, was smouldering all over with a hideous and foetid exhalation. Eddie was not to be put off, and had come by bus (all leave being stopped and invasion imminent) to decide on the final order of my poems which he was preparing for the press, and to argue a few outstanding points in Horace. The gunner at my side on the look-out for paratroops stood spell-bound, gazing fixedly at the intruder while the thought in his mind took shape. 'Blimey!' he said at last, under his breath.

A week later he called on one of the directors of Messrs. Macmillan, who 'spoke in a tone which made me think he meant to take my Odes', but next day he heard that the publishers' windows had been blown in, so rather illogically, as he confessed, he delayed posting his manuscript. Knowing that one set of the Odes, though probably not three, was bound to be blown up, he sent duplicate copies to Fuller, his pianist friend Joseph Cooper who was with a searchlight unit in comparatively safe open country, and myself. This was done just in time, by the margin of a few hours, for his typing agency in Chancery Lane was hit, a time-bomb landed within a few yards of Raymond Buildings, and he was ordered out of his rooms.

He moved a mile or two away to Brooks's but on October 20 experienced a mental black-out as he was crossing Bond Street, a taxi ran over him, and he was taken to a nursing-home in Queen's Gate. There he spent his first good night for weeks, sat up next morning, apparently recovered from his concussion, and began revising the Odes which happened to be in his pocket. 'Yours indestructibly' he ended a letter of that day. Among his first visitors was a new acquaintance who was in London on short leave from a gun-site in Essex. John Guest had already begun writing the journal letters which he was to edit and bring out eight years later under the title *Broken Images*, but now his visit was serving à dual purpose. He was making a new friend and obliging me by collecting material for a first-hand report on the patient's condition. The bed was strewn with pages of corrected typescript, and Eddie was sitting up with a white loosely-knitted shawl thrown over his pyjamas. His face wore 'a bright, expectant look' which was reassuring. One could hardly see the counterpane for the Odes, and the general conversation was brief, for most of the precious minutes were taken up with a reading aloud of all the verses within reach, not one word of which was intelligible to the visitor, who was unable at such short notice to attune his ear to a style of delivery so tremulous and withdrawn.

Meanwhile his old friends were anxious. 'I have thought of you all through the waking hours of the night,' wrote Desmond MacCarthy. 'I trust you are not so injured and shaken that you cannot take pleasure in your accomplished mind and love of literature.' Lady Desborough wrote to cheer him with a sheaf of anecdotes, and succeeded admirably with a story passed on from Sir Evan Charteris, the biographer of Gosse, who was in a dark air-raid shelter when an A.R.P. official looked in. 'Are there any expectant mothers here?' No answer. He repeated the question, and a young cockney shouted, 'Give us time, gov, we've only been here ten minutes.' Gordon Bottomley, ever solicitous in his friendship, offered consolation of another sort.

> You must feel in a unique position in these overwhelming days when your life-long friend of friends has become the master of all our fates —and when your close association with him in the first war must have given you an insight into his intentions and an intimacy with the way his thought moves that can still feel like vivid daily companionship.

From the nursing-home Eddie sent Charles Morgan an appreciation of his new novel *The Voyage*, and confided in Fuller: 'Ch. like you urged me most strongly to leave London, and I must think seriously about it, if only to please him, but where to go is a problem.' Nancy Maurice had moved into Raymond Buildings so that he wouldn't feel he was deserting Mrs. Elgy. Nothing would budge her from Gray's Inn. Eddie's immediate problem was solved when the Duke of Devonshire called and at a bedside conference took everything in hand. The books and furniture at Gray's Inn were to be moved to Compton Place, his house at Eastbourne, and when Eddie was fit to travel he was to go straight to the country-house at Churchdale, in Derbyshire. He left London on November 1, and a month afterwards finally steeled himself to send off his Odes to the printer.

The Duke and Duchess were old friends. He was happy at

Churchdale, but his misfortunes were not over. He celebrated the new year 1941 as my wife's guest at Highgate and by blessed chance was staying the night under our roof when Raymond Buildings was seriously damaged by blast, the floors strewn with lumps of plaster, and the furniture shifted as by magic away from the walls into the middle of the rooms. The mahogany sideboard for instance had waddled into collision with the dining-table. The intrepid Nancy Maurice was shaken but unhurt. Soon after his return to Churchdale the place was looted. 'All of what Mrs. Elgy is pleased to call the silver' was stolen, also his decorations, and his bundles of papers were kicked around the floor and trampled. Mrs. Elgy called to salvage what she could, but in May a stick of bombs laid waste the Gray's Inn Chapel, Hall, and Library. Almost alone, Raymond Buildings stood up gaunt and prominent among the rubble, more than ever like the Ark stranded on Ararat as it had appeared to the eyes of Paul Nash many years before.

When this disaster occurred, *The Odes of Horace*, dedicated to 'The Three Ronalds' (Fuller, Storrs, and Knox), had been on sale for a month. Among the letters heralding publication-day none touched him so closely as the note from Mrs. Elgy, who was still in Holborn, calling each morning to keep an eye on the remaining books and pictures.

> i am so plesed your book is to be published and i do hope it will go of with a bang for you have spent sum hours at it you do disserve sum thing for your Trubbil.

Within eight weeks it was reprinted. Its character was so inappropriate to the times that it overshot the mark and, coming full circle, was found to be exactly what was needed. 'It really does me good in these times to read something so cultivated and urbane,' wrote Maugham. At Heytesbury Sassoon stopped work on *The Old Century* to send a tribute of snowdrops from his garden and a rhyme.

> Hail to thee, blithe Eddie,
> Bard thou never wert!
> But on your sweetly steady
> Translations I am ready
> To bet my blooming shirt.

'What takes my breath away,' Charles Morgan asserted, 'is precisely that, for once, a translation does take away my breath.

Live happy in the moment, take no thought
For hidden things beyond, be firm to test
And turn the edge of troubles with a jest;
For bliss unmixed was never earthly lot.
Young, but illustrious, Achilles died:
Tithonus in immortal age decays;
And Time, who knows? may grant my lowlier days
Good gifts to yours denied.
For you, the neighing of your chariot mares
And countless lowing of Sicilian Kine;
For you the precious dye the murex bears,
A. jewels of the Indian mine:
With me kind Fate has kept her word;
My little farm she gives me, country peace,
A strain of music from the hills of Greece,
A mind made strong to flout the envious herd.

Edward Marsh

From *Otium divos* ·
Horace, Odes II xvi

A fair copy by Edward Marsh of the concluding lines of his
translation of Horace's Ode XVI, Book II

Eddie at Walton Street, 1952

I began very soon to understand that you had written a book of poems that men would read with pleasure and honour long, long after we were all gone.' Richard Church considered it 'the fruit of a lifetime of cultural delight at a perpetual feast'. Edith Sitwell, too, found that the grace and restraint of the poems gave her 'a strange feeling of permanence and mental comfort. And when there is sorrow there is no horror—after all, I suppose that all ugliness passes, and beauty endures, excepting of the skin.' MacCarthy hailed 'the prince of translators. Horace I count among the Consolers. I thought once of writing a little book of six essays on Consolers. He was one, Montaigne another, Hume another.' De la Mare was struck by their freshness: 'How dreadfully *solemn* most people are about such things, as if they must be in the deepest crepe when the dead languages are about.' Robert Nichols approved the English craftsmanship but had no patience with the Latin original. He found Horace 'a trifler'. This wasn't good enough for the translator. He rose to the bait.

> The trouble with you is that you have no feeling for Beauty as such, and that if you don't like what a poet *says* he may speak with the tongues of men and of angels and you have no ear for him, not realizing that an exquisite work of art is just as well worth having as what you call 'a moving and enlightening reference to the world at large'. . . . Furthermore if Horace is a 'club-wiseacre' I suppose I am too. I wonder you put up with *me* as you do.

Since the English poet has at his disposal a much narrower range of metres than his Latin forerunner, Eddie's concern to find equivalents which reproduced something of the movement and tone of the original resulted in a book of poems technically more varied and interesting than his La Fontaine; and the *Romanitas* of Horace gave him opportunities of exercising the elevated Miltonic 'tune' for which he had an ear so peculiarly sensitive and assured. The unrhymed stanza of Milton's own translation of *Quis multa gracilis* (I, 5) is used more than once; elsewhere the pitch and rhythm of *Love in a Valley* is heard (*Laudabunt alii*, I, 7) and *The Book of Thel* (*Te maris*, I, 27), and a poem in Sapphics (*Impias parrae*, III, 27) appears in the guise of an idyll in blank verse. 'Exact fidelity, when by a lucky chance attainable, is a great virtue,' he wrote in the Preface, 'but it comes second to ease and naturalness.' The metrical liberties he took obliged him to make the effort of as it were recreating each poem from the ground upwards. It was here that his own personality, quite apart from his scholarship, proved a special asset. He was already Horatian in English terms. No wonder the eighteenth-century peasants in Horace's Sabine valley came to suspect that the poet must have been an Englishman, so numerous were the English pilgrims who asked the way to the site of the poet's villa. Something of Gray, Matthew Prior (even Horace Walpole), and the eighteenth-century imitators of Milton combined in Eddie to make of him a natural conductor for the work of his Augustan poet. The one adverse review implied that Horace had been diminished to a Georgian or minor Victorian poet. There is no trace of either quality in these Odes. Rather do they belong to an earlier age of our literature when neo-classic statues were erected in formal gardens to terminate the prospect. At such a time, when he would have been the obliging and esteemed friend of William Shenstone, an English Horace might have flourished. Into that age, which was still alive within him, Eddie sank the shaft of his poetical feeling and expression. His footnotes, as with La Fontaine, were sometimes quaintly objective, as if he were smiling over the reader's shoulder. 'Can I hope to forestall criticism by owning that my version of this Ode illustrates the proverb "Milton helps them who *help themselves*"?' Or, accounting for the omission of some verses, 'If Horace did not write them, it is only fair to leave them out: if he did, it is only kind.'

He owned to a particular fondness for his versions of the lighter Odes, and certainly he had a knack for starting them off with spirit: 'How long, old madam, will you carry on This monstrous racket?' or 'Tibullus, pull yourself together.' But one returns to the book chiefly for sake of those graver passages where Horace has moved his translator to such smoothly elegiac numbers . . . 'sole tree of all thy woods shall Cypress follow thee'.

> Young, but illustrious, Achilles died.
> Tithonus in immortal age decays. . . .
>
> At that blest hour when the departing sun
> Changes the mountain shadows one by one,
>   Disyokes the weary ox, and sheds
> The pleasant cool of evening on the meads. . . .

It was May 1941. Within a few months he would be sixty-nine, with his vigour unimpaired. In the retired peace of Churchdale he looked through the letters and cuttings that acclaimed a worthy sequel to the Fables. And with that sense of achievement the penultimate chapter of his life came to an end.

Since January 1940 he had been deputy chairman of the Trustees of the Tate Gallery. In a few weeks' time this, the last of his official obligations, would cease. There would be nothing to draw him back to London. As for Gray's Inn, much of it was now rubble, and Fuller had been injured that same night. Eddie decided never to return. Even Mrs. Elgy had at last consented to find refuge with relatives in Nottingham. She prepared to leave London, somewhat consoled, one hopes, by the thought of her generous pension. On May 25, after forty years' exemplary service, a masterpiece of her own, she wrote to Churchdale:

> i no you must of felt as greved as i do myself for i never thought we wood of parted in such a sad way it is braking my heart to have to leve the Place i have loved so meney years i feel i cannot geve it up as it is like taking my life away will you please thank the Duchess verrey much for offering to store my furniture . . . i cannot express my greatful thanks for all the kindness you have geven to me my one greif is i cannot do henny thing for you in return oh i am so sad about it all i doant no hough i am goin to bear it . . . i will try to bear it hoping you are well all the best yours greatfully H. Elgy.

Then she had Micky, and Judy the dog, put to sleep, and wrote from the Midlands:

> i kept them to the last you will no what that means to me i wood rather of stayed in the Ruins and kept them . . . there is a dog here but I doant like it he bit me on sunday he is verry snapey.

Chapter Nineteen

DOMINIQUE
(*June 1941–January 1953*)

A T Churchdale, for the first time in his life, Eddie Marsh saw the seasons round in the countryside, but after a year he was obliged to seek shelter elsewhere. Living space out of town was limited, and his room was wanted. Although he had ample warning he showed himself peculiarly lacking in resource, and such exertions as he made to fend for himself were ineffectual. In January 1942 he moved to a hotel off St. James's Street, which was practically deserted and had already been damaged. It was obviously imperative that he should settle somewhere in the country. At this time my military office was the boiler-room of a house in a Kentish village, and there seemed no way of solving Eddie's problem except by getting him into the Army billet at Walton-on-the-Hill near Tadworth from which I had recently been posted away. Fortunately the elderly widow whose home it was could play bézique. Using this as a bait on both sides negotiations came to a point where Eddie was invited to go, on approval, as a paying guest. Surrounded by complicated luggage, he arrived in late January. He was soon making notes on the manuscript of Brett Young's poem *The Island*, settled at last in an upper room of the small villa, overlooking a magnificent Calvary Thorn which glowed a fiery and dishevelled copper beneath his window.

This lasted a month. Then a letter from the hospitable lady showed that all was not going as one could wish. She had much enjoyed the readings aloud after supper, and had acquired quite a taste for Latin poetry, but the management of a house in wartime was difficult enough without a guest who declaimed verses in the small hours, played cards with unflagging persistence, helped himself to all the jam, delayed meals by sending out the maid with registered letters, and seemed incapable of doing anything for himself. Together we devised an excuse about a sudden influx of relations, and an appeal to my commanding officer gave

630

me access to the military telephone reserved for priority calls. After checking over a long inventory of Eddie's friends, all of whom seemed to be in Africa, France, or the grave, I had but one suggestion left. In the vicarage at Stonegate near Tunbridge Wells lived Mr. and Mrs. Andrew Young. Since they had barely met the proposed lodger, and were already overworked in the parish, my telephone call must have sounded like an offer of the last straw. To Stonegate, however, went the miscellaneous luggage, and the evacuee was given welcome. The Youngs took him on a visit to Viola Meynell at Greatham, and he was so contented in their company that when his sister died in April, and his brother-in-law, Sir Frederick Maurice, wrote asking for his companionship, he was reluctant to uproot himself again, even though his new destination was to be in West Road, Cambridge.

Staying with Sassoon at Heytesbury in July he listened to some chapters of *The Weald of Youth*, and in his correspondence he passed on to Bottomley what had struck him as perhaps the best *bon mot* of the war. The Chief Rabbi of Jerusalem was asked who in his opinion was going to win. 'I think, on the whole, the British,' came the reply, 'either naturally or miraculously.' On being asked what he meant by this he said, 'They might win by the help of God, which would be natural, or by their own efforts—which would be miraculous.' 'I told this to Winston,' Eddie concluded. 'He was *much* amused. I wondered what would have happened to anyone who had told an analogous story to Hitler.'

Eddie was becoming increasingly fascinated by his dreams. After this visit Sassoon was favoured with a good example. 'I woke up the other day from a dream in which I had been reading some modern poet, I don't know who, and found myself saying, "It seems as if a vocabulary had been wandering over the page and at a signal given each word had sat down wherever it happened to be."'

Mr. Churchill must have been told the anecdote of the Rabbi when Eddie lunched with him earlier in July. On his return to Cambridge Eddie wrote to tell me of 'a very good luncheon at 10 Downing Street'.

Winston was in great form, looking very well and vigorous, and said some quite good things. Talking of the difficulties among the Free French, he said, 'When a country collapses, the chaos reproduces itself in every microcosm'. . . He also said how wonderful it was that the country should be so united behind him, 'when I'm admittedly the biggest defeat-merchant in English history' . . . Edward Halifax also looked extremely well and beanful. The moment when Winston went to see Roosevelt and was told on his arrival of the fall of Tobruk must have been one of the most painful of his life. At first he couldn't believe it.

At Cambridge there were G. M. Trevelyan, George Rylands, and John Hayward; also Robert Nichols working on a drama about Don Juan, and above all Frances Cornford, who welcomed him into the bosom of her family at Conduit Head. In his time he had seen all too little of family life, so he was glad of the daughter-in-law and small grandson who accepted him as an uncle. Mrs. Cornford herself was at work on her book *Poems from the Russian*. She took him into her poetical workshop, and was continually submitting her rough drafts to his criticism. Once more he had the joy of being useful to someone he loved. One of his minor occupations, meanwhile, was curious in the extreme. Noel Langley on war service in Canada had asked for scholarly information for use in his new novel *Lysistrata*. 'I consulted the eminent Greek scholar Dr. F. M. Cornford, who has lately published a superlative translation of Plato's *Republic*,' wrote Eddie. 'I asked if there were any improper Greek words that you could use for naming characters—but it's a melancholy fact that my generation of Greek scholars were remarkably pure-minded—and tho' both of us from time to time must have met with many such words, neither of us could remember any of them except the obvious ones. I've been meaning to read some Aristophanes in hopes of finding more.' He had just celebrated his seventieth birthday at Brooks's and drunk a bottle of Paul Roger which was all the more delicious for being the last in the cellar.

The year 1943 passed agreeably at Cambridge. There were occasional dinners at Trinity or King's, proofs to correct, the composition of various prize-winning entries for the *New Statesman* competition page, and the constant diversion and solace of Mrs. Cornford's companionship. His letters were full of Cambridge anecdotes like the story of a royal visit to Trinity. 'When the Duchess of Kent was to lunch there at the Lodge two or three weeks ago George Trevelyan sent to ask the Food Office if he could have anything extra, they told him he could have some rice and two pennyworth of meat—so he went out and shot two partridges which saved the situation.' In September a letter from Langley, deprecating the tendency on the part of some people to 'enjoy' the war, moved him to reflect on the prevailing climate of opinion:

I know that I live an unduly sheltered life, also that I'm by nature naive and gullible, nor do I move among politicians and business men but almost everybody I know seems to take an unexceptionable line— loathing the War, but calm and patient and enduring and looking forward with stoical goodwill to the Better World that is to follow, however little its prophesied shape may appeal to them personally. 'The World of the Common Man!' it makes me shudder, but I prepare myself to greet it with a cheer (not that I shall survive to see much of it!).

Soon after Christmas he visited my home in Surrey, and I was given an insight into the troubles which had led to the hurried departure from Tadworth. During his travels he had certainly developed his powers of self-entertainment. Wine, talk, music, books, children—one would have thought the guest had been sufficiently amused and worn out. But long after midnight my wife was disturbed by voices in the spare bedroom raised in altercation. Puzzled and alarmed, I tip-toed on to the landing. There was a light under Eddie's door, and now it sounded like a party in full swing. 'Oh well *played!*' came the familiar voice. 'Don't be a fool—play the King and—damn—now you've done it! You're left with a miserable Three of Clubs. Oh God, Oh Montreal. . . . Ah well, better risk it. . . .' Not to be done with the agreeable day too soon, he was playing cards against himself, and was also his own spectator. In the minute villa at Tadworth such dramatic monologues in the dead of night must have sounded like robbery with violence.

With the new year 1944 he was back at Cambridge, corresponding with Baring about Meredith, whose work was the subject of a new monograph by Sassoon. 'Has it ever struck you,' wrote Baring, 'that all the catastrophes which happen in his books would not have happened had there been such a thing as a telephone? This is not true about Shakespeare.' Eddie was also pursuing an argument with Bottomley, whose recent plays were showing a tendency to use the present indicative in the subjunctive sense. 'I'm quite *sure* there is no difference in sense between "as though you were being watched" and what you *mean* to mean by "as though you are being watched".' Such use of the indicative, Eddie protested, was 'all part of the general blunting of the language'. Another correspondent was the poet Martyn Skinner, whom he had not yet come to know personally but whose *Letters from Malaya* (sent him in proof by MacCarthy in 1941) had started a lively and learned exchange that was to last for the rest of his life. Skinner was the first to be given one of his important notes on Milton's text. 'The only emendation I passionately want to make is in *L'Allegro*, which he [Milton] could see through the press himself. "Of Cerberus and blackest midnight born." Why should Cerberus give birth to Melancholy? I think he *must* have meant to put Erebus.' In March the seven-year term as a Trustee of the Tate Gallery came to an end. 'You are, if I may humbly say so, the ideal 20th-century patron of art,' wrote Jasper Ridley on behalf of the Committee, 'and we all know it.'

Now and again he would travel up from Cambridge for what he called 'a theatre cure'. The London stage had recovered from the Blitz, and *The Dancing Years* which was now at the *Adelphi* looked like becoming the *Chu Chin Chow* of the second world war, the show that nobody on leave should miss. He had recently taken Mrs. Churchill to see it before a special performance, given in aid of her Russian Fund, and had supped afterwards at Downing Street, where he found Mr. Churchill playing bézique with Averil Harriman. Novello was doing a lot for war charities and his song *Rose of England*, a revival from one of his pre-war plays, was being reissued. He had just composed a new patriotic song, in anticipation of an Allied push through France, when all thought of work was driven from his mind. It was April 1944. When Eddie rushed up to London having heard that Novello was to stand his trial at Bow Street for an alleged offence against the regulations governing the use of petrol he had no real fears. He knew that Novello would have had neither time nor inclination to enter into the squalid little conspiracy in which he was supposed to be involved. For years he had delegated to others the tedious routine of his administrative affairs. If anything were irregular, thought Eddie, it could only be an oversight, an omission to look into some matter or other which did not happen to interest him. 'If I were *conscious* of anything wrong,' Novello remarked to him, 'surely you know I would have told *you*'; and then, 'How can anyone suppose I would have knowingly run such a risk for so little?' He was advised to plead 'guilty through inadvertence', but he would not hear of it. If there was a shadow on his name, he would plead the innocence which he felt, and so be acquitted and cleared of the slightest imputation. Out of his element, he lost his nerve. He had no idea how to conduct himself under the ordeal of cross-examination, and was altogether at a loss when confronted with facts, figures, quickfire questions, and other aspects of the panoply of the law which he had never met with before. Between his conviction and the appeal on May 16 Eddie made personal calls on every individual, office, or department of the legislature that was in any way involved. He did the one thing he had sworn never to do. He broke his oath never to take advantage of personal affection by asking the Prime Minister to give a preferential thought to one of his friends. He called at Downing Street and, getting no immediate satisfaction, beat with his fist on Mr. Churchill's desk. It is not easy to imagine what he thought the Prime Minister could do beyond give assurance of his sympathy, which of course he did. At the London Sessions, Newington Butts, Eddie was called to give evidence of the appellant's character. Lewis Casson and Sybil Thorndike accompanied him and did likewise. The prison sentence was not revoked, but it was reduced from eight to four weeks. So gruelling was the strain of these times, so shocked was he by what in his view was the savagely rigid application of the letter of the law combined with the outrage of its spirit, that his normally firm handwriting began to wander uncertainly over the page as he relived his trouble each evening in the daily reports to his friends. Paul Nash was the first to condole. In his time he had benefited from Novello's patronage. 'It was certainly the most painful thing in my life,' Eddie replied. 'He had certainly been most imprudent and far too happy-go-lucky, but if there's one thing in the world I'm certain of it is that he had neither intention nor consciousness of doing anything wrong, and now he bears his misfortune with exemplary courage and fortitude.'

'Dear Paul,' he ended, 'It is true that I didn't keep up with you in *all* your developments, but there was never a time when I lost touch with the body of your work; even when I didn't under-stand there was often much that I admired and enjoyed.' He was at last beginning to feel old. 'I've never been one for living in the past,' he had written to Langley, 'but every now and then I get quite Tennysonian about the days that are no more.' He was in a

front stall for the anxious moment of the curtain rise on Novello's
return to the Adelphi. The astonishing demonstrations of enthusiasm showed that the general public were in accord with his
own view of the affair. The anxiety was over, but the state of
shock remained. Sometimes when walking he would have to
stop to get his breath.

The proofs of essays by MacCarthy, Raymond Mortimer,
Peter Quennell, some war-time speeches of Churchill, *A Prospect
of Flowers* by Andrew Young, and new verses by Brett Young,
were lying neglected on his table at Cambridge. He was weary and
had suddenly grown thin. Relief came from an unexpected
quarter. Late in July a scathing diatribe against things in general
from Langley in Canada had the rousing effect of a tonic on his
spirits. He threw off his lethargy and was duly grateful:

> There's been nothing like your letters since Rabelais and *The
> Anatomy of Melancholy*, no such rolling and varied rhythm, and wealth
> of weltering words and pregnant nonsense. When I die I must leave
> the bundle to Ch. against the day you hope for when Art will regain
> a scrotum and revive under a new Priapus, and your flame will blaze
> in a shocked but enchanted sky. Even your most woe-begone letters
> never depress me, because I know that such valorous writing could
> not be bred by despair.

For some months Eddie had been aware that his brother-in-law
was counting on him to look for a new abode, and he had so far
proved no more resourceful than on previous occasions. One may
imagine that he had been getting hold of *The Times* first and spending too long over the crossword puzzle, or slamming the bathroom
door, not now and then but constantly. For whatever the reason,
the waters at West Road were not unruffled. 'Why this is so, I've
never been able to understand,' Eddie confessed to his friend in
Canada. 'He is a most excellent and admirable man, in a high
degree able and intelligent, interested in literature and the arts,
and at bottom very good-natured—so why? but the fact remains
that we are "allergic"—I've never hinted this to a soul (except
once to Ivor)—not even to Ch., as it would have distressed him,
so keep it eternally under your hat.' The time was drawing
uncomfortably near for his room to be taken over by the newcomer
when a total stranger stepped out of a Rolls-Royce and rang the
doorbell. 'A *deus ex machina* all to myself!' Eddie remarked, 'and

what a machina!' It was an unknown admirer, Dr. Bernard
Armitage, who had heard of the urgent problem and come in the
nick of time to make an offer of a place under his roof at Kew.
Amazed with his luck, as well he might be, Eddie accepted at
once and, as he put it, 'began to lay the foundations' of his packing.
During these labours he took himself off for a 'theatre cure' and a
luncheon at Downing Street, and on August 27 sent his comment
to Gordon Bottomley.

> When I was in town three weeks ago I lunched with the Hero and
> found him in most excellent case, somehow more impressive than
> before. For the bodily man *dodu*[1] seemed the best word (you remem-
> ber *'Didon dîna dit-on du dos d'un dodu dindon'*) and there was a new
> augustness about him—an air of power and dignity, but still the old
> ribald twinkle—like a Louis Quatorze or even mediaeval archbishop
> —master of his world, and at the same time *gaguenard*[2] and above all
> benevolent. He must be the greatest example in history of the stone
> that the builders rejected. I wish I could remember in which of the
> Thirties it was that he told me he would quit politics if he didn't
> still think there might be a faint chance of being Prime Minister
> after all. 'What a hope,' I thought at the time, but 'the good stars
> met in his horoscope' must have already decided that every seeming
> setback and obstacle should in the end lead to his triumph. How
> fatal it would have been if he had got back into politics before he
> did—his loyalty would have entangled him in the errors that he
> would have been no more able to prevent than he actually was—
> but when his moment came he had a clean sheet instead of a white
> one to stand in. Now you are able to convert even Sidney St. which
> was for so long thought a blot on his record, into an augury! I was
> there, you know,—alas, I shan't be (if your prophetic soul is justified
> and history repeats itself) at Berchtesgaden.

As the names and events of the past kept recurring in his mind
he tended to withdraw into himself more and more. The quality of
agelessness was gone. There was an autumnal air about him.
'Desmond MacCarthy once observed that half the disasters in
human relations came about because people want to be loved in
the way that suits *them* and won't be satisfied with the kind of love
that it suits the other person to give,' he wrote to Langley in
September, 'and you seem to have realized this and acted upon
it—and in so doing to have become a bigger, better, and wiser
man.' The tones of a gentle sage were to grow more frequent.

[1] Plump.   [2] A man of caustic and sardonic wit.

In October the Kew house was under repair, so it was to Dr. Armitage's property on Yarnell's Hill, two miles from Oxford, that Eddie moved with his belongings. 'It's in a lovely situation among autumnal woods,' he reported to Langley, and gave news that he shared the little place with a family of refugees from Plymouth. The mother, a woman of German birth, held two degrees in Philosophy and Domestic Economy, 'the latter of which is to me the more important'. He was teaching her bézique, and was happy enough in spite of the slight congestion. Also in the house were two golden retrievers, which accompanied him on his strolls into the neighbouring woods. During this autumn of 1944, when he was rediscovering the countryside in his solitary walks and looking about him at the waning year in a spirit of acceptance after suffering, Eddie Marsh was becoming the perfect translator of the novel *Dominique* by Eugène Fromentin, if only someone should put the idea into his head.

ii

On leaving Yarnell's Hill at the end of December he moved for a few weeks to St. Fagan's Castle, Cardiff, where he re-arranged a section of the library with his thoughts overshadowed by the death of Robert Nichols. 'It's tragic to think of his last moments,' he wrote to Charles Morgan, 'if he realized that he would never live to trace the shadows of the symbols that crowded his brain. I never had much belief in *Don Juan*, but some of his projects were very fine—if only he had been able to concentrate on one of them!' When the time came to move again he booked himself a room at the Goring Hotel, near Grosvenor Gardens. He had not seen London for six months, and even the promised refuge at Kew seemed too far out of town. The only problem was how to pay his bills. Reluctantly he visited the vaults of the Tate, picked out one of his treasures, *The Vale of Aylesbury* by John Nash, sold it, and sent half the proceeds to the artist, who was serving as a staff officer at Portsmouth. Nash was surprised by the windfall and saddened to hear that he would never again climb the stairs to breakfast at Gray's Inn. 'There was that lovely fresh morning air and the delightful look of the tops of the trees. . . . I think I remember a cooing of doves and a sense of peace and beauty which has always surrounded you in my memory.'

A day or two after settling in the hotel at the end of January, Eddie wrote to me saying that the chief event recently was 'a delightful half-hour with Winston'.

> I went to No. 10 on Thursday, with a batch of proofs, and hearing that I was there he sent for me—I found him in bed, after his great speech, with a bad cold, for which he was 'inhaling'—but it hadn't impeded his delivery. He told me he had spent three days in bed composing the oration, damning and cursing all the time and hating it more and more—but that when he was on his legs he found himself coming round to it, till in the end he thought it quite good. He was over the moon about the Russian offensive, which he thought might have enormous, incalculable results. One thing that pleased me: he spoke unprompted of the sentence on Ivor, which he said had grieved him very much . . .

Eddie had been translating La Fontaine's *Invocation* for Bernhard Berenson, who was urging him to undertake some new task of magnitude. 'As for my doing any more translations,' he replied, 'I'm afraid my day is past. Horace and La Fontaine were the two authors I knew best. I felt I knew more or less how they ought to go, and there's so much that seems to me English in them both. I should be afraid of saddling them with bastard brothers.' He would soon be changing his tune. Meanwhile there were proofs to correct. Maugham's *The Razor's Edge* had been finished in the autumn, and now the same author's *Then and Now* was arriving in instalments. Between 1935 and 1951 Maugham received many hundreds of pages of critical notes on fourteen of his publications.[1] The correcting of printer's errors was the least part of their bulk, since it was Eddie's custom to identify himself with the author's purpose and challenge the slightest deviation in expression from the writer's meaning. 'I know what I want to say, and I say it,' Maugham once remarked, 'then Eddie comes along and tells me I haven't.' In 1939 Maugham published an article on Eddie Marsh called *Proof-reading as an Avocation*.[2] He told the story of their meeting in London when he was at work on *Don Fernando*, and how he diffidently broached the subject of his proofs. 'He is a highbrow, and has always mixed with highbrows,' Maugham wrote, 'and I was humiliatingly conscious that they did not look

[1] See Appendix III for examples of his notes on *The Summing Up* (1938).
[2] *The Publisher's Weekly* (the American Book Trade journal), Vol. CXXXVI, No. 16, 1939.

upon me as fit to belong to their august body; I was afraid he would not think it worth his while to waste pains over work that was so popular.' He was embarrassed by the cordiality with which Eddie acceded to his request. 'He spoke as though I were positively doing him a favour.' On that day in 1935 Eddie himself referred to the incident in his diary. He did indeed regard it as a favour. 'There's glory for me!' he noted with satisfaction. When at last the first batch of notes arrived Maugham was taken aback. 'Here were not the few casual corrections I had expected, but an imposing series of remarks on punctuation, grammar, style, and fact.'

> I must add that if Edward Marsh in his relations with people somewhat overflows with the milk of human kindness, he makes up for it when he corrects proofs; for then his comments are by turn scornful, pained, acid and vituperative. No obscurity escapes his stricture, no redundance his satire, and no clumsiness his obloquy. I think few authors could suffer this ordeal and remain persuaded that they wrote tolerably well.

In *A Number of People* there is a chapter entitled Diabolization. It begins by describing how when writing to me soon after our meeting in March 1934 Eddie had asked me to regard him as an *Advocatus Diaboli*, in the sense that he was a critic whose declared aim was to find fault and be as carping as possible for the eventual benefit of the work in hand. Since his avowed function was to be disagreeable, the crumbs of his approval were all the more precious and his rare praise a real encouragement. From his Latin style I coined the word 'diabolization' to describe his particular brand of criticism. The noun and its verb 'diabolize' have been used by Maugham and others, so it may almost be said to have entered the language. There were other terms which were coined for our private use. A session in which one challenged certain of his objections—the process of counter-diabolization—was called a 'battlefield'; postponing the settlement of a point so as to visit the London Library was 'defence-in-depth'; and the final session when minor differences were disposed of was a 'skirmish'. He liked being challenged, and would grow shrill and heated, his most powerful weapon in a skirmish being his sense of the ridiculous. The counter-diabolizer had only one possible defence as a last resort. When hard pressed, you could shift your ground and say that you hadn't really meant to say *quite* what he was *supposing* you had intended to say, so he might as well stop beating his wings in vain. But this was unfair. He would break off at once, fascinated, and softly launch the dreaded shaft, 'I see; then in that case what *did* you mean to say?' the answer to which required quick thinking. At the luckiest one would disengage from the skirmish bearing the scar—'But how *could* you have imagined that (meaning what you *now* say) you had already *said* it or anything *like* it?' When all was over, and he had been exasperated, and the counter-diabolizer had grown irritable, he would go to the side-table for the whisky, and turn, glass in hand, remarking in the tones of a giant refreshed, 'What a simply *splendid* skirmish!'

In the early years of the war Maugham was out of reach of his diabolizer so he made up for it by offering him the dedication of *Strictly Personal*. In the dedicatory epistle he spoke of the pleasure he had taken in Eddie's 'acidity, mitigated fortunately by humour . . . and humanized by a pleasant weakness for the colon. . . . The future (if it is concerned with us at all) will find that many of the best writers of English of our generation are indebted to you for such proficiency as they have acquired in the practice of writing our difficult language.' It must have been after *Don Fernando*, or another of the earlier books to be diabolized, that Maugham wrote: 'I scampered hurriedly through your notes, and then I went straight down to the Bath Club to look you out in *Who's Who*. I heaved a great sigh of relief. Thank heaven you'll last my time, for what I should do without you I can't imagine.' After getting the notes on *Catalina* he wrote: 'I think you have been harsher than I have ever known you before, but I have kissed the rod.' Among Eddie's papers was a shabby brown envelope which he called the Vanity Bag. It contained certain letters which had especially gratified him, and among their number were several records of Maugham's generous thanks.

I sometimes read in the papers (A) that I write well and (B) that I am modest. They little know, the people who say this, that it is not I but you who write well; and as for modesty, those pages of corrections of yours are iron heels on great Nazi boots that grind my face into the dust; each time I say to myself—Now *this* time I'm sure he won't see much to find fault with, and then the proofs come back . . . all my conceit has got to be hurriedly packed away again. So it is not only the correctness of my language that I owe to you, but also the beauty of my character.

The Vanity Bag also contained Maugham's charmingly extravagant tribute, 'If now I am widely used in foreign countries, even as far way as Japan, in the teaching of English, I am sure that I owe this largely to you.' Throughout the war he sent Eddie food-parcels from abroad. They were appreciated far more than he could have realized at the time. Certain of the luxuries puzzled the recipient. 'What *am* I to do with these?' he would say, holding up a tin of something. 'Isn't Willie a dear? but how in heaven's name does one cook them? I suspect that the secret is to *soak* them. One can but try and see what happens.' He was apt to be rather secretive about these parcels, knowing that if he consulted a stranger on how to deal with the contents he might feel obliged to give a lot of them away. When he was settled at the Goring Hotel, food being still rationed, one can understand why a caller was surprised to find the wash-hand basin in the bed sitting-room afloat with sodden apricots.

In November (1945) he saw Paul Nash's *Sunflowers* at Tooth's and wrote in excitement to the artist, who was already afflicted with his last illness. He was not again in touch with Nash before his premature death in July 1946. He had recently come upon a poem of Dylan Thomas, he said, and had been obliged to give it up in a spirit of 'uncomprehending respect. . . . When I see something I ought to but cannot admire,' he confessed, 'I always quote Crabb Robinson's diary—"Took Landor and Wordsworth to see the Elgin Marbles which Wordsworth confessed he wasn't up to."' Soon after this his Christmas letter to de la Mare, congratulating him on the perpetual freshness of his recent verse, moved the poet to remember former times.

> Coming from you, out of the old Georgian days, as it were, when you did so much for me, the kindness of it and as one lover of poetry to another: Well, there we are. . . . The last time we met was in Piccadilly (all my sense of time is in hopeless confusion) and the streets and the shops and the people faded out as we talked.

It was now full winter for the Georgians. Bottomley's Christmas letter came from his old home in the Lakes.

> Dear Eddie, be ageless and continuing, I beg you: the men of our time were a rich company, and we were rich in them, and they have been going down lately like spires and campaniles before the guns of Fate. Even I am incredibly seventy-two. But change does not touch you. Don't let it, Eddie. Stay and console us.

He stayed, and was happy so long as he was being useful to someone he respected. As the year 1946 came in he was copying out poems in his clear script for John Hayward's anthology *Seventeenth Century Poetry*. While staying with his brother-in-law at Cambridge he had been a regular caller on John Hayward who was living at Merton Hall during the war. So far the chief result was that he had lost a good deal of his prejudice against the poetry of T. S. Eliot. When *The Dry Salvages* first came out as a pamphlet Hayward insisted on reading aloud the first section and, at sight of the tears gathering on the lower lids of his visitor's eyes, knew he had won his point. In January Hayward became literary adviser to the Cresset Press and editor of the Cresset Library, a new series containing a number of new English translations of foreign classics. The proofs of his preface and selection of seventeenth century poems left Eddie's table at the Goring Hotel in March, accompanied by the usual sheaf of notes. 'I'm sure I shall not reject your good advice,' wrote Hayward, 'except in one or two insignificant places where my *amour-propre* would be glad of an excuse to do so. O dear (or should it be Oh! dear) it is mortifying, though doubtless salutary. . . .' It must have been shortly after this that Hayward found Eddie one evening in the billiard-room at Brooks's, sitting alone in the dark listening to the Club's wireless set. It occurred to the intruder that a fine and scholarly mind might perhaps be suffering for want of active occupation. He was right, and with that thought *Dominique* came a stage closer.

iii

Meanwhile Eddie Marsh was trying his hand at house-hunting, and some of the places he considered seriously only proved that, food and drink apart, he had no instinct for physical comfort. Economy had become an obsession. More than once I followed him up a frowsty stairway only to be shown into an attic such as Chatterton would have scorned to die in. After weeks of disappointment some rooms were found on the first and second floors of 86 Walton Street, Knightsbridge. Next door lived Leonard Appelbee (some of whose work was already in the Marsh collection) and his wife, Frances MacDonald, who had at last found this place which would serve tolerably well, small though it was. Of one thing Eddie was now certain, he must sell his library. The Duke of Devonshire's house in Eaton Terrace was unoccupied, so the drawing-room floor was borrowed for displaying the books which came up in vans from Eastbourne. A system of lanes was devised, so that one could walk up and down among them, while the few that might be needed for future use were put aside in one corner of the parquet floor. 'Will you be wanting this?' I asked, holding up a dishevelled copy of the *Aeneid*, doubtless a relic of Westminster. 'How do you expect me to get on without a Virgil?' he answered petulantly from his chair at the central point of the radiating lanes. 'Can *you* imagine anybody living without a Virgil?' I said I could name one or two, and happened to ask why the poet's name was sometimes spelt with an 'e'. '*Nothing* makes me so angry as spelling Virgil with an "e"!' he cried in exasperation. His hair was unkempt, his hands and clothes grey with dust, he was dog-tired. He looked as if he had suddenly been turned into a very old man.

The relief of having a place of his own at last quite overcame the disadvantage of restricted space. When more packages from Eastbourne arrived at Walton Street and were dumped on the floor of the empty dining-room he was almost alarmed by the quantity of glass which had accrued to him over the years, enough for a banquet of thirty with all varieties of wine, all dulled with dust and looking as far removed from their days of Edwardian good cheer as the drinking bowls in a museum from their bygone feasts of Dionysus. Disconsolate, he sat among scrolls of news-paper, silver ladles, and ornamental sauce-boats, wondering what on earth to do with these relics of better days. While Mrs. Appelbee conducted interviews for a daily help, her husband worked with hammer and wire, hanging pictures as directed, till the very doors rumbled when opened with the infant thunder of colliding frames. Eventually the pictures overflowed into the hallway shared in common with the occupant of the flat below. By the door into the garden a rusty nail stuck out from the wall barely five inches from the floor. Beside it the long-suffering tenant of the ground-floor flat scribbled in pale pencil, 'Please hang no picture *here*.' It was some months before this was noticed and pointed out to the great patron. 'Is that,' he said, 'perhaps the *quietest* little joke you've ever seen?'

It was now imperative that one touring exhibition should overlap with another, for were the whole family to come home at once the place would be uninhabitable. 'What *am* I to do?' he would exclaim, distracted, when threatened with an invasion. In the end he loaned his pictures out to friends. Many remained in the vaults of the Tate Gallery, in particular several Alexander Cozenses which he looked upon as a supplement to the 'murder money'. 'X is at his wit's end again, poor fellow, and he's painting so well these days. He really has come on. I must do something to keep the wolf from his door. Let's meet for tea next week. Monday any good? Then we can go to the Tate and pick out another Cozens.'

The kitchen and bathroom were combined in the adjoining room, the head of the bath alongside the sink, and the William Morris writing-table from Gray's Inn, piled with superfluous crockery, was pushed against the fireplace. High over the gas oven a Paul Nash painting was hung where the bather could contemplate its vista as he lay and meditated in comfort. The bath itself was overshadowed by an enormous geyser which looked as if it were hatching sinister designs. On two occasions it disgorged its boiling contents over the floor, so that the flat below received a cascade through the ceiling. 'There's no getting away from it,' was Eddie's comment, 'that thing really hates me.'

The blue Sickert presided over the dining-room chimney-piece; the same painter's *New Bedford* gleamed in the recess at one side and Duncan Grant's *Harlequin* in the other. The chimney-piece itself was an orderly muddle of his favourite oddments: a small terracotta head of a goddess which Ronald Storrs had sent from Cyprus; an ancient tear-bottle of opalescent glass from a tomb at Heliopolis, a present from Mrs. Flecker; a miniature figurine in bronze by Gaudier-Brzeska, given by T. E. Hulme; a thick silver coin of Athens at the time of Pericles; a diminutive bust of Walter Scott in white marble; a locket of Brooke's hair in its leather case; a framed snapshot of Bridges as an old man, sitting on a stone seat beneath a mullioned window; and invitation cards to private views of picture exhibitions, variously coloured and propped up, exposed, or slipped in here and there, according to whether they were reminders of pleasures yet to come or mementos of the past. Between the windows overlooking the street stood the mahogany cabinet which still contained most of the Horne collection, and on the top were arranged numerous little china emus and prancing horses (most of them presents from Mrs. Elgy) with their centre-piece a massive bull carved in Spanish serpentine by John Skeaping; and once the two glass-fronted book-cases were in position the place was furnished, and there was only just room to walk round the table. The present of a wireless set from Frances Cornford served a dual purpose, performing its normal function and screening the cat's saucer which otherwise would be displaying its unsightly morsel of neglected fish.

The room above was used as the living-room (less heavily furnished because the stairs were so narrow) until it had to become the bedroom for a manservant. The back room where Eddie slept was minute. Over the fireplace, where it could be easily admired from the bed, hung the portrait of an unknown lady which he had bought as a Lely many years before, but which has since been attributed to Pieter Borssler—the head and shoulders of a tired, plain woman of exalted birth, in premature middle age. After Wilson's *Cader Idris* (which by now had been presented to the National Gallery as a thank-offering for V.E. Day) it was the most treasured painting of the whole collection. The soft and pendent brown curls of her wig touched her breasts, which just showed above a brown silk dress, and they framed a narrow, angular face, ashen pale, with a pointed, slightly protruding chin, suggesting an uneven bite. The mouth, set firm, was depressed at the corners, the eyebrows highly arched over wide-open but languid eyes, the face wore that far-away regard of someone who does not see what she is looking at, and in her right hand which rested on her knee she held a flower, absently, as if it were nothing of hers but had been put into her hand for sake of the composition and she had forgotten about it. One could gaze at her for minutes together, wondering what elegiac seventeenth-century thought she was turning over in her mind, letting it soften those chilly, almost sexless features. 'She is supposed to be a member of the Ashley-Cooper family,' was all that Eddie knew of her. He hung her portrait where it would be the last thing he saw at night and the first on waking.

The back-garden was his own domain, and in the centre he set up the small Gill statue of a naked girl from Raymond Buildings. He took his gardening seriously, and bought a roller which had to be pulled round almost the moment it was got in motion, so confined was the area of manœuvre. 'Come and look at the garden first,' he would say on one's arrival. 'Do you remember that pathetic little shoot only last week? Look at it now. And what about the lawn? I've been clipping it with scissors. Would you have guessed?' And then the undersized black-and-white cat with the end of one ear bitten off, conscious that the social moment of the day had begun, would streak by, chasing an imaginary leaf; on all sides the backs of grey brick Victorian houses; at one angle a glimpse of somebody's washing on the line, and all around the rumbling murmur of traffic from the neighbourhood of Brompton Oratory.

It had been difficult to persuade him to have the stairs carpeted or the walls repainted, but the sale of his books had brought him enough extra cash to prevent him indefinitely regarding these necessities as an extravagance. Several of his painters wrote to greet him in his new home. 'I call it an honour indeed to have had you sitting in my studio in your shirt sleeves,' wrote one of them. 'You must know,' wrote another, 'that without your real help when I most needed it years ago, I would never have had the strength to plod on.' None of this gratitude was wasted on him. It was now early August, and for three weeks he had been settled in. All he wanted was something to engross his mind. It was then that a letter from John Hayward of the Cresset Press suggested a translation of the novel *Dominique* by Eugène Fromentin, which had first begun to appear in the *Revue des Deux Mondes* in April 1862.

iv

Eddie was diffident about undertaking another major translation at the age of seventy-four. Most of La Fontaine and Horace he had known by heart. Now he would have to make the acquaintance of a comparative stranger, but it was worth trying, for there were occasions when he had to admit that for one whose habitual place was in the swing of things he was being left behind by the times. He had discovered boredom. There was also the thought that he had already been associated with John Hayward and had taken pleasure in busying himself in his service. Moreover Fromentin was a painter and *Dominique* was his solitary essay in fiction. This roused his curiosity. There was reason enough at least for borrowing the book and glancing through it. And now the deaths of Maurice Baring and Paul Nash, following the loss of Robert Nichols, were making him look around for something to keep his mind from dwelling on the transitoriness of life.

While he is still a boy Dominique falls in love with Madeleine, the cousin of a school-friend, who is a little older than himself. He does not become conscious of the full intensity of his feelings until he discovers that she has made an eligible but loveless marriage. She then learns the truth from Dominique, and in her solicitude for him, which takes the form of helping him try to convert his love into friendship, she is herself infected with his passion. Both suffer while their relationship develops towards the critical point where circumstances are such that Dominique, if he wished to pursue his advantage, could become her lover. Instead, after agonies of indecision, he walks away from her door in a spirit of resignation and acceptance, resolved never to see her again. We have already learned something of his subsequent history. A prologue which describes the French countryside in mellow October has shown him settled with a wife and children on his own estate at La Rochelle on the French Atlantic coast, and to that scene we are returned at the end. The story of love renounced is set in an autumnal frame. The outward incidents are few and relatively slight but the introspective drama of the mind is continuous and on occasion intense, evoked rather than stated, the whole plan being carried out with something of that strictness of economy which a poet accepts along with the advantages of an arbitrary form in verse. In subjecting the romantic confessional mood of fiction, which was fashionable, to the discipline of classical restraint, which was native to him, Fromentin evolved a modest and pellucid style appropriate to his story of love at odds with morality, and like a poet he made a virtue of necessity. This was something of a counterpart in letters to what Eddie Marsh had done with life. In Fromentin's writing the result was a model of fastidiousness, suggesting great reserves of emotional power held under control, such as one may feel in the music of his fellow-countryman Gabriel Fauré. Like a poem, too, the details are of a piece with the whole; even the passages of natural description, observed with a painter's careful eye, are found to be reflections of the climate in the mind of his principal character, and the season of falling leaves established at the start seems never to be absent, so that even the ardours of youth seen in retrospect are bathed in an autumnal glow. It was inevitable that such a style should wear a bloom which could not be translated, though it might, in exceptional circumstances, be created afresh.

'The first time I met him was in the autumn,' says the narrator, speaking of Dominique in the prologue. 'Chance brought us together at the season he loves best and talks about most often, perhaps because it typifies the tempered way of life which pursues its course and comes to its end in a natural framework of serenity, of silence, and of regrets.' The first glimpse of Dominique's home and its neighbourhood seems by analogy to portray the man himself.

> Evening was at hand. It was only a few minutes before the sun would reach the cutting edge of the horizon, and its long rays were lighting up with streaks of shine and shadow a wide, dreary, woodless plain, chequered by vineyard, fallows, and marshland, with scarcely an undulation, and here and there a vista opening on the distant sea. Only a whitish village or two, with flat-roofed church and Saxon belfry, rising from a bulge of the plain, and a few small lonely farms, each with a thin clump of trees and a huge stack of fodder by its side, gave life to this vast and monotonous landscape, whose picturesque poverty would have seemed complete but for the singular beauty conferred on it by the weather, the hour, and the season.

Not only in the central figure did Eddie Marsh discover something of himself. There were also Dominique's friends: Augustin the scholar-tutor, who summarized his creed as 'Believe in life, be sensible, and don't cry for the moon', and advocated 'the daily practice of sound ideas, of logical feelings, and of attainable affections'; Olivier, the man of sensibility and pleasure who declares, 'Do you know my chief object in life? It's to kill boredom. The man who could do his fellows this service would be the real dragon-killer.' Among these characters, including their author, were the ingredients of a composite self-portrait of their translator. Of course there were omissions, chief among them the qualities of a devoted aesthete who pines to be creative and allays his disquiet by giving his life-blood to others in the hope that one or more of them will achieve a masterpiece in his stead. Even this was not entirely omitted. At any time before the present juncture he might have felt his sympathies too little engaged. His admiration of Fromentin would have been profound but purely literary in character. This might not have been enough to stimulate him. He would certainly have been less well qualified. As it was, this book came into his hands at the psychologically autumnal moment. He was able to add Fromentin to the list of painters and writers whom he had served with self-denying zeal. So complete and effortless was the identification with his new author that he was able for once to serve him as well as perform a creative act of his own.

Alike in life and art he believed in the virtue of obedience to external laws. In its core *Dominique* contains a view of life which Fromentin might have preached overtly had he not been a pure artist. It was no less Eddie Marsh's own for his being a confessed hedonist of Horatian breed. Human nature would be less interesting if it were less paradoxical. Writing of *Dominique* Charles Morgan has ably expounded the meaning at its heart. 'He [Fromentin] assumes the existence and the everyday validity of an absolute value which is not happiness. He assumes further that happiness itself cannot be obtained except by those who recognize this over-riding value.'[1] Life, he went on, would be unlivable in a world reduced to chaos by everyone supposing that any impediment to their personal satisfaction was an intolerable injustice to be fought against. Fromentin seems to say, 'Your unhappiness, even though it spring from no fault of yours, does not entitle you to take sides with chaos.' So Morgan points out that when Dominique turned away from Madeleine's door he acted not out of expedience or a sense of conventional honour but in submission to an absolute law. When Sainte-Beuve argued that if Madeleine did not despise Dominique thereafter, she could only have mistaken his natural timidity for stoicism, the great French critic showed that he had missed the underlying attitude to life which gives the book its tone, pace, and style. Eddie Marsh was so constituted that he could not make the same mistake. The philosophy of liberation through acceptance must have been the basis of his sympathy with Fromentin and his novel. For eleven months he worked on the translation in the upper room at Walton Street, reading the new pages aloud each week, and relishing every minute of the labour. He felt strongly about it, and for reasons of editorial responsibility and scholarship, so did John Hayward. It was hardly to be wondered at that over certain textual points

[1] *The Hibbert Journal*, April 1949.

where opinions differed these two scholars should have come into sharp collision. The counter-diabolizer's term of 'battlefield' was especially apt in this instance, and over three minute points of dictionary meaning in particular there was a considerable expense of spirit in their intellectual skirmish. By June 1947 the task was accomplished, and both were satisfied.

v

As the year 1947 came in, it was Desmond MacCarthy who was reminding Eddie Marsh of Time's winged chariot. MacCarthy was ill and beguiling his sleepless nights with the Odes: 'Thus I was often in your mind and you were often in mine; and some-times after being delighted by your skill I would recall the bits of life we have spent together. . . . I used to read Herrick with Horace, they go well together.' To Martyn Skinner Eddie con-fessed that he was busy enough, but the gay days were gone for good. 'One might as well be living in the Thebaid for any chance there is of social life.' The refusal of a certain London theatre management to reserve him his usual pair of front stalls at first nights did nothing to better the situation, but *Dominique* was then still on the stocks. He was too much engrossed to be depressed, and he was still capable of launching his barbed shafts in the old style, such as the postcard to a young poet—'I can't remember if I've told you before that you remind me of Humpty-Dumpty in *Alice* who made words mean just what he liked and that I hope that like him you pay them extra on Saturday nights.' As a relaxation from French he was diabolizing *The English Festivals* for Laurence Whistler.

Life had not yet altogether lost its savour. There were even two or three public engagements. He appeared on the stage of the Lyric theatre, Hammersmith, as *compère* of a poetry recital, having himself compiled the programme, and he opened a show of flower paintings in characteristic style.

Ladies and gentlemen, Boswell tells us that one of the explanations current at the time of the suicide of the great Lord Clive was that he was 'weary of Still Life'; and every now and then, after a surfeit of pots and pans, or even guitars, I have been induced to think there might be something in this theory. But I feel sure that no one will be tempted to any rash act by the present exhibition.

There was only one real interruption in the progress of *Dominique*. Work on the last chapter was broken off to answer Maurice Browne, who had written from New York. The subject was Brooke. 'You knew him, almost certainly, better than anyone else living today, and it is highly probable that you alone know the *facts*.' Browne had picked up a rumour in America that Brooke was homosexual and had died of syphilitic infection. On both these heads Eddie considered Geoffrey Keynes (a much older friend of Brooke's and an authority in the medical profession) to be by far the best qualified person to speak. Keynes' answer to Browne left no grounds whatever for any such rumours in the future, but before passing on the enquiry Eddie sent a comment of his own:

First of all, let me say most positively that during all the years when I knew him I never saw the slightest reason for thinking that he had a 'homosexual streak'. I can't of course answer for him as a school-boy, but there is nothing I am more certain of than that if he ever had one he had completely outgrown it by the time I got to know him. Moreover the only time I ever saw or heard it suggested was in a review in some yellow rag or other which turned out to have based itself on the phrase in *The Great Lover* about 'the rough male kiss of blankets'!

As for the syphilis, this is the first I've heard of that too, and I don't believe a word of it. Anyhow I am still old-fashioned enough to think that even geniuses have a right to a reasonable privacy about their sexual affairs, though I recognize that there is a case for the contrary; but what is quite certain is that 'revelations' should not be made on the flimsy kind of evidence that your letter suggests is all that exists for these stories. . . .

As for your idea that 'thinking people' find death from strepto-coccus 'merely picturesque' but death from syphilis 'truly tragic'— you must forgive me for saying that it is best described by Hazlitt's phrase about *The Broken Heart*—'the very false gallop of sentiment'.

'Once Mrs. B.'s will was read,' he concluded, 'I disappeared once and for ever from the scene.' Then he handed the problem over to Keynes, and turned back with relief to the last pages of *Dominique*.

For the first time he had asked Mr. Churchill to withhold his proofs a short while until he was free to give his mind to them. The first two chapters of *The Second World War* had been sent back several months ago. On July 1, when *Dominique* had just left the flat, three more chapters arrived, and two days later the previous chapters came back with disconcerting speed 'in accordance with your corrections', requiring a double check. On July 14 Mr. Churchill wrote again:

> I sent you five or six chapters today which form the beginning of Book III of Volume II called *Their Finest Hour*. The first chapter about the formation of the National Coalition is comparatively unfinished and unworthy, but the others form a' consistent military narrative, which has been checked by high military authorities.
>
> All the comments and corrections that you make are of the utmost value, and there is hardly one which I do not accept and incorporate. But would you also very kindly express your opinion with great freedom on what is boring?

The answer given with great freedom was by word of mouth, but for some weeks the discussion on lesser points continued, as is shown by Mr. Churchill's letter of August 30.

MY DEAR EDDIE

1. I am still balancing between 'Goering' and 'Göring' and 'Fuehrer' and 'Führer', etc. Whatever we do must be uniform. It will be quite easy to change the text throughout by a general direction to the Printer. Curiously I like some one way and some t'other. Let us talk about this.

2. On the whole I am against *commas*. They should only come in when it is absolutely necessary, to make b.f.'s understand. We have already eliminated them in the 'however's and 'therefore's, etc. Now they are getting very plentiful. Sometimes you pass passages which are without them on your principle of punctuation, and yet one can quite understand what is meant. I think they should be an *aid* and not a rule. Within limits we can do what we like, so long as the same policy is made effective throughout the work. Personally I shy off a comma when three things are mentioned when there is the 'and' before the last. I like the 'and' as a substitute for the comma. However we have sprinkled them in these places. On the other hand I am very much in favour of the semi-colon; and think that blighter should have a good run for his money in the text.

3. We are both agreed that capitals should be reduced as much as possible. Will you think out the principle of capitals and talk to me about them. For instance must the 'A' in 'Ally' always be cap?

I delight in all your notes and comments.

Yours ever

W.

In November Messrs. Eyre and Spottiswoode brought out what Eddie Marsh called 'a collection of minor opuscula' called *Minima*. Here was a curious farrago: undergraduate translations of Verlaine, a translation of Wordsworth into Latin, a song lyric for Ivor Novello, two imitations of Milton (one of them an addition to the Banquet in Book II of *Paradise Regained* of which he was especially proud), an exercise in triple-rhymed blank-verse in the style of Hood:

> ... And gaze upon some harum-scarum arum
> Or meconopsis of the true blue hue,
> Or flaring salvias like a red bed-spread,
> Whose gaudy tints the floppy poppy copy ...

and so on, with a footnote to the arum, 'I apologize to this most orderly plant'; a quatrain to the tune of 'When first I saw your face' addressed to the author of *Anna Livia Plurabelle*:

> When first I read your works I resolved
> To honour and renown you;
> But now your style has grown so involved,
> The time has come to down you.

Several items were winners or runners-up in weekly competitions. None gratified him more than the 'Escapist Epigram' submitted to the *New Statesman* and, as he said, 'accepted, much to my surprise; for that journal makes world-disgust a *spécialité de la maison*'. The literary editor retaliated adroitly by setting an answer to the epigram as the subject of his next competition. Intrigued by the thought of carrying the war into his own camp, Eddie himself competed and won the prize. The challenge and the riposte are best read in sequence:

> I
>
> Bard, you are evidently much distressed,
> Your world-disgust appears in every line,
> No doubt you're right to get it off your chest
> But don't, for God's sake, put it on to mine.

> 2
>
> Old crusty denizen of ivory towers,
> How dare you mock such agony as ours
> Who, since we know 'some life of men unblest',
> Like Thyrsis, cannot rest?

Another quatrain on a related theme was sent to the *Spectator*.

> 'The sound is forced, the notes are few'
> Said Blake. The first four words are true.
> Not so the next, the poor reviewer
> Must sometimes wish the notes were fewer.

The early months of 1948 were workless, so he subscribed to a lending library in order to catch up with contemporary literature without the discomfort of knowing that he was making an addition to the piles of books which were already encumbering his chairs. He also began a systematic re-reading of the works of Peacock. For his midday meals he generally took a bus to Brooks's. Catering had become a nuisance without Mrs. Elgy.

He was relying more than ever on the post to keep him in touch with his friends. De la Mare's seventy-fifth birthday fell in April. '"Smiled on your little prelude",' the poet began, echoing a phrase in Eddie's greeting. 'I nearly wept. . . . I have thought of you so often since then, before writing. Do *you* remember that you ploughed through the proofs of *Memoirs of a Midget* for me? Do you remember our little altercation with a strong-headed bus-conductor one night? my coming to see you and Rupert one Sunday morning at Raymond Buildings—he might be in the room now.' There was also a revival of correspondence with Sassoon, who was finishing his book on Meredith. 'I sent Winston my Collected Poems,' Sassoon wrote, 'which gave me an excuse to thank him for saving England. . . . What's the world going to do with itself? The damage done seems beyond repair.' The chief diabolization of the year was Peter Quennell's *John Ruskin*, begun after polishing off the proofs of *Dominique*, and work had started on James Pope-Hennessy's *Monckton-Milnes: The Years of Promise*, when *Dominique* was at last given to the public early in November. The reception was all that he could have wished. Although it was acknowledged that a work of such quietism might never enjoy the popularity of the Odes or Fables, more reviewers than on those former occasions were moved to commit themselves to the word 'masterpiece'.

Throughout January 1949 the rooms in Walton Street were being inundated with over three thousand sonnets entered for a *Sunday Times* competition. He was to judge the best translation from the French of a sonnet on the fall of Icarus by Philippe

Desportes. The prize was eventually given, he explained in his report, 'for the greatest closeness to the original compatible with ease and elegance'. During this ordeal, which he found 'absolutely gruelling' (he was in fact only too glad to have something to complain of other than the cost of living), he was cheered by a particularly discerning review of *Dominique* which had appeared in the *Irish Times*. Its author, the poet Monk Gibbon, had strolled into the newspaper office one day, in search of publications to review, and had noticed a new translation from the French lying unclaimed on the editor's table. This had a sequel of some consequence. For the present it led to a 'selling notice' and a lively exchange by post.

The translator was soon giving Monk Gibbon his views on the future of literature. 'The prospects are among the things that make me glad I'm not long for this world. There are plenty of good elements still, but how long can they survive? In poetry, people now seem to have been born without ears, and in painting, without either sense or senses. It's like the end of the *Dunciad* (but that's a cheering thought, because Universal Darkness didn't finally prevail that time, so perhaps it won't now).' Then Gibbon started a new train of thought by referring to what he called the 'artificiality' of Horace. Eddie replied:

> You set me, I won't say thinking, because that is too grand a word for my mental processes, but wondering at haphazard what artificiality in poetry consists in beyond consummate craftsmanship (which I hope you don't follow the modern heresy of mistaking and sniffing at)—and finally deciding that whatever it is, I like it. The only other instance you name is Pope. To my mind the *Epistle to Arbuthnot* is as 'natural' a poem as ever was written (it was natural to Pope to be witty). I can see that *The Rape of the Lock* (one of my best-loved poems) is artificial, but is it any the worse for that? To me 'A sparkling cross upon her breast she wore Which Jews might kiss and infidels adore' is no less poetical than Tyger, tyger. How about Milton? I could understand your saying that *L'Allegro* is more natural than, say, the Great Consult in the 2nd book of *P.L.* but I see no reason for preferring it—both are perfect. Are the Odes to the Nightingale and the West Wind artificial? I really don't know. I'm in wondering mazes lost.

He returned to the theme of Pope in his next letter.

The only thing I'm pleased about in my own way with books is that I think I read them for what they are, without considering whether they might have been better or greater if they had been something else. For instance I know quite well that Aeschylus, Milton & Co are grander creatures than Pope, but I read the *Rape of the L.* with complete enjoyment and don't in the least mind it not being cosmic.

Then a new biography of Tennyson sent him back to the poems.

Who was it in *Our Mutual Friend* who confessed that he had never read Gibbon slap through? I don't believe I'd ever read *In Memoriam* slap through before, and I don't wonder. It's full of the most glorious things, but really there are deserts of what seems vast Eternity—and such extraordinary naiveté. Do you remember his dream, when he's living in a 'hall' with 'maidens'? One day a dove arrives with a 'summons', and Tennyson and the maidens obediently troop down to the river where they all embark in a small 'shallop' and eventually come upon a 'great ship', on the deck of which Arthur Hallam is standing *three times life size*! Up the side of the ship Tennyson shins, and apparently up Arthur's side too, for the climax is that he falls on his neck.

In July Monk Gibbon dined at Walton Street, drank sherry supplied by Sir Gerald Kelly, and brandy, the gift of Somerset Maugham, seated at one end of the dining-room table, the other half now being used as a writing-desk heaped with books and papers. There had been a big change in the household. In the winter, some months before this, Novello had called. 'I think,' he remarked afterwards, 'I should be congratulated on having reached the North Pole,' and he got the impression that Eddie should no longer be living without someone else in the house at night. For some time a daily help had governed the domestic scene with temperamental ferocity. 'She was rather bewildered at first,' Eddie had admitted, 'and seemed to be moving about in worlds not realized.' Longer acquaintance, however, had not enabled her to settle down. An appeal to his competent and obliging neighbour, Frances Appelbee, to make different arrangements, was long overdue. His incapacity in domestic affairs was absolute. He was also no easy employer. How could Mrs. A. from the mews round the corner be expected to know that the shaving tackle must be packed on the opposite side from the proofs and the Milton, or that the pyjamas must be *under* the Milton and *both* under the evening trousers? It never struck him that such duties might not have been considered part of her bargain. And he suffered chronic inconvenience through having a 'right place' for everything. If the thing he sought was not 'there', he concluded it must be nowhere, in the sense that it might be anywhere, so there was no point in looking for it, the chances of laying hands on it being so small. 'I was using it as a marker in the Freya Stark book'—'Oh, and where *should* you have put it?'—'Where I *did* put it, in the right place, on the end of the chimney-piece, along with the other invitations'—'And it isn't there?'—'Of course it isn't, that's why I'm asking you'—'Then it might be anywhere' —'That's *just* it! Now you have a positive *nose* for such things.' . . . The limited space, where so many things had to be placed beneath others instead of alongside, meant that nothing short of constant vigilance would keep confusion at bay.

The overcrowded table where he sat, read, and ate his meals, provided material for one of his letters at this time. John Guest had just brought out *Broken Images*, his book of war-time reminiscences. Eddie had barely finished reading it, and was about to write a note of glowing enthusiasm to the author when a presentation copy arrived. 'Xtopher lent me his copy at luncheon-time on Sat.,' he wrote to Guest. 'I put all other books aside and finished it last night. I was expecting a good deal, and I've never been less disappointed—it's pure delight from beginning to end.' He referred to the episode of the singing barber, calling it 'a little masterpiece, as memorable as anything in *The Sentimental Journey* —how Dickens would have enjoyed it! . . . All your descriptions of nature are admirable, so evocative and so beautifully written, reminding me of my beloved Fromentin.' Then the table at Walton Street occasioned a digression.

> Now I have an appalling confession to make. I was reading Christopher's copy at dinner last night and was helping myself to a cutlet—suddenly it jerked up in a most unexpected way, and shot a large dollop of gravy on to p. 200 and the grease soaked through all the last pages. I simply can't face Xtr with it and I must throw myself on your mercy. Could you possibly let me bring it one of these days so that you could copy the *dédicace* (which gives him so much pleasure) into another? It's a lot to ask, but I'm really desperate.

He considered *Broken Images* to be one of the best books to have come out of the war, but his praise was never absolutely unmixed.

In a postscript he made a small critical point, returning to his defence of the subjunctive which he had argued so often and unavailingly with Gordon Bottomley.

> There's just one point of style I should like you to consider—the use of 'as though' with the present indicative—'as though it is' instead of 'as though it were'. This is a horrible corruption of the language, and *quite* new—but spreading everywhere—I do beg you to avoid it in future.

Guest was prompt to cheat the malicious cutlet of its triumph, but there was another occasion, less easily remedied, when Eddie, lost in thought, ceremoniously, as it seemed, plunged his pocket Milton into a plate of vegetable soup, not realizing that the first course had been put before him without comment while he was reading. These were difficult times. Mrs. Elgy was still alive, but getting on for her ninetieth year, living on her pension in a tenement flat in Holborn, and nothing could be expected of her beyond her monthly tea-time visit, when she would produce the tribute of a peach or a couple of bananas from her hand-bag, and sit hunched at the table, unable to hear a word, content merely to smile and have her being for an hour in her master's company.

Then came the early morning when the autocratic daily help, incensed afresh, threw *The Times* down on the bed, pointed to a photograph, which she happened to know was one of her employer's most gifted and distinguished friends, and snapped out, 'Well, that's an idiotic face for a *start*!' Obviously this sort of thing couldn't go on. There was nothing for it but to find a manservant to occupy 'Rupert's bed', then convert the dining-room into the study. With the eventual arrival on the scene of an agreeable young Irishman (who seemed to have no objection to ladies of quality such as Mrs. Churchill being brought in during his siesta and invited to lean over his prostrate form, the more closely to admire the pictures over his bed) the impasse came to an end. Patrick was out when Monk Gibbon came to dinner and the host forgot to put on the second course to warm up in advance, so there was an entr'acte of twenty minutes between the soup and the meat. This was invariably the way, but such was the talk no one could have wished it otherwise.

In August Eddie travelled to Manchester for the opening of Novello's new musical play *King's Rhapsody*, arriving early so as to enjoy the pandemonium of the last rehearsals. He took with him an absorbing piece of home-work. He had first met Princess Marthe Bibesco in Lady Leslie's house in London, and during subsequent encounters in company with Lady Oxford or Philip Sassoon they had made fast friends, finding much in common, and in particular French literature, especially the work of her friend Marcel Proust. She had recently so much enjoyed the good talk at an evening party given by Lady Colefax that she missed her train, so Eddie took her back to share his supper at Walton Street. After she had assured him that she didn't at all mind the cat eating its dinner on the table at her elbow the conversation turned on her own literary work. She was finishing a book in French, *The Sphinx of Bagatelle* (the first *jardin à l'anglaise* to be laid out in France was called Bagatelle), which by drawing upon family traditions and papers shed a new light on a familiar episode in history centred in the romance of Louise de Polastron and the Comte d'Artois. No pressure was needed to make Eddie Marsh its translator. Addressing him in a prefatory letter which praised his Fables, she described how after reading *Dominique* in English she had recalled Claudel's inspired interpretation of the word *reconnaissance*—'to be re-born through another'.

Back in London his friend Clifford Dyment's suggestion that he should be one of the editors of a new anthology revived the question of his attitude to the youngest writers of verse. 'On the one hand I'm all for the young poets getting a hearing, whether I can follow them or not: on the other, as I must have confessed to you more than once, I am at sea with almost all of them, and if I were challenged to name any in whose work I could reasonably expect readers to take "pleasure" I should be at a loss. . . . It would always be an honour to be associated with de la Mare, but such is his angelic nature that he seems capable of enjoying almost anything. Of course the fact is that it's "not my choice, but my necessity in being old"—I cannot learn the new tricks. But I do feel a curmudgeon.' As usual he was leaving it to others to do him justice. There were newcomers who had certainly caught his interest. Notable among them was Christopher Fry. Writing to Monk Gibbon he confessed that *The Lady's not for Burning* which he was now reading 'baffled me when I saw it and still does'. All the same he was bound to admit that he found it 'chockfull of humour and beauty! but to use a pedantic word I'm fond of—autoschediastic'.[1] All the passages he most liked happened to be scannable, he maintained, and he copied out the nine lines beginning 'Out here is a sky so gentle',[2] adding, 'This seems to me quite lovely!' Although he never came to know Fry personally he expressed a wish that on his death a drawing by Algernon Newton of the canal near Paddington overlooked by Fry's window should be given to the poet as a token of his blessing.

In February 1950 he told Princess Marthe Bibesco that he had at last disposed of Mr. Churchill's proofs and was now ready to consider the translation of a second book of hers which she had put before him. The new manuscript was a biographical study of the Comtesse Adehaume de Chevigné, described by the authoress as 'the woman in whom the genius of Marcel Proust, divining her perfect essence by the light of his worship, found the archetype of his Duchesse de Guermantès'. Of this book, entitled *Proust's Oriane*, he was more than usually diffident.

> I've finished reading the MS, it's certainly a most charming book, but whether I shall be able to make anything of it remains to be seen! I think it will be almost desperately difficult to put into English, it's so extremely personal and subtle and so utterly French. . . . I've never been able to get you to believe how *stupid* I am—or if you do, you don't show it—also the MS is here and there almost illegible. . . . So all I can say is that in the course of next week I will make a start and see what happens. Very likely I shall have convinced myself within the week that it's beyond me—and even if I begin by seeming to make headway I daresay I should find later on that there are things I can't manage—especially Proust's own letters, which are so very elusive, even with your elucidations.

He soon recovered from this sharp attack of modesty. The work beguiled much of his solitude in the months to come, with pleasant interludes at luncheon with the authoress in the Grill Room of the Ritz, where he would always ask for his favourite dish, known on the bill of fare as *blanchailles diablées*, quote Verlaine and Musset over the wine, or discuss the work in progress.

It was this summer that he walked away from a dinner of the Horatian Society, quoting Horace and Catullus, and discussing Latin pronunciation with Patrick Leigh Fermor, a new acquaintance whose books and letters from abroad introduced a fresh

[1] Impromptu in character.
[2] Spoken by Thomas Mendip in Act II.

interest into his life. The poet Paul Dehn, a near neighbour, Lady Kilbracken, Eleanor Kelly, James Pope-Hennessy, and John Synge were also among his companions these days; but had it not been for *Proust's Oriane* this would have been another year with too little work on hand at home. He was still Chairman of the Contemporary Art Society, which was now his chief link with the painters; and he was an active Vice-President of the Royal Society of Literature, attending the monthly meetings of its Council at Hyde Park Gardens and gracing the front row at its lectures. Although he paid autumn visits to Lord Bute at Rothesay, and to Beaufront Castle, several of the great houses where he used to recreate himself so strenuously among the rhododendrons were closed, fallen into other hands, or were show-places open to the public. The Brett Youngs had moved to South Africa. In February 1951 Jessica Brett Young was surprised to receive an admission of advancing age. 'It's as if all my past had been recorded in pencil and was now faded away.' He was finding the world 'still just tolerable, but I wonder how long that will last'. Within a few days he was to suffer a grievous blow.

Early in the morning of March 6 his telephone was out of order. It was important to spare him the shock of first hearing from the wireless the news of Novello's sudden death from a heart-attack, yet he was filled with misgiving at sight of a caller on his doorstep at such an hour. It seemed best not to say why I had come until we had mounted the stairs to the sitting-room, lest he should be unable to retrace his steps. I was conscious that no matter how gently the blow was delivered he could not long survive it. His reaction was unexpected. After the first impact of realization, on which he bowed his head very low, he clenched his fists in rage. He was angry that Fate should have granted him so many years of almost empty existence, as he put it, yet had cut short in its prime another life so much more useful and, to his way of thinking, more gifted than his own. He was disgusted with himself for having lived so long. There was something formidable in this tearless passion of disgust held grimly under control. There was of course no Christian consolation he could turn to, but for a while he put me in mind of Prometheus in the Caucasus, emblem of humanity that will not submit even to the edict of Zeus, courageously and unavailingly hurling defiance at whatever gods may be. He confided in Monk Gibbon that he was 'knocked endways', adding, 'This is one of the worst blows that could have befallen me.'

Soon came news of the death of R. C. Trevelyan. Bottomley and Victor Lytton were already gone. He was all the more glad to have the proofs of *Aspects of Provence* and the second volume on Monckton Milnes, both by James Pope-Hennessy, lying on his table ready for treatment at the hands of the diabolizer. While he could be useful life was still worth the bother of living, and Monckton Milnes, the biographer of Keats and friend of Swinburne, was a subject after his own heart. Yet another agreeable distraction was his work on the proofs of *The Youthful Queen Victoria* by his friend Dorothy Colston-Baynes (Dormer Creston), whom he had first met in 1946. She was now his neighbour, living round the corner in Ovington Square, and Eddie was often to be found at her tea-parties, regaling the guests with his impersonation of Henry James, and making the saucers dance as he brought down his fist to point the climax of an involved peroration. There were distractions enough, but it was impossible to avoid all reminders of his recent loss. In June he paid his last visit to Redroofs, made an inventory of the pictures which were there on loan and returned with many of them piled in the car, including Paul Nash's *September Moon*, which became the pride of the sitting-room at Walton Street. On January 28, 1952, when unveiling a bust of Novello at Golders Green, he recalled that he was there by right of his 'thirty-six years of affection', and paid his tribute by using as a text a couplet from his own translation of La Fontaine:

> Some few there be, spoilt darlings of high Heaven,
> To whom the magic grace of charm is given.

And on May 2, at the Theatre Royal, Drury Lane, he was present at the unveiling of the bust by Clemence Dane which had stood on a writing-desk in the Aldwych flat. Here was the man who more than any other had benefited from the 'murder money' and Eddie's ever vigilant affection, honoured in a niche of the Rotunda in London's most historic theatre! It was impossible for him not to feel that he had made some contribution to this achievement, although none but he knew of its extent, nor was he unaware that there had been benefits that worked the other way. It was not only Novello's 'brilliant gifts', as he had said at Golders Green, 'his gallant spirit, and the fun it was to be with him', but the naturalness of his charm which 'though he thoroughly enjoyed the exercise of it, was no deliberately cultivated embellishment of his personality, but sprang from the roots of his being. He had a genius for happiness, and for spreading happiness around him, and it was remarkable that neither the greater nor the lesser pleasures of his life ever palled on him, as on so many they do; to him his successes, his popularity, his possessions, never grew stale or flat or unprofitable—he turned naturally to the light like a flower.'

vi

Since the end of the war it had been Eddie's custom to call every Saturday morning at the Aldwych flat. Now the only regular event of the week was my appearance at tea on Tuesdays, when the cat was allowed on the table to wrinkle an exploratory nose at the cake or cautiously elongate her neck towards the crumbs on Eddie's plate. Another visitor was the young painter Harold Drury, whose first acquaintance had been made informally a few months earlier in a lift at the Burlington Galleries. Within a few months Eddie was the means of Drury selling pictures to the value of over eighty pounds, while the Perceval fund enabled the painter to occupy a studio in Paris.

On the bookcase by the door were propped the letters he had received during the week, and I would be expected to produce a similar collection from my pocket. This was called an 'exhibition', a term we adopted for the material of any conversation which needed documentary support. In this manner he was able to share the obscure concerns of my existence which it pleased him to take as seriously as if they were his own.

His eyes were larger nowadays, or such was their effect, their lustre somehow veiled, and his brow above the wrinkled and slightly shrunken cheeks looked more than ever domed. He was less the type of ripe old man for whom 'ripeness is all', rugged and mellow, all trace of the previous 'ages of man' sloughed off, than a man of not more than middle age who had never entirely outgrown the brilliant undergraduate, but was nevertheless bone-tired, and frail, and a little dispirited. At home he was generally dressed in a maroon-coloured dressing-gown over his pyjamas with a silk scarf at the neck secured in the manner of a stock with an opal-headed pin. Max Beerbohm has recalled him in his prime—

'With his tufted eyebrows and his sharply chiselled features and his laconic mode of speech, he was not, one would have thought, unalarming.' The 'alarm' could never have lasted very long, and if his appearance had now quite lost the power to intimidate, even for a moment, the patrician *hauteur* was still there, though softened and withdrawn; and he still carried himself stiffly erect, walking with the usual measured deliberation, or sat bolt upright in his chair, turned sideways from the table towards his guest, still avoiding the upholstered armchair as if it were a piece of furniture reserved only for the guest who might happen to be an invalid. His gentleness was if anything more pronounced. This was no negative quality, no mere lack of that gnarled ruggedness which is common to old men, but a positive attribute of his own, and it emanated from him, as it seemed, in rays of solicitude, giving his companion the sensation of being the focus of an ardent but curiously cool light—a soft light, but invigoratingly unsentimental, for there was about him habitually an air of critical and debunking humour, and nothing—neither his neighbour's logic, syntax, house, ox, ass, nor anything that was his—was so sacred as to be altogether immune, if a chance presented itself. Especially when listening, he loved to get his joke in edgeways. It was as if he watched the moving target of one's discourse passing across his mental vision, then took a pot shot, and knew he had scored if the thread was broken by a laugh.

Charles Morgan has described a luncheon-party at Gray's Inn as resembling a conversation-piece by Zoffany. Yet when there was only one guest, the casual informality of the host, and the atmosphere around him of slippered ease, gave one the impression that his window no longer overlooked a busy street in London but the College quad at dusk, and only the functional bars of the electric fire dispelled the illusion of anchovy toast and a bowl of mulled claret standing ready in the grate. Often there were silences. Perhaps he had consulted his watch, and with a perceptive twinge of pleasure observed that another cigarette was overdue, and had fitted it pensively into the holder, and was now exhaling luxuriously, reining his head away from the smoke, his eyes fixed on nothing in particular somewhere about half-way up the window curtain.

By now the meal was over, and the moment had come for the 'exhibition' and its accompanying monologue. 'Remember that man who wrote about the Odes?' he might begin, picking the first envelope from the pile. 'Well, he's written again. You must tell me whether you think he's a lunatic. The bit where he says I'm "undeniably a classic" is all right, of course, but he rather spoils it by seeming to imagine Horace was a Frenchman. And now what *do* you think? Another batch of poems from that person at Hove. I can't have been nearly rude enough about the first lot. Must one sink to downright abuse? At last one really knows what Pope was feeling in the *Epistle to Dr. Arbuthnot*. Well, it's nice to be in good company. But don't you think *you* might have a go at them this time? I may be in my dotage, of course, and you'll discover a genius, but I rather suspect you won't. Here's another Private View. I'll have to go for sake of my conscience. It certainly won't be out of self-indulgence. Anyway, it will be quite a change *not* to feel tempted to buy anything. Only the other day I had that *terrible* struggle with myself, remember? Do you realize I haven't set foot out of doors for a whole week? It's getting serious. I suppose you wouldn't like to come too—to these drawings? Or are they "not a very inviting thought"?' (This was a stock phrase of his which did service, like *num* in Latin, when he anticipated a negative reply.) 'Here they're offering a pair of seats at Wembley. One ought to go before one dies, like the man in Dickens who while in Canterbury thought it would be a pity not to have seen the Cathedral. Oh look, I can't —it's the 15th—that's dear little Miss Kelly's birthday—I haven't the heart to—but wait— False alarm. I could do both with a squeeze. Should one change for Ice? . . .' and so on, until it was his visitor's turn. This would begin with a string of questions on the well-being of my wife and family, when I often discovered he had been worrying over some petty ailment I had forgotten to worry about myself.

At strategic points on the staircase, where he would pause for breath on the way up, special drawings were hung for refreshing contemplation; among them an Italian wine-flask in pencil by Richard Wilson, Paul Sandby's *Richmond Bridge*, and Cotman's *The Tanning Mills at Norwich*. It was my custom to pay each the tribute of a glance on the way down. If I forgot, it was: 'You haven't noticed the Cotman today. You may not have another chance till next Tuesday.' His pictures were part of him, and not to take note of his favourites was to leave something of him still unvisited. After a last look at the contemporary paintings in the hall he would come out as far as the top step and stand waving till one was round the corner, when he would turn back and, more often than not, slam the door with such vehemence that pictures would be shocked sideways or dislodged from their nails in the hall next door.

'I don't mind Eddie taking all the cream,' Novello once remarked to me, 'or expecting Ellen to pack for him on Monday morning, or taking his siesta with his boots on the counterpane, but with the best will in the world I can't stand the detonations that go on as he moves from room to room.'

It was as difficult to induce him to wear an overcoat in midwinter as to take a taxi in the rush-hour. Whenever he did consent to step out of a bus queue for a taxi one had to be prepared to double the tip so as to avert a brawl. 'Wouldn't you say that taxi drivers in our Welfare State were growing rather *more* coarse than otherwise?'—'No wonder, you slammed the door.' 'Not again? Anyway, if a door is *open* and you require it *shut* . . .'—'Yes, but surely *brute* force isn't called for'—'Oh Chris, that reminds me of Maurice Baring once when we were in Germany . . .' His promptness of anecdote for all occasions gave him absolute freedom of manœuvre in the evasion of a tiresome issue.

He had first got to know Patrick Hamilton when his play *Rope* appeared in 1929, and now in 1951 they were corresponding about that author's novel *The West Pier*. Hamilton has since recalled how 'after a warm and gloriously stimulating evening with him, he would escort you to the door and suddenly slam it on you with *ferocious* vigour! At first I used to think that I had in some mysterious way offended him at the last moment, but later I began definitely to look forward to it, as another little engaging manifestation of his abundantly engaging personality.'

Life at Walton Street had become Spartan. 'I sometimes wonder how much longer I can *afford* to go on living,' he remarked, and although such strict austerity was hardly warranted by the state of his finances, he was doggedly convinced of the contrary. He took a perverse and defiant pleasure in conforming with the customs of the altered times no more than was absolutely essential. There was some consolation, however, in the closer relationship with Walter de la Mare. 'What ages it is since we've exchanged even a word,' wrote the poet, 'apart from a great many on my side despatched via the

Celestial Telepathic Union.' Eddie had written about his new book of poems, *Winged Chariot*. 'I'm pretty certain there is no positive "train of thought" in it,' de la Mare explained, 'not much more at any rate than a light engine and a guard's van.' And again, in April of this year—'I hope you realize that you glide as soundlessly into the orbit of my mind (and heart) though I know not with what punctuality, as does any terrestrial planet.' He had just come upon an old batch of Eddie's critical notes and 'a fountain of gratitude welled up in me: for so much that it is really of course impossible to thank you for'. The warmth of this acknowledgement prompted an immediate reply.

> Our friendship is one of my few survivals from those old happy times —and very precious to me—I blush to think how blithely I accepted the office of 'Kindly Correct My Grammar' (you know how the Australians used to interpret K.C.M.G.?) to the Midget, but you have forgiven me! May I come and quote Aristophanes to you next Sunday afternoon?

De la Mare had become the spokesman of the poets, as had John Nash for the painters. On May 31, Nash wrote in connection with his painting *The Cornfield* which Eddie had retrieved from Novello's flat. It had reminded him of bygone days, for it was the first picture he had painted after being demobilized in 1918. He recalled old kindnesses to himself 'as well as to many others, then and subsequently. I hope none of us will ever forget that. Rather formal, my dear Eddie, and a little involved, but I've long felt it was due to be said.' On top of this came good news about his La Fontaine. It was about to appear in the Everyman series of classics. 'Once there,' he wrote to Leigh Fermor in satisfaction, 'it *can't* go down the drain!'

Edward Shanks wrote in July, wanting his help in the making of an anthology drawn from the five volumes of the Georgian series; he said he was getting more and more 'militantly disgusted' by current references to the movement. 'No one knows what it did for the poets represented in it and for the public appreciation of contemporary poetry in general.' The Introduction, written in a 'belligerent manner', would tell the story of how the whole thing came into existence. He was however extremely doubtful whether he would succeed in rousing the founder's interest. He did not know that the recent broadcast which had finally provoked him to action, had also been heard by 'E.M.' Eddie himself took a more lenient view. 'I do think it was rather out of proportion,' he wrote to Frances Cornford, 'to regret that Rupert hadn't died in 1910 because "the disaster of Georgian Poetry would *thus* have been averted".' At the Savile Club he had recently met the latest and last of his poets and had taken him to tea with Edith Sitwell. The young American W. S. Merwin quickly became a close friend whose correspondence was a joy to Eddie at a time when the project put to him by Shanks was reviving memories of the days when all his poets were as young as he. Another of his callers was Elizabeth Lady Kilbracken. They were standing in the garden: 'What would you say,' she asked, 'if you were told you were going to die tomorrow?' Eddie's reply was unhesitating, 'I'd say "Thanks for the party."' Characteristically he had answered and yet turned the question by a literary allusion. In a flash he must have recalled his own version of La Fontaine's *Death and the Old Man*.

> . . . Here Death spoke true. When we are old as he
> We should get up from life as from a feast,
> And take our leave as fits a thankful guest,
> Not clamour for reprieve that cannot be.

In August he wrote to Max Beerbohm on behalf of the Contemporary Art Society 'to find out whether there is any chance that you would fall in with a strong desire they have formed (prepare yourself for a shock) to commission Graham Sutherland to paint your portrait—I expect you have heard of his portraits of Willie Maugham and Max Beaverbrook, both of which seem to me masterpieces. . . . I understand that in continental opinion he now ranks with Henry Moore, who for the first time has put English sculpture on the map of Europe.—Besides which he is a most charming fellow.' The reply was in the gentle negative. 'My dear Eddie, I, with my pencil, have been in my time a ruthless monstrifier of men. And the bully is, proverbially, always a coward. . . . I had no notion that you were anywhere near the age of 80. The news makes me feel that *I* must be about to be 90. . . . "Henry Moore," you say, "has put English sculpture on the map of Europe!" This being so the younger Pitt would not now say "Roll up that map!" It has been squashed down flat for ever.' Eddie's reply, for the sake of a laugh, concealed his genuine admiration for the sculptor.

As to Henry Moore, I agree with you in part. I'm quite certain that he's an extremely gifted sculptor, but why *does* he? It fell to me as Chairman of that same C.A.S. to present his 'Group of 3 standing figures' to the London County Council in Battersea Park, and I was longing to say 'Ladies and Gentlemen, these figures are gift horses, but I cannot ask you not to look them in the mouth, because they haven't got any'—but as H.M. was present I contented myself with whispering in my own ear

> There was a little Pole
> And she had a little hole
> Right in the middle of her forehead.

On September 24 the Contemporary Art Society decided to persuade their retiring Chairman to take Beerbohm's place and sit for his portrait. Raymond Mortimer addressed the committee, paying so generous a tribute that Eddie copied it out and slipped it into the Vanity Bag. It ended—'His services to the Arts, literature as well as painting and sculpture, have been prodigious, improbable, fabulous. He has offered incessant and practical sacrifice to the Muses; poets, and painters, and all of us who love the Arts, are immeasurably in his debt.' Honours were crowding thick upon him. 'Oh that Vanity Bag!' he exclaimed, referring to the shoddy brown envelope where he kept the more gratifying items of his correspondence. 'Don't think me swollen-headed, but I think we shall have to buy a trunk. Isn't it extraordinary?' Then on October 9 a note from Harold Nicolson heightened the air of expectation.

The rumour is circulating in London that somewhere towards the middle of November you attain your eightieth birthday. Alan Pryce-Jones, James Pope-Hennessy and I would like to join with some other of your admirers and friends and offer you a dinner on the occasion.

The idea was that we should get some ten various men together and ask you to dine with us in a private room at the Travellers Club. . . . I have been instructed to ask you whether you would be glad to be our guest of honour on that occasion.

Shortly before this he had taken Merwin to *Henry VI*, Part 3, at the Old Vic. 'I've started reading the play,' he wrote, when the plan was made, 'which is so far quite frightful.' In the same month he saw *Romeo and Juliet*.

I sat in the front row and kept my hands ready during the Montagu-Capulet brawl at the beginning, to shield my eyes in case a sword flew off the stage by accident, such was the violence of the swashing blows. Also those witticisms of the young gallants, so frigid in the reading and usually so boring in the delivery, were spoken with such pace and gusto that I found myself roaring with laughter.

He had just come back from a few days at Skipwith Hall, in Yorkshire, where he was happy destrigulating the rhododendrons on what was to be his last country excursion. On his return he wrote to Merwin saying he was disconcerted to have found his cat 'estranged'. 'When I called her as she sat on the roof in the garden next door, "Come down, O maid, from yonder mountain height", she started washing her face with pointed apathy.'

As November 18 drew near he was making his selection of the Georgians. 'I'd rather treat my birthday as a movable feast,' he wrote to Miss Horatia Seymour, an old friend who had been one of Mrs. Churchill's bridesmaids, 'as when a man-of-war has to coal on a Sunday and the Captain announces that next Sunday will be a Monday. . . . I've been ageing rapidly in preparation for octogenarianism.' And now he received from Harold Nicolson his plans for the birthday dinner-party.

> There are to be no speeches and we shall all wear black ties. Alan Pryce-Jones, James Pope-Hennessy and I have more or less organized the dinner but all the others will be paying their share, and thus everybody present, except yourself, will be acting as host. We have tried to get a small party together consisting of some of your oldest friends and also representatives of literature and the arts. The following will be present: The Duke of Wellington, Mr. T. S. Eliot, Sir Gerald Kelly, Mr. Clive Bell, Mr. Christopher Hassall, Mr. Peter Quennell, Mr. Alan Pryce-Jones, Mr. James Pope-Hennessy, and myself.

With unwonted fatalism Eddie wrote to Frances Cornford, 'It will, I presume, be my last happy day.'

There was a coal fire burning genially, the only other light in the room coming from the two silver branch-candlesticks on the polished round table. The guest of honour sat with the Duke, his oldest friend among those present, on his right, and Nicolson on his left. There was an extraordinary air of convivial benediction, only once interrupted when a waiter came in with a telephone message. An evening newspaper was on the line, 'wanting to know if anything particularly witty or amusing had been said so far'. Pryce-Jones has written his own account of the occasion.[1]

> I looked across the table. It was absurd I thought that we should be celebrating Eddie's eightieth birthday, for really he was almost exactly the same Eddie whom I had first seen twenty-five years before. Most of us, even in the benevolent candlelight, had changed quite a lot in those years; we had to undo the top button of our trousers after meals; the birthday champagne, we knew, would either give us a fleeting anemone-coloured flush or a waxen pallor; as we got tireder our standards of conversation would flag. But not Eddie's. His ideas, like his tie and his manners, were in perfect order. Whatever he needed to his purpose was there. It might be a situation, or it might be a sharp verbal image fished out of the past. . . . For the great point about Eddie's conversation was his quickness on the draw. He did not even take time to speak from the throat, but threw out his comment high from the palate, widening his mouth a little as if to make more room for the right words.

Alan Pryce-Jones continued his reminiscence, reminded of an occasion at Whitehall in 1928.

> He was bringing in some papers for the Chancellor (and the Chancellor at that time was Mr. Churchill), but at the same time he could not resist wondering why on earth the Chancellor had sent for me to talk about Venizelos. Like a juggler he kept both balls in the air at once: Crete and the surtax, Madame Venizelos and a most tiresome point of Treasury procedure. Oh yes, and how well did either of us know the work of Christopher Wood? You can only talk in that saltatory fashion if your mind obeys a discipline as strict as that of the trapeze-artist. . . . No doubt he *was* 80. . . . But the candles shone upon him kindly; they lent the right note of flickering gaiety to his utterance, and above all from us, and I hope for him, if only for one evening they hid the dark.

When the port began to circulate Harold Nicolson turned to his guest of honour and without the formality of rising to his feet addressed him in terms of affection and gratitude, then most of the others took their turn to follow his example. They were all familiar friends except one, the representative of poetry, whose gesture in being present at all was matched by the kindliness of his remarks. Neither I nor Mr. Eliot himself kept any record of what he said, but the general drift was to the effect that for some

[1] *Eddie Marsh, Sketches for a Composite Portrait* (Lund Humphries, 1953).

time people had regarded the two of them almost as antagonists. And yet they had both worked to the same end—each in his own way. 'Schools' and fashions might give rise to heated differences of opinion, but they came and went, while Poetry remained. The only real distinction was 'good' and 'bad' verse. They both knew the 'good' when they saw it, each in his own aspect of poetry, so that all along, above any controversy there may have been, they had, in fact, been colleagues in one cause. 'I salute you,' he said, 'and drink your health.' No one was so wanting in tact as to press for a reply, for the guest of the evening was too deeply moved to speak.

The party broke up very late. By then it had sorted itself out into a rather noisy group by the fire, where the loudest laughs were coming from Bell and Kelly, and two smaller conversation pieces on either side of the table, centred on the Duke and Mr. Eliot, Eddie moving from one to the other, joining in at least three topics of conversation like a champion chess-player at a tournament. It was long after midnight when I escorted him in a taxi back to Walton Street. He was dazed with happiness and the deleterious effects of good living. 'Wasn't it good of Mr. Eliot to come?' I remarked, as we swung out of Pall Mall. 'Very,' was the bemused reply. 'Oh *very*!' he said again more emphatically, and at intervals repeated the same word pensively to himself, adding nothing more until he was fumbling for his latch-key. He was emotionally exhausted, utterly content, and for the time being sustained only by the artificial and temporary support of plentiful champagne.

Next morning he could not move without palpitations and great difficulty in breathing. The doctor came and the patient was ordered a complete rest. On that day, still buoyant in spirit, he wrote an unusual number of letters. Everyone must know what had happened, both of good and ill. 'My shortness of breath has got worse and is now a real nuisance,' he wrote to Miss Horatia Seymour, and told her of the party and the circle of his hosts which included 'T. S. Eliot (rather a surprise, as I always supposed he didn't take me seriously), I *can't* get over it!' He was actually declining invitations. 'Don't think hardly of me if I can't come and see the Brangwyns,' he wrote to Gerald Kelly. 'The fact is I'm none the better (*physically*) for my wonderful dinner, my breathing has gone all to pot. I think I *must* stay at home all day (I'm getting out of a delightful dinner!), the doctor is coming to see me.' It was Kelly who recorded Eddie saying, 'I buy pictures by the pricking of my thumbs, but I *know* about poetry.'

Meanwhile the Vanity Bag was beginning to overflow. Messages from Raymond Mortimer and Rose Macaulay especially gratified him, and he was touched by John Lehmann taking 'the opportunity to say how much I always have admired what you did for the poets who were starting to write forty years ago, and how much I think we are all in your debt today, whatever changes time and fashion may have wrought'; which prompted Eddie to reply with 'a thousand thanks. I've been terribly spoilt all this week. . . . It's specially pleasant to be approved of by juniors whom one is apt to think of as having left one far behind!'

On the second day after the dinner nothing would keep him indoors. For some while he had been awaiting with pleasant alarm a lecture on his translation of *Dominique* which Monk Gibbon was to deliver to the Royal Society of Literature. 'I look forward to your lecture with palpitation,' he had written as far back as July. 'It will be a great event in my life. How you are going to talk about me for a whole hour is a mystery.' On November 20 he sat with Frances Cornford in the front row at Hyde Park Gardens. Lord Dunsany opened the proceedings. Not only was the substance of the lecturer's discourse illuminating but Gibbon was blessed with a gift rarer among men of letters than learning, a lucid and arresting style of delivery. Although Eddie's hearing was unimpaired he was apt nowadays to nod off if the slightest effort of concentration was demanded of him. A technique of gently mounting pressure on the knee, so slight that when he opened his eyes he did not know that he had been roused, was by now brought almost to perfection, and for all the qualities of the lecturer, and the appeal of his subject, it had frequently to be resorted to if no word of what Coventry Patmore would have called 'the harrowing praise' were to be missed in an interlude of coma. Gibbon related how he had overheard a woman exclaim to the translator, 'What I want to know is where did you get your beautiful style?' and the answer came, 'From Fromentin, my dear.' 'No,' Gibbon commented, 'some of it, without a doubt, must have been found elsewhere, in the man whom his friends call Eddie Marsh.' He was right, of course, but he could not have realized how right he was.

With the assurance that he was 'one of the great translators' still ringing in his ears, he went home and acknowledged a message of greetings from Max Beerbohm.

> Your telegram was a *bon mouvement* which made me very happy. It is of course only right that our age-group should hang together, but there is no member of it that could cast more reflected glory on the others than you.
>
> I had a very gratifying birthday on Tuesday, and this afternoon my head was still further turned by a lecture on my translation of *Dominique* at the R.S.L. by my Irish friend Monk Gibbon; but I don't mention this fact for its own sake. I think you may be amused by a true story of Dunsany who took the Chair. Five minutes before the lecture began he hurried up to me and said '*You* will be able to tell me who wrote *Mozambique*—and what is it? A long poem?' But no one could have exercised more charmingly a function for which he was so little prepared. Well, dear Max, thank you again from my heart.

It was like old times when on December 3 there arrived galley proofs referred to as 'Vol. 6 of Book ii' of Churchill's *History of the English-Speaking Peoples*. How welcome was this new summons to duty can be inferred from the letter to Merwin of the 7th.

> . . . But oh my dear Bill, don't wish me *too* many 'returns'. I did really become eighty, as you'll find when we meet again, and the very day after the great one I lost my wind and with it my power of locomotion. . . . I seem to have lost the passion for pleasure which Wilde said was the secret of keeping young. I sit at home sometimes for days at a time dozing over disappointing books and not bothering to go and see plays or pictures, I hope it's partly this bloody winter.

Next day he wrote to the Prime Minister.

> This is a miserable harvest. I've hardly found anything to criticize. I've marked the few notes that seem to call for your attention in any way. . . . As for punctuation: I don't find the new system entirely consistent, but I've shown extreme self-restraint about commas, and only put in about a dozen where they seemed obligatory on *any* principle. I regret the almost entire suppression of the semi-colon, but I suppose we must move with the times.

He enclosed a list of thirty-two points requiring special notice, so he had lost nothing of his thoroughness in spite of his disconsolate admission. The Prime Minister replied that he looked forward to studying the notes during the Christmas Recess. He was planning to take his holiday on the Prospect Estate, Jamaica, where he would enjoy the necessary leisure.

In mid-December Eddie attended a meeting of the Contemporary Art Society. He had now served on the committee for nearly forty years. A message from Graham Sutherland was read out. He was eager to paint the portrait but regretted that he could not start on it until the next autumn. 'In a voice that arrested by its intense melancholy,' so John Rothenstein has written,[1] 'Eddie exclaimed—"The sands are running out." In the silence that followed could be read his friends' mournful recognition that he had spoken the truth.'

Five days later he was the guest of honour at a Foyle's Literary Luncheon. 'Compton Mackenzie said I was the Great Mother of all young writers etc., apologising afterwards for the sex which he had been forced to give me by the facts of Greek Mythology.' His Christmas was spent at home, unshaven and in his pyjamas. When my wife brought the children to see him and deliver their presents, they could not stay long. It was clearly an effort for him to focus his mind, and the proximity of such animal health and youngness was like the door of a hot oven opened in his face. He exclaimed happily, but inwardly recoiled. It was a long time since he had suffered a mental black-out, but merciful Nature was already beginning to visit him with an attack in slow motion, so gradual and unalarming that what was normally a cataclysm of three or four seconds was to develop by almost imperceptible degree over a period of three weeks. Merwin had recently sent him his latest poems. Eddie wrote to him on January 5.

Before my birthday I looked on myself as a youngish 70; on Nov. 19 I woke up at least 85. Desmond MacCarthy used to say that people didn't get gradually older, but now and then fell off a ledge, and this was what happened to me. . . . I couldn't go upstairs without wishing I'd never been born, or turn over in bed, panting. There were other physical tiresomenesses such as a cough, but worst of all was a violent attack of stupidity. I couldn't take in the meaning of the printed word, or read for half an hour without dropping asleep. For instance I've long been hankering after a fourth reading of *Tristram Shandy*, and now that I'm ⅔rds through I'm as often as not unable to see what he's driving at. I tell you all this not to arouse your sympathy but to excuse myself for another failure to enter into your

[1] *Eddie Marsh, Sketches for a Composite Portrait* (Lund Humphries, 1953).

Kingdom. Of course it isn't so bad as with the short poems—I can follow the order of events but my present crassness is only superimposed on a natural incapacity for understanding allegories. . . . I see heaps of incidental beauties in the descriptions, and I can manage your ruleless prosody with a fair degree of comfort. Don't give me up. I dare say I shall improve in course of time.

On the same day he wrote to Frances Cornford: 'I'm much too stupid to attempt a proper letter. I do believe I'm entering on the stage of life when one is affected by the weather, a frightful comedown!' It was a particularly raw winter, but he still went out when the temptation to do so was too much for him. He went to a first night at the Old Vic on the 6th, rounding off his theatregoing as it began, with *The Merchant of Venice*. Next day, his affection for the speaker and her subject induced him to attend the lecture on de la Mare's recent poem *The Traveller* which was given by Vita Sackville-West at the British Academy in Burlington Gardens. My vigilance over his involuntary sleep must have been seriously impaired by my interest in the speaker's exposition, for Eddie was twice most rudely and truculently nudged awake by a crusty old scholar seated on his other side, who had been disturbed by his laboured breathing. Even so, the special technique was successfully put into action at least twenty times. While walking away after the lecture he remarked under his breath, 'I shouldn't be seen in public.' I had not before heard this note of bitterness, and it was very difficult to make light of the affair. 'After all,' he said, when at last he was feeling in better spirits, 'I only dropped off twice.' There was nothing to do but agree that twice was nothing.

He spent the morning of January 12 in his maroon dressing-gown, reading the second volume of *Tristram Shandy*. After lunching alone at the end of the table cleared of books, he was having his usual cup of black coffee and a cigarette when he began to cough and rang the hand-bell for Patrick. Because he was unable to make himself understood he reached for a pencil, scribbled something on the back of an envelope, and pointed to the pot of white heather which stood in the middle of the table. Patrick poured him a glass of water, looked at the envelope and saw he had written, 'The pot is talking.' As the coughing fit was soon over, the servant excused himself on the pretext of going back to his kitchen. Instead, he ran next door where he would not be overheard telephoning the doctor. While he was out Eddie located his pen, ink, and paper, and wrote a short letter. It was Monday, and my next visit was arranged for Friday. Normally he held his pen as I have seen an artist guide his pencil, high up, well clear of the nib, and jutting it forward at an acute angle as if trying to push it into a succession of minute corners; but now he had lost command, and the wavering characters were barely legible.

I got so much worse, so abruptly, yesterday, mainly locomotion, but also mental force, appetite, etc. Last night I really thought I must be mad. I got tremendously involved in a plot of the Marlborough family about the Crown Jewels, so convincing that it must be true, but yet so unnaturally nonsensical and *un*true that I couldn't believe in it seriously. I thought I must be mad! This hand-writing is the best I can manage, which will give you a line on my condition.* I don't want you to come before Friday tea, because there's no joy in seeing or being seen like this! If you ring up, aim at Patrick as telephoning is a misery!

Of course 'it ain't serious'

All love

E.

* It has suddenly got better! Typical.

There was no need to persuade him to go upstairs and lie down. He had always taken a nap after luncheon, in fact he claimed that his sole contribution to the Allied victory lay in his having prevailed upon Mr. Churchill to adopt the same habit. He went briskly upstairs, taking with him Arthur Grimble's *A Pattern of Islands*, his latest pick from the lending library, and never once paused for breath. Such a thing had not happened for weeks. He complained that the dog in the next-door garden was talking, and someone had got their wireless on too loud. A dog was certainly barking, but there was no sound of a wireless. By about 3 o'clock there was a dense fog gathering outside, and the doctor was delayed. On just such another day, at a crucial stage of the battle of El Alamein, Mr. Churchill was poring over the maps in his operations room in London, when he glanced up. 'This sort of weather won't do Eddie Marsh any good,' he said, thinking aloud, then turned back to his battle. Now there was less resistance. Patrick was on the telephone, listening to me giving what little first-aid advice I could think of on the spur of the moment, when at last the doctor arrived. His patient seemed in a deep coma, but he rallied, took notice of him, and asked if it was 'serious'. On seeing his grave expression, he uttered his last coherent remark, 'Well, I can take it.'

He was apparently quite unconscious when I looked in an hour or so later, but on the nurse telling him who had called he opened his eyes with a look of brilliant and instantaneous recognition, then seemed to sink back infinitely far into his private world. A little later he sat up and, frowning, spoke animatedly in a commanding voice, but the look that held one so fixedly was not his, and it was not possible to distinguish any intelligible words. The cat which was curled asleep on his feet remained blissfully undisturbed. I noticed that the sash window had jammed a fraction short of the top, and the fog was feeling its way in through the crack in a dismal yellow smoulder. An attempt to plug the gap with twists of newspaper was doing little good when Nancy Maurice, Eddie's niece arrived, and was later joined by his nephew Michael. He recognized them and was glad of them, but this time their uncle was lost in a wilderness more confounding than ever was met with on the island of Corsica.

Michael stayed with him through the night, and shortly after 3 A.M., still unconscious, Eddie Marsh died aged eighty years and two months. The funeral service was held at the church of St. Mary the Virgin, Sloane Square. Mr. Churchill was represented by Brendan Bracken, and Mrs. Elgy, now in her nineties, was seated at the front. That afternoon, at Putney, alone on the coffin was a plain wreath of poet's bay. And then the ashes were strewn along the wind.

The only unpublished manuscript on his table was an article on Winston Churchill which had been asked for by a French magazine. 'Whether or not it be true that no valet can make a hero of his master, it is certainly not so of a Private Secretary,' he had written. 'I do not propose to write about his achievements as a statesman,' he went on. 'Are they not written in the books of the Chronicles? It is enough to say that to my mind he is indisputably the greatest figure in English history, with the possible exception of King Alfred, about whom I do not know enough to form an opinion.' On January 13, that illustrious friend and patron of 'the last of the great patrons' heard the news while still on

holiday in Jamaica. Next day *The Times* published the message
he had sent by cable:

> *The death of Edward Marsh is a loss to the nation, and a keen personal grief to me. Since we began working together at the Colonial Office in 1905 we have always been the closest friends. Apart from his distinguished career as a Civil Servant he was a master of literature and scholarship and a deeply instructed champion of the arts. All his long life was serene, and he left this world, I trust, without a pang, and I am sure without a fear.*

Appendix I

GEORGIAN POETRY *1911–1912* AND THE CRITICS

THE Georgian anthology appeared almost simultaneously with Quiller-Couch's *Oxford Book of Victorian Verse* and in several journals they were reviewed together. The first article to appear was written by Lascelles Abercrombie for the *Manchester Guardian* (January 8). He worked his way to the Georgian book with a bitter attack on the companion volume. 'What it most conspicuously accomplishes is a monstrous degradation of the standards by which poetry ought to be judged.' He believed that the Georgians had broken away completely from Victorianism in manner as well as matter. 'But the book is not a collection of merely revolutionary efforts,' he wrote. This was shown by the dedication to 'the man who has kept the classical tradition of English poetry nobly alive and vivid among us'. He saw no signs of a new school or even a movement. 'Poetry does not willingly classify itself when it has vital business in hand . . . it is enough that the book gives us a chance of judging whether the poetry of today is able to accept the significance of its own time without refusing, or trying to refuse, the unalterable traditional nature of its art.' He thought that Gibson most fully illustrated this dual aim in substance and style, for his work dealt 'frankly and uncompromisingly with familiar workaday life, using a language which is charged indeed with the race of common speech, but severely indifferent to the supposed requirements of customary ornament, effecting the transformation of reality into art by the extraordinary certainty of its whole formality— formality comparable to that of classical music', and he ended by saying that the anthology was important 'not because the poetry in it is entirely satisfactory, but because it is unmistakable evidence of poetry's determination to undertake new duties in the old style'.

Two days later (the same day as Henry Newbolt gave the inaugural address at the opening of the Poetry Bookshop in

Devonshire Street) the *Daily News* carried an article by Ellis Roberts headed 'Poets of the Hour'. According to this writer the main break with the late Victorians lay in the abandonment of poetical egotism, and a veering away from ornate diction towards a refreshing simplicity and concern for the poem as a whole. His principal objection was the book's incompleteness. Where were Belloc (whom Brooke was apparently following), Colum, Freeman, Middleton, Anna Bunston, and Gerald Gould? Brooke and Monro himself, on the other hand, were 'so young it seems a pity they were not left ungathered'.

On January 14 Edward Thomas reviewed the Georgians in the *Daily Chronicle*. He regarded Bottomley, Masefield, and Gibson ('whose *Queen's Crags* in the current *English Review* is a fine thing and his best work') as the most characteristic writers of a recognizable new school which also included Abercrombie, Brooke, Lawrence, Sargant, and Stephens. 'Messrs Brooke, Lawrence, and Sargant are, as it were, the core of the group.' Like Roberts he was conscious of omissions. 'There are writers more Georgian than half a dozen of these, and as worthy of inclusion.'

> But the volume is more representative and striking than if twice the number of poets had been drawn from. It shows much beauty, strength, and mystery, and some magic—much aspiration, less defiance, no revolt—and it brings out with great clearness many sides of the modern love of the simple and primitive, as seen in children, peasants, savages, early man, animals, and Nature in general. Everyone, except Messrs Davies and de la Mare, is represented either by narrative or by meditative verse, and by practically nothing else.

A. C. Benson's review came out in the *Cambridge Magazine* on the 18th. After welcoming 'a fine touch of personality about the *flair* of the collector, which adds zest to the book' he found fault with the title. 'One thinks of George II's horror of "Boetry" and George III's complaints of all the "sad stuff" there was to be found in Shakespeare.' Like Abercrombie he perceived no sign of a 'school'. 'Each of these poets seems to be working wholly on his own line, without deference or subservience yet without anarchical experiment. There is no sense of a revolt, no hint of a desire to arrest or impress at any cost.' He considered Abercrombie and Sturge Moore the most distinctive of the contributors, analysed Brooke's *The Fish*, numbering it among the best of the individual pieces, and was the first critic to suggest a sequel to the present volume.

At this early stage the idea of a series was by no means a foregone conclusion in the editor's mind. Since the outbreak of war was to prevent the succeeding two years from yielding their Georgian harvest, and indeed brought the whole venture to an end, or so it seemed, it is all the more necessary to regard the first anthology as a thing on its own. With the fourth volume (1919) the very term 'Georgian' came to mean something different. Yet the germs of that later sense of the term (a combination of false rusticity and simplicity, glibness of feeling and a studied lucidity of style that was merely modish) had already been detected, one feels, in this initial stage, if only dimly, by Edward Thomas.

The main critical event was of course the review by Edmund Gosse entitled 'Knocking at the Door' which appeared in the *Morning Post* on January 27. He began by pointing out that this selection was the first critical attempt to sort out the 'latest generation' of poets by drawing attention to its most characteristic members.

> *Georgian Poetry 1911–1912*, therefore, though put forth with great modesty, deserves the careful attention of all who desire to contemplate without prejudice the moving spectacle of literature. It takes us a step further in the progress of poetry than any previous publication has done, and future historians may place it, if not quite with *The Germ* of 1850, at least with the Oxford Garlands of the Eighties and with the first 'Book of the Rhymers' Club' of 1892. It was high time that we should receive another landmark of this sort.

He then argued that the book would have made a clearer impression if such seniors as Chesterton and Sturge Moore had not been included. (Marsh, who was now coming to realize the serious implications of a venture which had been embarked upon without any critical pretensions on his part, saw the wisdom of this, and three years later dropped these two contributors, together with Trevelyan, on grounds of seniority.) Gosse was in favour of artists living and working in association.

> The effect of poetry depends on a great many things besides the formal merit of the verse as it strikes a reader for the first time. It is modified by the effect of 'reverberation', and hence the great importance to a new school of poets, of being presented by a graceful choragus such as 'E.M.' who is with them but not of them.

He perceived no distinct uniformity of purpose but an unconscious unity of attitude.

> Recognizing that what is always to be feared and jealously to be guarded against in any revolution is absurdity, the new poets are careful not to be preposterous. . . . I seem to detect, as the leading principle of the action of them all, a desire to render the texture of poetry more plastic, more sensitive, more independent of mediocrity. . . . Not one of these writers but abandons the loud bassoon. They are haunted, more than their predecessors, by the poignant and feverish hopes of individuals. They exchange the romantic, the sentimental, the fictive conceptions of literature, for an ingenuousness, sometimes a violence, almost a rawness in the approach to life itself.

Looking back, the 'violence' and the 'rawness', which Gosse was quick to detect, seem characteristic of the first Georgians whose typical figures were Abercrombie, Bottomley, and Brooke. The 'violence' in Flecker's *Hassan* and Brooke's play *Lithuania* is of the same early Georgian order. The 'rawness' of *The Everlasting Mercy*, in which the last shreds of late-Victorian 'decadence' were vigorously thrown off, is perhaps the early Georgian archetype. In one important respect Gosse's opinion was in opposition to Ellis Roberts'. He believed that there was traceable in the work of these poets a conviction, or a vague belief, that the aspects of Nature as seen in the external world and the mind of Man were parallel, to an extent which could be partly discerned by the senses when quickened by the sympathetic imagination. 'This is a curious feature of the new school, and stamps them as Pan-psychical.'

> They are mysterious and discreet, as though for ever eavesdropping in the courts of life. In short, they are willing to stretch to its extremest limit the emotional consciousness of the intellect. It is obvious that this distinguishes poets of the Georgian group from their predecessors, and leads them to an excess of subjectivity which is in direct opposition to the objectivity which marked the poets of the close of the Victorian age.

He ended with a warning that 'the fatal rock' ahead of these writers was the dislocating of their verse forms into a state little better than rhythmic prose. 'From this the pilot of their genius must deliver the Georgian generation.'

The Times Literary Supplement (February 27, 1913) devoted its leading article to what it called 'this quaintly named anthology'.

'It is boldly decreed that we may already speak of a new *Georgian* period, and we accept the licence with alacrity. The word was wanted, and it sufficiently meets our need.' It was difficult to define any new movement in England because there was no orthodoxy, no central academic tradition. 'It may be pleasing to an English poet to reflect how free he is born. . . . A poet defies the public from the very start, by the mere act of writing poetry. No agreement relevant to the poet's case is really discussable between them. . . . The only body with which an excited poet can join direct issue is a constituted literary authority in possession of the ground which he claims.' The critic maintained that the only poetic authority of any sort which had been in England for nearly a hundred years was the personal domination of Tennyson, which had exerted no very wholesome influence on poetry, including Tennyson's own. What was wanted, however, was some sort of Academy or association vaguely respected by the public as an official institution, 'and fiercely attacked by every poet (until he becomes a member of it) as an obstruction to all light and liberty. Then indeed we should feel that poetry had every chance in its favour.'

> For the present our Georgians have to make the best of their misfortune that nobody wishes to interfere with them, and we, too, have to put up with the difficulty that they cannot be defined by a common antagonism.

They did, however, represent a reaction from a mood characteristic of late Victorian verse, a 'pale and uncertain mood', conscious of the failure of the cheerful mid-Victorian individualism, yet somehow content to do no more than 'sing its blighted faith'. Above all the old style was notorious for its 'timidity in confronting experience. . . . To refuse to be confronted is to take the line of least resistance, and an art which amuses itself with isolated moments and detached fancies is rightly called decadent. . . . It is curious to think that a disdainful rejection of philosophic consolation was at one time a characteristic of youth. A poet who is afraid to use his brains seems nowadays to be as rare as was a poet twenty years ago who trusted anything but his sensibilities.' These new writers, the critic argued, all showed a desire to clarify and shape experience, instead of sitting back and receptively awaiting its impact. 'The tendency of poetry today is thus almost exclusively towards drama', not necessarily the drama of the stage but the dramatic handling, in some form or other, of life and character. The danger in this was that their sense of beauty might suffer and become coarsened. The new direction of poetic literature brought with it a duty of fastidiousness. 'The degeneration of beauty towards prettiness is not in these days to be feared; where that happens it means that art is travelling between narrowing walls.' (This is a good analysis of what was to happen in traditional verse during the course of the war, and at length come to critical notice when the fourth Georgian book appeared.) The writer in the *Literary Supplement* found himself drawn to agree with Gosse on the question of 'violence'. 'The temptation is great to think that life and strength and energy are enough, and that an art which is conscious of enjoying these advantages had better let itself be guided entirely by them.' The 'affected and self-conscious brutality' to which writers could easily succumb, according to this perceptive critic, was the very quality which D. H. Lawrence was to censure in connexion with Abercrombie in his correspondence with Marsh. Nevertheless this article considered Abercrombie the leading Georgian figure. 'Of all the poetic talents which have appeared since the beginning of the century his is the most conspicuous union of breadth and intensity.' After placing Bottomley second in importance to Abercrombie, the writer came to Brooke, who had so far attracted little notice except in the Cambridge journal. 'Finally, we have Mr. Rupert Brooke, who occupies in such a company as this a very curious position. He is literally the only one, so it seems, who takes the immemorial advice to the poet—"Fool, said my Muse to me, look in thy heart, and write!" exactly as it has been understood in all ages and as Sidney himself understood it. His poems are written in just that emotional simplicity which the other poets have eschewed, and passion is to be heard in them, even if it is a little shrill.'

The critic of the *Nation* (March 8) was most impressed by Abercrombie as a 'vehement, imaginative thinker. If he were a race-horse he might be described as by Browning out of Elizabethan drama. . . . He does not harangue the reader personally like Browning. . . . His language is not like brilliant talk; it has the elaborate compact force of the written word.' Brooke's imagination struck him as 'ecstatic and harsh. . . . He is an intellectual poet; bygone criticism would have dubbed him metaphysical, and he would have met with readier appreciation in the seventeenth century.' Of de la Mare this writer remarked: 'There is a tincture of Coleridge in the temper of his imagination. He can touch us with a ghostly finger.' Davies too was aptly noticed. 'Only quite a simple mind could have wanted to say that, and only a delicate mind could have found that way of saying it.' Gibson's *The Hare* showed that his style was 'the perfection of colloquial poetry', and Bottomley's *Babel* was 'a Doré picture, but translated into words with a massive thoroughness of imagination'.

D. H. Lawrence's review appeared in the March number of *Rhythm*. 'This collection is like a big breath taken when we are waking up after a night of oppressive dreams. The nihilists, the intellectual, hopeless people—Ibsen, Flaubert, Thomas Hardy—represent the dream we are waking from. It was a dream of demolition. . . . The first song is nearly a cry, fear and the pain of remembrance sharpening away the pure music. And this is the book.'

What are the Georgian poets, nearly all, but just bursting into a thick blaze of being? They are not poets of passion, perhaps, but they are essentially passionate poets. The time to be impersonal has gone. We start from the joy we have in being ourselves, and everything must take colour from that joy.

Appendix II

THE SPEAKING OF DRAMATIC VERSE

LIKE his friend R. C. Trevelyan, and his acquaintance W. B. Yeats, Marsh's own practice as a speaker of verse showed that he was always at pains to emphasize rather than conceal the metrical artifice in the passage he was delivering. Since the poem was conceived and written in an artificial convention, then doubtless, he contended, the poet aimed at certain advantages of measure and loftiness of style which should be no less apparent when the poem was received through the ear than through the reading eye. Owing to the vogue for naturalism in acting, especially in the films, there was a danger that the craft of speaking dramatic verse might be lost along with the other crafts depending on the human body which had been outmoded by Science. If the 'secret' (the candid delivery of verse as verse) were forgotten, then the function itself of verse in the theatre would be misunderstood. In the part of Romeo, for instance, there were places where for the sake of realistic effect the modern actor skilled in naturalism might all too easily be tempted to sacrifice truth to the character (as a creation in verse) to the more familiar kind of truth—that of common humanity. Marsh maintained that the persons in a poetic drama were all equally, and at all times, abnormal or 'unnatural' in one respect, and one only—their expressiveness; so he wanted a compromise, neither the rhetorical 'spouting' of a lay-figure, nor the workaday utterance of an Ibsenite, but a judicious blending of the two within a convention which should establish an order of naturalness all its own.

In October 1935 he attended a performance of *Romeo and Juliet* at the New Theatre which received an enthusiastic review from Mr. St. John Ervine in the *Observer*. On November 3 Marsh wrote to the critic.

> I agree with all your praise of Larry Olivier's acting, and I am glad indeed that you have given him his due; but the opinion which you

appear to hold about the proper way of speaking Romeo's verse seems to me so strange and so erroneous that I am going to put my head in the lion's mouth, and contribute to the postbag which gives you weekly opportunities for argumentative triumph.

Shakespeare's pen, you say, when he wrote that verse, was 'clogged with mumness'—and by 'mum', you say you mean 'inarticulate'; therefore, to give its full value, the actor who delivers it should be mum, or inarticulate, too. Do you really hold that Shakespeare was 'mum' when he wrote the lines about the 'wondering white-upturned eyes', and 'Death's pale flag', and the 'yoke of inauspicious stars', and all those others which are commonly held to reach the limit of verbal beauty and melody? If you do, alas you are tone-deaf, and there is no arguing with you. But of course this is not so. Romeo, you must think, being an impetuous young man in love, would naturally and necessarily 'fumble for words in which to say his love'; and this propensity to fumbling is so much the most important thing about him that all Shakespeare's art of words must be sacrificed to the exhibition of it. But this is realism gone mad. Why should Shakespeare have been at pains to write such heavenly poetry, if the actor is to halt, or count the syllables on his fingers? Dramatic verse is a convention; and if an actor cannot within its bounds convey the essence of the character he is playing, he has not perfectly mastered his job.

But what, you will wonder, does this captious person know of verse, that he speaks about it so slickly? Upon my head be it.

In his reply Mr. St. John Ervine explained that by 'mumness' he meant to convey that comparative lack of facility and crafts-manship which Shakespeare showed in his earliest plays when he was still uncertain of his form and in almost servile awe of Marlowe. 'The servitude did not disable him from writing the lovely lines you cite, nor am I suggesting that he was "mum" in the sense that he could not produce them. Of course he produced them, just as Rupert produced lovely lines while he was still at Cambridge, but you won't disagree will you? when I say that Rupert's last poems were those of a mind not only more profound than it was when he was an undergraduate, but also a mind more articulate, more capable of saying with accomplishment and ease what it contained.'

He did not wish Romeo to stumble over his words, but he did expect him to give the impression that his head and heart were so flooded with love that he could not utter his feelings as he felt them. Olivier gave him this sense of an overwhelming passion,

'Other actors have made me feel that they had their answers pat to every remark that Juliet might make. They delivered their lines as if they were saying to themselves, " Even if you do miss your cue, I shan't miss mine. I know my part! . . ." '

> Somehow, it seems to me, Olivier has caught not only his character's mood, but his author's. I am ready to believe that if Shakespeare read his play to a party of friends in your rooms, as I heard Rupert read *Lithuania* there to you and Cathleen Nesbitt and my wife and me, he would have read it as badly as Rupert did. Some shyness or constraint would have embarrassed his speech. By the time he had written *Twelfth Night* that embarrassment had disappeared, and he would have read it to us, had that been possible, as easily as Rupert would have read the War Sonnets.

Marsh replied next day:

> Many thanks for your interesting answer; but I see that we shall each be of the same opinion still; our views of Romeo's *utterance* are exactly opposite. To me the effect of his love upon him is not embarrassment but liberation: he glories in his new-found powers of expression, and rides the wind of rhythm like a young god. I am sure that for this ideal representative there is a mean between mumness and patness. It is hard to hit. . . . One can't argue from the way poets read their own verses. I never, as you may suppose, heard Shakespeare or Shelley, but Rupert was certainly no hand at it. Gosse's imitation of Tennyson was convincing, and very funny; and de la Mare does it as if he were his own spinster aunt who had been told by the village clergyman that her nephew's poems had merit.

This brought the discussion to a close. The rival claims of naturalism and convention in the verse drama will never be finally resolved, but it is necessary that from time to time the nature of the problem should be restated.

Appendix III

DIABOLIZATION

I N Chapter 19 (p. 640) 'diabolization' has been defined as
the act of a critic whose declared aim is 'to find fault and be
as carping as possible for the eventual benefit of the work in
hand'. If the book was in proof this included all the duties of the
conventional proof-reader, but Edward Marsh always took it
upon himself to challenge the motive behind a passage, as well as
the syntax or the matters of fact which it contained, so that his
special function warranted the creation of a special term. He
dealt with problems in the shape and cadence of a sentence, the
precise meaning to be conveyed, and the logical unfolding of
thought within a paragraph.

Mr. Somerset Maugham's *The Summing Up* (Heinemann, 1938)
was the fourth of his books to be criticized in proof by Marsh.
Many pages of textual comment were pasted inside the back
cover of the page proofs when they were bound and given by
Maugham to Sir Gerald Kelly. This form of book-doctoring took
up so great a part of Marsh's life in his latter years that at least a
rough impression of the 'diabolizer' at work should be included
here to show his method and complete the picture of his contribution to English letters. A special debt of thanks is due to Mr.
Maugham for allowing these private notes to be offered as an
illustration. Out of a great number of points in the notes on *The
Summing Up* I have selected the following examples. First the
original proof (*a*) is quoted in italics, then Marsh's comment (*b*),
then the author's revision (*c*) is indicated. When the comment
alone is enough there is no alphabetical letter to introduce it, and
unless the contrary is stated the suggestion was adopted by the
author. The page numbers have been adjusted to conform with
the first edition, and the critical points have been numbered so
that the reader can the more easily distinguish them from one
another. *The Summing Up*, a statement of the author's personal
conclusions on the function of literature and the nature of the

good life, was naturally of special interest to Marsh, and his study of the proofs was among the first tasks which he undertook after his official retirement.

1. p. 8   (a) *I can decide what they* [the creatures of his invention] *would think more readily than I can decide what I think myself. The one has always been a pleasure to me; the other,* [*even when it has amounted to no more than making a note in a commonplace book,*] *has been a labour that I have willingly put off.*

(b) Does the sentence about 'the one and the other' work out? 'The other' can only be deciding what you think yourself; but it seems odd to say without explanation that this process may amount to putting a note in a commonplace book.

(c) The clause in the second pair of brackets is cut.

2. p. 10   (a) *In the course of Rousseau's Confessions he narrates incidents that have profoundly shocked* . . .

(b) I should slightly prefer 'Rousseau in the course of his Confessions narrates . . .'

3. p. 13   (a) . . . *there is only one thing about which I am certain, and this is that there is very little about which one can be certain.*

(b) Isn't this inconsistent with what you say at bottom of p. 11 'Time generally makes the truth obvious'? (which I rather boggled at when I read it).

[p. 11 ran: *I have a modest confidence in my instinct. Time generally makes the truth obvious. I am willing to change my mind.*]

(c) The solution was to leave p. 13 as it stood, and on p. 11 substitute 'certain' for 'modest' and cut the 2nd sentence 'Time etc.'

4. p. 14   (a) *I wish I had* [read his grandfather's essays], *for I might from it have learnt something of the kind of man he was.*

(b) See my suggested transposition—or you might say 'for from it I [might] have learnt'—as it stands it's a bad rhythm.

(c) I wish I had, for I might have learnt from it . . .

5. p. 16   Shouldn't it be 'Beauty and the Beast', not *the* Beauty? In the fairy story Beauty is a proper name.

6. p. 17   'The papers of my uncle' sounds rather Ollendorfian, why not 'my uncle's'?

7. p. 28   Has 'massivity' any advantage over the usual 'massiveness'?

8. p. 31   I would put 'Few people have written' . . . to avoid beginning two consecutive sentences with 'There are'.

9. p. 33 'too profound for it to be possible to express them' is rather clumsy, why not 'too profound to be expressed'?

10. p. 34 (a) *I have aimed at it* [simplicity] *because I had no gift for richness.*

(b) Either 'I have aimed at it because I have' or 'I aimed at it . . .'

(c) the former suggestion adopted.

11. pp. 35, 36 I think the order in which you have arranged the discussion of 'simplicity' gives it an appearance of confused thought. If your thesis is to be that the *native* English style represented by Sir T. More was *corrupted* by the style of the Bible, it seems wrong to *start* with saying that 'English is a naturally poetic language' etc. To solve this the author deleted 'English is a naturally poetic language and its writers of prose have always singing in their ears the rhythm and language of verse. The good prose word is constantly being displaced by the poetic one.' Thus he let stand his point about More and the Bible, but cut the previous general statement on the naturally poetic qualities of the language.

12. p. 37 One wouldn't think from this that de Quincey was contemporary with Shelley. I would at any rate put him before Carlyle. I've always understood that what Buffon himself said was '*Le style c'est de l'homme*' and that '*Le style c'est l'homme*' was a popular corruption of this. If this is so, perhaps better say 'The dictum'.

The author reversed the order of Shelley and Carlyle, and dropped the reference to Buffon by name, so that the sentence ran 'The dictum that the style is the man is well known'.

13. p. 38 It seems wrong to say first 'Poetry is baroque' and then (after 3 sentences in between) 'Baroque is essentially poetical'. [The author deleted the latter phrase.]

14. p. 39 (a) *It was in this period* [18th-century Rococo] *that for the first time conversation was pursued as an art.*

(b) You might be taken to mean that conversation was not practised as an art before the 18th century, but surely the Restoration drama is proof to the contrary, and the process began still earlier in France.

(c) The sentence is deleted.

15. p. 41 I don't think it's euphony to begin two consecutive sentences 'One of the differences' and 'One difficulty'— say, in the latter case, 'It is a difficulty in writing English.'

16. p. 42   (a) . . . *though I think you may without misgiving make this concession* [use of a special word] *to pleasant sound, I think you should make none to sense.*

(b) 'I think you should make no concession to sense' seems to me the exact opposite of what you mean, which is that you should make no sacrifices of sense. And 'It is the sound of water' etc., no doubt the alliteration here is appropriate, but I do think it's overdone—'*so sooth*ing that you *soon cease* to be *sens*ible of it'.

(c) 'sense' is cut, and 'what may obscure your meaning' substituted. Also 'soon' is changed to 'presently'.

17. p. 45   (a) *I would sooner a writer were vulgar than refined; for life is vulgar, and it is life he seeks.*

(b) I can't help boggling at the last sentence of 1st para. To say that an author should be vulgar in his search of vulgar life lays you open to Dr. Johnson's 'who drives fat oxen must himself be fat', and to make your point I think you need some more definitely derogatory word than 'refined' which doesn't necessarily mean the same as 're-faned'! refinement has a sense in which it is a good quality.

(c) 'mincing' is substituted for 'refined'.

18. p. 46   (a) *We cannot, however much we would, escape* . . .

(b) I don't think 'however much we would' is possible grammar. You couldn't say 'I would very much'. 'however willingly we would' would be grammar.

(c) 'willingly' is substituted for 'much'.

19. p. 50   (a) . . . *sometimes the stars shine more brightly from the gutter than from the hilltop.*

(b) The sense is clear, and the sentence may stand, but I can't help observing that stars don't shine *from* the gutter or the hilltop.

(c) 'seen' is added after 'brightly'.

20. p. 59   I think 'seeing things from another point of view' is rather a faculty than a quality?

'Faculty' is accepted.

21. p. 66   'humankind' jingles uncomfortably with 'open mind'— say 'human beings'.

22. p. 71   In giving Stendhal this pride of place, should you not glance at Montaigne, and perhaps at Shakespeare? (Perhaps not, as I see you say the 'first *novelist*'.)

23. p. 95   This clashes a little with what you said before, that you couldn't be an hour with anyone without getting material for a possible story.

Resolved by a considerable cut and a transposition.

24. p. 99 (a) *It is all very well to say that poetry is emotion remembered in tranquillity; but the poet cannot cut himself into two halves, his emotion is a poet's emotion and it is never quite so entire as the ordinary man's. . . . This dichotomy prevents the writer from entering into perfect communion with men.*

(b) I don't quite catch your drift here, and certainly the expression is obscure. The fact that the poet *cannot* cut himself into 2 halves is strangely described as a dichotomy and as *preventing* his emotion from being entire. I can't help thinking that you meant 'A poet cannot (but) cut himself . . .'

(c) After 'tranquillity' the remainder is cut and recast as 'but a poet's emotion is specific, a poet's rather than a man's, and it is never quite disinterested'.

25. p. 102 (a) '*a pure gemlike flame*'.

(b) Pater's phrase was 'a hard gemlike flame'.

26. p. 103 'A young thing'·in line 1, 'pretty little things' in line 6; this repetition of 'thing' is jejune?

27. p. 107 Why do you succumb to the Americanism [stage] director for producer?

Footnote inserted: 'I use the American word director rather than the English one producer because I think it describes what should be the function of the person in question.'

28. p. 110 (a) *Indeed I should never have gone to see my plays at all, on the first night or any other, if I had not thought it necessary in order to learn how to write them to see the effect they had on the audience.*

(b) Surely three infinitives are too many?—to learn—to write—to see. I think the awkwardness arises from the separation of 'necessary' from 'to see', and it would be all right it you transposed 'in order to learn how to write them' to the end of the sentence.

29. p. 113 (a) *. . . the exhibitionism which is usual in them* [actors] *and which of course has induced them to go on the stage gives them a dualism of personality that is very similar to the writer's.*

(b) Your argument here is tantalizingly incomplete, you begin by saying that you—a writer—can't quite look on actors as human beings, and then you admit that their dualism (which I take to be the same thing as their 'amorphousness' which is up to that point the only thing you have alleged against them) is 'very similar to the writer's'. Surely you are bound to explain why in that case a writer is a human being and an actor is not!

(c) The whole clause is cut and the following written in its place '. . . their character, like his [the novelist's] is a harmony that is none too plausible; they are all the persons they mirror, while he is all the persons he can beget.'

30. p. 124 Half-way down, I would leave out 'of' after 'cynicism' as there are two more 'of's' to come in the sentence.

31. p. 129 'It is here that it may serve him.' I am pedantic in my dislike of two unrelated 'it's'.

32. p. 129 I feel that unless there were something wrong with the adverb 'difficultly' it would be commoner (I don't think I ever met with it before). Wouldn't 'laboriously' be better? or reluctantly or coyly? P.S. When you used 'difficultly' three times I was driven to the Dictionary which I find *does* recognize it, tho' without giving an authority. ['Reluctantly' accepted.]

33. p. 132 (a) . . . *individuals will laugh at a joke they do not see because others who see it do.*
(b) The 'do not' and 'do' with different references are inelegant. Perhaps 'they have not seen' for 'do not see'?

34. p. 132 (a) *It* [the audience] *likes ideas, so long as they are put in dramatic form but, they must be ideas that it has itself had, though, for want of courage, has never expressed.*
(b) 'though has never expressed' isn't grammar. I suggest 'only they must be ideas . . . itself had, but for want of courage has never expressed'. No commas after 'but' and 'courage'.

35. p. 138 'I can think of no serious prose play that has survived the generation that gave it birth' . . . I suppose you are confining yourself to English plays, but as a general principle is involved I think you should guard yourself against being taken to have overlooked Molière. (Personally, tho' this is neither here nor there, I disagree strongly about the English comedies. I could never look at *The School for Scandal* as a museum piece—and when Edith Evans played *The Way of the World*, or when *She Stoops* or *The Country Wife* were given at the Old Vic, the audience did not laugh with politeness or embarrassment.) [No change.]

36. p. 139 (a) . . . *once they* [dramatists] *have got a number of persons into the playhouse, they have become an audience* . . .
(b) Am I too pedantic about pronouns? 'once *they* have got . . . *they*'—would you hate to put 'these' instead of the second 'they'? Also I should prefer (for balance) 'the

reactions by which an audience is governed' at the *end* of the sentence. Last line, here comes Molière at last but I think belatedly.

37. p. 142   It may be worth observing that English did not *invent* the word uxorious, but adopted it from Latin—Virgil and Horace use it in our sense.

38. p. 145   (a) *He is forced to drop asides because people do not naturally talk to themselves out loud.*

    (b) I think 'drop asides' is ambiguous, cf. 'drop a remark'—better 'forgo'?

39. p. 147   'I am conscious that the cinema can do better whatever the spoken theatre can do.' This raises an interesting point. When Ivor [Novello] put on an earthquake in his last play and a railway smash in the present one, several people made the remark that one would have thought beforehand that such effects were obsolete in the theatre, but that it turned out to be the contrary; since people had become *blasé* about such things in the Cinema just because they knew of the great resources to which everything seemed possible—but were still capable of being pleased and *épaté* by them in the theatre just because they were still conscious of the difficulty of producing them. I think this point of view is worth considering.

40. p. 148   'willing suspension of belief.' When this occurred before, I altered it *sub silentio* to disbelief, because I thought it was a slip of the pen, but it seems you attach a meaning to it, tho' I don't know what. Certainly what Coleridge said was 'disbelief'. I shouldn't be in the least grateful to an audience which suspended belief in my play, willingly or not!

41. p. 158   (a) *I grew tired of the absurdity that admits in conversation all manner of facts that it denies on the stage.*

    (b) It is not the absurdity which 'denies'—say 'that must be denied on the stage.'

42. p. 159   (a) *I have always had a dislike that managers should lose money over me.*

    (b) 'dislike that' is an unusual construction.

    (c) 'dislike to managers losing.'

43. p. 161   (a) *It* [naturalism] *has lessened his themes* . . .

    (b) The word 'lessened' is ambiguous, and may mean either 'diminished the importance of' or 'restricted the number of'. It seems to me that either would be possible here, and I don't know which you mean. Next sentence, I think this is a case for a double 'which'—'Comedy

which depends on verbal wit, which in turn depends . . .'
is really more logical.

(c) 'restricted' and the double 'which' accepted.

44. p. 162 (a) *During rehearsal I found that the actors, unused any longer to speeches of this sort . . .*

(b) I think it should be either 'no longer used' or 'unused by now'.

(c) The former suggestion adopted.

45. p. 181 'achieves this' doesn't match the sentence before where it is his public that has 'achieved' the discovery—the sense would be given by saying that 'it takes him time to convince his public that'. Next sentence, I would omit 'of this' which has only rather a vague reference.

46. p. 182 Wouldn't 'writing' sound better than 'to write'? Next sentence, '*those* countries'—no country has been mentioned. I think you will have to repeat 'English speaking', and wouldn't 'the cultivation of the arts' be better than an infinitive?

47. p. 182 (a) *In France and Germany to write is an honourable profession.*

(b) Here is this substantial infinitive again, I do think it's awkward.

48. p. 182 I expect you wrote *the* sensibilities to avoid another 's', but I think that is the lesser evil. If you say 'his imagination' you *must* say 'his sensibilities'.

49. p. 185 I would put the sentence 'By essential . . . word' in brackets, as the next sentence carries on from the one before. I think also 'implication' would be better than 'meaning'.

50. p. 186 I still hold out for 'lunch' being the verb and 'luncheon' the noun, but I know it's old-fashioned. (In my time 'lunch' as a noun was a horrid vulgarism.) End of para. as 'useful' and 'serviceable' mean the same thing, I would substitute 'advantageous' for one of them.

51. p. 188 I entirely agree that as a general rule success doesn't make people vain, but I think you ought to admit that there are exceptions.

52. p. 192 (a) *The writer's only safety is to find his satisfaction in his own performance. If he can realize that in the liberation of soul which his work has brought him and in the pleasure of shaping it in such a way as to satisfy to some extent at least his aesthetic sense, he has got an ample reward for his labour and can afford to be indifferent to the outcome.*

(b) The last sentence [of the page] is incomplete, it's all one long 'if' clause without an apodosis. It could be mended by putting 'he can afford' instead of 'and can afford' but that would be intolerably awkward after 'he has got'. I can't suggest a good correction, as I'm not sure how you mean it to go. (You might say '. . . his own preference, and to realize'—but that would make a very long and cumbrous sentence.)

(c) The first sentence is let stand. In the second, after 'aesthetic sense', the clause is recast to read 'he is amply rewarded for his labours, he can afford' etc.

53. p. 193 'The art.' Unless I am mistaken Aristotle was dealing with the art of tragedy, with which you are not here exclusively concerned. Better make it general and say 'which Aristotle tells us is the object of art'. (I don't think you could be meaning 'the art' to refer to 'the tragedy' at the beginning of the sentence which you are using in the metaphorical sense.)

54. p. 194 '*it* was a natural reaction from *it*'—substitute 'success' for the second 'it' and I would have a colon before 'I was' as the sentence is getting rather invertebrate.

55. p. 206 Is 'unaccustomed' the right word? surely some at least of the 'characters' you met in the South Seas were accustomed to their environment. You have the right word on p. 210—'alien'.

56. p. 208 'sociability'—'amiability' so close together are not euphonious. Could you say 'an inestimable social gift' or 'gift as a mixer'? (vulgar, but such a good word). [First suggestion adopted.]

57. p. 209 (a) *The fact that 'characters' have been a popular form of letters since Theophrastus* . . .

(b) 'The fact that' throws the sentence off its balance. I would say 'The "characters" which have been a popular . . .'

58. p. 210 (a) *I concluded that I had come to the end of my capacity for seeing people in the circumstances in which I sought them with individuality.*

(b) I think the sentence beginning 'I concluded' has gone wrong—'with individuality' goes in grammar with 'sought them' but in meaning with 'seeing people' and the phrase 'in the circumstances in which I sought them' conveys to me no definite meaning.

(c) I concluded that I had come to the end of my capacity for seeing with passion and individuality the people I went so far to find.

59. p. 226 I think 'Pheidias' is a pedantry. You might as well say
'Horatius'. 'Phidias' is the English form.

60. p. 233 Wasn't Matthew Arnold a creative writer as a poet?

61. p. 235 (a) *It is because he is so many that he can create many and the*
measure of his greatness is the number of selves that comprise him.
(b) Should be either 'that compose him' or 'that he comprises'. Do you remember a letter of Keats in which he
dwells on this very point—the one about the poet having
no personality, with the account of his identifying himself
with the sparrow picking up crumbs outside his window?
(c) 'he comprises' adopted.

62. p. 239 (a) *Others may despise us because we do not lend a hand with*
a bucket of water; we can do no more, we do not know how to
handle a bucket.
(b) 'do no more'. The point is not that you 'can do no
more', it is that you can't even do *that*, i.e. lend a hand
with a bucket.
(c) 'can do no more' becomes 'cannot help it'.

63. p. 241 (a) *I wrote of what by practice I had some cognizance.*
(b) You've made an 'of' do double duty, with 'wrote' and
with 'cognizance'.
(c) 'of' added after the last word.

64. p. 249 I think the semicolon you have put in after 'faculty'
(segregating as it does a 'though' clause from the statement it qualifies) darkens rather than clears up this long
sentence—a comma would be better.

65. p. 259 I can't follow your reasoning here—surely if you were
'achieving the ambition that consumed you' you were
'seeking your own gratification'. You weren't denying
your inclinations because it was *right* to do so—so where
is the inconsistency? [This resulted in a big cut of seven
lines.]

66. p. 277 I think in *good* modern English 'infer' should be distinguished from 'imply' (they are often confused).

67. p. 303 I am accustomed to the form '*Toute vérité n'est pas bonne à*
dire' which is a little terser. [Not accepted.]

68. p. 305 Unless I fail to take your point, the analogy of the roses
seems rather sketchy. True we cannot smell the actual
blooms our ancestors smelt—nor can we read the
Antigone in Sophocles' autograph. But the flower Rose
remains the same, and so does the text of *Antigone*. But
so far as we know, the pleasure our ancestors took in their
roses was the same that we take in ours; whereas no
doubt their sense of *Antigone* was very different from ours.

This for the analogy of the roses. On the general argument I shouldn't go as far as you do. I expect that in our feelings towards *Antigone* and those of the Periclean Athenians the identity is far greater than the discrepancy. I agree however that for the reason you give (among others) beauty can't be analysed.

69. p. 306 (a) *It is usual enough to talk of the aesthetic instinct, which seems to give it a place among the mainsprings of the human being, like hunger and sex, and at the same time gives it a specific quality that flatters that philosophical craving for unity.*

(b) 'to talk of the aesthetic instinct, which' doesn't quite work out. I should say 'It is usual enough to talk of the aesthetic instinct: the term seems to give it a place.' Also '*seems to give* it' and at the same time '*gives* it' isn't very elegant. Could you say 'and at the same time to endow it with'?

70. p. 305 Surely there is here a confusion of thought. You seem to speak as if the process of adding emotion *to* the odes [of Keats] must in some strange way end in wringing all emotion *out* of them and leaving them empty husks. Apart from the apparent contradiction in terms I can't follow your idea that the beauty of a work can be exhausted by being enjoyed—granted that an individual, or even a generation, might be satisfied with it, the work itself remains intact for future individuals to enjoy afresh.

71. p. 314 (a) ... *there are few things that cause greater wretchedness than to love with all your heart someone whom you know is unworthy of love.*

(b) Either 'who you know is' or 'whom you know to be' (otherwise you are landed with 'whom is').

(c) 'who' substituted for 'whom'.

72. p. 317 (a) *It is not action that aims at happiness; it is a happy chance if it produces it.*

(b) Here are three 'it's', all different in meaning. You could get rid of *two* by saying 'it is a happy chance if happiness results'.

When Maugham's *The Vagrant Mood* came out, long after *The Summing Up*, Eddie Marsh, who had been unable to see it in proof, assured the author that he could find in it practically nothing to cavil at. Recalling this in his letter which so generously allowed me to quote the foregoing analysis, Mr. Maugham remarked, 'I think I must have improved in time'; and he drew attention to a matter of some biographical importance which is best disposed of

in his own words, 'I trust that in your biography you will not fail
to mention that Eddie looked upon this job . . . not, as one might
have expected, as a colossal bore, but as something very like a
delightful recreation.' Indeed he not only took delight in it, but
pride. The reader may recall the entry in Marsh's diary when
Maugham first invited him to look through one of his manuscripts—'There's glory for me!'

If the mastery of textual emendation which he acquired under
Verrall brought Marsh several new friends, his habit of caustic
comment also lost him a few. To the list of contemporary writers
he diabolized (without loss of mutual esteem) should be added Mary
Borden, Geoffrey Dennis (first brought to Marsh's notice by his
novel *Mary Lee*), Martin Armstrong, J. D. Beresford, A. A. Milne,
Dorothy L. Sayers, Ethel Smyth, Edward Shanks, Robert Byron,
Derek Patmore (*Portrait of My Family*) and Cyril Stott, the playwright. He also made notes on *Family Record* by Lady Wemyss;
and it was probably in connection with her memoir, *Haply I May
Remember*, that Lady Cynthia Asquith had the happy thought of
sending him a presentation copy with the inscription '*To the onlie
begetter of the ensuing commas*'.

The shots and counter-shots of critical skirmishes occur throughout his letters. 'Thank you for your grammatical exposition,' he
wrote to Bottomley, who had been trying to defend himself, 'but
I cannot say that it penetrates my obtuse Southern mind. Why the
indicative should be more applicable than the subjunctive to an
individual as opposed to a tube, is a mystery to me!' And on
returning proofs to another author he exclaimed: 'I can't make out
your punctuation at all! I once said the same thing to X about
something I read for her, and she told me the punctuation had
been put in by two friends who had conflicting ideas on the
subject!—and I wonder if anything of that kind has happened
here!' While he was at work on the proofs of *Orientations* by
Ronald Storrs he received a letter from the author commiserating
with him on the dryness of his labours. Reminded of the Gram-
marian in Browning's poem, Marsh replied that, contrary to what
many might suppose, it was a pleasure. 'I find something attractive
in pedantry,' he asserted, 'and feel a sneaking admiration for the
man who spends his life in properly basing οὖν.'

In 1907 at Brooke's suggestion he entered for a *Westminster
Gazette* competition and won the first prize for his choice of the

six best sentences in English prose. His examples were taken from
the *Song of Solomon*; a speech of Falstaff's in *Henry IV*, Part I;
Swift's *Tale of a Tub*; de Quincey's *Suspiria de Profundis*; the
concluding words of *Wuthering Heights*; and a sentence from *The
Stones of Venice* where for thirteen lines Ruskin sustains his description of the channel at low-tide which divides Venice from the
mainland. In later life, discussing contemporary literature, Marsh
declared that Aldous Huxley would be the most difficult author to
'diabolize', if he were given the chance. 'His English is certainly
the most correct,' he remarked, then added, 'even so, that isn't
everything, of course.' He regarded the ear as final arbiter. 'You
would never have let that pass if you had *listened* to it,' he would
say. The nature of his contribution to contemporary letters in this
kind was summed up by Harold Nicolson in his acknowledgement
of some critical notes on the proofs of his *Tennyson* (1923). 'They
show me,' he wrote, 'in a way that heartens rather than humiliates,
how wide a gulf is fixed between writing and good writing.'

ACKNOWLEDGEMENTS

THE reader will be aware that my indebtedness to all those who have helped me bring this chronicle into being must be considerable and widespread. First, I must acknowledge with warm thanks those whose contribution has been of an essential kind: Lady Churchill for her encouragement and interest from the start, allowing me to quote the passages from Sir Winston's letters and checking throughout the references to her family; Lord Bridges for his work on the papers of Robert Bridges and for his researches connected with the late Mrs. Laura Denniston; the late Baroness Wentworth for her hospitality at Crabbet Park and for giving me access to the important letters addressed to herself and Neville Lytton; Lady Cynthia Asquith for valuable comment on the proofs, much encouragement and helpful advice, and permission to quote from her own memoir; Sir Geoffrey Keynes for approving on behalf of the Brooke Trustees the passages relating to Rupert Brooke; Mr. Julian Hoare and Mr. Norman Edyvean-Walker, executors of the poet's mother, for most kindly entrusting to my discretion the correspondence of Mrs. Brooke; the late Mr. John Middleton Murry for especially writing his reminiscences of Marsh, Brooke, and Katherine Mansfield; Mr. W. Somerset Maugham for use of his letters and the proofs of *The Summing Up* with Marsh's critical notes; Messrs. William Heinemann for certain illustrations in *A Number of People* here reproduced, as well as various kinds of material for which that book is the chief authority; Sir Harold Nicolson for his guidance at the outset concerning the papers relating to Marsh's official life and for permission to quote from his own correspondence; Miss Nancy Maurice for her constructive criticism during her reading of the proofs and for approving the work as a whole on behalf of her family who are the next-of-kin; and my secretary Miss Gillian Patterson for her assistance in research and for her watching brief over every aspect of this enterprise from its inception to the end.

For allowing me to consult them personally, as well as supplying letters and granting permission to quote, I am most grateful to: Mrs. Lascelles Abercrombie, Mr. Leonard Appelbee, Mr. David Balfour and Mrs. Sheppard (*Reggie Balfour*), Princess Marthe Bibesco, Mr. Edmund Blunden, Lady Violet Bonham Carter, Mrs. Frances Cornford, Miss Clemence Dane, the late Professor E. J. Dent, Mrs. John Drinkwater, the late Mrs. Elgy, Mr. Wilfrid Gibson, Mr. Michael Gibson, Dr. Philip Gosse, Mr. Rupert Hart-Davis, Mr. John Hayward, Mr. William James (*executor of Henry James*), Sir Gerald Kelly, Elizabeth Lady Kilbracken, Mr. James Knapp Fisher (*Messrs. Sidgwick & Jackson*), Pamela Countess of Lytton, Miss Frances Macdonald, the late Mr. Walter de la Mare, Sir Francis Meynell, the late Mr. Charles Morgan, Miss Cathleen Nesbitt, Mr. James Pope-Hennessy, Lady Reid, Dr. E. V. Rieu, Sir John Rothenstein, Earl Russell, the late Mr. Michael Sadleir, Mr. Siegfried Sassoon, Mrs. George Shield (*literary executor of General Sir Ian Hamilton*), Mrs. Oswald Sickert, Miss Naomi Royde Smith, the late Sir John Squire, the late Mr. Dudley Ward, Mr. Laurence Whistler, the Hon. C. M. Woodhouse, Mrs. Annie Wynick, the Rev. Canon Andrew Young, and Mrs. Francis Brett Young.

I am also indebted to the following who have provided valuable material or helped in other ways by correspondence: Mr. Fred Allen, Mr. Robert Andrews, Mr. Martin Armstrong, Mrs. Raymond Asquith, Sir George Barnes, the late Mr. James Strachey Barnes, the late Sir Max Beerbohm and Lady Beerbohm, Lady Violet Benson, Mr. Bernhard Berenson, Mr. Anthony Bertram, Dr. R. W. Chapman, Lord David Cecil, Miss Dorothy Colston-Baynes, Mr. D'Arcy Cresswell, Mr. Basil Dean, Mr. Geoffrey Dennis, Mrs. Mary Denniston and Mrs. Fred Holland, Miss Christabel Draper, Lady Juliet Duff, Mr. Clifford Dyment, Mr. H. S. Ede, Mr. T. S. Eliot, Mr. St. John Ervine, Lord Esher, Mr. Patrick Leigh Fermor, Mr. E. M. Forster, the late Mr. Barnett Freedman, Mr. Ronald Fuller, Mr. Monk Gibbon, Mr. Robert Graves, Mr. Patrick Hamilton, Mr. Laurence Haward, Mr. Tristram Hillier, Mr. Ivon Hitchens, Mr. Richard Hughes, Mr. Constant Huntington, Lady Keeble, Mr. Denis Kelly, the late Miss Eleanor Kelly, Mr. Noel Langley, the late Mrs. Frieda Lawrence, Mr. John Lehmann, Sir Shane Leslie, the Earl of Lytton, the late Dame Rose Macaulay, Mr. Malcolm MacDonald, Sir Compton Mackenzie, Mr. John Masefield, Mr. W. S. Merwin, the late Professor G. E. Moore, Mr. Harry T. Moore, the late Mr. A. A. Milne, Mr. Raymond Mortimer, the late Dr. Gilbert Murray, Mr. John Nash, Mr. Sean O'Casey, Mr. Derek Patmore, Mr. Ezra Pound, Mr. Alan Pryce Jones, Mr. Peter Quennell, Dr. Robert Ross (of U.S.A.), the Rev. Raymond Roseliep (*concerning Lionel Johnson*), Miss Flora Russell, Mr. Roger Senhouse, Miss Horatia Seymour, Mr. Lance de G. Sieveking, Mr. Martyn Skinner, Dame Edith Sitwell, Mr. Cyril Stott, Mr. Graham Sutherland, Dr. G. M. Trevelyan, the Duke of Wellington, Miss Vita Sackville-West, and Mr. G. M. Young.

In connection with the names given in brackets (in those cases where the grounds for acknowledgement are not self-evident) I am much obliged to the following executors, trustees, or owners of copyright: Professor Claude Colleer Abbott (*Gordon Bottomley*); Lady Cynthia Asquith (*Sir James Barrie*); Mrs. K. Auchterlonie (*T. E. Hulme*); the Society of Authors as the literary representative of the James Joyce Estate; Mr. Thomas Balston and Mrs. Kostenz (*Mark Gertler*); Signora J. S. Barnes and Messrs. Eyre & Spottiswoode (*James Strachey Barnes*); Lord Bruce (*the 9th Earl of Elgin*); Mr. Derek Clarke of the Brotherton Library, Leeds (*for access to the Gosse papers*); Mrs. Lionel Curtis; Mr. Rupert Hart-Davis (*Sir Hugh Walpole*); Mrs. Pamela Diamand (*Roger Fry*); Lady Dunsany (*Francis Ledwidge*); the Hon. Mrs. A. St. Clair Erskine (*F. S. Kelly*); Lord Fisher of Kilverstone; Mrs. James Elroy Flecker; Mr. John Sherwood (*J. E. Flecker*); Mrs. John Freeman; Messrs. Macmillan (*John Freeman*); the late Mrs. John Galsworthy; Dr. Mary Grierson (*Sir Donald Tovey*); Mr. Laurence Housman and the Society of Authors (*A. E. Housman*); Mr. Vyvyan Holland and Rupert Hart-Davis Ltd. (*Oscar Wilde*); Mr. Rex de C. Nan Kivell (*Christopher Wood*); the Rev. J. S. D. Mansel (*W. Denis Browne*); the Estate of the late Mrs. Frieda Lawrence, Messrs. Wm. Heinemann, Messrs. Pearn, Pollinger & Higham, and The Viking Press, Inc. (*D. H. Lawrence*); Professor A. W. Lawrence on behalf of the Trustees of T. E. Lawrence; Lady Lovat (*Maurice Baring*); Mr. Michael MacCarthy (*Sir Desmond MacCarthy*); the literary Trustees of Walter de la Mare; Miss Riette Sturge Moore (*T. Sturge Moore*); Mrs. Alida Monro (*Harold Monro*); Mrs. Charles Morgan; Mr. C. D. Medley (*George Moore, Charles Morgan*); Mrs. Paul Nash; Mrs. Kathleen Nevinson (*C. R. W. Nevinson*); Mrs. Robert Nichols; the Directors of the Ivor Novello Charities Ltd. and the Executors of the Novello Estate; Mr. Denys Parsons (*Viola Tree*); Lord Ponsonby of Shulbrede; Mrs. B. G. F. Richards and Messrs. Dawson & Co. (*Maurice Hewlett*); Mr. John Russell and Mr. Robert Gathorne Hardy (*Logan Pearsall Smith*); the Duke of Rutland (*Lady Violet Granby*); Mrs. Helen de G. Salter (*A. W. Verrall*); Mrs. Elliott Seabrooke; Mr. George Scott Moncrieff (*Charles Scott Moncrieff*); the Oxford University Press and Lord Bridges for the passage from the memoir of Digby Mackworth Dolben; Miss Katharine Shaw-Stewart (*Patrick Shaw-Stewart*); Mrs. Frank Sidgwick; Mr. Robert Speaight and Sir John Rothenstein (*Sir William Rothenstein*); Mrs. James Stephens; the Duke of Sutherland (*Millicent, Duchess of Sutherland*); the Trustees of the copyright of the late Dylan Thomas; the late Mrs. R. C. Trevelyan and Mr. Julian Trevelyan; Mrs. D. Mewton Wood (*W. J. Turner*); Mrs. Annie Wynick and Messrs. Chatto & Windus (*Isaac Rosenberg*); Mrs. W. B. Yeats; Mr. and Mrs. Ralph Hodgson; and Mrs. Igor Vinogradoff (*Lady Ottoline Morrell*).

For commenting most helpfully on the typescript I am obliged to Mr. Bertram Rota and Miss Una Simmons, also to Mr. John Schroder for his examination of the proofs. I must thank Messrs. A. P. Watt & Son for their good offices in connection with several problems, and I am similarly indebted to Mr. David Higham. I acknowledge with thanks the kind service done me by the Curator of the Houghton Library of Harvard University, U.S.A., and the courtesy of Dr. John D. Gordan, Curator of the Berg Collection, New York Public Library, where the greater part of the Marsh papers is deposited. I much regret having been unable to trace the executors of A. C. Benson, Lady Lavery, St. John Lucas, and Robert Ross, and will study to make amends for these omissions should I succeed at length and opportunity serve. For the present I am only conscious of an obligation which I would like to discharge but cannot.

Finally am I put in mind of those numerous friends of Eddie Marsh who for one reason or another, whether through enemy action or the vicissitudes of peace, have hunted in vain for the letters I asked for. Sometimes, I am afraid, they were involved in a good deal more trouble than certain others of my correspondents who met with more success. I cannot bring these acknowledgements to a close without at least setting on record my appreciation of these many obliging people who are no less deserving of thanks for their having to remain anonymous.

C. H.

INDEX

A.E. (George Russell), 95

Abercorn, 2nd Duke of, 107

Abercrombie, Catherine, 251, 261, 281, 333, 460

Abercrombie, Lascelles, 178 and n., 191, 192, 201, 226n., 241–2, 506, 684, 686; Maurice Hewlett on, 205; on D. H. Lawrence, 214; *The End of the World*, 242, 268, 273, 288; *The Staircase*, 242; in Italy, 251, 261; introduction to London life, 272, 274; *The Olympians*, 266; *Speculative Dialogues*, 282; on Robert Frost, 285; financial straits of, 293; stays in 1914 with Marsh, 302; on *King Lear's Wife*, 369; as inspector of shells, 379; *Witchcraft, New Style*, 461; at the Brooke medallion unveiling, 460; and Brooke annuity, 460; *Theory of Poetics*, 483; *Phoenix*, 518; *Witchcraft, Old Style*, 518; on Mrs. Brooke's Will, 569; and Presentation Dinner to Marsh, 596, 599; on Marsh's mind, 614; on *Georgian Poetry*, 681; A. C. Benson on, 682; the *Nation* on, 686

Academy, the, on Brooke, 355

Agadir incident, 173

Aga Khan (1877–1957), 562

Agate, James, 483, 553, 606; and Presentation Dinner to Marsh, 599

Aiken, Conrad, 287

Ainley, Henry, 203, 221, 276, 285n.; readings of J. E. Flecker's poems, 239, 246; reading of *King Lear's Wife*, 279; in *Hassan*, 511

Ajaccio, 224, 225, 557, 560

Albert (France), 431

Aldington, Richard, 575

Alexander, Sir George, 48

Alexandra Hospital for Children with Hip Disease, 10, 14

Alexandra, Queen, 156

Allgood, Sara (Sally), 273

Alma-Tadema, Sir Lawrence, 84, 111

Alsace, 145

Amiens, 431

Ampthill, Lord, 102

Amyot, Etienne, 589

Anderson, Sir John, 77

Andrews, Robert, 550, 553

Anglesey, Marjorie, Marchioness of, 230

Apostles Society, the, 142, 144, 199, 228

Appelbee, Frances, 643, 657

Appelbee, Leonard, 551, 643

Archangel, British troops at, after World War I, 488–9

Archer, William, 42; and Ibsen's seventieth birthday, 81

Arlette (operette, adapted from the French), 434

Armitage, Dr. Bernard, 637

Armstrong, John, 551

Armstrong, Martin, 702; in *Georgian Poetry V*, 497; *Miss Thompson Goes Shopping*, 506

Arras, 450

Art, Marsh's appreciation of, 109ff.

Arthur, Sir George, 553

Asquith, Arthur, 460; in World War I, 298, 301, 304; leave in Cairo, 315–16; wounded, 332; account of Brooke's death and burial, 341; death, 616

Asquith, Lady Cynthia, 128, 211, 253, 535; letter from Marsh, 138; in Canada, 143; friendship with D. H. Lawrence, 219, 235–6; Marsh confides in, 352; *Haply I May Remember* (memoir), 702

Asquith, Elizabeth. *See* Bibesco, Princess Elizabeth

Asquith, H. H. *See* Oxford and Asquith, 1st Earl of

Asquith, Herbert, 219, 241, 235

Asquith, Margot. *See* Oxford and Asquith, Countess of

Asquith, Raymond, 125, 213, 303; engagement to Katharine Horner, 129; A. A. Milne's opinion of, 202

Asquith, Mrs. Raymond (Katharine), 124, 129–30, 561

Asquith, Violet. *See* Bonham-Carter, Lady Violet

Assisi, 116

Astor, Nancy, 2nd Viscountess, 396–7, 547

Athenaeum, the, 465; on modern poetry, 473, 476, 477

Athens, 223, 225

Auden, W. H., 610, 611

Index